PHP

Black Book

Peter Moulding

President and CEO
Roland Elgey

Publisher
Al Valvano

Associate Publisher
Katherine R. Hartlove

Acquisitions Editor
Jawahara Saidullah

Development Editor
Jessica Choi

Product Marketing Manager
Tracy Rooney

Project Editor
Jennifer Ashley

Technical Reviewer
Richard Luck

Production Coordinator
Peggy Cantrell

Cover Designer
Laura Wellander

PHP Black Book

The Coriolis Group, LLC
14455 N. Hayden Road
Suite 220
Scottsdale, Arizona 85260

(480) 483-0192
FAX (480) 483-0193
www.coriolis.com

Library of Congress Cataloging-in-Publication Data
Moulding, Peter
    PHP black book / by Peter Moulding.
        p.   cm.
    Includes index.
        ISBN 1-58880-053-9
    1. PHP (Computer program language) I. Title.

QA76.73.P224 M68 2001
005.13'3–dc21   2001047423

Printed in the United States of America
10 9 8 7 6 5 4 3 2 1

The Coriolis Group, LLC • 14455 North Hayden Road, Suite 220 • Scottsdale, Arizona 85260

A Note from Coriolis

Coriolis Technology Press was founded to create a very elite group of books: the ones you keep closest to your machine. In the real world, you have to choose the books you rely on every day *very* carefully, and we understand that.

To win a place for our books on that coveted shelf beside your PC, we guarantee several important qualities in every book we publish. These qualities are:

- *Technical accuracy*—It's no good if it doesn't work. Every Coriolis Technology Press book is reviewed by technical experts in the topic field, and is sent through several editing and proofreading passes in order to create the piece of work you now hold in your hands.

- *Innovative editorial design*—We've put years of research and refinement into the ways we present information in our books. Our books' editorial approach is uniquely designed to reflect the way people learn new technologies and search for solutions to technology problems.

- *Practical focus*—We put only pertinent information into our books and avoid any fluff. Every fact included between these two covers must serve the mission of the book as a whole.

- *Accessibility*—The information in a book is worthless unless you can find it quickly when you need it. We put a lot of effort into our indexes, and heavily cross-reference our chapters, to make it easy for you to move right to the information you need.

Here at The Coriolis Group we have been publishing and packaging books, technical journals, and training materials since 1989. We have put a lot of thought into our books; please write to us at **ctp@coriolis.com** and let us know what you think. We hope that you're happy with the book in your hands, and that in the future, when you reach for software development and networking information, you'll turn to one of our books first.

Coriolis Technology Press
The Coriolis Group
14455 N. Hayden Road, Suite 220
Scottsdale, Arizona
85260

Email: ctp@coriolis.com
Phone: (480) 483-0192
Toll free: (800) 410-0192

Look for these related books from Coriolis:

Perl Black Book, 2nd Edition
by Steven Holzner

C++ Black Book
by Steven Holzner

XML Black Book, 2nd Edition
by Natanya Pitts

Also published by Coriolis Technology Press:

Java 2 Black Book
by Steven Holzner

Kylix Power Solutions
by Don Taylor, Jim Mischel, and Tim Gentry

Open Source Development with CVS, 2nd Edition
by Karl Fogel and Moshe Bar

Linux System Administration Black Book
by Dee-Ann LeBlanc

About the Author

Peter Moulding is a Web site developer, programmer, and system engineer experienced with many computer languages on mainframes, PCs, and Web servers. He is a trainer in information management and technology for major insurance companies, banks, government departments, and oil companies, and in conferences worldwide. Peter's writing on Information Technology helps people use and, more important, understand technology. Readers respond to his articles with "Exactly what I need to know" and "Many thanks for the clearest instructions I have found to date." Peter is also experienced with architectural and financial issues, regularly presents projects to management, and ghost writes articles for people who need to explain technology to business people.

Peter's father, an engineer, recommended *listening* to machinery. If the machine produces noise, the machine is wasting energy on the noise instead of applying that energy to the machine's task. That same systematic approach to careful testing is evident in both Peter's writing and code. He makes sure code does what the code is designed to do and builds in the means to prove the code works. His own Web site, **http://petermoulding.com**, contains many pages that test variations of database design, HTML, and PHP code.

More than 50 Web sites benefit from Peter's work, including many built from the ground up using PHP. **http://PHPSydney.com** demonstrates what he achieves in an afternoon of PHP coding. His large-scale commercial work is often buried behind the scenes. Some projects involve converting existing static HTML sites to dynamic pages totally database driven through PHP, thus completely removing maintenance headaches while leaving the site looking exactly the same. Other projects include developing a single interface to many applications and bringing together diverse databases using the power of PHP.

For 20 years Peter has presented papers showing how to select and use the right technology—the easiest to use, most practical technology. Sometimes he is the keynote speaker predicting the future of technology. Often he presents practical, detailed "how to" sessions. He will most likely ask you about local history, national parks, and seafood restaurants. You can talk with Peter at major conferences including ApacheCon and the International PHP Conference—just look for the friendly Australian with the Akubra hat.

Acknowledgments

Thank you to Kevin D. Weeks for talking me into writing this book, to my wife Carolyn for taking care of the world while I was buried in the book, and to my children, Louise and Christopher, who said "Go dad" when I was hesitant.

Rasmus Lerdorf deserves a special thank you for making PHP open source so this whole opportunity could open up.

There are many people to thank at Coriolis including Jennifer Ashley, Project Editor, Jessica Choi, Developmental Editor, Brian MacDonald, Copy Editor, Richard Luck, Technical Editor, Tracy Rooney, Marketing Specialist, Adrienne Dueck, Publicist, Peggy Cantrell, Production Coordinator, April Nielsen, Layout Designer, and Laura Wellander, Cover Designer.

—*Peter Moulding*

Contents at a Glance

Table of Contents

Chapter 4

Chapter 5

Immediate Solutions

Introduction

Thank you for buying *PHP Black Book*. PHP is both the most useful programming language for Web sites and the most cost effective. You will enjoy using PHP, and the people who spend money on Web sites will enjoy saving money with PHP. Expect a long and prosperous career using PHP.

If you work with Web sites, PHP is the technology you need now, and this is the book you need with PHP. Start with a Linux, Unix, or Windows workstation and add PHP. You will also need a working Web server (Apache is included on the CD). You will benefit from using a database, so you will find MySQL included on the CD. You can use any browser to run the examples, and for most you do not need an Internet connection.

Is This Book for You?

PHP Black Book was written with the intermediate or advanced user in mind. You already have some experience with a scripting or programming language and know the basics of HTML. This book adds PHP to your arsenal of power tools for conquering every Web site project.

You can read the In Depth theories and explanations anywhere, any time, on the train or on the plane. You can work through the examples in the Immediate Solutions sections on your notebook or desktop PC. Among the topics covered in this book are:

- The PHP language, data, constructs, arrays, functions, and objects
- The Web server environment and network
- File access
- Databases: MySQL, PostgreSQL, DB2, ODBC, and every database you need
- Images: GIF, JPEG, PNG, Flash, and PDF
- Mail, News, IMAP, and LDAP
- XML

All the Web site technologies are included here, with emphasis on the ones you need now. All the important Web server operating systems—Unix, Linux, NT, and

Windows 2000—are covered plus the most widely used workstation operating system, Windows from 98 onward. You can install a practice Web server on a Windows 98 or later notebook and practice your skills any time. The same notebook-based Web server can be used for presentations and demonstrations, becoming an active working proof of your skill.

How to Use This Book

Start with Chapter 1 for an overview of PHP. If you are new to PHP and programming, read Chapters 2, 3, and 10, then 8. Read the rest in any order you like. Most of the remaining chapters need a data source, and reading Chapter 8 will help you produce or diagnose files based data sources.

If you are new to databases, read Chapter 5 and work through the MySQL examples. ODBC from Chapter 6 should be your second database assignment. Noting how employment advertisements read these days, I believe the database chapters (5 and 6) are the most important in the book. Based on experience, a sound, in-depth knowledge of one SQL database is more useful than light knowledge of many databases. MySQL is the easiest database to learn at home, and the SQL skills are transferable to all the popular databases.

When you want to know everything that PHP can do, read the In Depth section of each chapter. Read the In Depth sections on your way to work, over lunch, or while your partner is off shopping for a car or having a baby. The In Depth sections will teach you all the PHP key features and buzzwords in 24 hours.

Object-oriented programming is introduced in Chapter 17, and builds on Chapters 1, 2, 3, and 10.

XML is a popular buzzword few people understand. Chapter 20's In Depth section explains the important aspects and uses of XML. Work through arrays, files, functions, and objects (Chapters 3, 8, 10, and 17) and then go through Chapter 20's Immediate Solutions.

Practice your way through the Immediate Solutions in all the chapters as you need them.

The *Black Book* Philosophy

Written by experienced professionals, Coriolis *Black Books* provide immediate solutions to global programming and administrative challenges, helping you complete specific tasks, especially critical ones that are not well documented in other books. The *Black Book*'s unique two-part chapter format—thorough technical overviews followed by practical immediate solutions—is structured to help you use your knowledge, solve problems, and quickly master complex technical issues to become an expert. By breaking down complex topics into easily manageable components, this format helps you quickly find what you're looking for, with the code you need to make it happen.

I welcome your feedback on this book. You can either email The Coriolis Group at **ctp@coriolis.com** or contact me directly through my Web site **http://petermoulding.com**. Errata, updates, and more are available at **http://petermoulding.com/phpblackbook**.

Chapter 1

PHP Overview

In Depth

Welcome to PHP. If you currently program in any other scripting language, you are about to enjoy the world's best scripting language for Web sites. Readers starting from languages a long way away from scripting languages, such as Assembler and C, are about to gain the speed improvement Captain Kirk gained when he swapped his push bike for the Starship Enterprise.

I started using PHP because Perl can be tedious to write, and Visual Basic was available on only one platform. PHP removed both limitations. Visual Basic was the world's most popular programming language at the end of the twentieth century; it even let dentists write applications for dental practices. Visual Basic is related to the Basic language, but all the relatives in the Basic family are different, and even Visual Basic has many incompatible variations.

PHP has just two variations in widespread use: PHP3 and PHP4. PHP4 is quickly replacing PHP3 on computers all over the world.

Perl has advantages over PHP when writing utility programs to run outside of a Web server; however, there are ways to stretch PHP to replace many of those utilities. After you write PHP for a while, you will find it easier to stretch PHP than to revert to Perl.

I used to write programs in Assembler and Cobol for mainframe servers. Some Assembler diehards wanted to write everything in Assembler for speed of execution. Cobol diehards wanted to write everything in Cobol for speed of programming. Back then, computers were sufficiently slow and expensive that speed of execution was an issue; a large-scale processor speed jump cost about the same as hiring 20 programmers for a year. Now a massive processor speed jump costs about the same as hiring one person to program for one week. Speed of execution is rarely an issue today.

PHP3 was slow enough that competent Perl programmers had an excuse to stick with Perl, but Perl is no longer needed for performance.

C is the only other language needed for programming, and C is needed only for writing the operating system and compiler used to create PHP. If you are an expert with the ANSI C used to write PHP, you can grab the source code to PHP and add new features or improve existing code.

For the 99.75 percent of us who do not know C, we can expand PHP's utility by building a collection of code, functions, and objects. Several Web sites publish collections of prewritten applications and components for your use. Freshmeat (**freshmeat.net**) and Sourceforge (**sourceforge.net**) are good starting points. If you want PHP-based email clients or managers, search Freshmeat for "php email". At the time of writing, this search returned 56 items containing applications, objects, and beta versions of code under development.

Programming 101

If you are moving directly from editing HTML to programming in PHP, the history of scripting languages and their evolution into PHP will be helpful. If you are a programmer arriving here from another language, the information on either GML or open source will help you understand PHP.

A Little History

In 1833, Charles Babbage started building a computer out of brass and pewter wheels. That seemed a little primitive to me when I started writing programs in Assembler, but now Assembler seems as much of a step backward from modern programming languages as brass is from the silicon chips in modern computers.

I worked with over 30 computer languages and wrote a couple, but I ran into the limitations of what one person can write into a language and the restricted growth of proprietary languages developed by single companies. Open source software development essentially removed those limitations.

When one person develops a language, they have great control of the language and are able to pioneer computing in new directions. In 1969, Dr. Charles Goldfarb led the team at IBM that invented Generalized Markup Language (GML), and then went on to invent Standard Generalized Markup Language (SGML). SGML is the parent of Hypertext Markup Language (HTML) and Extensible Markup Language (XML). His leadership took computing in a new direction.

Proprietary products from big companies usually go the opposite direction. I worked with two products from IBM, both competing for the same market, and both limited by the fact they could not interface with the full range of other products from IBM. People at IBM were playing politics with development projects, and the politics eventually killed off both products. Open source development removes the political limitations because open source development lets many people compete with different ideas and it lets the users vote for the product they want. Eventually, the less-useful products are merged with other products, or abandoned, as the developers move to help develop more popular products or move on to completely new ideas.

Enter Open Source

In 1992, Linus Torvalds made open source software viable by writing Linux, a free operating system you can run on cheap PCs. Thousands of people donate their time to the development of Linux, and millions of people use it free of charge.

In 1994 Rasmus Lerdorf invented what became PHP/FI and, through open source development, grew into PHP4. PHP4 is the open source language of choice for new Web developers and is steadily replacing older languages like Perl.

Compiling and Language Development

The original programming languages were compiled on paper and then typed in binary formats. Next came automatic compilers that could translate a human-readable language into the binary language the computer could understand. Compilation saved processing time in the long run, but produced long delays for programmers.

Scripting languages replaced the process of one-off compilation with an interpretation process that occurred every time the computer read the script. Programming became faster, but the scripts were slower.

In the early 1980s, script language developers experimented with compilers. Some script interpreters actually compiled the script into memory, so that parts of the script that were used many times could be compiled once and would therefore run faster. Some script language developers went on to provide a way of saving the compiled memory image to disk so subsequent uses would be faster.

During the late 1990s, Web server languages went through the same evolution. Perl and the first PHP were interpreted line-by-line, as were HTML pages. Developers later moved to systems that compiled into memory. The huge performance improvement from PHP3 to PHP4 reflects a move from interpretation to a compilation process.

There are now various cache mechanisms for Apache and PHP that save compiled memory images for subsequent use. Depending on how your scripts work, your Web server might speed up a lot using the cache software, or might slow down slightly because the extra software overhead outweighs any savings.

Cost

The first servers behind big networks were IBM mainframe servers costing $10,000,000 or more. I had the pleasure of negotiating 60 percent off one of those beasts by pitting the supplier of the first IBM mainframe clone head-to-head with IBM.

Now you can set up a server with a $400 second-hand 486 PC fitted with lots of memory. Of course, if you want to have any sort of success, you need a current model PC fitted with the maximum memory you can squeeze in. If your Web site really takes off, you might need 10,000 PCs or more.

Using Open Source

When you use open source software, read the license conditions. You will find hundreds of sites offering PHP-based open source applications with all sorts of licenses. Usage conditions vary from "This is something I did in college. Here, have it free" to "This is copyrighted. You can use it only if …" where the conditions might require you to keep the original code in the original package, complete with all documentation and copyright notices.

There are *memorialware* (you have to mention the code is dedicated to the programmer's dead friend or relative), *postcardware* (you have to send the author a postcard), *charityware* (you have to estimate the value of the software and donate that amount to charity), and yettobeinventedware where you write some code, publish the code, and invent your own unique license. The common standard license is the GNU General Public License (GPL) license defined at **www.gnu.org/copyleft/gpl.html**.

Diagnostics

When languages are compiled, the compiler picks up many simple errors. Compiled programs are usually clean and easy to diagnose. The move to interpreted scripts means some computer-detectable errors will not be detected until a specific part of the script is interpreted, and that might not occur until the script is in production for a few months. Interpreted scripts are hard to test. A whole industry grew up around building software to systematically test interpreted languages, and systematically tested scripts still fail. PHP3 suffered this problem.

The move to "compile into memory" script interpreters is a step back toward syntax checking a whole script in one hit. PHP4 checks the syntax of the whole script before use, then compiles all the functions, and then works through the main part of the script. If your PHP4 script successfully produces any HTML, that means the whole script is free of syntax errors and all the functions compiled properly, a far better check than in PHP3.

Advantages of PHP

PHP is clearly the *one true language*, but some people need facts; following are facts that clearly show PHP is the scripting language for today's Web sites. Based on experience, PHP is easier to teach than other mixtures, like Visual Basic and IIS, but more schools teach Visual Basic than PHP, so in the short term, Visual Basic looks more appealing to IT Managers.

Interpret versus Compile

Think of computer languages as lists of instructions. Then think of instructions you regularly use, such as recipes or a note on how to find a friend's new house. Imagine that the person typing the instructions skips some parts because they seem obvious, and mistypes a few words. The result is that you cannot follow the instructions.

Now apply computer compilation to the problem. As soon as the typist finishes typing, the computer can look up the spelling of names, and it can check that each instruction starts where the previous instruction finishes. (However, the computer cannot check if you meant salt or sugar, because both are valid ingredients.)

Compiled languages have a disadvantage: You have to write the whole program before you can compile, because any missing parts will cause compilation errors. Interpreted scripts can be developed line-by-line, because the interpreter will process the lines one at a time without caring that many lines are missing.

Apply computer interpretation to the problem of a mistyped name. As soon as the typist finishes typing, the computer does nothing. The computer leaves the instructions unchecked until you start using the instructions. The computer does not look up the spelling of a name until you get to the line in the instructions that contains the name. In the middle of the recipe with a half-made cake mix, the computer tells you there is no such thing as "csdter sugar". You have to throw out the work in progress and start again another day.

PHP has a near-perfect blend of compilation and interpretation. It checks about as much as a good compiler will check and still gives you all the advantages of interpretation.

Parts versus Programming

You can assemble applications out of included files, functions, objects, and all sorts of code scraps, but none of them replace writing your own code. If you have never written code to access a PostgreSQL database, you cannot verify another person's PostgreSQL-based code. Lots of free PHP objects and applications are available for download, and many contain deadly coding traps that make them difficult to maintain and unsuitable for a business site.

Code exists out there that was never updated to use important features of PHP4, like ===, code that does not validate input, and code that uses a database but not the correct data types for each field. For example, consider MySQL: A lot of people use phpMyAdmin to set up tables in MySQL and never notice that phpMyAdmin defaults to setting fields to **NOT NULL**. Those people then publish their code on the Web, and someone else uses that code on tables set up with ordinary SQL, which in MySQL lets fields default to **NULL**. If you fall into that trap, you will have null values causing strange results in SQL output pages.

By writing your own code, you will learn enough to test, verify, and fix all the code you download. If you keep using downloaded code, please feed your changes back to the authors (or recommend this book to them) so they may improve their code and the next 25,000 people downloading the code can all benefit.

Output Control

You can code HTML pages in two ways with PHP. Here is the first way to add a date to a line of text using PHP:

```
<p>Today's date is <?php print(date("l F j, Y")); ?>.</p>
```

This method works, and it is supposed to be quick to code and process because you just insert little bits of PHP into existing HTML pages. PHP-based applications using this approach are available free for download all over the Web. However, they usually need lots of messy changes to suit a Web site, and they make minimal use of databases.

The following example, with little bits of text inserted in to PHP code, lets you take control of everything and better suits large database-driven applications:

```
<?php
print("<p>Today's date is " . date("l F j, Y") . ".</p>");
?>
```

As you develop more sophisticated applications, the percentage of code will increase and text will migrate out of your scripts and into databases. This second style of coding is the end point of the evolution, so you might as well start all new pages at the end point. The second example is where I start all the code in this book, so you can develop powerful applications that work with any browser.

PHP4

PHP4 introduces speed: speed of execution for long scripts, and speed of development for PHP4 functions. One of the Open Source advantages is the opportunity to add what is missing, and those programmers who do add functions report that it is far easier to add things to PHP4 than to PHP3. Listed here are the new things in PHP4 that have an immediate advantage to my customers.

New Functions

PHP4 brought an explosion of new functions. Many are aimed at helping you manage PHP and large applications. Because some ISPs restrict your access to the php.ini configuration file, PHP4 offers a range of functions to test and set PHP configuration values.

PHP3 let you dabble with dynamically generated functions, but PHP4 includes the full range of functions needed to manage dynamically generated functions. PHP4 made function development so easy and popular that the only current list of PHP functions is the one at **php.net**, but even their documentation struggles to keep current. There are simply not enough examples of what PHP functions do in real-life use. I maintain a small list of examples for programmers at **PHPtect.com** (short for "PHP and Web site architecture"). I thought I would use the examples when writing this book, but every time I use PHP, I find new functions, extra parameters in existing functions, and better ways to use the functions and a growing list of peculiarities, so all the code in this book is caught fresh daily at my workstation. Keeping current with PHP is like clothing children. By the time you walk from the changing room to the clothes rack and back, they grow another size.

New Name

People used to give HTML pages the file name extension .html and pages containing PHP3 the extension .php3. The PHP4 developers set up PHP4 to use the extension .php. The two file types, PHP3 and PHP, let you process some pages with PHP3 and some with PHP4. I find it is generally quicker to convert a small Web site straight from PHP3 to PHP4 than to use the two in parallel, so I rarely use the dual-name system. The dual-name system is more suited to servers serving multiple Web sites and applications written by outside organizations.

As you grow your Web site, you convert more HTML pages to PHP, so why not start off by giving all pages the .html extension and running them all through PHP? Your Web server can be set to run every page through PHP with little overhead, and you can immediately begin standardizing headings and navigation with PHP code.

Speed

PHP4 is much faster than PHP3 because the code is compiled once. In loops, your code saves time the second and subsequent time through the loop. The bigger your programs grow, the more time you save compared to PHP3.

PHP4 is so fast that your Web site speed will depend on everything except PHP. You will gain more advantage from adding indexes to your databases than even the most intensive analysis of PHP code speed.

Lots of code speed hints that were true in PHP3 are not true in PHP4. For example, some people recommend using single quotes around strings if you do not need to perform the type of substitution allowed in double quotes. I tested single quotes versus double quotes in PHP4 and found single quotes to be marginally slower than double quotes, although by an amount so small as to be irrelevant. In PHP4, use double quotes for consistency.

The one real slowdown I was able to produce I did by using multiple nested functions in big loops. If you have a process that walks through a 100,000-entry array and calls one of your functions from within the loop, you can gain a small speed advantage by moving the processing code out of the function and directly into the loop. The saving is still trivial against what you save if you use the 100,000-entry array in place of repeated passes through a disk-based file or database.

PHP Debugger

Some exciting developments are happening in the area of PHP debuggers, but at the time of writing, none are ready for large scale application development. I suggest a code editor with really good syntax checking and an application development plan with the tests designed alongside the applications.

On Windows NT, I use Homesite for editing. There are lots of similar products for Windows and Unix, and your choice depends on the exact mix of languages you use. Some will syntax-check HTML or PHP, but not at the same time.

Once the syntax is checked, I test using local copies of Apache, PHP, and MySQL. For PostgreSQL and other databases, I first test the code locally, and then upload to a server with the right database. Once it's running on the target server, I continue there because there are just too many special cases related to databases to jump back and forth.

COM for Windows

COM is the Component Object Model, and it lets you perform a wider range of functions, such as opening Microsoft Word documents from PHP scripts. There are lots of other things you can do with COM, but COM is available only on Windows systems, so any use of COM immediately restricts your application's portability.

PHP COM support provides several functions to let you access COM objects: **com_get()**, **com_invoke()**, **com_load()**, **com_propget()**, **com_propput()**, **com_propset()**, and **com_set()**. In Chapter 7, I show an example of COM. I could not think of a good reason to access a Windows-only file until I remembered you could use COM to open a Word document, and then save the document as a HTML or RTF document so everyone can read it in any operating system.

Regular Expression Functions

PHP supports two types of regular expressions, POSIX and Perl compatible. You can find some regular expression examples in the "Regular Expressions" section under "Immediate Solutions" in this chapter. You can get more information and tutorials about POSIX regular expressions by visiting **www.alltheweb.com** and performing an exact-phrase search for "POSIX 1003.2 Regular Expressions". POSIX extended functions include **ereg( )**, **ereg_replace( )**, **eregi( )**, **eregi_replace( )**, **split( )**, and **spliti( )**.

Perl programmers will be more comfortable with the Perl-compatible regular expression functions, include **preg_match( )**, **preg_match_all( )**, **preg_replace( )**, **preg_replace_callback( )**, **preg_split( )**, **preg_quote( )**, and **preg_grep( )**.

PHP and Apache

Which Web server should you use? Apache or Apache? Straight up, I have to admit to a bias toward Apache. It is so easy to install, so easy to use, and so reliable, that I recommend Apache first and then discuss the operating system to support it. In the unlikely event you are stuck with Netscape's Web server or Microsoft's IIS, or any other Web server that is not Apache, you are probably stuck with a whole Web-site development environment that does not include PHP, and will not be reading this book anyway.

Sure, Apache release 1 was not perfect—that's why Apache release 2 was developed—but Apache is perfect for PHP and perfect for your first Web site. And Apache 2 has an architecture that makes it easy for Apache developers to make it perfect for those rare occasions when it is not yet perfect. If you are using an odd operating system, such as AIX, Apache 2 can be easily be made into a perfect fit.

Apache on Any Platform

A few years ago, most people recommended Sun's Solaris for fast, reliable Web servers. FreeBSD became a popular choice, and Debian's Linux the choice of the price-conscious. Then came hundreds of thousands of people experimenting with FrontPage, and many Internet Service Providers (ISPs) switched to Windows NT as the only easy way to cope with FrontPage. Eventually, Red Hat's Linux became another popular choice.

Apache runs on all of these servers and more. If you do not know which operating system to use, choose Apache so that you are free to change as you wish. If someone else is setting up your Web server, let them choose Apache (and be suspicious of anyone who does not choose Apache). The only things you need change when moving to a new computer or operating system are the directory names in the Apache configuration file, httpd.conf.

Installing Apache on Windows NT is reliable and easy: Download the Win32 binary version of Apache from **apache.org** or a local mirror site, or from the CD-ROM that accompanies this book, and then click on the apache_1.3.20-win32-no_src-r2.msi file to install it. (The 1.3.20 number varies from release to release.) If MSI is not installed on your computer, download InstMsi.exe from the same location, install InstMsi.exe, and then install Apache. MSI is contained in Windows (from Windows 2000 onward), but not in NT 4 or in early versions of Windows.

If you are installing Linux using the Mandrake distribution, you just select the Web server option, and Apache is working. Each distribution of Linux has a different option list, but most will install Apache if you click on anything labeled "Web server". The Mandrake distribution, from **www.linux-mandrake.com**, is the easiest.

PHP installs everywhere Apache installs. The PHP installation details vary across platforms, but the parts in Apache relating to PHP are the same. Most Linux distributions default to installing Apache with languages like Perl but leave PHP as an optional extra. You end up having to install everything or digging around in options menus (or expert mode) to get PHP installed.

As a general rule, if you do download an update to either Apache or PHP, download the latest update for the other product at the same time, update Apache, and then update PHP a short time after Apache. For production sites, I install the latest PHP about 30 days after release on **php.net**; on the few occasions that there is a fault in a PHP release, a fixed version is posted within that time.

Module or CGI

Apache lets you run PHP as Common Gateway Interface (CGI) or as a module. The fine details are covered in the installation instructions supplied with Apache and PHP. Both may eventually be replaced with something named Internet Server Application Programming Interface (ISAPI).

CGI is ideal for testing PHP and Apache. Apache and PHP do nothing until you run a script, and then everything happens from scratch. Under CGI, PHP does not read the php.ini file until Apache hands your script to PHP. The one disadvantage of CGI is speed, because Apache and PHP have to repeat the setup work every time you run a script.

When you run PHP as an Apache module, Apache and PHP can perform some tasks once when Apache starts up, and every script execution runs that little bit faster. For efficiency, make sure your production Web servers run PHP as a module.

When you run PHP as an Apache module, there are a small number of extra functions available but nothing you are likely to use in your first scripts. After you practice with PHP or finish reading this book, you will have the perfect php.ini setup. You will no longer need to experiment with changes to php.ini, and you will be ready to upgrade your test Apache server from running PHP as CGI to using PHP as a module.

The Zen of PHP

You can use any style of programming with PHP, but some things work better than others—I will try to hit all the quirks in this section. Most of the problems stem from PHP not having strong data typing. Strong data typing annoys beginners writing 100-line scripts but is an important safety factor for professionals writing 1,000-line scripts. Some of the important changes in PHP4 are purely to improve PHP's use of data types and type testing.

Syntax

You can insert PHP in to a HTML file by typing the first line of code shown here. The second line shows a one-line PHP script that includes a **print** statement; lines three through six show a multiple-line PHP script:

```
<?php ?>

<?php print("Hello"); ?>

<?php
$message = "Hello";
print($message);
?>
```

<?php starts PHP code. You can start it anywhere in a HTML page and the code is XML compatible, so always use the syntax **<?php**. You can also use things like **<?**, but that does not work with XML. **?>** ends the PHP code.

When you include a PHP file within a PHP file, PHP starts reading the included file as HTML, so be sure to start the included file with **<?php** to get straight into PHP.

Every statement ends with a semicolon, **;**, and statement blocks are surrounded with braces, **{ }**, as in:

```
if("a" == "a")
    {
    print("true");
    }
```

You can leave out the semicolon and braces in certain circumstances, but it makes code hard to understand and leads to mistakes when you modify code.

You can add a comment to the end of a line with *//* as in:

```
print("true"); // This is a comment.
```

You can add blocks of comments with */** and **/* as in:

```
/* This is a comment that goes all over this line
and another line and in fact uses up a whole three
lines. */
```

Variables are created by adding **$** to the front of a name, and the variable name is case-sensitive. When you add the following two lines to your code, you can print out **$a** and get the value assigned to **$a**, not the value assigned to **$A**:

```
$a = "the contents of a variable";
$A = "contents of a different variable";
```

Numeric variables do not require quotes. If you use quotes, the variable will be stored as a string, but will be converted to a number when needed as a number.

```
$a = 33;
```

You can also use names defining logical values, including the following:

```
$a = null;
$b = true;
$c = false;
```

Functions are described in Chapter 10. Function names are not case-sensitive. If you define **hero( )**, and then try to define **Hero( )**, you get a parse error.

If, Then, Else

You know a binary field can have only one of two values: 0 or 1, true or false, yes or no. I used to write Assembler programs to process binary fields as true or false because I had absolute precise control over the code and data, and the compiler would warn me about any changes. When I started writing higher-level languages, I found strange things happening. I would use a binary field, and then find it could have more than two values. I would make a field binary, then the next programmer would change the field type, and the compiler or interpreter would not complain. That was when I started adding **else** to everything.

PHP has fewer data types and automatically converts between types, so testing data becomes more important. Consider the following sections of code (irrespective of language):

```
if($a == 0) {…}
if($a == 1) {…}
```

In a language with strong typing and a binary field, the code will work perfectly because **$a** can contain only 0 or 1, and the code has an action for each value. The following code also works for that type of language:

```
if($a == 0) {…}
else {…}
```

What if another programmer comes along and defines the type as integer? The test using **if else** will most likely work as intended, because any value over 1 will work as 1. The code using the two **if** statements will not work, because it will ignore any value greater than 1. What if the subsequent programmer uses a negative number; should –1 be treated like +1 or as a special case? If there is no logical **else**, add a warning message, like this:

```
if($a == 0) {…}
elseif($a == 1) {…}
else
    {
    print("Warning message…");
    }
```

PHP is more liberal with data types, and PHP4 added the **===** comparison to let you check values by type; but you still cannot lock in data types, so you have to be careful when interpreting data. Here is an attempt at defining all the possibilities for what you might think is a simple binary field:

```
if(!isset($a) {…some sort of warning…}
elseif($a === false) {}
elseif($a === true) {}
elseif($a == 0) {…}
elseif($a < 0) {…}
else {…}
```

First, you have to check that a field exists, because PHP replaces missing fields with an variable of the same name. The alternative I suggest in the "PHP Configuration" section in "Immediate Solutions" is to turn on all warnings so you will be warned about any attempts to read a field that does not exist.

The next test is to check if a field is true or false. You have to replace **==** with **===**, because **==** lets PHP convert numeric and string fields to true or false, whereas **===** checks that the field is the correct type in the first place.

PHP treats 0 as false and everything else as true, whereas some other languages treat negative values as false. When you have data arriving from another system or any file created by software other than PHP, you need to check for negative values, and check how the creating software treated negative values.

Making Data the Right Type

When you first receive data from any source, you might want to start your script with code to test and display the values in every field in the first record, and then display any record that varies from the first record.

Databases are applications that interfere with your data, because they convert your data to their internal storage format and then return a representation of their stored format. You have to convert your data to a format that fits SQL and the database, and then the database software has to translate from the SQL representation to the binary format that uses the least storage space, and return the data in the closest format that PHP can handle. The most common errors are with values that can so easily be converted to other values, such as false and null.

At this time of writing this paragraph, the MySQL database does not have a true binary field type (one is promised soon), so you have to use something like MySQL's **TINYINT** to store binary values. **TINYINT** can confuse your SQL and PHP code by containing null values, so you have to turn them off by setting **NOT NULL**. The field can also contain negative values. Negative values are interpreted as true in PHP, but as false in some other languages, so set the field to **UNSIGNED**. Only then are you safe across all languages.

Make the Entrance Small and the Exit Large

The safest programming strategy in any language is to restrict the entry of incorrect data, and then program so anything can get through. When your visitor fills in a form, does an empty field mean "I do not know" or "I do not care"? Does the answer translate to null or false or 0 or ""? Your validation routine should help the visitor define exactly what they mean, your documentation should define exactly what value should be stored, and the code between the form and the database should ensure that the database receives only the documented values no matter what else can fit in the database field.

Once data is in the database, you need to define a processing path for every possible value, even those not allowed by your input routines. If your program has to display postal codes, convert null and false to a zero-length string. If the output is headed for a HTML table, convert zero-length strings to ** ** because some browsers drop empty table cells. Convert unknown values to a value that will let the output page work, and append a note or message to indicate the error.

Remember that other people will work on your code, and they may not be as detailed or accurate (or good-looking) as you are. They might drop **NOT NULL** from a field, and lots of "Them" are working on Web sites without any training or experience. You want your code to survive their mistakes.

Immediate Solutions

Apache Configuration

When you configure Apache for PHP, add the following code to Apache's configuration file, httpd.conf. Where you see **DirectoryIndex**, add **index.php** or **index** plus any other extension you want for PHP pages. Use the same method with **AddType**: Add one for each page extension you want processed by PHP. The **LoadModule** line points Apache to the ISAPI version of PHP4, and you need to change the directory name to the directory where you installed PHP. The last line has a **#**, which indicates a comment. I commented out the line to run PHP as CGI instead of a module, which would replace the **LoadModule** line:

```
DirectoryIndex index.html index.php
LoadModule php4_module "c:/Program files/php/sapi/php4apache.dll"
AddType application/x-httpd-php .html
AddType application/x-httpd-php .lib
AddType application/x-httpd-php .php
AddType application/x-httpd-php .php3
AddType application/x-httpd-php .php4
#Action application/x-httpd-php "/cgi-bin/php.exe"
```

Specific Apache Functions

The function examples shown here return information about Apache, HTTP, or the environment surrounding Apache. For a description of each item returned by these functions, refer to a good book on Apache or HTTP, such as *Apache Server Commentary*, by Greg Holden and Nick Wells (The Coriolis Group, Inc.) or *Apache Server for Windows Little Black Book*, by Greg Holden (The Coriolis Group, Inc.).

Keep this code handy to display the lists returned by some of these functions:

```
function list_list($list)
    {
    $text = "";
```

```
while(list($k, $v) = each($list))
   {
   $text .= "<br>" . $k . ": " . $v;
   }
return($text);
}
```

apache_lookup_uri()

You can find information about Internet resources through **apache_lookup_uri( )**. The function works when PHP is installed as a module, but not when PHP is run through CGI. The **apache_lookup_uri( )** function returns an object, so use this code to test the function and look at the output:

```
print(list_list(apache_lookup_uri($PHP_SELF)));
```

Here is the result:

```
status: 200
the_request: GET /phpblackbook/apache_lookup_uri.html HTTP/1.0
method: GET
content_type: application/x-httpd-php
uri: /phpblackbook/apache_lookup_uri.html
filename: i:/petermoulding/web/root/phpblackbook/apache_lookup_uri.html
path_info:
no_cache: 0
no_local_copy: 1
allowed: 0
sent_bodyct: 0
bytes_sent: 0
byterange: 0
clength: 0
unparsed_uri: /phpblackbook/apache_lookup_uri.html
request_time: 987732253
```

apache_note()

Apache's note system lets you pass messages between Apache modules. If you write your own Apache module to process a page before PHP sees the page, you can set a note containing data for PHP. Within PHP, you can set notes containing messages for modules that process the page after PHP.

If I were writing a preprocessor, such as an Active Server Pages (ASP) translator, I would have the preprocessor pass messages to the PHP script by simply generating PHP variable assignments. I cannot think of a reason for processing pages after PHP, because PHP lets you do everything you need in a Web script, so you may never need to pass notes from PHP to other modules.

You set an Apache note with this code:

```
apache_note("visitor", "Peter Moulding")
```

You get an Apache note with the following:

```
print(apache_note("visitor"));
```

ascii2ebcdic() and ebcdic2ascii()

If you happen to be writing scripts for use under Apache on IBM mainframes using OS390 or Fujitsu Siemens mainframes using BS2000, you can use **ascii2ebcdic( )** or **ebcdic2ascii( )**. They connect to Apache functions to translate from ASCII to EBCDIC and back, but they work only on OS390 and BS2000. If you have to translate a file from EBCDIC to ASCII, do it on the EBCDIC machine before sending the file to an ASCII machine.

getallheaders()

The **getallheaders( )** function displays the HTTP headers that arrived with the request for the page you are generating with your script. The function works when PHP is installed as a module, but not when PHP is run through CGI. The function returns an object, so use this code to test the function and look at the output:

```
print(list_list(getallheaders()));
```

The output will look like this:

```
Accept: image/gif, image/x-xbitmap, image/jpeg, image/pjpeg, image/png, _
    */*
Accept-Charset: iso-8859-1,*,utf-8
Accept-Encoding: gzip
Accept-Language: en
Connection: Keep-Alive
Host: test.petermoulding.com
Pragma: no-cache
Referer: http://test.petermoulding.com/phpblackbook/
User-Agent: Mozilla/4.76 [en] (WinNT; U)
```

PHP Configuration

PHP configuration issues are disappearing: The default installation is useful, and many installation parameters can now be set within your scripts. This section is oriented toward runtime configuration, where possible, because runtime configuration can be used when your system administrator or hosting ISP prevents you updating the PHP's configuration file, php.ini.

dl()

After you configure PHP using php.ini, you might be missing one PHP extension, and you may want to load that extension from your PHP script. If you use an ISP that is slow to make changes, you might have to load a new extension yourself. You might also find a monster of an extension that chews huge amounts of memory, but is only ever needed for one script. All of these issues can be handled by the **dl( )** function.

The **dl( )** function accepts a file name, and the file name needs the appropriate directory information. By default, **dl( )** loads from the **extension_dir** specified in php.ini. To load **gnu_gettext** in Windows using **dl( )**, write:

```
dl("gnu_gettext.dll");
```

To load **gnu_gettext** in Unix using **dl( )**, write:

```
dl("gnu_gettext.so");
```

extension_loaded()

Before you use **dl( )** to load an extension, you can use **extension_loaded( )** to check whether the extension is loaded. **extension_loaded( )** uses PHP's internal module name, usually the file name without the .dll or .so extension, as shown here. **Extension_loaded( )** returns true when an extension is loaded and false when the extension is not loaded:

```
extension_loaded("gnu_gettext");
```

Diagnostics

The best way to diagnose problems in scripts is to flood the scripts with tests and messages from the start. When you add a test, add a message to show the data being tested and the result of the test.

In fact, you should write up your tests when you document your data before coding the script. Is customer number always an integer, or will you allow mixed names and numbers? What will you enter for prospects who are not yet customers?

Once you are past the design stage and faced with really tricky problems, you might have to resort to the diagnostics that follow.

assert()

The **assert()** function is equivalent to **if(eval())**, where the only action is to produce a message if the result is false. **assert()** accepts any string for evaluation, so you could use it for diagnostic checking, but do not use it for validating user input because you have little control over the result. The following statement is false, and so produces the message shown immediately after the statement:

```
assert(25 == 92);
Warning: Assertion failed in /petermoulding/assert.html on line 5
```

assert() is strictly for diagnostic purposes and, after building 50 Web sites, I have never used **assert()** for anything. Follow these three rules regarding **assert()**:

1. Do not use **assert()**.
2. Before using **assert()**, read the documentation at **php.net**.
3. See rule 1.

assert_options()

The **assert_options()** function gives you a little control over the outcome of using **assert()**. The first code line shown here returns the current value of an option related to **assert()**; the second line shows you how to set the option to a new value, in this case 1:

```
$setting = assert_options(ASSERT_ACTIVE);
$setting = assert_options(ASSERT_ACTIVE, 1);
```

Table 1.1 shows **assert()** options as set in php.ini and through **assert_options()**.

die()

The **die()** function stops your script dead in its tracks. **die()** can output a message as the last gasp of your script. Some people like to write scripts that send cryptic messages and then stop. Never do that to a customer. For productions sites, test everything carefully, log problems, and send useful messages.

Table 1.1   assert() options.

Php.ini option	Default Value	assert_options()	Usage
assert_active	1	**ASSERT_ACTIVE**	Enable **assert()**
assert_bail	0	**ASSERT_BAIL**	Terminate if assertion failed
assert_callback	null	**ASSERT_CALLBACK**	Call function if assertion failed
assert_quiet_eval	0	**ASSERT_QUIET_EVAL**	Disable **error_reporting** during assertion
assert_warning	1	**ASSERT_WARNING**	Issue warning for failed assertion

Here is killer code to stab your script and the message it produces:

```
die("This script is suffering acute bad programming");
This script is suffering acute bad programming
```

die() can also accept a function to clean up files. If you have a cleanup function named **clean_up_files()**, here is the code to run the function and then die:

```
die(clean_up_files());
```

Errors

In php.ini, PHP defaults to

```
error_reporting = E_ALL & ~E_NOTICE
```

Immediately change this setting to:

```
error_reporting = E_ALL
```

The main difference between these settings is that the default lets you use missing variables without warning, whereas the changed version warns you. That helps you avoid using missing data due to simple typos. (Php.ini contains comments describing the settings.)

You can override the error reporting setting in php.ini using **error_reporting()**, but you should never need it. If your ISP will not let you alter php.ini, ask them to set up .htaccess files. If they do not help you with .htaccess files, change your ISP.

When you need to suppress errors, you can add **@** to the start of function names to stop the functions producing errors, and then pick up the errors later. MySQL functions produce error messages when the SQL is in error, but you do not want end users seeing the messy MySQL errors. So, suppress the errors with **@**, and then test the MySQL-generated error fields for errors. Errors from other functions can be found in **$php_errormsg**, the global PHP error field.

Logs

PHP produces an error log, and you can direct the log to PHP's own log, a system log, or a file using the **error_log** configuration line in php.ini. You can add your own messages to the error log using

```
error_log("this is a message", 0);
```

The 0 indicates that the message should go where the **error_log** setting points. You can also send the message via email by changing the 0 to 1 and adding extra headers similar to those used in **mail( )**. The **mail( )** function is covered in Chapter 15, so read that chapter before tackling error messages by email.

Output Control

There are times when you want to write your HTML output without sending the output to the browser, and then decide to cancel the output. PHP's output buffering lets you control when output is actually sent to the browser. To stop output going to the browser, type:

```
ob_start();
```

When you are ready to send output to the buffer, type:

```
ob_end_flush();
```

If you decide not to send output to the buffer, type:

```
ob_end_clean();
```

If you want to read the buffered output and perhaps save it to disk, type:

```
$x = ob_get_contents();
```

Some Web servers buffer the output from PHP, and you cannot control that from PHP. Some browsers buffer their input, and you cannot control that from PHP either. Most releases of Netscape will not display a table until Netscape receives the table end tag, **</table>**, so long tables seem to take forever to display no matter what you do.

Security

The main security problem with PHP occurs when **eval( )** is used to process something typed in by a visitor. Never run user data into **eval( )**, because the user can include any PHP code they like, and damage your system. If you want to give users the ability to enter text with fancy formatting controls, make the input an XML stream and process only the tags that you approve.

The PHP XML processing functions are explained in Chapter 20. If XML is overkill for the type of facilities you want to give users, plenty of PHP string-handling functions exist to process their text in useful and strange ways. You can also resort to the complexity of regular expressions, something I have so far managed to avoid, thanks to the rich range of standard PHP string functions.

Related solution:	*Found on page:*
String Functions	63

Regular Expressions

Regular expressions let you search for strings within strings, and replace strings within other strings. PHP has a number of functions to let you use regular expressions in a variety of ways.

ereg()

The following code prints *true* because **ereg( )** finds the string *pear* within **$x**:

```
$x = "apples and pears are fruit";
if(ereg("pear", $x)
    {
    print("true");
    }
```

Note that **ereg( )** would not find *Pear* in **$x** because **ereg( )** is case-sensitive.

Table 1.2   ereg() special characters.

Character	Description	Syntax	Result
^	Indicates the search string must be at the start of the searched string	**^pear**	pear
$	Indicates the search string must be at the end of the searched string	**pear$**	pear
*	Searches for the string followed by any number of characters	**an***	ann or annn or annnnnnnnn
{ }	Searches the string for the specified number of characters within the brackets	**an{3}**	annn
{,}	Searches the string for either of the specified number of characters within the brackets	**an{3,4}**	annn or annnn

Table 1.2 lists special characters that can be appended to the **ereg( )** search.

You can use a lot of other symbols to control the result of a regular expression (**www.phpbuilder.com/columns/dario19990616.php3** contains a good article on regular expressions), but I'll move on to other PHP regular expression functions.

ereg_replace()

The **ereg_replace( )** function adds replacement to **ereg( )**. The following code replaces *pear* with *orange*:

```
$x = "apples and pears are fruit";
ereg_replace ("pear", "orange", $x);
```

eregi()

The **eregi( )** function is the case-independent version of **ereg( )**. If **eregi( )** searches string **$x** for *Pear*, **eregi( )** would find *pear*, because **eregi( )** ignores case differences. You could think of **eregi( )** as:

```
ereg (strtolower("pear"), strtolower($x));
```

eregi_replace()

The **eregi_replace( )** function is the case-independent version of **ereg_replace( )**.

split()

The **split( )** function returns an array of strings containing the parts of the target string split up by the delimiter. The following code splits **$x** in to an array **$a**, and then prints the array. The result is *pears,apples,oranges,*:

```
$x = "pears and apples and oranges";
$a = split(" and ", $x);
while(list($k, $v) = each($a))
    {
    print($v . ",");
    }
```

spliti()

The **spliti( )** function is the case-independent version of **split( )**, and it works even if one of the *and*s in the previous code example is typed as *And*.

Chapter 2

Data

In Depth

Data is the foundation of your program. If you define your data the wrong way, the program will run, but it will produce the wrong results, which can be absolutely frustrating. PHP has an automatic type conversion that can increase the difficulty of diagnosing problems. Fortunately, PHP4 contributes an extra level of functionality to help you easily test data.

This chapter is about defining data, creating data, testing data, and converting data. The chapter contains references to specific data sources and destinations, including the database MySQL. The examples will help you prepare for reading data from your sources, and writing data to your database. Chapters 5 and 6 cover the specific details of each database.

Data Types

PHP lets you define data as strings, integers, floating-point numbers, logical values, and compound mixtures of types. It also provides two sets of special mathematical functions to handle complex mathematics. Here is a simple string:

```
$a = "any alphanumeric characters";
```

In the "Variables" section that follows, you will see how to control data types, which PHP does automatically. In the "Working on Data" section, you will see how to compare and change data. Chapter 3 contains an in-depth coverage of arrays, but I will slip a few simple arrays into this chapter's examples, because arrays give you easy ways of working with data collections. In fact, the sample string **$a**, shown in the previous code, is an array; here is how you access the fifth element in **$a**:

```
$fifth = $a[4];
```

You will find PHP counting from zero in strings, arrays, and all sorts of functions, so the fifth element of **$a** is referenced as **[4]**. If you get unusual results with PHP data, check all indexes and references, such as the starting character number in the function **substr( )**, in case you counted from 1 where you should have used 0.

Variables

$a is a variable because you can change its value at any time. Constants cannot be changed, and you cannot change a variable in a different scope. Both those conditions are described later in the chapter.

Variables have a defined type, such as integer or string; but PHP automatically changes the type when needed, so you can get unexpected results if you make assumptions about a variable's type. A string containing zero characters, as shown in the first line of the following example code, is a string, but can be converted to null, false, or zero. A string containing one character, the number 0, as shown in the second code line, can be converted automatically to the value zero, and the value zero can be converted to null or false:

```
$s = "";
$t = "0";
```

When the data type is important, you have to replace the **==** operator with the **===** operator, or use a type-testing function like **is_integer()**, all of which are described in the following sections.

All variables have a case-sensitive name, which means the variable **$peter** is different from the variable named **$Peter**, and both are different from the variable named **$PeTeR**. The variable **$Peter_The_Great** is different from the variable **$PeterTheGreat**, and a lot easier to read. Use the underscore character (_) sparingly—you can use it to build long variable names, but you will get tired of typing. The underscore character works in MySQL, but not in all databases; likewise it works in some operating systems when used in a file name, but not in all of them. Trying to remember what accepts which is hard, so I do not use the underscore for external names.

Variables have a maximum length, but that length is almost unlimited for a string (limited only by memory), and anything else can be converted to a string, thus giving you a length from the string representation. If you are working with numbers and storing the numbers in databases, you will find that the length indicated by a PHP function does not help you work out the space the number will occupy in a database on disk.

Automatic Creation

PHP automatically creates missing variables. In the following code example, the variable name is typed as **$metre** in the variable definition line, and then as **$meter** in the **print()** statement. By default, PHP will create an empty variable **$meter** for the **print** statement. If you have warning messages turned on, PHP will issue a warning message when it does this. I perform all testing with warnings turned on, so I can detect and correct this type of error:

```
$metre = 35;
print($meter);
```

The **isset( )** function tests if a variable exists, and the **unset( )** function removes a variable completely. **unset( )** might be used in situations where your code uses **isset( )** to check if a variable exists. Be careful about using **unset( )** to indicate a special value, because another person may not use **isset( )** as rigorously as you do; if the php.ini values are not set the correct way, you can end up missing the warning messages about missing variables, which would otherwise alert programmers of the need to use **isset( )**. Chapter 1 discusses the required php.ini settings.

Constants

A *constant* gets defined once when you type:

```
define("a", "any alphanumeric characters");
```

The **define** command creates a constant with the name provided in the first parameter and gives the constant the value from the second parameter. In the previous code example, constant **a** has the value *any alphanumeric characters*.

The **define** command can be used anywhere, and the defined constants have a global scope, as described in the next section, so your constants are useable inside functions and all sorts of places where variables do not reach. The **define** command accepts simple data definitions, so it does not handle complex data structures like objects. You could use **define** to store a name, use the name when you create an object, and then use the defined name to reference the object indirectly, but the resulting application will fry the brain of the next programmer.

Scope

Scope defines where your data is visible. Data defined outside of functions is not visible within functions, and data within functions is not visible outside of functions. This means you can write a function almost independently of the surrounding code. The scope of individual data representations does vary and can be changed: Defined constants cross function boundaries, and ordinary variables can be allowed to cross into a function, if the function has the variables defined as global. More details on scope and functions appear in Chapter 10, and the full details of scope in relation to objects are found in Chapter 17.

Because PHP automatically creates missing variables, you can be easily confused by variables that are empty when you know they contain data. If you create variable

$whiskey in your main code, and then refer to **$whisky** within a function, **$whisky** will be empty. You will be confused, and if you are panicking while fixing a broken production application, you will probably be in need of a stiff drink.

First calm down with a cup of warm relaxing chamomile tea, and then change your php.ini from

```
; error_reporting = E_ALL & ~E_NOTICE
```

to the following:

```
error_reporting = E_ALL
```

Removing **~E_NOTICE** makes PHP warn you about missing variable definitions and other devilish traps.

Working on Data

PHP offers many expressions, operators, control and structure, functions, classes and objects, and ways of handling data for databases and HTML.

Expressions

Everything in PHP is an expression. Type my age, 29, on a line by itself, and you have an expression with the value 29. Expand the line to "$age = 29;" and you have three expressions with the value 29: the original 29; **$age**, which is now set to 29; and the statement as a whole. The following line will print *29* because the **print( )** function prints the value of the expression, and the value of the expression is effectively the value assigned to the left hand side of the expression:

```
print($age = 29);
```

PHP allows multiple equal signs and evaluates them from right to left. In the following example, **$age** is set to 29, then **$number** is set to 29, and then 29 is returned to the **print( )** statement and printed:

```
print($number = $age = 29);
```

You can also use the value of an expression in control functions, such as **if( )**, as shown next. Although this example is trivial, you can use the feature by wrapping **if( )** and **while( )** control functions around file and database functions, graphics functions—and almost every other function—to control the flow of processing based on what is returned from a function:

```
if($age = 29)
   {
   print("Age is true");
   }
```

The next example uses **mysql_fetch_row( )** to read a row of data produced by an SQL query on a MySQL database. (The full explanation of database functions is in Chapter 5.) **mysql_fetch_row( )** returns data until the rows run out, and then it returns false. When false is assigned to **$row**, false also becomes the value of the whole expression (**$row = mysql_fetch_row($query_result)**), so false is the value passed to **while( )**. The **while( )** loop loops back to the expression until the expression turns false, and then drops through to the rest of the program. In your program, you would have more than the example **print** statement within the loop; you would have code to process **$row**:

```
while($row = mysql_fetch_row($query_result))
   {
   print("Another row from the SQL query");
   }
```

PHP goes to extraordinary lengths to evaluate expressions in useful ways. In Chapter 3, you will see the following **while( )** structure used to step through arrays. **each( )** returns an element of an array, steps to the next element, and returns false when it hits the end of the array. **list( )** splits the element into key and value, and returns true. While **each( )** is feeding data to **list( )**, **while( )** interprets the expression as true and continues looping. When **each( )** passes false to **list( )**, **list( )** passes false to **while( )**, and the **while( )** loop ends:

```
while(list($key, $value) = each($array))
```

Early PHP functions did strange things to indicate the end of a process, but PHP functions now almost universally return false at the end of the data, or on encountering an error. That means expressions can differentiate between instances where a function works and returns no data versus instances where a function fails. PHP4's new **===** operator, explained in the next section, is crucial to handling expressions and functions.

Expressions are mixtures of variables, values, and operators, so there is little more I can tell you without including operators. In the following section on operators, I cover everything you can do without using control statements. Then you can proceed to the "Control and Structure" section to learn everything that controls process flow. If you know Perl or C, you already know enough to make the right guess most of the time and become really frustrated at other times because PHP picks the best out of both languages without picking up all the arcane tricks and traps of either language. Some of your favorite tricks may not work, but the majority that do work are the ones understandable by mere humans.

Operators

Start memorizing **=, ==, ===, !=, !==, +=, .=, +, -, *, /, $, &**, and all the other characters on the keyboard that require awkward hand movements. They are your PHP operators. In this section, I step through them in the order you need to learn them and build examples on the way. Rather than show you the result of each statement as a separate line, I will add the result to the end of the line as a comment.

Assignment Operator: =

Start by assigning my age to a variable using the assignment operator, the equal sign, **=**, which sets the left-hand variable to the value of the right-hand side. This example shows **$age** set to 25. The result, 25, is shown after the **//** (the **//** starts a single-line comment, so this code will work in your script):

```
$age = 25;        // 25
```

You can use several assignment operators in one statement, as shown next. This example sets the variable for each of my birthdays to the same value I have used for the last 10 or so years:

```
$age_2004 = ($age_2003 = ($age_2002 = ($age = 25)));      // 25
```

The next line is an example of a common trap with the equal sign, the mistake of using the equal sign to test the equality of two values. This problem most often happens to people who were brought up coding in other languages. The following code always produces true, because the equal sign sets **$width** to the same value as **$height**. **$height** is usually a positive value, and **if( )** interprets the positive value as true. One of the symptoms of the problem is an unusual value in **$width**:

```
if ($width = $height);       // true
```

Comparison Operators: == === != !==

Here is the correct way to code the comparison of **$height** to **$width**. In my case, **$width** is not equal to **$height**:

```
if($width == $height);       // false
```

The comparison operator **==** compares two values, and with PHP's automatic conversion of data types, you can end up with errors. If a function returns a record count and can return false to indicate an error, code using **==** will convert a record count of zero to false and indicate an error where there is none. The most common examples are database functions where a SQL **select** statement works and selects zero records, but the poor programmer spends days trying to work out why there is an error in the SQL statement, because the **if( )** statement interprets zero as false. Replace **==** with **===**, as shown next, to get a comparison of value and type that distinguishes false from zero. The **mysql_num_rows( )** function returns a row count, but returns false if **$result** has the wrong value or is the wrong variable:

```
$rows = mysql_num_rows($result);
if($rows === false)      // true if MySQL error, false if row count zero
```

The reverse of **===** is **!==**, and the reverse of **==** is **!=**. Table 2.1 offers a quick summary of comparison operators.

In some languages, **=>** works the same as **>=**, but not in PHP. There are no **>==** or **<==** operators, but you can use **!** in places other than shown here. More examples of uses for **!** appear in the following sections.

Arithmetic Operators: + - * / %

Do the PHP operators add up? Yep, sure do. You can add with **+**, subtract with **-**, multiply with *****, and divide with **/**; and **%** will return the remainder of a division. These operators all return a floating-point number if the input is floating-point, and may convert integers to floating-point if an integer field cannot hold the results.

The math is performed by calls to the operating system, and the operating system calls the hardware in your computer, which means the accuracy of these operations depends on your hardware and how your operating system handles the hardware's results. You can get integer mathematics of unlimited accuracy from the GMP (an open source math package) math functions described in

Table 2.1   Comparison operators.

Operator	Meaning	True	False
==	Of equal value	8 == 8	8 == 4
!=	Not of equal value	8 != 4	8 != 8
===	Of equal value and type	0 === 0	0 === false
!==	Of unequal value or different type	0 !== false	0 !== 0
<	Less than	4 < 8	8 < 4
>	Greater than	7 > 6	7 > 8
<=	Less than or equal	4 <= 4	8 <= 4
>=	Greater than or equal	7 >= 6	7 >= 8

the following sections, if you have GMP installed. If you want an integer from a floating-point number, **floor( )** returns the floating-point number rounded down to the nearest integer, and **ceil( )** rounds the floating-point number up to the next integer.

String Operators: . .=

You can concatenate two strings with a dot (.) and append a string to the end of another sting by using the combination of a dot and equal sign: **.=**. In the following two lines of code, the first sets **$x** to "open source" by concatenating the string "open" with a space and a string containing "source". The second line then adds " software"; **$x** ends up containing "open source software":

```
$x = "open" . " " . "source";
$x .= " software";
```

Document Entry: <<<

I do not know the official PHP name for the **<<<** operator, but I use it all the time. If you want to enter a block of text, complete with line breaks, such as the body of an email, use the **<<<** operator as shown in the following code. The example loads **$x** with the text between the first line and the last line. The **anytext** in **<<<anytext** is matched up with the **anytext** in **anytext;** to delimit the data, and everything in between goes into **$x**. The **anytext;** has to start on a new line, and the text can contain any character except **$**, which must be escaped with \ just like a **$** in a double-quoted string:

```
$x = <<<anytext
Dear Coriolis Editors,
The PHP Black Book is proving truly magnificent and worth every cent.
It lives permanently next to my copy of Coriolis's Linux Core Kernel
Commentary.
B. Gates III
anytext;
```

Another use for this operator is testing code when you want to both display the code in a page and run the code so you can see the results. Load the code into **$x** the same way the example email was loaded into **$x**, display **$x** on the page using **print( )**, execute the code using the function **eval( )**, and then display any variables set by the code. The following is a simple example that sets **$c** to a value, displays the code first, then evaluates the code, and then displays **$c**. For those who want to verify the results from the code, **$c** should end up containing 4.

Because the code contains **$** characters, change all instances of **$** to **\$** (they will be stored as **$** within **$x**). To make **$x** safe to display in an HTML page, wrap

$x within **htmlspecialchars( )** within **print( )**. Each line of code ends with an invisible newline character, **\n**, which is ignored by HTML, so use **str_replace( )** to replace **\n** with **
\n**, because **
** will force a line break in the HTML page:

```
$x = <<<codedelimiter
\$a = 2;
\$b = 2;
\$c = \$a + \$b;
codedelimiter;
eval($x);
$x = str_replace("\n", "\n<br>", $x);
print(htmlspecialchars($x));
print("<br>c: " . $c);
```

Incrementing/Decrementing Operators: ++ - -

The **++** and -- operators can be used before or after a variable to increment or decrement it, much like the equivalents in the C language. If you set **$b** to 7, and then type "print(++$b);", **$b** will be incremented from 7 to 8, and then printed. Typing "print($b++);" works in the reverse sequence: **$b** prints as 7, and then is incremented to 8 after the printing. If you use **$b** in an invoicing application to contain the current invoice number, you could use **++$b** to return the next invoice number.

The -- operator decrements variables, so **--$b** decrements **$b** and then returns the decremented value, whereas **$b--** returns the current value and then decrements **$b**. If **$b** contains a count of the paper in a printer, at the end of each page print, you could use **--$b** to decrement the count of available paper and return the number of sheets left.

Error Control: @

The **@** operator suppresses errors from functions and various expressions, which is a good thing to do in production Web sites because the default error messages are cryptic and generally useless to your Web site visitors. It's better to suppress the basic messages, detect the errors yourself, and substitute useful, meaningful error messages. When you use MySQL functions, you can add **@** to the start of the function name, test the result, and then decode errors using MySQL's error fields. (MySQL is covered in Chapter 5.) If a function does not have a specific error-reporting mechanism like MySQL does, you can look in PHP's **$php_errormsg** to get PHP's version of the error.

The next code example is taken straight from a MySQL-based page. It checks the result of an insert query, in **$sql**, fed through the MySQL function **mysql_query( )**, and prints a message if the result is false. Some functions need more complicated tests because they can return both false and a valid value of zero, which PHP can also interpret as false unless you code the test using the magic comparison operator **===**. Check the descriptions of individual functions to find exactly what they return:

```
if(!$query_result = @mysql_query($sql))
   {
   print("Error in query:" . $sql . "<br>Error number: ". mysql_errno()
      . ", error text: " . mysql_error());
   }
```

Bitwise Operators: & | ^ ~ << >>

I presume you know that characters are stored as binary stings, and integers are stored as binary strings, and everything in a computer is stored as binary strings of various lengths. So how do you bite into those bits with PHP? Bitwise operators!

The first example uses the numbers 1 and 2, either as simple integers or stored as the single characters *1* and *2*. Both the integer forms and the character forms have binary representations that end in binary 01 for 1 and 10 for 2. In binary form on a 32-bit platform like current PCs, 1 would be 31 zeros followed by a one, and the character *1* would be 00110001.

If you merge the bits using the logical **AND** process, by coding **$b = 1 & 2;**, the bits in **$b** are set on where the equivalent bits in both 1 and 2 are on, whereas all other bits are off. The 01 in 1 and the 10 in 2 combine with **AND** to form 00, so **1&2** makes 0 and **"1"&"2"** makes *0*. PHP automatically converts from character to integer and back, so you can get the same result from **1&"2"**.

The logical **OR** process, coded as **$b = 1 | 2;**, sets the bits on in **$b** where the equivalent bits in either 1 or 2 are on, whereas all other bits are off. The 01 in 1 and the 10 in 2 combine with **OR** to form 11, so **1 | 2** makes 3 and **"1" | "2"** makes *3*.

The logical **XOR**, also called the "exclusive Or", coded as **$b = 1 ^ 2;**, sets the bits on in **$b** where the equivalent bits in either 1 or 2 are on, but not on in both, and all other bits are off. The 01 in 1 and the 10 in 2 combine with XOR to form 11, so **1^2** makes 3 and **"1"^"2"** makes "□" (the character used to indicate characters that cannot be displayed). Oops, what happened to **"1"^"2"**? *1* in character form is 00110001, and *2* in character form is 00110010, so **XOR** turns off the first 11 because the bits are on in both characters. That leaves **$b** containing 00000011, and 00000011 is a nondisplay character that could appear as anything in your browser, including a space or a little box to indicate a display error.

The logical **NOT**, coded as **$b = ~ 2;**, inverts all the bits, setting the bits on in **$b** when the equivalent bits are off in 2; all other bits are set to off. The 10 in 2 is inverted to form 01, and that long string of 0s in front of the 10 are set to 1s, so **~2** becomes –3. **~"2"** produces 11001101, which is the accented capital i, *Í*.

Having fun yet? There are just two bitwise operators left, shift right, **>>**, and shift left, **<<**. Both move bits the number of positions you specify, from one to the length of the field you are working on. Both drop the bits off the end, and add zeros at the other end. I notice some people suggesting the dropped bits are rotated around to the other end of the binary field, but that does not happen on the systems I use. If **$b** is set to 4, **$b = 4;**, and you shift the bits one position to the right, **$b >>= 1;**, **$b** then contains 2. The next shift right produces 1, the next shift 0, and then **$b** remains at 0. Starting again at **$b = 4;**, a shift left of one bit, **$b <<= 1;**, produces 8, and a shift left of 2, **$b <<= 2;**, changes 4 to 16. If you shift the bits left far enough, you can end up with a negative number because you have moved a 1 bit to the sign position. After that, you will get zero, because all the 1 bits have moved out of the field. The bitwise operators can also be used in the form **$a = $b >> 1;** and with numbers, as in **$a = 126 >> 1;**.

Execution Operator: '

Up in the top left hand corner of your keyboard is the lonely, underused backtick key, '. Backtick wants to be important, but everyone confuses it with a single quote, except PHP. PHP treats it like the **system( )** function, and anything found between backticks is sent to the operating system for execution. Anything returned by the operating system is placed in a string you can process or display. Although backticks are similar to **system( )** and **exec( )**, the backtick is the only one to return all the output for your convenience.

The example uses the Unix/Linux **ls** command to list file names and place them into **$list** for later display or perhaps analysis. You would be better off using one of PHP's file functions to get the simple file-name list shown in this example, but you may find a particular command that has no exact or easy equivalent in PHP

```
$list = 'ls';
```

References: & =&

References are aliases for variable names. If you set **$x** to the value 5, **$x** is a name that points to the value 5 stored in an integer field, and PHP lets you point other names at the same integer field. You can set **$f** to point at the same integer field by using **$f =& $x;**. The integer field containing 5 remains untouched and **$x** remains pointing at the integer field. All you did was add an extra name in PHP's symbol table pointing to the same integer field. If you add 3 to **$f**, the integer field changes to 8, and **$x** returns the value 8 when you use **$x**.

You cannot use references to change another reference, so in the example discussed so far, you cannot point **$x** to a new field by pointing **$f** to a new field. If you have field named **$b**, and you point **$f** to the same field as **$b** by using **$f =&** **$b;**, all you change is **$f**. **$x** remains pointing at the same field. The same rule applies to unsetting references: When you unset **$f**, **unset($f)**, you remove **$f**, but leave **$x** and the integer containing 5 all intact.

Line one of the following example does not work. Line two is the start of the error message you will get if you try the code. The code is trying to add a reference to a value, but PHP does not know how. PHP can only add references to fields created by a normal assignment statement:

```
$a =& 5;
Parse error: parse error, expecting 'T_NEW' or 'T_STRING'
```

Some languages let you add references to parts of fields or an aggregation of fields, but not PHP. When I tried **$b =& $a[15];**, PHP produced a parse error, and when I tried aggregation with **$a =& $b . $c;**, PHP created a reference to just the first field **$b**.

You can add the single ampersand, **&**, to parameter names in functions to make the parameter a reference to a field outside a function, rather than a copy of the external field. In the following example, the function **plus_one( )** accepts a variable, adds one, and then prints the variable. Because the example starts with **$x** set to 11, the function returns 12, and the first **print** statement prints 12. However, the second **print** statement prints 11, because it prints the original unmodified **$x**:

```
$x = 11
function plus_one($value)
    {
    return($value + 1);
    }
print(plus_one($x));
print($x);
```

Now add one character to the example, an **&** on the front of **$value**. The second **print** statement now prints 12 instead of 11, because **&$value** becomes a reference to the same field that **$x** points at, instead than a copy of the field that **$x** points at:

```
$x = 11
function plus_one(&$value)
    {
    return($value + 1);
    }
print(plus_one($x));
print($x);
```

You can also use **=&** to create aliases for references returned by functions. If the previous code had **$a = &plus_one($x);**, **$a** would be a reference to the value returned by the function, and therefore would be a reference to the variable **$x**. References can be to objects as well as to variables.

Other references are created by the **global** statement in functions and **$this** in object methods. Functions are described in Chapter 10, and objects are covered in Chapter 17. The next example shows a function, **find_variable()**, returning a reference instead of a value because there is an **&** in front of the function name in the function definition. If **find_variable()** returned a reference to an internal field, the field would disappear when the function finished, so **find_variable()** needs external fields. You supply these external fields by placing an **&** in front of the parameter names, or via a **global** statement. Once you have references going in, and the function is defined to return references, you can perform any processing you like to select the reference to return. In this short example, **find_variable()** simply returns the input. **$b** is set to 5 to produce a test field and is fed into **find_variable()** so **find_variable()** returns a reference to **$b**. **$a** is set to reference the result of **find_variable()** by **=&**, and because the result is a reference to **$b**, **$a** now refers to the same field as **$b**. If you then change **$a**, (the example increments **$a** by one), **$b** points to the same incremented field and the last line prints "a: 6, b:6":

```
function &find_variable(&$parameter)
    {
    return($parameter);
    }
$b = 5;
$a =& find_variable($b);
$a++;
print("a: " . $a . ", b: " . $b);
```

Operator Precedence

The following list has the operators listed in their order of priority (or precedence) from highest to lowest. Operators of equal precedence are evaluated from right to left. You can use brackets, ( ), to override the precedence:

- **new**
- **[**
- **! ~ ++ -- (int) (double) (string) (array) (object) @**
- __* / %__
- **+ - .**
- **<< >>**

- < <= > >=
- == != === !==
- &
- ^
- |
- &&
- ||
- ? :
- = += -= *= /= .= %= &= |= ^= ~= <<= >>=
- **print**
- **AND**
- **XOR**
- **OR**
- ,

Control and Structure

This section covers all the statements you use to control the flow through your script, including making decisions with **if( )**, **else**, and **elseif( )**, and then talks about an alternative syntax. The **switch( )** statement can be a great replacement for long sets of **if( )** statements and is similar to the **select** statement available in other languages. The **while( )** and **for( )** statements let you loop through code based on certain conditions and seem to work like **while( )** and **for( )** in other languages.

The **include( )** and **require( )** statements let you include code from other files, and both work like their equivalents in C. There are a couple of traps to be aware of when using them in PHP, and the new **require_once( )** and **include_once( )** statements help to reduce the common problem of including files more than once.

if()

Coding with **if( )** in PHP is similar to coding with **if( )** in other languages. This section will describe the shortcuts for coding with **if( )** in PHP, plus show you some traps to avoid. The next example is a short piece of code to test the value of **$a** and print "ok" if **$a** is greater than zero:

```
if($a > 0)
   {
   print("ok");
   }
```

PHP interprets zero as false, everything greater than zero as true, and everything less than zero as true. Some other languages consider negative numbers to be false, so that can be a trap if you are processing data from other systems. Because PHP automatically converts character data to integer, 0 is also treated as false, as is the zero-length string. If you coded **if($a == false)**, 0 and "" would both produce false results, so you have to code **if($a === false)**, as discussed in the "Operators" section.

PHP converts fields straight to logical values, so you can reduce **if($a != 0)** to **if($a)** and PHP will convert **$a** to true or false for **if()**. You can also code **if** statements in the form **if(!$a)** to perform something when **$a** is false. All these variations can expose you to unintended results, so consider using the formal comparison of value and type as in **if($a === true)** and **if($a === false)**.

The **if** allows for multiple conditions joined by **and**, or **and** structured with parentheses **()**. Because the conditions are evaluated from left to right, you can check if a variable exists before testing for a value in the variable. The following example will stop at the **isset()** if **$a** is not defined, so it will not generate an error message for a missing **$a**. This is a short example of the code you can use when testing for optional variables that may not exist, such as a field from a form:

```
if(isset($a) and $a > 0)
    {
    print("ok");
    }
```

else

The **else** statement gives you a great way to cover all values, and it works the same as in all other languages. You use it after an **if()**, as shown in the following example:

```
if($a == $b)
    {
    print("equal");
    }
else
    {
    print("not equal");
    }
```

elseif()

The **elseif()** statement lets you step through various conditions using **if()** statements and is similar to **elseif()** and **else if()** in other languages:

```
if($a == "hot")
   {
   print("Turn on air-conditioner");
   }
elseif($a == "warm")
   {
   print("Enjoy the weather");
   }
else
   {
   print("Turn on heater");
   }
```

switch()

The code example in **elseif( )** can be represented as a multiple selection using **switch( )**. The code based on **switch( )** is easier to maintain when there are many possible values and actions. Here is the code from the previous section redone using **switch( )**:

```
switch($a)
   {
   case "hot":
      print("Turn on air-conditioner");
      break;
   case "warm":
      print("Enjoy the weather");
      break;
   default:
      print("Turn on heater");
   }
```

The **switch( )** statement tests a variable or expression, in this case **$a**, against the expression in the first **case** statement, "**hot**", and on a successful comparison, starts executing the code following the **case** statement. On failure, **switch( )** jumps down to the next **case** statement and tries another comparison.

The **default:** statement is equivalent to the **else** statement with **if( )**—it is the action that will be executed if all the **case** statements fail. The **default:** statement is not compulsory, just as an **else** is not compulsory after an **if( )**.

After **switch( )** completes the code in a **case** statement, **switch( )** keeps on going down the code, running the code unless you have a **break** statement to jump execution out of the **switch( )**. (Some languages always jump out of their equivalent to **switch( )** without the equivalent of a **break**, which means you cannot use the equivalent of the next example.) In the previous example, you might want

"hot" to both turn on the air-conditioner and display the message about enjoying the weather. All you need to do to accomplish the change is leave out the **break** at the end of **case "hot"** as shown here:

```
switch($a)
   {
   case "hot":
      print("Turn on air-conditioner");
   case "warm":
      print("Enjoy the weather");
      break;
   default:
      print("Turn on heater");
   }
```

Sometimes you want multiple values to cause the same action, and many languages allow the equivalent of multiple values on a **case** statement. PHP requires a **case** statement for each value, which makes it easier to document each value (with a comment on each line). In the following example, the programmer likes the weather "hot", and so leaves the air-conditioner off:

```
switch($a)
   {
   case "hot":
   case "warm":
      print("Enjoy the weather");
      break;
   default:
      print("Turn on heater");
   }
```

while()

When you are reading an array or a file or rows returned from a database, you might like to use **while()** to control the program execution flow. The only competitor in PHP is **for()**, but I tend to use **while()** the most because **while()** fits better than **for()** with many PHP functions and constructs.

Many languages give you variations of **while()** to allow testing of conditions before or after a loop, so you can loop through your code at least once. PHP supplies a **do while()** statement for those occasions. The following example shows a standard **while()** loop that will run zero times because **$a** is already equal to **$b**. The second part of the code shows the **do while()** equivalent that runs at least once before testing for **$a == $b**. The first part prints zero lines, and the second part prints one line:

```
$a = $b = 5;
while($a != $b)
    {
    print("This will never print");
    }

do
    {
    print("This will print at least once");
    }
while($a != $b);
```

The **while( )** loop works extremely well with **list( )** and **each( )** for stepping through arrays, as shown in the next example. The example builds a short array, resets the array pointer to the start of the array, and then uses **while( )** to step through the array. The **each( )** statement returns one array entry at a time, moves the array pointer to the next entry, and returns false at the end of the array. The **list( )** statement takes the data from **each( )** and places the array entry key in the first field, **$k**, and the array entry value in the second field, **$v**:

```
$white_crystalline_substance[] = "C12H22O11";
$white_crystalline_substance[] = "C8H10N4O2.H2O";
$white_crystalline_substance[] = "NaCl";
reset($white_crystalline_substance);
print("Warning, the most abused and addictive substances are:");
while(list($k, $v) = each($white_crystalline_substance))
    {
    print("<br>" . $v);
    }
```

Note that you do not need to provide an index value when creating an entry for an array; when PHP sees the empty square brackets, PHP automatically uses the next available index number. See Chapter 3 for the full details about arrays.

When **while( )** steps through the example, it loops through the code three times, once for each entry, and stops when **each( )** returns false:

```
Warning, the most abused and addictive substances are:
C12H22O11
C8H10N4O2.H2O
NaCl
```

for()

On some occasions, **for( )** is a better choice than **while( )**, such as when you are stepping through a list where you need to count or display a sequence number for each entry. The **for( )** statement accepts three expressions separated by semicolons, as in C, and evaluates each expression the same way as does C. Here is a quick example that prints the numbers from one to three:

```
for($i = 1; $i <= 3; $i++)
   {
   print($i);
   }
```

The first expression is run once at the start of the **for( )** processing and creates your index with the correct starting value. You may leave out the first expression if your index field already exists with the correct value, but remember to leave the semicolon there so **for( )** knows what to do with the next expression.

The second expression is evaluated once per loop through the code at the start of the loop. This could result in no loops through the code, if the index field has already reached the limit specified in the second expression. You can leave out the second expression, which means **for( )** will loop infinitely, and then break out of the **for( )** loop using a **break** statement, but this is dangerous, because changes to the code can prevent the process reaching the **break** statement. If there is a known limit on the passes through the loop, put that in the **for( )** statement, and reserve **break** statements for breaking out of the **for( )** loop early.

The third expression is evaluated once per loop at the end of the loop. You can leave out this expression, and it can be something like a **print** statement. You normally use expression three to increment the index field, so that the index field will eventually reach the limit set in expression two, but you might not do this if part of the code in the loop has the effect of incrementing the index. An example might be the use of **each( )**, **next( )**, or **mysql_fetch_row( )**, all of which move to the next row or entry in the input.

The following **for( )** example uses the previous **while( )** example and prints the array with items numbered from one upward, the way you might number a top 10 list:

```
print("The most addictive substances are (in order of addictiveness):");
for($i = 0; $i < count($white_crystalline_substance); $i++)
   {
   $n = $i + 1;
   print("<br>" . $n . " " . $white_crystalline_substance[$i]);
   }
```

Although this code may not be the most elegant-looking solution, it is the most practical, and I will run through the advantages and alternatives. Arrays count from zero, so the **for( )** statement starts with an index set to zero, **$i = 0**, and runs

2. Data

to one less than the count of the number of elements in the array, incrementing by one, **$i++**. The code does not use the array pointer, so you do not have to reset the array pointer at the start. The code does not use the key of the array, so it works if entries are deleted from the array, or if the array is sorted in a way that does not resequence the key. In fact, the key could be a number, such as kilograms used per year.

The array is numbered from zero, but the list has to be numbered from one, so the code sets up **$n** as a discrete field **$i + 1**. This means that **$n** can be used in a variety of ways in the **print** statement, although the example just places **$n** at the start of the row. This code is easier to change if you need to modify the **print** formatting.

require(), require_once(), include(), and include_once()

When you are writing a script as big as this chapter, it is time to get out the chainsaw and cut up the script into bite-sized chunks. To help you manage the process, I will cover the types of cuts you want to inflict, and which PHP **include( )** or **require( )** statement is appropriate.

I could cut this section, on **require( )** and **include( )**, out of the main document and edit this part separately, because there are no cross-references between this section and the rest. You can easily and reliably cut out sections of PHP code when there are no connections of the type I call *dependent connections*. What is a dependent connection and how do you test the dependencies? Pick any section of code, cut the code out of its current location, and then paste the code into another location. Does your script still work?

If your script still works, you have an independent section of code that is suited for placement in a separate include file. Functions and object definitions are good choices for include files, because they can be included in your main script at any location (in PHP4; that was not true for PHP3). Start cutting.

If your site sells farm machinery, and the script displays power tools, the first consideration is where you can reuse the functions. Suppose your power tool page is named powertoolpage.html, and you have five functions that are only used in powertoolpage.html. You might place these five functions in powertoolpagefunctions.html. Formatting functions that can be used in other pages might go in formattingfunctions.html, and the database access functions that are only used for pages displaying product lists might go in productdbfunctions.html. Because all the functions can be included anywhere and are most useful if included right at the start, you can start your page with:

```
require("powertoolpagefunctions.html");
require("formattingfunctions.html");
require("productdbfunctions.html");
```

The **require( )** statement takes a file name and includes the file right at the start of PHP processing, during syntax checking and before script execution, so **require( )** cannot be controlled by **if( )** statements or similar control logic. That makes **require( )** faster, but less flexible; so use **require( )** for files you always include, but not for files needed only occasionally.

The **include( )** statement accepts the same file name but does not include a file until program execution reaches the **include( )** statement. If you have a section of code that is used on only a few pages, put the bulk of the code in a separate include file. Then, use an **include( )** in your main document and wrap the **include( )** in an **if( )** statement that decides if the extra code is needed. Suppose some of your power tool pages have a feedback page that asks customers about their recreational uses of power tools. You could set **$ask** to true when the questionnaire is needed, save the questionnaire in questionnaire.html, and then use the following **if( )** and **include( )** statements to include the questionnaire:

```
if($ask)
    {
    include("questionnaire.html");
    }
```

Included files can contain **include( )** and **require( )**, which leads to the possibility of page a.html including b.html and c.html, and then b.html including c.html. If this happens, c.html will be included twice, and your script will fail because of the duplicate code. The **include_once( )** and **require_once( )** statements solve the problem by checking if a file is already included before including the file again. In this example, b.html will not include c.html if a.html has already included c.html. For this to work, you must change all **include( )** statements for c.html to **include_once( )**, because a stray **include("c.html")** will still include c.html.

Functions

Functions are explained in detail in Chapter 10 and do not have any special requirements to do with data. In the "References: **&=&**" section of this chapter, I covered the use of references with functions, and in the "**require( )**, **require_once( )**, **include( )**, and **include_once( )**" section, I covered easy ways to separate common functions into include files.

Classes and Objects

Objects are explained in detail in Chapter 17 and do not have any special requirements to do with data. They can be managed the same way I suggest for functions in the previous section. Objects are a class of data and can often be used where you can use strings and numbers, such as entries in arrays. You can check if a data item is an object with the function **is_object( )**.

Data for Databases

With most relational databases, you add data to the database using SQL, and SQL delimits strings with quotes. That means that to make a string acceptable to SQL, you have to change a single quote within the string to something else. The **addslashes( )** statement does exactly that. The **addcslashes( )** statement gives you an extra level of control so you can escape any character via a character list that defines which characters are changed. The **addcslashes( )** statement performs a C-like conversion with nondisplay characters converted to octal representation. MySQL requires **addslashes( )**. I have not had to use **addcslashes( )** for anything.

The **stripslashes( )** and **stripcslashes( )** statements perform the reverse function, and you may need them one day. When you add slashes to data headed for MySQL, MySQL converts the data back to the correct format before storing the data in the database. MySQL then presents the data in the right format when you retrieve the data, which means you do not need **stripslashes( )**. Check your database before using **stripslashes( )**.

Data for HTML

Suppose you write a tutorial on HTML and want **
** to display as the characters *
*, and not as a line break. Just wrap **htmlspecialchars( )** or **htmlentities( )** around the string containing **
** to convert **<** to **<** and **>** to **>**. The **htmlspecialchars( )** statement changes the characters <, >, ', "", and &, whereas **htmlentities( )** changes every character that has an HTML equivalent. Both functions accept a second parameter to change the way they handle quotes, but the default works fine on every occasion when I need the functions.

Date and Time

PHP includes more date and time functions than a gadget-laden watch. Use this section as a quick guide to when you would use the functions. More detailed examples follow in the "Immediate Solutions" section.

Julian Date

The *Julian date* is different from the Julian calendar described in the following section. The Julian date is a format that has one special feature: no months. You will use two Julian dates.

The *Julian day count* date is used in PHP for calculating dates, and is a day count starting at 4000 B.C. When PHP converts a date from one calendar to another, PHP converts from the original calendar to the Julian day count, and then converts to the desired calendar. The **unixtojd( )** function converts a Unix timestamp to a Julian day count, and **jdtounix( )** converts a Julian day count back to a Unix timestamp.

The *IBM Julian* date format presents the year followed by the day of the year (as three digits), so a Julian day remains constant no matter how you organize months and conventional dates. Monday, May 2, 2001 as a Julian date is 2001122. Functions including **date( )**, **getdate( )**, and **localtime( )** can return the year and day of year, letting you build a Julian date.

Time

You know about 8:00 A.M. and 7:00 P.M., and how 7:00 P.M. can be represented as 19:00 when clocks are set to 24-hour mode. You might not know why your Web server returns funny times, or how to get the correct time, so here is a quick explanation.

GMT

Greenwich Mean Time (GMT) was the basis of all international time when the British Navy ruled the world. (The town of Greenwich, near London, is also a lovely place to visit in Spring, complete with a good display about time and the history of time. If you want some links about time or tips about visiting London and Greenwich, drop me a note through my Web site, **petermoulding.com**.)

The time shown on Windows-based computers is GMT plus your local time offset. Australia, being ahead of the rest of the world, is 10 hours ahead of GMT, and New York is 5 hours behind.

UTC

Of course, the Americans could not live with the British Navy dominating the world or time, so the United States invented Coordinated Universal Time (UTC). Coordinated Universal Time lets you synchronize your computer to the U.S. Navy's atomic clock at their observatory in Washington, D.C., using a protocol named Network Time Protocol (NTP) that communicates by the User Datagram Protocol (UDP, something special you have to set if your computer is behind a proxy server). UTC counts from the international date line in the Pacific and is verified by comparing the time on a lot of atomic clocks all over the world.

Depending on your operating system and date/time settings, the dates and times displayed and used on files might be UTC or local time. Workstations are usually set to use local time, and usually are set to adjust for things like daylight savings time; however, some are not, and you can get unexpected date/times as a result. Most servers are set to UTC, with some functions returning local time, but some servers are wrong, or are set to the wrong location. I have worked on networks of servers where all servers were set to the same time even though some servers were in different time zones or at least serving customers in different time zones. PHP lets you get at both local and UTC dates and times.

If you are synchronizing transactions across databases and get times a fraction of a second off, that is network propagation delay. If you get a time that is a few minutes off, the time was set from someone's watch, so ask the network people to make the servers synchronize properly. Times one hour off are caused by one machine having a daylight savings time adjustment turned on and the other machine having the adjustment turned off.

To compare unadjusted UTC dates and times on servers, use PHP's **time( )** function, and use **date( )** or **getdate( )** to get the local time that includes the time zone adjustment and any settings for daylight savings time.

Calendar

The old Roman Empire used a calendar based on lunar cycles. Julius Caesar changed all that. In fact, the many Roman emperors filled chronology with fascinating bouts of vanity, politics, and the trappings of a good detective novel. Pope Gregory upstaged Julius Caesar with an even more accurate calendar. PHP supports more calendars than just the Roman calendars. If you need to build a Web site for a historian, PHP is the perfect scripting language.

Jewish Calendar

The Jewish calendar is the oldest calendar handled by PHP. The calendar dates from 3761 B.C., was originally a lunar-based calendar, and gained all sorts of formal rules to keep the year in sync with the sun. PHP's date conversions use a system that works back to 4000 B.C., so PHP can handle the Jewish calendar. The **jdtojewish( )** function converts a Julian day count to the Jewish calendar, and **jewishtojd( )** converts a date back to the Julian day count.

Julian Calendar

Julius Caesar created the Julian calendar in 46 B.C., complete with 12 months, 365.25 days per year, and a leap year every fourth year to handle the 0.25 of a day. He also named the month July after the person he admired most, himself. The **jdtojulian( )** function converts a Julian day count to a Julian calendar date, and **juliantojd( )** converts a Julian calendar date back to a Julian day count.

Gregorian Calendar

By the sixteenth century, the Julian calendar was 11 days off, despite the occasional fiddle with dates by various Roman emperors. Pope Gregory XIII changed the leap years so that centennial years would not be leap years, unless they were also a multiple of 400. This change brought the average year down to 365.2425 days, just .000411 days off. The **jdtogregorian( )** function converts a Julian day count to a Gregorian date, and **gregoriantojd( )** converts a Gregorian date to a Julian day count.

French Republican Calendar

The French Republican calendar was adopted by the French on October 24, 1793, a year after the republic was formed. This calendar featured 12 months of 30 days and some other attempts at calendar reform, and then disappeared in 1806. The **jdtofrench( )** function converts a Julian day count to the French Republican calendar, and **frenchtojd( )** converts back to a Julian day count.

Easter

If you need to know on what date Easter falls for any year between 1970 and 2037, feed the year to **easter_date( )**, as shown in the "Easter" section in the Immediate Solutions. For other years, use **easter_days( )**, as shown in the same Immediate Solution. **easter_date( )** uses a Unix timestamp and so is restricted to the same narrow range of years covered by the Unix timestamp, whereas **easter_days( )** uses a Julian day count to cover a wider range of years.

ICAP

The Internet Calendar Access Protocol and PHP ICAP functions let you access and share Internet-based calendars. There are more details on Internet protocols and proposals for calendars at places like **www.ietf.org/** and **www.imc.org/**, and they may all become standards at **www.w3.org/**. ICAP can plug in to MCAL, which I describe next.

MCAL

MCAL is the Modular Calendar Access Library, a system that lets you plug in modules to connect to and process calendars, including a module for ICAP. MCAL code, documentation, and modules are available at **http://mcal.chek.com/**.

The calendars can be on your machine, your LAN, ICAP servers out on the Internet, or other types of servers that have an **mcal** plug-in module. You can query calendars, see events, set alarms (called triggers), and build reoccurring events. PHP's documentation of MCAL functions at **www.php.net/manual/en/ref.mcal.php** includes functions like **mcal_open( )** to open a connection to an MCAL service. MCAL looks and works a lot like IMAP, which is covered in Chapter 15, so if you have experience with IMAP, MCAL should be easy to understand.

Math

PHP lets you easily use integer and floating-point math functions up to the limitations of the standard math functions on your computer, and then provides access to extended math software for working with larger numbers. GMP gives you access to larger integers, and BCMath gives to access to whatever GMP does not cover.

Integer Math

The standard integers on PCs are limited to 32-bit numbers and are treated exclusively as signed numbers, so you get a range from minus 2 billion to plus 2 billion. You cannot store an unsigned 32-bit number (like CRC32 numbers and MySQL key fields defined as "int unsigned") as integer; you have to use string or floating point for those numbers. GMP is the alternative and gives you integers of unlimited length. (CRCs are Cyclical Redundancy Checks, commonly used to verify files and network transmissions. CRC32 is described in Chapter 8.)

GMP is GNU MP, an open source math package from **www.swox.com/gmp/** that can be hooked into PHP to give you integers of unlimited length. To quote from the GMP site, "GMP is a free library for arbitrary precision arithmetic, operating on signed integers, rational numbers, and floating-point numbers. There is no limit to the precision except the ones implied by the available memory in the machine GMP runs on."

To use GMP, you need to download the code, compile the code, and add the right option to PHP. GMP was not available for Windows last time I looked, so you might have to search for more information, or you might find GMP added to PHP as standard by the time you read this.

How do you use GMP? You can convert numbers and strings containing numbers to GMP numbers using **gmp_init( )** like so:

```
$gmp_number = gmp_init(1234567890987654321);
```

In most cases, PHP will automatically convert PHP integers and strings containing numbers to GMP numbers, so **gmp_init( )** is just for emergencies. You can get the same result by using the following value in GMP functions:

```
$gmp_number = "1234567890987654321";
```

The next example shows the addition of two very large numbers. Experiment with GMP and read the manual at **www.swox.com/gmp/**:

```
$gmp_number = "1234567890987654321";
print(gmp_add($gmp_number, "9999999999999999999"));
```

Floating-Point Math

Most computers use the IEEE 64-bit floating-point standard, which uses 14-digit numbers. To use larger numbers, move on to Arbitrary precision math functions or GMP.

Floating-point numbers cannot give you exact representations of some decimal numbers (instead of 8, you might get 7.9999999), so the best plan is to keep integers as integers and use floating-point numbers only where exact decimal values are not needed. When you get a number that is not exactly what you need, there are PHP functions such as **floor( )** to round down and **ceil( )** to round up, although neither will solve the problem of working out how many decimal places are accurate and how many are inaccurate. If you are working out a percentage and want an answer to one decimal place, and you start with numbers accurate to five decimal places, you can maintain good accuracy because the example 7.9999999 will round up to 8.0 if you use the function **round( )**. Problems are more likely to occur when you perform exact comparisons. For example, 7.9999999 will never be exactly equal to 8. You might have to compare floating-point numbers using something like the next example, where the floating-point numbers on both sides of the comparison are first rounded to four decimal places:

```
if(round($a, 4) == round($b, 4));
```

Arbitrary Precision Math

Arbitrary precision math is math where you make up the precision you want, and the software, in this case BCMath, struggles to cope with huge numbers by whatever means necessary. The result is that some calculations will take a little longer than the standard math functions, because the large number is split into smaller bits, calculated in parts, and then brought back together. Other functions will grind on for a long time as the math software tries to emulate a giant calculation by performing millions of little additions or subtractions.

PHP uses the BCMath library from Phil Nelson, currently released under the LGPL license that lets PHP include BCMath in a standard distribution. However, this was not always the case, so older PHPs may require an upgrade. The next example shows the **bcadd( )** function from BCMath. Two long numbers are defined in **$a** and **$b**, and they are added in **bcadd( )** without an optional precision parameter. The result, 367, is displayed in the last line:

```
$a = "256.5858957598759587500498240924820944";
$b = "111.00000000000000000000000000000000011";
$c = bcadd($a, $b);
print($c);
```

367

The default in BCMath is a precision of zero digits, so the next example has the same two numbers fed through the same **bcadd( )** function, but with a precision specification of 34. The last line shows the result to 34 decimal places:

```
$c = bcadd($a, $b, 34);
print($c);
```

367.5858957598759587500498240924820955

Immediate Solutions

Creating Data

The examples in this section show how to create data of all the types mentioned in this chapter.

String Data

String data is easy to create, and you can have fun with various ways to join strings together to create useful data. In the code that follows, **$a** accepts a string surrounded by double quotes that includes a single quote, something common in text input. **$b** accepts a string surrounded by single quotes that includes double quotes, something you want to do when your text input includes quotations. **$c** accepts a three-line poem made famous in the movie *Dead Poets Society*; the **\n** characters insert new lines, something you can do in double-quoted strings, but not single-quoted strings:

```
$a = "The cat's dinner smells fishy.";
$b = 'The cat said "meow".';
$c = "The cat\nsat on\nthe mat.";
```

Single-quoted strings accept single quotes if they are preceded by a backslash, as shown in **$d**. Because the backslash is used as a special character, a backslash requires a backslash as well, as shown in **$e**:

```
$d = 'Single quote \' in a single quoted string.';
$e = 'Backslash \\ in a single quoted string.';
```

Double-quoted strings accept double quotes if they are preceded by a backslash, as shown in **$f**. Because the backslash is used as a special character, a backslash requires a backslash as well, as shown in **$g**. Double-quoted strings accept variables for substitution, and **$i** will end up containing "The cat likes tuna for dinner.", because **$h** contains "tuna". Double-quoted strings accept **\n** to generate newline characters (used in all operating systems) and **\r** to generate return characters (used in various ways in some operating systems):

```
$f = "Double quote \" in a double quoted string.";
$g = "Backslash \\ in a double quoted string.";
```

```
$h = "tuna";
$i = "The cat likes $h for dinner.";
```

You can join two strings(**$j** and **$k**, in this example) using either of the following methods. In **$l**, two variables are joined by substitution within double quotes. In **$m**, **$j** and **$k** are joined using a period, which is PHP's string concatenation operator. The result is "catfish", a fish cats would love to catch:

```
$j = "cat";
$k = "fish";
$l = "$j$k";
$m = $j . $k;
```

You can join all the strings in an array using **implode( )** which is used in the database examples in Chapter 5 to build SQL strings. The following example array **$n** contains the words for a sentence, and **$o** gets the sentence built from the words in **$n** via **implode( )**, plus a period, which is added via concatenation. The **implode( )** function inserts a space between each word, so the result is "cats drop fur everywhere.":

```
$n = Array("cats", "drop", "fur", "everywhere");
$o = implode(" ", $n) . ".";
```

The function **serialize( )** can turn a collection of data items into a string that can be stored in a database or a session record, as described in Chapter 19. The **unserialize( )** function converts the string back to the individual elements. The following example converts array **$n** to a string, and then converts the string back to an array in **$m**:

```
$string = serialize($n);
$m = unserialize($string);
```

Integer and Floating-Point Data

Integers and floating-point numbers are created automatically. In the following example, **$p** becomes integer, and **$q** becomes floating point. If you want to force an integer to be floating point, you can, as shown in **$r**, where the specification of **(double)** overrides PHP's default type. All the types are returned by **gettype( )**, displayed by the **print** statement. The last line shows the result:

```
$p = 111;
$q = 11.1;
$r = (double) 111;
```

```
print("Types: p: " . gettype($p) . ", q: " . gettype($q)
  . ", r: " . gettype($r));

Types: p: integer, q: double, r: double
```

You can also use the function **settype( )** to force a change of type for a variable, and **settype( )** will return false if the conversion fails. The following example shows **settype( )** forcing **$p** into type double:

```
settype($p, "double");
```

However, I do not trust direct changes of type, so do not use **settype( )**. If you do want to change type, set a new variable to the new type; during testing, you can compare before and after.

Testing Data

You can test data with comparison operators and functions. The list that follows shows a set of test variables that will be used in all the tests:

```
$a = "";
$b = "0";
$c = 0;
$d = 22.55;
$e = false;
$f = null;
$g = "no new taxes";
$h = "30 May, 2002";
```

The standard comparison operator, **==**, checks that two items of data have the same value, and fails when PHP automatically converts values from one type to another, as shown in the first line in the following code, where PHP converts the string "0" to zero (or the integer zero to the string "0") before the comparison. The second line shows the new PHP4 comparison operator that checks that the variables are of the same type before the comparison and returns false if their type does not match:

```
if($b == $c)      //  true
if($b === $c)     //  false
```

The following function examples display variable attributes. The result of each function is shown as a comment, beginning with **//**, after the function (**1** is interpreted as true; the blank result is interpreted as false):

```
print(empty($a));        //    1
print(empty($b));        //    1
print(empty($c));        //    1
print(empty($d));        //
print(empty($e));        //    1
print(empty($f));        //    1
print(empty($z));        //    1 and Warning: Undefined variable: z
```

The **empty( )** function is a quick way of testing if a variable is empty, but it indicates empty for a string containing 0, which can be a problem. If a variable should not be considered empty when the variable contains 0, use the following function to detect empty. The function results are shown after the function:

```
function is_empty($field)
   {
   if(!isset($field) or !strlen($field))
      {
      return(true);
      }
   else
      {
      return(false);
      }
   }
print(is_empty($a));        //    1
print(is_empty($b));        //
print(is_empty($c));        //
print(is_empty($d));        //
print(is_empty($e));        //    1
print(is_empty($f));        //    1
print(is_empty($z));        //    1
```

Listed next are more useful functions, with results supplied as comments. If you misuse an item, PHP will often insert a comment to help you work out the error. If you place an array in a **print** statement instead of a string, PHP will replace the array with the word **array**:

```
print(gettype($a));        //    string
print(is_array($a));        //
print(is_bool($e));        //    1
```

```
print(is_double($d));    //    1
print(is_long($c));      //    1
print(is_null($f));      //    1
print(is_numeric($h));   //
print(is_numeric($b));   //    1
print(is_object($d));    //
print(is_string($g));    //    1
print(isset($b));        //    1
print(isset($z));        //         (Because there is no $z defined)
print(strlen($g));       //    12
```

The functions **is_int()** and **is_integer()** are aliases for **is_long()**, and both **is_float()** and **is_real()** are aliases for **is_double()**. The function **is_scalar()** tests if a variable is integer, floating point, string, or Boolean:

```
print(is_scalar($a));        //    1
print(is_scalar($b));        //    1
print(is_scalar($c));        //    1
print(is_scalar($d));        //    1
print(is_scalar($e));        //    1
$i = array("Coke", "Pepsi", "Jolt");
print(is_scalar($i));        //
print(is_scalar($z));        //    Warning: Undefined variable: z
```

The function **is_numeric()** ignores the 30 in **$h**, but **intval()**, discussed in the following section, will extract the 30 as an integer.

The **print_r()** and **var_dump()** functions print information about variables and could be used in diagnostics. The following example prints information about the array **$i**:

```
print_r($i);
Array ( [0] => Coke [1] => Pepsi [2] => Jolt )
```

WARNING! *if print_r() prints an array that contains a reference to the same array, print_r() will go into a print loop. If you try to print the array $GLOBAL, you will get a loop, because $GLOBAL contains an entry for $GLOBAL.*

var_dump() provides more information. The following example displays the same array as used in **print_r()** and returns a count of entries in the array and the length of each string (something that will reduce confusion if your strings have trailing spaces). **var_dump()** can go into a loop, just like **print_r()**, if it processes an array that has a reference back to the same array:

```
var_dump($i);
```

```
array(3) { [0]=> string(4) "Coke" [1]=> string(5) "Pepsi" [2]=> _
    string(4) "Jolt" }
```

var_dump( ) output can be messy if you have arrays within arrays. **var_dump( )**
includes **newline** characters in the output; the next example uses HTML tags to
force the browser to interpret the **newline** characters as breaks. The resulting
display is easier to read when displaying complex data:

```
print("<pre>");
var_dump(\$i);
print("</pre>");
```

```
array(3) {
  [0]=>
  string(4) "Coke"
  [1]=>
  string(5) "Pepsi"
  [2]=>
  string(4) "Jolt"
}
```

Converting Data

The function **intval( )** looks for integer values and chops off values after the decimal point. It can also extract integers from strings if the integer is at the front
of the string. The following example shows **intval( )** extracting values, with
the results shown at the end of the line. Note that **intval( )** extracts the 30 from
"30 May" but not from "May 30":

```
intval(22.45)              22
intval("30 May, 2002")     30
intval("May 30, 2002")     0
```

The **base_convert( )** function converts numbers from one base to another for
bases in the range of 2 to 32. Base 2 is the ever-popular binary, base 8 the occasionally used octal, base 10 the standard decimal system, and base 16 the hexadecimal system. The following examples show **base_convert( )** converting the
decimal number 30 to binary, decimal 30 to hex, hex 3 to binary, hex 0 to binary,
and hex 30 to binary, with the results of each shown in the right column. Note that

hex 0 ends up as a single 0, but the 0 in hex 30 ends up as 0000 in the result because **base_convert()** leaves off leading zeros. The truncated numbers make sense in some situations but would be a trap if the output is concatenated into a larger number:

```
print("<br>" . base_convert("30", 10, 2));        11110
print("<br>" . base_convert("30", 10, 16));       1e
print("<br>" . base_convert("3", 16, 2));         11
print("<br>" . base_convert("0", 16, 2));         0
print("<br>" . base_convert("30", 16, 2));        110000
```

The **decbin()** function is a quick way to convert a decimal number, up to 2 billion, to binary. The **bindec()** function is a quick conversion of a binary number of up to 31 bits back to decimal. The **dechex()** function is a quick way to convert a decimal number, up to 2 billion, to hexadecimal. The **hexdec()** function is a quick conversion of a hexadecimal number up to 7fffffff back to decimal. The **decoct()** and **octdec()** functions provide the same type of conversion between octal and decimal.

The **deg2rad()** function converts data from degrees to radians, and **rad2deg()** converts radians to degrees. In fact, PHP has a massive list of data conversion functions. Table 2.2 is a quick run-through of the mathematical conversions.

Table 2.2   PHP mathematical conversions.

Result	Function	Purpose
$integer_or_float =	abs($int_or_float)	Gets the absolute value
$float =	acos($another_float)	Gets the arc cosine in radians
$float =	asin($another_float)	Gets the arc sine in radians
$float =	atan($another_float)	Gets the arc tangent in radians
$float =	atan2($float_1, $float_2)	Gets the arc tangent of two variables
$float =	cos($another_float)	Gets the cosine in radians
$float =	exp($afloat)	Raises *e* to the power of **$afloat**
$float =	lcg_value()	Combined linear congruential generator
$float =	log($afloat)	Gets the natural logarithm of **$afloat**
$float =	log10($afloat)	Gets the base 10 logarithm of **$afloat**
$value =	max($array)	Gets the maximum value in the array

(continued)

Table 2.2   PHP mathematical conversions *(continued).*

Result	Function	Purpose
$value =	max($value1, $value2 ... $value*n*)	Gets the maximum value in the list of parameters
$value =	min($array)	Gets the minimum value in the array
$value =	min($value1, $value2 ... $value*n*)	Gets the minimum value in the list of parameters
$string =	number_format($float, $decimal_places, $decimal_point, $decimal_separator)	Formats a number with a decimal point and thousands separators
$float =	pi()	Gets the value of pi to about 13 places
$floata =	pow($floatx, $floaty)	Raises **$floatx** to power of **$floaty**
$float =	sin($another_float)	Gets the sine in radians
$float =	sqrt($afloat)	Gets the square root of **$afloat**
$float =	tan($another_float)	Gets the tangent in radians

NOTE: *If you want to know too much about linear congruential generators, read* **http://crypto.mat.sbg.ac.at/results/ karl/server/node3.html**.

The **max( )** and **min( )** functions can accept either an array or a list of two or more parameters (an unlimited number of parameters). The **number_format( )** function accepts one, two, or four parameters: the number you want formatted, the number of decimal places, the character you want to use for the decimal place if you want something other than a decimal point, and the character you want to use for the thousands separator if you do not want to use a comma. Some European countries that swap the decimal point and the comma would use:

```
$string = number_format($float, 2, ",", ".");
```

String Functions

String functions are fun to use in PHP and a valuable way of handling data. Most string functions handle binary data, and PHP readily converts numbers to strings for input to these functions. Table 2.3 provides a summary of string functions.

Table 2.3   PHP string functions.

Result	Function	Purpose
$string =	addcslashes($string, $characters)	Adds backslashes, C style, to any characters listed in **$characters**.
$string =	$addslashes($string)	Adds backslashes to quotes, double quotes, backslashes, and null characters, so the string can be inserted into a database via SQL.
$string =	bin2hex($string)	Returns a hexadecimal representation of the binary data in the input string.
$string =	chop($string)	Removes trailing whitespace, including spaces, **\r**, **\n**, **\t**, and **chr(13)**.
$string =	chr($integer)	Returns the ASCII character equivalent to the number (the opposite of **ord()**).
$string =	chunk_split($string, $length, $end)	Inserts the **$end** characters (default **\r\n**) into the string every **$length** (default 72). Used with base64 encoding for attachments to email.
$string =	convert_cyr_string($string, $from, $to)	Converts the string from one Cyrillic character set to another.
$array =	count_chars($string, $mode)	Returns an array containing the frequency of each character in the string. **$mode** is optional and controls what is counted.
$int =	crc32($string)	Calculates the CRC32 value of a string (see Chapter 8).
$string =	crypt($string, $key)	DES encrypts a string, using an optional key.
	echo($string)	Outputs one or more strings and is similar to **print()**.
$array =	explode($separator, $string)	Creates an array from a string split at each occurrence of **$separator**.
$string =	get_html_translation_table($table, $quote)	Returns the translation table used by **htmlspecialchars()** or **htmlentities()**. The optional **$quote** specifies how you want quotes handled.
$array =	get_meta_tags($file_name)	Returns an array of meta tag content from the named file.
$string =	hebrev($hebrew_text, $chars)	Converts Hebrew text within the input string to displayable text with **$chars** per line.
$string =	hebrevc($hebrew_text, $chars)	Version of **hebrev()** that converts **\n** to ** \n** for use in HTML.

(continued)

Table 2.3   PHP string functions *(continued)*.

Result	Function	Purpose
$string =	htmlentities($string)	Converts <, >, ', ", &, and difficult-to-display characters to HTML entities.
$string =	htmlspecialchars($string)	Converts <, >, ', ", and & to HTML entities.
$string =	implode($separator, $array)	Joins array elements to form a string. Opposite of **explode()** (see Chapter 3).
$string =	join($separator, $array)	Alias for **implode()**. Use **implode()**.
$int =	levenshtein($string, $string)	Calculates the Levenshtein distance between two strings, an indication of similarity. See also **metaphone**, **similar_text()**, and **soundex()**.
$string =	localeconv()	Returns formatting information for a location set by **setlocale()**(see Chapter 12).
$string =	ltrim($string)	Strips spaces, **\n**, **\r**, **\t**, **\v**, and **\0** from the beginning of a string.
$string =	md5()	Returns the MD5 hash of a string. (See **www.faqs.org/rfcs/rfc1321.html** for more on MD5.)
$string =	metaphone($string)	Calculates the metaphone value of a string, an indication of how the string sounds, for use in "sounds like" searches. Similar to **soundex()**.
$string =	nl2br($string)	Returns a string with HTML line breaks (** **) inserted before all **newlines** (**\n**).
$integer =	ord($string)	Returns the ASCII value of the character (the ordinal number of the character within the character set).
	parse_str($string, $array)	Parses the string into variables as if the string were a URL. If the optional second parameter is supplied, the values are stored in the array instead of the variables.
$boolean =	print($string)	Outputs a string and returns true on success, false on failure.
$boolean =	printf($format, $variables)	Prints variables formatted via the string **$format**.
$string =	quoted_printable_decode($string)	Returns a quoted-printable string converted to an 8-bit string.

(continued)

Table 2.3   PHP string functions *(continued)*.

Result	Function	Purpose
$string =	quotemeta($string)	Returns a string with backslashes in front of the meta characters . \\ + * ? [^] ($ and). **htmlspecialcharacters()** is the better choice if the string will be used in SQL, and **htmlentities()** is the better choice is the string will be used with HTML.
$string =	rtrim($string)	Strips spaces, **\n**, **\r**, **\t**, **\v**, and **\0** from the end of a string. An alias for **chop()**.
$array =	sscanf($string, $format)	Returns an array with values parsed from a string using **$format**.
$string =	setlocale($category, $string)	Sets the locale information specified by category to the value **$string**.
$int =	similar_text($string, $string)	Calculates the similarity between two strings. Similar to **levenshtein()** but uses more processing time.
$string =	soundex($string)	Calculates the soundex value of a string, an indication of how the string sounds, for use in "sounds like" searches. Similar to **metaphone()**.
$string =	sprintf($format, $variables)	A variation of **printf()** that returns a string instead of outputting directly to the page.
$int =	strcasecmp($string1, $string2)	Binary-safe, case-insensitive string comparison that returns 0 if **$string1 == $string2**, -1 if **$string1 < $string2**, or 1 if **$string1 > $string2**.
$int =	strncasecmp($string1, $string2, $length)	Variation of **strcasecmp()** that compares the strings up to length **$length**.
$int =	strchr($search, $string)	An alias for **strstr()**.
$int =	strcmp($string1, $string2)	The case-sensitive version of **strcasecmp()**.
$int =	strcoll($string1, $string2)	Version of **strcmp()** that performs comparisons modified by settings in locale.
$int =	strcspn($string, $chars)	Returns the length of the initial segment in **$string** that has no characters matching characters in **$chars**.
$string =	strip_tags($string, $tags)	Returns the string with HTML tags removed except for those listed in **$tags**.

(continued)

Table 2.3   PHP string functions *(continued).*

Result	Function	Purpose
$string =	**stripcslashes()**	Removes backslashes added with **addcslashes()**.
$string =	**stripslashes()**	Removes backslashes added with **addslashes()**. If you use **addslashes()** and then store data in MySQL, MySQL will remove the backslashes and return the data ready to use.
$int =	**stristr($search, $string)**	Case-insensitive version of **strstr()**.
$int =	**strlen($string)**	Returns the length of the string.
$int =	**strnatcasecmp($string1, $ string2)**	Case-insensitive string comparison using a *natural order* (discussed in Chapter 3) when sorting arrays.
$int =	**strnatcmp($string1, $ string2)**	Case-sensitive version of **strnatcasecmp()**.
$string =	**strncmp($string1, $string2, $length)**	Case-sensitive version of **strncasecmp()**.
$string =	**str_pad($string, $length, $pad, $mode)**	Returns **$string** padded to the right with spaces to length **$length**. If the optional **$pad** string is supplied, that is used instead of spaces. The optional **$mode** lets you switch the padding to the left or split it between both ends.
$int =	**strpos($string1, $string2)**	Returns the position of the first **$string2** with **$string1**.
$string =	**strrchr($string, $char)**	Returns the string from the last **$char** to the end of **$string**.
$string =	**str_repeat($string, $integer)**	Returns a string containing the input string repeated **$integer** times.
$string =	**strrev($string)**	Returns the string reversed character by character.
$int =	**strrpos($string, $char)**	Returns the position of the last **$char** with **$string**.
$string =	**strspn($string, $char)**	Returns the length of the first segment of **$string** that contains only characters in **$char**.
$int =	**strstr($search, $string)**	Returns the position of the first occurrence of **$search** within **$string**.

(continued)

2. Data

Table 2.3   PHP string functions *(continued)*.

Result	Function	Purpose
$string =	strtok($string, $separator)	Splits the string at **$separator** and returns one segment at a time. You are better off using **explode()**, and then looping through the array from **explode()**.
$string =	strtolower($string)	Returns the string converted to lowercase.
$string =	strtoupper($string)	Returns the string converted to uppercase.
$string =	str_replace($find, $replace, $input)	Returns a string with all occurrences of **$find** replaced by **$replace**. From PHP 4.0.5, the input and output can be an array.
$string =	strtr($string, $from, $to)	Returns a string with characters translated from **$from** to **$to**.
$string =	substr($string, $start, $length)	Returns part of a string from **$start** for length **$length**. If length is missing, it returns to the end of the string.
$int =	substr_count($string, $char)	Returns the number of **$char** in **$string**.
$string =	substr_replace($string, $replace, $start, $length)	Returns a string with the text from **$start** for **$length** replaced by **$replace**. If **$length** is not supplied, it replaces up to the end of the string.
$string =	trim($string)	Strips spaces, **\n**, **\r**, **\t**, **\v** ,and **\0** from the beginning and end of a string. Equivalent to **ltrim(rtrim())**.
$string =	ucfirst($string)	Makes the string's first character uppercase; useful for formatting sentences.
$string =	ucwords($string)	Change the first character of each word to uppercase; useful for formatting headings.
$string =	wordwrap($string, $length, $char)	Returns the string with **newline**s inserted to make the string wrap into lines of length **$length** when printed. The default is 72 characters per line if **$length** is not supplied. If **$char** is specified, **$char** replaces the **newline**.

rand(), srand(), and microtime()

The **rand( )** function provides a random number. The **mt_rand( )** function is supposed to supply a better random number, as explained at **www.math.keio.ac.jp/ ~matumoto/emt.html**. The **mt_rand( )** function is also faster, although speed is rarely of importance unless you are using **rand( )** several times per page.

Both **rand( )** and **mt_rand( )** require a *seed*, or a starting point. The following line of code is the way to supply the seed. With **rand( )**, you must run **srand( )** once before the first use of **rand( )** in your script, but not anywhere else in the same script. With **mt_rand( )**, you must run **mt_srand( )** once with the same input:

```
$srand((double) microtime() * 1000000);
```

Both **rand( )** and **mt_rand( )** accept range parameters. If you want to find the maximum value that can be used in the range, you can get it from **getrandmax( )** or **mt_getrandmax( )**. On an NT workstation using PHP 4.0.5, **getrandmax( )** returned 32767.

If you want to get a random number between 1 and 99, use the following code. When you leave out the second parameter, the maximum value, **rand( )** uses the maximum returned by **getrandmax( )**. When you leave out the first parameter, **rand( )** uses zero. In most cases you will want a specific range of values, so you will specify both parameters:

```
$integer_number = rand(1, 99);
```

If you want a number between 1.00 and 2.00, you can ask for a range from 100 to 200, and then divide by 100. If you want a number larger than that returned by **getrandmax( )**, you can get several random numbers and add them together or multiply them together.

Have another look at **microtime( )**, the ideal script timing function. **microtime( )** returns two numbers separated by a space, such as 0.62186100 988888118. The second number is a Unix time in seconds, and the first is the fraction of a second. The following is the code to convert the result of **microtime( )** to a usable date and time. The **explode( )** function separates the two fields based on the space, **date( )** formats the Unix time into a date and time, **substr( )** removes the leading zero on the micro portion of the time, and the second **date( )** supplies the "pm":

```
$mstart = explode(" ", $m);
print("The date and exact time is:<br>"
   . date("l F j, Y h:i:s", $mstart[1])
   . substr($mstart[0], 1)
   . date(" a", $mstart[1]));
```

```
The date and exact time is:
Thursday May 3, 2001 09:08:38.62186100 pm
```

You can run **microtime()** before and after a process to time the process but remember two little things. Displaying the time adds time to the process, so at the start of the process, save the **microtime()** value to a variable. Then perform any time calculations or display after you save the second **microtime()** value at the end of the process. Also note that the size of the two parts of **microtime()** exceeds the normal integer range for PHP, so use either BCMath or GMP functions to perform the calculation.

The next code shows BCMath subtracting **microtime()** value **$a** from **microtime()** value **$b**. The **explode()** and **substr()** functions are the same as before. The parts of the array are then joined to make string inputs for **bcsub()**, and the result is printed:

```
$a_array = explode(" ", $a);
$b_array = explode(" ", $b);
$a_array[0] = substr($a_array[0], 1);
$b_array[0] = substr($b_array[0], 1);
$a_string = $a_array[1] . $a_array[0];
$b_string = $b_array[1] . $b_array[0];
print(bcsub($b_string, $a_string));
```

```
0.00325400
```

Calculating the Date or Time

PHP has a rich variety of date and time functions, which are summarized in Table 2.4. I will cover performing date/time calculations using the values from these functions or for formatting with these functions.

The Unix timestamp is the number of seconds from January 1, 1970, and will run up to some time in 2037, sort of like a Unix Y2.037K. (If you do not remember, some computers had date systems that would not handle the year 2000, so the problem was called the Y2K problem. Unix will need the same type of change before 2037.) You can perform calculations on the Unix timestamp by adding or subtracting seconds.

Suppose you want to add 20 hours to the current time. 20 hours is 1,200 minutes or 72,000 seconds, so you could add that number to **time()** with the next simple

Table 2.4   PHP date and time functions.

Function	Purpose
checkdate()	Checks that a Gregorian date is correct
date()	Returns the local date/time formatted
getdate()	Gets the local date/time as an array
gettimeofday()	Gets the current time as an array
gmdate()	Same as **date()**, but uses GMT instead of local date
gmmktime()	Converts a date to a Unix timestamp
gmstrftime()	Formats a GMT date and time
localtime()	Gets the local time as an array of parts
microtime()	Gets a Unix timestamp with fractions of a second
mktime()	Gets a Unix timestamp from a date
strftime()	Same as **gmstrftime()**, using local time
time()	Gets a Unix timestamp
strtotime()	Converts text date/time to a Unix timestamp

code sample. The result could be formatted with **date()**, just like any other date/time:

```
$new_time = time() + 72000;
```

What if you want to add 3 days, 4 hours, and 22 minutes to the current time? The **strtotime()** function converts text dates and times to a Unix timestamp, which can then be added or subtracted from **time()**. You can use this function for any sort of date/time calculation using Unix timestamps. The following line of code sets **$seconds** to a value that can be added to the value from **time()** or a value from a database. The **strtotime()** function can also perform some calculations for you; the second line of code shows **strtotime()** adding the 3 days, 4 hours, and 22 minutes to "now", which is the **strtotime()** equivalent to **time()**:

```
$seconds = strtotime("+3 days 4 hours 22 minutes");
$seconds = strtotime("now +3 days 4 hours 22 minutes");
```

The **strtotime()** function currently requires dates in the American format of mm/dd/yyyy, as in 03/04/2002, and can perform calculations from dates as shown in the following example. The second line shows a **print()** statement formatting the Unix timestamp with **date()**, and the last line is the result:

```
$seconds = strtotime("03/04/2002 +3 days 4 hours 22 minutes");
print(date("l F j, Y  H:i:s", $seconds));
Thursday March 7, 2002 04:22:00
```

Easter

If you are looking for the date of Easter between 1970 and 2037, **easter_date( )** is perfect. The function produces a Unix timestamp you can feed in to a date formatting function, such as **date( )**. You can print the result as shown in the next example, complete with the result on the second line. The **easter_date( )** function returns the time of midnight on that date and is limited to the years covered by a Unix timestamp:

```
print(date ("F d, Y", easter_date(2003)));
April 20, 2003
```

For years outside this range, use **easter_days( )** to get the number of days between March 21 and Easter for the given year. Then use the appropriate date functions to calculate the date. In the following example, **easter_days( )** returns the number of days from March 21 till Easter, **gregoriantojd( )** supplies a Julian day count for March 21 of the same year, the next line adds the two results together and then feeds the number to **jdtogregorian( )** to get a Gregorian date for Easter, and the following line prints the result, which is 3/28/1703. The result is a messy date format that does not let you distinguish between 4/1/2002 and 4/1/2002 where one is an American date in April and the other is a European date in January. Line five in the code splits the Gregorian date into components. Line six defines an array of month names with the entry zero set to blank, so each month name lines up with the month number. Line nine replaces the month number, in **$m**, with the month name. The last line prints the result, which is the internationally understandable March 28, 1703:

```
$e = easter_days(1703);
$j = gregoriantojd(3, 21, 1703);
$g = jdtogregorian($e + $j);
print("<br>" . $g);
list($m, $d, $y) = explode("/", $g);
$months = array("", "January", "February", "March", "April", "May",
    "June", "July", "August", "September", "October", "November",
    "December");
$m = $months[$m];
print("<br>" . $m . " " . $d . ", " . $y);
```

Chapter 3

Arrays

In Depth

PHP arrays are easy to use, provide great flexibility, and have few traps. You can use PHP arrays like mini databases in memory, as there is a rich range of functions for sorting and processing arrays. Data stored in text files, print files, XML files, and databases can be loaded into an array and then processed without disrupting the original file. I will step through the building of simple lists in arrays, the building of complex lists, and all the ways to process and sort the various lists.

Sometimes you get faster performance by replacing complex SQL with a simple select and a little in-memory processing. If you have not used SQL, Chapter 5 includes examples for use with MySQL and PostgreSQL. Coriolis also publishes *SQL Server 2000 Black Book* for SQL Server users; and if you really want to know way too much about SQL, there is *SQL: The Complete Reference* by Groff and Weinburg (McGraw-Hill). You can perform excessively complex actions in SQL. Way back when I was young, single, and stupid, and IBM employed a young, single, beautiful, female, database guru, I sent her a romantic poem written entirely in SQL. The SQL worked but required an unusual database structure.

Now that I have outgrown being young and graduated from single, I tend to use far simpler SQL and let PHP take care of formatting data. In SQL, you can and should select the minimum data so that the database can reduce disk IO. You can sort data into a useful sequence, if you need the data in just one sequence; the database might be able to save a sort by retrieving the data in that sequence via an index. If you have a page reading the same data several times, and the only difference is the sequence of the data, you can read the data into an array and then use one of the PHP array sort functions to get the other sequences.

You can also use SQL to transform data and perform calculations using a variety of functions, but the range of functions varies across databases. Also, where two databases have the same function, they may use a different name and have the parameters in different sequences. This is another good reason to get the data from the database with the minimum SQL and transform the data in PHP.

Simple Arrays

Let's start with single-dimension arrays. They work like the simple lists you write when you go shopping, and array functions are easily applied to single-dimension arrays. The section "Multiple Dimensions" tackles multiple-dimension arrays; you can consider multiple-dimension arrays as "arrays of arrays" and often work through multiple-dimension arrays as a series of nested single-dimension arrays.

The World's Simplest Array

To begin with, here is a simple array:

```
$a = "abc";
```

In PHP, strings are arrays of characters, which you can access like this:

```
print($a[0] . " " . $a[1] . " " . $a[2]);
```

The resulting string, in this case, would be:

```
a b c
```

Elements in an array are accessed by adding the element number in square brackets **[ ]** after the array name.

Arrays Are Numbered from Zero

In some languages, elements in an array are numbered starting from 1, or you can set the base; but PHP array elements start from 0 by default and let you set the base, so they can begin anywhere. You can create a new array or a new entry in an existing array by simply typing something like the following:

```
$a[] = "fruit";
```

Then you can access the array like this:

```
print($a[0]);
```

The result would be:

```
fruit
```

You can create an array starting from 1 (or any other number) by inserting the base number, as follows:

```
$b[1] = "pear";
```

You can create subsequent entries with empty brackets, as shown next. The value **apple** will end up in $b[2]:

```
$b[] = "apple";
```

PHP stores only the entries you create. So, for example, if a fast-food chain started numbering its branches at 1, opened a lot of branches, and then had to subsequently close down most of its branches, its branch location list might look like the following:

```
$branch[25] = "Boston";
$branch[42] = "Sydney";
$branch[98] = "London";
$branch[145] = "Wahroonga";
```

No space is wasted on nonexistent elements. Of course, that also means you cannot merely step through the elements using a simple loop starting at 0 and going to the maximum element; you would need to use some smarter techniques, like the **while( )** loop mentioned in the section "The Array Pointer."

Array Elements Can Be Named Anything

Array elements can be named instead of numbered, making them types of arrays referred to as *associative arrays*. Building on the fast food chain example from the previous section, a branch staff count could look like the following:

```
$branch_staff["Boston"] = 22;
$branch_staff["Sydney"] = 45;
$branch_staff["London"] = 18;
$branch_staff["Wahroonga"] = 72;
```

You could mix both arrays, like this:

```
$silly_array[25] = "Boston";
$silly_array[42] = "Sydney";
$silly_array[98] = "London";
$silly_array[145] = "Wahroonga";
$silly_array["Boston"] = 22;
$silly_array["Sydney"] = 45;
$silly_array["London"] = 18;
$silly_array["Wahroonga"] = 72;
```

When you get a plain array from a database function, such as **mysql_fetch_row( )**, you get an array in which each field is in a numbered entry representing the field's position in the table or the SQL select statement. If you switch from **mysql_fetch_row( )** to **mysql_fetch_array( )**, you get an associative array in which each field is present as both a numbered entry and an entry created with the field name.

If you have a SQL statement containing "select country, city from cities" and the first entry is for Sydney, **mysql_fetch_row( )** creates the same array that you would create with the following:

```
$array[0] = "Australia";
$array[1] = "Sydney";
```

For the same SQL, **mysql_fetch_array( )** would create the array shown next. The numbered entries are separate entries from the named entries, so they can be processed and changed without affecting the named entries. If you happen to write SQL that produces duplicate field names, only the last occurrence of the field will be in a named array entry, whereas all occurrences will be in the numbered entries:

```
$array[0] = "Australia";
$array["country"] = "Australia";
$array[1] = "Sydney";
$array["city"] = "Sydney";
```

In effect, all PHP arrays are associative arrays. Even the normal numbered entries work like associative indexes. Associative arrays are so popular and easy to work with that many PHP functions are moving toward associative arrays as the main form of array usage. For example, **mysql_fetch_array( )** gained an optional second parameter to produce named entries, without numbered entries, and the new parameter was used so often that someone added **mysql_fetch_assoc( )** to create just the named entries without having to type in the second parameter.

Array Creation Functions

array( ) creates a normal array or an associative from a list, and **explode( )** creates an array from a delimited string. Array creation functions are demonstrated in "Creating Arrays" in the "Immediate Solutions" section.

Potential Problems

I found only two problems with PHP arrays: sorting and case sensitivity. Sorting problems, like sorting data without sorting keys, can be avoided by working through examples of all the sort functions before selecting the function you need. All the sort functions are demonstrated in this chapter's "Immediate Solutions" section.

Case sensitivity is a problem if you are moving from a case-insensitive language to PHP. Some languages are case-sensitive and give you options for turning off case sensitivity when needed; other languages are case-insensitive everywhere.

PHP has a curious mixture in the middle, where function names are not case sensitive, but variable names are. In arrays, the element keys are case-sensitive. The following array elements are all different entries in the array because the array element keys have characters in different cases:

```
$branch_staff["Boston"] = 22;
$branch_staff["boston"] = 45;
$branch_staff["bosTon"] = 18;
```

Don't just believe me; test everything for yourself. You can demonstrate the case-sensitivity of arrays by printing the array using the following code. The practice will help you remember case sensitivity, and it's an easy way to investigate arrays:

```
reset($branch_staff);
while(list($k, $v) = each($branch_staff))
    {
    print("<br>key: " . $k . ", value: " . $v);
    }
```

The code moves the array pointer (explained in the "Array Pointer" section) to the front of the array; then **each( )** steps through the array elements, returning each element, and **list( )** saves the element's value and key in variables for the **print( )** statement. The result is the following:

```
key: Boston, value: 22
key: boston, value: 45
key: bosTon, value: 18
```

If you need to store a list of mixed-case words or names, PHP arrays will let you do it. When case is not important and is likely to lead to duplicates, I suggest converting all the keys to lowercase, using **strtolower( )**, or documenting the case definition next to the array definition. In the example using city names, I would translate all the keys to lowercase if they are never used for display, or document the use of the initial capitals, if the keys will be used for display.

Multiple Dimensions

PHP arrays accept any number of dimensions and can have any number of elements in every dimension. In fact, a huge array would make your script run out of memory before you ever hit a PHP limit. PHP's option file, php.ini, contains one setting you need to increase for large arrays. Change **memory_limit** from the default 8MB to something several times the size of your largest array.

You can create and refer to multiple dimensions by just adding extra references inside square brackets, as in the following example. The **$travel_comment** array is indexed by country, state, and town. I am creating one entry for Carmel, California:

```
$travel_comment["USA"]["California"]["Carmel"] =
   "Scenic town";
```

You can create as many array dimensions as you need to keep your data structured in useful ways, and the example has the travel comments structured by country, state, and city. You could add suburb, street, building, restaurant, and barista, if you wanted to guide people to exactly the right coffee maker in each restaurant in every building in Carmel, although I doubt doing so would help them find coffee as good as that in San Francisco or Sydney. (If you do not know the term *barista*, visit **www.scaa.org/barista/** and read about the formal certification process for people who operate espresso machines.)

Elements in an array can be anything, including other arrays, so that you can build an array with an asymmetrical structure. Consider, for instance, an array of cities in which larger cities are classified by municipal areas and smaller cities have just one entry. You might want to list population figures by area when there are areas and by city when a city does not contain areas. The following example inserts some made-up population figures into an array of areas in Sydney, Australia:

```
$Sydney["Chatswood"] = 51,000;
$Sydney["Parramatta"] = 145,000;
$Sydney["Wahroonga"] = 12,000;
```

Add to that an invented list of populations, classified by area, for San Francisco, as follows:

```
$San_Francisco["Castro"] = 55,000;
$San_Francisco["Chinatown "] = 50,000;
```

To include **$Sydney** and **$San_Francisco** in an array containing populations by city, you would enter them as follows:

```
$city["Dayuanjiadun"] = 5,000;
$city["Islip"] = 200;
$city["San Francisco"] = $San_Francisco;
$city["Sydney"] = $Sydney;
$city["Ulaanbatar"] = 38,000
```

When you access the **$city** array, processing is a little bit tricky because you have to check each value to see if that value is also an array. If you had to add up the populations from all the cities, you could use a recursive function to add the numbers at the top level and to call itself when a value is an array. See "Looping through Multidimensional Arrays" in the Immediate Solutions section for more information.

The Array Pointer

The *array pointer* is a feature that is available in only a few languages, and PHP has the best implementation I found in over 30 languages. It lets you keep track of where you are when stepping through an array. Each array has a separate array pointer, so you can work on any number of arrays completely independent of one another. Several functions let you use the array pointer to aid navigation through an array.

When you create an array by adding elements, the array pointer points to the last element added so you can add another element to the end of the array. When the array is built, you will want to go back to the start of the array so you can read the array.

reset() sets the array pointer back to the start of the array, and you should use this command before stepping though an array of unknown status. An array's pointer is set back to the start of the array when the array is sorted, and copies of an array are created with the array pointer at the start of the array. For example, when **$y** is an array and you set **$x = $y**, **$x** will have its array pointer set to the start of the array.

When you pass arrays to functions, the default is to pass by value, which means the function gets a copy of the array, and the copy has its array pointer set to the start of the array. If you pass the array by reference, the array retains the original pointer in an unknown position.

NOTE: *You can pass a variable to a function by prefixing the variable with* **&**, *which is described in Chapter 10.*

You can find out the current position of an array pointer with the function **current()**, and you can move an array pointer with the functions **next()**, **prev()**, and **end()**.

The function **each()** returns the key and value of the current element in an array, and then moves the array's pointer to the next element. **each()** lets you step though an array using a simple **while** loop. To loop through the array using **while()**, first reset the array to make sure the pointer is at the first element, and then request each element using **each()**. The **each()** function returns the key of the element and the value of the element, and then performs a **next( )** to move the pointer to the next element, as in:

```
reset($array);
while(list($k, $v) = each($array))
    {
    }
```

In this example, **list( )** saves the element key and element value as separate variables so you can process the results easily. If the array has multiple dimensions, the variable **$v** will be an array containing a subset of **$array**, and the array pointer for **$v** will be at the start of **$v**.

Sorting Arrays

You can sort PHP arrays just about any way you want to, with functions that sort in any of the following ways:

- By value

- By key

- In straight alphabetical order

- In various "natural" and special orders

NOTE: *The term* natural *is used for sorting techniques designed to emulate the way a human being would sort things when a straight alphabetical sort does not produce the most logical result, and includes special processing for things like numerical suffixes on names. See the "Immediate Solutions" section for detailed examples on* **sort()**, **rsort()**, **asort()**, **arsort()**, **ksort()**, *and* **natsort()**.

One thing to watch for is the way in which sort functions handle the issue of case. Standard sorts treat each character as a binary byte containing anything; therefore, lowercase characters are sorted differently than uppercase characters. **natsort( )** and **natcasesort( )** are two sort functions that work in a different way because they contain extra code to process the data before the sorting of the data. **natcase( )** adds code to correct the sorting of numbers within names, and **natcasesort( )** enhances **natsort( )** with code to remove case sensitivity. Most of the other sort functions sort as follows. The list

```
a
A
b
B
c
C
```

would sort into:

```
A
B
C
a
b
c
```

Some of the array sort functions sort the values in an array (dropping associated keys and resetting numerical keys), whereas others sort the values by key, thus retaining the key associations in the array. This gives you heaps of organization options that let you store and sort data any way you like, almost like a relational database. Suppose you want to store a list of friends and information about them, and then display the data all sorts of ways online. To do this, you would first make a list of friends (just use a few for testing, but imagine you are planning to list all 500 people your parents invited to your wedding plus the 200 people you really wanted to invite):

```
$friend[] = "Cate Blanchett";
$friend[] = "Nicole Kidman";
$friend[] = "Kate Beckinsale";
```

Now add their telephone numbers. The original array makes little sense, but an associative array based on the friends' names makes more sense:

```
$friend["Cate Blanchett"] = "555 111 1111";
$friend["Nicole Kidman"] = "555 222 2222";
$friend["Kate Beckinsale"] = "555 333 3333";
```

Now you want to add their birthdays, so you make a two-dimensional array:

```
$friend["Cate Blanchett"] = array("number" =>"555 111 1111",
   "birth" => "1969-05-14");
$friend["Nicole Kidman"] = array("number" =>"555 222 2222",
   "birth" => "1967-06-20");
$friend["Kate Beckinsale"] = array("number" =>"555 333 3333",
   "birth" => "1973-07-26");
```

Next, you decide to sort the list by birthday, so you can call them on the right day and list them by telephone area code (and so you can call them off-peak). Why stop at one array? You could load the data as multiple arrays, write code to split the data in to multiple arrays, or make copies of the data before sorting. The current two-dimensional list could be split in two with the following:

```
while(list($k, $v) = each($friend))
    {
$birthday[$v["birth"]] = $k;
$number[$v["number"]] = $k;
    }
```

Now you have one list you can sort by birthday and another you can sort by telephone number. You can cross-reference both, because you know the names will match exactly. The next example assumes you know the telephone number but not the name or birthday (I was a bachelor once and often wondered what to do with telephone numbers that had no name attached). The example is as follows:

```
$b = array_search($number["555 333 3333"], $birthday);
```

$number returns a value that happens to be a name. **array_search( )** searches for that value in the other array and then returns the key, which is the birthday.

If you are processing one list lots of ways in one page, consider which fields will end up as keys in the arrays, and if it would be easier to have multiple arrays with one value each. Also, consider how you want to step through the arrays.

Push, Pop, Pad, and Merge

Many new PHP functions let you perform weird actions with or on arrays. I will give you a quick overview of the latest functions in this section.

Push and Pop

The **array_push( )** and **array_pop( )** commands are for people who like stack-based code. You use an array like a memory stack, meaning you use **array_push( )** to put things on the stack, and then use **array_pop( )** to pop the items back off. The first use that comes to mind are preference-based systems in which people select something like a holiday and add options on top. Subsequent code pops the options off as the options fail the selection criteria. The code might select all the flights to Port Douglas based on cost, and then, starting with the cheapest, delete the ones that have too many stops, followed by the ones that do not serve vegetarian meals. The following code shows array **$a** created by adding one element at a time, and array **$b** created in fewer lines of code using **array_push( )** to add a list. Both **$a** and **$b** end up with the same contents:

```
$a[] = "Bali";
$a[] = "Fiji";
$a[] = "Hawaii";
```

```
$b[] = "Bali";
array_push($b, "Fiji", "Hawaii");
```

The following example shows arrays **$a** and **$b** returning and losing the last element of each array using standard array functions and **array_pop( )**. **$x** is set to the value of the last element in **$a** by function **end( )**, and then **key( )** returns the key of the last element, and **unset( )** deletes the element of that key from **$a**. **array_pop( )** achieves the same result in one line of code. **$y** ends up with the same value as **$x**:

```
$x = end($a);
unset($a[key($a)]);
$y = array_pop($b);
```

You do not have to use **array_push( )** first, and then **array_pop( )**. You can build the array in any sequence, then push or pop, then sort, then push or pop, until you have exactly the array you want.

Pad

Suppose you have a top-10 list of something important, but you have only nine entries, or seven, or four. How do you guarantee 10 entries? The **array_pad( )** function does just that. You supply **array_pad( )** with the name of the array, the number of entries, and the value for the entries created by **array_pad( )**. If your top-10 list of sexy men is short a few entries, use:

```
$sexy_men = array_pad($sexy_men, 10, "Peter Moulding");
```

Why use **array_pad( )** to guarantee 10 entries (or any other number of entries) in an array? Imagine a top-10 list that will be placed in a voting form (using forms code from Chapter 9). You want to insert the five or six Oscar nominations for best movie, plus let people fill out the list with their own choices. The manual process is to loop through the array of nominations, create a form entry for every nomination, and then calculate how many empty entries are needed then create all the empty form entries with a second loop. By padding the original array with empty entries, you need just one loop.

Merge

The **array_merge( )** command merges two or more arrays. It uses one technique for associative arrays and another for ordinary arrays. Ordinary arrays with integer keys are appended together and then resequenced, whereas associative arrays are merged entry by entry, and a new entry with the same key as an existing entry replaces the existing entry. The following code shows two arrays, **$friends** and **\$more**, merged via **array_merge( )** into **\$x** and conventional **while( )** loops into **\$y**. Both **\$x** and **\$y** end up with the same entries: In both cases the second **Tom** will replace the first **Tom**, but the code using **array_merge( )** takes less time to write and less time to process:

```
$friends["Adam"] = "Hawaii";
$friends["Tom"] = "London";
$more["Alice"] = "Copenhagen";
$more["Tom"] = "Perth";

$x = array_merge($friends, $more);

while(list($k, $v) = each($friends))
    {
    $y[$k] = $v;
    }
while(list($k, $v) = each($more))
    {
    $y[$k] = $v;
    }
```

Immediate Solutions

Creating Arrays from Lists with **array()**

The function **array()** creates an array from a list. A simple numbered array can be built with something like the following:

```
$fruit = array("apple", "banana", "feijoa");
```

You can also build an associative array with **array()**. Note the use of **=>** to indicate the assignment of a value to a key in the following:

```
$fruit_weight = array("apple" => 35, "banana" => 29, "feijoa" => 25);
```

array() and the other functions described in this section can be nested to build multidimensional arrays, as shown by **$carbohydrate** and **$protein** in this example:

```
$carbohydrate = array("fruit" => array("apple", "banana", "feijoa"),
    "vegetable" => array("carrot", "potato"));
$protein = array("vegetable" => array("potato", "beans", "lentils"),
    "deadthings" => array("cow", "sheep"));
```

You can also use arrays within **array()** to build multidimensional arrays as shown in the following example:

```
$lunch = array("carbohydrate" => $carbohydrate, "protein" => $protein);
```

Now you can type any list as an array ready for processing and merge lists in to multidimensional arrays reflecting the structure of your data. Chapters 5 and 6 show you how to read your lists from databases, and some of the Immediate Solutions that follow show useful examples of processing your arrays.

Creating Arrays from Strings with **explode()**

The **explode()** function chops up a string (based on a delimiter) and makes each part of the string an entry in an array. In this example, the string has a comma in between the name of each fruit. The first parameter in **explode()** is the delimiter, and the second parameter is the string, as shown next. The **explode( )** code is followed by code showing the entries that go into the array:

```
$fruit = explode(",", "apple,banana,feijoa");

$fruit[] = "apple";
$fruit[] = "banana";
$fruit[] = "feijoa";
```

Creating Strings from Arrays with **implode()**

The **implode( )** function does the reverse of **explode( )** and joins all the elements of an array into a string optionally separated by a delimiter. In the following example, you can build SQL from lists of fields in arrays, a process that can be applied to building any string-based list, including dynamically generated functions, coordinated lists for graphics, and lists within HTML and XML tags.

Basic SQL

To illustrate building SQL, the basic SQL will be a **select** statement of the form shown next. The parts that lend themselves to lists are the field list after **select**, the condition list after **where**, the field list after **order by**, and the field list after **group by**:

```
select a, b, c, d from x where a = 'z' order by b, c group by b
```

NOTE: *If you're not familiar with SQL (Structured Query Language), it lets you select data from tables. When the table contains many fields, you want to select just those fields you need using a command such as **select fielda, fieldb**, and so on. If the table has few fields, it is just as fast to select every field using **select ***. If there are no **where** parameters, **order by** parameters, or **group by** parameters, you just leave out the whole clause.*

The example table contains a list of furniture for a local shop that provides supplies for home decorators. To make shopping simple, the shop organized everything by room. The table is named **furniture** and contains the following fields:

- room
- type
- style
- color
- brand

- height
- width
- depth
- weight
- material
- on_order
- shipping_time
- assembled
- options

select

First, you need the selection list, so you can build the **select** field list for your SQL. You need your list as an array for ease of processing. In this example, use the following array named **$select**:

```
$select[] = "room";
$select[] = "color";
$select[] = "height";
$select[] = "width";
$select[] = "depth";
```

where

Next, you need the **where** list so you can select the right rows from the database table. If you are shopping for shelves to store all your most important books, you need bookshelves, so create the following array named **$where**:

```
$where["type"] = "bookshelf";
```

order by

You want the list of bookshelves ordered by color, height, and depth so you can select the right wood color, and choose taller, deeper bookshelves to store really large books. **$order** contains the list of sort fields and will be built in to the **order by** list in the SQL:

```
$order[] = "color";
$order[] = "height";
$order[] = "depth";
```

group by

There is no need to split the list into groups, so there is no **group by** list for the bookshelf selection SQL. The SQL build code has to check if a **$group** array exists before using **$group** to build a **group by** list.

Building the SQL

Step 1 of building the SQL is to build the **select** part of the SQL in the string **$sql**, checking that the **select** list exists, and separating each entry with a comma and a space. If the **select** list does not exist, you want to use "*" as the default to select every field in the table. If **$select** is not an array, assume it is a preformatted list built in some other part of the code:

```
$sql = "select ";
if(isset($select))
    {
    if(is_array($select))
        {
        $sql .= implode(", ", $select);
        }
    else
        {
        $sql .= $select;
        }
    }
else
    {
    $sql.= "*";
    }
```

The code first defines the string **$sql** to contain the SQL, and inserts the keyword **select**. It then checks to determine if an array named **$select** exists and inserts "*" if there is no array. If **$select** exists, the code decides if it is an array using **is_array( )**, and then builds the selection list using **implode( )**.

The first parameter in **implode( )** is the separator; it can be any string, including a zero-length string if there is no need for a separator. The second parameter for **implode( )** is the array, which can be either a standard array or an associative array, because only the values in the array are used.

The **select** command is followed by the **from** clause of the SQL, and in the simple example, the **from** clause only ever names the one table listed here:

```
$sql .= " from furniture";
```

The **where** list is a little more complicated, because the list is an associative array, and the SQL needs both the array value and the array key. Luckily, all the values will be joined by **and**, in this case, so you can still use a simple **implode( )** to join multiple **where** values.

To keep the code simple by keeping this section similar to the **select** code, you should first convert the **where** list array from an associative value pair array to a simple array containing a list of strings so you can then use the list of strings in **implode( )**.

The following is the code to step through the **$where** array and join the keys with the values into another array named **$where_list**. First, check that **$where** exists, and then reset **$where** to place the array pointer at the start of the array. Next, step through the array. If **$where** is not an array, you should assume that it is a fully formatted **where** string and pass it through as a string, as in:

```
if(isset($where))
    {
    if(is_array($where))
        {
        reset($where);
        while(list($k, $v) = each($where))
            {
            $where_list[] = $k . " = '" . $v . "'";
            }
        }
    else
        {
        $where_list = $where;
        }
    }
```

This code is similar to the **$select** processing code previously shown and the following **order by** and **group by** code in that this code checks that the variable exists before using the variable, uses **is_array( )** to detect if the variable is an array, and treats the variable as a single string entry if it is not an array. The main difference is the **while( )** loop that steps through the **$where** array and creates **$where_list**, an array containing string entries that each contain one SQL selection condition that will be joined by **and** connectors in the **where** part of the SQL.

NOTE: *Some databases do not like single quotes (' ') around integers, so your **where** code might need to check the field type before creating the **$where_list** entry for a field.*

You can now convert **$where_list** to SQL using code similar to the **select** list code. Unlike the previous **select** list in the SQL, there is no default of ***;** to replace a missing list. The default for the **where** list is to leave out this segment of the SQL. Like the **select** code, this code assumes **$where_list** is a fully formatted list, if **$where_list** is not an array, as in:

```
if(isset($where_list))
   {
   $sql .= " where ";
   if(is_array($where_list))
      {
      $sql .= implode(" and ", $where_list);
      }
   else
      {
      $sql .= $where_list;
      }
   }
```

Next, create the **order by** SQL from **$order** using code similar to the **$select** processing code and the last part of the **$where_list** code. The default for the **order by** list is to leave out this segment of the SQL. Like the **select** and **where** code, this code assumes **$order** is a fully formatted list if **$order** is not an array, as in:

```
if(isset($order))
   {
   $sql.= " order by ";
   if(is_array($order))
      {
      $sql .= implode(", ", $order);
      }
   else
      {
      $sql .= $order;
      }
   }
```

The **group by** SQL is created from **$group** using code almost the same as that used for **$order**. The default for the **group by** list is to leave out this segment of the SQL. Like the previous code, this code assumes **$group** is a fully formatted list if **$group** is not an array, as in:

```
if(isset($group))
   {
   $sql .= " group by ";
```

```
if(is_array($group))
   {
   $sql .= implode (", ", $group);
   }
else
   {
   $sql .= $group;
   }
}
```

When you print **$sql**, you should get the following:

```
select room, color, height, width, depth from furniture
where type = 'bookshelf' order by color, height, depth
```

Specifying a Range of Elements with range()

When you want a list of numbers in an array ready for printing on labels or some other orderly process, **range()** builds the list starting at the number specified in the first parameter and ending at the number specified in the second parameter, as shown in the first line of the next code block. The remaining code shows what you would have to type if you did not have **range()**, followed by the array displayed in Figure 3.1:

```
$labels = range(5, 10);

for($i = 5; $i <= 10; $i++)
   {
   $labels[] = $i;
   }
```

Key	Value
0	5
1	6
2	7
3	8
4	9
5	10

Figure 3.1   Values in an array built by **range()**.

Specifying a Key Range with **range()** and **array_flip()**

When you want a list of numbers in an array ready for printing labels, such as asset register labels, you may want to put the range in the array key, so you can then add something (such as a date) as the value. **array_flip()** swaps values and keys in an array, moving the range of numbers built by **range()** into the key. The following code expands that in the "Specifying a Range of Elements with **range()**" section, creating the range in a work array, and then flipping the array into **$labels,** with the range in the key. After the two lines of **range()** and **array_flip** code, the code you would have had to write before the invention of **array_flip()** is listed. Figure 3.2 shows the resulting array:

```
$numbers = range(5, 10);
$labels = array_flip($numbers);

while(list($k, $v) = each($numbers))
    {
    $labels[$v] = $k;
    }
```

Key	Value
5	0
6	1
7	2
8	3
9	4
10	5

Figure 3.2   Values in an array built by **range()** and **array_flip()**.

Removing Duplicate Array Values with **array_flip()**

If you have a list in an array and want to remove duplicate values, consider using **array_flip()** twice, as shown in the code here. The sample array has **keyboard** entered twice:

```
$labels[] = "keyboard";
$labels[] = "mouse";
$labels[] = "keyboard";
$labels[] = "monitor";
$x = array_flip(\$labels);
$labels = array_flip($x);
ksort(\$labels);
```

Figure 3.3 shows the array before and after two flips. You can see that just one keyboard is left. The first flip moves the key to the value and the value to the key. As both keyboards have the same value, they end up going into the same key; the entry for the second keyboard replaces the entry for the first keyboard. When the second flip occurs, the array is back to its normal form, but in a different sequence than the original, so I added the **ksort()** to sort the array back to the original sequence. **Ksort()** keeps keys and values paired while sorting by key.

Key	Value		Key	Value
0	keyboard		1	mouse
1	mouse		2	keyboard
2	keyboard		3	monitor
3	monitor			

Figure 3.3   Array before (left) and after (right) two **array_flip()**s.

Randomizing an Array with **shuffle()**

Suppose you have a CD to play, but you are tired of listening to the tracks in the same sequence every time. Similarly, if you have a Web site with a list of banners for display, you might want to make the banners appear in a random sequence in order to generate fresh interest. The **shuffle()** function is the magic function to use to create a random list.

First you need a list to shuffle. Here is list of tracks from a blues CD:

```
$tracks[] = "Smokestack Lightnin'";
$tracks[] = "My Babe";
$tracks[] = "High Heeled Sneakers";
$tracks[] = "We're Gonna Make It";
$tracks[] = "I'm In The Mood";
$tracks[] = "Forty Four";
$tracks[] = "Help Me";
$tracks[] = "I'd Rather Go Blind";
$tracks[] = "Wang Dang Doodle";
$tracks[] = "I'm Your Hoochie Coochie Man";
$tracks[] = "Walkin' The Blues";
$tracks[] = "Walking By Myself";
$tracks[] = "When The Lights Go Out";
```

Shuffling the tracks is easy; you simply enter the following:

```
shuffle($tracks);
```

Now display the first entry in the array. The entry could be any one of the tracks.

If the order of the tracks looks less than random, it is because **shuffle( )** uses PHP's random number generator, and the random number generator is initialized with time. I found that hitting the Refresh button on a test page at a regular time interval of every 2 seconds produced a minimal movement of tracks, without the major changes you would expect in a truly random shuffle. In some circumstances, that may not be random enough, so you can initialize the random number generator with something other than the standard Unix timestamp (based on seconds) via the function **srand( )**. The **microtime( )** function is a good replacement for **time( )** in **srand( )** because **microtime( )** gives a result in microseconds, and it's unlikely that you will be able to achieve the same result twice. The details are explained with the function **rand( )** in Chapter 2.

The next example shows **srand( )**, **microtime( )**, and **shuffle( )** used together, and Figure 3.4 shows the play list shuffled twice in close succession. You use **srand( )** just once per script, no matter how many times you use **shuffle( )** or functions like **rand( )**. The use of **microtime( )** is purely to reduce repetition from script execution to script execution, by seeding the random number generator with a fraction of a second instead of a whole second:

```
srand((double) microtime() * 1000000);
shuffle($tracks);
```

High Heeled Sneakers	Walking By Myself
Help Me	Forty Four
I'd Rather go Blind	Wang Dang Doodle
My Babe	I'm Your Hoochie Coochie Man
Smokestack Lightnin'	We're Gonna Make It
I'm In The Mood	When The Lights Go Out
We're Gonna Make It	Walkin' The Blues
Fourty Four	High Heeled Sneakers
Wang Dang Doodle	I'm In The Mood
I'm Your Hoochie Coochie Man	Help Me
Walking By Myself	I'd Rather Go Blind
Walkin' The Blues	My Babe
When The Lights Go Out	Smokestack Lightnin'

Figure 3.4   Play list in two random shuffles.

Randomizing Banners with **array_rand()**

If you do not want to shuffle the whole list, and you only need one random entry (as you might when selecting just one banner to display at the top of a page), use **array_rand()**. The **array_rand()** function selects a fixed number of entries from an array and defaults to selecting one entry. It is almost perfect for selecting one banner from a list of banners.

First, you need a list of banners. You might not have heard of the following companies, but they just happen to have products I like:

```
$banners[] = "Coriolis";
$banners[] = "Coopers";
$banners[] = "Penfolds";
$banners[] = "Volvo";
$banners[] = "Compaq";
$banners[] = "AMD";
$banners[] = "PHP";
$banners[] = "Apache";
```

You can select and display any one of these banners with the simple code shown next. **srand()** runs just once per script before the first use of **array_rand()**. The **print()** statement is made more realistic by using the sort of centering and highlighting you might use for a banner:

```
srand((double) microtime() * 1000000);
$banner = array_rand($banners);
print("<p align=\"center\"><font color=\"339933\" size=\"+4\">"
    . \$banners[\$banner] . "</font></p>");
```

array_rand() returns the key of the selection rather than the value of the selection, so you can also use either the selection's key or the selection's value. If you were selecting a random music track from a CD (building on the example used in the previous Immediate Solution), you might want the value (the track name) when you want to display the track, but you might need the key (the track number) to feed the audio software that reads the CD and plays the track. In this banner example, I'll first look at the name of the banner, with the banner's file name consisting of the banner name plus the .jpg extension.

The following code example selects one random banner from the **$banners** array, and then displays the banner key so you can check the value returned by **array_rand()**. It then displays the banner name so you can check that the entry from **$banners** is valid, and then displays the banner file name the way you would insert the name into an HTML **<img>** tag:

```
$banner = array_rand($banners);
print("Banner number: " . $banner);
print("<br>Banner name: " . $banners[$banner]);
print("<br>Banner file name: " . $banners[$banner] . ".jpg");
```

On occasion, you might need another number of random entries. Some Web sites have three animated banners on every page. Here is the code to select three random banners from the **$banners** array:

```
$banner_list = array_rand($banners, 3);
```

Note that **array_rand( )** returns the array entry value when you select one entry and returns an array of values when you select more than one entry. To use the banner list, you could use code similar to the **while** loop shown next. The code uses the standard **while( )**, **list( )**, and **each( )** commands used in previous examples, and loops through a **print** statement that builds the HTML **<img>** tag using the file name from the **$banners** array:

```
while(list($k, $v) = each($banner_list))
    {
    print("<img src=\"" . $banners[$v] . ".jpg\" border=\"0\">");
    }
```

Because **array_rand( )** returns the array key, you can access more complicated arrays. In the case of the banner table, there is a good reason for making the banner table more complicated. The following, complete with extra information to help the banner display work better, demonstrates what an expansion of one entry in the **$banners** array looks like:

```
$banners[] = array("name"=>"Coriolis", "height"=>50, "width"=>200,
    "alt"=>"Check out their cool Black Books");
```

The following is a single banner display expanded with all the extra data in the **$banners** array to produce a far better banner display. The first line is the same random selection as in the previous example. The second line places the resultant selection into **$image**, because the selection is no longer a single string but an array of strings. The **print( )** statement is expanded to use each entry in **$image** in the appropriate tag within the **<img>** tag:

```
$banner = array_rand($banners);
$image = $banners[$banner];
print("<img src=\"" . $image ["name"] . ".jpg\" border=\"0\""
    . " alt=\"" . $image["alt"] . "\""
    . " height=\"" . $image["height"] . "\""
    . " width=\"" . $image["width"] . "\">");
```

In a production Web site, you would check that each array attribute existed before use and would set useful defaults. This code could be expanded with extra lines immediately after the creation of **$image** so you could be sure to get useful defaults. The next example makes sure you have a value for the image **alt** text, and it sets **$image["alt"]** to the name of the image if **$image["alt"]** is missing, or if **$image["alt"]** contains an empty string:

```
$image = $banners[$banner];
if(!isset($image["alt"]) or !strlen($image["alt"]))
    {
    $image["alt"] = $image ["name"];
    }
```

Reading a File into an Array with file()

To read a file into an array, start with a file named test.txt that contains several lines of text. Read the file into an array with the **file( )** function, as in:

```
$lines = file("test.txt");
```

Simple. The file could also be a Web page, such as:

```
$lines = file("http://petermoulding.com/index.html");
```

Each entry in the array ends with the **newline** character, **\n**, which delimits the line. You can remove the **newline** with an appropriate string function. Lines read from files from the Windows operating system may end with a return followed by a **newline**, **\r\n**, and files from Apple's Mac can end in **\n**, **\r\n**, or **\n\r**. Fortunately **file( )** leaves the **newline** in place so you can decide how to process the character.

Not all files contain lines ending with **newline** characters, but **file( )** will still read the files in as an array with one or a few giant elements, as I found when reading JPEG files. JPEGs contain some bytes that have the same value as **newline**, so **file( )** splits JPEGs into a small number of elements that you can count and process. However, there are better ways to read binary files such as JPEGs, as described in Chapter 8.

Sorting an Array by Value with **sort()**

To sort a list of photography film brands into ascending order, start by defining a standard array, naming the brand names, as in:

```
$film[] = "Konika";
$film[] = "Ilford";
$film[] = "Kodak";
$film[] = "Fuji";
$film[] = "a_name_in_lower_case";
```

Then you sort the list using the **sort()** function, as follows:

```
sort($film);
```

To print the list, use the following code:

```
while(list($k, $v) = each($film))
   {
   print("<br>" . $v);
   }
```

You will see the following list as a result:

```
Fuji
Ilford
Kodak
Konica
a_name_in_lower_case
```

NOTE: *The lowercase entry sorts out of alpha-order sequence because **sort()** is case sensitive. If you want a sort that handles case the way you would expect, see "Sorting an Array by Value Naturally with **natsort()**" later in the "Immediate Solutions" section.*

Sorting an Associative Array by Value with **asort()**

If you sort an associative array with **sort()**, you will find all the keys reset to numbers. The **asort()** function sorts an associative array by value and retains the original associated keys. The following example uses an array of film brands and their country of origin. Here is the sample array:

```
$film["Konika"] = "Japan";
$film["Ilford"] = "England";
$film["Kodak"] = "Mexico";
$film["Fuji"] = "Japan";
$film["a_name_in_lower_case"] = "anywhere";
```

You can sort the associative array with **asort( )** to get a list of film brands by their country of origin. As **sort( )** does, **asort( )** places lowercase letters after uppercase letters, because **asort( )** only sorts on the binary value of each character. The following code shows **asort( )** in action on **$film**:

```
asort($film);
```

You can print the list using the following:

```
while(list($k, $v) = each($film))
   {
   print("<br>" . $v . " " . $k);
   }
```

The result is the following list:

```
England Ilford
Japan Fuji
Japan Konica
Mexico Kodak
anywhere a_name_in_lower_case
```

Sorting an Array by Value in Reverse Order with rsort()

At some point, you might need to sort an array by value in reverse order. To sort a list of film titles in reverse (descending) order, use **rsort( )**. Like **sort( )**, **rsort( )** does not understand case, and sorts by binary values. First, start by defining a standard array naming the particular movie titles you want to sort, as follows:

```
$films[] = "Taxi Driver";
$films[] = "Heat";
$films[] = "Men of Honor";
$films[] = "The Adventures of Rocky & Bullwinkle";
$films[] = "Great Expectations";
$films[] = "Cape Fear";
$films[] = "any other film";
```

Next, sort the list using the **rsort( )** function, as in:

```
rsort($films);
```

You can print the list using the following:

```
while(list($k, $v) = each($films))
   {
   print("<br>" . $v);
   }
```

The result will look like the following list, complete with the lowercase entries listed before the uppercase entries:

```
any other film
The Adventures of Rocky & Bullwinkle
Taxi Driver
Men of Honor
Heat
Great Expectations
Cape Fear
```

Sorting an Associative Array by Value in Reverse Order with **arsort()**

To sort an associative list of film titles in reverse (descending) order, use **arsort( )**. Like **sort( )** and **asort( )**, **arsort( )** sorts on binary values. Start by defining an associative array, naming the films and their stars, as follows:

```
$films["John Travolta"] = "Swordfish";
$films["Mark Wahlberg"] = "Planet Of The Apes";
$films["Michael J. Fox"] = "Atlantis: The Lost Empire";
$films["Alcatraz"] = "Escape From Alcatraz";
$films["anyone"] = "any other film";
```

Sort the list using the **arsort( )** function, and then print the result with the following code:

```
arsort($films);
while(list($k, $v) = each($films))
   {
```

```
print("<br>" . $v . " " . $k);
}
```

The result is the following list:

```
any other film anyone
Swordfish John Travolta
Planet Of The Apes Mark Wahlberg
Escape From Alcatraz Alcatraz
Atlantis: The Lost Empire Michael J. Fox
```

Sorting an Associative Array by Key with ksort()

The **ksort( )** function sorts an associative array by key. A matching **krsort( )** sorts associative arrays by key in reverse order. The following example uses an array of films and their manufacturers. Here is the sample array:

```
$plastic["Saran Wrap"] = "Dow Chemical";
$plastic["GLAD Wrap"] = "Clorox Australia Pty Limited";
$plastic["Multix"] = "Multix Pty Limited";
$plastic["generic plastic wrap"] = "just about anyone";
```

To sort by key, sort the associative array with **ksort( )** to get a list of brands of plastic wrap ordered by their names. Like **sort( )** and **asort**, **ksort( )** places lowercase letters after uppercase letters. You would do this as follows:

```
ksort($plastic);
```

And you would be able to print the list using the following:

```
while(list($k, $v) = each($plastic))
    {
    print("<br>" . $k . " - " . $v);
    }
```

As a result, you would get the list:

```
GLAD Wrap - Clorox Australia Pty Limited
Multix - Multix Pty Limited
Saran Wrap - Dow Chemical
generic plastic wrap - just about anyone
```

Arrays
3. Arrays

Sorting an Array by Value Naturally with **natsort()**

The **natsort()** function sorts a list into a more natural ascending order than **sort()**. There are many definitions of natural sort orders, and they vary depending on the character set and language you use. **natsort()** happens to work very well with file names such as numbered images.

To use this, start by defining a standard array containing the file names of images, as in:

```
$image[] = "grease.jpg";
$image[] = "condensation.jpg";
$image[] = "grease03.jpg";
$image[] = "mildew4.jpg";
$image[] = "mildew040.jpg";
$image[] = "Mildew54.jpg";
$image[] = "MILDEW44.jpg";
$image[] = "slime.jpg";
$image[] = "butter.jpg";
$image[] = "rust 3 b.jpg";
$image[] = "rust3 a.jpg";
$image[] = "rust 3c.jpg";
$image[] = "rust3e.jpg";
```

First sort the list using the ordinary **sort()** to see what happens:

```
sort($image);
```

Then print the list using the following:

```
while(list($k, $v) = each($image))
    {
    print("<br>" . $v);
    }
```

As a result, you would get the following list:

```
MILDEW44.jpg
Mildew54.jpg
butter.jpg
condensation.jpg
grease.jpg
grease03.jpg
mildew040.jpg
mildew4.jpg
rust 3 b.jpg
```

```
rust 3c.jpg
rust3 a.jpg
rust3e.jpg
slime.jpg
```

NOTE: *Notice that* rust 3c *sorts before* rust3 a *because the space character sorts before the 3 does.*

Next, sort the list using the **natsort( )** function, by typing the following:

```
natsort($image);
```

The result is the following list:

```
MILDEW44.jpg
Mildew54.jpg
butter.jpg
condensation.jpg
grease.jpg
grease03.jpg
mildew040.jpg
mildew4.jpg
rust3 a.jpg
rust 3 b.jpg
rust 3c.jpg
rust3e.jpg
slime.jpg
```

As you can see, **natsort( )** managed to sort the rust images, 3a, 3b, 3c, and 3e in the correct sequence despite spaces mixed into various places. The rust images are sorted as if there were no spaces in their names; this feature is useful with files on computers based on Windows, NT, mainframes, or the Mac OS.

mildew040, you can see, is still sorted before mildew4 because **natsort( )** does not remove leading zeros when handling numbers. Although no option exists to do that in **natsort( )**, you can do it in **usort( )**, a sort function that lets you supply the sort comparison rules via a function, and which is discussed in the next section.

The lowercase entries sort after the uppercase entries because **natsort( )** does not understand case. The next example demonstrates exactly the same array but after it has been sorted with **natcasesort( )**, which is a case-independent sort. Here is the code to use **natcasesort( )**:

```
natcasesort($image);
```

The following shows the result from **natcasesort( )**, complete with the upper-case "mildews" sorted in the correct place in the list:

```
butter.jpg
condensation.jpg
grease.jpg
grease03.jpg
mildew040.jpg
mildew4.jpg
MILDEW44.jpg
Mildew54.jpg
rust3 a.jpg
rust 3 b.jpg
rust 3c.jpg
rust3e.jpg
slime.jpg
```

In the example, one file name ends with *4* and another ends with *040*, a situation where computers default to sorting the *040* before the *4*, but in which humans sort the *4* as if it were *004*. European characters are another example where sorting can be difficult: $\grave{E}$ (E grave accent) is a character with a binary value of 200 that sorts a long way after the standard alphabet, yet we expect it to sort like the letter *E*.

In certain situations, you will need to use phonetic sorting. The simplest sorting system is the Soundex system, which is supported by PHP's **soundex( )** function. A more accurate (and extensive) method is to use metaphones, via **metaphone( )**. Soundex generally uses a fixed four-character identifier, although MySQL uses a variable-length Soundex and is supported by databases such as Oracle. Metaphones are of variable length, use more rules about English language pronunciation, and are too new to be widely supported. **metaphone( )** and **soundex( )** are discussed in Chapter 12.

Sorting an Array Unnaturally with **usort()**

Sometimes you need to sort an array in a specific order, and the standard sort functions just do not give you the right option. The **usort( )** function lets you take complete charge. It accepts first an array to sort, and then the name of a function to perform the comparison between elements in the array. You supply the comparison function. Your function must accept two values for comparison and return a value to indicate the action the sort must take. You return any positive integer to indicate the two values are out of order, a 0 to indicate the two values are equal, and a negative integer to indicate the two values are in sequence.

The following example uses an array containing the file names of images. In this example, the images are of various types, and the user-defined sort will sort by file type. Within a type, the files will be sorted alphabetically, and the names will be translated to lowercase before comparison.

I will also throw in a step to change *jpeg* to *jpg* before the comparison, so both spellings of *jpeg* will sort together. And just to make sure those rust images sort the right way, I will remove all spaces before the comparison.

Here is the test array:

```
$image[] = "grease.jpg";
$image[] = "condensation.jpeg";
$image[] = "grease03.JPG";
$image[] = "mildew4.jpg";
$image[] = "mildew040.jpg";
$image[] = "Mildew54.jpg";
$image[] = "MILDEW44.jpg";
$image[] = "slime.gif";
$image[] = "butter.pgn";
$image[] = "rust 3 b.jpg";
$image[] = "rust3 a.jpg";
$image[] = "rust 3c.jpg";
$image[] = "rust3e.jpg";
```

usort( ) needs a function that will return –1 when the values are in sequence, +1 when the values are out of sequence, and 0 when the values are equal. The following function, **unnatural( )**, does just that. Take a look first at the function, then at the following example of the function's use, and then at the result. All this is followed by an explanation of the parts of the function:

```
function unnatural($x, $y)
    {
    $x = strtolower($x);
    $y = strtolower($y);
    $x = str_replace(" ", "", $x);
    $y = str_replace(" ", "", $y);
    $p = strrpos($x, ".");
    if($p === false)
        {
        $xf = $x;
        $xt = "";
        }
    else
        {
```

```
        $xf = substr($x, 0, $p);
        $xt = substr($x, $p + 1);
        }
$p = strrpos($y, ".");
if($p === false)
    {
    $yf = $y;
    $yt = "";
    }
else
    {
    $yf = substr($y, 0, $p);
    $yt = substr($y, $p + 1);
    }
if($xt == "jpeg")
    {
    $xt = "jpg";
    }
if($yt == "jpeg")
    {
    $yt = "jpg";
    }
if($xt < $yt)
    {
    return(-1);
    }
elseif($xt > $yt)
    {
    return(1);
    }
else
    {
    if($xf < $yf)
        {
        return(-1);
        }
    elseif($xf > $yf)
        {
        return(1);
        }
    else
        {
        return(0);
        }
    }
}
```

To sort the list using the **usort()** function and the **unnatural()** function, enter:

```
usort($image, "unnatural");
```

To print the list, use the following:

```
while(list($k, $v) = each($image));
    {
    print("<br>" . $v);
    }
```

The result is:

```
slime.gif
condensation.jpeg
grease.jpg
grease03.JPG
mildew040.jpg
mildew4.jpg
MILDEW44.jpg
Mildew54.jpg
rust3 a.jpg
rust 3 b.jpg
rust 3c.jpg
rust3e.jpg
butter.pgn
```

Notice that the result has sorted the GIF file first, then all the JPEGs, and finally the PNG file. The JPEG files are sorted the correct way no matter what the case of the file name is, or how JPEG is spelled.

unnatural() accepts the two values, **$x** and **$y**, presented by **ucase()**. Both values are immediately translated to lowercase by **strtolower()** to make all file names sort the same, no matter what the typist did with the case when creating the files.

The line **$x = str_replace(" ", "", $x);** and the equivalent line for **$y** remove spaces from the file names so all the rust images will sort logically. Although not every operating system allows spaces in file names, every operating system allows some space-like characters, including dash and underscore, that you can remove at this point in the processing.

The next part, reproduced here for **$x**, finds the last dot (.) in the file name using **strrpos()**, splits the file name at the last dot using **substr()**, and then places the text before the dot in **$xf** and the text after the dot in **$xt**. **$xt** is used for the subsequent type comparison, and **$xf**, the file name, is used if the types are equal, as in the following code:

```
$p = strrpos($x, ".");
if($p === false)
    {
    $xf = $x;
    $xt = "";
    }
else
    {
    $xf = substr($x, 0, $p);
    $xt = substr($x, $p + 1);
    }
```

The next two pieces of code for **$xt** and $yt, shown below, simply check for *jpeg* and replace it with *jpg*. Because *jpeg* is the full spelling of the file type, and most people write it as *jpg*, you can the make the two the same before comparing the file types, as follows:

```
if($xt == "jpeg")
    {
    $xt = "jpg";
    }
if($yt == "jpeg")
    {
    $yt = "jpg";
    }
```

The next code compares the file types, **$xt** and **$yt**, and then returns −1 if the values are in sequence and 1 if the values are not in sequence. The last **else** leads to the processing needed if the file types are equal:

```
if($xt < $yt)
    {
    return(-1);
    }
  elseif($xt > $yt)
    {
    return(1);
    }
  else
```

The file name processing is a copy of the file type processing using **$xf** instead of **$xt** and **$yf** instead of **$yt**. If the file names are equal, the code returns 0 to indicate equality.

Although the code is longwinded, it is quick and easy to document with comments. People wanting to save lines can easily place the **str_replace( )** inside the **strtolower( )** and chop out all the pretty spacing.

When I manage files with databases in image management applications and the like, I often chop the file type off the name very early on in the processing and store the file type as a separate field so I can select and sort with SQL instead of using **usort( )**.

Related solution:	Found on page:
String Functions	63

Looping through an Array Backward

You could loop through an array backward by sorting the array into reverse order and then working forward, but that would be a slow way of accessing an array if you only wanted to quickly find the last few entries. This section explains the quick way to start at the end and work backward.

First, take a look at this example array:

```
$mineral[] = "gold";
$mineral[] = "palladium";
$mineral[] = "iridium";
$mineral[] = "platinum";
$mineral[] = "ruby";
$mineral[] = "rhodium";
$mineral[] = "ruthenium";
$mineral[] = "indium";
$mineral[] = "tantalum";
```

Start by selecting the last entry in the array by using **end( )**, which returns the value in the last entry, as follows:

```
print(end($mineral));
```

Once you do this, you should see the following:

```
tantalum
```

You can access the array's previous entry with the function **prev( )**, which moves the array's file pointer back to the previous entry and then returns the value of that entry:

```
print(prev($mineral));
```

Once you do this, you should see the following:

```
indium
```

You can loop backward through the array using **while( )** and **prev( )**, because **prev( )** returns false when it runs past the start of the array, like this:

```
while($x = prev($mineral))
    {
    print($x);
    }
```

There is just one problem with **prev( )**: It also returns false for empty array elements. One alternative to **prev( )** is to reverse the array, and then use **each( )** to step forward through the array, because **each( )** does not return false for empty elements. Although reversing the array costs processing time, it does avoid problems with empty elements. The following is code to reverse an array and then step through the reversed array, with the function **array_reverse( )** performing the reversal and the **while( )** loop stepping forward through the reversed array:

```
$reversed = array_reverse($mineral);
while(list($k, $v) = each ($reversed))
    {
    print("<br>" . $v);
    }
```

You can also step through arrays using a **for( )** loop based on the **count( )** of an array, but **count( )** fails when your processing within the loop, adds or removes array entries. **prev( )** is the fastest way to step backward through the array, if you can guarantee no empty elements. **for( )** is the next choice for speed, if you are not adding or deleting entries from within the loop. **each( )** is the most reliable way of stepping through an array, because **each( )** works with empty elements, deletions, and additions.

Looping through Multidimensional Arrays

This example adds up the weights of all the items in an array of products. Some of the products are made up of other products, which also may be made up of other products, so the array has multiple dimensions. Because I do not know how many dimensions, and the dimensions also don't happen to be symmetrical, I cannot use a simple set of nested loops to loop through the array. Luckily, PHP has a simple way to access even the strangest of array structures.

First, start with some example products with weights in a one-dimensional array named **$weight**. This example uses only weights, but a real stock system would have quantities and other values:

```
$weight["nut"] = 50;
$weight["bolt"] = 550;
$weight["flange"] = 300;
$weight["gasket"] = 30;
```

Some of the products named in **$weight** are assembled from other products and instead of having a weight, have a list of products that have to be added up. Here is an example widget, made up of a nut, a flange, and a bolt:

```
$weight["widget"] = array($weight["nut"], $weight["flange"],
    $weight["bolt"]);
```

The company making the widgets has a flagship product, WidMAX, assembled from widgets and extra bolts. The next example is the entry in **$weight** for the WidMAX and includes references to widgets, which are also assemblies of other products:

```
$weight["WidMAX"] = array($weight["widget"], $weight["widget"],
    $weight["bolt"], $weight["bolt"], $weight["bolt"]);
```

Assume you own a moving van, and I asked you to move all my stock from Kotlik in Alaska to Brownsville in Texas. How do you calculate the total weight you would have to ship? Start with the following simple function to add up the numbers in a one-dimensional array (the code needs an addition, as explained in subsequent paragraphs, to work with the entry for **$weight["idMAX"]**):

```
function add_weights($weights)
    {
    $x = 0;
    while(list($k, $v) = each($weights))
```

```
    {
    $x += $v;
    }
  return($x);
  }
```

The simple array gets each value **$v** and adds the value to **$x**. For the multidimensional array, you need to check if **$v** is an array, and do something special if it is. The simplest thing is to call **add_weights( )** with **$v** to repeat the processing one level down in the array structure. The following is the one-dimensional function expanded to handle unlimited dimensions:

```
function add_weights($weights)
  {
  $x = 0;
  while(list($k, $v) = each($weights))
    {
    if(is_array($v))
      {
      $x += add_weights($v);
      }
    else
      {
      $x += $v;
      }
    }
  return($x);
  }
```

The previous **$x += $v;** is replaced by the code starting with **if(is_array($v))**, which calls **add_weights( )** if **$v** is an array and uses the same **$x += $v;** if **$v** is not an array. **add_weights( )** starts with a subset of the array, which is itself an array, and returns the weight of the subset. If elements in the subset are arrays, the processing of those elements calls **add_weights( )** again.

TIP: *One thing to consider when performing recursion like this is the possibility of an infinite loop. If you make a minor typing error when writing code like this, you can end up looping back to the same point, which will then run until PHP hits the time limit set in php.ini. The error message will not tell you where your script was when the timeout occurred. To test code like the last piece shown in this section, run the code once with the recursive line $x += add_weights($v); commented out.*

---

3. Arrays

Chapter 4

Credit Cards

In Depth

Some shoppers are paranoid when asked to type their credit card number into a Web page, but will then read the same number out over the telephone with no security of any sort. Other shoppers type in their credit card numbers without checking delivery terms or conditions, and then complain when an unexpected charge appears on the bill. Some Web sites make matters worse by misrepresenting the sale—for example, by providing a link to the manufacturer's Web page for a product but then delivering a different model or a kit with different accessories than those shown in the linked Web page. Your job is to make your Web site visibly safer and more reliable than the sites belonging to your competitors.

The paranoid have good reason to feel that Web sites are out to rip them off. You will have a hard time selling to those already burned by online shopping, so consider the alternative of not billing customers until delivery. If you are delivering fruit or groceries, the buyer will be home to accept delivery, so let them pay on delivery.

Consider the following real-world problems:

1. I purchased wine at an online auction, and entered my credit card information to ensure speedy delivery, but was charged more than twice what I bid. I did not find out until the statement arrived a month later. As a result I will not buy from an online auction that requires my credit card information before delivery, and owners of new online auctions will have a hard time convincing me that their auction site is safe. What went wrong with the online auction? The Web site developers set up the site to ensure that the sellers get the highest price by adding an automatic bid-increase function. The developers then made the automatic increase the default and made the Web pages turn the automatic feature back on every time I visited the bid page, even if I had originally turned off the automatic bid. I do not know if the developers were ignorant, cretins, insanely greedy, or pure evil. The end result was that my bid ended up with the automatic bid set on, I paid more than I wanted to pay, I will never use an auction site that has an automatic bid feature, and I will warn many other people to avoid Web sites like that.

2. A home delivery company lets shoppers provide a credit card number once, bills every delivery to the same card, and makes it very hard for the customer to change the credit card number. I cancelled an old card and

supplied my new card number, but they billed me on my old card. I will not buy through that particular company again because I do not trust their billing procedures.

3. I buy disk drives and other items from a supplier that lists current stock, back orders, and next delivery for all items. When I need something immediately, I buy something that is in stock. One day I purchased a mobile phone battery from a similar-looking site—a site that suggested that the supplier is a big, reliable warehouse. There was a slight problem ordering online, so I used their telephone contact. It turned out, after several weeks of waiting and many telephone calls, that the online sales part of the company was one young kid sitting at a telephone, and the company had no stock. The untrustworthy supplier eventually located someone who would ship me a battery at very low cost to them, but I was paying full retail, and the battery failed quickly because it was old stock and possibly second-hand or demo stock. As a result, I will not order those type of items unless the site lists stock on hand, reserves stock on receipt of an order, and delivers the goods sealed in the manufacturer's packaging.

If you are still up to the challenge of overcoming the problems listed so far, read on. You can overcome the few software problems, the many customer service problems, and all the fears of shoppers burnt by existing online sites. You can accept credit cards with orders. You just need to head in the right direction and test every step thoroughly.

Merchant Account

To accept credit card payments of any sort, you need a *merchant account*. The account lets you claim your money back from a bank or other business that processes credit card payment claims. You pay them a setup fee, a monthly minimum fee, a minimum transaction fee, and a percentage of the amount you are billing a client. Small customers might pay 6 percent of the transaction amount, and big customers might pay as little as 0.2 percent (this fee is often called the *merchant discount* or just *discount*). Transaction fees are from 10 to 20 cents. The monthly fee might be $10 for a paper-based account up to $35 for an electronic account, be it through the Internet or through a dial-up telephone.

You are paid after a delay, and the payment can be withdrawn for a period up to three months. Check the details with your bank and shop around for the best overall deal to match the volume and size of sales you make.

If you accept a payment online, and then ship the next day, you can reduce some problems by delaying the payment clearance until you are ready to ship. Think about the problem of the site taking a few weeks to find a battery. If it had accepted payment online, and I had cancelled the order after the first delay, the site would have had to refund my money and pay a refund fee. If the site has a lot of refunds, its discount fee will increase.

One Australian online shop uses a standard Visa/MasterCard merchant account from a bank for local sales, but accepts only American Express for international sales because American Express offers a higher level of credit card verification than the local bank. Most vendors of expensive items use some form of sales tracking to check prior sales of that item before clearing a sale. You can track prior sales to the same customer, prior sales to the same country, and sales of a certain value or type. People using stolen credit cards will often order products they can resell quickly, like Sony Walkmans, and order multiple units. Beware if you are a retail site and a brand new customer orders 10 Walkmans. One online retailer told me he gets many orders from addresses near tourist resorts in Indonesia that use American credit cards, yet he sells nothing a tourist would buy during a holiday. Visa announced that American pornography sites would stop accepting Visa cards from many countries because there were so many cases where people would sign up for a month of viewing pornography and then dispute the item on their bill.

There are lots of reasons for not clearing the payment online, but that does not eliminate credit card usage. If your site accepts donations to charity, you lose nothing through online clearance. When you sell software for online delivery, the immediate sale is more important than the odd failure of a payment from a remote country. You can add code to detect suspicious orders, defer delivery, and flag the order for hand checking. If an online grocery store receives an order for $1,000 worth of potato crisps and cola drinks, defer the delivery and call the buyer to confirm the order.

Children

If your site attracts children, you will get children shopping with their parents' cards, and parents disputing the charges. You can avoid some of these problems by deferring clearance of payments from new customers until you complete a verification check, such as calling the customer about large orders.

Billing Name

If your Web site is **custom-software-delevopment.com** and your bill appears on the customer's credit card statement as **internationalservices.com**, some customers will dispute the charge because they do not know who **internationalservices.com** is.

The moral of the story is to make sure your customer knows what to expect from your site and on their bill, track sales to highlight problem patterns, and ask your merchant account supplier for help preventing problems.

Security

The minimum security for transactions is Secure Sockets Layer (SSL) at the 128-bit level, and you need to lock down your server tight so the accepted credit card information cannot be stolen from your server. You can get more information on SSL at the open source SSL Web site (**www.openssl.org/**) and SSL implementation for the Apache Web server at **www.apache-ssl.org/**.

Some merchant account providers use clearance systems where the credit card information is never stored on your Web server. The information is just passed on to the merchant account provider, but a breach of your Web server will not be reported in the media as harmless. Once your Web site is mentioned in the press, your name will be surrounded by accusations and inferences of credit card losses.

Server

If your Web server is RedHat or Mandrake Linux, run the Bastille security script after every change. Find the equivalent for other operating systems. Bastille (**www.bastille-linux.org/**) is a script that goes through your Web server and operating system turning off options that compromise security. Some distributions of Linux are preconfigured for a higher level of security, and many people prefer freeBSD because of built-in security settings. Your Web server software is your first line of defense. Once someone cracks through the Web server, the operating system has to stop the cracker taking control of the whole server.

You can add a firewall in front of the Web server to filter out certain types of attacks on your server. As I type, the lights in my network router are blinking from code-red attacks, and the firewall in the router is dropping the offending packets without a single attack reaching my local network and servers. The code-red worm attacks Microsoft's IIS and uses IIS servers as the base to attack other servers. The worm attacks random IP addresses, and version 3 of code red is in enough IIS servers to cause an attack on my network every two seconds.

Hashing

A *hash* is what I make when my cooking turns food into a disaster. Hash also has some technical meanings in computing, and not all of them refer to my code when it turns out like my cooking. A hash is a code, usually a number, produced from a string and can be used to identify a long string with a short number. If you have a database containing recipes, you set up a hash based on major ingredients, such as 1 for potato and 2 for salt, and 9 for the method of cooking, such as frying. Hash browns (fried chopped potatoes, usually salted), would have a hash number of 129, whereas salt-free hash browns would have a hash of 19. Your database could file recipes for salted hash browns in record 129 and the healthier version in record 19. When someone searches for recipes featuring potatoes, frying, and no salt, you can instantly calculate that the hash is 29 and retrieve record 29 without searching the database. Various hash calculations are used in cryptography and other areas. Some are two way—the original value can be determined from the hash—but most are one-way hashes—the original value cannot be calculated from the hash.

PHP provides the **mhash_** functions to calculate various values loosely referred to as *hash values*. The **mhash_** functions are shown in action in the Immediate Solution entitled "Hashing Data," later in this chapter.

Hashes are used for verification and checking, but not for encryption. Hashes are generally one-way, so you cannot "unhash" to recover the original information. Hashes give you a way of validating data without sending two full copies of data and comparing the copies. The type of hash you use depends on your requirement. Cyclical Redundancy Checks (CRCs) are designed to verify every bit in a file or record, whereas other hashes may only use the first part of a string. CRC32 (described in Chapter 8) can store 4 billion values, so it can be used to identify one file out of thousands. (I had a directory containing 49,000 files of similar size and content, yet all had unique CRCs.) If you want to hide a string, like a password, and then retrieve the string later, you need encryption instead of a hash.

- *CRC32*—CRC32 is a 32-bit Cyclical Redundancy Check checksum used to detect errors on disks, when data is transmitted over a network, and to verify files like ZIP files. The **mhash_** functions support **MHASH_CRC32** (used in Ethernet) and **MHASH_CRC32B** (used in zip programs). CRC32 values can be displayed in hexadecimal or integer. PHP sometimes mangles the integer versions because PHP treats them as 32-bit signed integers, whereas they are really 32-bit unsigned integers. If you see a negative integer CRC32 displayed by PHP, you have to add 4 billion to get the correct value.

- *MD5*—The MD5 algorithm was invented by Ron Rivest at RSA, and is described in RFC 1321 (**www.faqs.org/rfcs/rfc1321.html**). **mhash** calls MD5 **MHASH_MD5**. MD5 is used to pass versions of passwords from browsers to servers, and for storage on disk. MD5 is not encryption—there is no decryption of MD5, and you cannot get a password back from MD5. When using MD5, you save the MD5 version of the password on disk, convert incoming passwords to MD5, and then compare the MD5 values to verify the password. When your customer calls and says they have forgotten their password, you cannot recover the password; you have to reset the password to a default, and make them change the password again.

- *MD4*—Think of MD4 as the Apollo 13 of encryption, a heroic effort that broke. Use MD5 instead.

- *SHA1*—The SHA algorithm is used by NIST (National Institute of Standards and Technology [**www.nist.gov/**]) as its Digital Signature Standard. **mhash** calls this algorithm **MHASH_SHA1**.

NOTE: *An interesting aside: NIST-F1, one of NIST's cesium-based clocks, counts 9 billion cycles per second and is accurate to one second in 20 million years. This is already old hat because NIST's new mercury-based clock counts 1 quadrillion cycles per second and is accurate to one second in 20,000 million years. Is your Web server set to the right time?*

- *HAVAL*—HAVAL is a modification of MD5. It allows values of various lengths and is defined in **mhash** as **MHASH_HAVAL256**, **MHASH_HAVAL224**, **MHASH_HAVAL192**, and **MHASH_HAVAL160**.

- *RIPEMD-160*—RIPEMD-160 is a 160-bit replacement for MD4, MD5, and RIPEMD, designed by Hans Dobbertin, Antoon Bosselaers, and Bart Preneel. RIPEMD was developed as part of the EU project RIPE (RACE Integrity Primitives Evaluation). **mhash** calls this algorithm **MHASH_RIPEMD160**.

- *Tiger*—Tiger, designed by Eli Biham and Ross Anderson, is said to be very fast on 64-bit computers. In **mhash**, this algorithm is defined as **MHASH_TIGER192**, **MHASH_TIGER160**, and **MHASH_TIGER128**.

- *GOST*—GOST is a 256-bit Russian Digital Signature Standard. **mhash** calls this algorithm **MHASH_GOST**.

Encryption

Encryption is half science, half art. Science proves that encryption works or fails. Selecting the correct implementation of encryption for your site is an art. You need something that is practical to the point where you can perform the encryption in a reasonable time using an economical Web server, yet is unbreakable by a hacker that has access to all the spare capacity of a few thousand networked computers at a company or university. The hacker can claim to be performing legitimate research into security on behalf of the company owning the computers, but not mention that he or she is trying to crack a password from the local bank or a Web site selling tickets to rock and roll concerts.

PHP includes the **mcrypt** functions, which access the mcrypt software from **http://mcrypt.hellug.gr/**, and give you the ability to use the encryption algorithms BLOWFISH, TWOFISH, DES, TripleDES, 3-WAY, SAFER, LOKI97, GOST, RC2, RC6, MARS, IDEA, RIJNDAEL, SERPENT, CAST, ARCFOUR and WAKE.

4. Credit Cards

Installing mcrypt

To install mcrypt, follow these steps.

Unix

To install mcrypt for Unix, follow these steps:

1. Download libmcrypt-x.x.tar.gz from **ftp://mcrypt.hellug.gr/pub/mcrypt/libmcrypt/**.

2. Follow the installation instructions included in the download.

3. Compile libmcrypt with the option **--disable-posix-threads**. Configure libmcrypt using superuser to avoid permission errors.

4. Compile PHP with **--with-mcrypt**.

Windows and NT

The PHP 4.0.6 Win32 binary does not include php_mcrypt.dll. I hope that a later release includes mcrypt as standard.

mcrypt Functions

The following sections list the **mcrypt_** functions with some examples.

mcrypt_get_cipher_name()

You can get the name of a encryption cipher (algorithm) from a cipher id using the following code. If the id is wrong, the function returns false:

```
print("<br>" . mcrypt_get_cipher_name(MCRYPT_DES));
```

The example's result is:

```
DES
```

mcrypt_list_algorithms()

The following code will list all the ciphers in the mcrypt library. You can supply an optional directory name to find all the ciphers in the directory:

```
$array = mcrypt_list_algorithms();
while(list($k, $v) = each($array))
   {
   print("<br>" . $v);
   }
```

mcrypt_list_modes()

This function lists all the modes available in the mcrypt library so you can check that the current library has the mode you want. You can supply an optional directory name to find all the modes in the specified directory. The encryption modes include CBC (cipher block chaining), CFB (cipher feedback), ECB (electronic codebook), OFB (output feedback with 8bit data), nOFB (output feedback with nbit datat), and STREAM (PHP does not yet support stream mode). The following code lists all the modes returned by **mcrypt_list_modes( )**:

```
$modes = mcrypt_list_modes();
while(list($k, $v) = each($modes))
    {
    print("<br>" . $v);
    }
```

mcrypt_get_block_size()

This function tells you the block size for a given algorithm. PHP currently supports encryption of strings, not streams or anything complicated, so the block size is only needed for setting up things like field sizes in tables:

```
print("<br>" . mcrypt_get_block_size(MCRYPT_DES,cbc));
```

mcrypt_get_key_size()

Use **mcrypt_get_key_size( )** when you need to know the size of a key for a specific encryption algorithm:

```
print("<br>" . mcrypt_get_key_size(MCRYPT_DES,cbc));
```

mcrypt_module_open()

mcrypt_module_open( ) opens an encryption module for use and should be run before **mcrypt_create_iv( )** or the encryption or decryption function. The result is a resource id that is used in some other functions. The module name is the name of a module that implements a specific encryption algorithm. The module for algorithm Blowfish can be entered as the string "blowfish" or using the defined name **MCRYPT_BLOWFISH**. The modules are in the directory pointed to by php.ini parameter **mcrypt.algorithms_dir**, which defaults to /usr/local/lib/libmcrypt. Once open, you close the module with **mcrypt_module_close( )** or **mcrypt_generic_end( )**. **mcrypt_module_close( )** is missing from the current documentation, and may be phased out. The following example opens DES, uses the default directory specified in php.ini, uses mode CBC, and gets CBC from directory **/usr/lib/mcrypt-modes**:

```
$cipher = mcrypt_module_open(MCRYPT_DES, "", MCRYPT_MODE_CBC,
   "/usr/lib/mcrypt-modes");
```

mcrypt_create_iv()

You need an *initialization vector* (IV) to start some forms of encryption, so **mcrypt_create_iv( )** creates the IV. Specify the size of the IV and the source of the randomness for the IV as follows:

```
srand ((double) microtime() * 1000000);
$iv = mcrypt_create_iv(32, MCRYPT_RAND);
```

Precede **MCRYPT_RAND** with **srand( )** (discussed in Chapter 2). The first parameter is the block size returned by **mcrypt_get_block_size( )**. The second parameter can also be **MCRYPT_DEV_RANDOM** to read data from /dev/random, or **MCRYPT_DEV_URANDOM** to read data from /dev/urandom.

mcrypt_get_iv_size()

mcrypt_get_iv_size( ) gets the size of the IV associated with the algorithm:

```
print("<br>" . mcrypt_get_iv_size(MCRYPT_DES,cbc));
```

mcrypt_cbc()

mcrypt_cbc( ) encrypts in cipher block chaining mode, a mode suitable for files:

```
$key = "Do not tell anyone the contents of this string";
$string = mcrypt_cbc(MCRYPT_DES, $key, $file_or_string, MCRYPT_ENCRYPT,_
   $iv);
```

The first parameter is the cipher, and the second is the key. Because keys have to be secret, the key is not shown in the example. The key has to be suitable for the cipher; some algorithms become stronger when the key string is long, whereas other algorithms use only a limited string length. The next parameter is the data to be encrypted or decrypted, and could be a string or a file read into a string using **file( )**. The fourth parameter is the mode, encrypt or decrypt. The optional fifth parameter is an IV from **mcrypt_create_iv( )**. The first parameter in **mcrypt_create_iv( )** needs to be the blocksize returned by **mcrypt_get_block_size( )** for mode CBC.

mcrypt_cfb()

mcrypt_cfb( ) accepts the same parameters as **mcrypt_cbc( )** and encrypts in cipher feedback mode, the best choice for byte-by-byte encryption. The following example decrypts a string:

```
$string = mcrypt_cfb(MCRYPT_DES, $key, $file_or_string, MCRYPT_DECRYPT);
```

mcrypt_ecb()

mcrypt_ecb( ) accepts the same parameters as **mcrypt_cbc( )** and encrypts in electronic codebook mode, the best choice for short strings, such as keys. The following example decrypts a string:

```
$string = mcrypt_ecb(MCRYPT_DES, $key, $file_or_string, MCRYPT_DECRYPT);
```

mcrypt_ofb()

mcrypt_ofb( ) accepts the same parameters as **mcrypt_cbc( )** and encrypts in output feedback mode, an 8-bit mode that is insecure and not recommended. The following example encrypts a string:

```
$string = mcrypt_ofb(MCRYPT_DES, $key, $file_or_string, MCRYPT_ENCRYPT);
```

mcrypt_encrypt()

mcrypt_encrypt( ) accepts almost the same parameters as **mcrypt_cbc( )** and encrypts in the mode specified by the fourth parameter. The optional fifth parameter supplies an IV for those modes that need an IV. The following example encrypts a string:

```
$string = mcrypt_encrypt(MCRYPT_DES, $key, $file_or_string,
    MCRYPT_MODE_CBC);
```

mcrypt_decrypt()

mcrypt_decrypt( ) accepts the same parameters as **mcrypt_encrypt( )** and decrypts in the mode specified by the fourth parameter. The optional fifth parameter supplies an IV for those modes that need an IV. The following example decrypts a string:

```
$string = mcrypt_decrypt(MCRYPT_DES, $key, $file_or_string,
    MCRYPT_MODE_CBC);
```

mcrypt_generic_init()

mcrypt_generic_init( ) accepts the cipher resource id returned by **mcrypt_module_open( )**, a key, and an IV. The function initializes all the buffers needed for encryption. If an error occurs, the function returns –1:

```
$int = mcrypt_generic_init($cipher, $key, $iv);
```

mcrypt_generic()

mcrypt_generic( ) accepts a cipher resource id from **mcrypt_module_open( )** and a string for encryption, and returns the string encrypted. Call **mcrypt_generic_init( )** before calling **mcrypt_generic( )**:

```
$encrypted = mcrypt_generic($cipher, $string);
```

mdecrypt_generic()

mdecrypt_generic( ) accepts a cipher resource id from **mcrypt_module_open( )** and an encrypted string, and returns the string decrypted. Call **mcrypt_generic_init( )** before calling **mdecrypt_generic( )**:

```
$string = mdecrypt_generic($cipher, $encrypted);
```

mcrypt_generic_end()

mcrypt_generic_end( ) closes all the buffers opened by **mcrypt_generic_init( )**, and closes the module opened by **mcrypt_module_open( )**:

```
if(!mcrypt_generic_end($cipher))
    {
    print("<br>mcrypt_generic_end() failed.");
    }
```

mcrypt_enc_self_test()

mcrypt_enc_self_test( ) runs a test on the module opened by **mcrypt_module_open( )**, and returns 0 if the test result is OK or 1 if the module fails the test:

```
if(mcrypt_enc_self_test($cipher))
    {
    print("<br>module failed.");
    }
```

If you use this test, use it before encrypting anything. In PHP 4.0.6, **mcrypt_enc_self_test( )** worked as a CGI module and a standard Apache module, but not as an Apache/Unix DSO (Dynamic Shared Object).

mcrypt_enc_is_block_algorithm_mode()

mcrypt_enc_is_block_algorithm_mode() runs a test on the current mode, and returns 1 if the mode works with block algorithms or 0 if the mode is for streams:

```
if(mcrypt_enc_is_block_algorithm_mode($cipher))
    {
    print("<br>mode is for block algorithms.");
    }
else
    {
    print("<br>mode is for stream algorithms.");
    }
```

mcrypt_enc_is_block_algorithm()

mcrypt_enc_is_block_algorithm() runs a test on the current algorithm and returns 1 if the algorithm works with blocks, or 0 if the algorithm is for streams:

```
if(mcrypt_enc_is_block_algorithm($cipher))
    {
    print("<br>block algorithm.");
    }
else
    {
    print("<br>stream algorithm.");
    }
```

mcrypt_enc_is_block_mode()

mcrypt_enc_is_block_mode() runs a test on the open mode and returns 1 if the mode outputs blocks, or 0 if the mode outputs byte streams:

```
if(mcrypt_enc_is_block_mode($cipher))
    {
    print("<br>mode is for blocks.");
    }
else
    {
    print("<br>mode is for streams.");
    }
```

mcrypt_enc_get_block_size()

mcrypt_enc_get_block_size() returns the block size used by the open algorithm:

```
$size = mcrypt_enc_get_block_size($cipher);
```

mcrypt_enc_get_key_size()

mcrypt_enc_get_key_size( ) returns the maximum key size used by the open mode. For modes that support variable key sizes, any key size up to the maximum is valid:

```
$size = mcrypt_enc_get_key_size($cipher);
```

mcrypt_enc_get_supported_key_sizes()

mcrypt_enc_get_supported_key_sizes( ) returns an array containing all the valid key sizes for the current algorithm. If the array is empty, all the key sizes from 1 up to the maximum are valid. The following code prints the list of key sizes when there is a list:

```
$size = mcrypt_enc_get_supported_key_sizes($cipher);
while(list($k, $v) = each($size))
    {
    print("<br>" . $v);
    }
```

mcrypt_enc_get_iv_size()

mcrypt_enc_get_iv_size( ) returns the size of the IV for the current algorithm. If the function returns zero, the algorithm does not use IVs:

```
$size = mcrypt_enc_get_iv_size($cipher);
```

mcrypt_enc_get_algorithms_name()

mcrypt_enc_get_algorithms_name( ) returns the name of the current algorithm:

```
$name = mcrypt_enc_get_algorithms_name($cipher);
```

mcrypt_enc_get_modes_name()

mcrypt_enc_get_modes_name( ) returns the name of the open mode:

```
$name = mcrypt_enc_get_modes_name($cipher);
```

mcrypt_module_self_test()

mcrypt_module_self_test( ) tests a module, and returns true on success or false on failure. The optional second parameter accepts a directory name where the module resides:

```
if(!mcrypt_module_self_test($module))
    {
    print("<br>module " . $module . " failed.");
    }
```

mcrypt_module_is_block_algorithm_mode()

mcrypt_module_is_block_algorithm_mode( ) runs a test on the specified module, and returns 1 if the module works with block algorithms or 0 if the module works with stream algorithm modes. The optional second parameter accepts the name of a directory containing the module:

```
if(mcrypt_module_is_block_algorithm_mode($module))
    {
    print("<br>block algorithm modes.");
    }
else
    {
    print("<br>stream algorithm modes.");
    }
```

mcrypt_module_is_block_algorithm()

mcrypt_module_is_block_algorithm( ) runs a test on the specified algorithm, and returns 1 if the algorithm works with blocks or 0 if the algorithm works with streams. The optional second parameter accepts the name of a directory containing the algorithm module:

```
if(mcrypt_module_is_block_algorithm($module))
    {
    print("<br>block.");
    }
else
    {
    print("<br>stream.");
    }
```

mcrypt_module_is_block_mode()

mcrypt_module_is_block_mode( ) runs a test on the specified module, and returns 1 if the module returns blocks or 0 if the module returns bytes. The optional second parameter accepts the name of a directory containing the module:

```
if(mcrypt_module_is_block_mode($module))
    {
```

```
    print("<br>block.");
    }
else
    {
    print("<br>byte.");
    }
```

mcrypt_module_get_algo_block_size()

mcrypt_module_get_algo_block_size( ) returns the block size used by the specified algorithm. The optional second parameter accepts the name of a directory containing the algorithm:

```
$size = mcrypt_module_get_algo_block_size($module);
```

mcrypt_module_get_algo_key_size()

mcrypt_module_get_algo_key_size( ) returns the maximum key size supported by the specified algorithm. The optional second parameter accepts the name of a directory containing the algorithm:

```
$size = mcrypt_module_get_algo_key_size($module);
```

mcrypt_module_get_algo_supported_key_sizes()

mcrypt_module_get_algo_supported_key_sizes( ) is a new function for releases after PHP 4.0.6 and will return an array containing all the valid key sizes for the specified algorithm. If the array is empty, all the key sizes from 1 up to the maximum are valid. The optional second parameter accepts the name of a directory containing the algorithm. The following code prints the list of key sizes when there is a list:

```
$size = mcrypt_module_get_algo_supported_key_sizes($module);
while(list($k, $v) = each($size))
    {
    print("<br>" . $v);
    }
```

Payment Software

When you launch into online payment acceptance and clearance, you will need software to talk with your merchant account provider. That software might be provided by your merchant account provider, by your ISP, or by a third party. Here are some third-party providers supported directly by PHP functions.

CyberCash

CyberCash is now owned by VeriSign (**www.verisign.com**), and CyberCash's software was sold to First Data Merchant Services (**www.firstdata.com/**). (First Data's Web site uses JSP instead of PHP, so would you really want to deal with them?)

To install CyberCash in Unix, compile PHP with **--with-cybercash**. To install CyberCash in Windows NT 4 or Windows 2000, do the following:

1. Copy php_cybercash.dll from c:/Program Files/php/extensions to c:/winnt/ system32.

2. Change one line in c:/winnt/php.ini from **;extension=php_cybercash.dll** to **extension=php_cybercash.dll**.

3. Restart your Web server (if PHP is running as a module).

In other versions of Windows, substitute c:\windows\system for c:/winnt/ system32.

Payflow is the alternative to CyberCash. Payflow is owned by VeriSign, the same company that owns CyberCash, so CyberCash is likely to disappear, or have its internals replaced by Payflow.

To use CyberCash, you register at the CyberCash Web site, and then you receive a user id, password, merchant id, and encryption key. When you want to process a payment, you encrypt the message to CyberCash using **cybercash_encr( )**, encode the encrypted message using **cybercash_base64_encode( )**, and then send the message to CyberCash via **fopen( )** and a CGI script. **fopen( )** returns the results of the transaction. The results have to be split up, decoded using **cybercash_base64_decode( )**, and then decrypted using **cybercash_decr( )**.

Documentation for CyberCash is at **www.cybercash.com/cashregister/support/ docs/**. You can make life a little easier by reading about objects in Chapter 17, and then downloading Nathan Cassano's CyberClass at **www.cjhunter.com/~nathan/ class.cyberclass.txt**. **fopen( )** is described in Chapter 8.

cybercash_encr()

cybercash_encr( ) encrypts the request message using triple DES encryption. Read the CyberCash documentation for the message format. The merchant key will arrive with your merchant id. The session key is an identifier you build that is unique to the session, perhaps a string containing the session id and the current date/time:

```
$session_key = session_id() . " " . date("Y-m-d H:i:s");
$encrypted = cybercash_encr($merchant_key, $session_key, $message);
```

```
if($encrypted["errcode"] === false)
   {
   print("<br>output buffer: " . $encrypted["outbuff"]
     . "<br>output length: " . $encrypted["outLth"]
     . "<br>mac buffer: " . $encrypted["macbuff"]);
   }
else
   {
   print("<br>error code: " . $encrypted["errcode"]);
   }
```

cybercash_base64_encode()

cybercash_base64_encode( ) base64 encodes an encrypted message for inclusion in a URL:

```
$outbuff = cybercash_base64_encode($encrypted["outbuff"]);
$macbuff = cybercash_base64_encode($encrypted["macbuff"]);
```

fopen()

In between **cybercash_base64_encode( )** and **cybercash_base64_decode( )**, you need to build the encoded strings into a URL, feed the URL to a CGI script at CyberCash via **fopen( )**, slice up the results, and then feed the results to the decode. You will need error checking and code to handle network timeouts. (**fopen( )** is described in Chapter 8.) The following code provides an example (the URL will change as VeriSign relables CyberCash's products):

```
$file = fopen("http://cr.cybercash.com/cgi-bin/", "r");
```

cybercash_base64_decode()

cybercash_base64_decode( ) decodes a base64 encoded message:

```
$output = cybercash_base64_decode($result_output);
$mac = cybercash_base64_decode($result_mac);
```

cybercash_decr()

cybercash_decr( ) decrypts the message from CyberCash using the merchant and session keys:

```
$decrypted = cybercash_decr($merchant_key, $session_key, $output);
if($decrypted["errcode"] === false)
   {
```

```
    print("<br>output buffer: " . $decrypted["outbuff"]
      . "<br>mac buffer: " . $decrypted["macbuff"]);
  }
else
  {
  print("<br>error code: " . $decrypted["errcode"]);
  }
```

Payflow

VeriSign's (**www.verisign.com/payment**) Payflow Pro provides a range of financial transactions including credit card clearances. To install Payflo in Unix, compile PHP with **--with-pfpro** and download the software development kit (SDK) from VeriSign (you have to register with VeriSign first). Payflow appears to be missing from the PHP 4.0.6 Win32 binary.

pfpro_init()

pfpro_init( ) starts a Payflow process. If you forget this function, the next Payflow function will automatically start this process:

```
pfpro_init();
```

pfpro_version()

pfpro_version( ) returns the version number of the Payflow library and can be used to warn your system administrator if a new version is installed without suitable testing:

```
if(pfpro_version() != "L211")
  {
  print("<br>Warning, payflow library wrong version.");
  }
```

pfpro_process()

pfpro_process( ) processes a transaction and returns the result in an array. The following code processes one transaction and prints the result with **print_r( )**:

```
$test = array("USER" => "fredsmith", "PWD" => "fs123",
  "TRXTYPE" => "S", "AMT" => 49.95, "TENDER" => "C",
  "ACCT" => "1234123412341234", "EXPDATE" => "0904");
$server = "test-payflow.verisign.com";
$port = 443;
$timeout = 30;
```

```
$sslproxy_host = "192.168.32.45";
$sslproxy_port = 123;
$sslproxy_logon = "securetran";
$sslproxy_password = "sec123";
if($array = pfpro_process($test, $server, $port, $timeout,
   $sslproxy_host, $sslproxy_port, $sslproxy_logon, $sslproxy_password))
   {
   print_r($array);
   }
else
   {
   print("<br>pfpro_process() failed.");
   }
```

The first parameter is required and the rest are optional, but you will almost always specify the server. Ask your network administrator for any proxy settings.

pfpro_process_raw()

pfpro_process_raw( ) performs the same action as **pfpro_process( )**, and has just two differences in use. The first input parameter is a string with all the key-value pairs encoded similar to URL encoding, and the output is a string. **pfpro_process( )** is easier to use, and will give more reliable results because you will not make string encoding errors.

pfpro_cleanup()

pfpro_cleanup( ) ends a Payflow process. If you forget this function, the Payflow extension will automatically start this process at the end of your script:

```
pfpro_cleanup();
```

CCVS

You can read about Red Hat's Credit Card Verification System (CCVS) at **www.redhat.com/products/software/ecommerce/ccvs/**. The system costs money for an access key and support. Instead of a free test facility, there is a 30-day trial for $95. The key is for a single merchant and a single server, so it will cost more as you expand. Unfortunately, there is no indication of the extra cost on Red Hat's site.

The CCVS software sits between your Web site and the credit card clearing houses. Red Hat's Web site says CCVS works with "most" clearing house protocols, so decide who you will open your merchant account with and who they clear through, and then check if CCVS works with the right protocol. If CCVS does not work, you can probably use PHP's network and encryption functions to communicate with the clearing house of your choice.

Red Hat's sales pitch claims CCVS works well with online real-time clearances happening at the same time as bulk batch file transfers. That means you could have customers buying new subscriptions online while you put through your monthly renewal of existing subscriptions, which is hard to do with some credit card clearing systems.

CCVS works in the United States, Canada, and some other countries. CCVS uses a specific protocol, Visa 2nd Generation K Format, so look for the protocol at your local bank or merchant services provider.

The documentation suggests that the protocol was written for dial-up modems and a language less sophisticated than PHP. If Red Hat wants to make this product a winner, they need a good rebuild for PHP4.

Installing CCVS in Unix

To install CCVS in Unix, follow these steps:

1. Download and install CCVS from **www.redhat.com/products/software/ecommerce/ccvs/**.

2. Point PHP at the CCVS directory with **--with-ccvs**.

3. Start a **ccvsd** process for the configuration you want to use with PHP.

4. Make the PHP processes run under the same user id as the **ccvsd** process.

Windows and NT

There is no CCVS in the PHP 4.0.6 Win32 binary. RedHat says that CCVS is POSIX-compliant, so CCVS should work under native Windows NT or Windows NT with the addition of Cygwin. PostgreSQL (discussed in Chapter 5) is installed on Windows NT using Cygwin, and Red Hat could easily copy the PostgreSQL approach.

Functions

There is old documentation for PHP3 CCVS functions at **www.redhat.com/products/software/ecommerce/ccvs/support/docs/ProgPHP.html**.

4. Credit Cards

Immediate Solutions

Hashing Data

This solution makes use of the **mhash** functions. **mhash( )** is the one that performs the real work, and the rest could be of use in an administration facility where you want information about available hashes.

mhash()

mhash( ) produces several hashes. To test that the hashes work with a range of data, this solution tests them with the following string, integer, floating-point number, special characters, and non printable characters:

```
$data[] = "gfgfgfdgfsdgs";
$data[] = 125;
$data[] = 125.986;
$data[] = "special ÂÈÇ";
$data[] = "non print" . chr(13) . chr(10);
```

CRC32

CRC32 is the normal 32-bit CRC used for networks and disks, whereas CRC32B is a special 32-bit CRC used in ZIP files. The following code steps through the test data producing a CRC32 and a CRC32B string from each data item. The input data and results are output to a table for side-by-side comparison. Because the CRCs are 32-bit binary values, the code displays the CRCs in hexadecimal via **bin2hex( )**:

```
reset($data);
print("<table><tr><td>Data</td><td>  </td>"
    . "<td>CRC32</td><td>  </td><td>CRC32B</td></tr>");
while(list($k, $v) = each($data))
    {
    $hash = mhash(MHASH_CRC32, $v);
    $hashb = mhash(MHASH_CRC32B, $v);
    if($hash === false)
        {
        print("<br>made a hash of " . htmlentities($v));
        }
```

```
      else
         {
         print("<tr><td>" . htmlentities($v) . "</td><td> </td>"
            . "<td>" . bin2hex($hash) . "</td><td> </td>"
            . "<td>" . bin2hex($hashb) . "</td></tr>");
         }
      }
   print("</table>");
```

The following table shows the result, always 32-bit, and spread evenly across the full range of 32-bit values. CRCs are discussed further in Chapter 8.

```
Data              CRC32      CRC32B
gfgfgfdgfsdgs     7478b178   20859599
125               29432b3c   e7c62b61
125.986           b50d8790   b8cf7900
special ÂÈÇ        46243921   f5cbe007
non print         f5cd130c   7dd5c4c7
```

Related solution:	Found on page:
Calculating CRCs for Files	321

MD5

MD5 is a quick way to store passwords when you are not after the highest level of security. The following code is a version of the CRC32 code changed to use in MD5:

```
reset($data);
print("<table><tr><td>Data</td><td>  </td><td>MD5</td></tr>");
while(list($k, $v) = each($data))
   {
   $hash = mhash(MHASH_MD5, $v);
   if($hash === false)
      {
      print("<br>Error with " . htmlentities($v));
      }
   else
      {
      print("<tr><td>" . htmlentities($v) . "</td><td> </td>"
         . "<td>" . bin2hex($hash) . "</td></tr>");
      }
   }
print("</table>");
```

The first change just replaces CRC32 with MD5 in the heading. The second change replaces the two **mhash( )** functions with a single **mhash( )** containing **MHASH_MD5**. The word *hash* is replaced in the error message, and then the final **print( )** is changed to print the single result from **mhash( )**.

The following list shows the result with the 16-byte MD5 string displayed in hexadecimal:

```
Data           Hash
gfgfgfdgfsdgs  d8b32ce730bd0d5463a85d1c2a44b708
125            3def184ad8f4755ff269862ea77393dd
125.986        f3b22c8513875add521ef724a53a5c79
special ÂÈÇ    ff5e791248822257f8a279c4b72c88f4
non print      80b5da917ee85d4e797831633a0d760d
```

Notice the list shows unprintable characters like **0d** and **08**. When you store MD5 in a database, you need to use a binary-safe field or a representation, like hexadecimal. When you transmit MD5 through a URL or email, you need to use base64 encoding.

The Rest

Here is a quick run-through of the other **mhash( )** hashes. I used the following code and just replaced the string *SHA1*, in the highlighted code, with the names of the other hashes:

```
print("<table><tr><td>Hash</td><td>  </td><td>Result</td>"
  . "</tr>");
print("<tr><td>SHA1</td><td> </td>"
  . "<td>" . bin2hex(mhash(MHASH_SHA1, $data[0])) . "</td></tr>");
 print("</table>");
```

The results are as follows (lines are wrapped to fit the layout of this book):

```
Hash         Result
SHA1         36c02443ad02211bb93825e2ab0570fe7599b0bf
HAVAL256     b0e777d66725441baaf19dff51d8e4e94b56be0ad61605d8d81405b2c6
             a777e0
HAVAL224     323323ae1e7550f323527ac689188855574a9d94c1c1465188e28c20
HAVAL192     7d4dbefa3b15b45ea4dd91580301df1e88f2b1a6b0b1a3db
HAVAL160     dfbbab634967ab93ab868223de90ec2c83d70c63
RIPEMD160    631b594ffdb75af20e14a62585f8d400a0209642
GOST         bc10c57f8931759eafe871e68f72f248273bda56018d98732a0b7b1a48cc
             6394
TIGER        424e4610167e4d1aa587eff90d76ccbe14877424a0ddecb0
```

mhash_get_hash_name()

If you have a hash id, such as **MHASH_CRC32**, and want to know the official name of the hash, use this code:

```
print("<br>" . mhash_get_hash_name(MHASH_CRC32));
```

The result is:

```
CRC32
```

mhash_get_block_size()

If you have the id of a hash and want to calculate the space required for the hash, use the following code:

```
print("<br>" . mhash_get_block_size(MHASH_CRC32));
```

The result, shown next, is the length required for a hash of the specified type. You could use this calculation when you're automatically building a database table and need to calculate field sizes:

```
4
```

mhash_count()

mhash_count() returns the highest id allocated to a hash and lets you write code to step through all available hash ids. The following code steps from the first hash id, **0**, through to the value returned from **mhash_count()**, and returns both the name and block size for each in a neat table:

```
$hashes = mhash_count();
print("<table><tr><td>Hash</td><td> </td>"
    . "<td>Block Size</td></tr>");
for($h = 0; $h <= $hashes; $h++)
    {
    print("<tr><td>" . mhash_get_hash_name($h) . "</td><td> </td>"
        . "<td>" . mhash_get_block_size($h) . "</td></tr>");
    }
print("</table>");
```

Here are the results, including two ids that have no name or block size. The results will vary as new hash types are added and obsolete hashes are dropped (causing the empty entries):

```
Hash         Block Size
CRC32        4
MD5          16
SHA1         20
HAVAL256     32
             0
RIPEMD160    20
             0
TIGER        24
GOST         32
CRC32B       4
HAVAL224     28
HAVAL192     24
HAVAL160     20
```

mhash_keygen_s2k()

mhash_keygen_s2k( ) helps you generate a key from a user-given password using the salted S2K algorithm specified in the OpenPGP RFC 2440. The function requires the name of a hash, the password data, a salt value, and a length. The following code uses MD5 for the hash, the first value in table **$data** as the password, a not very random **turkey** as the salt, and **32** as the length:

```
$hash = mhash_keygen_s2k(MHASH_MD5, $data[0], "turkey", 32);
print("<br>" . htmlentities($data[0]) . "  " . bin2hex($hash));
```

NOTE: *A salt value is an initial value used to start a process and may be random or the same value each time. If you use the same salt string and password, you end up with the same key. If you change the salt value, you get a different key even using the same password. When you let your users enter a password to generate a key, they may enter the same password on several other sites, so you need to make the key for your site unique by entering a salt value unique to your site.*

Here is the result from the example code. The 32-byte result, displayed in hexadecimal, wrapped at the end of the line to fit this book's layout:

```
gfgfgfdgfsdgs b2a1f1ba22319592b739557ae118c2ee747c053732005c335c43a008eb
      b0e0e8
```

The salt field is just a random starting point for the generation process. Make the salt random to the point that people cannot guess it. **mhash( )** could produce a hash from a random string, like the string returned by **microtime( )**, and the hash could become the salt. You need the salt when checking keys, so save the salt when you save the key.

The salt is restricted to 8 bytes, and the following is the message you get when the salt exceeds 8 bytes. PHP 4.0.7dev also terminates abnormally when trying to process oversized salt fields:

```
Warning: The specified salt [13] is more bytes than the required by the
    algorithm [8]
```

Chapter 5

Databases: MySQL and PostgreSQL

In Depth

MySQL and PostgreSQL are both open source databases ideal for small and medium-sized Web sites. Both have similarities that make them equally good choices for most Web sites, and both have special features that will make one the best choice for some projects. The first part of this chapter covers the similarities and differences that will help you choose one of the databases, and the second part, the "Immediate Solutions" section, shows you how to perform the most common and important tasks with both MySQL and PostgreSQL. In addition, I will build toward code that is similar for both databases, so you will have minimal conversion work if you have to change from one to the other.

MySQL is available already set up for Windows and Windows NT, so users of either operating system can start with MySQL. If you want to use PostgreSQL on Windows, you are currently facing a complicated installation of several products plus compilations. For all versions of Unix and Linux, both MySQL and PostgreSQL are equally available, equally easy (or difficult) to install, and have about the same level of support.

In the past, I developed Web sites on Windows NT and then distributed the sites to Windows NT, Solaris, Linux, or FreeBSD as required, so I would always start with MySQL and use PostgreSQL only when there was a need for some specific feature of PostgreSQL. Starting with the Mandrake 8 distribution of Linux, Linux gained the same ease of installation and user interface as Windows NT, so I may switch over to Linux for everything.

MySQL used to perform faster than PostgreSQL for the simple read-intensive databases used on many Web sites because MySQL did not carry the overhead of transaction processing. Now MySQL has transaction processing, and PostgreSQL has started to match MySQL for update-intensive databases, so the performance of the two is no longer a real consideration unless you aim to use one big database of a very specific design.

History

Open source software has two main streams of database evolution: the big, slow bulldozer that can go anywhere and do anything (Postgres) and the small, fast Porsche (MySQL). Postgres first grew out of a project at Berkeley that seemed destined to compete with Oracle feature for feature.

Over at Bond University in Queensland, Australia, programmer David Hughes attempted to connect an application to Postgres via SQL (Postgres did not have SQL). David wrote his own SQL processor and called it miniSQL. David decided Postgres was too slow, so he added his own light, fast, database to miniSQL, and called it mSQL.

MySQL later replaced mSQL, but continued to be fast and light. Postgres eventually expanded into PosgreSQL.

The popular vote, so far, is for the Porsche over the tractor.

MySQL

The following quote is from the MySQL documentation and explains the ownership of MySQL: "MySQL AB is the Swedish company owned and run by the MySQL founders and main developers. We are dedicated to developing MySQL and spreading our database to new users. MySQL AB owns the copyright to the MySQL server source code and the MySQL trademark. A significant amount of revenues from our services goes to developing MySQL." MySQL used to have an odd license arrangement, but it is now issued under the standard open source GNU General Public License (GPL). The developers started by experimenting with mSQL, and then decided to write a database that could scale up to large Web sites better than mSQL. Monty Widenius is the principal MySQL developer, and he clearly aimed MySQL toward practical day-to-day use, which ensures MySQL's ongoing popularity.

PostgreSQL

PostgreSQL is an update of Postgres95, which is derived from Postgres, software developed at University of California at Berkeley beginning back in 1986. Postgres was developed commercially by Illustra Information Technologies; Informix bought Illustra, and then IBM bought Informix, so a little bit of Postgres may seep into IBM's DB2. Starting from release 7 of PostgreSQL, a number of MySQL users report good performance and predictability from PostgreSQL in medium-sized Web sites, so expect to see PostgreSQL usage expand as people gain the database experience needed to make use of the extra features in PostgreSQL.

PostgreSQL is still a pain to install in an operating system other than Unix, and that will force the millions of Web developers using Windows to learn MySQL first, which will keep MySQL in the lead. Before you can install PostgreSQL in Windows, you have to install various components of Unix, each with a different installation procedure. I tried to find you an up-to-date, comprehensive, and accurate tutorial on installing PostgreSQL under Windows or Windows NT, but I did not succeed. The problems with Windows suggest PostgreSQL will also be slow in reaching other platforms and MySQL's simple, robust construction will let MySQL beat PostgreSQL to each new platform.

The PostgreSQL code in this chapter is tested with PostgreSQL 7.1.1 on Windows NT 4 Service Pack 6a using cygwin 1.3.1 from **http://cygwin.com** and cygipc 1.09-2 from **www.neuro.gatech.edu/users/cwilson/cygutils/V1.1/cygipc/**. Cygipc and cygwin are prerequisites for PostgreSQL on Windows NT and provide an extended POSIX environment within Windows NT, complete with a Unix bash shell. If you are baffled by terms like *bash shell*, do not try installing PostgreSQL on Windows NT. Try to get some experience with Linux first, or get a person with Linux experience to walk you through the installation and startup procedure.

Some Differences

MySQL and PostgreSQL are close to the ANSI/ISO SQL92 standard with PostgreSQL throwing in some SQL99. Both are improving release by release, so there is little point in selecting either database based on standards compliance. Just be aware of the differences and document the differences in your code. Major feature differences will outweigh your need for standards compliance; most variations from the standards and differences in features are listed here, with some differences, such as data types, covered later in this chapter.

MySQL has some SQL coding variations that I hope will be cleaned out one day. SQL is just another language, complete with peculiarities that are what I would call nonstandard, and in some cases the MySQL developers chose to be more standard than the people developing SQL. One example is the way comment lines are indicated: The most common approach across all languages is a # symbol at the start of the line. The ANSI/ISO/SQL people chose the symbol -- for comments. MySQL chose the # symbol, and also supports the -- symbol; whereas the PostgreSQL developers stuck to the -- symbol. I believe, for most existing programmers, both SQL and PHP would be easier to learn if they permitted # at the start of a line to indicate a comment, and all languages would be easier for future programmers to learn if they switched to just one standard comment delimiter.

MySQL's nonstandard SQL allows # for comments (and also allows the standard --), uses ' to delimit system identifiers (which most programmers rarely use), uses " to quote strings (and also allows the standard ' that is used in all examples in this book), and uses || to mean **or** instead of string concatenation. You can avoid the misuse of || by always writing **or** when you need the logical **OR**, and spelling out terms like **or** and **and**. This is the safest way to program in most languages.

Dates

PostgreSQL and MySQL have slightly different date handling, but then again, every database seems to be different; the most popular commercial databases are the worst, with their insistence on the American date format of mm/dd/yyyy, a format that is too easily confused with the European dd/mm/yyyy. If you print a date like 02/06/2002, the date is indistinguishable from 02/06/2002: One date is Waitangi Day in New Zealand (February 6), and the other is Republic Day in Italy (June 2). The SQL standard is yyyy-mm-dd, and both databases accept that format.

Case Sensitivity

PostgreSQL uses a case-sensitive string comparison and provides functions to perform a case-insensitive comparison, whereas MySQL starts out case-insensitive and lets you choose case sensitivity. MySQL uses case-insensitive comparisons for string types **char**, **text**, and **varchar**, whereas **blobs** use binary comparisons (case-insensitive), and **char**, **text**, and **varchar** can be changed to case-insensitive by defining them with the **binary** attribute. MySQL also provides functions to translate string fields to upper- or lowercase for manual comparisons.

PostgreSQL field, table, and database names are case-insensitive but can be specified with a specific case if you want to make life difficult. MySQL database definitions become directories in the underlying file structure, whereas table names become individual files, and both have their case sensitivity determined by your operating system. If you start MySQL with the parameter **lower_case_table_names=1**, you can force all table names to lowercase and avoid case-sensitivity traps. Because MySQL stores databases as separate directories and tables as separate files, you have greater flexibility, but you will crash into operating system restrictions on the characters you can use in directory and file names; so leave out all characters that are not lowercase letters or numbers.

Transactions

PostgreSQL has always had transactions, and MySQL recently added a new table type that lets you use transactions, a choice that makes sense because transactions do have a performance overhead. If you want big read-only tables for reference information in a Web site, choose MySQL's standard tables without transaction support, and choose either MySQL's new table format or PostgreSQL for tables requiring updates. There is nothing to stop you running both side by side, and in a multiserver Web site, you can have your primary reference database transaction enabled to guarantee clean updates, and then replicate the data to reference servers with no transaction support—an ideal structure for search engines with thousands of servers.

Stored Procedures

Twenty years ago, stored procedures were the savior of databases, because stored procedures let you encapsulate business rules in one definition locked in step with the data, instead of being duplicated across many programming languages and buried deep in code. Stored procedures should process many times faster because the processing is performed within the database code, thus reducing traffic between the database and your program. Today, *Star Trek* is more believable.

Stored procedures solved a multiple-language problem when people wrote procedural code in COBOL, reports in RPG, and data format conversions in an Assembly language, but introduced the problem of learning another language, the stored procedure language, that is limited to just one database. Today you can write programs, reports, and data conversions in PHP, which in turn means you can have a business rule stored in one place as a function or object in an include file named businessrule01.html, and include the rule in any script that accesses your database. Stored procedures are no longer needed to solve a multiple-language problem and actually create one by making you learn a language other than PHP.

If your system contains a database on a database server and your PHP scripts on a separate Web server, you have a classic client/server network traffic problem that can be solved by good SQL design. Stored procedures can prevent some accidents with SQL design, but reliance on stored procedures can also increase problems when one person develops sophisticated stored procedures and all the other developers have insufficient SQL design experience.

PHP's code inclusion, its ability to easily use functions and objects, and PHP4's speed mean there are few reasons to adopt stored procedures. In a smaller development environment, you save the overhead of having a person specialize in yet another language. Stored procedures are needed for protecting databases shared among multiple applications written in diverse languages.

Triggers

Triggers, like transactions, slow down processing but provide a function difficult to build into your code; so, if your Web site has a need for triggers, dive into PostgreSQL, because MySQL has no equivalent. Do look carefully at your need for triggers before implementing anything, because the client-driven nature of Web sites removes the need for some traditional uses of triggers. If you have not used triggers, they are database-dependent; so study PostgreSQL's documentation and tutorials, especially the parts related to triggers, at **postgresql.org**.

Views

The best initial view of data is a clean view unobstructed by stored procedures or any other tricks database software provides. Once you understand the database structure and content, there are uses for limited views of the content, such as letting all your staff see staff names and contact telephone numbers, but not salaries. You might want to take the control a little farther by letting all your staff see everyone's day and month of birth, so they can celebrate birthdays, but not see anyone's year of birth, so the staff member who spent $20,000 on cosmetic surgery will not have his secret exposed. You can write SQL to provide a limited view of data, but the next programmer can drop in another field and corrupt the SQL view. PostgreSQL's view feature lets you lock the view into the database and use PostgreSQL's security to control access, with each view behaving like a separate table with all the access restrictions of a separate table. If you have a database administrator and many programmers, and you use views, your database administrator is the only person able to spy on staff salaries.

Data Types

When you store data, you want to store bits, bytes, integers, floating-point number, strings, binary objects, and very large binary objects. Everything else is stored in one of these data types, or stored in an external file with a reference stored in one of these data types. How do PostgreSQL and MySQL compare across all these data types?

Bits

MySQL's **set** is a special-case binary object for storing lists of options. PostgreSQL has an SQL99-standard **boolean** field type that could be used for each option stored by **set**, and PostgreSQL has two **bit** string types that act like **char** fields but store only ones and zeros. Although MySQL's **set** saves programming work for some types of data, PostgreSQL's **boolean** is the best selection for the future, and the developers at MySQL have promised **boolean** in a future MySQL.

The PostgreSQL **bit** and **bit varying** fields store a string of ones and zeros with no constraints on content or interpretation and no bits interpreted as signs or given any other special meaning. **Bit** is a fixed-length field; you specify the length, and it is zero-filled (filled with zeros to the specified length). **Bit varying** is variable length and of unlimited length if you do not specify a maximum length.

When I set up applications for the long term and use MySQL, I store boolean-style data in **tinyint** or **set** fields via functions, so some time in the future I can easily replace the **tinyint** and **set** fields with fields of type **boolean**. SQL standards compliance is more important in the long term than a little processing overhead or disk space, but you are more likely to choose a database based on your operating system, use of transactions, or a the need for referential integrity.

Integers

PostgreSQL and MySQL integer types are listed in Table 5.1. Both databases are close to the ANSI/ISO SQL92 standard for numeric data, and I see little reason to choose one database over the other based on integers. MySQL does provide the optional **unsigned** parameter to let you store larger positive numbers in integers, and that is of use mainly with **int**, when you want 32-bit unsigned integers for fields like CRC32, and when you use **int autoincrement** for key fields (described later in the chapter).

PostgreSQL's **bigint** may not be available on every platform, so be prepared to use another format; and **money** is obsolete, so choose another field format like **decimal**. MySQL's **dec** is an alias for **decimal**, and **int** is an alias for **integer**.

Decimal and Numeric

Decimal and **numeric** store numbers as strings so you can store any length number. Both MySQL and PostgreSQL have limitations on how they handle these data types, so any large number stored for use in BCMath or GMP is best stored in a conventional string. If you do use these types in a database, you can specify them with a maximum length and a precision, as in **decimal(11,2)**.

Serial

PostgreSQL's **serial** and MySQL's **int autoincrement** are used for automatically incremented numeric identifiers in tables, and can be used for things like invoice number and transaction number. MySQL lets you add **unsigned** to integer fields to double their range when used for **autoincrement** fields. A later

Table 5.1   Integer data types in MySQL and PostgreSQL.

Type	Bytes	Range	MySQL	PostgreSQL
tinyint	1	-128 to +127	Yes	No
smallint	2	-32768 to +32767	Yes	Yes
mediumint	3	-8388608 to +8388607	Yes	No
integer	4	-2147483648 to +2147483647	Yes	Yes
bigint	8	17 to 18 digits	Yes	Yes
decimal	Variable	No limit	Yes	Yes
numeric	Variable	No limit	Yes	Yes
serial	4	0 to +2147483647	No	Yes
money	4	-$21,474,836.48 to +$21,474,836.47	No	Yes

section, "Inserting Ids," discusses the use of automatically incremented integers as key identifiers.

Floating-Point Numbers

MySQL and PostgreSQL have similar floating-point numbers of four or eight bytes, with the eight-byte type matching PHP's internal eight-byte format; so make all your floating-point fields of type **double precision** unless you can guarantee that the results will fit in to a smaller field, and you are happy with the truncation of numbers containing fractions that do not fit exactly into the smaller fields. The floating-point types are listed in Table 5.2.

MySQL's **double** is an alias for **double precision**. MySQL's **float** lets you specify an optional precision, which is not an SQL92 standard; there are few times when you need to set a precision for this type of data, so, for compatibility, avoid **float**.

Strings

MySQL has a better range of field types for storing small strings, and could be the best choice for applications that can make good use of short text fields. As disk storage costs drop, there is less reason to save one or two bytes per string field. The string types are listed in Table 5.3.

Table 5.2   Floating-point data types in MySQL and PostgreSQL.

Type	Bytes	Range	MySQL	PostgreSQL
float	4	6 decimal places	Yes	No
real	4	6 decimal places	Yes	Yes
double precision	8	15 decimal places	Yes	Yes

Table 5.3   String data types in MySQL and PostgreSQL.

Type	Length field (bytes)	Data (bytes)	MySQL	PostgreSQL
char	0	1 to 255	Yes	No
varchar	1	1 to 255	Yes	No
tinytext	1	1 to 255	Yes	No
text	2	1 to 65535	Yes	No
mediumtext	3	1 to 16777216	Yes	No
longtext	4	1 to 4294967295	Yes	No
text	4	1 to 4294967295	Yes	Yes
character	4	1 to 4294967295	No	Yes
character varying	4	1 to 4294967295	No	Yes

MySQL's **varchar**, **tinytext**, **text**, **mediumtext**, and **longtext** are variable-length fields that store just the data you supply plus a small length field, as shown in Table 5.3. PostgreSQL's **text** is equivalent to MySQL's **longtext**. PostgreSQL's **character varying** is equivalent to MySQL's **text**, with a maximum limit, or MySQL's **varchar** expanded from a maximum length of 255 to a maximum of 4294967295. **Character varying** has an alias of **varchar**. PostgreSQL's **character**, also called **char**, is equivalent to PostgreSQL's **character varying**, with spaces filling out the field to the specified length, or MySQL's **char** with a much longer maximum length.

Enum

MySQL's **enum** lets you store a number representing a keyword defined when you define the **enum** field, and is perfect for selection boxes in forms where you ask the visitor to select one of many choices. Suppose your Web site is storing votes for the world's 10 most popular people, and you really want to save space because all 800,000,000 internet users will vote. You could define an **enum** field containing the names, and the field will use just one byte instead of the number of characters required to store a name, because the names are stored just once in the table's field definitions, and the field stores only an index in to the name list. The index for lists from 1 to 255 names fits in one byte, the entry for lists up to 65,000 names fits in two bytes, and data may be entered using the name defined in **enum** or directly as the index number. The following code example is the **enum** definition for a field named **person** that will store the name of a person from the top 10 list in table **votes**:

```
create table votes (person enum('Nicole Kidman', 'Peter Moulding',
   'Hannibal Lecter', 'Janet Jackson', ' Kevin Spacey',
   'Cuba Gooding Jr.', 'Rasmus Lerdorf', 'Madonna', 'Yoda',
   ' _ insert your name here _ '))
```

Set

MySQL's **set** lets you store a binary string with a bit that is set on for each keyword value supplied in the input. Suppose your Web site is accepting votes for people as described in the "**Enum**" section, you want voters to check off why they selected the person they voted for, and you let them select attributes such as "caring," "handsome," and "has the right DNA for breeding." The following code shows how to define a field named **features** to store the list of attributes checked off by the voter. One bit in **features** is set on or off for each attribute, and because **set** fields have a maximum length of eight bytes (or 64 bits), you can specify up to 64 attributes in one **set** field. **Set** suits checkbox selections in HTML forms where people can select several of many choices, up to 64 choices per **set** field, and reduces the need for the PostgreSQL **boolean** field type (MySQL promises **boolean** in a future release):

```
alter table votes add column features set('intelligent', 'handsome',
    'caring', 'sharing', 'DNA')
```

Blobs

Binary Long Objects (**blobs**) let you store images and other binary data in databases, something that is sometimes very good, and sometimes very bad. Very good examples are things like encrypted passwords that are perhaps only 32 bytes in a database, but would chew up a large amount of disk space if stored as a discrete file—8,192 bytes in Linux's ext2 file system. Storing full-sized images in databases is the exact opposite: 100,000-byte images are best stored in the file system with just a reference stored in your database.

Dates and Time

PostgreSQL and MySQL have similar date and time fields for the most common dates and times you will store. Both accept similar input and produce similar output to the point where your PHP code for one database could move to the other database without converting the SQL. Table 5.4 lists the mostly similar field types.

MySQL's **timestamp** is a standard Unix timestamp, which is valid from 1970 to 2037 in one-second increments, whereas PostgreSQL's **timestamp** counts from 1903 in one-second increments. MySQL's **timestamp** is updated when you insert a record, change a field in a record, or set the field to **null**. PostgreSQL does not seem to update its **timestamp**, so you have to write a stored procedure or use one of the other PostgreSQL special features to perform the same task. PostgreSQL does allow you to specify time zones, which would let you accept a local time and translate back to a GMT/UCT time.

Table 5.4   Date and time data types in MySQL and PostgreSQL.

Type	Length (bytes)	Format	MySQL	PostgreSQL
date	3	yyyy-mm-dd	Yes	Yes
datetime	8	yyyy-mm-dd hh:mm:ss	Yes	Yes
timestamp	4	yyyymmddhhmmss	Yes	Yes
time	3	hh:mm:ss	Yes	Yes
year	1	1901 to 2125	Yes	No
interval	12	−178000000 to +178000000	No	Yes

PostgreSQL's **year** is from 4137 B.C. to A.D. 32767, whereas MySQL covers 0000 to 9999 and allows both **month** and **day** to be zero, so you can store partial dates such as 0000-11-04 (a person's birthday without giving away their age) or 1857-00-00 (when you know the year your ancestor was born but not the month or day).

PostgreSQL's **interval** looks like a very long version of a Unix time expanded to a time scale suitable for astronomy or perhaps the tax department. **Interval** stores 356,000,000 years in one-second increments, and, because the number of seconds per year changes every few years (the earth is slowing down), **interval** must use an approximation of seconds per year.

PostgreSQL Specials

PostgreSQL has a few special format fields that may be of use to you, although the use of special format fields can be a trap. Australia uses four-digit postal codes, and every year the post office talks about changing to six-character postal codes; so in Australia, using a special database field designed for postal codes could be a real trap. Table 5.5 has the special PostgreSQL types lists.

cidr holds Internet Protocol version 4 (IPv4) addresses (the Internet community is already deploying IPv6) in the format $x.x.x.x/y$ where y is the number of bits in the subnet mask used with the address. **inet** is a variation of **cidr** that allows non-zero values in all address positions so you can store individual host addresses. **cidr** is the one you use to store the prefix for your network, such as 192.168.3/8, and **inet** is the one to store addresses of individual computers, such as 192.168.3.4. **macaddr** accepts media access control (MAC) addresses in various formats,

Table 5.5   Data types exclusive to PostgreSQL.

Type	Length (bytes)	Value
cidr	12	Any IPv4 network address
inet	12	Any IPv4 network or host address
macaddr	6	Any network adapter MAC address
point	16	A point in two-dimensional space
line	32	An infinite line in two-dimensional space
lseg	32	A finite line in two-dimensional space
box	32	A rectangular box in two-dimensional space
path	Variable	An open or closed path in two-dimensional space
polygon	32	A polygon in two-dimensional space
circle	24	A circle in two-dimensional space

including 01:03:44:0a:f3:92. The letters can be upper- or lowercase and the colon, :, can be a dash, –, on input, and is output as :.

point stores an x,y coordinate for two-dimensional geometry; **line** stores two x,y coordinates from an infinite line; **lseg** stores the starting and ending x,y coordinates from a finite line; **box** stores the two opposite x,y coordinates defining a rectangle; **path** stores multiple x,y coordinates to form an open or closed path (much like **polygon**); **polygon** stores multiple x,y coordinates to form a polygon; and **circle** stores the center (as x,y coordinates) and radius of a circle. All the fields contain multiple eight-byte floating-point numbers, so you need to make sure all your numbers are entered using a matching scale.

Inserting IDs

When you insert records that have an **auto_increment** field (**serial** in PostgreSQL), you may want to get the value of the **auto_increment** field from the insert. If you insert an invoice and use the **auto_increment** number as the invoice number, you want to use the invoice number when you insert the item entries for the invoice. You can get the **auto_increment** value a variety of ways. MySQL has the SQL function **last_insert_id( )**, and PHP includes the MySQL function **mysql_insert_id( )**. If you insert your invoice into a table of invoices, you could run this SQL:

```
select last_insert_id() from invoices limit 1
```

You can also use this PHP code for MySQL:

```
$invoicenumber = mysql_insert_id();
```

mysql_insert_id( ) gets the most recent value of any **auto_increment** field in the current thread, so you have to place **mysql_insert_id( )** immediately after the successful **insert** and before any other databases accesses that will trigger **auto_increment**s. When getting an **auto_increment** value from any database, get the value immediately and check the database's documentation about what happens if several scripts insert into the same table at the same time. With some databases, you have to lock the table for update and insert, then retrieve the id, and then unlock the table.

The PostgreSQL equivalent is shown next and is a little different because PostgreSQL's nearest equivalent to **mysql_insert_id( )** is **pg_getlastoid( )**, a function that returns an internal PostgreSQL identifier, **oid**. You cannot use **oid**s long-term because **oid**s are reset by things like table reloads. What the code does is request the **oid**, and then use the **oid** to request the sequence field, in this case named **invoice**, from the row identified by the **oid**. **pg_exec( )** is equivalent to **mysql_query( )**; it takes a database link identifier and an SQL statement, and returns a result identifier. The result identifier is used in **pg_fetch_array( )** to get the one row that matches the **oid**. The row is an array with fields identified by their field name, similar to **mysql_fetch_array( )**, and you can set **$invoicenumber** to the right value. There are other ways to perform this action in PostgreSQL, including a way to get the sequence field before the **insert**, but this way is closest to what you can do in other databases, and is the one least likely to cause problems when several programmers, all new to PostgreSQL, work on the code:

```
$oid = pg_getlastoid($result);
$result = pg_exec($link, "select invoice from invoices"
    . " where oid = " . $oid);
$row = pg_fetch_array($result);
$invoicenumber = $row["invoice"];
```

PHP allows integers up to 2 billion. If your **auto_increment** field goes over that, PHP changes to using a long numeric field. MySQL and other databases allow for huge **auto_increment** values, but they may not convert correctly to PHP's long numeric format. You can get around the problem by using SQL to retrieve the id and keeping the id in the form returned by the SQL query.

Could you ever have such a big number? Image setting up a system so customers could analyze their view rates on the top 25 Web sites. There is one record per view, and several banners per page, so there are several view records per page, tens of millions of pages per site, and 25 sites, which means around 100,000,000 records per day into the database. Even if you continually deleted records older than seven days, the **auto_increment** number would keep growing.

Platform Independence

PostgreSQL is available on every version of Unix and Linux I have looked at. MySQL is available on the same versions of Unix and Linux, and is available on Windows and Windows NT. Therefore, MySQL is more platform-independent and is the best choice for applications you want to use on any server. MySQL appears to be available on every platform on which you can install Apache, which means MySQL is also available everywhere you can install PHP.

MySQL has one anomaly across platforms: Database names become directories and table names become file names, so you are restricted to whatever file-naming convention is allowed by your operating system and any other operating system you plan to use. I suggest you use lowercase names, with no spaces, underscores, dashes, or special characters, and keep the names short so they will work on every operating system.

Platform independence also requires SQL that works anywhere and the ability to read and produce any format data. Both MySQL and PostgreSQL handle the very large binary objects, **blob**s, that cause problems on some computers, and both have efficient ways of storing data, which is a problem with some databases on small computers with limited storage.

Turning Raw Data into Databases

SQL provides a variety of ways to read external files directly via SQL **insert** statements, and PHP is the perfect language to reformat files if the input files do not quite fit the requirements of SQL **insert** processing. A standard SQL **insert** is described in "Inserting a Row of Data" in the "Immediate Solutions" section. The **mysql.com** and **postgresql.org** Web sites provide documentation describing what format files their **insert** statements can read, and Chapter 8 describes how to read files with PHP when you have to manually format data for placement into SQL **insert** statements.

Arrays and Databases

PHP arrays, described in Chapter 3, provide a rich range of storage formats and key structures to let you load any relational data into memory and process it from memory, which is ideal when you access the same data several times in one script. Instead of reading the same data in several formats or sequences via different SQL, read the data once, and then sort and process the data from arrays.

To Index or Not to Index

Database indexes make some reads faster because the database software can go straight to the required data, and can make some writes slower because extra indexes mean extra records to write. Most databases provide a way to work out when an index would help a particular query, and a way to add and delete extra indexes. PHP supports all the special features of both MySQL and PostgreSQL. You will have to dig into logs to find out things like "which query is used most?" and PHP can read just about any file format, including log files. You will have to calculate the merits of extra speed for reads versus extra overheads for each write, and PHP will help you automate the calculations once you decide which calculations are most important for your site. With both MySQL and PostgreSQL, you can easily create an index, watch the Web site performance, and then delete the index.

Relationships

PostgreSQL's support for relationships is what makes a database a relational database, and is of immense use in certain situations. Relationships lock tables to other tables to keep entries in related tables in step, but a bad relationship rule creates data-entry headaches. If you are just starting out with databases or with brand-new data, you are better off skipping relationships, reading the data into tables, verifying that the data matches all criteria, and then experiment with adding relationships. Once you have a feel for the data and experience designing relationships, you can judge the value of relationships for your data, and then decide if the extra overheads justify any increase in data integrity you gain from PostgreSQL.

The quickest way to load and inspect data is to use the prewritten phpMyAdmin, available at **www.phpwizard.net**, and phpPgAdmin, from **www.greatbridge.org**. They both work off the shelf (but use frames) and both let you type in raw SQL if the precoded options do not fit exactly what you want.

ODBC

Object Database Connectivity (ODBC) gives you some database independence when accessing several types of databases; the cost is extra overhead for each access. If you are working with one database, such as MySQL, and are converting to another, such as PostgreSQL, the best approach is to use PHP's native functions for each database and carefully check that each access runs at optimum speed. If you work most of the time with one database and occasionally access other databases of different types, ODBC access to the other databases makes sense, because the ODBC overhead will not occur on your main database and you can quickly plug new databases in to the ODBC connection. You'll find more information on ODBC in Chapter 6.

Immediate Solutions

Connecting to a Database

The minimum code you need to connect to a local MySQL database is shown in the first example line that follows, and the rest of the lines show a connection to another server on the same network. A connection is made to a server via **mysql_connect( )**, which requires the server name as the first parameter and defaults to **localhost** if you don't supply the server name. You can also add a port number to the server name, in the form **sqlserver:3306**. **mysql_connect( )** defaults to 3306, so it is not necessary unless your network administrator gives you another port number. The user name defaults to the name of the user that owns the Web server process, and the password defaults to empty, so you can usually leave this out for MySQL on the same machine when your Web site is the only Web site on the machine. All the values are grouped in the array **$database** so you can load the values from a common file.

The **@** in front of **mysql_connect( )** simply disables the default error messages so you can intercept the error and produce a message that is more useful to you and less confusing to your Web site visitors. The message I included is a basic message for illustration purposes only. In practice, you would include contact information or a redirection to a feedback page or an email to the Web site administrator:

```
$connect = mysql_connect();

$database["server"] = "sqlserver";
$database["user"] = "sqluser";
$database["password"] = "tx04dd";
if(!$connect = @mysql_connect($database["server"],
   $database["user"],
   $database["password"]))
   {
   print("MySQL problem. Connect failed to server: "
      . $database["server"]);
   }
```

The previous code connects MySQL to a server; the following code connects MySQL to a database using **mysql_select_db( )**. The database is **movies**, the first parameter in **mysql_select_db( )** is the name of the database, and the second parameter is the optional connection identifier returned by **mysql_connect( )**. The connection identifier is an optional parameter in many MySQL functions, and if you leave the parameter out, the functions use the most recent connection, which is all you need in scripts that use just one connection. **mysql_select_db( )** returns false on failure so you can produce a useful error message:

```
$database["database "] = "movies";
if(!@mysql_select_db($database["database"], $connect))
   {
   print("MySQL problem. Failed to select " . $database["database "]);
   }
```

PostgreSQL has a function, **pg_connect( )**, equivalent to MySQL's **mysql_connect( )** and **mysql_select_db( )** combined, that accepts all parameters in one connection string. The following example connects to a database named **template1** (**template1** is built in during installation of PostgreSQL) on the local server as user **peter** with a **password**, **host**, and **port** specified. When I tested this with a PostgreSQL server running on the same computer as my test Apache Web server, I had to specify **host**, but not **password** or **port**:

```
$database["database"] = "template1";
$database["host"] = "localhost";
$database["port"] = "5432";
$database["user"] = "peter";
$database["password"] = "tx04dd";
$connect = pg_connect("dbname=" . $database["database"]
   . " host=" . $database["host"]
   . " port=" . $database["port"]
   . " user=" . $database["user"]
   . " password=" . $database["password"]);
```

Note that I left the **@** off the front of **pg_connect( )** and left out the error checking. **@** suppresses PostgreSQL's error messages. On the version I used to test this code, the **pg_errormessage( )** function did not return an error message, which means you are stuck with making sure your PostgreSQL connections are 100 percent perfect and letting end users see the occasional ugly message when the PostgreSQL connection fails. How ugly? Figure 5.1 shows the error message. **pg_errormessage( )** works once a connection is established, and reports the last error message to occur on that connection.

> **Warning**: Unable to connect to PostgreSQL server: connectDBStart() -- socket() failed: errno=0

Figure 5.1   Ugly error message from failed pg_connect().

Both MySQL and PostgreSQL support persistent connections, which reduces overhead by letting your script reuse a previous connection for the same user, password, and server. Persistent connections seem 100 percent safe with MySQL, but can cause occasional problems with PostgreSQL if PostgreSQL is restarted without a restart of Apache. In MySQL, you replace **mysql_connect( )** with **mysql_pconnect( )**, and in PostgreSQL, replace **pg_connect( )** with **pg_pconnect( )**.

Listing Databases

When you want to know what databases are available on your server, MySQL supports the SQL **show databases** command, shown in the first code line that follows, to show you all the databases you are authorized to see. This command may include databases you are authorized to see, but not read. The code assumes you made a connection to the database as shown in the previous "Connecting to a Database" section:

```
$database["sql"] = "show databases";
if($result = @mysql_query($database["sql"]))
    {
    while($row = mysql_fetch_row($result))
        {
        print("<br>" . $row[0]);
        }
    }
else
    {
    print("Query error: " . mysql_errno() . ", " . mysql_error()
        . " using sql " . $database["sql"]);
    }
```

The code places the SQL in a general database access array and then presents the SQL to **mysql_query( )**, which returns a result indicator or false on error. **mysql_fetch_row( )** reads one row at a time from the result, and returns false after the last row is read. If you get an error in the database access, the code returns the error message; but if the access works and zero lines are returned from the SQL, there will be no error message and no data lines printed. The result from my workstation is shown next, complete with the **movies** database used as an example in a few Immediate Solutions, the **mysql** database used by MySQL for administration, and the **test** database set up by MySQL for your testing:

5. Databases: MySQL and PostgreSQL

```
movies
mysql
page
test
```

PostgreSQL has all the databases on a server named in table **pg-databases**, a table hidden in an administrative database, and lets you see the list of databases with the SQL **select** statement, shown first in the following code. PostgreSQL's administrative tables list the tables in PostgreSQL's administration database, so people accessing PostgreSQL with administrative rights see the extra tables, which you can exclude by using the second **select** statement shown in the following code. The example code is similar to the MySQL query with **pg_exec()** performing the query and **pg_fetch_row()** returning the results row by row. PostgreSQL has one error message function, **pg_errormessage()**, replacing MySQL's **mysql_error()** and **mysql_errno()** functions:

```
select datname from pg-databases
select datname from pg-databases where tablename not like 'pg%'

$database["sql"] = "select datname from pg_database";
if($result = @pg_exec($database["sql"]))
    {
    $rows = pg_numrows($result);
    if($rows)
        {
        for($i = 0; $i < $rows; $i++)
            {
            $row = pg_fetch_row($result, $i);
            print("<br>" . $row[0]);
            }
        }
    else
        {
        print("<br>Zero results. Error: " . $error
            . "<br>from sql: " . $database["sql"]);
        }
    }
else
    {
    print("Pg_exec() error: " . pg_errormessage()
        . "<br>using sql: " . $database["sql"]);
    }
```

PostgreSQL's **pg_fetch_row( )** requires a row index entry. All rows are indexed from zero, so you have to access **pg_fetch_row( )** with a **for( )** instead of a **while( )**, and you can prime the **for( )** with the number of rows via **pg_numrows( )**. The previous code is also expanded to differentiate between those occasions when the **pg_exec( )** strikes an error and those occasions when **pg_exec( )** works but returns zero rows. The **if($rows)** detects the zero-rows situation and outputs a special error message so you can check your SQL for logic errors. The following list is the result returned from PostgreSQL—the **test** and **movies** databases I set up plus two **template** sets copied in by the PostgreSQL installation process:

```
test
template1
template0
movies
```

PHP's MySQL functions include a special function, **mysql_list_dbs( )**, to list databases as shown in the following code. **mysql_list_dbs( )** reads the optional parameter, **$connect**, to connect to a MySQL server, and returns the pointer to the results list; then **mysql_num_rows( )** returns the number of rows to read, and the **for( )** loop steps through the rows. Each row is returned by the function **mysql_db_name( )**, a function written specifically to return the database name:

```
$result = mysql_list_dbs($connect);
$rows = mysql_num_rows($result);
for($i = 0; $i < $rows; $i++)
    {
    print("<br>" . mysql_db_name($result, $i));
    }
```

You can also return the rows into an object named **$x** via **mysql_fetch_object( )**, and then access the database name as **$x->Database**. Note that object property names are case-sensitive, so **Database** has to have a capital *D*. Here is the code:

```
$result = mysql_list_dbs();
while($x = mysql_fetch_object($result))
    {
    print("<br>" . $x->Database);
    }
```

You can now connect to a MySQL or PostgreSQL server and get a list of all the databases available from the server. The following Immediate Solutions take you through finding tables, finding fields, and creating new tables and data.

5. Databases: MySQL and PostgreSQL

Displaying Database Tables

When you want to know what tables are in a database, MySQL supports the SQL **show tables** command, shown in the second code line that follows, to list the tables in a database. The code assumes you made a connection to the database as shown in the earlier Immediate Solution, "Connecting to a Database," and the database is named **movies**:

```
$database["database"] = "movies";
$database["sql"] = "show tables from " . $database["database"];
if($result = @mysql_query($database["sql"]))
   {
   while($row = mysql_fetch_row($result))
      {
      print("<br>" . $row[0]);
      }
   }
else
   {
   print("Query error: " . mysql_errno() . ", " . mysql_error()
      . " using sql " . $database["sql"]);
   }
```

The code passes the SQL through **mysql_query( )**, which returns a result or false on an error, and then **mysql_fetch_row( )** reads one row of results at a time and returns false after the last row is read. A database access error returns the error message, and no error message or data lines are printed if there are no tables in the database. The result from the **movies** database is shown next; these tables are used as examples in later Immediate Solutions:

```
cast
director
movie
person
producer
title
```

The PostgreSQL equivalent is shown next. The selection is from the administration table **pg_tables**, a table that is not really a table but a view of table **pg_class.** Note that no database is specified. **pg_class** contains a range of definitions, including tables and indexes, but does not directly relate the definitions to databases the way tables are related to databases in MySQL.

The rest of the code is similar to the code used to display database names in the preceding "Listing Databases" section but dissimilar to the equivalent MySQL code.

Although you could write common code for both databases, some of their differing concepts would be hard to understand if buried in common code. The PostgreSQL functions **pg_fieldname( )** and **pg_fetch_row( )** both use an index into the result returned from **pg_exec( )**, so both require a **for( )** loop instead of a **while( )** loop, and both require a count to terminate their loop. **pg_fieldname( )** requires the number of fields from **pg_numfields( )**, and **pg_fetch_row( )** requires the number of rows from **pg_numrows( )**. The table formatting is the same as that used in the previous Immediate Solution:

```
$database["sql"] = "select * from pg_tables";
if($result = @pg_exec($database["sql"]))
    {
    $rows = pg_numrows($result);
    if($rows)
        {
        print("<table border=\"1\"><tr>");
        $fields = pg_numfields($result);
        for($f = 0; $f < $fields; $f++)
            {
            print("<td><em>" . pg_fieldname($result, $f) . "</em></td>");
            }
        print("</tr>");
        for($i = 0; $i < $rows; $i++)
            {
            $row = pg_fetch_row($result, $i);
            print("<tr>");
            for($f = 0; $f < $fields; $f++)
                {
                print("<td>" . $row[$f] . "</td>");
                }
            print("</tr>");
            }
        print("</table>");
        }
    else
        {
        print("<br>Zero results. Error: " . $error
            . "<br>from sql: " . $database["sql"]);
        }
    }
else
    {
    print("Pg_exec() error: " . pg_errormessage()
        . "<br>using sql: " . $database["sql"]);
    }
```

PHP also supplies **mysql_list_tables()** to return a list of tables in a database. **mysql_num_rows()** returns the number of rows to read, and the **for()** loop steps through the rows; each row is returned through the function **mysql_tablename()**, a function written specifically to return the table name. The **for()** loop is used instead of a **while()** loop because **mysql_tablename()** requires the index value, **$i**. Everything else is the same as the previous example:

```
$database["database"] = "movies";
$result = mysql_list_tables($database["database"]);
$rows = mysql_num_rows($result);
for($i = 0; $i < $rows; $i++)
    {
    print("<br>" . mysql_tablename($result, $i));
    }
```

Another way to list tables from MySQL is to wrap a **while()** loop around **mysql_fetch_row()**, shown next, and access the contents of the row using **list()**. This technique is closer to the technique used for listing databases in the previous Immediate Solution, and seems to make **mysql_tablename()** obsolete. But you never know what future PHP and MySQL releases will return from **mysql_list_tables()**, so **mysql_tablename()** may provide an extra measure of release independence:

```
$database["database"] = "movies";
$result = mysql_list_tables($database["database"]);
while(list($table) = mysql_fetch_row($result))
    {
    print("<br>" . $table);
    }
```

Displaying Table Fields

When you want to find all the fields in a database table, the SQL **show fields** command in MySQL will show you all the fields in the table, as will **show columns**. *Column* is the correct term for relational databases, although the words *field* and *column* are interchangeable in most databases. The first example that follows shows the two general SQL ways of requesting field information, followed by the MySQL version, and then the PostgreSQL version. The database is **movies**, the table is **person**, and the results are from a MySQL test database used to prototype a new Web site:

```
show columns from person from movies
show fields from person from movies
```

To list tables from MySQL, connect to MySQL as shown in the first Immediate Solution in this chapter, and then run the following code. **mysql_list_fields( )** returns a result for a table within a database; **mysql_num_fields( )** supplies the number of fields to read from the result; then **for( )** loops through the result. Individual field attributes are returned with **mysql_field_name**, **mysql_field_type**, **mysql_field_len**, and **mysql_field_flags**.

```
$result = mysql_list_fields("movies", "person");
$rows = mysql_num_fields($result);
for($i = 0; $i < $rows; $i++)
   {
   print("<br>" . mysql_field_name($result, $i)
      . " type: " . mysql_field_type($result, $i)
      . ", length: " . mysql_field_len($result, $i)
      . ", flags: " . mysql_field_flags($result, $i));
   }
```

The result is:

```
entry type: int, length: 10, flags: not_null primary_key unsigned
auto_increment
updated type: timestamp, length: 14, flags: not_null unsigned zerofill
timestamp
name type: string, length: 60, flags: not_null
realname type: blob, length: 255, flags: not_null blob
born type: date, length: 10, flags: not_null
comment type: blob, length: 65535, flags: not_null blob
```

The next example is a clearer way to display the information by wrapping the information in **<table>** tags. To delineate the columns in the table, the code uses borders in the HTML **<table>** tag, **border="3"**. Before printing the first row of data, the code prints a **<table>** tag and a row of headings, loops through the rows of data, and then prints a closing **</table>** tag. Within the loop, the code prints a table row with all the fields from each row:

```
$result = mysql_list_fields("movies", "person");
$rows = mysql_num_fields($result);
print("<table border=\"3\"><tr><td><em>Field</em></td>"
   . "<td><em>Type</em></td>"
   . "<td><em>Length</em></td>"
   . "<td><em>Flags</em></td></tr>");
```

```
for($i = 0; $i < $rows; $i++)
  {
  print("<tr><td>" . mysql_field_name($result, $i) . "</td>"
    . "<td>" . mysql_field_type($result, $i) . "</td>"
    . "<td>" . mysql_field_len($result, $i) . "</td>"
    . "<td>" . mysql_field_flags($result, $i) . "</td></tr>");
  }
print("</table>");
```

The table appears as shown in Figure 5.2.

The equivalent PHP PostgreSQL function is more complex, because PostgreSQL stores field names in a generic class table, field types in a separate type table, and field attributes in a separate attributes table. First look at each of the three tables to see the type of data they contain: Grab the PostgreSQL example from the previous Immediate Solution and run the sample three times, each time changing the table name to one of the three tables mentioned here. A sample of the **pg_class** table is shown in Figure 5.3. **pg_type** appears as shown in Figure 5.4, and **pg_attribute** is shown in Figure 5.5.

Clearly you do not want to work through the raw data, so use PostgreSQL's powerful SQL to pull the data together from all the tables and present the data just the way you want. The following code uses the same code as used in the previous three table displays, and replaces the SQL with the following SQL that selects fields from all three tables. In SQL, **from** lets you specify multiple table names

Field	Type	Length	Flags
entry	int	10	not_null primary_key unsigned auto_increment
updated	timestamp	14	not_null unsigned zerofill timestamp
name	string	60	not_null
realname	blob	255	not_null blob
born	date	10	not_null
comment	blob	65535	not_null blob

Figure 5.2   Fields in MySQL table **person**.

relname	reltype	relowner	relam	relfilenode	relpages	reltuples
pg_type	71	1000	0	1247	2	126
pg_attribute	75	1000	0	1249	8	575
pg_shadow	86	1000	0	1260	1	1
pg_class	83	1000	0	1259	2	80
pg_toast_1215_idx	0	1000	403	17213	1	0

Figure 5.3   Sample of PostgreSQL table **pg_class**.

typname	typowner	typlen	typprtlen	typbyval	typtype	typisdefined	typdelim
bool	1000	1	1	t	b	t	,
bytea	1000	-1	-1	f	b	t	,
char	1000	1	1	t	b	t	,
name	1000	32	32	f	b	t	,
int8	1000	8	20	f	b	t	,

Figure 5.4   Sample of PostgreSQL table **pg_type**.

attrelid	attname	atttypid	attdispersion	attlen	attnum	attnelems	attcacheoff
1247	typname	19	-1	32	1	0	-1
1247	typowner	23	1	4	2	0	-1
1247	typlen	21	0.19229	2	3	0	-1
1247	typprtlen	21	0.198765	2	4	0	-1
1247	typbyval	16	0.518141	1	5	0	-1

Figure 5.5   Sample of PostgreSQL table **pg_attribute**.

and **where** lets you select records that match up between the rows. In this case, the **oid**, an internal PostgreSQL identifier, in **pg_class** has to match **attrelid** in **pg_attribute**, and the **oid** in **pg_type** has to match **atttypid** in **pg_attribute**. In relational terms, **pg_attribute** joins **pg_type** to **pg_class**, and without that join, the parts are meaningless:

```
$database["sql"] = "select pg_attribute.attnum,"
  . " pg_attribute.attname as field,"
  . " pg_type.typname as type,"
  . " pg_attribute.attlen as length,"
  . " pg_attribute.atttypmod as variablelength,"
  . " pg_attribute.attnotnull as notnull,"
  . " pg_type.typprtlen as printlength,"
  . " pg_class.relname"
  . " from pg_class, pg_type, pg_attribute"
  . " where pg_attribute.attrelid = pg_class.oid"
  . " and pg_attribute.atttypid = pg_type.oid"
  . " order by pg_attribute.attnum";
```

The output from this SQL is shown in Figure 5.6 and is still not right. There are **attnum** values that are negative; they are rows not relevant to our table definitions. You will find many fields in PostgreSQL administration tables that have negative numbers to indicate special values; –1 is often used to indicate false or not used, something that conflicts with PHP's approach of all numbers other than zero meaning true, so you want to test those fields for less than zero.

5. Databases: MySQL and PostgreSQL

attnum	field	type	length	variablelength	notnull	printlength	relname
-7	tableoid	oid	4	-1	f	10	pg_ipl
-7	tableoid	oid	4	-1	f	10	pg_toast_1216
-7	tableoid	oid	4	-1	f	10	pg_group
-7	tableoid	oid	4	-1	f	10	pg_toast_17058
-7	tableoid	oid	4	-1	f	10	pg_attribute

Figure 5.6   Sample of the first join between pg_class, pg_type, and pg_attribute.

Add an extra term in the SQL's **where** to return rows with **attnum** greater than zero, and then add an extra term to select the entries for the right table, which you can do with **pg_class.relname**, as shown in the next SQL. Because this code will work, you can throw away the display of **attnum** and **relname**. Run it once to verify that it works, and then read all the documentation supplied with PostgreSQL and experiment with displaying other values from the administration tables:

```
$database["table"] = "person";
$database["sql"] = "select pg_attribute.attname as field,"
    . " pg_type.typname as type,"
    . " pg_attribute.attlen as length,"
    . " pg_attribute.atttypmod as maximumlength,"
    . " pg_attribute.attnotnull as notnull,"
    . " pg_type.typprtlen as printlength"
    . " from pg_class, pg_attribute, pg_type"
    . " where pg_class.relname = '" . $database["table"] . "'"
    . " and pg_attribute.attnum > 0"
    . " and pg_attribute.attrelid = pg_class.oid"
    . " and pg_attribute.atttypid = pg_type.oid"
    . " order by pg_attribute.attnum";
```

Figure 5.7 shows the final working list, although it still does not indicate which field has the primary index or all the attributes possible in PostgreSQL. When you are happy with the SQL, you can load the data access rules from the working SQL into PostgreSQL as a view, and then just access the view using simple SQL. Setting up views in PostgreSQL is outside the scope of this book, and the PostgreSQL

field	type	length	maximumlength	notnull	printlength
entry	int4	4	-1	t	10
updated	timestamp	8	-1	t	47
name	varchar	-1	64	t	-1
realname	varchar	-1	259	t	-1
born	date	4	-1	t	10
comment	text	-1	-1	t	-1

Figure 5.7   List of fields in PostgreSQL table person.

developers seem to be busy developing more administrative views with each release. A view of fields within a table might be their next project.

You now have code to display any table in PostgreSQL, SQL to join tables, and experience with the administrative tables—many of the things you need for a long and happy career using PostgreSQL. Plus, you have the equivalent for MySQL.

Displaying Table Data

You want to find all the data in a table, but you do not know the names of the fields, so you want all the fields in the table included automatically. SQL supplies **select *** to select all fields from a table, and most databases return the data with the fields in the order in which the fields were defined. The example (and all the examples in this Immediate Solution) assumes the database **movies** and the table **person**, a table I first defined in MySQL and then defined in PostgreSQL using the closest standard field types I could find in PostgreSQL (PostgreSQL lets you define your own types, which is something you might tackle after reading this book, experimenting with PostgreSQL for a few months, and then reading all the documentation created by PostgreSQL during installation):

```
select * from movies.person
```

Notice the two names connected by the dot in this SQL; the first is the name of the database and the second is the table name. With database accesses, you can specify the database in the SQL or the PHP function that accesses the database. MySQL provides **mysql_select_db( )** to select a database before using the standard **mysql_query( )**. PHP used to provide **mysql_db_query( )**, in which you can specify a database as a parameter, but **mysql_db_query( )** was deprecated in favor of the separate **mysql_select_db( )** and **mysql_query( )**. If you see the old style code hanging around, please update the code.

Once you are happy with a display of all the fields in a table, you can move to selecting individual fields by replacing * with a field list, as shown next. No matter how you specify the fields or which database you use, the functions returning the fields follow a few simple rules: The fields come back in the sequence you specify in the **select**, or, for *, they come back in the sequence the database lists them (usually the sequence in which they were added), so you can predict the sequence, grab the rows as numerically indexed arrays, and display the fields with the correct titles and usage:

```
select name, born from movies.person
```

The only problem with accessing fields by numbers is changing the numbers when you change the fields in the database (when you are using *) or when you are using a field list and change the list. The code in this Immediate Solution is aimed at automating the retrieval of data. In the next example code, **mysql_query( )** selects all fields from table **person** and displays the data in a raw table with no headings:

```
$database["database"] = "movies";
$database["table"] = "person";
$database["sql"] = "select * from ";
if(isset($database["database"]) and strlen($database["database"]))
    {
    $database["sql"] .= $database["database"] . ".";
    }
$database["sql"] .= $database["table"];
$result = mysql_query($database["sql"]);
print("<table border=\"1\">");
while($row = mysql_fetch_row($result))
    {
    $fields = mysql_num_fields($result);
    print("<tr>");
    for($i = 0; $i < $fields; $i++)
        {
        print("<td>" . $row[$i] . "</td>");
        }
    print("</tr>");
    }
print("</table>");
```

The result of this code is Figure 5.8, and it is not pretty. One improvement is to add headings to the columns, so that is the first enhancement to the code.

When you want field names as column headings, you could create unique code for every display, but I recommend building as much code as possible into

1	00000000000000	Tom Berenger	Thomas Michael Moore	1949-05-31	
2	00000000000000	Mimi Rogers	Miriam Spickler	1956-01-27	
3	00000000000000	Lorraine Bracco		1955-10-22	
4	00000000000000	Jerry Orbach	Jerome Bernard Orbach	1935-10-20	
5	00000000000000	John Rubinstein		1946-12-08	
6	00000000000000	Ridley Scott		1937-11-30	
7	20010422203132	Russell Crowe	Russell Ira Crowe	1964-04-07	The world's greatest actor.
11	20010423083731	Christopher Walken	Ronald Walken	1943-03-31	

Figure 5.8   Displaying table **person** before making the display pretty.

reusable functions; the following example function will help with table displays. The function, **mysql_result_fields()**, accepts the result id and gets all the information MySQL supplies about each field in the result. The functions, like **mysql_field_name()**, require the result id and the field index number, so **mysql_num_fields()** supplies the number of fields, and the **for()** loop steps through the fields grabbing the information. The field attributes are stored in the output array, and just in case there are no fields, a line sets the output to false if the array is not created. The code gets a set of flags in a string from **mysql_field_flags()**, splits the string up using **explode()**, and then places each flag in the output array as a field of the same name as the flag:

```
function mysql_result_fields($result)
    {
    $num_fields = mysql_num_fields($result);
    for($i = 0; $i < $num_fields; $i++)
        {
        $flags = mysql_field_flags($result, $i);
        $flag_array = explode(" ", $flags);
        while(list($k, $v) = each($flag_array))
            {
            $array[$i][$v] = true;
            }
        $array[$i]["length"] = mysql_field_len($result, $i);
        $array[$i]["name"] = mysql_field_name($result, $i);
        $array[$i]["type"] = mysql_field_type($result, $i);
        }
    if(!isset($array)) {$array = false;}
    return($array);
    }
```

Now that you have the information about the fields in an array, you can set the array at the start of the loop through a result set, print a heading using the array, and use the array to control other functions, like formatting. The following code starts at the **while()** statement in the previous table display and inserts nine lines of code to use **mysql_result_fields()** to set up a heading. The result is shown in Figure 5.9. **mysql_result_fields()** places an array in **$field_array**, and so you will not repeat the same code on every row, the code is wrapped in an **if(!isset())** to let the code happen only when **$field_array** does not exist. The **if()** also makes the code the perfect place to print the heading, because it occurs only on the first row, and will not happen if there are no rows in the results:

entry	updated	name	realname	born	comment

Figure 5.9   Heading for display of table **person.**

```
while($row = mysql_fetch_row($result))
   {
   if(!isset($field_array))
      {
      $field_array = mysql_result_fields($result);
      print("<tr>");
      while(list($k, $v) = each($field_array))
         {
         print("<td><em>" . $v["name"] . "</em></td>");
         }
      print("</tr>");
      }
```

Another useful thing to do at this point is to dump unwanted fields, starting with **updated** and **realname**, using code that can be easily changed and reused. First list the fields you do not want, as shown next:

```
$exclude = array("updated", "realname");
```

Now build **mysql_table_fields()**, a function that returns the names of all the fields in an array ready for use in a **select** statement, but that excludes any fields named in the array supplied as the third parameter. The function, shown next, uses **mysql_list_fields()** to return a result containing all the fields in a table, much the same as running a query using **select** *; then the code steps through the result with **mysql_field_name()** to build the output array of names. Each name is checked against **$exclude** using **in_array()**, a function that returns true if the first parameter is an entry in the array named in the second parameter, and only names not excluded will go into the output array:

```
function mysql_table_fields($database, $table, $exclude="")
   {
   $result = mysql_list_fields($database, $table);
   $result_fields = mysql_num_fields($result);
   for($i = 0; $i < $result_fields; $i++)
      {
      $name = mysql_field_name($result, $i);
      if(!is_array($exclude) or !in_array($name, $exclude))
         {
         $array[] = $name;
         }
      }
   if(!isset($array)) {$array = "";}
   return($array);
   }
```

Now you can transform the table display code in to the elegant form shown in Figure 5.10, complete with headings and fields excluded. **implode()** is used to grab the array returned by **mysql_table_fields()** and join the elements to make a list for use in the SQL **select** statement. The parameter **", "** provides the comma and space needed between each element in the list. There is one last change: The figures so far were prepared using Netscape Navigator 4.76 because that browser highlights most of the problems found scattered over the dozens of browsers littering the Internet, and you may have noticed that empty table cells do not get a border. To avoid that and several other problems with browsers, I added one line of code to check if the output field is a zero-length string and replace the zero-length string with a single HTML non-breaking space, ** **. The changes from the previous listing of this code are all highlighted:

```
$database["database"] = "movies";
$database["table"] = "person";
$exclude = array("updated", "realname");
$select = mysql_table_fields($database["database"], $database["table"],
   $exclude);
$database["sql"] = "select " . implode(", ", $select)
  . " from " . $database["table"];
mysql_select_db($database["database"]);
$result = mysql_query($database["sql"]);
print("<table border=\"1\">");
while($row = mysql_fetch_row ($result))
   {
   if(!isset($field_array))
      {
      $field_array = mysql_result_fields($result);
      print("<tr>");
      while(list($k, $v) = each($field_array))
         {
         print("<td><em>" . $v["name"] . "</em></td>");
         }
      print("</tr>");
      }
   $fields = mysql_num_fields($result);
   print("<tr>");
   for($i = 0; $i < $fields; $i++)
      {
      if(!strlen($row[$i])) {$row [$i] = " ";}
      print("<td>" . $row[$i] . "</td>");
      }
   print("</tr>");
   }
print("</table>");
```

entry	name	born	comment
1	Tom Berenger	1949-05-31	
2	Mimi Rogers	1956-01-27	
3	Lorraine Bracco	1955-10-22	
4	Jerry Orbach	1935-10-20	
5	John Rubinstein	1946-12-08	
6	Ridley Scott	1937-11-30	
7	Russell Crowe	1964-04-07	The world's greatest actor.
11	Christopher Walken	1943-03-31	

Figure 5.10   Displaying table **person** with columns excluded.

Inserting a Row of Data

When you want to add data, you need a data source, and that is usually a form. To save paper, I will quickly outline a form using functions developed in Chapter 9, and then use data as it appears in the script receiving input from the form.

Related solution:	Found on page:
Creating a Form Using Functions	344

Assume a page named people.html asks for names of actors, directors, and producers. Using the functions from Chapter 9, you can create a form with:

```
$question[] = array("name" => "person", "type" => "text",
   "question" => "Please enter the screen name of the person:");
$question[] = array("name" => "real", "type" => "text",
   "question" => "Enter the person's real name if their"
   . " screen name is fake:");
$question[] = array("name" => "born", "type" => "text",
   "question" => "Enter their date of birth as yyyy-mm-dd:");
$question[] = array("name" => "comment", "type" => "text",
   "question" => "Enter any comments:");
form("people.html", $question);
```

On screen, the form appears as shown in Figure 5.11.

When the form filler clicks the Submit button, the page will receive data about an actor. For this exercise, we will work with this data:

Please enter the screen name of the person: _____

Enter the person's real name if their screen name is fake: _____

Enter their date of birth as yyyy-mm-dd: _____

Enter any comments: _____

[Submit]

Figure 5.11   A form to input an actor's name.

```
$person = "Russell Crowe";
$real = "Russell Ira Crowe";
$born = "1964-04-07";
$comment = "The world's greatest actor.";
```

There are two other fields in table **person**, and both those fields are automatically updated by MySQL. The primary key field is an integer set to **auto_increment**, so MySQL will allocate the next available number. The field named **updated** is set to **timestamp** so MySQL will update the field each time the record is updated and show you when the record was last changed. Unfortunately, MySQL does not set timestamp fields to a useful value when the record is first inserted, a problem you can fix that by adding **updated** to the insertion SQL with a value of **null**. This is the SQL for the insert:

```
$sql = "insert into person set updated=null"
   . ", name='" . $person . "'"
. ", realname='" . $real . "'"
. ", born='" . $born . "'"
. ", comment='" . addslashes($comment) . "'";
```

Note the **addslashes( )** function. **addslashes( )** adds a backslash (\), as an escape code to certain characters to stop the characters breaking the SQL. In a SQL string, fields are delimited by a single quote, so any single quote in the string has to be preceded by a backslash. The backslashes arc not stored in the database, so you do not have to remove the backslashes when reading the data from the database.

Now for the code to perform the insert. This is the simplest code:

```
mysql_select_db("movies");
$result = mysql_query($sql);
```

The simple code will produce crude error messages, so add **@** to the front of **mysql_query( )** and wrap the function in error-checking code, as shown next. Then work on nice error messages to replace my cryptic message:

```
if($result = @mysql_query($sql))
   {
   print("Success!");
   }
else
   {
   print("Error: " . mysql_errno() . ", " . mysql_error()
      . " in sql: " . $sql);
   };
```

The code works and displays:

```
Success!
```

To let you see an error, I changed **name** to **nname** and reran the code. **mysql_errno( )** returns an error number, and **mysql_error( )** returns an error message. You can make use of these functions any way you want, because you now control the error message display process. This is the result of the deliberate error:

```
Error: 1054, Unknown column 'nname' in 'field list' in sql: insert into
person set updated=null, nname='Russell Crowe', realname='Russell Ira
Crowe', born='1964-04-07', comment='The world\'s greatest actor.'
```

Note the comment value contains a single quote, which was backslashed.

You can do one more thing when you insert records: Report the insert id if you have an **auto_increment** field. Imagine creating one page to enter a star and the star's greatest movies. Your page would insert the star's name into **person**, and then insert the person's entry number in the cast list for each movie so you can match the star to the movies. There is an **auto_increment** field in table **person**, so you can grab that using the function **mysql_insert_id( )** with this code:

```
$personentry = mysql_insert_id();
```

The only option for **mysql_insert_id( )** is a connection if you have multiple connections active. **mysql_insert_id( )** gets the most recent value of any **auto_increment** field in the current thread, so you have to place **mysql_insert_id** immediately after the successful **insert**. Therefore, you would place it like this:

```
if($result = mysql_db_query("movies", $sql))
   {
   $personentry = mysql_insert_id();
```

Creating a Database

When you want to create a new database in MySQL, PHP provides **mysql_create_db( )**, as shown in the next code example. The example assumes you have connected to MySQL using the connect code shown in the first Immediate Solution in this chapter. To force an error (so you can see the error message), the code tries to create a database, **movies**, that already exists on my test machine. **mysql_create_db( )** returns true on success and false on failure, **mysql_error( )** returns the most recent error reported by MySQL, and the code prints a confirmation message to ensure you know if the request succeeded or failed:

```
$database["database"] = "movies";
if(mysql_create_db($database["database"]))
   {
   print("<p>Created database " . $database["database"] . "</p>");
   }
else
   {
   print("<p>Failed to create database " . $database["database"]
       . ", error: " . mysql_error() . "</p>");
   }
```

So you can see what **mysql_error( )** returns, the next example is the message printed when the database already exists:

```
Failed to create database movies, error: Can't create database 'movies'.
Database exists
```

Other errors you might get include a failed connection, if you are accessing a new server that is not yet set up the correct way; an authorization error if you do not have permission to set up databases; and a not-so-obvious failure because you tried to create a database with a name that is not acceptable to the underlying operating system. The invalid database name occurs because MySQL tries to create a new directory of the same name as the database, and the operating system rejects the directory name.

When you create databases and tables through SQL, you can easily forget which server and what operating system you are using. It is easy to make a mistake (such as including a space in a table name), and then spend hours trying to understand the misleading error message returned by the database. The only things you need to remember are: a database becomes a directory, and a table becomes a file. Both database names and file names are subject to the operating system restrictions.

Creating Tables

There is not much difference between the programming required to create a table and any other SQL query. For MySQL, you use **mysql_query()**; and for PostgreSQL, you use **pg_exec()**. Both databases have their own special features, but PostgreSQL has support for tablelike constructs, such as views; in some cases, a view might be a viable alternative to a new table.

In the following example, **mysql_select_db()** uses the connection you opened in the first Immediate Solution, "Connecting to a Database," and selects the database. **mysql_query()** accepts the table creation SQL and returns true if the SQL works and false if the SQL does not work. The rest of the code, the error message section and **mysql_error()**, is the code used and explained in the previous Immediate Solution, "Creating a Database":

```
$database["database"] = "movies";
$database["table"] = "director";
$database["sql"] = "create table " . $database["table"]
    . " (movieentry int(10) unsigned default '0' not null,"
    . " directorentry int(10) unsigned default '0' not null,"
    . " updated timestamp(14),"
    . " personentry int(10) unsigned default '0' not null,"
    . " comment text not null,"
    . " primary key (movieentry, directorentry));";
mysql_select_db($database["database"]);
if(mysql_query($database["sql"]))
    {
    print("<p>Created table " . $database["table"] . "</p>");
    }
else
    {
    print("<p>Failed to create table " . $database["table"]
        . ", error: " . mysql_error() . "</p>");
    }
```

Now you can create tables from your scripts, and use the same code with SQL, like **drop table director**, to remove tables and fill Web sites with tricks like dynamically creating a new table for each product line in a shop. You can also create tables as a temporary accommodation for intermediate data when converting systems from one file structure or database to another.

Using Databases for Sessions

PHP's session management works well using files, but database records are more efficient for very large numbers of sessions. You need to do some things before you can use sessions, and there are additional steps to use a database for sessions. The steps are listed in the sequence you would perform them when setting up a Web server with PHP.

If you are compiling PHP, during the PHP installation, you need to include **--enable-trans-id** in the compile, so PHP can add session ids to URLs when browsers do not accept cookies. This option is already included in the compiled binary versions of PHP for Windows, Windows 2000, and NT.

You need two options turned on in php.ini: **track_vars**, which is turned on automatically from PHP 4.0.4 onward, and **register_globals**, an option that is useful even when you are not using sessions. If you run PHP as CGI, PHP will read php.ini once for every script execution, so php.ini changes are instant—whereas an Apache module installation requires you to stop Apache, change php.ini, and then restart Apache to make PHP read the updated php.ini.

You can start sessions automatically by setting **session.auto_start = 1** in php.ini or manually in your script by using **session_register()** or **session_start()**. You would start a session automatically if you want to track all visitors to your Web site, and start a session manually if you want to use sessions only when a person logs in to your site. When sessions are related to logging in, you can destroy the session during logout by using **session_destroy()**.

When a session starts, a new session id is allocated and kept until you destroy the session with **session_destroy()** or when the session times out. The session id is carried from page to page using cookies or URLs. The session information is saved to disk at the end of your script, and read back into memory at the start of the next script for the same session. Because the session id is unique within your Web site, you can use the session id as a key to the session database, and then use information in the session data to point to any other database, like the customer profile or the current order in progress.

You have a choice of using cookies automatically, by setting **session.use_cookies = 1** in php.ini, or manually. Manual control lets you test cookies on your Web site before upsetting your visitors. If you already use cookies for something else, dive into automatic cookies and look at linking your current use of cookies to session management so you can move data out of cookies and into session records. Cookies are named **session.name = PHPSESSID**. You can change the name, and a lifetime, **session.cookie_lifetime**, with the default, **0**, meaning the session lasts until the browser is closed. While you are changing php.ini, make sure to set **session.save_handler = user** so you can supply session-handling routines.

Define a database named **sessions**, using code from the previous Immediate Solutions or a prewritten database administration application, and a table named **session**; for MySQL, use the following SQL to save time:

```
create table session
    (
    id varchar(32) binary not null,
    updated timestamp(14),
    data text not null,
    primary key (id)
    );
```

The rest of the examples are based on MySQL, but can be translated to PostgreSQL or any other database mentioned in Chapter 6 using the code examples in previous Immediate Solutions.

To save a variable in a session, simply register the variable using **session_register( )**, and the variable will be saved to the session record at the end of your script and restored at the start of your script. If you want your visitors to select a category and have that retained by sessions, name the variable **$category**, and then include the following line of code in your script:

```
session_register("category");
```

You can create **$category** at any time, but remember that it is restored at the start of your script, and will override any variables created by forms. If you want your visitor to supply a new category via a form, you have to name the field something else in your form, like **$newcategory**, and then add some code to transfer the category from **$newcategory** to **$category**, such as the following code example:

```
if(isset($newcategory) and strlen($newcategory))
    {
    $category = $newcategory;
    }
```

You can unregister variables no longer needed with **session_unregister ("category")**, which you might do with customer profile variables when they log out. You can also choose to not register them but instead write the variables to dedicated fields in the session record, which you might do with **$category** if you wanted an online page to list the number of current visitors to each category. When a variable is buried in PHP's session record, you cannot use SQL to select, sort, and summarize the data they way you can when the data is stored in a discrete database field.

You need several functions to make session records, store the records in the database, retrieve the records, and delete expired session records. Session processing starts with the definition of the processing functions, and then the registration of the functions; then you can start a session with **session_start( )**, or have it started when you first use **session_register( )**. If you have automatic processing turned on in php.ini, the session processing will start with **session_set_save_handler( )**, as shown in the following code. **session_set_save_handler( )** goes after your function definitions, before your **session_start( )** or your first **session_register( )**, and before the first use of the variables you registered on previous pages in the same session:

```
session_set_save_handler("mysql_session_open",
    "mysql_session_close",
    "mysql_session_read",
    "mysql_session_write",
    "mysql_session_destroy",
    "mysql_session_gc");
```

When your session starts, you may get error messages like the following, which indicate the session is trying to send cookies too late, or your session code is preventing the rest of your script from sending headers:

```
Warning: Cannot send session cookie - headers already sent by…
Warning: Cannot send session cache limiter - headers already sent
Fatal error: Failed to initialize session module
```

Cookies are HTTP headers, and HTTP headers have to go first before any other output, including stray characters you may not notice leaking out of your scripts; so make sure every page starts in PHP mode, **<?php**, and stays that way until the session starts. If your session code produces warning messages, those messages will stop the rest of your script from producing headers, so make sure all other header production on your page is pushed up to the top of the script immediately after the session starts. If your script is producing headers to prevent caching of the page, you can drop your code as PHP session code outputs headers to prevent page caching.

Before you use **session_set_save_handler( )**, you have to create the functions it calls, and if you do not, or if you type an error somewhere, you will get the error message shown next. PHP4 syntax checks all the code before execution, so you should have clean functions by the time you get to an error like this:

```
Fatal error: Failed to initialize session module
```

PHP's session management requires a function to open a session and, for MySQL, the example code shown next simply opens a persistent connection to a MySQL server. You can have sessions in databases that are not on your Web server and might open a persistent session when you have multiple servers, with several Apache Web servers sharing one server dedicated to a session database and all other database activity spread over other database servers. **$session** is a list of session-related information in an array so it can be accessed by functions with one global definition, which means that code can access parts of **$session** with either an ordered or structured method. PHP supplies the function **mysql_session_open( )** with a file path and a session name because that is what is usually required for file-based sessions. You could make either the database name and the other the table name, but it is cleaner to keep everything using standard fields in **$session**:

```
$session["database"] = "sessions";
$session["table"] = "session";
$session["host"] = "localhost";
$session["log"] = "t:\mysqlsessionlog.txt";
$session["user"] = "";
$session["password"] = "";
function mysql_session_open($path, $name)
    {
    global $session;
    mysql_session_log("mysql_session_open");
    if($session["connection"] = @mysql_pconnect($session["server"],
        $session["user"], $session["password"]))
        {
        if(!isset($session["fields"]))
            {
            $result = mysql_list_fields($session["database"],
                $session["table"], $session["connection"]);
            $result_fields = mysql_num_fields($result);
            for($i = 0; $i < $result_fields; $i++)
                {
                $session["fields"][mysql_field_name($result, $i)] =
                    mysql_field_type($result, $i);
```

```
            }
         }
      return(true);
      }
   mysql_session_log("Connect failed to server: " . $database["server"]
      . ", MySQL error: " . mysql_error());
   return(false);
   }
```

If you analyze the code in **mysql_session_open( )**, you will notice it is code from earlier Immediate Solutions: specifically, code to make a connection, from the first Immediate Solution, plus code to retrieve field names, from a later Immediate Solution. I added the code to collect the field names and field types so both could be used in the read and write functions to manage the data in the session records when you start adding discrete fields to the session table.

mysql_session_log( ), used in the preceding code and shown next, was written because you cannot write diagnostic messages to the screen from within the session write and session close functions, because both functions occur after the last data is sent to your page. **mysql_session_log( )** writes messages to a separate file you can browse at any time, and because it is not buried in Apache or PHP logs, you do not have to fight with an ISP to get access (as some times happens with hosted sites). The log record has a date and time at the front to let you see which test produced each message, and a **newline** character is added to the end of each line to separate the lines when you browse the text file in an editor:

```
function mysql_session_log($message)
   {
   if($file = fopen($session["log"], "a"))
      {
      fwrite($file, date("Y-m-d H:i:s  ") . $message . "\n");
      fclose($file);
      }
   }
```

Everything that opens must be closed, and **mysql_session_close( )** closes the session, except there is nothing this function need do when using a database. The MySQL connection need not be closed, and in fact it was opened as persistent to deliberately reduce both opens and closes. This function has one log message to help you through testing, and then you can delete the message (if you want to conduct performance tests on your Web pages, you could replace the log time with PHP's **microtime( )**, and then use the time from the **mysql_session_close( )** log entry as the time the script ends):

```
function mysql_session_close()
   {
   mysql_session_log("mysql_session_close");
   return(true);
   }
```

The following code is **mysql_session_read()**, which uses **mysql_query()** as shown in several earlier Immediate Solutions, starting with "Displaying Table Data," and does just a few new things. **mysql_fetch_array()** has **MYSQL_ASSOC** added to force the production of any array with key names, but no integer indexes (the default is both), a trick that lets you loop through a row as an array with the key being the field name. The field named **data** is returned in the **return** statement, and all other fields are placed in **$session**, indexed by field name. The extra code means you can add any number of fields to the session table and have them retrieved automatically without having to change **mysql_session_read()**:

```
function mysql_session_read($id)
   {
   global $session;
   mysql_session_log("mysql_session_read");
   $session["sql"] = "select * from " . $session["table"]
      . " where id='" . $id . "'";
   mysql_select_db($session["database"]);
   if($result = @mysql_query($session["sql"], $session["connection"]))
      {
      if($row = mysql_fetch_array($result, MYSQL_ASSOC))
         {
         while(list($k, $v) = each($row))
            {
            if($k != "data")
               {
               $session[$k] = $row[$k];
               }
            }
         return($row["data"]);
         }
      else
         {
         return(""); // This point means there is not yet a record.
         }
      }
   else
      {
      mysql_session_log("Session read query error: " . mysql_error()
         . " using sql " . $session["sql"]);
```

```
        return("");
        }
    }
```

The session write function, **mysql_session_write( )**, receives the session id and session data, and then tries to update an existing record. If the update fails, **mysql_session_write( )** assumes it is the first write to the database for the session, and inserts a new record. The query processing is the same as used earlier in this chapter: **addslashes( )** makes the character data safe to insert via SQL, and the code uses the field list, created in **mysql_session_open( )**, to build the SQL dynamically. The SQL build code grabs a copy of the field list; deletes the field **updated**, because **updated** is updated by the database software; deletes the field **data**, because **data** is separately inserted in to the SQL; and deletes **id**, because **id** is not inserted during an update:

```
function mysql_session_write($id, $data)
    {
    global $session;
    mysql_session_log("mysql_session_write");
    $session["id"] = $id;
    $fields_sql = " set data='" . addslashes($data) . "'";
    $fields_list = $session["fields"];
    unset($fields_list["data"]);
    unset($fields_list["id"]);
    unset($fields_list["updated"]);
    while(list($k, $v) = each($fields_list))
        {
        if(isset($session[$k]))
            {
            $fields_sql .= ", " . $k . "='" . addslashes($session[$k])
                . "'";
            }
        }
    $session["sql"] = "update " . $session["table"]
        . $fields_sql . " where id='" . $id . "'";
    mysql_select_db($session["database"]);
    if($session["result"] = @mysql_query($session["sql"], _
        $session["connection"]))
        {
        if(mysql_affected_rows($session["connection"]))
            {
            mysql_session_log("mysql_session_write update using sql: "
                . $session["sql"]);
            return(true);
            }
```

```
        else
            {
            // Update failed so insert new record:
            $session["sql"] = "insert into " . $session["table"]
                . $fields_sql . ", id='" . $id . "'";
            if($session["result"] = @mysql_db_query($session["database"],
                $session["sql"], $session["connection"]))
                {
                mysql_session_log("mysql_session_write insert using sql: "
                    . $session["sql"]);
                return(true);
                }
            else
                {
                mysql_session_log("mysql_session_write insert error: "
                    . mysql_error()
                    . " using sql " . $session["sql"]);
                return(false);
                }
            }
        }
    else
        {
        mysql_session_log("mysql_session_write update error: "
            . mysql_error()
            . " using sql " . $session["sql"]);
        return(false);
        }
    }
```

mysql_session_destroy( ) uses **mysql_query( )** to delete the session record for the supplied session id. If the record is accidentally left in place by this code, the record will be deleted by the garbage cleanup function that follows:

```
function mysql_session_destroy($id)
    {
    global $session;
    mysql_session_log("mysql_session_destroy");
    $session["id"] = $id;
    $session["sql"] = "delete from " . $session["table"]
        . " where id = '" . $id . "'";
    mysql_select_db($session["database"]);
    if($session["result"] = @mysql_query($session["sql"], _
        $session["connection"]))
        {
```

```
        return(true);
        }
    else
        {
    mysql_session_log("Session destroy error: " . mysql_error()
        . " using sql " . $session["sql"]);
    return(false);
        }
    }
```

PHP's session management includes a garbage cleanup function to remove any session records left lying around by people who never logged off a site, and those who went overseas for three weeks with their browser still browsing the same page through their permanent Internet connection. Every record has a field called **updated**, which is updated by the database software, so you can delete any record where **updated** is too old; the definition of too old is the current time minus the session **lifetime** specified in php.ini. The functions **time()** and **date()** and the session **lifetime** all work in units of one second, so you can simply subtract **lifetime** from **time()** and feed the result into **date()** to get a date/time formatted for MySQL. You could also use MySQL functions to provide and calculate time, but performing the calculation in PHP lets you see the result. The only problem you are likely to get with this calculation occurs if a server is set to local time and a database is working off GMT or the other way around. PHP has functions to return both local and GMT time, so you can match any server or database setup:

```
function mysql_session_gc($lifetime)
    {
    global $session;
    mysql_session_log("mysql_session_gc");
    $session["gcdate"] = date("YmdHis", time() - $lifetime);
    $session["sql"] = "delete from " . $session["table"]
        . " where updated < '" . $session["gcdate"] . "'";
    mysql_select_db($session["database"]);
    if($session["result"] = @mysql_query($session["sql"], _
        $session["connection"]))
        {
        return(true);
        }
    else
        {
        mysql_session_log("Session gc error: " . mysql_error()
            . " using sql " . $session["sql"]);
        return(false);
        }
    }
```

Now you have magic session code that works with MySQL, can be modified for other databases, and gives you the option to easily add discrete fields to session records so you can manage your sessions and analyze the records. You can find out who is using your site, where they are browsing, and what they are looking for. If you have a search facility, instead of burying the visitor's search string in the session data, make the search string a separate field in the session record, so you can write a query to show you online the latest and greatest search requests.

Cleaning Up Code

The quickest way to start administering MySQL or PostgreSQL is to install a prewritten application such as phpMyAdmin or phpPgAdmin. They help you define your first databases, tables, and fields so you can experiment, provide example code and SQL, and provide help with importing data from other sources. You can find applications like these by looking at my recommendations at **petermoulding.com**, or searching **freshmeat.net** or **sourceforge.net**.

Once you have the code, you will want to clean it up; this section is about scrubbing code, using phpPgAdmin 2.3 as the example. You can apply these changes anywhere, including contributing the changes back to the developers so that off-the-shelf PHP code will evolve from the level of a Ford to a Mercedes.

When you clean up code, you often need to find functions, but most code has a mix of functions written like the first sample line of code that follows, complete with a space between the function name and the bracket, (. You need to perform a global search of the code for " (", check if any of the occurrences are spaces after function names, and remove the spaces so the code looks like the second line. Once you apply this fix to code, you can then safely search for functions and apply some of the global changes shown later in this section:

```
include ("footer.inc.php");
include("footer.inc.php");
```

Off-the-shelf code assumes you can access a secure PHP include directory, but many ISPs do not provide the access you need; so to get started using code like phpPgAdmin, you need to include files from the local directory. If the included files are created the correct way, they will not offer a security or reliability problem directly through the browser, and, with some ISPs, it is easier to create a small administration subdirectory with password access than it is to get a private PHP include directory.

To access the included files from the local directory, you need to change the **include** (and **require**) statements from the form shown here

```
include("footer.inc.php");
```

to the form shown here:

```
include("./footer.inc.php");
```

Because a manual change like that means you will have many changes to make every time you change your Web site configuration, take the code a step further and change the code to the format shown here. The name **include_prefix** is concatenated in front of the file name, so you can have the prefix defined in one place, and change every occurrence in one hit:

```
include(include_prefix . "footer.inc.php");
```

You can take the code another step forward and plan for the day when you stop using .php as a file name suffix or change to .php5 (that is planning ahead). Simply replace the **.php** with the field **include_suffix** as shown here:

```
include(include_prefix . "footer.inc" . include_suffix);
```

When you change **include()**, remember to change all occurrences of **include_once()**, **require()**, and **require_once()**. **require()** is the same as **include()**, but much earlier in PHP's processing and before the evaluation of conditional statements, such as **if()**. **include()** can be controlled by **if()**, but **require()** will include a file no matter what code is wrapped around **require()**.

include_prefix and **include_suffix** have to be defined somewhere, so create a small file named **include.html** (or **include.php** if your Web server is not set up to process .html pages with PHP), and then define the fields in include.html as shown in the following block of code:

```
<?php
define("include_prefix", "./");
define("include_suffix", ".php");
?>
```

You can add any of your local configuration information in include.html. You can use the file across all your applications, and I recommend you use this approach whenever you are faced with changing all the file name suffixes in an application. One example I tackled this way was a set of code that had all pages named .php3;

another set of code was a prerequisite, and the other set of code had all pages named .phtml. Rather than manually change one set of code to match the other, and then face manually changing the code again to match other Web sites, I changed all the **include** statements to use **include_suffix**.

Now you need to perform a one-time **insert** to include your standard definitions at the top of every PHP page, as shown in the next set of code. I start all my Web pages in PHP mode, but some people start in HTML mode, and then jump back and forth. The example three lines will fit at the start of any page no matter how the rest of the page is coded:

```php
<?php
require_once("./include.html");
?>
```

If your Web server does not interpret **.html** as PHP, you will have to use **.php**, and if your Web server is set up the wrong way, you might have to replace **<?php** with **<?**. **require_once( )** is only found in PHP4, but there are ways to code an equivalent to **require_once( )** in PHP3, and these are shown next.

To make your include.html file compatible with versions of PHP that do not have **require_once( )** or **include_once( )**, set a variable in the include file, as shown next, that follows a standard naming convention and indicates that the include file is included. I use the name of the include file plus **_included**, so include.html gets **$include_included**. The **include** of include.html changes to the conditional include shown after include.html, and uses **include( )** instead of **require( )** because **require( )** does not work within **if( )** statements. I use a variable for **include_included** because constants create a problem when you test the constant, **isset( )** does not work with constants, and the equivalent for constants, **defined( )**, produces an error message if the constant is not defined:

```php
<?php
$include_included = "yes";
define("include_prefix", "./");
define("include_suffix", ".php");
?>

<?php
if(!isset($include_included))
    {
    include("./include.html");
    }
?>
```

phpPgAdmin, phpMyAdmin, and most other code is tested with warnings turned off in php.ini, so the code assumes a missing variable is not wanted and allows all sorts of typographical and logic errors. You will run with warnings turned on, so you will get heaps of messages about undefined variables. One change you can make when you get a warning message is to add **isset( )** to **if( )** statements. Replace lines like this one

```
if(!printview)
```

with the expanded version shown here:

```
if(!isset(printview) or !printview)
```

Some free code assumes you can easily see variables buried in strings, but not many editors do a good job of highlighting the buried variables, so you might as well make life easier for yourself and everyone else by unburying the variables. When you are changing code and find a buried variable, like **$HTTP_HOST** shown here

```
$short_realm .= "$HTTP_HOST:local";
```

you can extract the variable and leave the code like this:

```
$short_realm .= $HTTP_HOST . ":local";
```

This example code was copied from **lib.inc.php** in phpPgAdmin 2.3, and the code just assumes the variable, named **$short_realm**, exists, so there is a warning message when the code tries to concatenate new data onto a missing variable. To remove the error message, I inserted code to create an empty variable if the variable is missing:

```
if(!isset($short_realm)) {$short_realm = "";}
```

You will get other warnings and have to replace many programming shortcuts to produce reliable code. If you try an open source application like phpMyAdmin, and continue to use the application, volunteer a little of your time to feed your changes back to the developers so you will have less to clean out of future releases. When you work your way through this book, you will be ready to clean up all PHP applications or create your own, and become an open source hero.

5. Databases: MySQL and PostgreSQL

Chapter 6

Databases: Commercial
and Unusual

In Depth

You can use many databases to serve your Web site, and many file types with structures similar to databases serve niche applications. If MySQL is not quite right, and PostgreSQL is too complicated, you can choose from databases much smaller than MySQL, up to databases that make PostgreSQL seem like a beginner's tool. This chapter is about the databases not discussed in Chapter 5.

Oracle stands out as the first database suitable for large systems and available across many brands of large systems. IBM's DB2 stands out as the first choice among IBM's biggest customers, which, in the past, meant the world's largest computer systems. Microsoft's SQL Server cashed in on the millions of system administrators who went straight from breastfeeding to MCSE training.

There are lots of other choices, with features that favor special uses, from databases that fit on a floppy disk to databases designed to sing when filled with MP3 files or shine when storing movies. This chapter will help you choose from those databases already supported in PHP, and help you understand more about how databases work and how to choose the perfect base for your data.

SQL

SQL is to databases what HTML is to Web pages. SQL92 is the oldest SQL standard; it has international recognition and is supported by most databases the way early browsers supported HTML standards, which makes SQL92 better than nothing, but not a complete solution. Important things are missing from the standard; so, to write a normal application, you have to use nonstandard SQL extensions. However, SQL92 has no requirement to make database vendors tell you exactly what is standard and what is not. It reminds me of a Ford advertisement in Australia for an economy model; although Australian laws make windshield wipers compulsory, Ford listed windscreen wipers among the "free extras."

The SQL99 standard is the replacement for SQL92, and a small number of database developers, like the team behind PostgreSQL, are working toward SQL99. I recommend looking for databases with some SQL99 compliance, as an indication the developers are planning for the future.

To Index or Not to Index

Indexing tables can increase their performance for reads and slow down updates. Nothing in PHP directly influences index use, and the whole question comes down to how your database software will interpret your SQL. The two things you can do in PHP are to install an easy-to-use database management interface, such as phpMyAdmin or phpPgAdmin, to let you quickly create and delete indexes; and wrap PHP's **microtime( )** around SQL so you can compare retrieval times before and after you add or delete indexes. The "Timing Retrieval: A Path to Performance" section in the Immediate Solutions shows effective logging of retrieval times.

Relationships

Relationships create as many problems as they solve; ask anyone who is married. If you want more order and more control, but less flexibility, dump MySQL, get to know PostgreSQL, and build your databases with relationships. Your applications will work more reliably, even if the relationships stop you performing clever tricks with data. You will feel happier and more relaxed and you won't wake up in the morning wondering what those strangers were doing with your data.

Think of all the rules you live by daily—wash your hands before eating, put on your safety belt when driving, and so on—and then think about the same type of rules applied within a database. Relationships let you lock rows of data together so you process all related data or none. They provide rules that make the deletion of an invoice also delete all invoice line-items for that invoice or, the reverse, that do not let anyone delete an invoice if invoice line-items exist. This type of software safety belt is required for applications like accounting, where extreme financial penalties and jail terms punish mistakes both fraudulent and stupid. Why risk being hurt by a software crash? Develop your application from the start with reliable relationships.

Persistent Connections

I have yet to see detailed measurements of resource savings from persistent connections across all sorts of databases, so your results may vary from what I observe out in the field. Persistent connections let PHP reuse database connections when the connection is for the same server, user, password, and every other parameter required to connect to a particular database. PHP can use persistent connections only when run as an Apache module and when a few other things fall into place, like time between transactions and database software. Persistent connections tie up resources, and so need lots of memory (but then again, reconnecting uses up resources and requires lots of memory).

If you specify a persistent connection, and anything prevents a persistent connection, the result will be a conventional connection. If this happens, you may never notice what is happening, and you may not know that most of your connections are not persistent. There are reports of technical reasons why you should not use persistent connections, and plenty of people specify persistent connections without any problems. If in doubt, ask your Web server administrator if there is a reason not to use persistent connections on the server; if not, specify persistent connections and let PHP figure out if it can reuse a connection. A persistent connection is based on user ID; therefore, a Web site with 10,000 visitors, each logged on by a unique ID, and each accessing the database using its unique ID, means 10,000 persistent connections—an inefficient condition that will swamp a Web server. If those 10,000 visitors use their unique IDs just to log on, and then share one database ID for all subsequent accesses, they can share one connection, which is efficient and exactly what persistent connections are designed for. In reality, 10,000 users might have their page requests processed by 50 *child processes*, each with a separate connection. Fifty persistent connections are still a lot better than 10,000 individual connections. (Child processes are explained in any good book about Apache.)

If you start a transaction with a persistent connection and then forget to close the transaction, or your script aborts before closing the transaction, the resources could be locked up in the transaction until the Web server is restarted. Given that modern hard disks have a rated life of 300,000 hours, and everything else should last longer, those resources could be locked up for a long time. If you use transactions and persistent connections, register a PHP shutdown function to roll back any open transactions.

ODBC

Object Database Connectivity (ODBC) reduces the complexity of connecting to several databases by providing a database-independent interface and some features especially suitable for accessing databases across networks. If you are accessing more than one type of database from your Web site, consider using ODBC to access all the databases. The downside to ODBC is that, in some situations, ODBC will increase network traffic.

Figure 6.1 shows my interpretation of the Schulman/Gartner model of client/server processing; the critical line in the middle represents the network traffic. The problem has not changed in the many years since I first presented this consideration to the heads of big companies spending tens of millions of dollars per mainframe. If you place all your processing on the server and have little more than presentation on the client (exactly the way a single-server Web site works), you have little network traffic. If you place all your processing on the client with

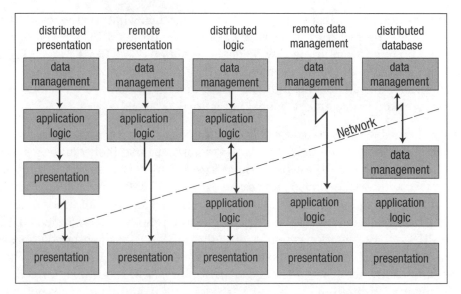

Figure 6.1   Schulman/Gartner model of client/server processing.

the bare minimum of data processing on the server (the way your Web site works when picking up images from an image server but caching most images locally), you have high initial network traffic with little subsequent traffic The worst case is usually when the work is evenly divided between two servers, because the connection between the two halves of a process carries a massive amount of traffic; this is the distributed logic system shown in the middle of the diagram.

If your PHP scripts run on one server and are an ODBC client to a database server, a single script generating one page for the browser may send seven SQL requests to the database server with some of the requests retrieving 100 or more rows from the database. That one page might require 500 row retrievals; some database APIs make the situation worse by requiring a separate request for each field in each row, which turns those 500 row requests into 5,000 field requests. ODBC makes one stab at cutting back the network overhead between your script and the database server: **odbc_fetch_row()** brings a whole row back to PHP, and then lets you step though the row by field, using **odbc_result()** on the locally cached row. In effect, your 5,000 field requests are limited to 500 row requests by the design of the ODBC interface.

You still have the problem of 500 rows travelling across the network one by one. If you send SQL to retrieve 500 rows, you need the 500 rows, so ODBC should return them in one network transfer. If you want just some of the rows, like the first 10, you should be able to use SQL facilities, such as **LIMIT**. The network traffic is increased because ODBC in trying to guess what your application needs, changes the unit of data transfer to something other than what you request. ODBC would become perfect for transnetwork operations if the ODBC interface were tightened up to allow multiple-row requests, to match SQL's **LIMIT** and **START** parameters. You would have one data transfer across the network for each SQL request. ODBC would become more like SQL, and the system would be closer to the "remote data management" model in Figure 6.1.

If ODBC is the best way to access lots of different databases, it makes sense for database suppliers to minimize the work required to use their databases with ODBC, and to minimize the work required to build interfaces, by building just one: an ODBC interface. It also makes sense for ODBC software builders to build their software so they can minimize the work required for each interface and just plug in a module for each database. The end result, referred to as Unified ODBC, is that PHP's ODBC functions connect directly to IBM's DB2 and other databases, because those databases have standard APIs that are in the ODBC format. Where there is no ODBC interface, PHP uses iODBC, an ODBC interface that accepts small plug-ins for different databases. In the long term, more databases will have either an ODBC interface or an iODBC plug-in to let you use ODBC with every database on every platform. The only things not unified are the formats for data fields, such as dates, and the way databases respond to requests for advanced features. Some software, when faced with a request it cannot handle, replies with a polite no, false, or zero; other software generates an error; and some software does the worst thing possible—it replies with a valid-looking answer that is totally misleading.

DB2

DB2 started as a mainframe-based successor to IBM's earlier mainframe databases and then spread to IBM's other platforms, including AIX-based Web servers. Linux then started spreading through IBM's platforms right up to the mainframe, so IBM ported DB2 to Linux. IBM's DB2-everywhere policy gave the company one-third of the commercial database market, neck-and-neck with Oracle. DB2 was first with a range of database technology improvements, and it is the database you are most likely to find in large companies, like banks, that use IBM mainframes.

IBM recently purchased the Informix database, so DB2 will gain some Informix technology, and Informix will be connected to DB2 in various ways. If you are working on Informix-based systems, the choice will be an upgrade to DB2 because DB2 has great multitier client/server facilities, or a step sideways to the open source PostgreSQL or perhaps the more-popular and less-advanced MySQL.

DB2 is currently available for AIX, AS/400, HP-UX, Linux, OS/2, OS/390, Sun Solaris, Windows, Windows NT, VSE, and VM, which covers the useful operating systems and servers used to serve large volumes of data across the Internet. PHP provides access to DB2 through *Unified ODBC*, a system in which the native application programming interface (API) of the database looks like ODBC, so you can access the database without the overhead of ODBC. From the PHP programming perspective, you can mix DB2 databases with any other ODBC or Unified ODBC database without changing code.

SAP DB

SAP is a well-known set of applications from Germany, popular among mainframe users and targeted at logistics, accounting, and human resources teams. SAP DB is the database used by SAP; it is SQL-based with some support for objects, XML, and unstructured data; it can be accessed through ODBC; and it was recently released under the open source GPL license. You can download the source code at **www.sap.com/solutions/technology/sapdb**.

Although SAP DB sounds great, the code looks to be a mixture of C++, Pascal, and Python, and you have to use SAP development tools to build components and assemble the result. I do not know anyone who is an expert in C++, Pascal, and Python, so the long-term development of SAP DB will require diverse teams or the rewriting of the Pascal and Python components in another language. In my opinion, SAP's developers should immediately replace all user interfaces with a PHP-based administration application like phpMyAdmin, convert all Pascal to C++ or Python, and then begin a long-term move toward using the variant of C used for Gnome, and the conversion of all Python to C or PHP. In fact, I think SAP should work toward a merger with PostgreSQL, so PostgreSQL gains anything of value from SAP DB and SAP saves the cost of maintaining SAP DB.

If you already use SAP, using the open source SAP DB for non-SAP applications gives you one database for all situations, but limits your long-term flexibility. Using SAP DB via ODBC gives you more flexibility, but still leaves you with code dependent on SAP DB features. Experiment with other databases, such as PostgreSQL, so you can judge which applications need features specific to SAP DB and which applications can be written to be compatible with other databases.

Other Databases

The following databases have special features and reasons why you might use them, but they are best accessed through ODBC or replaced with databases like MySQL and PostgreSQL. You will have to work with some of these databases, and if you can make every connection through ODBC, you will save major rewrites of your code each time you are confronted with a new database.

Adabas

Adabas, from Software AG (**http://softwareag.com**), is, in Internet years, a grandparent of the database family. Adabas was battling IBM's IMS database before IMS was displaced by IBM's new baby, DB2. I do not know of an advantage of Adabas over Oracle or DB2, but visit Software AG's Web site, and look at the company's new database, Tamino.

Tamino seems to be a new incarnation of the hierarchical databases that preceded relational databases, this time as a repository of XML documents. Instead of storing XML documents in text fields within a relational database and using SQL for access, Tamino lets you aggregate your XML documents into a giant XML-based structure. I cover XML in Chapter 20.

Reading filePro

filePro is from fP Technologies, Inc. (**www.fptech.com**), and my first observation is that fP's Web site uses JSP instead of PHP. filePro seems to come from an old side branch of database development where the database developers also supply a report generator, and then try to make the report generator do everything in the world—a genetic line that is dying out. I have listed the PHP functions available for filePro but do not recommend them, except for a conversion from filePro to something modern, like MySQL or PostgreSQL:

- **filepro( )**—Reads and verifies the map file
- **filepro_fieldname( )**—Gets the field name
- **filepro_fieldtype( )**—Gets the field type
- **filepro_fieldwidth( )**—Gets the field width
- **filepro_retrieve( )**—Retrieves data
- **filepro_fieldcount( )**—Gets the number of fields in a database
- **filepro_rowcount( )**—Gets the number of rows in a database

The functions provide read access, and, because there are no file locks in filePro, an online update from Web pages would be dangerous. For the same reason, do not use other facilities, such as batch programs, to update filePro files while they are accessible through your Web site.

filepro( ) takes a string with the name of a directory containing a FilePro database; checks that the database will work; retrieves information, like the number of fields; and seems to open an internal connection for subsequent filePro functions. **filepro_retrieve( )** takes a row number and a field number, and returns a field. At this point, you might realize filePro databases are sounding like sheets from a spreadsheet, not much more than a table from a relational database, and MySQL is sounding so much better. **filepro_rowcount( )** and **filepro_fieldcount( )**

provide the numbers you need to loop through all the rows and fields in a database. While looping through the fields in the first row of the database, you can use **filepro_fieldname( )**, **filepro_fieldtype( )**, and **filepro_fieldwidth( )** to get the information you may need to format the output.

Accessing FrontBase

FrontBase is available at **www.frontbase.com** and is new to PHP 4.0.6—so new that I do not have a test system handy and can only list the functions here. The functions look very much like ODBC; FrontBase would have saved a lot of the end user's time by making its API ODBC-compatible:

- **fbsql_affected_rows( )**—Gets the number of rows affected by the previous query
- **fbsql_autocommit( )**—Enables or disables autocommit
- **fbsql_change_user( )**—Changes the user id in the connection
- **fbsql_close( )**—Closes the connection
- **fbsql_connect( )**—Opens a connection to a server
- **fbsql_create_db( )**—Creates a database
- **fbsql_data_seek( )**—Moves the result pointer to the next row
- **fbsql_db_query( )**—Executes a query
- **fbsql_drop_db( )**—Deletes a database
- **fbsql_errno( )**—Returns the number of the latest error message
- **fbsql_error( )**—Returns the text of the latest error message
- **fbsql_fetch_array( )**—Fetches the result row as an array
- **fbsql_fetch_assoc( )**—Fetches the result row as an associative array
- **fbsql_fetch_field( )**—Returns column information as an object
- **fbsql_fetch_lengths( )**—Gets the lengths of fields in the result
- **fbsql_fetch_object( )**—Fetches a result row as an object
- **fbsql_fetch_row( )**—Gets a result row as array
- **fbsql_field_flags( )**—Gets the flags for the field
- **fbsql_field_name( )**—Gets the name of a field in the result
- **fbsql_field_len( )**—Returns the length of a field
- **fbsql_field_seek( )**—Sets the result pointer to a field offset
- **fbsql_field_table( )**—Gets the name of the table containing the field
- **fbsql_field_type( )**—Gets the type of the field in a result
- **fbsql_free_result( )**—Frees result memory

- **fbsql_insert_id( )**—Gets the id from the previous insert
- **fbsql_list_dbs( )**—Lists the databases available on the server
- **fbsql_list_fields( )**—Lists the result fields
- **fbsql_list_tables( )**—Lists the tables in a database
- **fbsql_num_fields( )**—Gets the number of fields in the result
- **fbsql_num_rows( )**—Gets the number of rows in the result
- **fbsql_pconnect( )**—Opens a persistent connection to a server
- **fbsql_query( )**—Sends a query
- **fbsql_result( )**—Gets result data
- **fbsql_select_db( )**—Selects a database
- **fbsql_tablename( )**—Gets the table name of a field
- **fbsql_warnings( )**—Enables or disables warnings

Hyperwave

Hyperwave was first developed at the Institute for Information Processing and Computer Supported New Media (**www.iicm.edu**), and it was then made into a commercial product at Hyperwave (**www.hyperwave.com**). There are PHP functions for using Hyperwave, but Hyperwave does cost money, and I do not see much advantage in using it for new applications. Hyperwave, in essence, stores documents alongside identifying information, similar to the meta information you store in Web pages. Imagine taking a standard Web page, storing the text in a long text string, and then storing all the tags in other related tables. You could use the information to reassemble the Web page, plus use SQL to select all the pages containing *fish* in the title. You can add any identifying information and have the information linked to the text as a whole or a location within the text.

Today you would automatically use XML, perhaps an XML-aware database like Tamino, or just leave the XML as tags in the text in a long text field, have the identifiers as conventional related data (and switch to PostgreSQL so you could enforce relationships), and then read the document into PHP using PHP's XML or DOM XML functions. Back when Hyperwave was designed, the predecessors to XML, PHP's XML support, and open source databases were less than ideal for building document storage, so Hyperwave was a step forward; but now it is a step sideways into proprietary software that does not fit in a small development environment, because it requires understanding and maintaining at least two databases.

The PHP developers did a good job of documenting how to fit a Hyperwave server into Apache, so Hyperwave becomes transparent, and the people visiting your site see just the pages you generate through PHP. You may have to use Hyperwave if you receive documents already in a Hyperwave database, and Hyperwave may be a good long-term choice if the Hyperwave developers move it to an open standard format and current technologies.

Informix

IBM purchased Informix's database, so the future of the Informix database is uncertain. Also, at the time of writing, the people developing the PHP Informix functions are busy adding Informix release 9 support to code designed for Informix release 7. If I included a list of Informix functions and function parameters here, it would be out of date before the ink is dry. When you need to use Informix functions, send an email to **informix@petermoulding.com** and tell me the release of Informix you want to use, and I will write an up-to-date Immediate Solution for that release of Informix using the latest PHP release of the functions.

Ingres II

Ingres is another database that started at Berkeley; the name was originally an acronym for Interactive Graphics Retrieval System. An old, free version of Ingres exists in the public domain, and a new, modern Ingres II is available from Computer Associates (**www.cai.com/products/ingres.htm**). See the Immediate Solution "Accessing Ingres II" for examples of working with Ingres II.

InterBase

InterBase is from Borland (**www.borland.com**) and has a dedicated Web site at **www.interbase.com**. InterBase has an ODBC interface, so you do not have to use special functions for access, and it has dedicated PHP functions listed in this section.

InterBase uses Sybase-style single quotes for escaping characters in SQL (Sybase is discussed later in this chapter). When you enter the SQL string "Ted's great adventure", most databases look for "Ted\'s great adventure" but Sybase and InterBase look for "Ted's great adventure". InterBase does other strange things: **create table stock (brand varchar(60))** creates a field named **BRAND**, and you have to use **BRAND** when accessing the field; but **create table stock ("brand" varchar(60))** creates a field named **brand**.

ibase_connect() and **ibase_pconnect()** create connections and persistent connections to databases, similar to the equivalents for other databases. The parameters are the path to the database, and then the optional user name, password, and other parameters you do not need in a test environment. The database path name can contain network prefixes for databases on other machines, and the form **hostname:**, for TCP/IP, is the most important. **ibase_close()** closes the connection when you are finished and is not used with persistent connections.

ibase_query( ) accepts a connection id and SQL statement and executes a query immediately, whereas **ibase_prepare( )** and **ibase_execute( )** work like their equivalents in ODBC and are used when you want to perform one query many times, changing the values for each execution. **ibase_free_query( )** frees the memory allocated to a query by **ibase_prepare( )**.

ibase_fetch_row( ) accepts a query result id and returns a standard array of fields, the same as **mysql_fetch_row( )**, and **ibase_fetch_object( )** returns the row as an object. When you are finished with a result set, you can reduce resource usage by freeing the memory allocated to a result set with **ibase_free_result( )**. If your query requires transactions, you can use **ibase_trans( )** to start a transaction, **ibase_commit( )** to commit an update at the end of the transaction, and **ibase_ rollback( )** to remove updates when you want to cancel a transaction. If the query produces an error, you can use **ibase_errmsg( )** to return the latest error message from InterBase.

ibase_field_info( ) accepts a result id and a field number, and then provides information about the fields so you can vary your processing based on field type or name. Like MySQL, InterBase fields are numbered from 0. So many other things are like MySQL, you can slip InterBase functions into the MySQL examples in Chapter 5. **ibase_num_fields( )** returns the number of fields in a result set, so you can step through the fields with a **for( )** loop; and **ibase_timefmt( )** sets the format for fields of type date, time, and timestamp, when returned from a query.

Microsoft Access

MS Access is probably the best database in the world for single-workstation, single-user use. You can build the relations within a database just by a few mouse clicks on a picture of your database. I know a few people who model huge databases in Access and then struggle to get "full size" databases to provide the same level of functionality.

To keep MS Access from pushing MS SQL Server off small intranets, MS Access is limited to one user updating the database and a small number of users reading the database. You can easily plug MS Access into PHP through ODBC, so you can demonstrate an MS Access-based prototype to the world, and then transfer the same code, ODBC setup, and SQL to another database. If you use all the features of MS Access and then need to move to a database that allows multiple-user updates, you will have to use PostgreSQL (or its equivalent) instead of MySQL. Expect future development work in PostgreSQL to be many times harder because of the primitive user interface in PostgreSQL. (phpPgAdmin makes PostgreSQL easier but is still crude next to MS Access.)

As a guide, in a site with a huge, powerful server running basic business applications on Microsoft SQL Server, I developed administration applications in MS

Access because I saved days compared to setting up the databases in SQL Server. A daily log process and analysis program ran for just one hour on a spare, slow, cheap PC using MS Access, but required four hours when run in SQL Server with all the other applications and the overhead of transaction locking. The MS Access databases died when they hit 2GB (because of Microsoft's programming) but never missed a beat before that.

Once you hit the 2GB limit in MS Access, the best replacement for speed of execution and reliability is MySQL under Apache and PHP4, with phpMyAdmin for initial administration. If you want relationships in your database and want to stay on Windows, MySQL is out and all the other options are, by comparison, painful to install and painful to administer.

Microsoft SQL Server

In case you have not heard of Microsoft, they are the people who wrote Windows, so their SQL server should be great for use within Windows. Well, MS SQL Server has advantages, but it has disadvantages that are equally great. MS SQL Server started out as Sybase (**www.sybase.com**), and then was given Bill Gates's special treatment on Windows and Windows NT. Although Sybase developed across all the important Web server platforms, MS SQL Server is limited to Windows NT servers.

The two databases are still compatible to the point that you can use Sybase Unix components to access MS SQL Server from Unix, but it is easier and more reliable to use ODBC. In fact, it is easier and more reliable to access MS SQL Server through PHP's ODBC functions than to use PHP's MS SQL Server functions, even when your Web server is on Windows NT. For that reason, I skipped the MS SQL Server functions and recommend that MS SQL Server users jump to the Immediate Solution titled "Accessing Databases with ODBC."

mSQL

mSQL, or MiniSQL, is from Hughes Technologies Pty Ltd (**www.hughes.com.au**) and is best described as a smaller, lighter MySQL. The developers of MySQL actually started out using mSQL, and then decided to write a new database because they though mSQL would not scale up to the size required. I have not used mSQL, because MySQL is available for all the platforms I use. MySQL is available under the open source GPL license, and, if I wanted to change databases, I would probably move up to the fuller-function PostgreSQL.

If you have mSQL and want to access mSQL from PHP, you can read about MySQL in Chapter 5, use the code from there, and substitute the mSQL function names where I use MySQL functions. Hughes Technologies, which sells mSQL, sells a book on mSQL, but the few differences can be picked up from the PHP pages describing mSQL functions. To add to the problem, Hughes Technologies is about to roll out a whole new release of mSQL, and if the new release is a genuine leap forward, PHP's mSQL functions may have to change to match.

Oracle

Oracle, the company, produces Oracle, the database, and a range of commercial applications, such as financial software, based on the Oracle database. Oracle has one-third of the commercial database market, neck-and-neck with IBM's DB2. Oracle was the first commercial database widely available across multiple platforms, and it became the product of choice for Unix vendors trying to sell to mainframe-based IT departments.

PHP provides functions prefixed with **ora_** for older versions of the Oracle database, from Oracle Corporation (**http://oracle.com**), and newer functions, prefixed **oci8_**, for Oracle releases 7 and 8. Based on listening to problems with accessing Oracle through the specialized functions, I see no reason to use anything other than the ODBC interface. Getting the ODBC interface working is no more difficult on Linux, much easier on Windows NT, and somewhere in between on other platforms.

Oracle is a great choice for use across many types of platforms, mostly variations of Unix. Oracle has frequently topped the charts for the largest active commercial database, or the fastest, or the busiest. IBM's DB2 and NCR's Teradata lead with the biggest in the area of spatial data, and IBM's DB2 tends to perform best on IBM-proprietary platforms but is relatively new to Unix. You will end up on projects using Oracle, but not all will use Oracle's native API. You will find customers running Oracle behind applications like SAP, even though SAP comes with its own database, because large corporations can plug Oracle into the back of any application and use Oracle to share data between applications.

When you do strange things with data, the way you do it limits your future options. One customer had a database that stored the year as two digits, and instead of buying an upgrade to the latest release of the database, complete with four-digit years, they tried to write a procedure to encode the four-digit years to fit in the space of two digits. If they had succeeded with their stored procedure date conversion, they would have locked themselves into one database and made a move to open source databases all the more difficult. In the end, their stored procedure was unreliable, and the only way they could fix the stored procedure code was to upgrade the database to the latest release.

If you lock data processing into a stored procedure within a database, you limit yourself to databases with stored procedures. The most freely available alternative to Oracle, with stored procedures, is the open source PostgreSQL. The latest

Oracle has excellent features for spreading large databases over multiple servers in a way that lets the database survive the failure of individual servers. Use the power of Oracle to meet that type of challenge for large sites, but do not write code that prevents small sites using a lower-cost database.

If you perform all your strange processing in PHP and keep the database representation simple, you can input the simple representation from any data source, database file, or HTML form, and output to any data source. The **ora** functions work just like the ODBC functions and require all the strange processing to happen in PHP (a good thing), SQL (not so good but OK), or stored procedures (generally a bad thing). The newer **oci8** functions let you use the interface to perform strange things, which is extremely limiting (and limits you to Oracle), and they are definitely the worst choice.

Ovrimos SQL Server

Ovrimos SQL Server, from Ovrimos S.A. (**www.ovrimos.gr**), is the only Greek product mentioned in this chapter. Ovrimos is small and fast, and it competes more with MySQL than PostgreSQL. Ovrimos has transaction support, which used to give it an advantage over MySQL, but no longer.

The full Ovrimos Web Server application combines a Web server with a database, so it may be a smaller, less resource-intensive alternative to installing something like Microsoft's IIS and SQL Server. I do not know how it stacks up against a combination like Apache and MySQL, but more people are available with Apache and MySQL experience, so you are better off setting up your own Web server with Apache and MySQL. Ovrimos is used preconfigured in some Web appliances, and you have to access the database in the server as a remote database—a situation where ODBC is usually the best choice.

There is an ODBC interface for Ovrimos, so you do not have to use any special PHP functions or installation settings; just skip to the ODBC part of this chapter. There is also a set of PHP functions for Ovrimos, prefixed **ovrimos_**, and they look almost the same as the MySQL functions, so you could use the MySQL code examples from Chapter 5 and substitute Ovrimos functions. Ovrimos has transactions, like the latest MySQL, and the Ovrimos **commit** function looks just like the ODBC **commit** function—another reason to use ODBC.

SESAM/SQL-Server

SESAM/SQL-Server, from Fujitsu Siemens Computers (**www.fujitsu-siemens.com**), is a SQL-based database written for the BS2000 operating system, an operating system that is now ported across a range of Fujitsu computers from small-risk systems to large mainframes. If you are stuck with BS2000, you are stuck with SESAM, and you can access SESAM either using the PHP SESAM function or via an ODBC extension for SESAM and PHP's ODBC functions. The ODBC extension for SESAM costs extra, and it comes from another company, one of Fujitsu Siemens' business partners.

When you install the native interface to SESAM, you install the main part in Apache and a small link in PHP—a nonstandard approach that is difficult to get working, slow for the first access, and then fast for subsequent accesses. The SESAM interface supports *sequential* and *scrollable* cursors; the first is fast, and the second is flexible. Sequential cursors let you step through the cursor once, and presumably drop data from the cursor once you move past the data; they probably reduce resource usage further by not retrieving each row until you request the row. If you use sequential cursors for long lists, you will save resources, and you can always save the data in a PHP array if you need to step backward. Scrollable cursors let you jump around a cursor, perform seeks, and do all sorts of things that do not make sense in cursors. If you select a lot of data via SQL and then perform a seek within the cursor, you have failed to make effective use of SQL. Most uses of scrollable cursors made sense for online systems in use before Web sites, but not for the style of access currently used with Web sites; look carefully at scrollable cursors and replace them with better SQL or data cached in PHP arrays.

Because there is an ODBC interface for SESAM, I recommend ODBC ahead of the native interface provided by the PHP functions prefixed with **sesam_**. But if you are not allowed to buy the extra software for the SESAM ODBC interface and can find someone to set up the SESAM software in Apache, use the SESAM functions in PHP. The SESAM functions are almost the same as ODBC functions, with one extra—**sesam_diagnostic( )**—that returns a status array containing the number of rows in the cursor, any error messages, and other information.

Solid

Solid Information Technology (**www.solidtech.com**) focuses on software for embedded systems. Its Web site lists customers such as Nokia and Nortel, so its products fit into telephones and routers. One day you might get to write a Web site that fits into a handheld device, using PHP, Apache 2, and the Solid database, but if you are using ODBC for database access, you may not notice any difference between the Solid database and any other database.

Sybase

Sybase, from Sybase, Inc. (**http://sybase.com**) is similar to MS SQL Server (because MS SQL Server is based on Sybase), and has the advantages of running on many platforms, an ODBC connection, and many years of development. The native PHP functions for Sybase; allow a couple of things that an ODBC connection does not, mainly to do with error handling, but nothing I would call important, and ODBC functions are increasing in range and capability all the time.

Database Abstraction Layers

Abstraction layers disconnect databases from your code and should let you concentrate on your application logic and data, instead of the detailed technical needs of external software. In practice, one problem that database abstraction layers run into is that databases have their own field formats, local variations of SQL, and different ways of handling features such as **auto_increment** fields. PHP contains more than one database abstraction layer, because more than one group of developers are trying to solve the same problem.

DBA Functions

PHP's Database Abstraction layer (DBA) functions let you access a group of databases with one set of functions, listed here:

- **dba_close( )**—Closes a database
- **dba_delete( )**—Deletes an entry specified by a key
- **dba_exists( )**—Checks if a key exists in the database
- **dba_fetch( )**—Fetches a record specified by the key
- **dba_firstkey( )**—Fetches the first key in the database
- **dba_insert( )**—Inserts a new record
- **dba_nextkey( )**—Fetches the next key in the database
- **dba_open( )**—Opens a database
- **dba_optimize( )**—Optimizes a database by removing unused space
- **dba_popen( )**—Opens a database with a persistent connection
- **dba_replace( )**—Replaces a record
- **dba_sync( )**—Synchronizes a database

The databases include Berkeley DB from Sleepycat Software (**www.sleepycat.com**) (Berkeley DB was formerly called DB2, but is not related to IBM's DB2), and cdb from **http://cr.yp.to/cdb.html** (a server in the Department of Mathematics, Statistics, and Computer Science at the University of Illinois at Chicago). DBM functions, described in the next section, are similar, and are used for Sleepycat's Berkeley DB products (DBM is the name of the predecessor to Berkeley's DB).

The PHP functions let you do anything the underlying database allows and let you submit requests to perform actions that the underlying database may not provide. It is up to you to read the database documentation or construct tests to determine exactly what the database software does with your requests.

dba_open( ) is halfway between a database connection and a file-handling function. It accepts as parameters a file path, a mode of **r** for read access, **w** for write access, **c** to create a database and then provide read/write access, and **n** to create, truncate, and provide read and write access. The third parameter is the name of the actual file-handler module, and you can add other parameters that will be passed to the file handler. Because you have to nominate the file handler, the **dba** functions start to move away from true database abstraction. **dba_open( )** returns a database handle, similar to a file handle or database connection, for use in other **dba** functions, including **dba_close( )**.

dba_popen( ) provides a persistent version of **dba_open( )**. If you want to read more about persistent connections, read about **odbc_pconnect( )** earlier in this chapter. **dba_close( )** accepts the handle returned by **dba_open( )** or **dba_popen( )** and closes the database.

dba_fetch( ) accepts a string containing a key to a record and a database handle. It retrieves the record attached to the key and returns the record on success or false if the key is not found. If you want to search the database by key before fetching the record, **dba_firstkey( )** accepts a database handle and returns the first key of the database, and **dba_nextkey( )** returns subsequent keys.

dba_insert( ) accepts a string containing a key to a record, a string containing the record, and a database handle. It inserts the record and returns true on success or false if the key is already in the database. **dba_delete( )** accepts a string containing a key to a record and a database handle. It deletes the record attached to the key and returns true on success or false if the key is not found. **dba_replace( )** accepts a string containing a key to a record, a string containing the record, and a database handle. It replaces the record that the key refers to, and returns true on success or false if the replace fails. **dba_exists( )** accepts a string containing a key to a record and a database handle. It checks if the key exists and returns true on success or false if the key is not found.

dba_sync( ) accepts the database handle and forces a write to disk of all buffered records, which you have to perform after a write to databases like Sleepycat's DB2. You can test your database by running a script that writes to the database without **dba_sync( )**, and then running another script to read the data you wrote. **dba_optimize( )** accepts a database handle and performs some sort of optimization on the database. I presume the minimum would be to remove free space left by deletes or updates of uneven size, so you might want to schedule **dba_optimize( )** once per day or once every 1,000 deletes.

DBM Functions

The DBM functions let you access a group of databases with one set of functions, listed here:

- **dblist( )**—Describes the DBM library in use
- **dbmclose( )**—Closes a database
- **dbmdelete( )**—Deletes a record
- **dbmexists( )**—Checks if a key exists in a database
- **dbmfetch( )**—Fetches a record from the database
- **dbmfirstkey( )**—Retrieves the first key from the database
- **dbminsert( )**—Inserts a record
- **dbmnextkey( )**—Retrieves the next key from the database
- **dbmopen( )**—Opens a database
- **dbmreplace( )**—Replaces a record

The databases include Berkeley DB from Sleepycat Software (**www. sleepycat.com**) and gdbm from GNU (**www.gnu.org/directory/gdbm.html**). DBA functions, described in the "DBA Functions" section, are similar and are described as "used for Sleepycat's DB2," which is an old name for Berkeley DB (not related to IBM's DB2). I suspect Sleepycat dropped the name DB2 because IBM's DB2 is now available on Unix and the PHP documentation is a little slow in catching up with name changes.

The PHP functions let you request actions that the underlying database may not provide, so read the database documentation and construct tests to make sure a function works with your database the way you expect. Where a database can be used with both DBA and DBM functions, like gdbm, test both interfaces to determine exactly what you need.

dbmopen( ) accepts a file path and a mode of **r** for read access, **w** for write access, **c** to create a database and then provide read/write access, and **n** to create, truncate, and provide read and write access. **dbmclose( )** accepts the handle returned by **dbmopen( )** and closes the database. **dbmfetch( )** accepts a database handle and a string containing a key to a record, retrieves the record attached to the key, and returns the record on success or false if the key is not found. If you want to search the database by key, **dbmfirstkey( )** accepts a database handle and returns the first key of the database, and **dbmnextkey( )** returns subsequent keys.

dbminsert( ) accepts a database handle, a string containing a key to a record, and a string containing the record. It inserts the record and returns true on success or false if the key is already in the database. **dbmdelete( )** accepts a database handle and a string containing a key to a record. It deletes the record attached to the key and returns true on success or false if the key is not found. **dbmreplace( )** accepts a database handle, a string containing a key for a record, and a string containing the record. It replaces the record the key refers to and returns true on success or false if the replace fails. **dbmexists( )** accepts a database handle and a string containing a key to a record. It checks if the key exists and returns true on success or false if not found. **dblist( )** lists the DBM library used by the DBM functions.

DBX Functions

DBX is documented at **www.guidance.nl/php/dbx/doc/** and provides functions to give you simple access to a group of databases with one set of functions (listed here). The databases include MySQL, PostgreSQL, and ODBC-based databases, and the documentation includes instructions on how you can add more databases (if you can program in C):

- **dbx_close( )**—Closes a connection or database
- **dbx_connect( )**—Opens a connection or database
- **dbx_error( )**—Gets the latest error message
- **dbx_query( )**—Executes a query
- **dbx_sort( )**—Sorts the query's result
- **dbx_cmp_asc( )**—Compares rows for sorts in ascending order
- **dbx_cmp_desc( )**—Compares rows for sorts in descending order

These PHP functions seem primitive compared to the existing MySQL, PostgreSQL, and ODBC functions (discussed in Chapter 5 and this chapter), so check **php.net** for any updates that extend this function set before committing to commercial use of the functions. I find the MySQL functions simple and easy with ODBC adding a few niceties for accessing remote databases, so I would wait for the **dbx** functions to match either the MySQL functions or the ODBC functions before using **dbx**.

dbx_connect( ) accepts a module name, server name, database, user, password, and persistence indicator, and returns a handle for the connection to the database, a bit like **mysql_connect( )** and **mysql_select_db( )** rolled into one. The module name can be **mssql**, **mysql**, **odbc**, or **pgsql**, depending on what is installed. **dbx_close( )** accepts the database handle returned by **dbx_connect( )** and closes the database and the connection.

dbx_query( ) accepts a database handle, SQL, and optional flags that are too complicated to explain here. It executes the query, retrieves any rows from the query, and returns an object containing the rows, information about the rows, information about the columns (fields), information identifying the database handle, and optional extra information depending on the flags. **dbx_error( )** accepts a database handle and returns the most recent error message. The functions **dbx_sort( )**, **dbx_cmp_asc( )**, and **dbx_cmp_desc( )** let you sort the result set before retrieval, but I do not see the advantage of doing that when your SQL can include a sort. In fact, if you are using SQL's **limit**, **start**, or **group by**, you need the sort to occur before the creation of the result set, so you cannot use the DBX sort functions as many ways as you can use SQL's sort.

6. Databases: Commercial and Unusual

Immediate Solutions

Accessing Databases with ODBC

PHP's ODBC functions provide access to several databases through conventional ODBC mechanisms, and also to databases like Adabas, IBM's DB2, Solid, and Sybase whose native APIs are written to emulate ODBC. iODBC, from **www.iodbc.org**, plugs into PHP's ODBC functions and accepts iODBC plug-ins that let you access additional databases.

PHP 4.0.5's php.ini file contains the ODBC options shown in the following code. Some settings can be overridden by PHP's ODBC functions, which is extremely useful if your ISP does not give you access to php.ini, or for those occasions when you access more than one type of database, and each database requires different settings:

```
[ODBC]
;odbc.default_db    =  Not yet implemented
;odbc.default_user  =  Not yet implemented
;odbc.default_pw    =  Not yet implemented
; Allow or prevent persistent links.
odbc.allow_persistent = On
; Check that a connection is still valid before reuse.
odbc.check_persistent = On
; Maximum number of persistent links.  -1 means no limit.
odbc.max_persistent = -1
; Maximum number of links (persistent + non-persistent).
; -1 means no limit.
odbc.max_links = -1
; Handling of LONG fields.  Returns number of bytes to variables.
; 0 means passthru.
odbc.defaultlrl = 4096
; Handling of binary data. 0 means passthru, 1 return as is,
; 2 convert to char. See the documentation on odbc_binmode
; and odbc_longreadlen for an explanation of uodbc.defaultlrl
; and uodbc.defaultbinmode
odbc.defaultbinmode = 1
```

SQL is the standard language for ODBC, but not many databases speak pure SQL. The British refer to a medium size beer as a *pint*, even if the quantity is not a pint, and no matter how it is packaged, whereas Australians happily mix the terms *beer*, *glass*, *schooner*, and *pint*, in reference to beer by the glass, *stubbie* for a small bottle, and *can* for canned beer (except in Sydney, where many people call a can a *tinnie*). If beer drinkers cannot agree on standard terminology, how do you expect database makers to agree? Microsoft uses single quotes (') around dates in some software and a hash (#) (called *pound* by some people) around dates in MS Access, as shown in the first example code line that follows. To add complexity to SQL's misery, some databases require fields specified in display format and others require fields in internal format. If you set up a date field as YYYY-MM and use YYYY-MM in your SQL, and if your SQL fails with strange messages about the date, try the full date format as shown here—the database may want the ODBC SQL to deliver the date matching the internal format of the database. The second code line below shows the **date( )** format for MS Access:

```
$sql = "select * from stock where updated >= #2002-04-20 00:00:00#";
$formatted_date = date("Y-m-d H:i:s");
```

odbc_connect( ) connects to a database server, much like **mysql_connect( )** and **pg_connect( )**, and then returns a connection id for use in queries, commits, rollbacks, and **odbc_close( )**, or returns false (zero) if the connection fails. **odbc_pconnect( )** creates a persistent connection that reduces overhead, uses the same parameters as **odbc_connect( )**, and works when PHP is run as an Apache module, but not when PHP is run through CGI. The following examples show a variety of connections, the first using the minimum parameters of **dsn**, user, and password. **dsn** can be any identifier you use in your ODBC software, so read the documentation for the software.

Related solution:	Found on page:
Connecting to a Database	159

TIP: *If you are using Windows ODBC, use a type of **SYSTEM**, not user or file, because the Web server runs as system and will not see the user or file ODBC definitions.*

odbc_connect( ) lets you specify the type of cursor used with ODBC, and the four types are shown in the third through sixth examples that follow. If you have any weird errors on your first query, try cursor type **SQL_CUR_USE_ODBC**, and use the others based on the documentation supplied with your ODBC software. The manufactured examples are typical of what you end up with in Web portals where all the facilities, such as news and auctions, come from other suppliers using different types of databases. The last example connection is the way some ODBC software accepts the connection string:

```
$connection["vitamins"] = odbc_connect("vitamins", "", "");
$connection["stolen goods"] = odbc_connect("auctionsite", "bill",
   "zz15zz");
$connection["nuclear weapons"] = odbc_connect("NSAserver", "georgew",
   "w", SQL_CUR_USE_ODBC);
$connection["erotica"] = odbc_connect("everywhere", "peter",
   "over21", SQL_CUR_USE_IF_NEEDED);
$connection["stolen goods"] = odbc_connect("auctionsite", "peter",
   "zz15zz", SQL_CUR_DEFAULT);
$connection["music"] = odbc_connect("napster", "peter",
   "b1b6b12", SQL_CUR_USE_DRIVER);
$connection["vitamins"] = odbc_connect(
   "DSN=chemicalfactory;UIS=peter;PWD=b1b6b12");
```

odbc_exec( ), and the synonym **odbc_do( )**, take as parameters a connection id and a query, and return a result id or false if the query failed. The next example code shows an SQL statement, **odbc_exec( )**, executing the SQL statement and returning a result identifier. **odbc_prepare( )** and **ocbc_execute( )** work together to perform the same as **ocbc_exec( )**, with one slight change and a trap. The SQL passed to **odbc_prepare( )** can have question marks (**?**) in place of values, and **odbc_execute( )** will pass an array of parameters to match up to the question marks. With some databases, the database software will precompile the SQL to reduce overhead, and each **odbc_execute( )** will run a little faster, which saves time if your script runs the same SQL many times with slightly different parameters:

```
$sql = "select brand, item, price from prices where item = 'b12'";
$result = odbc_exec($connection["vitamins"], $sql);

$sql = "select * from prices where item = ? and price < ?";
$sql_result = odbc_prepare($connection["vitamins"], $sql);
$selection = array("b12", "5.00");
$result = odbc_execute($sql_result, $selection);
$selection = array("C", "3.50");
$result = odbc_execute($sql_result, $selection);
```

So, is precompiling SQL really useful? When writing a batch process, you might read 300,000 input records and run the query once per input record, at one-tenth of a second per execution, a total saving of 8 hours, 20 minutes. If you run the same query online with just one execution per page, the combination of **odbc_prepare( )** and **odbc_execute( )** will probably be slower than a single **odbc_exec( )**. You may find your database does not accept **odbc_prepare( )**, or the documentation says the database does not precompile. And, with some databases, frequently used

SQL transactions can be made faster by inserting them into the database as a view or using a special precompiler supplied with the database.

odbc_commit( ) commits all transactions in a connection, whereas **odbc_rollback( )** cancels all transactions and rolls back all changes made by those transactions (assuming the database can perform a rollback). **odbc_rollback( )** returns true if all transactions are rolled back and false if anything goes wrong:

```
$status = odbc_commit($connection["vitamins"]);
$status = odbc_rollback($connection["vitamins"]);
```

odbc_close( ) closes one connection to a server, requires the connection id returned by **odbc_connect( )**, and will not close a connection that has active transactions. Here, it is shown closing the connection for the vitamins server:

```
odbc_close($connection["vitamins"]);
```

odbc_close_all( ), shown here, closes all ODBC connections in one hit, except those with open transactions:

```
odbc_close_all ();
```

Results

At this stage, you have all the code to open a connection, close a connection, and execute a query, but you have not retrieved a result, so this section is all about results.

odbc_num_rows( ) accepts a result id and returns the number of rows in the result cursor from a **select** statement, or the number of rows changed by **insert**, **delete**, and **update**. **odbc_num_rows( )** returns –1 for an error (because zero can be a valid result); there are reports of some databases always returning –1, presumably due to an error in the database software. The following code shows how to step through a result cursor using **odbc_num_rows( )** (assuming it works for the database) and **odbc_fetch_row( )**. The rows count from 1, so the **for( )** loop counts from 1; and **odbc_fetch_row( )** returns false on error, so I put in a test for errors:

```
$sql = "select * from prices";
$result = odbc_exec($connection["vitamins"], $sql);
$rows = odbc_num_rows($result);
for($r = 1; $r <= $rows; $r++)
    {
```

```
if(odbc_fetch_row($result, $r))
   {
   // Process result with odbc_result()
   }
else
   {
   // Insert error message here
   }
}
```

When **ocdb_fetch_row( )** fetches the row, the row is transferred across the network from the database server to ODBC's local memory, and you access the row with **odbc_result( )**. You can also use a **while( )** loop with **odbc_fetch_row( )** to save overhead. The **while( )** loop is shown next. Note the second parameter, the row number, is left out. **odbc_fetch_row( )** defaults to reading the current row, and then moves the row pointer to the next row for the next fetch, much the same as **each( )** does with an array (explained in Chapter 2):

```
$sql = "select * from prices";
$result = odbc_exec($connection["vitamins"], $sql);
while(odbc_fetch_row($result))
   {
   // Process result with odbc_result()
   }
else
   {
   // Insert error message here
   }
```

You could use **odbc_fetch_row( )** to step through a result cursor several times, but you would chew up network resources. You would be better off reading the cursor into a PHP array and making the multiple passes over the array.

odbc_result( ) accepts a result id from **odbc_fetch_row( )** and a field identifier, and returns one field from the result cursor. The field identifier can be a field number, counting from 1, as shown below in line five, or a field name as shown in line six:

```
$sql = "select brand, item, price from prices where type='D'";
$result = odbc_exec($connection["vitamins"], $sql);
while(odbc_fetch_row($result))
   {
   print("<br>Brand: " . odbc_result($result, 1)
      . " , price: " . odbc_result($result, "price"));
   }
```

If you are retrieving fields from multiple tables, and you have the same field name in several tables, assign an alias to the second and subsequent occurrence of each name so you can identify them by name in the result, as shown in the SQL that follows:

```
$sql = "select brand, price, prices.updated, quantity,"
   . " stock.updated as datestockchecked"
     . " from prices, stock where stock.item = prices.item";
```

There are endless reports of problems with ODBC where a field is too long, a field is of an unusual type, or you have too many fields in your result; so be selective, which will reduce your network overhead, and read your database's documentation on how that database feeds very long fields through ODBC. *If in doubt, cut it out.* When you have problems with SQL, remove suspect fields from your SQL and retry until you have working SQL. Perhaps start from scratch with the bare minimum SQL to get the query going, and then add one field at a time.

odbc_result_all( ) accepts a result id from a query and an optional format string, and prints the contents of the cursor. The cursor contents are inserted into an HTML table. The field formatting string can be any parameters you want added to the **<table>** tag. Because the print is immediate, you cannot place the output into a string. No formatting options are available for table cells or the cell contents, so **odbc_result_all( )** is limited to use in tests and diagnostics. The following examples dump the test tables, **stock** and **prices**, using the sample code shown next. The results from **stock** appear in Figure 6.2 and the results from **prices** appear formatted in Figure 6.3:

```
$sql = "select * from stock";
$result = odbc_exec($connection["vitamins"], $sql);
$result_all = odbc_result_all($result);

$sql = "select * from prices";
$result = odbc_exec($connection["vitamins"], $sql);
$result_all = odbc_result_all($result, "border=\"5\"");
```

ID	brand	item	quantity	updated
1	generic	A	2	2002-04-19 00:00:00
2	generic	C	5	2002-04-19 00:00:00
3	Nature's pills	A	1	2002-04-21 00:00:00
4	Nature's pills	B	4	2002-04-21 00:00:00
5	Nature's pills	C	3	2002-04-21 00:00:00
6	Nature's pills	b12	7	2002-04-21 00:00:00

Figure 6.2   **Stock** table printed with **odbc_result_all()**.

ID	brand	item	price	updated
1	generic	A	2.9500	2002-04-19 00:00:00
2	generic	C	2.9500	2002-04-19 00:00:00
3	Nature's pills	A	29.9500	2002-04-21 00:00:00
4	Nature's pills	B	38.9500	2002-04-21 00:00:00
5	Nature's pills	C	35.9500	2002-04-21 00:00:00
6	Nature's pills	b12	182.5000	2002-04-21 00:00:00

Figure 6.3   Price table printed with **odbc_result_all()** and a format string.

There are times you want to know the number of fields (columns) in a result returned from **odbc_exec()**, and **odbc_num_fields()** supplies that number. Because rows are returned as arrays in most scripts, you can process the results without knowing the number of fields, so I expect you will be more likely to use this number for those occasions when you just want the number of fields and will not proceed to reading the results. The next example shows **odbc_num_fields()** in action immediately after one of the **odbc_exec()** statements from an earlier example:

```
$sql = "select * from stock";
$result = odbc_exec($connection["vitamins"], $sql);
$number_of_fields = odbc_num_fields($result);
```

odbc_fetch_into() accepts a result id, a row number, and an array, as shown in the following code, and returns a row from the result set in the array. Although the function sounds like a few other row retrieval functions, some slight differences need to be explained. The array is accessed by reference, so **odbc_fetch_into()** simply writes new content into the array, replacing everything that was already in the array and converting the variable to an array if it was in any other format before. Instead of returning an array, like other row retrieval functions, **odbc_fetch_into()** returns the number of fields placed in the array or false if there is no row to retrieve. The function accepts a row number, so you can retrieve any row, or zero, so you can step through a set of rows, as shown in the example, and increments the row pointer:

```
$sql = "select * from stock";
$result = odbc_exec($connection["vitamins"], $sql);
if($result)
    {
    print("<table border=\"3\">" );
    $array = "";
    while($result_all = odbc_fetch_into($result, 0, $array))
        {
```

```
        reset($array);
        print("<tr>" );
        while(list($k, $v) = each($array))
            {
            print("<td>" . $v . "</td>" );
            }
        print("</tr>" );
        }
    print("</table>" );
    }
else
    {
    print("<br>No result" );
    }
```

The output of this example is shown in Figure 6.4.

When I tested this function, using the PHP 4.0.5 Win32 binary, **odbc_fetch_into()** was replacing the array's content but not resetting the array's internal pointer to the start of the array, and the test code would print just one line. I inserted the **reset($array)**, included in the example code, and suddenly everything printed perfectly. Most array functions either add each row to the end of the array or create a new array and reset the array pointer, so I reported the anomaly to **php.net**.

NOTE: *If you suspect the behavior of a PHP function, check the error reports at **http://www.php.net/bugs.php**. Read the PHP documentation first, read the FAQs on **php.net**, search existing bug reports thoroughly, and write extensive test code to show every possible variation, all before reporting a bug. Then be brave and report the behavior. Your contribution might improve PHP's code or documentation.*

Errors

What happens when there is an error within ODBC or the database? **odbc_error()** returns a string containing a six-digit ODBC error indicator, and **odbc_errormsg()** returns an error message. Both return an empty string if there was no error. Both

1	generic	A	2	2002-04-19 00:00:00
2	generic	C	5	2002-04-19 00:00:00
3	Nature's pills	A	1	2002-04-21 00:00:00
4	Nature's pills	B	4	2002-04-21 00:00:00
5	Nature's pills	C	3	2002-04-21 00:00:00
6	Nature's pills	b12	7	2002-04-21 00:00:00

Figure 6.4 **Stock** table printed with **odbc_fetch_into()**.

functions accept a connection id and return error information for that connection, but you can use them without a connection id, and they will return the last error that occurred on any connection. The following code example shows how you might print the error information after a query:

```
$sql = "select brand, item, price from prices where type='b12'";
if(!$result = odbc_exec($connection["vitamins"], $sql))
    {
    print("<br>ODBC error number " . odbc_error($connection["vitamins"])
        . ", message: " . odbc_errormsg($connection["vitamins"]));
    }
```

MS Access exhibits behavior typical of certain types of databases, so I used it here both as an illustration of problems with MS Access and to demonstrate some things to look out for with other databases. MS Access lets many people look at data, but only one person can update the data at any one time. If you try to access the data while the database is open for update, you will get a message like the following:

```
Warning: SQL error: [Microsoft][ODBC Microsoft Access Driver] Could not
    use '(unknown)'; file already in use., SQL state S1000 in SQLConnect
```

Information about Fields

When you retrieve results and want to vary your processing to suit the results, it is nice to have a list of field names, lengths types, and other information. The following code retrieves all the information about results in fields, so you can process each field exactly how you want. The one real difference between the ODBC version and similar code for other databases is that the index counts from 1 instead of 0. The code also shows you all the ODBC functions you use to gather information about fields:

```
function odbc_fields($result)
    {
    $number_of_fields = odbc_num_fields($result);
    for($i = 1; $i <= $num_of_fields; $i++)
        {
        $array[$i]["name"] = odbc_field_name($result, $i);
        $array[$i]["column"] = odbc_field_num($result,
            $array[$i]["name"]);
        $array[$i]["type"] = odbc_field_type($result, $i);
        $array[$i]["length"] = odbc_field_len($result, $i);
```

```
//    $array[$i]["length"] = odbc_field_precision($result, $i);
      $array[$i]["scale"] = odbc_field_scale($result, $i);
   }
   if(!isset($array)) {$array = false;}
   return($array);
   }

$sql = "select * from stock";
$result = odbc_exec($connection["vitamins"], $sql);
if($result)
   {
   $fields = odbc_fields($result);
   }
```

odbc_field_name( ) returns the name of a field given the column number, and **odbc_field_num( )** returns the field number given the field name, so the preceding code has the artificial example of setting **$array[$i]["column"]** using **odbc_field_num( )** even though the number is known. **odbc_field_precision( )** is a synonym for **odbc_field_len( )**, so it is shown as a comment in the preceding code. **odbc_field_scale( )** returns the scale of a floating-point number.

Other Functions

odbc_autocommit( ) changes the **autocommit** setting for a connection from the default of **on** to **off** and back **on** if needed. Setting **autocommit** to **off** starts a transaction and requires **odbc_commit( )** or **odbc_rollback ( )** to end the transaction. In the following sample code, the first line returns the current status, the second line turns **autocommit** on, and the third line turns **autocommit** off:

```
$status = odbc_autocommit($connection["vitamins"]);
$status = odbc_autocommit($connection["vitamins"], true);
$status = odbc_autocommit($connection["vitamins"], false);
```

odbc_binmode( ) sets an option for the conversion of binary data to the character representation used to feed binary data through ODBC. The first parameter is the id for the result set you are accessing, and the second parameter is your choice of three options shown in the next example code. **ODBC_BINMODE_PASSTHRU** passes binary data untouched, **ODBC_BINMODE_RETURN** requests that data be returned as retrieved from the database, and **ODBC_BINMODE_CONVERT** requests the conversion of binary data to a hexadecimal string representation. If you want to set a default binary mode before creating results sets, use **odbc_binmode( )** with the result id set to zero, and remember that your setting is also affected by **odbc_longreadlen( )** (**odbc_longreadlen** is described later in this solution):

```
$status = odbc_binmode($result["vitamins"], ODBC_BINMODE_PASSTHRU);
$status = odbc_binmode($result["vitamins"], ODBC_BINMODE_RETURN);
$status = odbc_binmode($result["vitamins"], ODBC_BINMODE_CONVERT);
```

odbc_cursor( ) takes as a parameter the id of a result set, and returns a name for a cursor, shown in the following code:

```
print("<br>Current cursor: " . odbc_cursor($result["vitamins"]);
```

odbc_free_result( ) frees up resources and may be useful with long scripts that build many cursors or very long cursors. This function is shown next freeing a result set after a processing a result (the processing is left out for brevity). If you turn off **autocommit**, start a transaction, and then use **odbc_free_result( )**, the active transaction will be rolled back; so be decisive, and use **odbc_commit( )** or **odbc_rollback( )** first. Your resource savings with **odbc_free_result( )** will vary; the longer the cursor, the more resources saved, and the longer the scripts, the greater the savings:

```
$sql = "select brand, item, price from prices where type='D'";
$result = odbc_exec($connection["vitamins"], $sql);
while(odbc_fetch_row($result))
    {
    // process result in here…
    }
odbc_free_result($result);
```

A central database server, feeding many applications and users, is usually the bottleneck on any Web site running an online shopping application; so, every cursor freed early is an extra shopper who can shop. Every cursor left open, especially ones with transactions uncommitted, means a shopper leaving your slow Web site and buying from your competition (unless your competition is even sloppier at committing transactions and freeing resources). With some databases, one update transaction left open can block, or severely slow down, all read transactions. In scripts that read long cursors, consider reading the cursor straight into an array, freeing the cursor, and then processing the data from the array.

odbc_gettypeinfo( ) returns a cursor containing all the data types available from the source database and all the attributes of each data type. The following sample code was used to get the data type table shown in part in Figure 6.5 from MS Access and had 18 columns of attributes, with some columns applying to only one data type. The sample code was also used to get the data type table shown in part in Figure 6.6 from PostgreSQL and had 14 columns of attributes. This result has significant differences from MS Access and serves as a demonstration of the

TYPE_NAME	DATA_TYPE	COLUMN_SIZE	LITERAL_PREFIX	LITERAL_SUFFIX
GUID	-11	36	'	'
BIT	-7	1		
BYTE	-6	3		
LONGBINARY	-4	1073741823	0x	
VARBINARY	-3	255	0x	
BINARY	-2	255	0x	
LONGCHAR	-1	2147483647	'	'
CHAR	1	255	'	'
CURRENCY	2	19		
INTEGER	4	10		
COUNTER	4	10		
SMALLINT	5	5		
REAL	7	7		
DOUBLE	8	15		
DATETIME	11	19	#	#
VARCHAR	12	255	'	'

Figure 6.5   Type info from MS Access with ODBC and **odbc_gettypeinfo()**.

TYPE_NAME	DATA_TYPE	PRECISION	LITERAL_PREFIX	LITERAL_SUFFIX
int8	-5	19		
char	-7	1	'	'
char	1	254	'	'
date	9	10	'	'
numeric	3	1000		
float8	8	15		
float8	6	15		
int4	4	10		
lo	-4	-4	'	'
text	-1	8190	'	'
numeric	2	1000		
float4	7	7		
int2	5	5		
time	10	8	'	'
datetime	11	19	'	'
int2	-6	5		
bytea	-3	254	'	'
varchar	12	254	'	'

Figure 6.6   Type info from PostgreSQL with ODBC and **odbc_gettypeinfo()**.

6. Databases:
Commercial
and Unusual

differences between databases, especially with data formats that are not solved by ODBC:

```
$result = odbc_gettypeinfo($connection["vitamins"]);
if($result)
    {
    $result_all = odbc_result_all($result, "border=\"3\"");
    }
```

odbc_longreadlen( ) works with **odbc_binmode( )** to control the handling of long fields, such as **text** in some databases, **memo** in MS Access, and any field marked **long** or **long binary** or **blob**. The first parameter is a result id and the second is the maximum length for any field to be passed from the database. Zero has the special meaning of passing long fields without truncation. The following example, the first part of previous code to read results, has **odbc_longreadlen( )** inserted after **odbc_exec( )** and limits long fields to 200 characters:

```
$sql = "select * prices";
$result = odbc_exec($connection["vitamins"], $sql);
odbc_longreadlen($result, 200))
while(odbc_fetch_row($result))
    {
```

odbc_setoption( )is equivalent to opening up your tape-cleaning kit and placing a large steel hammer alongside the cotton buds: Do not use it until you know exactly what you are doing. **odbc_setoption( )** lets you set options for connections and SQL statement execution, but the results are unreliable, unpredictable, and occasionally antisocial because the possible settings vary by database and by the release of the database software. What works for you may be disastrous for anyone who tries to use your code. The first parameter is a connection id or a result, the second parameter is 1 for connections and 2 for results, the third parameter is an option number you have to get from your ODBC software documentation, and the fourth parameter is the option's value. The following example will, with some ODBC software and databases, set the timeout to 60 seconds. With other software, it may not work, or it may set a disastrous value in a different parameter:

```
odbc_setoption($result, 2, 0, 60);
```

odbc_tables( ) returns a cursor containing all the tables in a database. It requires at least a connection and accepts a variety of optional string parameters named **qualifier**, **owner**, **name**, and **types**. The **owner** and **name** fields let you use

SQL-style search patterns using % to match zero or more characters and _ to match one character. The **types** field can contain a list of comma-separated types, such as **"TABLE, VIEW"**, but the database can ignore any option it does not like. (For example, PostgreSQL supports views, but when I asked PostgreSQL for views, it returned zero rows.) The code I used to request and display the table list is shown next, and the output is shown in Figure 6.7:

```
$result = odbc_tables($connection["vitamins"]);
if($result)
    {
    $result_all = odbc_result_all($result, "border=\"3\"");
    }
```

odbc_tableprivileges( ) lists any privileges associated with tables. It accepts the same parameters as **odbc_tables( )** and produces the same type of output. **odbc_tableprivileges( )** does not list tables without privileges, so when you need a list of all tables, listing privileges for those tables that have them, you have to run **odbc_tables( )** first, and then merge in the result from **odbc_tableprivileges( )**.

New Functions

This section lists new ODBC functions that will be useful, but did not work with the databases I tested through ODBC; so look to **php.net** for updated documentation on the use of these functions. Check the documentation that comes with your database, because the database may not supply the appropriate data through ODBC.

odbc_primarykeys( ) identifies the primary key fields in your table, and **odbc_foreignkeys( )** identifies the foreign keys in your table, or the foreign keys in other tables that refer to the primary keys in your table. Both are important when you are building scripts that dynamically update tables, and a mistake with either could break relationships between your table and other tables.

If your database allows stored procedures, PHP has two new functions: **odbc_procedures( )** to list stored procedures, and **odbc_procedurecolumns( )** to help you identify the fields (columns) used in the stored procedure. You might need these functions when writing code to dynamically select the right stored

TABLE_QUALIFIER	TABLE_OWNER	TABLE_NAME	TABLE_TYPE	REMARKS
		prices	TABLE	
		stock	TABLE	

Figure 6.7   Tables list from PostgreSQL displayed with **odbc_tables()**.

procedure for a task. Few databases support stored procedures, and when you do find them, several stored procedures may be accessing the same fields with slightly different strategies designed to optimize certain queries.

odbc_specialcolumns( ) is another new function, aimed at identifying fields (columns) that uniquely identify a table or are automatically incremented. You might want to use this when dynamically building table access routines. When you build a data entry screen from table information, you need to know the fields that make the primary key unique so you can make the fields compulsory. When you build an update screen, you need to exclude automatically updated fields from user-updated fields and the update SQL.

odbc_statistics( ) retrieves statistics for a table, but not all databases collect statistics. Some collect statistics only when you run special utilities, and those that do collect statistics may or may not use them to optimize queries. When you can get statistics, you can use them to decide whether to add indexes to fields or remove existing indexes, and how often you should compact the database.

Accessing Databases with DBA Functions

The following code is a sample update, using gdbm, that shows a search for a key, **$search**, and the replacement of the attached record with a new value, **$new_value**. The database open uses **c** to allow creation of the database if the database does not exist, and there is one token error message if the replace fails but no error messages if anything else fails. The file name has forward slashes (/) because the code was written on NT. NT can use either / or a backslash (\) Unix and Linux require /, and Windows requires \. Note the **while** loop that has nothing within its brackets. The loop is looping to step through the keys using **dba_firstkey( )**. The only requirement is to end the loop at a match or end of file:

```
$search = "frog";
$new_value = "Frogs are small, wet and some have fat juicy legs"
    . " that are a great source of protein for birds and some humans.";
$db = dba_open("t:/test/db.dbm", "c", "gdbm");
$key = dba_firstkey($db);
while($key != $search and $key = dba_firstkey($db)
    {
    }
If($key == $search)
    {
    if(dba_replace($key, $value, $db))
```

```
      {
      print("<br>Replace worked.");
      }
   else
      {
      print("<br>Replace failed.");
      }
   }
dba_close($db);
```

Accessing Databases with DBM Functions

The following code is a sample update using gdbm. It shows a search for a key, **$search**, and the replacement of the attached record with a new value, **$new_value**. The database open uses **c** to allow creation of the database if the database does not exist, and there is one token error message if the replace fails but no error messages if anything else fails. If you looked at the preceding Immediate Solution using DBA functions, you will notice the DBM functions are almost identical to the DBA functions; therefore, the code ends up much the same:

```
$search = "dog";
$new_value = "Dogs are small, have wet noses and fast legs,"
   . " eat a deal of protein and are eaten by some humans.";
$db = dbbopen("t:/test/db.dbm", "c", "gdbm");
$key = dbmfirstkey($db);
while($key != $search and $key = dbmfirstkey($db)
   {
   }
If($key == $search)
   {
   if(dbmreplace($db, $key, $value))
      {
      print("<br>Replace worked.");
      }
   else
      {
      print("<br>Replace failed.");
      }
   }
dba_close($db);
```

Accessing Databases with DBX Functions

The following code is a sample update using MySQL. It shows a simple query and code to print the first field from the results:

```
$sql = "select * from fruit";
$connection = dbx_connect("mysql", "", "food", "peter", "xx00yyy");
$result = dbx_query($connection, $sql);
print("<table border=\"3\">");
for($r = 0; $r < $result->rows; $r++)
    {
    print("<tr>");
    for($c = 0; $c < $result->cols; $c++)
        {
        print("<td>" . $result->data[$r][$c] . "</td>");
        }
    print("</tr>");
    }
print("</table>");
dbx_close($connection);
```

Accessing Ingres II

You can read about Ingres II at **www.cai.com/products/ingres.htm**. There are reasons why someone would have purchased Ingres in the past, but now Ingres is owned by Computer Associates, a company that seems to have purchased a lot of databases and dropped several. Ingres is also limited to one query or transaction per connection, so you cannot use it for some types of applications, which is another reason to choose PostgreSQL instead. If you still want to access Ingres, perhaps for a conversion to another database, you have to switch on Ingres support in php.ini and use the functions described in this section.

ingres_connect( ) accepts a database name, user name, and password, and then returns a connection ID or false on failure. All three parameters will, if missing, default to values set in php.ini. Subsequent Ingres functions will default to the most recent connection, so there is no need to supply the connection id unless you want to use several connections. **ingres_pconnect( )** provides a persistent connection using the same parameters as **ingres_connect( )**. **ingres_close( )** closes the most recent connection so, like MySQL, you do not have to specify a connection id.

ingres_query( ) accepts an SQL query string and an optional connection id and returns true for success and false if the query fails. **ingres_fetch_row( )** gets the result rows on success, but there is no equivalent to **mysql_error( )** to get an error message when the query fails. **ingres_query( )** automatically adds the query to any existing open transaction, or starts a new transaction. You can end transactions with **ingres_commit( )** or **ingres_rollback( )** or make all transactions automatically commit with **ingres_autocommit( )**. **ingres_autocommit( )** accepts an optional connection id, which defaults to the most recent connection id, and switches **autocommit** on (or off, if **autocommit** is on). Both **ingres_commit( )** and **ingres_rollback( )** accept an optional connection id and commit or roll back pending updates.

You can get the number of rows and number of columns in the result using **ingres_num_rows( )** and **ingres_num_fields( )**, respectively. However, **ingres_num_rows( )** reportedly closes the query cursor and leaves you with no results; so do not use these functions, or else test them carefully. To get the rows in a result, just place one of the fetch functions in a **while** loop as shown next. **ingres_fetch_row( )** fetches a row as an ordinary array, **ingres_fetch_array( )** returns the row in an associative array, and **ingres_fetch_object( )** returns the row in an object. **ingres_fetch_row( )** is used in the example:

```
$sql = "select * from vegetables";

if(ingres_connect("database", "username", "password"))
   {
   if( ingres_query($sql))
      {
      print("<table border=\"3\">");
      while($row = ingres_fetch_row())
         {
         print("<tr>");
         while(list($k, $v) = each($row))
            {
            print("<td>" . $v . "</td>");
            }
         print("</tr>");
         }
      print("</table>");
      }
   ingres_close();
   }
```

You can get information about fields in a query result using any of the functions listed next. Just supply them with the field number, counting from 1, and an optional connection id if you have more than one connection open, and then print the result. The functions seem the same as the equivalents in the ODBC functions—so similar that I wonder why Computer Associates did not simply make the interface ODBC-compatible like IBM did with DB2:

```
ingres_field_name( )
ingres_field_type( )
ingres_field_nullable( )
ingres_field_length( )
ingres_field_precision( )
ingres_field_scale( )
```

Timing Retrieval: A Path to Performance

This solution is all about timing the microscopic differences between different functions, different SQL, and database changes, like adding an index. All these things can add up to huge savings when multiplied by thousands of page accesses. This approach assumes you will not time SQL using database utilities because their timings represent only part of the total time, or you will use the database tuning tools to recommend changes, and then you will verify the changes in your script. You can time page response at a browser, and that is great for other aspects of script tuning, but it does not give you the details of each database access.

The first thing you need to do is read up on **microtime( )**, explained in Chapter 2; but for now you only need the following code, which returns a Unix-format time string appended with several decimal places (usually six) of microseconds or whatever is available on your server for high-resolution timing. The first line shows the absolute simplest way of using **microtime( )**, the second line shows the string produced, the subsequent lines show how to format the string into a readable date/time for subsequent display, and the last line shows the result:

```
$microtime = microtime( );
0.52291300 989829487
list($seconds, $microseconds) = explode(" ", $microtime);
$display_time = date("Y-m-d H:i:s", $seconds)
    . substr($microseconds, 1);
2001-05-14 06:38:07.52291300
```

Now you need to wrap the timing around a database function in a meaningful way with minimum disruption to the function, because any overhead caused by the timing function makes the timing less accurate. I will pinch the code examples from ODBC in the first Immediate Solution, starting with the connection code:

```
$micro_start = microtime();
$connection["vitamins"] = odbc_connect("vitamins", "", "");
$micro_stop = microtime();
$event[] = array("description" => "odbc_connect vitamins",
    "start" => $micro_start, "end" => $micro_stop);
```

Notice the code simply saves the time in memory immediately before and after the **odbc_connect( )** and then puts the time in an array, a method that minimizes the overhead required to time the database event and defers the time management overhead to later. To verify the ratio between the time required for the connection and the overhead of timing, add a second recording of time, as shown next, to give you the processing overhead of **microtime( )** and add it to the array:

```
$micro_start = microtime();
$connection["vitamins"] = odbc_connect("vitamins", "", "");
$micro_stop = microtime();
$event[] = array("description" => "odbc_connect vitamins",
    "start" => $micro_start, "end" => $micro_stop);
$micro_extra = microtime();
$event[] = array("description" => "microtime overhead ",
    "start" => $micro_stop, "end" => $micro_extra);
```

The next step is to wrap the microtiming around the query execution; the only thing a little different is the setting of an extra time, **$query_start**, that will be used to time the overall query processing. Notice how PHP lets you place several variables in a row and propagates the one value over all of them. In effect, **$query_start** is set to the value of the rest of the statement, which is the value assigned to **$micro_start**:

```
$sql = "select * from stock";
$query_start = $micro_start = microtime();
$result = odbc_exec($connection["vitamins"], $sql);
$micro_stop = microtime();
$event[] = array("description" => "odbc_exec " . $sql,
    "start" => $micro_start, "end" => $micro_stop);
```

Wrap the microtiming around the row fetch code, shown next. Because the fetch is in the middle of a **while( )** statement, you have to set the start time just before the **while( )** statement for the first loop, and again right at the end of the **while( )**

loop to have a valid start time for subsequent loops. To minimize overhead during the fetch, the code saves the fetched rows to an array for later processing. If you have a heavily loaded database server and many long cursors active, you can reduce your server workload by quickly reading the cursor's contents into an array, freeing the cursor resource with **odbc_free_result( )**, and then processing from the array:

```
if($result)
   {
   $array = "";
   $micro_start = microtime();
   while($row = odbc_fetch_into($result, 0, $array))
      {
      $micro_stop = microtime();
      $event[] = array("description" => "odbc_fetch_into",
         "start" => $micro_start, "end" => $micro_stop);
      $rows[] = $row;
      $micro_start = microtime();
      }
   }
```

The query is complete, so the next code records a time for the whole query, and then frees the cursor resources and records a time for the function that frees the resources. Because resources are freed at the end of the script processing, you might not want to manually free resources near the end of a short script; it is more likely to be of use near the start of a long script or a script with many queries:

```
$micro_stop = microtime();
$event[] = array("description" => "whole query: " . $sql,
   "start" => $query_start, "end" => $micro_stop);
$micro_start = microtime();
odbc_free_result($result);
$micro_stop = microtime();
$event[] = array("description" => "odbc_free_result",
"start" => $micro_start, "end" => $micro_stop);
```

After the query is finished, you can print the timing results or write the times to a disk file for later analysis. You could log the times to a database, but that would slow down the database server and interfere with the times recorded by other pages. The next block of example code loops through the saved array and builds a table formatted for easy reading. Note the use of the BCMath function **bcsub( )** performing the one calculation with the times, because PHP integer arithmetic does not cope with the large numbers, and floating-point arithmetic tends to produce numbers in hard-to-read notation. BCMath, or GMP if you have GMP installed, handles the huge numbers easily. BCMath is included as standard in the latest PHP Win32 binaries and requires PHP compiled with **–enable-bcmath** in the Unix versions:

```
print("<table border=\"3\">"
   . "<tr><td><em>description</em></td><td><em>time</em></td></tr>" );
while(list($k, $v) = each($event))
   {
   list($start_microseconds, $start_seconds) =
      explode(" ", $v["start"]);
   $start_time = $start_seconds . substr($start_microseconds, 1);
   list($end_microseconds, $end_seconds) = explode(" ", $v["end"]);
   $end_time = $end_seconds . substr($end_microseconds, 1);
   $time = bcsub($end_time, $start_time, 8);
   print("<tr><td>" . $v["description"] . "</td>"
      . "<td>" . $time . "</td></tr>" );
   }
print("</table>" );
```

Figure 6.8 shows the times from two tests so you can see variations between similar measurements. The connection time varied 5 percent between the two tests, the **microtime()** overhead varied 18 percent, and individual fetches of rows varied more than 100 percent. There are clearly variations that you need to consider, and some that are a surprise.

The connection chewed up the most time, so it would be worth comparing with a persistent connection. Persistent connections are not always possible and, with

description	time	description	time
odbc_connect vitamins	0.01920600	odbc_connect vitamins	0.01837900
microtime overhead	0.00009800	microtime overhead	0.00008300
odbc_exec select * from stock	0.00535100	odbc_exec select * from stock	0.00439200
odbc_fetch_into	0.00027500	odbc_fetch_into	0.00025500
odbc_fetch_into	0.00023600	odbc_fetch_into	0.00021100
odbc_fetch_into	0.00018700	odbc_fetch_into	0.00011000
odbc_fetch_into	0.00014200	odbc_fetch_into	0.00010200
odbc_fetch_into	0.00012500	odbc_fetch_into	0.00009600
odbc_fetch_into	0.00012500	odbc_fetch_into	0.00009600
whole query: select * from stock	0.00692000	whole query: select * from stock	0.00567400
odbc_free_result	0.00039000	odbc_free_result	0.00036100

Figure 6.8   ODBC retrieval times.

some databases, do not save time. In this example, the time savings would not be significant in a page containing many queries; but on the example test page of all the possible database-related changes, the connection has the most potential to save time.

The whole query ran a little faster the second time, so it would be worth running the test several times to see if the change is a result of disk blocks being cached in memory (something that suggests the database or file system makes good use of memory). Try the test again with an update query and see how fast updates work. Some file systems, such as XFS, NTFS, and Reiser, log updates to enable recovery after a crash; that logging slows down some databases, such as PostgreSQL, because the databases are performing their own logging to enable transaction rollbacks. Heavily cached and highly developed file systems typically speed up reads and slow down some types of updates to the point where you might want to look at placing your database on a separate partition with a different file system.

You could split **odbc_exec( )** into **odbc_prepare( )** and **odbc_execute( )** to see if the database can make use of SQL preparation. If the database is on another server, you can watch the consistency of the fetch times and compare them with network activity on the link between the servers.

Related solution:	*Found on page:*
rand(), **srand()**, and **microtime()**	69

Chapter 7
Environmental Considerations

In Depth

Have you ever felt the need to grab your computer and give it a good shake, to wake it up and make it do what you want? This chapter gives you the tools to reach beyond Web pages, bypass your Web server, delve into your computer's internals, and perform surgery on the really obstinate parts of your system. You can add security at a finer level than offered by your Web server. You can give primitive command-line programs a civilized user interface by running the programs within a PHP script so users see a clean, helpful, and readable Web page.

Apache

Apache is a great Web server, and you can extend Apache to work harder for you on a script-by-script basis. There are ways to grab special features of Apache, if they are installed on your system, and you can use those features to enhance your PHP scripts. Apache also sets up a whole range of special variables for your use. Other Web servers set up similar variables, but not necessarily as complete a range.

Chapter 1 has examples of looking up URIs with **apache_lookup_uri( )**, communicating between Apache modules with **apache_note( )**, conversions between ASCII and EBCDIC, getting all the HTTP headers with **getallheaders( )**, and using non-PHP pages through Apache's CGI interface via **virtual( )**. Apache's note system lets you communicate from one module to another for the same script execution. If you want to communicate between multiple uses of the same module, you can use Apache's shared memory as explained later in this chapter.

When a browser requests your page, the browser sends a set of HTTP headers to your Web server, the Web server interprets the headers and passes some to PHP, and then PHP runs your script. Within your script, most of the information from the headers is available from environmental variables, and you can read the original headers using **getallheaders( )**. Figure 7.1 shows a typical set of headers.

Accept lists the types of files the browser will accept; */* indicates the browser will attempt to display anything. The same field is available through PHP environmental variable **$HTTP_ACCEPT**. You could use this list to decide if you can send an image in Flash format or if you should resort to a simple JPEG for older and smaller browsers, such as those on hand-held devices. Unfortunately, the lists supplied by browsers tend to be inaccurate and include the */*, misleading

Header	Value
Accept	image/gif, image/x-xbitmap, image/jpeg, image/pjpeg, image/png, */*
Accept-Charset	iso-8859-1,*,utf-8
Accept-Encoding	gzip
Accept-Language	en
Authorization	Basic cDV0ZXIfakeZYMAG3
Connection	Keep-Alive
Host	petermoulding.com
Referer	http://petermoulding.com/phpblackbook/environmental/index.html
User-Agent	Mozilla/4.77 [en] (WinNT; U)

Figure 7.1   HTTP headers returned by **getallheaders()**.

you to believe the browser will handle anything. If you do include special format content like Flash, and have a simpler format like JPEG available, include a link to the simpler version near the complex content so the end user can choose which version to view.

Accept-Encoding gzip means the browser will accept compressed files, so you can use PHP gzip functions (see Chapter 16) to compress files and Web pages to reduce transmission times to your customers. The same field is available through the PHP environmental variable **$HTTP_ACCEPT_ENCODING**. Gzip compression can also be invoked by the Apache Web server, to automatically compress all output from the Web site to compatible browsers. If Apache is configured to apply gzip, do not double up by applying gzip from within your scripts.

Accept-Language en means the browser was set to request pages in English, or defaults to English, and Apache can be configured to deliver different pages based on language, an approach that is ideal for sites mixing PHP with other pages. If all your Web pages are PHP, you can handle languages within PHP. Approaches to handling international issues, including language, are in Chapter 12. The language is also available through **$HTTP_ACCEPT_LANGUAGE**.

The **Authorization** field indicates the type of security used for logons, but it is usually handled by the Web server for small numbers of users, so it is of limited interest. When you move to coding your own security, you will probably use the user ID and password gathered by the Web server; so, again, you do not need to know the authorization type. Note that I modified the authorization string in case someone tries to hack the site.

The **User-Agent** field, also in **$HTTP_USER_AGENT**, tells you which browser is visiting your site, although the browser may be other software, such as a search engine, pretending to be a browser. Some people use the Agent field to work out if a browser supports options like cookies; but they forget that many browsers let the user switch off options, thus making the Agent field an almost useless indicator.

phpinfo( ) gives you an instant display of everything related to PHP and Apache: versions, configuration information, and all the environmental variables passed to your page. A sample appears in Figure 7.2. To see how this works, run up a page that includes just **<?php phpinfo( ) ?>** and browse the result. **phpinfo( )** writes HTML output directly to the screen, so there is no point in including it in a fancy screen layout. The display includes information helpful to hackers, so do not make the screen public.

PHP Configuration

You configure PHP with php.ini, but there are times when you want to make a change for one script, or when you're using a script for a special task. The following sections describe some things you can change from within your script.

Some of the things set in php.ini can only be set in php.ini, so you will not find functions to override the php.ini settings. Some can be locked, so even though they can be set at some sites, you may not be able to set them at every site.

Extensions

You can load extensions from within a script, which can help you reduce overhead. Imagine a news delivery server that delivers everything from a fast, read-oriented server. Now add one script that once per day contacts a Microsoft SQL Server to collect news releases from Microsoft. Why keep the php_mssql.dll module loaded all the time if it is used for only a minute per day? You can load a module from within your script using **dl( )**, as shown here:

```
dl("php_mssql.dll");
```

PHP Variables	
Variable	Value
PHP_SELF	/admin/phpinfo.html
HTTP_GET_VARS["v"]	12974
HTTP_COOKIE_VARS["cookie"]	1064996159
HTTP_SERVER_VARS["COMSPEC"]	C:\WINNT\system32\cmd.exe
HTTP_SERVER_VARS["DOCUMENT_ROOT"]	i:/helpnet/web/root
HTTP_SERVER_VARS["HTTP_ACCEPT"]	image/gif, image/x-xbitmap, image/jpeg, image/pjpeg, image/png, */*
HTTP_SERVER_VARS["HTTP_ACCEPT_CHARSET"]	iso-8859-1,*,utf-8
HTTP_SERVER_VARS["HTTP_ACCEPT_ENCODING"]	gzip
HTTP_SERVER_VARS["HTTP_ACCEPT_LANGUAGE"]	en

Figure 7.2   Part of the display returned by **phpinfo()**.

php.ini Settings

You can read a setting from php.ini using **ini_get()**, as shown next, alter the setting, and restore the setting to the original setting in php.ini. When you alter the setting, the alteration applies just to your script, starting from the time you make the change.

ini_get() accepts the name of any parameter from php.ini and returns the current value. **ini_set()** accepts a parameter name and a new value for the parameter. **ini_alter()** is an alias of **ini_set()**, so you may occasionally see **ini_alter()** mentioned in older code. **ini_restore()** accepts the name of a parameter and restores the parameter to the setting in php.ini. In the example, 0 means false and 1 means true or on. The example turns off error logging, displays the change, and then resets error logging and displays the results:

```
$setting = ini_get("log_errors");
print("<br>" . $setting);
ini_set("log_errors", 0);
$setting = ini_get("log_errors");
print("<br>" . $setting);
ini_restore("log_errors");
$setting = ini_get("log_errors");
print("<br>" . $setting);
```

The code was tested on a server where php.ini was edited to change error logging from the default of off to on. The results are as follows:

```
1
0
1
```

Time Limit

Your script will time out unless you set the time limit to zero, a setting that lets your script run forever. You do not want scripts to run forever if they are just in a loop chewing up CPU cycles, so consider some safe options.

The way to set the time limit is shown next, with the example using **set_time_limit()** to set it to a limit of 20 seconds:

```
set_time_limit(20);
```

The limit counts from the time you set it, so if the script has already run for 5 seconds, it can run for a total of 25 seconds. The times are not cumulative, so you do not get a 60-second limit if you set the limit to 20 seconds in three successive code lines.

To use the feature without getting into an infinite loop, make sure you do not set the time within a loop. Imagine a script that performs a slow network access, checks the data returned from the network, and then loops back to get more data. If you set the limit to 10 seconds within the loop, the network access takes 9 seconds, and then it goes back to get another 1,000 records from the network, the script could run for 9,000 seconds, or 2.5 hours. You would be better off setting the time limit before the loop, setting it to a test time, like 100 seconds, and including a record count to indicate how far the process progressed before timing out.

Environmental Variables

The environmental variables available within PHP contain values from many sources: PHP, Apache, the network, and incoming HTTP headers. You can access the variables a few ways, including through the function **getenv( )**, and you can set variables through **putenv( )**.

The following example retrieves the value of the URL query string with **getenv( )**. Most of what is available through **getenv( )** is also available as predefined variables if the php.ini **track_vars** parameter is set:

```
$q = getenv("QUERY_STRING");
```

You can also set environmental variables using **putenv( )**, but doing that serves no purpose for your current script, and everything is reset for the next script. Why use **putenv( )**? When you call an external program using **exec( )** or **system( )**, those programs may read environmental variables, and you can set the values for the variables for those external programs.

Security

Your work is important, and your data is valuable. Do you really want some obnoxious 14-year-old kid to break in and mess up all your files? No. Here is how you keep the creeps, the cheats, and the outright clumsy out of your files.

HTTP Authentication

HTTP authentication is available when PHP runs as an Apache module, not as CGI. People using PHP as CGI are restricted to using Apache's .htaccess and .htpasswd files for security; so, your plan of attack, as mentioned in Chapter 1, is to get PHP running as CGI for initial testing, and then move to an Apache module for advanced features on your production Web site. You can keep the Apache security for closing off an administration directory from the public, and use the PHP HTTP authentication to give your customers individual logons.

NOTE: *If you want too much information about HTTP and headers, read* **www.w3.org/Protocols/rfc2616/rfc2616**.

Authentication starts with **header( )**, to send an "Authentication Required" header, followed by a 401 header, which makes the browser pop up a message asking for the user id and password. **header( )** requires a *realm*, a name associated with the authorization, so you can have several areas of a Web site, each with a different logon. The realm is displayed in the logon screen as part of the prompt. The user id ends up in **$PHP_AUTH_USER** and the password in **$PHP_AUTH_USER**.

CHMOD

chmod( ), **chgrp( )**, and **chown ( )** let you set the access permissions, group, and owner of a file or directory, and are explained in Chapter 8. The functions work on Unix, not Windows or NT, so on Unix, you can set up a new user with a private directory and exclusive access to that directory. On other servers, you need to look at running an external program to set security, or storing all user data in a database and using the database's security to control access. PHP can change permissions for files that it owns and files where PHP is a member of a group that has permission to change access rights.

PHP in Batch Mode

Web pages are important, but why limit your skill and knowledge to Web pages, or force yourself to remember a special language just to write batch programs, when you can use PHP for everything? Here are the special extras you need to make PHP work from a command-line console instead of a browser.

The line of code that follows is the execution of a PHP page in the command console on a Windows NT workstation. Figure 7.3 shows the result:

```
"c:/program files/php/php" i:/petermoulding/web/root/test/test.php
```

```
Command Prompt
X-Powered-By: PHP/4.0.5
Window-target: _top
Content-type: text/html

<br>
<b>Warning</b>:  Undefined variable:  HTTP_HOST
```

Figure 7.3   PHP page run from a command prompt.

You can apply this to any installation of PHP by just pointing the command to the CGI executable of PHP. If your PHP is compiled only as a module, follow the installation instructions for a compilation as CGI. The Win32 binary installation installs both module and CGI versions by default, so it does not need a compilation.

Those first three lines of headers in Figure 7.3 can be dropped by adding **-q** to the command, as shown in the next code line:

```
"c:/program files/php/php" -q i:/petermoulding/web/root/test/test.php
```

The fifth line in Figure 7.3 shows HTML output to the command prompt. Drop all the HTML in your batch execution pages, because the only useful formatting is a **newline** character, **\n**. The last line of the PHP page execution shows an error where the page tries to read environmental variables normally created by Apache, so drop all the Apache-related code.

How do you get data into the batch program? I define everything in files that can be updated from a Web page and read by the batch program using normal file functions. If you use Unix, you can try **readline( )**, a function dependent on the GNU Readline project (**cnswww.cns.cwru.edu/~chet/readline/rltop.html**). **readline( )** has a set of supporting functions including **readline_add_history( )**, **readline_clear_history( )**, **readline_completion_function( )**, **readline_info( )**, **readline_list_history( )**, **readline_read_history( )**, and **readline_write_ history( )**. All these functions are described in the PHP documentation that you can download with PHP.

Scheduling PHP

Once you have a PHP page ready to run as a batch file from the command line, you can schedule the job to run once per hour, overnight, or whenever it is needed. If you do not want to watch the job running at 3:00 A.M., place all the input information in files instead of command prompts, and direct all the output to files so the output is not lost at the command-prompt window.

When you want to run a job that collects input—say, groups of files—you can set up directory A to receive the files, set up directory B as a backup directory, and schedule your job to run at regular intervals, via **cron** or another scheduling package. Make your job read directory A to find every input file, process each file, and move each completed file to directory B. When your job runs, it will pick up only the new files in A, so you can run it as often as you like. To keep useful and accurate records of each run, you need to record dates, the times records are read, and a heap of other information, and you need to make the information readily readable.

I suggest storing everything in MySQL tables, as described in Chapter 5, so you can display the logs and results in Web pages visible from home. Make the batch job send you an email if anything goes wrong, so you can log in from home to correct things. If you want real freedom, make all the processing parameters configurable from a secure Web page, so at 3:00 A.M. in a trendy Internet Café, you can reconfigure the batch job while sipping coffee with some delightful person.

COM

Everyone has their favorite programs (I love Excel), and everyone has one program they use above all others. Because 90 percent of people are tapping away on Windows-based computers, 90 percent of those favorite programs, and all the documents they produce, are Windows-based. That's why you need Microsoft's Component Object Model (COM). COM lets you grab those 90 percent of programs and all their data for any purpose, including converting the data from the closed proprietary format to open, platform-independent formats. In this chapter, the example opens a Microsoft Word document in Word, and then saves the file in RTF format for distribution to people using Unix.

COM, as an interface, is the next step up from Microsoft's old Dynamic Data Exchange (DDE), and it's alongside ODBC as a fashionable technology, but not quite as clean as ODBC. Microsoft has also had several variations of COM, named OLE (object linking and embedding) and ActiveX, that make COM development a mess compared to the neat, clean ODBC approach. (ODBC is for databases and is discussed in Chapter 6.) A quick example of COM is in the Immediate Solution "Converting Word Documents to RTF Using COM," and you can use the example as a base for other COM-compliant applications, but you will either need good, current documentation of the target application's methods and properties or a lot of patient testing.

I used to work with Microsoft Access, Excel, and Word, and I have driven all three from other applications, using first DDE and then COM, so I find the whole approach easy for those applications. What can be difficult is finding reliable, current documentation for other applications, and trying to work out finicky differences between what you can do with those applications from a keyboard and what is allowed via the application's COM interface.

There is one thing to watch out for with COM when used with older COM-compliant applications: Many applications were never designed to run in a server mode (unattended with no one to immediately respond to all error messages). If you use them with COM on Windows, they pop up error messages all over the place, and you can see the error messages and fix your COM code. When the same applications are used in Windows NT from a Web server running as a service, the applications do not know where to send their error messages. You can end up with an application that just stops mysteriously, because it wants to pop up an error message but is not allowed to.

In some cases, the answer is careful research and extensive testing. In some cases, you might be better off upgrading to a later release. When people are recommending an expensive upgrade, ask to see the newer release running with COM on the same configuration you use, or ask for a money-back trial period. The problems can be configuration- and usage-specific, so that a demonstration on another person's machine is unlikely to show the same results you will get on your system. Microsoft distributed 120-day trial CDs of their latest Office products, and that is plenty of time to work through problems with COM.

File and Directory Names

People want your files, but they may not have a computer as good as yours, so please help the mere humans of this world by naming your files in ways your users and their computers can understand. It is much easier to rename a file at your end, and if your file names have a deep and special meaning for you, you can always copy the file, rename the copy, and then send users the copy.

Short names are easier to handle and are all that some computers can process, but they can be cryptic to the point of being misleading. Imagine sending in your expense claim in a file named "Expenses claim for the week ending January 6, 2002". Clearly something like s01062002 is easier to type and does not contain characters likely to upset operating systems. The problem is, s01062002 is June 1, 2002 to most of the world; so, when using dates, pick an internationally safe format like s20020106, because everyone will recognize the YYYYMMDD format and no one uses a YYYYDDMM format. If you want PHP to produce that file name with today's date, try the following code, or refer to Chapter 2 for more information on dates:

```
$file_name = "s" . date("Ymd");
```

Leave out spaces, and do not use underscores as a substitution. Although Expenses claim translates easily to Expenses_claim, in some situations the underscore will be lost, especially when people transcribe the file name from a link or a heading highlighted with an underline. Expensesclaim is easy to read but still has the problem that some operating systems will not find the file when a person searches for expensesclaim; so, reduce the file name to the internationally safe expensesclaim. The characters hyphen (-) and period (.) are safe in all the operating systems I use, but I have not used BeOS and some handheld devices.

Linux and Unix

The main problem with Unix is the inability of the operating system to understand case, and the lack of tools that will perform a case-insensitive search for a file. Developers seem to delight in using mixed uppercase and lowercase letters in file names and then being inconsistent within their own files. I recommend sticking to lowercase everywhere.

Windows NT

Windows NT lets you type anything into a file name, because Windows NT uses both an internal name and a presentation name, and you can use either to access a file. Unfortunately, although Windows NT accepts anything from anywhere else, it does not accept anything in return; so stick with the basics of lowercase letters and numbers.

Macintosh

The old Mac operating systems produce files with names that include unintelligible characters that do not display on other computers. Fortunately, Apple replaced the Mac OS with Unix and a Mac GUI glued on top. Apple called the pretty-looking Unix *OS X*. I hope you will be able to specify that all files and all removable media, like Zip disks, are formatted for Unix.

POSIX

The Portable Operating System Interface (POSIX) gives you the most reliable way to talk with operating systems from any application that will be used on multiple operating systems. Although not every operating system supports POSIX or has the facilities required by every one of these POSIX functions, you will have more chance of these functions working on a new operating system than if you use operating-system-specific commands through something like PHP's external program interface. Consider POSIX the ODBC of operating system interaction (if you have not used ODBC, scc Chapter 6).

In Unix, your program runs in a process; and under Apache, every Web page process has a parent process. If your software explodes and kills your process, the main Apache process does not care; it continues creating new processes for new pages. **posix_getpid( )** gets your process id so you can do things for or against your process, like killing your process via **posix_kill( )**. The nasty can use **posix_getppid( )** to get the process id of the parent process and kill that instead.

Security is controlled by user ids and groups, so **posix_getuid( )** lets you get the numeric id of the real user id used by your process. **posix_getpwuid( )** accepts the numeric user id and returns an array listing information about the user, including their name and an encrypted password. Processes can be associated with an effective user id; **posix_geteuid( )** returns the numeric id of the effective user id, and **posix_setuid( )** sets the effective user id. Under Apache, PHP usually runs as user **nobody** with no permissions. When someone logs on, they gain permissions from Apache's security, and suddenly you start getting useful values from all these functions. **posix_getlogin( )** returns the user's login name, and **posix_getpwnam( )** returns information about a user based on their name.

The **posix_getgid( )** and **posix_getegid( )** functions find out about a process's group, **posix_setgid( )** sets the group ID, and **posix_getgroups( )** gets a list of all the groups associated with the current process. In the resource area, you can get time used so far with **posix_times( )**, the system name with **posix_uname( )**, and a list of system resource limits with **posix_getrlimit( )**. A few other POSIX functions are described at **www.php.net/manual/en/ref.posix.php**.

If you are using Windows NT and need to extend its POSIX compliance, there is a product named Cygwin from RedHat (**http://sources.redhat.com/cygwin**). Cygwin is used by PostgreSQL to port its Unix code to Windows NT. The developers of PostgreSQL use the Cygwin tool set on Windows NT to start and manage the PostgreSQL server. You could potentially port a lot of Unix code to Windows NT by using Cygwin. Although many products would have a problem with the Windows interface, and many Windows users would have problems with the Cygwin/Unix interface, you do not have to port the whole GUI from Unix to Windows. PHP can provide the user interface!

Think of the opportunity. Take a Unix-based program that does something unique, replace the user interface with PHP and HTML forms, and then publish the program on Windows using PHP and Apache as the operating environment. Cygwin lets you compile the application on Windows, and PHP's external file-handling functions let you execute the file under PHP. Apache release 1.3.20 for Windows has a special interface to Cygwin preinstalled, and I am looking forward to testing it to find out how far the combination can be pushed.

Helping Programs Talk with Each Other

What do you do when you want to tell every program in your Web site the current exchange rate between the Andorran Franc and the Malawi Kwacha? Use a file, a database, or something faster? Shared memory is the fastest option, and if you need to synchronize updates, you can use semaphores.

File access is usually fast for small files, and if everyone is reading the same file, the operating system will cache the file in memory where access can be almost instantaneous. File systems slow down when updates occur; in fact, any update to any file can slow down all accesses to all files. Files are not the best choice if your site has lots of files actively updated; speed can be compromised when you have many people updating one file.

A database of exchange rates sounds great, but databases take time, and not every database can cache frequently used information. MySQL has good read access times and special database tables that reside in memory, but if you are not using all the features of a database, you still have unnecessary CPU overhead.

Shared Memory

Shared memory gives you power, flexibility, and a powerful statement of skill on your résumé, mixed with equal parts security holes, reliability problems, and expansion limitations. Here is a quick outline of how to scale a Mount Everest of computing without slipping on ice.

Shared memory is derived from a Unix System V facility, so it is well tested; but unrestricted access to the shared memory means any of your scripts can read and change the data. Shared memory is also available to C, Perl, and other programs, so not only can they update the data, they can accidentally format the data into a structure your script will not understand. Up to PHP 4.0.3, shared memory functions were prefixed with **shp_**, and from PHP 4.0.5 onwards, they are prefixed with **shmop_**.

shmop_open( ) accepts a key, an access/create flag, an octal access mode (the same as you use in **chmod**), and a size, and returns a shared memory segment id that is just like a file handle. The access key is a long variable, up to 8 bytes, so it could be a randomly generated number or a key generated by incrementing a key count somewhere else in shared memory. The access/create flag is **c** when you create the shared memory and **a** when you subsequently access the memory. The access is most often something like **0755** when you create the shared memory and **0** when you access the memory. The size is **0** when you access the shared memory and somewhere between 1 byte and 131,072 bytes when you create the shared memory.

shmop_close( ) accepts the shared memory segment id from **shmop_open( )** and closes access to the segment, but does not delete the segment. At that point, other programs can read the segment. When you finally want to delete the segment, you must open the segment, issue **shmop_delete( )**, and then close the segment. **shmop_delete( )** accepts the segment id and marks the segment for deletion. From that point on, no other process can open the segment. The actual deletion occurs when all current users close their access. The segment may stay in memory forever if you do not delete it, or if someone forgets to close their access. Only the segment owner or a user with root access can delete the segment. In the exchange rate example, be one user would create, update, and delete the shared memory segment, and all others would read the segment.

What can you do with an open segment? You can find out its size with **shmop_size( )**, write to it with **shmop_write( )**, and read from it with **shmop_read( )**. **shmop_read( )** needs the segment id; a starting location, counting from zero; and a length to read (0 seems to read everything, and **shmop_size( )** can tell you the maximum size). **shmod_write( )** needs the segment id, a string to write to shared memory, and an offset for the start of the write.

Now you have the equivalent to files in memory, which can be shared, protected from deletion, and protected from overwriting, but cannot be safely updated. There are limits to shared memory size, the number of segments, and segments opened by a process, so plan carefully and look at memory database tables, like those provided by MySQL, before flooding shared memory. Multiple update protection is provided by semaphores, and is covered next.

Semaphore

Semaphores let you control updates to shared memory segments. Before you open a segment for update, you use **sem_get( )** to request a semaphore ID based on the key of the segment, perform the update, and then use **sem_release( )** to release the semaphore. In **sem_get( )**, you specify the key, then a usage limit of **1** (so your process will be the only one accessing the related segment), and a chmod-style octal mode to stop other people from updating the segment. If other processes have the semaphore, issue **sem_aquire( )** to stop new processes from accessing the semaphore and then wait for existing processes to release the semaphore.

In effect, you end up writing database-style access management, and suddenly in-memory database tables look better. If you are already inserting your exchange rates into a database table for audit purposes, it is very easy to copy the latest rates into the in-memory table and not convert them to an entirely different format for use in shared memory. Database tables do not lock you into Unix or the special programming required to share the data with other applications.

External Programs

Here is where you rip open a Pandora's box of secret system commands and either destroy your Web server or thoroughly impress everyone with your consummate computing skills. This short section of simple steps will launch a thousand new commands and let you choose which are safe or appropriate.

exec( ) accepts a string command, much the same as you type into the command prompt, an optional array name, and an optional variable for a returned result. It then executes the command and returns the last line of output from the command. If you want a conventional return status, you have to supply a variable as the third parameter, and then check that variable (clearly this function does not fit the standard form of PHP4 functions). If you want all the output from the command, supply an array as the second parameter. **passthru( )** and **system( )** are variations of the command and are in the Immediate Solution "Executing an External Program."

escapeshellarg( ) accepts a string and returns the string with single quotes around it, with single quotes or backslashes added to single quotes and special characters within the string. This lets you format a parameter string for inclusion within a command like **exec( )**, as shown next. If you let users type in raw string data, and feed the data into commands, the users can include commands within their data and break into your system. **escapeshellarg( )** reduces the chance of a break-in by ensuring that the string is processed as one single string. In the following example, you could add the quotes and slashes to the string yourself, but in real life, the string might come from a database or another source where you cannot change the data:

```
$parm = "-Tt /dev/hda";
exec("hdparm " . escapeshellarg($parm));
```

The string returned by **escapeshellarg( )** is:

```
'-Tt /dev/hda'
```

escapeshellcmd( ) is an older function designed to do what **escapeshellarg( )** does but apparently not so well. I have not compared the two at the source code level, and I design Web sites so users cannot type strings directly into commands.

Extra Information

PHP is continually gaining extra helpful information. If you use a resource id as a string in a display, as shown next, you used to see a single integer, like **3**, that did not help you diagnose the mistake in the print statement. Now you see a message of the form **Resource id#3**, and you can instantly spot that you printed the resource id instead of retrieving a row and displaying the row:

```
$result = mysql_query("select * from countries");
print($result);
```

JPEG files can contain fields to tell you the settings used on the camera that captured a digital image. PHP now has a function to display those fields, **getexif( )**. See Chapters 8 and 11 for examples of displaying information about JPEGs and from JPEGs.

mnoGoSearch Functions

The mnoGoSearch software from MnoGoSearch (**www.mnogosearch.ru**) is free for use on Unix and costs money for the Win32 binary version, which restricts deployment of mnoGoSearch. The company supplies indexing software to gather information about files, pages, and sites, stores the information in any ODBC database, and supplies a PHP interface to search the databases. These functions could be of use on your site if your site is on Unix and will only ever be on Unix. The following list of functions includes a short description of each. (The software is not yet installed on my site so, I included no examples there. Go to the mnoGoSearch site to test the search).

- **udm_alloc_agent( )**—Starts an mnoGoSearch session.
- **udm_free_agent( )**—Ends the session.
- **udm_add_search_limit( )**—Adds limits to a search, so the search does not run forever.
- **udm_clear_search_limits( )**—Removes the search limits.
- **udm_find( )**—Performs the search.
- **udm_get_res_field( )**—Fetches the result field.
- **udm_free_res( )**—Frees the resources allocated to the result.
- **udm_cat_path( )**—Gets the path from the-top level category to the current category. (Categories are like the categories you can select when browsing **Yahoo.com**.)
- **udm_cat_list( )**—Lists all the categories on the same level as the current category.
- **udm_api_version( )**—Lets you see the version of the search API, so you can make sure you have a current version.
- **udm_errno( )**—Returns an error number.
- **udm_error( )**—Returns an error message so you can diagnose problems.
- **udm_get_doc_count( )**—Gives you the number of documents in a database so you can check if the number of documents is reasonable for the sites you index.
- **udm_load_ispell_data( )**—Loads spelling data (ispell).
- **udm_free_ispell_data( )**—Removes spelling data.
- **udm_set_agent_param( )**—Sets parameters in the search agent.
- **udm_get_res_param( )**—Returns result parameters.

Immediate Solutions

Cleaning Out Old Files

You want a healthy environment for your Web site, so clean out your old files. Your operating system will have utilities and methods for cleaning up some files, but not your precious Web site files. You will reach a stage when you need a custom clean-up application. This solution is the gritty bit, which you can place in as pretty an interface as you like.

The code starts with a list of files in an array and then deletes the files. You could read Chapter 5, and then set up a database to hold the list and a nice form to update the list. The database can also provide user access control, so other Web site contributors can include their deletion requirements in the list. In fact, you could add a deletion date so files can be set up for removal when they are added.

Start with the list of files to delete. The examples that follow name a test file and a test directory in a temporary directory, which you would use when testing, and then move on to more appropriate files, like images and banners used for date-dependent advertising. When your online shop is adding the images for your Fathers Day sale, you could set up the list to run at the end of Fathers Day and to clean out all the pictures of Fathers Day socks, shirts, and slippers:

```
$delete[] = "t:/Copy of New Text Document.txt";
$delete[] = "t:/Copy of temp";
```

The code prints a lot of messages in the same format via the **ptr( )** function, which accepts two fields and outputs them in an HTML table row:

```
function ptr($v, $m)
  {
  print("<tr><td>" . $v . "</td><td>" . $m . "</td></tr>");
  }
```

The next code reads the deletion list, deleting files and reading directories to find further files and subdirectories for deletion. You cannot easily delete a directory that contains subdirectories, so the code sets up individual deletion of each subdirectory. When the code finds a subdirectory, the subdirectory is added to the end of the deletion list. This process builds a list from the top directory down.

In a subsequent section of the code, the list is reversed, and each directory is deleted from the lowest subdirectory up to the original request.

The first line of the following code resets the array in case the array pointer is not at the first entry. Then the code prints the start of a HTML table, prints additional rows throughout the code, and ends with the printing of the HTML table **end** tag.

The **while( )** loop steps through the array entry by entry. By using the **each( )** approach to stepping through the array, the process is not adversely affected by the code's adding and deleting lines from the table during the loop. The first **if( )** tests for the existence of the file in case the file never existed or has already been deleted. The second **if( )** checks if the file is a directory. A matching **elseif( )** checks if the file is a file, and an **else( )** covers the case where an entry is neither a file or a directory entry. If the entry is a file, the file is deleted via **unlink( )**. If the file does not exist, is neither a file nor a directory, or has been deleted, the entry is deleted from **$delete** via **unset( )**.

Directories are read via **opendir( )**, **readdir( )**, and **closedir( )** (see Chapter 8). Every item from **readdir( )** is added to the array for subsequent deletion, except for the items containing **.** or **...** The single period is a pointer to the current directory, and the double stop is a pointer to the directory one level up:

```
reset($delete);
print("<table border=\"3\">");
ptr("<em>Item</em>", "<em>Result</em>");
while(list($k, $v) = each($delete))
    {
    if(file_exists($v))
        {
        if(is_dir($v))
            {
            $dir = opendir($v);
            if(substr($v, -1) != "/")
                {
                $v .= "/";
                }
            while($file_name = readdir($dir))
                {
                if($file_name != "." and $file_name != "..")
                    {
                    $delete[] = $v . $file_name;
                    }
                }
            closedir($dir);
            }
```

```
    elseif(is_file($v))
       {
       if(unlink($v))
          {
          ptr($v, "deleted");
          }
       else
          {
          ptr($v, "not deleted");
          }
       unset($delete[$k]);
       }
    else
       {
       ptr($v, "not a directory or file");
       unset($delete[$k]);
       }
    }
else
   {
   unset($delete[$k]);
   ptr($v, "not found");
   }
}
```

After your script completes the preceding code, **$delete** contains all the directory names from the top down; the final code has to process from the bottom up. **array_reverse()** solves the problem by reversing the array:

```
$delete = array_reverse($delete);
```

The next code steps through **$delete** deleting the arrays. Because of **array_reverse()**, it deletes the directories from the lowest level subdirectory up to the top level originally requested in **$delete**. **rmdir()** removes a directory, provided the directory is empty and you have appropriate permission:

```
while(list($k, $v) = each($delete))
   {
   if(file_exists($v))
      {
      if(is_dir($v))
         {
         if(@rmdir($v))
            {
            ptr($v, "removed");
            }
```

```
        else
          {
          ptr($v, "not removed");
          }
        }
      }
    else
      {
      ptr($v, "does not exist");
      }
    }
print("</table>");
```

Figure 7.4 shows the deletion report from the small test list, and Figure 7.5 shows the result from a second run, so you can see the file-missing messages. The list could be made shorter by modifying it to not display the deletion of lower-level entries. The entries created by traversing the subdirectories could be entered into a second array to be processed in parallel. When testing a system like this, it is better to display everything and look for selection errors.

TIP: *Here's a special tip for Windows users: When you are testing this code, and decide to use Windows Explorer or the equivalent to browse the test directories and view the progress of deletions, you can lock* **rmdir()** *out of a directory.* **rmdir()** *will not delete a directory that is open in a file browser window. Applications like Microsoft Word can also leave stray file locks on your test files. If you use Word to create a test file, and then you cannot delete the file or the directory containing the file, close the application used to create the test file.*

Item	Result
t:/Copy of New Text Document.txt	deleted
t:/Copy of temp/hs~1.tmp	deleted
t:/Copy of temp/Copy (2) of temp/hs~1.tmp	deleted
t:/Copy of temp/Copy (2) of temp/New Text Document.txt	deleted
t:/Copy of temp/Copy (2) of temp	removed
t:/Copy of temp	removed

Figure 7.4   File list showing the deleted files and directories.

Item	Result
t:/Copy of New Text Document.txt	not found
t:/Copy of temp	not found

Figure 7.5   File list from a script run on a directory that has already been deleted.

In modern computers, disk space is cheap, but it is also easy to fill a disk with the rapid deployment of large graphics and audio/visual files. You need to give your contributors the facilities to clean out their own obsolete files, and the best time to have them decide on the useful life of a file is when they upload the file. You can combine this information with a clean-up application to help your Web site users find and delete their obsolete files. The icing on the cake would be to add a field where they could describe the use of each file and a field where they could specify the date or conditions when the file can be deleted.

Related solutions:	Found on page:
Listing Databases	161
Reporting Disk Space	298
Listing Images	431

I found another use for this clean-up code when testing PHP's COM facility with various Microsoft Office applications. The Office applications would stop mysteriously and leave all sorts of temporary files and test files half created, so I had to clean out the files by hand. I copied the clean-up code into the start of my test script and used that to clean up. Adding an extra file to the array was far easier than either deleting the file by hand or typing it into code inside a file function.

The next step in extending the test file clean out was to add a **$copy** list to copy original test files from a source directory into the test directory, so I could replace damaged files with undamaged files. Although this copying and deletion seems a bit simple and obvious with PHP, I've worked on projects where people spent more than $50,000 on software that did little more than delete and copy files based on user created lists. The most expensive software did not even have online forms for entering parameters; it was all based on text files that had to be edited by hand. When you set up a file-management system for your Web sites, please give the end users easy-to-read and easy-to-use forms for entering the data.

Executing an External Program

Some things even PHP does not do, so you may need to run the occasional external program. Here is an example of how to run an external program using one of the world's simplest programs, ping.

If you have never used ping, it sends requests to IP addresses or URLs and lists the time taken by the responses. Figure 7.6 shows a ping from a workstation in

```
Command Prompt
Microsoft(R) Windows NT(TM)
(C) Copyright 1985-1996 Microsoft Corp.

r:\Peter>ping petermoulding.com

Pinging petermoulding.com [61.8.3.32] with 32 bytes of data:

Reply from 61.8.3.32: bytes=32 time=20ms TTL=244
Reply from 61.8.3.32: bytes=32 time=20ms TTL=244
Reply from 61.8.3.32: bytes=32 time=20ms TTL=244
Reply from 61.8.3.32: bytes=32 time=70ms TTL=244

r:\Peter>
```

Figure 7.6   Ping in a command prompt.

Sydney to a Web site hosted in another part of Sydney, which takes 20 milliseconds to complete the round trip. Pings from Sydney to **Yahoo.com** in the United States used 171 ms, a good time for an international trip, and pings to other sites in the United States dragged out over 500 ms, way too long for commercial interactive sites.

To run ping from a script, use **exec( )** as shown in the following code. The string is the name of the program you want to execute. If the program is not in a system directory, you have to include the path to the program. **$result** is the last line of the information returned by the program, and is displayed with the **print( )** statement. Unfortunately, the last line from ping is a blank line:

```
$result = exec("ping");
print("<br>" . $result);
```

To get all the output from a program, add the name of an array as the second parameter in **exec( )**, as shown next, and then loop through the array with **while( )** and **print( )** to see the output:

```
$result = exec("ping", $output);
while(list($k, $v) = each($output))
    {
    print("<br>" . $k . ": " . $v );
    }
```

The output from this code is shown here. It consists of a help page, because no target IP address or URL was specified (some of the lines were left out to save space):

```
0:
1: Usage: ping [-t] [-a] [-n count] [-l size] [-f] [-i TTL] [-v TOS]
2: [-r count] [-s count] [[-j host-list] | [-k host-list]]
3: [-w timeout] destination-list
4:                            .
5: Options:
6: -t Ping the specified host until interrupted.
<cut>
17: -w timeout Timeout in milliseconds to wait for each reply.
18:
```

Try the same ping again, in the same script, with the addition of a Web site name. The name can be a domain name or the name of a server. Feel free to experiment:

```
$result = exec("ping petermoulding.com", $output);
while(list($k, $v) = each($output))
    {
    print("<br>" . $k . ": " . $v);
    }
```

The new output presents the response times for requests to the server in a neat layout, which you could display to the Web page or split up with PHP string commands for analysis:

```
19:
20: Pinging petermoulding.com [61.8.3.32] with 32 bytes of data:
21:
22: Reply from 61.8.3.32: bytes=32 time=20ms TTL=244
23: Reply from 61.8.3.32: bytes=32 time=30ms TTL=244
24: Reply from 61.8.3.32: bytes=32 time=20ms TTL=244
25: Reply from 61.8.3.32: bytes=32 time=60ms TTL=244
```

Now add the extra code, shown next, to the same script:

```
reset($output);
while(list($k, $v) = each($output))
    {
    print("<br>" . $k . ": " . $v );
    }
```

The **reset( )** sets the array pointer back to the start of the array, and the surprising result is all the output from both **exec( )** statements. **exec( )** appends new

7. Environmental
Considerations

output to the end of the array so you can accumulate a set of outputs as a log and then process the accumulated output in one hit:

```
0:
1: Usage: ping [-t] [-a] [-n count] [-l size] [-f] [-i TTL] [-v TOS]
2: [-r count] [-s count] [[-j host-list] | [-k host-list]]
3: [-w timeout] destination-list
4:
5: Options:
6: -t Ping the specified host until interrupted.
<cut>
17: -w timeout Timeout in milliseconds to wait for each reply.
18:
19:
20: Pinging petermoulding.com [61.8.3.32] with 32 bytes of data:
21:
22: Reply from 61.8.3.32: bytes=32 time=20ms TTL=244
23: Reply from 61.8.3.32: bytes=32 time=30ms TTL=244
24: Reply from 61.8.3.32: bytes=32 time=20ms TTL=244
25: Reply from 61.8.3.32: bytes=32 time=60ms TTL=244
```

passthru( ) is an alternative to **exec( )**, and here is a quick demonstration. The code that follows pings **yahoo.com** and supplies an optional second parameter to receive a return code from the program. There is no option to receive all the output into an array, like in **exec( )**, nor is the last line returned. All the output goes straight to the screen. In the version I tested, the output was sent twice, complete with a help screen in the middle:

```
passthru("ping yahoo.com", $return_code);
print("<br>return_code: " . $return_code);
```

Because **passthru( )** sends uncontrolled, unformatted output to the screen, the main use of **passthru( )** is for programs that produce binary data, like graphics and movies. Send the correct header for the binary output, and then run the program with **passthru( )**. The binary output must follow the header with no HTML or other output in between.

system( ) is an alternative to **exec( )** and **passthru( )**, and the following is a quick demonstration. The following code pings **yahoo.com** and supplies an optional second parameter to receive a return code from the program. There is no option to receive all the output into an array, as there is in **exec( )**. **$result** received the last line of the output. **$return_code** received **0** from a successful ping and **1** if an error occurred:

```
$result = system("ping yahoo.com", $return_code);
print("<br>result: " . $result);
print("<br>return_code: " . $return_code);

result: Reply from 216.115.108.243: bytes=32 time=171ms TTL=244
return_code: 0
```

Converting Word Documents to RTF Using COM

This example can be used with any Microsoft Office product or any COM-compatible application under Windows or Windows NT. The only difficulty is working out how to make each application perform exactly the functions you want.

First you need a COM identifier for the target application, which may be documented within Visual Basic for Applications (VBA) documentation, and can be found from the Windows Registry. Use **regedit** to browse the Registry under **HKEY_CLASSES_ROOT**, as shown in Figure 7.7, or search for **CLSID**. Figure 7.7 shows **regedit** open at **HKEY_CLASSES_ROOT** and the Find box containing CLSID at the start of the search. Figure 7.8 shows a CLSID entry for Word (there are many CLSID entries in the Registry). The name you need is the folder name one level up, which in this example is **Word.Application**.

I wondered what options would work with **saveas,** so I created **saveas** in VBA, shown next, and then tested the equivalents in PHP. Word was version 97 SR-2, and the PHP version was 4.0.4pl1. **FileName** worked as the first parameter, and **FileFormat** worked as the second parameter, but **ReadOnlyRecommended** had no effect as the seventh parameter. PHP's COM is developing rapidly, so you may find a lot more options working and documented by the time you use COM in PHP:

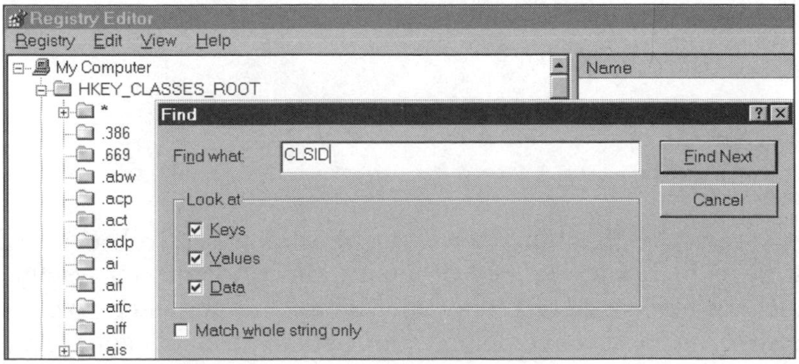

7. Environmental Considerations

Figure 7.7   Windows Registry HKEY_CLASSES_ROOT.

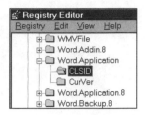

Figure 7.8   Windows Registry CLSID entry.

```
ActiveDocument.SaveAs FileName:="comtest.rtf",
    FileFormat:=wdFormatRTF,
    LockComments:=False,
    Password:="",
    AddToRecentFiles:=True,
    WritePassword :="",
    ReadOnlyRecommended:=False,
    EmbedTrueTypeFonts:=False,
    SaveNativePictureFormat:=False,
    SaveFormsData:=False,
    SaveAsAOCELetter:= False
```

If you want to experiment yourself, go to the Microsoft Office product of your choice and select Tools|Macro|Record New Macro. Perform the actions you want to perform in COM, stop the macro recording, and then view the macro in the Visual Basic editor supplied with Microsoft Office. You will, in some cases, be able to work out the translation from VBA to COM yourself. The Visual Basic editor will also list definitions, like **wdFormatRTF**, so you can get the actual value for use in your script or create PHP versions of the definitions. The following code is a list of file format definitions:

```
define("wdFormatDocument", 0);
define("wdFormatTemplate", 1);
define("wdFormatText", 2);
define("wdFormatTextLineBreaks", 3);
define("wdFormatDOSText", 4);
define("wdFormatDOSTextLineBreaks", 5);
define("wdFormatRTF", 6);
define("wdFormatUnicodeText", 7);
```

The code to perform COM actions, shown next, looks deceptively simple. The traps tend to be related to how individual applications work on your system. The first line creates a new instance of the object **com**, with the name **$w**, for the application **word**, and opens a communication path to the application. The **if( )** checks for success or failure. On my test machine, Word failed to respond a few times when it already had a document open for editing. The Microsoft Office applications will fail if you have the application running and the application has an open dialog box, such as the file Save As box. The applications will also fail if they are already accessing the file you are trying to access via COM, and will occasionally fail to remove their association with a file. If you edit a file in Word, you may have to physically close Word before you can open the file in other applications.

The **$w->Visible = 1** is supposed to make the application visible in a window so you can see the COM actions happening while you are testing. It works for some people but not others.

$w->Documents->Open( ) will open a document within Word, and is roughly equivalent to choosing File|Open in the Word menu structure. **$w->Documents[1] ->saveas( )** saves the file and accepts as its second parameter a document format from the earlier list. **$w->Quit( )** ends the application:

```
if($w = new com("word.application"))
   {
   print("<br>Opened Word version " . $w->Version);
   if($w->Visible = 1)
      {
      print("<br>Word should be visible.");
      }
   else
      {
      print("<br>Visible failed.");
      }
   if($w->Documents->Open("t:/comtest.doc"))
      {
      print("<br>Document opened.");
      }
   else
      {
      print("<br>Open failed.");
      }
   $w->Documents[1]->saveas("t:/comtest3.rtf", wdFormatRTF);
   $w->Quit();
   }
else
   {
   print("<br>Word failed to open");
   }
```

The following is a list of the COM functions not shown in the previous section. Their use varies by application. Some were still buried deep in bug reports when I tried to use them:

- **COM( )**—COM class
- **VARIANT( )**—VARIANT class
- **com_load( )**—Creates a new reference to a COM component
- **com_invoke( )**—Calls a COM component's method
- **com_propget( )**—Gets the value of a COM component's property
- **com_get( )**—Gets the value of a COM component's property
- **com_propput( )**—Assigns a value to a COM component's property
- **com_propset( )**—Assigns a value to a COM component's property
- **com_set( )**—Assigns a value to a COM component's property
- **com_addref( )**—Increases the component's reference counter
- **com_release( )**—Decreases the component's reference counter

HTTP Authentication Example

This example shows simple HTTP authentication applied to a demonstration page, but you could apply it to all the pages in a site or to a complex structure of administration panels and options. The essence of the authentication is the logon screen and a check for a user id and password. Once the HTTP authorization is working, you can apply it freely to any combination of pages.

First you need PHP's **header( )** function, which sends any HTTP header. You want to send an "Authentication Required" header, followed by a 401 header, because these will make the browser pop up a message asking for the username and password, as shown in Figure 7.9. A realm associates a name with the authorization,

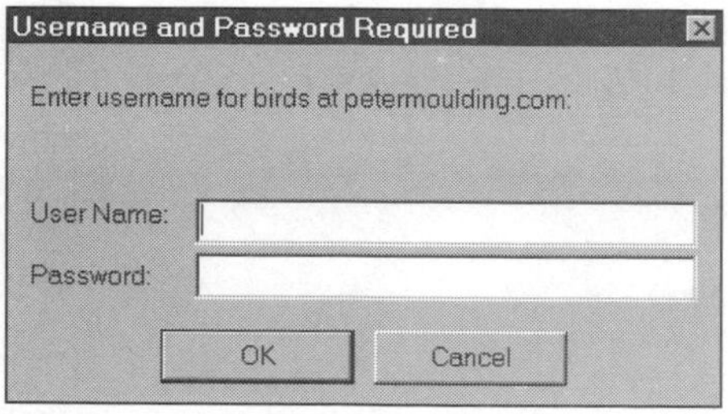

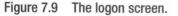

Figure 7.9   The logon screen.

and is displayed in the logon screen as part of the prompt. In Figure 7.9, the realm is **birds,** and is followed by the domain name.

The following code shows a simple logon page at **petermoulding.com/birds/**, ready for your testing. The code first checks for the existence of **$PHP_AUTH_ USER**, and then lets you in or produces the logon prompt by sending the two headers. If you cancel out of the logon or click OK, the browser sends the information back to the same page that sent the headers, so your script runs a second time. The second time, your script sees the user id or skips past the logon prompt and performs the code after the logon prompt. Figure 7.10 shows the browser window after a failed logon attempt:

```
if(isset($PHP_AUTH_USER))
    {
    print("Hello " . $PHP_AUTH_USER
        . ",<br>You are logged on with password " . $PHP_AUTH_PW);
    if(isset($PHP_AUTH_TYPE))
        {
        print("<br>You are using authentication type " . $PHP_AUTH_TYPE);
        }
    print("<p>Here is my first pretty bird, a King Parrot, sitting on"
        . " a branch outside my office window. The King Parrots arrive"
        . " when the noisy Eastern Rosellas are not covering the"
        . " branches.</p>");
    }
else
    {
    header( "WWW-authenticate: basic realm=\"birds\"");
    header( "HTTP/1.0 401 Unauthorized");
    print("If you want to see my pictures of pretty birds, please type"
        . " in your username and password, and click OK. Here is a sample"
        . " of what you are missing:<br>");
    }
print(img("kingparrot.jpg", 250, 500, "King Parrot"));
```

This level of security is suitable for demonstrating the headers and nothing else. In real life, you would compare the user id and password with entries in a database. To stop people reading the password from the database, you would encrypt the password before saving it in the database. When someone logs on, encrypt the incoming password with the same key, and check to see if the two encrypted passwords match. You can use JavaScript in the browser to encrypt a password before the password is passed to the server. That reduces the chance of someone reading the password as it travels around the network.

Figure 7.10   The screen from a failed logon.

Once a person is logged on, their session is maintained with a cookie or session id in URLs, both of which can be copied; so you need to encrypt a secret, place the secret in the cookie, and then check that incoming requests have the correct secret. The secret could contain something that will be unique for every logon, like the time returned from **microtime()**, plus something that will differentiate between two browsers, like their IP address. (Getting the right IP address for a browser behind a proxy can be tricky; some send the original IP address as a **HTTP_X_FORWARDED_FOR** header.) You also need to provide short time-out durations for user sessions to cover the situation where someone goes to lunch and leaves his or her browser open.

You can do a few other things, ranging from the paranoid to the delusional. In the end, making your site bomb-proof is of little use if your site is one of many virtual servers on one host server and all the other sites share one database product with loose security, or if the server has security holes, like FTP access.

Modifying Code to Suit the Environment

You can view the PHP environment with the function **phpinfo( )**, but you cannot modify the way your code works based on **phpinfo( )**. Here are the functions to help you modify your code to suit your environment.

Error Logging

First you need to log any script changes you make so you can see the results of your tests. Some changes may be dependent on a user's browser, so you should check the results each day to see if someone with an odd browser has visited your site. Some changes will occur before the page is displayed, after the page is displayed, or on pages that never display, like redirect pages, so you should record your messages from anywhere.

The easiest way is to record to PHP's log via **error_log( )**, shown next. **error_log( )** writes to PHP's log or the system log, depending on the settings in php.ini, and can optionally write to a disk file or send an email. I found that **error_log( )** messages do not always reach the log if PHP or Apache suffers an internal error, so I wrote a discrete log function:

```
error_log("Changed code to fit odd browser");
```

logtofile ( ) accepts any string, opens a file for logging, appends the date, time, and string to the file, and then closes the file. This always works because there is no buffering of records once the file is closed. The time is from **microtime( )** instead of the normal time function, so you can use the file to note the time between multiple entries from one script, and detect cases where part of a script consumes an unusually large amount of time. In **logtofile( )**, in the **fopen( )** function, name a directory that you own, so that you have unlimited access and can at any time delete the file to remove older entries. The **a** in **fopen( )** will make **fwrite( )** append to an existing file; if the file is missing, **fopen( )** will create a new file.

The function is shown in the following code. When you are testing a script, put a log message right at the start, and then a log message before and after parts of the script that use external resources, like database calls, so you can get an idea of the normal time for each portion of the code. Look at the times after environmental changes, like adding an index to a database, and compare the times to measure the effect:

```
function logtofile($text="")
    {
    $self = "";
```

```
    if(isset($PHP_SELF))
       {
       $self = $PHP_SELF;
       }
    if($log = fopen("t:/log.txt", "a"))
       {
       list($m, $t) = explode(" ", microtime());
       fwrite($log, date("Y-m-d H:i:s", $t) . substr($m, 1)
          . " " . $self . " " . $text . "\n");
       fclose($log);
       }
    }


logtofile("New test");
```

A sample result is as follows:

```
2002-06-07 16:11:05.61830400 New test
```

User Aborts

Does your Web site have one page that has a very long, slow display with the main information at the top? Pages like that often result in a visitor's reading the first few lines and then clicking the Back button. You can split your page into display segments and check the user's reaction at each point. First you have to tell PHP that you want to ignore user aborts, as shown in the first line of code:

```
ignore_user_abort(true);
logtofile("Start of very long database search page");

if(connection_aborted())
   {
   logtofile("User left the page");
   }
else
   {
   // continue with code
   }
```

ignore_user_abort( ) gives you script immunity from user aborts. You can tell PHP to ignore all user aborts by changing a setting in php.ini, but that is not a good idea because your Web server will spend a lot of time serving pages that people are not viewing. Once you have an individual script ignoring aborts, **connection_aborted( )** lets you check the abort status whenever you like.

Where should you place the checks? Between controllable points of large resource usage, like database queries. If your script displays the top 10 products by sales volume, followed by all products by category, you most likely use two database queries, and both probably use significant resources. Visitors who leave probably do so after seeing the top-10 list, so place a check between the queries. If you are using a slow database connection, like ODBC, you can place a check before retrieving a row, so you can determine if it is worth proceeding.

Script Timeouts

Sometimes the script runs out of time to process all the data, and PHP aborts the script. You can detect and record those instances with the following code. First write a function to log a message when the page shuts down. The example, named **logshutdown( )**, uses **logtofile( )** to record a message. The message is based on **connection_timeout( )**, a function that returns true if the script times out. The function will be useful only if the function runs after PHP terminates the script, so you have to tell PHP to run the script after everything else, by nominating the function in **register_shutdown_function( )**:

```
function logshutdown()
    {
    if(connection_timeout())
        {
        logtofile("The script timed out");
        }
    else
        {
        logtofile("The script shut down normally");
        }
    }

register_shutdown_function("logshutdown");
```

Choice of Database

If your code runs with PostgreSQL at one site and MySQL at another, you can test which database is installed by using **extension_loaded( )**. This check can be used with all sorts of PHP extensions, like graphics and math functions, to find out what you can use on the server where your script is executing. You need to know the name of the extension, as defined in php.ini. Windows uses a file extension of .dll, whereas Unix uses .so, so you may have to test for both, as shown in the following code:

```
if(extension_loaded("php_mysql.dll")
or extension_loaded("php_mysql.so"))
   {
   $database = "my";
   logtofile("Using MySQL");
   }
elseif(extension_loaded("php_pgsql.dll")
    or extension_loaded("php_pgsql.so"))
   {
 $database = "pg";
   logtofile("Using PostgreSQL");
   }
elseif(extension_loaded("php_mssql.dll")
    or extension_loaded("php_mssql.so"))
   {
   $database = "ms";
   logtofile("Using Microsoft SQL Server");
   }
```

The example code sets a value into **$database**. **$database** can be used in **if()** and **switch()** statements to select which code will be used to access a database. The code could just as easily be deciding on BCMath versus GMP or Flash versus PNG. Make sure any decision has a fall-back process, like producing a warning message or email, if none of your options are available. You could end up in the situation where you install your application and walk out the door, and then the system administrator deletes an extension needed by your application.

Browser-Based Code

Here is the lazy way to modify your application to suit different browsers. Just insert the code shown here, depend on a file named browscap.ini to supply information about browsers, and regularly update the browscap file from a page like **www.cyscape.com/asp/browscap/**:

```
$browser = get_browser();

if($browser->javascript)
   {
   logtofile("Generating JavaScript");
   // create JavaScript here
   }
```

get_browser() returns an object containing a list of the options that are probably available in the browser reading your script. I say *probably* because the browscap file might mislead you if it is not up to date, it might be wrong about a specific browser, or it might identify the wrong browser. Browscap is based on the **$HTTP_USER_AGENT** string supplied by browsers, and a busy site receives hundreds of unusual agent strings every day—many totally undecipherable.

A fixed list of browser capabilities does not tell you if all the browser's options were installed, or if some were switched off after installation. Browscap files tell you that a browser supports CSS2, but do not tell you which parts of CSS2 work in that browser or give details of the disastrous results you get from some of the second-rate CCS2 implementations.

The following example is taken from the browscap file supplied with PHP 4.0.5. It says the browser supports cookies, but doesn't say if they are turned on or off. It does not tell you that WebTV displays are restricted in size and quality, and so require smaller images. As a general rule, if browscap says something is not available, you know it is not available and have to do without, whereas anything labeled as definitely available is just a probability. If your Web site is dependent on specific browser features, you need to inform the visitor of the requirement, give the visitor the option of testing the feature, and provide guidance for those occasions when the feature fails:

```
[WebTV 1.0]
browser=WebTV
Version=1.0
majorver=#1
minorver=#0
frames=FALSE
tables=TRUE
cookies=TRUE
backgroundsounds=TRUE
vbscript=FALSE
javascript=FALSE
javaapplets=FALSE
ActiveXControls=FALSE
Win16=False
beta=False
AK=False
SK=False
AOL=False
```

Checking Functions

Is every function available at every site? If your application needs a new function, you can check the PHP release or simply test if the function exists using **function_exists( )**, as shown in the following code. The example checks if one of the extended mathematics functions is available, and logs an error if it is not. A test for a function will work when the site has the right release of PHP and installs all the right options, but perhaps forgets to set the **include** options to include the right files:

```
if(function_exists("bcadd"))
    {
    // perform calculation using BCMath.
    }
else
    {
    logtofile("BCadd missing");
    }
```

Checking before Sending Headers

If your code is included within someone else's script, you cannot be sure that it is safe to send HTTP headers. Before you send redirection headers or cookies, check if it is safe to send headers with **headers_sent( )**:

```
if(headers_sent())
    {
    logtofile("Too late to send headers");
    }
else
    {
    // send the headers
    }
```

HTTP headers are sent in one group at the start of a page, and are sent the moment the page produces any output. Even a single accidental space before the first PHP tag, or a character after the last PHP tag in an included file, will make PHP send the headers. To prevent accidental sending of headers, check that there are no spaces or **newline** characters before the first **<?**, and delete any characters after the last **?>**.

Checking PHP

There are times when you need to check the version of PHP. PHP 4.0.4 had working COM support in the Win32 binaries, but version 4.0.5 had a problem in the same area. If you are writing code that uses a feature like COM, you might want to produce warning messages for certain versions of PHP.

phpversion( ) returns a version string containing something like 4.0.7-dev. You can test the result to include changes to your code for special release-related problems. The following example code grabs the version, logs the version for reference, and then tests the version to see if it requires special processing. One reason for logging everything, including the version, is to help you understand log files sent from remote sites that may have been updated by a local administrator:

```
$version = phpversion();
logtofile($version);
if($version == "4.0.5")
    {
    logtofile("Sorry, too COMplicated");
    }
else
    {
    // COM code here
    }
```

If your code has release dependencies, place a check for the PHP version in the installation and upgrade portions of your software so people can see the problem before the installation or update reaches a point where they cannot back out.

Testing Memory

Before you launch a new application, you want to thoroughly test everything. What happens if your test database has only 100 rows, or the largest image is of moderate size? How do you test your system performance in a way that is similar to many scripts accessing many big files?

Try **leak( )**, a function that deliberately leaks memory every time it is used. **leak( )** tests PHP's ability to clean up resources under duress. My test php.ini is set to 30MB, so the following example tests with a leak of 29MB. The test machine has 600MB of virtual memory, so I only need to run the test 25 times to find out if the PHP clean-up routines work. By running 25 scripts in parallel, I can test how well the virtual memory copes with the load:

```
leak(30408704);
```

Although it sounds funny to be testing memory from within an application, your script is bound inside multiple layers of software, including PHP, the Web server (which might include several layers), and the operating system, all of which impose limitations on memory size. Most of the layers also impose performance penalties as you approach the maximum memory size. Push the limit and see how far you can get (and watch how performance changes).

Outputting Unusual Formats

When you are experimenting with new content types, and your Web server is hosted by people who are slow to add new MIME types to their configuration files, you need a way to bypass the normal system and deliver whatever you want. This solution shows you how to deliver freshly generated content using **fpassthru( )**, and shares the approach with similar code and a similar function in the next solution.

The following code is a test page that accepts three variables from a database (or a form, or URL, or anywhere that is convenient for your tests). In the following example, the values are typed direct into variables. **fopen( )** opens the new file for writing and reading; and it will empty the file if the file already exists and create the file if the file does not exist. In the middle, your code generates the special new file format. **rewind( )** moves the file pointer back to the start of the file, and then **fpassthru( )** sends the file on the way to the browser and closes the file:

```
$directory = "/tmp/";
$name = "roo.jpg";
$type = "image/jpeg";
$file = fopen($directory . $name, "w+");

// lots of code to generate the new file

header("Content-Type: " . $type);
rewind($file);
fpassthru($file);
```

With this simple code wrapped around your test-file-generation code, you can see the output instantly in your browser. The only fly in the ointment is the requirement to send a header after you generate the test file. That means you can't send diagnostic messages to the screen, because they would block the header. You could add logic to output the header and test files only if there are no messages (see **headers_sent( )** earlier in this chapter), or you could split the generation and display into two pages. With two pages, you could display all the messages you need, and then display the test file in the second page using **readfile( )**, as described in the next solution.

Securing Images

There are times when you need to display an image (or other secret information) to just one user, and you do not want to use your Web server's standard security. You can do that by moving your secure files outside the Web server directory and passing the files to the user via **readthru( )**, a function similar to **fpassthru( )**, described in the previous Immediate Solution.

First, you need a page to accept an image name and display the image. The following code example does exactly that with the incredibly simple **readfile( )**. **readfile( )** accepts any file reference, including URLs, and even FTP references. For ease of testing, this example accepts the image name through an insecure URL query parameter, but for a production site, you would read Chapter 19, set up sessions, and pass the image name as a field in the session record. The end user cannot touch the session record, so the end user cannot trick the system into delivering the wrong file or delivering a file when there should be none.

The file type is included in the code, but could be passed with the session record. The content type has to go out in a HTTP header record, and here is hand-coded; but it could also be passed by the session record, which would make this a totally generic file for displaying anything:

```php
<?php
if(isset($image))
    {
    header("Content-Type: image/jpeg");
    readfile("i:/usr/home/petermoulding/secure/" . $image . ".jpg");
    }
?>
```

The image will appear on a page along with headings and needs just one HTML tag to display the image, which is shown next. For testing, the image name is passed via the URL query parameter **image=roo**, but in the secure system, you would pass the image name via a session record.

To form good HTML, the **<img>** tag needs a height, a width, and an **alt** parameter. When you input a special image (or any other file), you will most likely set up a database entry to describe the file, and include a price (for commercial entries); you should include the size and **alt** information at that stage. When you retrieve the description and price, retrieve the size and **alt** information, and then store the whole lot in the session record for retrieval by the display page:

```
print("<img src=\"./readfile.html?image=roo\""
    . " width=\"280\" height=\"250\" border=\"0\" alt=\"\">" );
```

Related solution:	Found on page:
Displaying Image Information	433

This technique can be applied to any file. Because the file type is stored in the database and delivered dynamically, you could deliver a file type that your Web server is not configured to deliver. If your Web server is not configured to recognize a file type, the file type will never appear in a browser as a result of a request from a browser.

The double security offered by a file type unknown to your Web server and all the files stored outside the visible portion of the Web server means that your security exceeds the level of many major Web sites. You can go one step further by having the page retrieve the files from another server locked behind a firewall, thus increasing your security to the level commonly called paranoid.

Chapter 8

Files

In Depth

Files are the basic unit of data storage in an operating system, and they have many variations of format and function across file types and operating systems. Files also have two levels of attributes, at the operating system level and within applications. This chapter covers basic file types, attributes common to all file types, PHP code to work with files, and the basis for file access in other chapters, like the sessions described in Chapter 19.

All files have attributes such as size, but not all files contain displayable graphics, so operating systems or applications have to figure out which application can accept a file. In Windows, that decision is based on the file extension, the small set of characters after the last dot in the file name. Other operating systems use other methods for identifying which application is used for a file, but they all can make mistakes, such as some of the tricks used to spread viruses via email: If a virus program has a name associated with executable files, some email programs will run the virus without thinking.

Directories

PHP provides the directory handling functions **opendir( )**, **readdir( )**, and **closedir( )**, and the file type testing function **is_dir( )**, to help you find and work with directories. PHP also provides **dirname( )** to extract directory names from paths to files. **pathinfo( )** provides the same information as **dirname( )** and other functions wrapped into one; **realpath( )** converts relative directory links to absolute paths; **mkdir( )** creates a new directory, and **rmdir( )** removes a directory.

Apache's View

When Apache, or whatever Web server you use, counts directories for Web pages, the Web server counts from the base directory for your Web site. My test machine has the Web site **test.petermoulding.com** in i:/petermoulding/web/root. Within that directory, the test pages for this book live in the directory /phpblackbook (according to Apache), and the test pages and files for this chapter live in /files under directory phpblackbook. The URL for the index to the Chapter 8 test pages shows **/phpblackbook/files/index.html**.

PHP's View

PHP interacts directly with the operating system file access routines, so it counts directories from the start of the server file structure. My test Web site is in i:/petermoulding/web/root, with the test pages for this chapter in directory /phpblackbook/files, and the path supplied to PHP file functions is i:/petermoulding/web/root/phpblackbook/files.

Changing Views

You can find PHP's *current working directory* with **getcwd( )** and change the directory with **chdir( )**. I do not know how often you would want to do this in real life, because all the commonly used PHP file functions accept a file path, and you can just work from the file path. You are more likely to change the directory when using a system function to run a process that cannot accept a path parameter.

File Types

In some operating systems, you can determine file types by their suffix; for example, a JPEG file ends in .jpeg or .jpg. Other times, the operating system has a separate set of rules. PHP gives you functions to find out if the file is a normal file, **is_file( )**; a directory, **is_dir( )**; a Unix-style link to a file, **is_link( )**; or an executable file, **is_executable( )**. You can also determine whether you can read the file with **is_readable( )**, whether you can write to the file with **is_writable( )** and **is_writeable( )**, or whether the file is the result of a HTTP POST file upload with **is_uploaded_file( )**. You can also check for image files, with functions from Chapter 11, and you can check for other special files by trying to open the files with various PHP functions. Remember to use **@** to suppress errors, and check if the function returns a valid result or an indication of error with a result of false.

Each operating system has its own mechanism for determining the use of a file; most of the PHP functions were originally written as calls to Unix functions, so they tend to work best on Unix, and may not translate to your operating system. Test each function first, and if you get unexpected results, retest each time PHP is updated, because someone may dive into the code and change the way the function interprets information from your operating system.

Displaying Files

Once you know a file's type, you can display the file with the most appropriate mechanism and, if in doubt, dump part of the file using the special hexadecimal display in the Immediate Solution "Displaying Any Data." This chapter describes file processing applicable to every file. Special files, such as images and databases, have their special requirements and functions explained in other chapters.

Creating and Changing Files

If a file is text or some sort of raw binary format, you can use PHP's file functions to create and change the file, whereas all other files are best created with the functions specific to the type of file you want to create. You could write your own routines to create JPEG or PNG files using binary writes, but you would be forever changing the code to allow for special cases and changes to the standards, so you are better of using the appropriate functions in Chapter 11. The same policy applies to databases, Flash files, mail attachments, and every other special-format file: Create or change a file with the software designed for that type of file.

Copying Files

copy(*a, b*) lets you copy a file from ***a*** to ***b***, and **unlink(*a*)** lets you delete a file. **copy( )** and **unlink( )** together let you perform a file move (unfortunately, PHP has no **move( )** function). There are endless discussions on what security should be applied to a moved or copied file, and the operating system of your Web server will determine what the outcome is, so create a test page for your operating system to see the exact result.

Temporary Files

A *temporary file* is a unique type of file because you never have to worry about the file name or delete the file. The file exists only while open, is deleted when closed, exists in a directory that only the operating system has to know, and has a name you never have to see. **tmpfile( )** opens a temporary file exactly the same as **fopen( )**, returns a file handle just like **fopen( )**, and is closed by **fclose( )**, just like **fopen( )**. You can perform all the PHP file reads, writes, and other functions using the file handle; the only difference is the longevity of the file. In fact, the file has the life expectancy of pizza at a PHP Sydney User group (**PHPSydney.com**) meeting. **tempnam( )** returns a temporary file name so you can create your own file name, but what happens if two scripts compete for the same temporary name? PHP, from 4.0.3 onwards, solves the problem by creating a placeholder file, which means you can immediately delete and reuse the temporary name, or use **tmpfile( )** from the start, which makes more sense.

Uploading Files

HTTP performs file uploads and places the uploaded files in a temporary directory defined in php.ini; the upload size is limited by the **upload_max_filesize** specification. The section of php.ini is included here:

```
file_uploads = On
upload_tmp_dir = t:\upload
upload_max_filesize = 8M
```

When your script receives the file upload information, your script has to copy the file to check the file, and move it to a permanent location, or the file will be lost. The function **move_uploaded_file()**, found in the latest releases of PHP, moves an uploaded file for you, and an example appears in the Immediate Solution entitled "Uploading Files."

The File List Cache

clearstatcache() is a special function that you need when rereading file directories and accessing attributes like file size, because all those file attributes are saved in a cache and read from the cache instead of disk. Depending on the operating system, the cache may hold results for minutes or days, but usually too long for a script that updates a file and then immediately tries to read the new file length. If you write to a file and then try to read the file's attributes, you need to perform the write, run **clearstatcache()**, and then read the file attributes.

Permissions

In many operating systems and file systems, you can simplify access management by assigning files to groups, and then connecting individual users to those groups. In fact, the most sophisticated systems have both resource groups and user groups to produce access management equivalent to a well-structured relational database. PHP's security functions, like **chgrp()**, are a direct connection to the C functions in Unix and Unix-like operating systems, so they miss out on the finer points of access management and only function on Unix or Linux. Perhaps in the long term, the PHP functions will gain the ability to use the equivalents in other operating systems, or the other operating systems will gain the ability to emulate Unix when talking with PHP.

chmod() lets you perform a Unix **chmod** action from PHP, to change a file's access mode. It requires a leading zero on the mode to force the mode to be interpreted as octal. If the mode value is beyond you, grab a good book on Unix or Linux and read up on **chmod**. **chown()** lets you perform a Unix **chown** from PHP to change the owner of the file, and will work only if you have an appropriately high level of access to the file. **chgrp()** moves a file from one user group to another. Because Unix does not have resource groups, changing a group of files can become boring when using **chgrp()** on one file at a time. I suggest writing an administration page that lets you submit lists of files or directory names for mass change from one group to another. The code within the page could apply **chgrp()** to every file in a list, or to every file within a directory.

umask() sets a default permission mode mask that is applied to permission strings using a logical **AND** (logical **AND** is applied bit by bit and returns 0 if either argument is 0, or 1 if both arguments are 1) for new files. **umask(011)** converts a permission mode of 0777 to 0766, which effectively wipes out execution access for everyone except the file owner. Because it takes a simpleton like me a few reads of a Linux manual to remember how **chmod( )** works, I stick to GUI-based applications that let you just check the boxes for the permissions you want.

Immediate Solutions

Listing Directories

This solution shows how to step through files and directories in a directory structure, shows variations on the code for different purposes, and is the base code for several of the following Immediate Solutions. To reduce duplication, I will show some code and functions in one Immediate Solution, and then refer back to the code from subsequent solutions that need the same function.

Common Code

All the Immediate Solutions in this chapter assume the files are in a test directory that you can set, and will use the variable **$path** to hold the path to the base directory. My test machine has the test Web site **test.petermoulding.com** in i:/ petermoulding/web/root, and within that, the test pages for this chapter are in the directory /phpblackbook/files; so, to the operating system and PHP's file functions, all the files live in i:/petermoulding/web/root/phpblackbook/files:

```
$path = "i:/petermoulding/web/root/phpblackbook/files";
```

The **is_dir()** Approach

The following code reads through the directory structure under the directory named in **$path**, counts the directories and files found, and then prints a summary. Although bland and seemingly unimportant, it is the simplest code to demonstrate the directory handling functions, **opendir()**, **readdir()**, and **closedir()**, and the file type testing functions, **is_dir()**, **is_file()**, and **is_link()**. The first lines create counters, the next code opens a directory, and then the code loops through the directory, testing the type of each entry in the directory. . and .. are excluded because they are references to the current directory and the parent directory:

```
$directories_found = 0;
$files_found = 0;
$links_found = 0;
$others_found = 0;
$path_id = opendir($path);
while($file_name = readdir($path_id))
```

```
        {
        if($file_name != "." and $file_name != "..")
            {
            if(is_dir($path . "/" . $file_name))
                {
                $directories_found++;
                }
            elseif(is_file($path . "/" . $file_name))
                {
                $files_found++;
                }
            elseif(is_link($path . "/" . $file_name))
                {
                $links_found++;
                }
            else
                {
                $others_found++;
                }
            }
        }
    closedir($path_id);
    print("<br>Directories found: " . $directories_found);
    print("<br>Files found: " . $files_found);
    print("<br>Links found: " . $links_found);
    print("<br>Others found: " . $others_found);
```

The result is shown next. I hope there will be no **Others** on any system where
you use this code; I included **other** just in case an operating system, such as
BeOS, has a brand new file type. You could make the code smaller and tighter by
replacing the multiple **if()** statements with a **switch()** and replacing the four
variables with an array, but both approaches can be confusing to people using
PHP for the first time:

```
Directories found: 2
Files found: 3
Links found: 0
Others found: 0
```

The filetype() Approach

The next code example replaces the individual **is_dir()** and equivalent functions
with a single **filetype()** function, a function that returns the file type as a string
containing **dir**, **file**, or **link**. This lends itself to storing the file type totals in an
associative array keyed on the value returned from **filetype()**, and then looping

through the array to print the list of file types found. Although this code is ideal for performing the same actions on each file type, the previous code allows a different action for all files type within each **if( )**:

```
$path_id = opendir($path);
while($file_name = readdir($path_id))
    {
    if($file_name != "." and $file_name != "..")
        {
        $file_type = filetype($path . "/" . $file_name);
        if(!isset($found[$file_type]))
            {
            $found[$file_type] = 0;
            }
        $found[$file_type]++;
        }
    }
closedir($path_id);
reset($found);
while(list($k, $v) = each($found))
    {
    print("<br>Found " . $k . ": " . $v);
    }
```

The result of this code is shown next and is obviously less descriptive, something you would use for an administration panel, but would not make public. You could read through the array examples in Chapter 3 and use the short name as an index into an array containing a more descriptive display name:

```
Found file: 5
Found dir: 2
```

The **get_directory_file()** Approach

The previous examples step through a single level of a directory, but you will often want to step through all the files in subdirectories within the chosen directory; the next code example moves to processing multiple levels without limit. The directory-read code from the previous solutions is encapsulated in a function named **get_directory_file( )**; the function accepts a path to a directory. There is little difference between this and the example that finds file attributes; the only file attribute returned is the file type, for auditing the code's accuracy, but you could add any other attribute you need, including file size and some of the image file attributes described in Chapter 11. Some of the later examples use this function to gather just the directory and file names, and then collect additional attribute information based on the entries in the array produced by this function.

Because the code will build a longer and longer path as the code steps through subdirectories, the first section of code removes any trailing slash, /, from the path. The subsequent code then concatenates the slash back in when the file name is concatenated on to the path. The removal of the slash makes the directory path look more readable when stored in the table, and is the way some functions need the path presented when used as a directory name. When **get_directory_file( )** finds a that file is a directory, **get_directory_file( )** calls itself to process the subdirectory, and the function **array_merge( )** is used to merge the array returned from the subdirectory with the main array **$found**. If the function finds the directory empty, **$found** will not be created, so the last few lines of code create an empty **$found** for the **return** statement to return:

```
function get_directory_file($path)
   {
   $path_id = opendir($path);
   while($file_name = readdir($path_id))
      {
      if($file_name != "." and $file_name != "..")
         {
         $file_type = filetype($path . "/" . $file_name);
         $found[$path][$file_name] = $file_type;
         if($file_type == "dir")
            {
            $file_array = get_directory_file($path . "/" . $file_name);
            $found = array_merge($found, $file_array);
            }
         }
      }
   closedir($path_id);
   if(!isset($found))
      {
      $found = array();
      }
   return($found);
   }
```

Formatted File List

The remaining code example takes the output from **get_directory_file( )** and prints the formatted file list shown in Figure 8.1. The first line of code calls **get_directory_file( )** with the path to the top directory, receives back the array **$found** keyed by directory and file, and then prints the results in the table shown

Directory	File	Type
i:/petermoulding/web/root/phpblackbook/files/	images	dir
i:/petermoulding/web/root/phpblackbook/files/	index.html	file
i:/petermoulding/web/root/phpblackbook/files/	listingdirectories.html	file
i:/petermoulding/web/root/phpblackbook/files/	listingfiles.html	file
i:/petermoulding/web/root/phpblackbook/files/	test	dir
i:/petermoulding/web/root/phpblackbook/files/images	london.gif	file
i:/petermoulding/web/root/phpblackbook/files/images	peters.jpg	file
i:/petermoulding/web/root/phpblackbook/files/images	php4-small.gif	file
i:/petermoulding/web/root/phpblackbook/files/images	santaclara.gif	file

Figure 8.1   List of directories.

in the figure. Because **$found** has two levels of index, there are two **while()**
loops, the first to step through directories, and the second to step through
file entries:

```
$found = get_directory_file($path);
reset($found);
print("<table border=\"3\"><tr><td><em>Directory</em></td>"
    . "<td><em>File</em></td><td><em>Type</em></td></tr>");
while(list($d, $dv) = each($found))
    {
    if(is_array($dv))
      {
      while(list($f, $fv) = each($dv))
        {
        print("<tr><td>" . $d . "</td><td>" . $f . "</td>"
            . "<td>" . $fv . "</td></tr>");
        }
      }
    else
      {
      print("<tr><td>" . $d . "</td><td>" . $dv . "</td>"
          . "<td> </td></tr>");
      }
    }
print("</table>");
```

You have a few formatting choices: You could step through the directory entries
and produce a list just of directories, or you could place a highlight on the first
directory name at the start of each subdirectory. The only unusual entry is the
subdirectory **test**, a directory that is listed in the file list for the main directory
but is not in the directory list as a directory because **test** has no content, no files,
and no subdirectories.

You get to decide how you will treat empty subdirectories by choosing to list directories as a summary of the entries in the directory key, or by listing the files with a type of directory. You have the tools and code to find any directory; you can add a directory search using the forms described in Chapter 9, and to help your search, the next solution gives you access to the extra attributes specific to files.

Other Directory Functions

dirname( ) accepts a path to a file and returns the directory part of the path, whereas **basename( )** returns the remainder, the file name. The three quick examples that follow show you the best and worst of both functions. The test using **$path** works exactly as you would expect:

```
print("<br>Dirname: " . dirname($path . "/index.html"));
```

The result is:

```
Dirname: i:/petermoulding/web/root/phpblackbook/files
```

The code

```
print("<br>Basename: " . basename($path . "/index.html"));
```

results in:

```
Basename: index.html
```

The tests with **/a/b** show **b** interpreted as a file name, but **b** could be either a directory named **b** or a file named **b**, and in **URLs**, **b** is more likely to be a directory than a file:

```
print("<br>Dirname: " . dirname("/a/b")
   . ", basename: " . basename("/a/b"));
```

The result is:

```
Dirname: /a, basename: b
```

The third test, **/a/b/**, is surprising because **b** is returned as a file instead of a directory. Try the test with the release of PHP on your site:

```
print("<br>Dirname: " . dirname("/a/b/")
   . ", basename: " . basename("/a/b/"));
```

The result is:

```
Dirname: /a, basename: b
```

pathinfo( ) provides the same information as **dirname( )** and **basename( )** combined. The first example that follows is the same as the first example in the previous code section. **$path . "/index.html"** is followed by a **while( )** loop to print the resultant array:

```
$info = pathinfo($path . "/index.html");
while(list($k, $v) = each($info))
    {
    print("<br>Pathinfo: k: " . $k . ", v: " . $v );
    }
```

The result shows the same entries for **basename** and **dirname** as in the previous section, plus an extension name for the file:

```
Pathinfo: k: dirname, v: i:/petermoulding/web/root/phpblackbook/files
Pathinfo: k: basename, v: index.html
Pathinfo: k: extension, v: html
```

The second example shows the same interpretation of **/a/b** and, of course, no extension:

```
$info = pathinfo("/a/b");
```

This results in:

```
Pathinfo: k: dirname, v: /a
Pathinfo: k: basename, v: b
```

The third test attempts to split up a URL into components, but fails to handle the query string, as follows:

```
$info =
  pathinfo("http://www4.ncdc.noaa.gov/cgi-win/wwcgi.dll?wwAW~MP~PUB");
```

The result looks like this:

```
Pathinfo: k: dirname, v: http://www4.ncdc.noaa.gov/cgi-win
Pathinfo: k: basename, v: wwcgi.dll?wwAW~MP~PUB
Pathinfo: k: extension, v: dll?wwAW~MP~PUB
```

realpath( ) converts relative directory links to absolute paths, which you want to do when you're using a file name from a URL, and you want to feed the file name into a PHP function. The following code example shows a relative file name, **./index.html** from a page request, converted to an absolute file name, ready to feed into any PHP file function:

```
print("<br>Realpath: " . realpath("./index.html"));
```

The result is:

```
Realpath: i:\petermoulding\web\root\phpblackbook\files\index.html
```

Creating and Deleting Directories

mkdir( ) accepts a directory name or a full path to a directory, creates a new directory, and returns true on success or false on failure. **rmdir( )** accepts a directory name or a full path to a directory, removes the directory, and returns true on success or false on failure. Here is a simple test of the two functions:

```
$new = "./anothertest";
if(mkdir($new))
   {
   print("<br>:-)  Created directory: " . $new);
   if(rmdir())
      {
      print("<br>:-)  Removed directory: " . $new);
      }
   else
      {
      print("<br>:-(  Failed to remove directory: " . $new);
      }
   }
else
   {
   print("<br>:-(  Failed to created directory: " . $new);
   }
```

The result is as follows:

```
Warning: Wrong parameter count for mkdir()
:-( Failed to created directory: ./anothertest
```

Note that **mkdir( )** failed because it did not have the optional second parameter, the permissions settings, which is used with Unix but ignored for other operating systems. In PHP 4.0.5, **mkdir( )** requires the second parameter under Windows NT but, as far as I can tell, does not translate the Unix-style permissions settings to their Windows NT equivalents. When you write this sort of code for distribution across customers' Web servers, you need to allow for PHP release changes by making the second parameter a variable you can set at the top of your script, or even in one common include across all scripts in your Web site, so you can set a default that will work with all operating systems. The following example uses a common setting of 0777, to give everyone access. The only code line shown is the one that was changed from the previous example:

```
if(mkdir($new, 0777))
```

The result is:

```
:-) Created directory: ./anothertest
:-) Removed directory: ./anothertest
```

Both run as user **nobody** within your Web server (unless the server configuration defaults are changed), and so should have few rights to create and delete directories, which creates a problem when you try to write a Web page to set up a new home directory for a new user. The best solution is to run PHP as an Apache module, install a security certificate and SSL, implement all the right Apache security options to store user information in a directory, such as LDAP, or in a database, such as MySQL, and then have your administration page accept a user name and password for a login. The shorter way, for a small number of users, is to use Apache's .htaccess and .htpasswd files. Once access to your Web site is secure, you can relax file permissions. To get either system working, you will need a good book on Apache, such as *Apache Server for Windows Little Black Book* (Greg Holden, The Coriolis Group, Inc.), and a good book on administering your operating system, such as *Linux System Administration Black Book* (Dee-Ann LeBlanc, The Coriolis Group, Inc.).

Listing Files with Attributes

This solution shows how to step through files in a directory structure, listing the file attributes. This solution is based on the code from the previous Immediate Solution, "Listing Directories."

Common Code

The first step is to decide where you want to start the report. To keep both the processing and report size down for testing, the start point, in **$path**, is well down in a subdirectory with few files. You could add a form, as described in Chapter 9, to let you type in the starting directory name:

```
$path = "i:/petermoulding/web/root/phpblackbook/files";
```

get_directory_file() Expanded

The function **get_directory_file( )** from the previous Immediate Solution is expanded here to return more file attributes, specifically all the attributes available via the standard PHP file attribute functions. The changed section is highlighted and includes functions like **fileatime( )** to return the time the file was last accessed (if the operating system and file system provide the information). **filemtime( )** provides the last time a file was changed in size, and **filectime( )** provides the last time a file had any record updated. **fileowner( )**, **fileperms( )**, **filegroup( )**, and **fileinode( )** provide information in Linux, but in Windows NT the functions do not return the equivalent Windows NT attributes:

```
function get_directory_file($path)
    {
    $path_id = opendir($path);
    while($file_name = readdir($path_id))
        {
        if($file_name != "." and $file_name != "..")
            {
            $file["type"] = filetype($path . "/" . $file_name);
            if($file["type"] == "dir")
                {
                $file_array = get_directory_file($path. "/"
                    . $file_name);
                if(isset($found))
                    {
                    $found = array_merge($found, $file_array);
                    }
                else
                    {
                    $found = $file_array;
                    }
                }
            else
                {
```

```
                $file["accessed"] = fileatime($path . "/" . $file_name);
                $file["changed"] = filectime($path . "/" . $file_name);
                $file["group"] = filegroup($path . "/" . $file_name);
                $file["inode"] = fileinode($path . "/" . $file_name);
                $file["modified"] = filemtime($path . "/" . $file_name);
                $file["owner"] = fileowner($path . "/" . $file_name);
                $file["permissions"] = fileperms($path . "/" . $file_name);
                $file["size"] = filesize($path . "/" . $file_name);
                $found[$path][$file_name] = $file;
                }
            }
        }
    closedir($path_id);
    if(!isset($found))
        {
        $found = array();
        }
    return($found);
    }
```

Formatted File List

The following section of code produces the list of files and attributes shown in
Figures 8.2 and 8.3 by reading all the directory and file names with the function

Directory	File	Type	Accessed
i:/petermoulding/web/root/phpblackbook/files/images	london.gif	file	2001-05-17 11:27:12
i:/petermoulding/web/root/phpblackbook/files/images	peters.jpg	file	2001-05-17 11:27:12
i:/petermoulding/web/root/phpblackbook/files/images	php4-small.gif	file	2001-05-17 11:27:12
i:/petermoulding/web/root/phpblackbook/files/images	santaclara.gif	file	2001-05-17 11:27:12
i:/petermoulding/web/root/phpblackbook/files/	index.html	file	2001-05-17 13:29:42
i:/petermoulding/web/root/phpblackbook/files/	listingdirectories.html	file	2001-05-17 13:15:29
i:/petermoulding/web/root/phpblackbook/files/	listingfiles.html	file	2001-05-17 13:28:25

Figure 8.2   List of files and attributes, part A.

Changed	Group	Inode	Modified	Owner	Permissions	Size
2001-05-17 11:27:12	0	0	2000-09-11 21:16:41	0	33206	21940
2001-05-17 11:27:12	0	0	2001-03-16 09:46:13	0	33206	6530
2001-05-17 11:27:12	0	0	2001-01-30 04:36:00	0	33206	4528
2001-05-17 11:27:12	0	0	2001-03-15 21:50:59	0	33206	25430
2001-05-17 07:14:39	0	0	2001-05-17 12:22:29	0	33206	483
2001-05-17 07:15:32	0	0	2001-05-17 13:15:29	0	33206	5365
2001-05-17 12:03:44	0	0	2001-05-17 13:28:25	0	33206	5342

Figure 8.3   List of files and attributes, part B.

get_directory_file( ), and then looping through the resultant array, **$found**, to print the table. The first **print** statement prints the column headings, the second prints the matching fields, the third prints just the directory and file names in the unlikely event the file entry is not an array of attributes, the fourth prints the directory entry in the unlikely event the directory entry does not have files entries, and the last completes the HTML table tag. The directory and file name are printed with plain tags, and the dates are formatted with the **date( )** function, described in Chapter 2.

The first **while( )** statement loops through **$found** at the directory level, and the second **while( )** statement loops through the directory entry at the file level. I include the **if(is_array( ))** tests in case the **get_directory_file( )** function returns a directory without files or a file without attributes. Although I have never found files without attributes, I have found directories without files:

```
$found = get_directory_file($path, "");
print("<table border=\"3\"><tr><td><em>Directory</em></td>"
   . "<td><em>File</em></td><td><em>Type</em></td>"
   . "<td><em>Accessed</em></td><td><em>Changed</em></td>"
   . "<td><em>Group</em></td><td><em>Inode</em></td>"
   . "<td><em>Modified</em></td><td><em>Owner</em></td>"
   . "<td><em>Permissions</em></td><td><em>Size</em></td>"
   . "</tr>");
while(list($d, $dv) = each($found))
   {
   if(is_array($dv))
      {
      while(list($f, $fv) = each($dv))
         {
         if(is_array($fv))
            {
            print("<tr><td>" . $d . "</td><td>" . $f . "</td>"
               . "<td>" . $fv["type"] . "</td>"
               . "<td>" . date("Y-m-d", $fv["accessed"])
               . " " . date("H:i:s", $fv["accessed"]) . "</td>"
               . "<td>" . date("Y-m-d", $fv["changed"])
               . " " . date("H:i:s", $fv["changed"]) . "</td>"
               . "<td>" . $fv["group"] . "</td>"
               . "<td>" . $fv["inode"] . "</td>"
               . "<td>" . date("Y-m-d", $fv["modified"])
               . " " . date("H:i:s", $fv["modified"]) . "</td>"
               . "<td>" . $fv["owner"] . "</td>"
               . "<td>" . $fv["permissions"] . "</td>"
               . "<td>" . $fv["size"] . "</td>");
            }
```

```
          else
            {
            print("<tr><td>" . $d . "</td><td>" . $f . "</td>"
              . "<td>" . $fv . "</td><td> </td><td> </td>"
              . "<td> </td><td> </td><td> </td>"
              . "<td> </td><td> </td><td> </td></tr>" );
            }
          }
        }
    else
      {
      print("<tr><td>" . $d . "</td><td>" . $dv . "</td>"
        . "<td> </td><td> </td><td> </td>"
        . "<td> </td><td> </td><td> </td>"
        . "<td> </td><td> </td><td> </td></tr>" );
      }
    }
print("</table>");
```

Additional Attributes

On some operating systems, you can get additional attributes from the functions shown next, but you have to remember that even when these attributes are returned by the function, they can still have meanings that differ from operating system to operating system—particularly what constitutes an executable file. Note that **is_writeable( )** is an alias for **is_writable( )**:

```
$file["executable"] = is_executable($path . "/" . $file_name);
$file["readable"] = is_readable($path . "/" . $file_name);
$file["writeable"] = is_writeable($path . "/" . $file_name);
$file["writeable"] = is_writable($path . "/" . $file_name);
```

You can now report any attribute from files, if your operating system provides the information, and PHP has a function to gather the information. From all reports, PHP4 is not hard to extend with new functions, so anyone handy with C can add extra functions to collect additional information from an operating system.

Reporting Disk Space

When you start a complicated resource-chewing file build, you do not want the whole process to crash at the last minute because there is not enough space left on your disk. Better to check the space available first, and defer the process until you can clean out the junk. The code in this solution helps you find the biggest directories and files, and you could easily modify it to find the oldest files, or delete unused files.

Your operating system keeps track of some file information, and it may or may not keep track of the last time a file was read. Your operating system will also report the number of bytes in a file, rather than the true file space consumed by a file, so the results reported by PHP are a guide to be adjusted according to your operating system and file system. Consider some quick examples. Linux's ext2 file system allocates files in multiples of 8,192 bytes (8KB), so 1,000 files of 200 bytes each will occupy 8,192,000 (8MB) instead of 200,000. File systems with variable allocation, like Reiser and NTFS, will use less space for small files, but still round up to some multiple of the 512-byte sector used on disk. All file systems have overheads for directories, as well as security and logging information. Most file systems record when a file was created, but good file management requires the date the file was last read, and few file systems record that date because of the overheads.

Common Code

All that the code needs is a place to start on a disk, and I shall use the start of the system partition on my workstation, **c:**, as shown in the **$path** statement that follows, because **c:** includes a range of large files and small files, large directories and small directories. You could easily add a table of partitions and drives to feed through this reporting, but be aware that some of the file functions will not work with network drives:

```
$path = "c:";
```

get_directory_file() Expanded

The examples use the function **get_directory_file()** built in the previous Immediate Solution, complete with the expanded file attributes. To save you reading the full description of the function, the input is **$path**, and the output is an array keyed by directory and then file name that contains the file size, which you use later in this example, the date last accessed, which you also use, and other attributes you do not need.

Finding Free Disk Space

How much space is left in a partition? The next code example displays the space remaining in a disk partition using PHP's **diskfreespace()** function. Figure 8.4 shows several results. The first row shows the raw number returned from the root directory of a partition, the second row shows the same number formatted

8. Files

diskfreespace("/")	1277777920
Disk free space for /	1,277,777,920
Disk free space for /mysql/bin	1,277,777,920

Figure 8.4   Free disk space.

with **number_format( )**, and the third row shows the free space returned when **diskfreespace( )** is pointed at a subdirectory—a result that is the same as for the main directory, because the free space applies to the whole disk partition:

```
print("<table border=\"3\">");
print(trow(tdl("diskfreespace(\"/\")") . tdl(diskfreespace("/"))));
print(trow(tdl("diskfreespace(\"/\")") . tdn(diskfreespace("/"))));
print(trow(tdl("diskfreespace(\"/mysql/bin\")")
    . tdn(diskfreespace("/mysql/bin"))));
print("</table>");
```

Table Functions

To reduce the typing of HTML table tags in the display portions of the code in the "Immediate Solutions" section, use the simple formatting functions shown here. **tdd()** displays a date in a table cell, **tde()** displays emphasized text in a cell for headings, **tdl()** displays text left-aligned in a cell, **tdn()** displays a number formatted and right-aligned in a cell, **tdre()** displays emphasized text right-aligned in a cell, and **trow()** wraps table row tags around a row of cells. If there is no input to a table cell, the code insets a nonbreaking space, ** **, to ensure the cell displays correctly in all browsers:

```
function tdd($text="")
   {
   if(strlen($text))
      {
      $text = date("Y-m-d", $text) . " " . date("H:i:s", $text);
      }
   else
      {
      $text = " ";
      }
   return("<td>" . $text . "</td>");
   }
function tde($text="")
   {
```

```
   if(!strlen($text))
      {
      $text = " ";
      }
   return("<td><em>" . $text . "</em></td>");
   }
function tdl($text="")
   {
   if(!strlen($text))
      {
      $text = " ";
      }
   return("<td>" . $text . "</td>");
   }
function tdn($text="")
   {
   if(strlen($text))
      {
      $text = number_format($text);
      }
   else
      {
      $text = " ";
      }
   return("<td align=\"right\">" . $text . "</td>");
   }
function tdre($text="")
   {
   if(!strlen($text))
      {
      $text = " ";
      }
   return("<td align=\"right\"><em>" . $text . "</em></td>");
   }
function trow($text="")
   {
   if(!strlen($text))
      {
      $text = tdl(" ");
      }
   return("<tr>" . $text . "</tr>");
   }
```

Formatting the File List with Space Used

File lists can be huge when run at higher levels in the directory structure or on a directory containing artwork (for one project, I had a single directory containing 49,000 images of sky, clouds, and sunrises), so the following code has a print limit, set in **$print_limit**, to limit the number of lines sent to the browser. You could easily send the output to a database (I recommend MySQL) and browse the results from the database, using SQL facilities to step through the results in manageable blocks.

Related solution:	*Found on page:*
Creating a Database	179

The code uses **get_directory_file( )** to collect the file names with attributes including space used, code similar to the loop in the previous Immediate Solution. It then loops through the resultant array, **$found**, and prints the rows of results using the table cell formatting functions defined earlier. There are two **while( )** loops through **$found**; the first loops through at the directory level (the first key), and the second loops through files within a directory. To limit the print length, the middle **print** statements are wrapped in **if($print_limit)** statements, and extra code adds file sizes to **$directory_total**, a field that is printed at the end of each loop through a set of files within a directory to give a total of the space used for the directory.

The code starting at **$parts = explode("/", $d)** takes the total space used within a directory and adds the space to the array **$size** at every level it can find within the directory string. A directory like **/usr/local/bin/** is split into **usr**, **local**, and **bin**, and then built into **/usr**, **/usr/local** and **/usr/local/bin** with the space added into the entries for all three directories. **$size** is used for later lists (the result is shown in Figure 8.5):

```
$print_limit = 10;
$found = get_directory_file($path);
print("<table border=\"3\">" . trow(tde("Directory") . tde("File")
   . tde("Size")));
while(list($d, $dv) = each($found))
   {
   if(is_array($dv))
      {
      $directory_total = 0;
      while(list($f, $fv) = each($dv))
         {
```

```
    if(is_array($fv))
        {
        if($print_limit)
            {
            print(trow(tdl($d) . tdl($f) . tdn($fv["size"])));
            $print_limit--;
            }
        $directory_total += $fv["size"];
        }
    else
        {
        if($print_limit)
            {
            print(trow(tdl($d) . tdl($f) . td($fv)));
            $print_limit--;
            }
        }
    }
$parts = explode("/", $d);
$acc_dir = "";
while(list($pk, $pv) = each($parts))
    {
    if(strlen($acc_dir))
        {
        $acc_dir .= "/";
        }
    $acc_dir .= $pv;
    if(isset($size[$acc_dir]))
        {
        $size[$acc_dir] += $directory_total;
        }
    else
        {
        $size[$acc_dir] = $directory_total;
        }
    }
    }
else
    {
    print(trow(tdl($d) . tdl($dv) . tdl()));
    }
}
print("</table>" );
```

Directory	File	Size
c:	boot.ini	289
c:	BOOTSECT.DOS	512
c:	COMMAND.COM	32,768
c:	IO.SYS	98,304
c:	MSDOS.SYS	32,768
c:	NTDETECT.COM	26,816
c:	ntldr	156,496
c:cygwin/bin	aclocal	10,253
c:cygwin/bin	addftinfo.exe	33,792
c:cygwin/bin	addr2line.exe	337,408

Figure 8.5   File list with space used.

Listing Space Used by Directory

The following code sorts and displays the array **$size** produced by the previous code, while printing the list of space used by file. **ksort( )** and the other array sort functions used in this and later code are explained in Chapter 3.

The first part of the code checks that the array **$size** exists and is an array, just in case the previous code has changed, then sorts the array with **ksort( )**, and then steps through the array using **while( )**. Because each directory has one entry, the list is simple, although it looks complex because of the extra code to limit the total number of lines printed during testing. Once in production, you could remove the limit, but first test with your browser on a very large number of files. Netscape 4.76 fails to complete a list of 10,000 files, and locks up all open Netscape windows:

```
if(isset($size) and is_array($size))
    {
    $print_limit = 10;
    ksort($size);
    print("<table border=\"3\">" . trow(tde("Directory")
        . tde("Size")));
    while(list($d, $s) = each($size))
        {
        if($print_limit)
            {
            print(trow(tdl($d) . tdn($s)));
            $print_limit--;
            }
        }
```

```
print("</table>");
}
```

The results are shown in Figure 8.6.

Listing Space Used by Largest Directories

The following code and list is a variation on the previous directory list with the main difference being the sort, **arsort( )**, a function that sorts associative arrays by key into reverse order, giving you the directories listed by space used, with the largest listed first. **$print_limit** lets you limit the display to the top 10 or top 100 directories chewing up your disk space.

The result, in Figure 8.7, shows three lines of aggregate directories containing many applications, then one directory, cygwin, which stands out as the largest single application directory, and another open source application, StarOffice, running a close second. Both products could benefit from finer control over what is

Directory	Size
c:	347,953
c:KPCMS	6,679,805
c:KPCMS/CMSCP	625,012
c:KPCMS/DCPDB	6,054,793
c:Program Files	437,524,776
c:Program Files/ACDSee32	2,060,879
c:Program Files/ACDSee32/Shortcuts	1,248
c:Program Files/Adobe	6,072,513
c:Program Files/Adobe/Acrobat 4.0	6,072,513
c:Program Files/Adobe/Acrobat 4.0/Help	350,478

Figure 8.6   Space used, listed by directory.

Directory	Size
c:Program Files	437,524,776
c:WINNT	210,260,683
c:WINNT/system32	151,858,259
c:cygwin	130,321,558
c:Program Files/StarOffice	126,229,469
c:Program Files/StarOffice/program	77,192,911
c:cygwin/usr	75,921,580
c:Program Files/TMG	50,275,431
c:Program Files/JavaSoft	43,485,512
c:Program Files/JavaSoft/JRE	43,485,512

Figure 8.7   Space used, listed by largest directories.

installed. Considering Cygwin is only installed on the test machine to help install PostgreSQL, the total space used is ludicrous. Based on this report, I would run through the Cygwin installation again and turn off everything I don't need. The bloated StarOffice installation will also be reviewed. The code is as follows:

```
if(isset($size) and is_array($size))
   {
   $print_limit = 10;
   arsort($size);
   print("<table border=\"3\">" . trow(tde("Directory")
      . tde("Size")));
   while(list($d, $s) = each($size))
      {
      if($print_limit)
         {
         print(trow(tdl($d) . tdn($s)));
         $print_limit--;
         }
      }
   print("</table>");
   }
```

Listing Space Used by Largest Files

Finding the largest files is as useful as finding the largest directories, and is the next project. The following code revisits the **$found** array to produce a new array called **$file_size** containing space used in a way that lets you easily sort and process the array. Two **while( )** loops step through **$found** by directory, and then file. At the inner level, each file entry is added to **$file_size** keyed by size, directory, and file. The data accessed is carried over so you can see the last time the file was used; but depending on the operating system, the date accessed may not indicate the last time the file was read, which is the date you really need:

```
reset($found);
while(list($d, $dv) = each($found))
   {
   if(is_array($dv))
      {
      while(list($f, $fv) = each($dv))
         {
         if(is_array($fv))
            {
```

```
            $file_size[$fv["size"]][$d][$f] = $fv["accessed"];
          }
        }
      }
    }
```

$file_size contains the files listed by size, and in the next code example, **krsort( )** sorts the array into reverse order of size so you can see the largest files first. The rest of the code is almost the same as the previous two array listing loops, with the main change being the extra **while( )** loop because the array has three keys instead of two. The outer loop and main sequence is keyed to size, so the inner **print** statement prints size first. The inner **print** statement is limited to 10 lines by **$print_limit** in this example, and the loop keeps on running through every file after the printing ceases, so you might want to add **and $print_limit** as an extra condition in each **while( )**:

```
$print_limit = 10;
krsort($file_size);
print("<table border=\"3\">" . trow(tde("Size") . tde("Directory")
  . tde("File") . tde("Last accessed")));
while(list($s, $sv) = each($file_size))
  {
  if(is_array($sv))
     {
     while(list($d, $dv) = each($sv))
        {
        if(is_array($dv))
           {
           while(list($f, $fv) = each($dv))
              {
              if($print_limit)
                 {
                 print(trow(tdn($s) . tdl($d) . tdl($f) . tdd($fv)));
                 $print_limit--;
                 }
              }
           }
        }
     }
  }
print("</table>");
```

The results are shown in Figure 8.8.

Size	Directory	File	Last accessed
18,103,692	c:Program Files/StarOffice/help/01	shelp.dat	2001-01-30 20:05:00
16,777,216	c:cygwin/usr/local/pgsql/data/pg_xlog	0000000000000000	2001-05-14 19:57:47
11,646,640	c:Program Files/JavaSoft/JRE/1.3.0_01/lib	rt.jar	2001-05-19 17:23:51
11,646,454	c:Program Files/JavaSoft/JRE/1.3/lib	rt.jar	2001-05-02 21:33:04
9,089,327	c:Program Files/Opera/Mail/Apachetect	Trash.MBS	2001-04-13 07:33:44
6,111,232	c:Program Files/Iomega/Iomegaware	IOGUREG.EXE	2001-01-17 22:45:44
6,094,848	c:Program Files/StarOffice/user/store	out.scs	2001-01-30 19:52:14
6,047,744	c:WINNT/system32	QuickTime.qts	2000-12-04 17:35:40
5,767,168	c:Program Files/StarOffice/program	applicat.rdb	2000-05-08 05:20:00
5,760,054	c:WINNT	Carolyn.bmp	2001-05-19 14:49:16

Figure 8.8   Space used, listed by largest files.

Listing Image File Attributes

This solution shows how to step through files, listing the attributes of files that are images. It uses both **$path** and the function **get_directory_file( )** from the previous Immediate Solution. The image file attributes are gathered using the image function **getimagesize( )**, which is fully explained in Chapter 11, along with all other image processing functions. Once you master the code in this solution, you can create pages to list and display your images, perhaps mixing the code with MySQL database code from Chapter 5 to create an image catalogue, and then add code from Chapter 11 to automatically build image thumbnails and add titles and copyright notices.

getimagesize( ) accepts a file name and an optional extra parameter, here named **$extra**, and returns an array, named **$att** in the example, containing information about the image. **$att** receives four standard values, plus two extras for JPEG images, but none of the test images had the extra information and only two of the standard values, height and width, are of use. Therefore, I included code to store all the values, but I displayed only height and width. **$extra** receives an array containing information stored within the image—information that is currently only in JPEGs, and there were no JPEGs in the test files. Although I included code to collect and place the information into a string ready for display, I did not place the string in the output HTML table. Tests across several servers found few JPEGs that have extra information, and then only noted that the image was from Photoshop.

Collecting Image Information

The following code looks like the file-processing loop used in the previous Immediate Solutions, and has a few changes to collect extra information for images. The first change is to change the central processing loop to read only images. The other change is to output the image attributes to array **$images**. The code actually mixes the new image attributes with the existing file attributes, so you can add other display columns, such as date created:

```
$found = get_directory_file($path);
reset($found);
while(list($d, $dv) = each($found))
    {
    if(is_array($dv))
        {
        while(list($f, $fv) = each($dv))
            {
            $x5 = strtolower(substr($f, -5));
            $x4 = substr($x5, -4);
            if($x4 == ".jpg" or $x5 == ".jpeg" or $x4 == ".gif"
            or $x4 == ".png" or $x4 == ".swf")
                {
                $att = getimagesize($d . "/" . $f, $fv["extra"]);
                if(isset($att[0])) {$fv["width"] = $att[0];}
                if(isset($att[1])) {$fv["height"] = $att[1];}
                if(isset($att[2])) {$fv["it"] = $att[2];}
                if(isset($att[3])) {$fv["html"] = $att[3];}
                if(isset($att[4])) {$fv["channel"] = $att[4];}
                if(isset($att[5])) {$fv["bits"] = $att[5];}
                if(is_array($fv["extra"]))
                    {
                    while(list($ek, $ev) = each($fv["extra"]))
                        {
                        if(strlen($extra))
                            {
                            $extra .= "<br>" . $ek . ": " . $ev;
                            }
                        else
                            {
                            $extra = $ek . ": " . $ev;
                            }
                        }
                    if(isset($extra) and strlen($extra))
                        {
                        $fv["extra"] = $extra;
                        }
```

```
                     else
                        {
                        $fv["extra"] = "";
                        }
                     }
                  $images[$d][$f] = $fv;
                  }
               }
            }
         }
```

The central loop runs when a file ends with .jpeg or one of the other file suffixes
listed in the **if( )** statement; all other files are ignored. If you were reading a lot of
files and only a few were images, you could move the file type test up to the
get_directory_file( ) function to reduce overhead. For some operating systems
that do not use file suffixes, to find out if a file is an image, you could run
getimagesize( ) against files, and then check if the function returns an array
or false.

Displaying Image Information

Now that the image attributes are in **$images**, you can loop through the array
with display code similar to the code used in previous Immediate Solutions, just
changing the fields that are printed. The code following checks that the array
exists before using the array, just in case someone changed the previous code;
then the code sets a print limit, 10 in this case, for testing, and then two **while( )**
loops loop through directories and files printing entries. If you wanted to find the
largest images, the smallest images or images with some other attribute, you could
add additional **if( )** statements or convert the array to some other sequence using
the tricks used to display the top 10 space users shown in the previous Immediate
Solution:

```
if(isset($images) and is_array($images))
   {
   $print_limit = 10;
   reset($images);
   print("<table border=\"3\">" . trow(tde("Directory") . tde("File")
      . tde("Size") . tde("Height") . tde("Width") . tde("Channel")
      . tde("Bits") . tde("Extra")) );
   while(list($d, $dv) = each($images))
      {
      if(is_array($dv))
         {
         while(list($f, $fv) = each($dv))
```

```
            {
         if(is_array($fv))
            {
            if($print_limit)
               {
               print(trow(tdl($d) . tdl($f) . tdl($fv["size"])
                  . tdl($fv["height"]) . tdl($fv["width"])
                  . tdl($fv["channel"]) . tdl($fv["bits"])
                  . tdl($extra)) );
               $print_limit--;
               }
            }
         }
      }
   print("</table>" );
   }
```

Figure 8.9 shows the results.

Directory	File	Size	Height	Width
i:/petermoulding/web/root/phpblackbook/files/images	bs.gif	255	22	61
i:/petermoulding/web/root/phpblackbook/files/images	copy.jpg	6530	100	80
i:/petermoulding/web/root/phpblackbook/files/images	kingparrot.jpg	60810	500	250
i:/petermoulding/web/root/phpblackbook/files/images	me.jpg	6530	100	80
i:/petermoulding/web/root/phpblackbook/files/images	notme.jpg	50024	250	280
i:/petermoulding/web/root/phpblackbook/files/images	peter.jpg	6530	100	80
i:/petermoulding/web/root/phpblackbook/files/images	php-syd.gif	6405	100	190
i:/petermoulding/web/root/phpblackbook/files/images	roo.jpg	50024	250	280

Figure 8.9   List of image files with attributes.

Displaying Any Data

The object of this example is to build code that will display any file on screen without blowing up your browser. The examples include a text file, php.ini; an HTML file, test.html; and an image file, me.jpg. With PHP file functions, you can read and display any file your operating system and security setup allow.

Common Code

To make the displays manageable, I will limit the display to 10 lines using **$print_limit**, as used in previous Immediate Solutions, and truncate lines to 70 characters, as set in **$line_limit**. The first example uses the function **file( )** to read a whole file into memory, and then applies **$print_limit** at the time of print, which is ideal when the code will drop some lines before print and you want the same number of lines printed. The second example assumes that the puny test file is a massive text file, reads the file one line at a time with function **fgets()**, and limits the reading, rather than the print, which is a good technique for sampling the start of large files. The line length is applied to contain large lines and gives you options, like sampling the start of each record in a file:

```
$line_limit = 70;
$print_limit = 10;
```

Displaying a Text File

PHP's php.ini file is about 50 lines of settings and many more lines of comments, so it is long enough to demonstrate text file display. Also, I know there are no special characters in the file that will upset your browser. The code uses the function **file()** to read the file into an array, with a new array entry starting after each **newline** character. The newline character is retained, so each entry, except perhaps the last, ends with a newline, and files that are not text may end up as one big entry containing every byte from the input file. The **while()** statement loops through the array until the end of the array or until **$print_limit** decrements to zero. The rest of the code is basic PHP for printing; the **substr()** function limits the line length to **$line_limit**, and the first **print** line produces a little heading to identify the list:

```
$file = "php.ini";
$line_limit = 70;
$print_limit = 10;
$text = file($path . "/" . $file);
print("<br><em>File: " . $path . "/" . $file . "</em>");
while(list($k, $v) = each($text) and $print_limit)
    {
    $v = substr($v, 0, $line_limit);
    print("<br>" . $v);
    $print_limit--;
    }
```

The result of this code is:

```
File: i:/petermoulding/web/root/phpblackbook/files/php.ini
[PHP]
; Language Options ;
engine = On
short_open_tag = Off
```

```
asp_tags = Off
precision = 14
y2k_compliance = Off
output_buffering = Off
output_handler =
```

The next code is the same as the previous code with one major difference: **fgets( )** replaces **file( )** to read the data, because **file( )** reads the whole file every time, no matter how big the file, whereas **fgets( )** lets you read just the records you want and then stops. **fgets( )** requires a three-step process: **fopen( )** opens the file for input and returns a pointer to the file, **fgets( )** reads a record from the file and returns false at end of file, and **fclose( )** closes the file when you are finished reading the file. The remaining examples will use **file( )** to keep the code short, but you can change any of them to use **fgets( )** or similar file functions to reduce overhead with large files. Because this type of file access is aimed at large files, an extra line, containing **filesize( )**, gets the file size for display in the heading:

```
$file = "php.ini";
$line_limit = 70;
$print_limit = 10;
$size = filesize($path . "/" . $file);
print("<br><em>File: " . $path . "/" . $file . ", size: " . $size
    . "</em>");
$pointer = fopen($path . "/" . $file, "r");
while($line = fgets($pointer, $size) and $print_limit)
    {
    $line = substr($line, 0, $line_limit);
    print("<br>" . $line);
    $print_limit--;
    }
fclose(\$pointer);
```

The output from this code is the same as the previous code, except for the heading, so the following is just the first line:

```
File: i:/petermoulding/web/root/phpblackbook/files/php.ini, size: 6301
```

Displaying an HTML File

The next code tackles an HTML file. The problem with displaying HTML files is the HTML you display from the file interferes with the HTML in your display page, so the solution is to use either **htmlspecialchars( )** or **htmlentities( )** to convert HTML and other characters into a string representation that will display on

screen without being interpreted as HTML by the browser. If you display the test
file without replacing the HTML tags with special characters, you get the result
shown in Figure 8.10; but by using the next block of code, you end up with the
result shown in Figure 8.11:

```
$file = "test.html";
$line_limit = 70;
$print_limit = 10;
$text = file($path . "/" . $file);
print("<br><em>File: " . $path . "/" . $file . "</em>");
while(list($k, $v) = each($text) and $print_limit)
    {
    $v = substr($v, 0, $line_limit);
    print("<br>" . htmlentities($v));
    $print_limit--;
    }
```

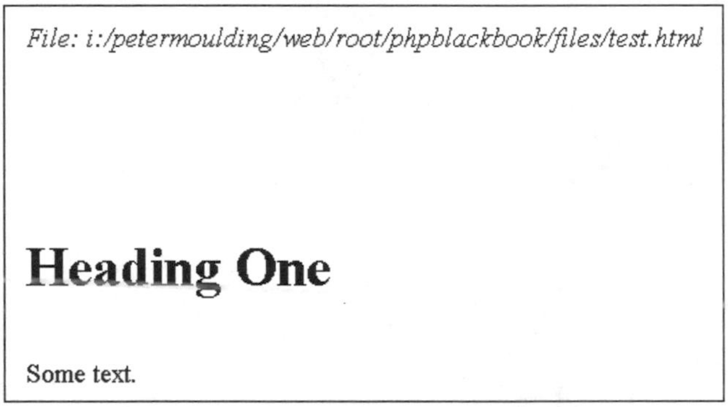

File: i:/petermoulding/web/root/phpblackbook/files/test.html

Heading One

Some text.

Figure 8.10   HTML file without tag replacement.

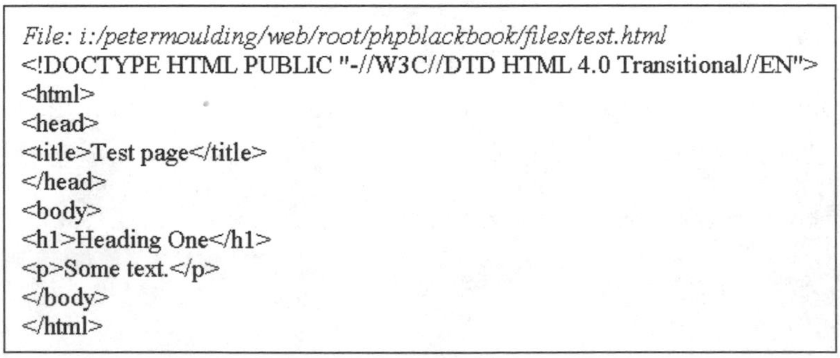

File: i:/petermoulding/web/root/phpblackbook/files/test.html
<!DOCTYPE HTML PUBLIC "-//W3C//DTD HTML 4.0 Transitional//EN">
<html>
<head>
<title>Test page</title>
</head>
<body>
<h1>Heading One</h1>
<p>Some text.</p>
</body>
</html>

Figure 8.11   The same HTML file with tag replacement.

Why two functions to perform the same work? I don't know; must be one of those secret PHP developer things. **htmlspecialchars( )** changes the bare minimum set of characters, mainly **<** and **>**, to let you display HTML without interpretation. **htmlentities( )** changes the same minimum character set, plus a whole set of special characters that are used mainly for accenting European characters. If you need to display special characters from a character set other than the European Latin character set, you could use **htmlspecialchars( )** to perform the basics, and then add your own translation for the other characters. There is an example of custom translation in the hexadecimal display that follows.

Displaying Any File

The next code is a significant expansion of the previous code, and it is all you need to print any file in existence. **$print_limit** sets the number of records to print, **$line_limit** sets the number of characters to print from a record, **$segment_length** defines the number of characters to print per line of output, **$current_record** is a record you could use to navigate through long files, and **$current_byte** is a field you could use to navigate long records. **get_html_translation_table( )** gets the table used in **htmlentities( )** so you can add extra entries and translate text manually with **strtr( )**, which gives you more control and the chance to translate spaces to ** **, a character that forces browsers to include a space when they might otherwise drop a space. The translation table goes into **$safe**, and the **while( )** loop adds extra entries for all characters from decimal 0 to decimal 32 (a space), so all the funny characters, like line breaks, will print as spaces instead of upsetting the HTML on the Web page. Each record goes into an array; each entry of the array goes into **$v**, is truncated to the **$line_limit**, and is split into segments; and each segment is printed on an individual line. **ord( )** converts individual characters to their decimal value, and **dechex( )** converts the decimal value to hexadecimal representation. Because some hexadecimal values lose their leading zero, a line of code adds the zero back, and a little loop adds spaces to the character representation of the segment so the segment will line up neatly in a column. The font specification forces fixed character spacing for the output so you can easily count through the characters on your screen:

```
$file = "./images/me.jpg";
$line_limit = 256;
$print_limit = 10;
$current_record = 0;
$segment_length = 16;
$safe = get_html_translation_table(HTML_ENTITIES);
```

8. Files

315

```
for($i = 0; $i <= 32; $i++)
    {
    $safe[chr($i)] = " ";
    }
$text = file($path . "/" . $file);
print("<br><em>File: " . $path . "/" . $file . "</em>" );
while(list($k, $v) = each($text) and $current_record <= $print_limit)
    {
    $current_record++;
    $current_byte = 1;
    print("<br><font face=\"'Courier New',Courier,monospace\">"
        . " Current record: " . \$current_record
        . ", current byte: " . $current_byte . "</font>" );
    $v = substr($v, 0, $line_limit);
    $current_byte += strlen($v);
    while(strlen($v))
        {
        $segment = substr($v, 0, $segment_length);
        $v = substr($v, $segment_length);
        $hs = "";
        for($i = 0; $i < strlen($segment); $i++)
            {
            $hex = dechex(ord($segment[$i]));
            if(strlen($hex) < 2)
                {
                $hex = "0" . $hex;
                }
            $hs .= $hex . " ";
            }
        while(strlen($segment) < $segment_length)
            {
            $segment .= " ";
            }
        print("<br><font face=\"'Courier New',Courier,monospace\">"
            . strtr($segment, $safe) . "  " . $hs . "</font>" );
        }
    }
```

You can modify the code to perform any task you need, including reading big files using **fgets( )** instead of **file( )**. If you want to print records 300 through 305, you can set **$print_limit** to 305, and add an equivalent statement to suppress printing prior to 300. Although PHP has a wide range of file functions, you need only a few to find data.

Creating Empty Files

It might seem strange to create an empty file, but it is a coding trick equivalent to creating an empty variable in a script. When you write a long script that randomly stores and reads a value, you usually define an empty variable for the value at the top of the script with a comment describing the variable's usage, and then let all the rest of your code assume the variable always exists. You can do the same with files—for example, all the files needed by a new user of your Web site. The new user might not have a list of favorites, but you can create an empty favorites file when you create the user's id, so there is no danger of a file allocation failure when the user logs in. An alternative is to create a script that creates all the default files the first time the user logs in, so every possible error occurs in one place and is out of the way with one support call.

The **touch( )** function accepts a file name and an optional date/time, and creates an empty file, or, if the file exists, just changes the date last modified and then returns true on success or false on failure. The optional date/time is a Unix timestamp, so you can set the date modified, as returned by **filemtime( )**. The default date/time is the current time, and you might use the default if you copy a set of default files for a new user and want to change the file dates to reflect the date the user was set up.

The following code changes the date/time on a file using **touch( )**:

```
$file = "./touchme.txt";
touch($file, strtotime ("+1 week"));
print("<br>File " . $file . " mtime: "
   . date("Y-m-d H:m:i", filemtime(\$file)));
touch($file);
print("<br>New mtime: " . date("Y-m-d H:m:i", filemtime(\$file)));
```

These two rows show the result using PHP 4.0.5 on a Windows NT system:

```
File ./touchme.txt mtime: 0
New mtime: 0
```

This line is the result on Linux with incorrect permissions for this function. If you do not have permission to access the file, you will get two errors, one for each **touch( )**. If you have permission to access the file, but not to change the file, you will get one error for the first **touch( )**, when you try to change the date/time:

```
Warning: utime failed: Operation not permitted
```

Uploading Files

This example starts with an extract of the code from Chapter 9's "Uploading Files" section. First check that your php.ini has **file_uploads** turned on; on Windows and Windows NT, you need to specify an **upload_tmp_dir** directory (and you must have access to it). Make sure that **upload_max_filesize** is larger than your largest file, and that **memory_limit** is at least twice as large as **upload_max_filesize**. Then, insert the HTML into a page that will ask the user for the file you want uploaded. In the HTML, **MAX_FILE_SIZE** must be at least as large as the file that will be uploaded:

```
file_uploads = On
upload_tmp_dir = T:\upload
upload_max_filesize = 8M
memory_limit = 30M
```

Insert the following code in your test page, here named uploadingfiles.html, set the **action=** form parameter to your page name, and then test the page. The **if( )** is to detect the **$uploadfile** field created by the upload; if the field does not exist, it shows the form, and when the field does exist, it displays the field contents. **$uploadfile** is the name set in the form **<input type="file">** tag and contains the name of the input file including the full path. **$uploadfile_name** contains the file name extracted from **$uploadfile**. **$uploadfile_size** contains the file size and is zero if the file upload fails. **$uploadfile_type** provides the MIME type of the file in case you want to perform special processing based on the file type:

```
if(isset($uploadfile))
    {
    print("<br>All set to upload a file." );
    print("<br>uploadfile: " . $uploadfile );
    print("<br>uploadfile_name: " . $uploadfile_name );
    print("<br>uploadfile_size: " . $uploadfile_size );
    print("<br>uploadfile_type: " . $uploadfile_type );
    }
else
    {
    print("<br>Please tell me which file I should upload." );
    print("<form enctype=\"multipart/form-data\""
        . " action=\"uploadingfiles.html\" method=\"post\">"
        . "<input type=\"hidden\" name=\"MAX_FILE_SIZE\""
        . " value=\"200000\">"
        . "<input type=\"file\" name=\"uploadfile\" size=\"60\">"
        . "<br><input type=\"submit\" value=\"Upload\"></form>" );
    }
```

When the form displays in your browser, you will get something like the form in Figure 8.12, taken from Netscape 4.76; most recent browsers handle the file upload in a similar manner, except browsers on Macs. One customer attempted to allow file uploads from Macs and received so many complaints about problems and errors that the file upload was removed from the site. Yes, you can get it working, but I strongly recommend you sit down in person at the Mac (or any other browser producing problems) and test everything yourself, rather than relying on other people's interpretations. For any file you upload, you should download the file to the same machine, or email the file back to the same machine, and compare the uploaded version to the original, to detect any modifications to the file.

TIP: *Macs have various compression routines active and no file extensions to indicate the format of a file; so, if you suspect a file is corrupt, try decompressing the file and compare the decompressed file to the original. Mac files may be zipped or, more likely, stuffed by Aladdin's StuffIt (**www.aladdinsys.com**).*

When your file uploads, you will get a display like the following four lines. php22.tmp is the temporary name assigned in the upload directory, and test.html is the original file name from the source computer. There is no way to find the original directory without resorting to unreliable JavaScript, and if you want to perform tricks, like spying on people by uploading files they did not select, you will have to use JavaScript so unreliable that it will get only files not worth uploading:

```
All set to upload a file.
uploadfile: T:\upload\php22.tmp
uploadfile_name: test.html
uploadfile_size: 183
uploadfile_type: text/html
```

When you try to upload a file that exceeds the size specified in the HTML **MAX_FILE_SIZE** (yes, some browsers or servers do need it in uppercase), you will see the following message:

```
Warning: Max file size exceeded - file [uploadfile] not saved
```

What do you do with the uploaded file? Insert the following code to save the file to a suitable directory for later use, or just open the temporary file to read the

Figure 8.12   File name form for file upload.

data into a database. **is_uploaded_file( )**, available in recent PHP releases, lets you check that the file is a valid uploaded file, and **move_uploaded_file( )** moves the file from the temporary directory to the permanent directory:

```
if(isset($uploadfile) and is_uploaded_file($uploadfile))
   {
   if(move_uploaded_file($uploadfile,
      $path . "/test/" . $uploadfile_name))
      {
      print("<br>Uploaded file saved." );
      }
   else
      {
      print("<br>Uploaded file save failed." );
      }
   }
```

NOTE: *move_uploaded_file()* *arrived in PHP 4.0.3.*

If you end up with hard-to-diagnose errors, the following two messages occur either because the target directory does not exist, or when the directory exists but has the wrong permissions:

```
Warning: Unable to create 'i:/petermoulding/web/root/phpblackbook/files/
   upload/test.html': No such file or directory
Warning: Unable to move 'T:\upload\php21.tmp' to
 'i:/petermoulding/web/root/phpblackbook/files/upload/test.html'
```

Another error to avoid is the incompatible file name error, caused by reading a file name, like "test file," on Windows and trying to write the same name on Unix systems, where spaces are not allowed in file names. You can also lose files when uploading the files TestFile and testfile from Unix, where the files are treated as two different ones (because, even though they have the same name, one is all lowercase and one contains caps), and then saving the files in Windows, Windows NT, or similar operating systems; the second file overwrites the first because the operating system, understanding case, assumes both files are the same.

If you try to upload a file that exceeds the HTML **MAX_FILE_SIZE**, you will get a network error at the browser, and the Web page script will not be invoked.

Calculating CRCs for Files

A good Cyclical Redundancy Check (CRC) lets you verify that a file is intact after transmission across a network, or compare two images that are otherwise difficult to compare, like two image files. The standard CRC32 produces a 32-bit identity that makes the chance of a mistake just 1 in 4 billion. This code example shows you how to create a standard PHP CRC32 and convert it to the more common integer and hexadecimal representations for comparison with CRCs generated on other systems, like the one that sent you the file you want to check. PHP uses a 32-bit signed integer with a range from minus 2 billion to plus 2 billion bits on most 32-bit based systems. The common CRC32 is expressed as an unsigned 32-bit integer with a range from 0 to 4 billion.

The following code looks at two files, **$a** and **$b**, finds and prints their sizes, and then finds and prints their CRCs. The files are different sizes, so you would not normally need to compare their CRCs, but just imagine both have the same size. The CRCs differentiate the two, and because of the way CRCs are calculated, the CRCs tend to accentuate small changes, so similar files produce wildly different CRCs:

```
$a = "/images/me.jpg";
$b = "/images/kingparrot.jpg";
$asize = filesize($path . $a);
$bsize = filesize($path . $b);
print("<br>Size a: " . $asize . ", b: " . $bsize);
$acrc = (double) crc32($path . $a);
$bcrc = (double) crc32($path . $b);
print("<br>CRC a: " . $acrc . ", b: " . $bcrc);
```

This code results in:

```
Size a: 6530, b: 60810
CRC a: 199407017, b: -40759560
```

The CRC produced here is fine for comparison between two files on the same system, but when you look at CRCs from another system, you will see unsigned 32-bit integers; so the next slice of code converts the CRCs to unsigned 32-bit notation. First, you need the value of 4 billion, and the easiest way I can remember to calculate that is to multiply 8 bits out four times. Hence the first line negative CRCs are subtracted from 4 billion to give the final result:

```
$thirtytwo = (double) 256 * 256 * 256 * 256;
print("<br>Thirtytwo: " . $thirtytwo);
if(\$acrc < 0)
```

```
    {
    $acrc = (double) $thirtytwo + $acrc;
    }
if($bcrc < 0)
    {
    $bcrc = (double) $thirtytwo + $bcrc;
    }
print("<br>CRC (unsigned) a: " . $acrc . ", b: " . $bcrc);
```

The result is:

```
Thirtytwo: 4294967296
CRC (unsigned) a: 199407017, b: 4254207736
```

The next slice of code converts the unsigned number to hexadecimal. Where the number loses a leading zero, the **if( )** code adds a leading zero:

```
$acrc = dechex($acrc);
$bcrc = dechex($bcrc);
if(strlen($acrc) < 8)
    {
    $acrc = "0" . $acrc;
    }
if(strlen($bcrc) < 8)
    {
    $bcrc = "0" . $bcrc;
    }
print("<br>CRC (hex) a: " . $acrc . ", b: " . $bcrc );
```

The result is:

```
CRC (hex) a: 0be2b5a9, b: fd920ef8
```

Chapter 9

Forms

In Depth

In PHP, forms are easy to create, and PHP arrays help you add long lists to forms. PHP's easy presentation of variables from cookies, URL queries, and **GET**- and **POST**-based forms means you can quickly move to multiple-page forms and specialized form features, such as file uploads. The forms' controls can also be used for things not associated with traditional forms, such as the alternative navigation mentioned in the next section. You can also use form submit buttons as an alternative to images and links for navigation.

Throughout this chapter, I will emphasize ways of creating questions in forms so you can quickly and easily deploy forms without having to rewrite code. The reusable form and question functions you will build in the "Immediate Solutions" section let you add questions and modify formatting without touching the code. After you work through Chapters 5 and 20, you might want to switch the input of the form functions to a database or an XML file. The database approach suits rapidly changing sites.

Alternative Navigation

The usual way to link pages is to use the anchor tag, **<a>**. The anchor tag passes variables via a URL, but URLs can get messy quickly when you load them up with variables. Forms can pass values by the cleaner-looking **POST** method, and **POST** works with both large values and long lists of values. (In fact, I have had a form **POST** pass 49,000 file names from one page to another.)

In forms, the <**form**> tag replaces the anchor <**a**> tag, <**input**> tags replace individual entries from the URL query string, and the form submit button replaces the text you place between the anchor start and end tags. The following example shows a standard link to a preformed query, followed by the same link accessed through a form. The query has a facility to exclude documents already viewed; in the first example, each excluded document is named via a field such as **exclude01**, whereas the example using the form uses a field named **example[]**, something that produces a simple array in PHP. By the time the searcher has viewed dozens of documents, the first form of this link will produce errors in most browsers, but the second form will handle far more document names than I could browse in one session:

```
$link = "<a href=\"query.html?"
    . "sortby=date&sortorder=descending&country=Suriname"
    . "&type=document&author=cia
    . "$exclude01=d1991122&exclude02=d3010304"
    . "&find=tropical+rain+forest+conservation">Find</a>

$link = "<form action=\"query.html\" method=\"post\">"
    . "<input type=\"hidden\" name=\"sortby\" value=\"date\">"
    . "<input type=\"hidden\" name=\"sortorder\" value=\"descending\">"
    . "<input type=\"hidden\" name=\"country\" value=\"Suriname\">"
    . "<input type=\"hidden\" name=\"type\" value=\"document\">"
    . "<input type=\"hidden\" name=\"author\" value=\"cia\">"
    . "<input type=\"hidden\" name=\"exclude[]\" value=\"d1991122\">"
    . "<input type=\"hidden\" name=\"exclude[]\" value=\"d3010304\">"
    . "<input type=\"hidden\" name=\"find\" value=\""
      . "tropical rain forest conservation\">"
    . "<input type=\"submit\" value=\"Find\">"
    . "</form>";
```

HTML or Pure PHP?

PHP mixes well with HTML, but the code becomes hard to read, and you lose the power of PHP every time you revert to HTML. You gain power and flexibility by building the whole form, every tag and every parameter, in pure PHP code. The scripts in this chapter generate every item in every HTML tag, so you have absolute control of content and format.

As browsers move to provide better support for Cascading Style Sheets (CSS), you can reduce the direct formatting of page content, but remember to first carefully assess your market before replacing the old **<font>** tags with something new. I once helped a marketing agency prepare a submission to the top boss in a very big company. The boss watched the presentation, picked up the agency's list of reference sites, and then went home to enjoy dinner with his children. Late that night, he used his children's old PC and slow modem to try out the agency's reference sites, and found that some sites were unreadable. The agency lost that sale.

Solving the problems of speed and compatibility is extra important for your site's registration form, the first form prospective customers see and use. Some sites lose thousands of customers because their registration form does not work in all browsers. Given the poor logging, reporting, and analysis used at many sites, companies never know how many customers they lose or why they lose them. When creating the initial registration form, inquiry forms, feedback forms, and problem-reporting forms, make absolutely certain the forms are easy to use and rock-solid reliable in every browser.

Your biggest fight might be with your marketing department to keep embarrassing, intrusive questions, distracting graphics, and convoluted text off your form. For some reason, some people feel free to ask questions online that customers would rarely answer on a printed form. Further, the form developers might make the answer compulsory and then wonder why people do not fill out the form.

Navigation through an online form is also affected by the speed at which you can change the pages; if you cannot make quick changes, the pages can become useless and misleading. You will find managers and marketing people requesting immediate changes about 10 minutes after the testing team has gone home; those changes might involve something as simple as removing a special price offer because the company has run out of stock, or as important as removing a page that is illegal and attracting fines of thousands of dollars per day. A couple of years ago, I was waiting at an elevator to go home, when I heard a shriek and went to investigate. The brilliant young marketing manager of a rapidly expanding online shopping site looked like he was about to have cardiac arrest, because their brand new product line, cigarettes, was displayed without the correct legal warnings. Luckily I had designed the Web site to accommodate quick changes and had the problem fixed before the elevator arrived.

One thing the code in this chapter will give you is consistency. The more consistent you make the format and layout of your questions and forms, the easier it will be for your customers to fill out the subsequent forms on your site. Consistency will help in the long run; and it is a good reason to use PHP code to generate everything, so that there are no stray HTML oddities.

Some of the code in this chapter handles multiple choice questions. Whenever you have multiple choice questions, consider providing an option for a free-form text entry as an alternative. For example, when some American sites made their first attempts to sell overseas, order forms demanded an address, but their state selection lists accepted only American states; so 5.6 billion of the 5.9 billion people on this planet could not enter a valid address. Now, most sites are better, and offer the option to list a different state, no state at all, a zip code not restricted to five digits, no zip code at all, and phone numbers with long dialing prefixes. Thankfully, in this wonderful age of email, fax numbers are no longer a required answer.

Minimum HTML

HTML forms require:

- A start tag, **<form>**
- Some sort of data tag, such as **<input>**
- An action tag, such as **<input type="submit">**
- An end tag, **</form>**

You can place these tags within page layout structures, like table cells, or wrap the **<form>** tag around a whole table and place individual **<input>** tags in individual cells, as in the following example:

```
<form action="page.html" method="post">
<input type="text" name="anything">
<input type="submit" name="doit">
</form>
```

In many browsers, the **<form>** tag will have annoying effects on spacing. The start of a form will, in some browsers, insert a break similar to the way tables insert a break. The end of a form can also insert a break or space.

Forms can include other formatting elements, such as a table to control the layout of individual elements in the form. You also can include paragraphs and a wide range of HTML formatting. There are rules about what can go inside a form and what can be wrapped around a form. Most browsers break these rules—some insert breaks where there should not be breaks, some ignore the more complex formatting options, some accept badly formed HTML—so take a conservative stance and use the minimum HTML required to lay out the form in a logical and readable manner. Test using several browsers, as your favorite browser may accept mistakes that destroy a page when viewed from other browsers.

You will have problems if you end a form at a different HTML tag level from that which starts the form. For example, if you start a form outside a table and then end the form inside a table cell, some browsers will be confused. You should make your structure uniform and symmetrical. I usually create **<input>**, then wrap it in **<td>** and **</td>** tags, then wrap that in **<tr>** and **</tr>** tags, then wrap that in table tags, and then wrap that in form tags. If I need to position the form in part of a page, I will then wrap a separate outer table around the form.

You can facilitate the neat nesting and symmetrical layout of forms and tables by making each layer a function, and then nesting the functions. I test sites with dozens of browsers and browser releases; and every browser on my top 30 list handles forms reliably when the form elements are laid out at matching levels in relation to other HTML tags. Creating forms with nested PHP functions is far more reliable than with Dreamweaver and other expensive page layout programs.

Bells and Whistles

HTML does not have a **<bell>** tag, and PHP does not have a **whistle( )** function. You need to consider carefully the level of complexity you add to a form to make the form conform to your marketing department's ideal look. PHP lets you build a form using simple functions, arrays, and complex objects. What you want is the simplest way of changing the form look when your testers report all the problems with forms.

A good approach is to separate formatting, sequence, and data so that you can change the sequence of the questions without changing the formatting, and so anyone can change the wording of a question without requiring you to edit the page. You can store the question sequence in an array and step through the array, as outlined in the next code example. (Chapter 3 covers all the details of using lists in arrays.) The sequence of the questions can be changed by simply moving the array entries up and down the list:

```
$question[] = "name";
$question[] = "address";
$question[] = "city";
$question[] = "country";
while(list($k, $v) = each($question))    {
    print("<br>The question is: " . $v);
    }
```

TIP: *You could use a **for()** loop in the above code, but the **while(each())** loop has a stack of advantages, including returning the correct next entry from an array even when you are inserting or deleting entries in the array from within the loop.*

If you have more complex names, you might find it easier to identify items by their entry numbers. When you are processing a list, you can use the index number of the item to find it again in the array. Consider the following list of items to go into a form:

```
$fruit[] = "Akee";
$fruit[] = "Black Sapote";
$fruit[] = "Durian";
$fruit[] = "Guaraná";
$fruit[] = "Otaheite Gooseberry";
```

Guaraná is a potent source of caffeine, and has an accent character to confuse people trying to type the name into a text box or code. You want this type of name in a selection list, so you don't have to process the characters. When you convert this list to a selection item, use the list entry number as the identifier.

Use PHP array processing to loop through the array list. First, reset the array to the start, and then use **while( )**, **list( )**, and **each( )** to process each entry. I'll give you plenty of examples in the "Immediate Solutions" section. The main aim is to avoid using an individual name as an identifier by processing each list as a whole and avoiding code that needs to identify an individual element.

Incidentally, PHP arrays are case-sensitive, so **$fruit["Apple"]** is different from **$fruit["apple"]**. Be careful mixing the names you use for display and the names you use for identification. I like this code trick to remove spaces from display names and convert everything to lowercase:

```
$display_name = "Macadamia nuts";
$id = strtolower(str_replace(" ", "", $display_name));
```

For ideas about changing the text on a page based on language, look in Chapters 12 and 20 to see how to input the text in a structured format. Both chapters offer ways you can use comprehensive lists of text edited by other people, techniques that can be used for your form questions. By divorcing the sequence and formatting from the content of the questions, you can concentrate on page construction and other issues, like the types of question you ask.

Form Questions

HTML gives you a variety of ways to ask questions and receive the answers, from simple checkboxes and radio buttons to extensive selection lists. You want a question that is easy for the user to understand and limits the user's answers to valid responses. You can mix types of questions, so you might give users three choices with radio buttons and then provide a text field where they can type comments if they need to.

Here, for example, are some mistakes common to forms on American Web sites of companies attempting to enter the Asian and Pacific market:

- Providing a fixed selection list of states without an option to enter Australian states
- Demanding the entry of a state without realizing many countries do not have an equivalent to American states
- Assuming every country has a postal code
- Assuming the postal code is a five-digit zip code

Every country has its own unique aspects that make form design interesting on international sites.

Yes/No Questions

The following types of questions suit HTML radio-style buttons:

- Do you eat fish? Yes/No
- Do you eat dairy products? Yes/No
- Would you like a window seat? Yes/No

Radio buttons are best used for any question in which you want only one answer out of multiple selections. In the browser, the question appears as shown in Figure 9.1. The answer appears as shown in Figure 9.2.

What is happening in the HTML and PHP code? The HTML is:

```
<form action="radiobutton.html" method="post">
Do you eat fish?   Yes
<input type="radio" name="fish" value="yes" checked>
   No<input type="radio" name="fish" value="no">
   <input type="submit" value="Test">
</form>
```

Note that the two radio buttons both have the name **fish**, and both have values assigned. The default value, which is **yes** in this case, is marked **checked**. PHP returns the selected value in a field named **fish** and, in the example, the value was displayed with the following code. Note the test for the existence of **fish**, **if(isset($fish))**, something important to remember when form pages link back to themselves to display results or errors. Add comments at the top of the page that explain what is displayed on first entry, what is displayed when an error occurs, and where the visitor will end up after clicking submit:

```
if(isset($fish))    {
   print("The value of \$fish is " . $fish);
   }
```

In a question, you can present as many answer choices as you like, so long as all choices have the same name. If you leave out the **name** field, some browsers will use the name of the previous radio button, but I would not trust all browsers to do the same.

If you leave out the **value** field, PHP returns the value **on**. You could give each selection a different name and search for the field with the value **on**, but that is generally the hard way to code a multiple-choice question. To illustrate this difficulty, the next code chunk contains two lines from the fish question example,

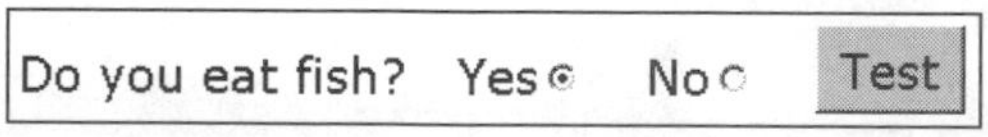

Do you eat fish?   Yes⦿   No○   Test

Figure 9.1   Yes/No question using radio buttons.

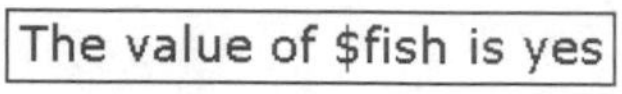

The value of $fish is yes

Figure 9.2   Answer from a Yes/No question.

with the first **<input>** tag given a name of **fishyes** and the second a name of **fishno**, to let you test for the presence of either field. This approach looks the easiest when each question has a small number of answers, but becomes hard to manage when a question has many answers:

```
<input type="radio" name="fishyes" value="yes" checked>
   No<input type="radio" name="fishno" value="no">
```

Make the **name** field different for each question and make sure the name does not conflict with any other PHP variable. You might find the best technique is to use the question sequence number, **$k**, as used in the example of sequencing in the **fish** example, and build the name using a common prefix, like *question* in the following code example. The fields returned to you from the form will be named **question0**, **question1**, **question2**, and so on:

```
$question = "<input type=\"radio\""
  . " name=\"question" . $k . "\""
  . " value=\"yes\" checked>";
```

One or Many Answers of Many

Many questions can have one answer, many answers, or no answer at all, questions that suit a HTML **<select>** tag. The **<select>** tag lets you choose one answer, and has an option to let you select multiple answers, although multiple selections may not work on every browser or operating system. Here are some example questions and the code, which results in the list shown in Figure 9.3:

- What are your favorite fruits?
- What should you pack when you travel to Sydney?
- Select your favorite Coopers beer.

```
print("<form action=\"query.html\" method=\"post\">"
  . "<select name=\"favorite\"><option>Sparkling Ale</option>"
  . "<option>Pale Ale</option><option>Dark Ale</option>"
  . "<option>Stout</option><option>Premium Ale</option>"
  . "<option>Vintage Ale</option><option>Old Stout</option>"
  . "<option>Special Old Stout</option>"
  . "<option>Genuine Draught</option>"
  . "<option>Light</option><option>DB</option></select></form>");
```

Consider a situation in which a customer cannot answer a question. I like the software companies that demand that you register a product before you can use

Figure 9.3   Select your favorite beer using <select>.

it, and then, when you're in the middle of the registration page, ask you for comments about their product. Surely the only honest answer would be:

```
So far, your product has cost me time and not produced anything
  useful!
```

The same problem happens when a shop sells you a stroller and asks how many children you have. Perhaps you are still in the planning phase or just like to pamper your dog.

Zero is a valid response. Let people skip the questions they cannot answer, capture the other answers to disk, and then consider how to ask the problem questions the next time the person visits your site.

When you get the results back from a form, you will receive a number of variables set with a yes/no answer or receive an array containing the list of items selected. It is up to you to choose exactly what you want in order to suit your programming style. I usually select a list approach, so I can easily add new items.

Consider a form that asks:

• Do you like bananas?

• Do you like oranges?

• Do you like apples?

The question list quickly becomes boring, so you change the format to have the "Do you like" question appear as a heading rather than a simple list of fruit. In your PHP code, you could have the form return **$bananas** containing true or false, then **$oranges** containing true or false, and so on. I prefer to have a list in an array, containing the fruits that go in the question's list, than to receive a simple list of selected fruit in another array. Anyone can add another item of fruit without requiring me to change even one line of code.

In the "Immediate Solutions" section of this chapter, you'll find code to let your customers select either one item or many items from a list. Look through the examples to see the exact style of question you want, and then try out the code.

Multiple Actions

A form ends with a submit button and a reset or cancel button, so that your customer can tell you, "Go ahead, bill me," or "Throw the order away." You are not restricted to just two options; you can present multiple actions, as shown in Figure 9.4.

In your PHP code, it is easy to handle multiple actions because you receive a different field from each submit button. If the Recalculate Fare button is named **recalc** and the others **book** and **save** respectively, your script will receive back either variable **$recalc**, **$book**, or **$save**, and can use code such as **if(isset($recalc))** to decide on an appropriate action.

The first HTML tag in a form is **<form>**, which contains **action="_page_name_"**, where **_page_name_** is the name of the page to be requested by the browser when the user clicks on a submit button or a reset button. The browser decides what to request, and then sends the request to the server. You choose which page and therefore which script the browser requests by placing the page name in the action parameter.

Do you want to send the user back to the same page or on to a new page? If you send the user back to the same page and perform your processing at the head of the page, you can then easily display the same page and form again, complete with error messages and requests for additional information. If you direct the user to another page, you have options, such as performing all the form data processing in a hidden page that displays nothing and then issues redirection headers to send the user's browser to the right page.

Sometimes you may want to direct people to more than one page, and you can do that by placing more than one form on a page. Consider a page containing only the three buttons shown in Figure 9.4; each button could be the submit button for a completely different form, each with a unique set of questions and actions. The Book The Trip button could point to a page on a secure server at your bank, Save For Later could point to a page that updates the customer's profile, and Recalculate Fare could simply jump back to the current page with a new fare calculation.

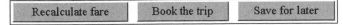

Figure 9.4   Multiple submit buttons.

The only problem with multiple forms is the lack of data coordination. You cannot collect data in the first form on the page if the user clicks the submit button for the second form on the page. To use multiple forms, you need to collect all the data first, and then have the separate select forms on a unique page.

JavaScript

Often, inexperienced developers using JavaScript for the first time plunge in with drop-down selection lists and complicated data verification. Inevitably, the site owners then pay me a lot of money to remove the very same JavaScript. Why? I'm paid to fix the forms because they do not work in some browsers and, even when they appear to work, the sites' databases end up full of invalid data. My tasks are to both make the forms work in more browsers and keep the useless data out of the databases. To accomplish this, I follow certain steps.

Removing Fancy Drop-Down Menus

Step one requires you to remove fancy JavaScript drop-down menus. The standard HTML **<select>** tag provides a drop-down menu that is not only easy to build in PHP, but is also one everyone understands. Anything more complicated will confuse some people, and you will either receive data entered into the wrong field, or find that the data is completely missing. A common symptom is a half-empty page because a click on a JavaScript controlled field in the middle of the page destroyed a series of unrelated fields.

Validating Fields at the Server

Step two requires that you validate every field at the server. No matter how good you make your JavaScript, people will get around the JavaScript and send you incorrect data. One trick is to make a copy of a page, change the JavaScript in the copy, and then have the copy reply from the browser. Many sites use incomplete and badly formed JavaScript that works only in Microsoft Internet Explorer, produces an error message in such browsers as Opera, and lets the person using the browser decide if the script will continue or stop. You can end up with data that was only partly verified by your script or completely manufactured by someone else's script, so you have to check everything, particularly prices and totals, in your PHP code. If you are checking a field at the server using PHP, then you do not save much time by checking the field in the browser with JavaScript.

TIP: *If you are hacking a JavaScript or cookie-based shopping cart, changing the total from $5,000 to $1,000 might work, but not to $10—someone always notices that.*

On one of your projects, someone will insist on using JavaScript to reject pages when compulsory fields are not filled in. If you stop prospective customers from returning the form, they might leave your site, never to return. By bringing the form back to the server and validating it at the server, you can record which fields people aren't answering, and feed that information back to the form designers.

Long Forms

Multiple-page forms are annoying if there is no real incentive to fill out the form. On a paper form, you spot the section headed "For People with Diabetes" and skip the section (or answer it) based on your need. The equivalent online is to ask the general question (Do you have diabetes?) in the first page, and then schedule or skip a page containing all the questions for people with diabetes.

The 2000 American Presidential election problem in Florida showed how easy it can be to confuse people using forms. Online, the problem is greater because it is hard for people to flip back and forth and compare sections of a form. Therefore, you must use common layout across pages to provide visual clues about each question and the type of answer required. The following sections offer you insights about how best to deal with multiple-page forms.

A good solution to long forms is to have one formatting function for all questions across all forms on your site. After a new visitor fills out one page of one form, he or she will be ready to tackle all the pages. By isolating the formatting from the questions, you can more easily rearrange the sequence of questions and the breaks between pages.

Breaking Up Long Forms

Plenty of shopping sites offer examples of overly long forms, registration pages, surveys, and competition entry forms, and the forms turn away prospective customers. The sites should break up the long forms in to related groups, offer an item of value with each group, and then place each group on a separate page.

Consider a food shopping site that wants customers to accept a weekly email and that wants to know the shopper's age, income, and sex. Some people will fill out such a form, many will simply leave the site and shop elsewhere, and many others will do what I do—click on grossly inaccurate answers to offensive and irrelevant questions. I always click No for email, because so many marketing people send out time-wasting, useless email; an age that is the highest or lowest option presented; and an income bracket that is something totally inaccurate for an impoverished author. Occasionally the question about sex will let me click Other.

What if you put the email question on a separate page and included a sample email? The email could be made interesting and useful by including a recipe or the like; the reader could then click a positive answer to the question "Would you like to receive email like this?"

Instead of asking a person's age directly, send them to a page that lists age-related features of your site, and then ask for their age and answers to other personal questions. For example, you could include pictures of smiling babies on a page that bragged about your unique range of baby foods, and then insert the question "To help us help you with your children, please tell us…" and ask for the ages of everyone in the family.

Try for one topic per page, a quick enticement to answer the question, the question, and then the supporting material. (It does not matter if the supporting material flows off the bottom of the screen.) It is better to get an accurate answer to one question than inaccurate answers to many questions.

Carrying Information from Page to Page

When you have multiple-page forms, you can carry information from one page to another via hidden fields, cookies, or session records. A typical strategy is to ask for a person's first name on the first page, and then display their name at the top of subsequent pages so the pages become more personal. A hidden field is the simplest way to carry the name, and a session record, if they have a session, is the best place to carry it, because the session record makes it available to every page in the Web site.

Using Hidden Fields

Hidden fields, **<input type="hidden">**, are easy to use for things like long lists; however, they do not work when a person filling out a form decides to leave the form halfway through and then tries to return to continue with the form later. Cookies can help in this regard, but they also have limitations.

Setting Cookies for Every Page

When you ask a user to fill out a multiple-page form, the values entered in the first page could be placed straight into a database or carried to the second page in hidden fields. If you are updating a customer's profile, you could enter every page of information into their profile immediately, and nothing would carry over from one page to another. In contrast, when you are collecting information to create a new profile, you might not want to save anything until the customer clicks on an agreement at the end of the last page.

For the new profile, you can carry variables from page to page with hidden fields, but adding new pages in the middle of a multiple page form means adding new hidden fields all the way through the subsequent pages, which can be boring and prone to cause mistakes. Cookies can be easier because you can throw anything in a cookie and set a new one for each page. Only the last script in a sequence has to look at each cookie. Cookies also have the advantage that they can stay on your customer's computer overnight and let the customer continue filling out the same form the next day.

The problem with cookies comes when you have built several pages of a long form. You run into a limitation of cookies and are forced to completely rethink your design. Each browser follows different rules for cookies, so this is just a guide. The cookie specifications say you can have only 20 cookies per domain, which precludes a 21-page form with one cookie per page. Cookies also have a maximum size of 4KB, so you cannot accumulate all the information from a long form in one cookie.

You will also run into problems if your customers have cookies turned off, have the browser set to forget cookies at the end of a session, or use software to clean out cookies each day. Cookies fail when the customer starts filling out a form on one computer at work and then tries to complete the form on his or her home computer. Because of this, you can see that the limitations of cookies mean that they should only be used to store a session ID so you can maintain active sessions.

Sessions are explained in Chapter 19, but here is a quick check of what you need (based on PHP 4.0.5). In php.ini, you need **use_cookies** turned on to use cookies (when available), **use_trans_sid** to automatically place the session ID in URLs when cookies are not available, and **rewriter.tags** set to the list of HTML tag parameters that can carry URLs. This is enough to get you started on a test site:

```
session.use_cookies = 1
session.use_trans_sid = 1
url_rewriter.tags =
   "a=href,area=href,frame=src,input=src,form=fakeentry"
```

Using Session Records

Session records can have unlimited size and unlimited entries. They are stored in a text field in a modern database, and they have a size limit of four billion characters, which means a form can be longer than my attention span and beyond my typing capabilities. If a session record is stored in a discrete file in a modern operating system, the record can be many terabytes. One session record could store all the text from every form filled out by every human on this planet. Using a cookie to store a session ID and a session record to store all other information is the ideal approach for page to page communication within a Web site.

The problem with session records, though, is their temporary nature. Session records disappear when you exit the browser, time out when you go to lunch, and depend on something, like a cookie or URL, to carry the session ID from page to page. You cannot easily reconnect to sessions, as any easy method would be a security risk; it would let people pirate your session; therefore, users cannot bookmark a page within a session, and then start up at the same place next day.

9. Forms

To allow people to reconnect to the same session the next day, you need a logon/logoff system that uses something like a userid and a password. You need to save all their session information in a user profile and then, the next day, create a new session populated with all the details from their profile. In theory, you could use the same session ID again, but that would let me pirate your session.

TIP: *How to pirate sessions on poorly coded sites: As soon as your coworker goes home, browse their cookie file (cookies.txt in Netscape), to find the name of a site and the related session ID. Turn off cookies in their browser to force the site to use URLs, log on to the same site using any other logon, and then cut and paste your coworker's session ID into your URL. Their session will remain in the server's file from 20 minutes to several hours, so you usually have plenty of time.*

Designing Good Long Forms

My retention span is two pages. In other words, I can remember what I typed on page one when I am typing page two, but not when I am typing page three. I try to use this span as a guide and consider possible retention spans of others as I design forms. If I have to set up a user profile or similar form, I aim to get the form user to provide his or her identification on the first page and use that as the base for subsequent pages.

Grab the Minimum First

If you cannot accept a visitor as a new customer until he or she has filled out a huge form, you will lose potential customers. I recommend getting the customer's name and email address and issuing this person's logon on the first page. Leave the marketing questions until later.

Design the form and the supporting code so you can save the essential email address before upsetting the visitor with intrusive questions or boring them with too many pages of questions. Design the site so they can leave halfway through the registration process and return later, though their login.

Make Marketing Pay for Its Intrusion

If your marketing manger wants to know a customer's age, get the marketing manager to provide an incentive or a prize of some sort. Capture the minimum contact information on the registration page, issue the customer's logon information, and then ask the other questions only after the customer has logged on. I have no idea why a site selling office stationery asks me if I am male or female—do they ship blue pens to men and only allow women to buy red pens?

If your site is not selling liquor, cigarettes, or pornography (or whatever else your government restricts by age), you do not need a person's age to let them shop. The question about age can be presented as a special bonus question, for example, and can be accompanied by an incentive, like a free product in their next delivery. You get their age and they get an incentive to buy something to get the free product—incentives to buy are always good business.

The same applies to questions about income and sex. Let your users register even if they do not answer the questions, and give them an incentive to answer. To obtain truthful answers, make sure the incentive does not induce a bias. If the incentive for young people was a DVD of the Xfiles and the incentive for elderly people was the DVD of the movie *Moulin Rouge*, I would give my age as 95!

Give Feedback

Once you have something you can use to identify the person filling out the form, place that information somewhere near the top of the page to remind the user that he or she is logged on. As you capture each section of the form, give the user feedback, something like Amazon's checkout screens, that list the steps completed and the steps yet to come on each page. A common problem with less well-designed forms is finding customers who are registered several times because they have either forgotten that they are already registered or they think their registration has failed.

You could easily keep an array listing the user's name and the form sections completed, and then place this information in one corner of the form. I sometimes make the whole form based on an array similar to this one:

```
$elements[] = array("name" => "firstname", "length" => 60,
    "question" => "First name", "complete" => false);
$elements[] = array("name" => "lastname", "length" => 60,
    "question" => "Family name", "complete" => false);
$elements[] = array("name" => "address", "length" => 60,
    "question" => "Address", "complete" => false);
```

I can cycle through the elements of the array building the form, set a limit of 10 questions per page, and mark each question as complete as the information is collected. If there is an error in a field, I can add an error element to that field's entry in the array. In the page handling the form, I can register the array once as a session variable, and then at the end of the processing, I can cycle through the array, saving things to a database. Other refinements you can include might involve adding an "always show" element to indicate files, like the customer's name, that you repeat on every page.

The Difference between Unasked and Unanswered

Once the data is in a database, you can use the database's facility to mark fields as empty, unknown, or null. In MySQL, you can have a string field return an empty string or null string, depending on a setting in the field definition (see Chapter 5 for details). You can apply this to questions such as "list your hobbies," and translate

MySQL's **null** to a PHP **false** to indicate the hobby field has never been asked, and should be presented to the customer the next time he reads his profile. Also, you can translate MySQL's empty string to PHP's "" to indicate that the hobby question has been asked but has not yet been answered. If it is too hard to distinguish **null/false** and "", as it is in some databases and was in PHP3, set up a separate field to indicate that the question was asked. You could even use a date to indicate when the question was asked and ask the question again every year.

Uploading Files

Forms can also let you upload files from your workstation to the Web server. There are a few small differences between upload forms and standard forms. In addition, the two types of forms act differently and display different things across browsers and operating systems. PHP makes the server processing easier, but does not help you explain to users how to use the upload facility in their browsers on their operating systems.

The first thing you need for an upload is a form tag with the **enctype** parameter set. Copy the example here or grab your *HTML Black Book* (The Coriolis Group, Inc., 2000) to read all the fine print about **enctype**. The form tag looks like this:

```
<form enctype="multipart/form-data"
action="apage.html" method=\"post\" >"

<input type="hidden" name="MAX_FILE_SIZE" value="200000">
```

You will need a text box to accept the file name, and HTML offers a special file name text box with a file selection facility, using type **file**. In this tag, **size** is the size of the file name text box, not the size of the file. It looks like this:

```
<input type="file" name="uploadfile" size="60">
```

Now you will finish with a standard submit tag and end of form tag, as follows:

```
<input type="submit" value="Upload"></form>
```

PHP has an options file named php.ini, which contains several parameters that will limit what your form can upload. You need **file_uploads** on, **upload_tmp_dir** pointing to a suitable directory, and **upload_max_filesize** set to a size at least as large as the largest file you want to upload. Some file operations are limited by the memory allocated to PHP, so set PHP's **memory_limit** to a value greater than **upload_max_filesize**. To do this, you might enter:

```
file_uploads = On
upload_tmp_dir = T:\upload
upload_max_filesize = 8M
memory_limit = 30M
```

file_uploads lets PHP process file uploads. Some people think it can be a security risk, and some consider it an unacceptable resource usage. Whatever you decide to do, you should limit file uploads to people who have logged on in some way so you can contact them about inappropriate uploads. Imagine the problems if your Web server is flooded with files containing pornographic images or a pirated Nirvana song.

When someone uploads a file, the file goes into the temporary directory named in **upload_tmp_dir** so you can check the file before moving it to somewhere secure. Make sure the temporary directory has plenty of space to allow for many parallel uploads, and is a directory that is cleaned out each night so your server is not swamped with old uploads.

The **upload_max_filesize** entry is an attempt to limit what is uploaded by limiting the size of individual files; but people can upload multi-gigabyte pirated movies using many files of a few thousand bytes each, and then reassemble them via readily available automated software. Limiting file size does not stop the nastier misuses of your server.

The **memory_limit** entry applies to PHP and limits the memory PHP will use. When you increase PHP's **memory_limit**, you may crash into a roadblock created by the Web server or operating system, so check their settings for memory size limits. If your script generates huge variables or arrays, increase **memory_limit** to at least double the size you will think you need. The largest image on my workstation is a 95MB landscape image. I also have PHP-based image management software that reads pairs of images for comparison. That 0.15MB script would need 191MB to compare two of my landscapes.

When your file arrives on the Web server, the name of the file will be in variables named after the **name** parameter in the **<input type="file">** tag. In the example, the **name** parameter contains **uploadfile**, so the uploaded file will be named in **$uploadfile**. **$uploadfile** contains the full path and file name needed for **copy( )** and other file functions so you can process the file. **$uploadfile_name** will contain the name of the file as supplied by the browser, **$uploadfile_size** will contain the size of the file, and **$uploadfile_type** will contain the file MIME type if the browser provided that information.

9. Forms

The file arrives at the server in a temporary directory, so you must copy the file to a safe spot if you want to keep the file. PHP 4.0.4 and later provides a special **move( )** function. In older versions of PHP, you can perform a copy, and then an unlink.

When you reach this point and still have problems with file uploads, the problems are usually a result of operating system permissions or browser or file-type problems. If you get file-type errors, print the **_type** field to see what the browser thinks the file is.

Access errors occur when the Web server operating system restricts your access to the directory that receives the uploaded file, reducing you to the level of having to beg and bribe the system administrator for access. Look at **upload_tmp_dir**, and then experiment with manual copies from the **tmp** directory to your target directory.

If all else fails and you cannot work out what PHP is doing with the file, run the page shown next to see every Apache parameter the way Apache sees them and PHP option the way PHP sees them:

```
<?php phpinfo(); ?>
```

Immediate Solutions

Creating a Form

Here is a basic form, in HTML, that asks your name and then links back to a page named createaform.html:

```
<form action="createaform.html" method="post">
Please enter your name:
<input type="text" name="name">
<input type="submit" name="submit" value="Submit">
</form>
```

Here is basic PHP code to build the form:

```
print("<form action=\"createaform.html\" method=\"post\">"
    . "Please enter your name:"
    . "<input type=\"text\" name=\"name\">"
    . "<input type=\"submit\" name=\"submit\" value=\"Submit\">"
    . "</form>");
```

Figure 9.5 shows the result in a browser.

In the createaform.html page, the data typed in by the user will be placed in a variable called **$name**. PHP grabs all the fields from forms, via **POST** or **GET**, and places the values in fields named by the **name** parameter in the HTML **<input>** tag. Here is the code to access the data in the createaform.html page:

```
if(isset($name)) {print("Your name is: " . $name);}
```

Figure 9.5   A basic form with one question and a Submit button.

Creating a Form Using Functions

The code shown in the "Creating a Form" section is hard to change when you have large forms, so a good remedy might be to split the code into a small number of functions and separate questions from the form. Here is basic PHP code to build the form tags, including questions entered as a string of text, via a function named **form( )**:

```
function form($page, $text)
   {
   return("<form action=\"" . $page . "\" method=\"post\">"
      . $text
      . "<input type=\"submit\" name=\"submit\""
      . " value=\"Submit\">"
      . "</form>");
   }
```

Function **form( )** accepts the name of the target page as the first parameter, and a string containing all the questions to go in the form. The form method defaults to **post**, because that is the best way to build forms. Every form requires a submit button, the **<input>** tag with the type of submit, so I included one hard-coded into **form( )**. You might also add a reset button.

Next is basic code to build a question using text input. The function needs a name for the question, the text of the question, and an optional default answer:

```
function form_text($name, $question, $default="")
   {
   if(strlen($default))
      {
      $default = " value=\"" . $default . "\"";
      }
   return($question . "  "
      . "<input type=\"text\" name=\"" . $name . "\""
      . $default . ">");
   }
```

The **<input>** tags can have a default value to prompt the person filling out the form. In **form_text( )**, the **if(strlen($default))** line checks for text in the default field before wrapping the **value** parameter text around the default text.

The **return( )** method in **form_text( )** returns the question, a few spaces, and the **<input>** tag with appropriate parameters. **$question** is required, because it is the only way to tell your customer what you want to know. **$name** is also mandatory, because you have no other way of identifying the answer when it is returned to your script.

Now you can create the form using code that is easy to expand and can be laid out with one question per line. The following code wraps the **form_text( )** function around one question to create an **<input>** tag, and then wraps the **form( )** function around the **form_text( )** function to turn the question into a complete form. **print( )** is wrapped around **form( )** to output the form to the browser:

```
print(form ("form.html",
    form_text("name", "Please enter your name:")
    ));
```

The code produces the form shown in Figure 9.6.

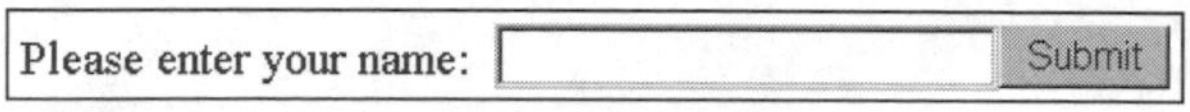

Please enter your name: [   ] Submit

Figure 9.6   Form with one question.

Creating a Long List in a Form

The form example used in the "Creating a Form" section becomes difficult to use for long lists of questions, so we will change the example to use an array for the questions. First, define an array containing questions in the sequence you want on the form:

```
$question["name"] = array("type" => "text",
    "question" => "Please enter your name:");
$question["address"] = array("type" => "text",
    "question" => "Address:");
$question["city"] = array("type" => "text",
    "question" => "City:");
$question["state"] = array("type" => "text",
    "question" => "State:");
$question["country"] = array("type" => "text",
    "question" => "Country:");
```

The array contains five entries, and each entry is an array containing elements **name**, **type**, and **question**, with **name** used as the key in the array. The **name** field identifies the field containing the answer to the **question** and so should comply with your naming standards for fields in the script that processes the answers. **type** tells **form()** to use the **<input>** tag formatting function named **form_text()**. **question** provides the readable text to go in front of the **<input>** tag, which is the part your visitor reads. **question** can also contain HTML highlighting, because **question** is output unmodified.

Next is basic code to build a question using text input. This is the function from "Creating a Form," with modifications. It uses a name to identify the answer to the question, the text of the question, and an optional default answer:

```
function form_text($name, $parameters)
   {
   if(!isset($parameters["default"]))
      {
      $parameters["default"] = "";
      }
   if(strlen($parameters["default"]))
      {
      $parameters["default"] = " value=\"" . $parameters["$default"]
         . "\"";
      }
   return($parameters["question"] . "  "
      . "<input type=\"text\" name=\"" . $name . "\""
      . $parameters ["$default"] . ">");
   }
```

This function accepts **$name** as a discrete parameter, accepts the remaining parameters in an array, creates **$parameters["default"]** if it does not exist, checks the length of **$parameters["default"]** to find out if there is a default answer for the question, and skips the generation of **value=** if there is no default text. The **return()** statement includes the **$parameters["question"]** unmodified (so the question can contain formatting tags), some spaces, and the **<input>** tag so your visitor can type in an answer.

NOTE: *The spaces are HTML nonbreaking spaces, ** **, instead of standard spaces, " ", because standard spaces tend to disappear in HTML (the HTML standard makes multiple spaces into a single space and ignores some single spaces).*

Now, take the basic form function from "Creating a Form" and expand the function to loop through an array of questions. The modified code uses the PHP functions **list()** and **each()** to return each question as a single array named **$v**. (See Chapter 3 for more information on **list()** and **each()**). The new code adds the question **type** to the prefix **form_** to create a function name, places the function name in variable function, and then executes the variable **$function** as a function. (Each time you add a new question type, you add a function with a matching name.) Try the following, as listed in the code:

```
function form($page, $question)
    {
    $text = "";
    while(list($name, $v) = each($question))
        {

        if(strlen($text)) {$text .= "<br>";}
        $function = "form_" . $v["type"];
        $text .= $function($name, $v);
        }
    return("<form action=\"" . $page . "\" method=\"post\">"
        . $text
        . "<input type=\"submit\" name=\"submit\""
        . " value=\"Submit\">"
        . "</form>");
    }
```

In **form()**, the **while()** statement loops through the list of questions (in the array **$question**) and places the formatted questions in **$text**. Because the array might be empty, **form()** starts by creating **$text** as an empty string.

Within the **while()** loop, the code checks to see if there is text in **$text** and if so inserts a break tag **
** so that each question will appear on a separate line. Next, the code builds a function name from the constant **form_** and the type element in the array. Then, you put everything together into **$text**.

If you have not read Chapter 10, you will be wondering about the **$function()**. When PHP finds a variable used where a function name should appear, PHP uses the value in the function name as the name of the function. This feature lets you build function names dynamically.

return() adds a submit button, **<input type="submit">**, to the end of the questions, and then wraps form tags around the whole thing. The alignment looks messy, but the next solution tackles neatness. The code produces the form shown in Figure 9.7.

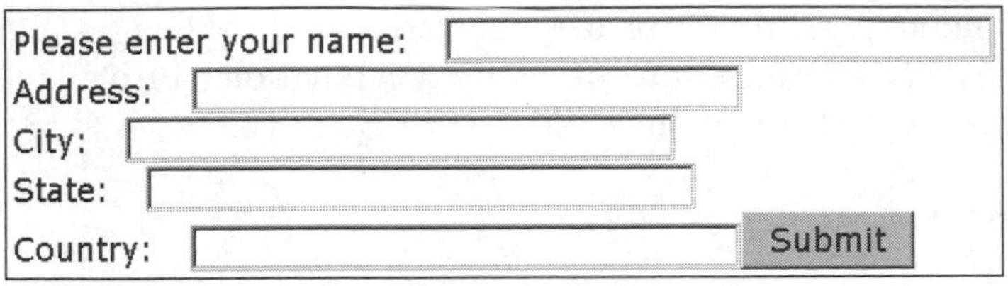

Figure 9.7   Form with multiple questions.

Aligning Columns

This solution adds code to the previous solution to align columns in forms and give you a head start on central control of form layout. The example makes all the questions run down the page because vertical scrolling is easier then horizontal scrolling. You could easily add an extra column on the right to include comments about questions just by adding the text to the **$question** array and generate an extra column in **form( )**.

Start with an array listing questions. This array offers just two as an example:

```
$question["name"] = array("type" => "text",
    "question" => "Please enter your name:");
$question["address"] = array("type" => "text",
    "question" => "Address:");
```

Each entry in the **$question** array has, as the key, the **name** to identify the answer from the question and an array containing two elements, the **type** to indicate the correct formatting function for this question, and the **question** text (including any HTML formatting tags you need for the text of the question).

The next code is the previous **form_text( )** function, from the "Creating a Long List in a Form" solution, with the question text removed so you can format the question text in the **form( )** function:

```
function form_text($name, $parameters)
    {
if(!isset($parameters["default"]))
        {
        $parameters["default"] = "";
        }
    if(strlen($parameters["default"]))
        {
        $parameters["default"] = " value=\"" . $parameters["default"]
          . "\"";
```

```
        }
    return("<input type=\"text\" name=\"""  . $name . "\""
        . $parameters["default"] . " >");
    }
```

The **form_text()** function checks for text in **$parameters["default"]** before wrapping the **value=** parameter around the text. If **$parameters["default"]** is empty, there is no need to generate the parameter.

The **return()** puts all the text into an **<input>** tag of type text.

Copy the **form()** function from the "Creating a Long List in a Form" solution, and move **$v["question"]** to the front of the question formatting function. **form()** accepts the list of questions in the array **$question**, steps through the array with **while()**, and passes the content of each question to a function named **"form_" . $v["type"]**, where **type** is the **type** element in each question array:

```
function form($page, $question)
    {
    $text = "";
    while(list($name, $v) = each($question))
        {

        if(strlen($text)) {$text .= "<br>";}
        $function = "form_" . $v["type"];
        $text .= $v["question"] . "  "
            . $function($name, $v);
        }
    return("<form action=\"""  . $page . "\" method=\"post\">"
        . $text
        . "<input type=\"submit\" name=\"submit\"""
        . " value=\"Submit\"></form>");
    }
```

The gory details of **form()**, are explained under "Creating a Long List in a Form," including a quick explanation of the variable as a function name. I give the full explanation of using variables as function names in Chapter 10.

In this version of **form()**, I simply took the question text out of the formatting function and formatted the question text within **form()** so all the text from all the questions gets the same formatting.

Now you can add formatting using a variety of techniques, including paragraph tags, break tags, and tables. I will use a simple three-column table with the middle column providing a small space between the question and the answer columns:

```
function form($page, $question)
   {
   $text = "";
   while(list($name, $v) = each($question))
      {

      if(strlen($text)) {$text .= "<br>";}
      $function = "form_" . $v["type"];
      $text .= "<tr><td>" . $v["question"] . "</td>"
         . "<td>  </td>"
         . "<td>" . $function($name, $v) . "</td>";
      }
   return("<form action=\"" . $page . "\" method=\"post\">"
      . "<table>" . $text . "</table>"
      . "<input type=\"submit\" name=\"submit\""
      . " value=\"Submit\">"
      . "</form>");
   }
```

This version of **form( )** has table row **<tr>** and table cell **<td>** tags wrapped around the components of the text generated within the **while( )** loop. That means each question will end up in a new row. The first column of the table holds the question text, the second column contributes a small space, and the third column contains the **<input>** tag where your visitor can type the answer.

The **return( )** statement wraps the table start and end tags around the questions so all the rows and cells get generated within the form. This symmetry prevents problems with certain browsers when form tags start outside a table and end inside a table, or vice versa.

The Submit button is outside the table, and therefore will not be aligned on the page by the table. Look at the browser display, and then I will suggest a slight modification that may interest you. The browser displays the form shown in Figure 9.8.

I do not like the Submit button where it is. I think the button should be directly below the area where the user types, so make one more minor adjustment manually. Replace the lines containing **<table>**, **$text**, **</table>**, and the Submit tag with the following code in order to align the Submit button:

```
. "<table>" . $text . "<tr><td></td><td></td>"
. "<td><input type=\"submit\" name=\"submit\""
. " value=\"Submit\"></td></tr></table>"
```

The new code places the Submit button in a new row within the table and places the button in the third cell of the row so the button is directly under the last

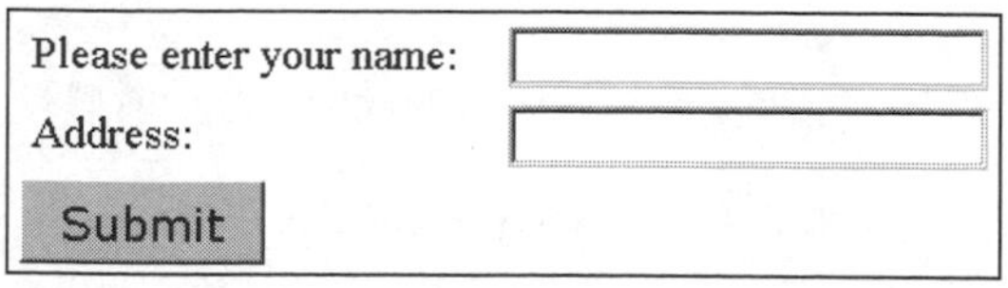

Figure 9.8 Form with multiple questions aligned in columns.

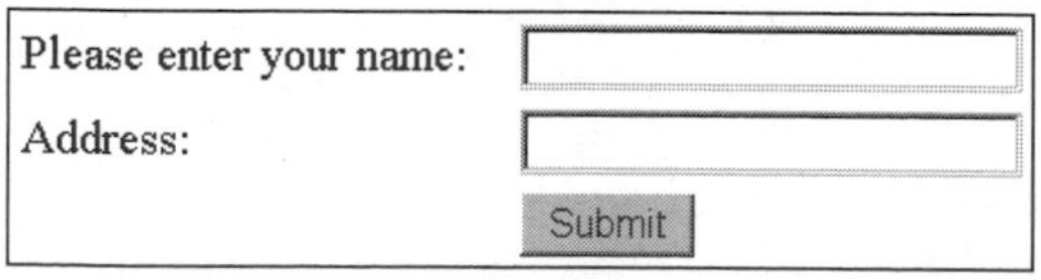

Figure 9.9 Form with fields and Submit button in a neat column.

<input> tag. When you run your eyes and mouse down the screen, all three (assuming you have two eyes and one mouse) will travel down to the Submit button. The browser now displays the form shown in Figure 9.9.

Selecting One of Many Choices

If you were to open your own travel agency and ask your customers online, "Which country do you want to visit?" you would need to have a form with a long selection list with which people could check off their desired destinations. Building on this scenario, this solution uses an array to contain the list of country names, the HTML form **<select>** tag to display the countries available for selection, and a variable to receive the selection.

To do this, you start with a list of countries in an array:

```
$country[] = "Australia";
$country[] = "Austria";
$country[] = "Azerbaijan";
```

You need a function to display questions with selection lists, and the function **form_select()**, shown next, does just that. It accepts a name for the array, a list of options to present in the selection list, and an optional default field in which you can specify the selection to be preselected as the default. Take a look at the following:

```
function form_select($name, $parameters)
    {
    $output = "";
    while(list($k, $v) = each($parameters["list"]))
```

```
         {
      if(isset($parameters["default"]) and $v == $parameters["default"])
        {
        $output .= "<option selected>" . $v . "</option>";
        }
      else
        {
        $output .= "<option>" . $v . "</option>";
        }
      }
    return("<select name=\"" . $name . "\">"
      . $output . "</select>");
    }
```

form_select( ) is similar to the question formatting functions in other Immediate Solutions in this chapter in that it accepts a name for the answer and a default value to prompt the user with the most likely answer. The rest is unique because it is creating a **<select>** tag.

The **<select>** tag lets you provide a list of selections to your visitor and lets the visitor select an answer from the list without having to type the answer. With some browsers and some operating systems, you can make multiple selections, but this only works if you allow multiple selections by adding the **multiple** parameter to the **<select>** tag.

In **form_select( )**, the list of answers is provided by **$list**. The **while( )** loop steps through **$list** generating individual **<option>** tags, each containing one answer. The default answer is marked by adding the keyword **selected** to the **<option>** tag. The **<option>** tags are added to the string **$output**, so I create **$output** before the first loop just in case there are no entries in **$list**.

The **return( )** function adds the name to the **<select>** tag and wraps the **<select>** tag around the list of **<option>** tags in **$output**.

How do you display your new question? Modify the question array used in the previous form examples, so the country array becomes a **list** parameter for a question of type **select**. After this, a small modification to the **form( )** function from previous solutions will handle this type of question with great ease:

```
$question["destination"] = array("type" => "select",
   "question" => "Which country do you want to visit?",
   "list" => $country);
```

Each entry in **$question** is an array containing the element's name, type, question. This entry, of type **select**, also contains the element list. The element list accepts an array containing a list of answers to be presented in the **<select>** tag generated by questions of type **select**.

The **$question** key value names the answer in the script receiving the answers, **type** specifies the function that formats the question, and the element **question** provides the text for the question.

You can add an optional element named **default** that provides the default answer for the question. In **<select>** lists, the default must match an entry in the list array, including the correct case. A safe way to add a default entry is shown next. When you add the entry "Anguilla" to the list **$country**, first add it to **$country_default** and then add **$country_default** to **$country**, as in:

```
$country_default = "Anguilla";
$country[] = $country_default;
```

When you add the entry to **$question**, include the **default** direct from **$country_default**. That way, you have the default added. The following example is the previous question with the default added:

```
$question["destination"] = array("type" => "select",
  "default" => $country_default,
  "question" => "Which country do you want to visit?",
  "list" => $country);
```

After this, you can take the **form( )** function developed in the previous solutions and use **form( )** unmodified with the new question type. In **form( )**, the question list is an array, and each entry is processed by a function specified by the array entry **type** value. Previous examples passed **name** and **default** to the function, and for **form_select( )**, you want to pass an extra parameter. **form( )** continues to work because all parameters, other than **name**, are passed in a single array.

An alternative to using an array for the parameter list is to use a fixed list of three parameters and change the existing **form( )** functions to accept a dummy parameter, so every function accepts exactly the three parameters.

Related solution:	Found on page:
Using Default Function Parameters	389

The following code extends the table an extra row and moves the Submit button to the extra row, so the Submit button will line up with the answer entry areas. Run the code in your page, and the browser should display the form shown in Figure 9.10:

Figure 9.10   Form with a drop-down selection list.

```
function form($page, $question)
   {
   $text = "";
   while(list($name, $v) = each($question))
      {
      if(!isset($v["default"])) {$v["default"] = "";}
      if(strlen($text)) {$text .= "<br>";}
      $function = "form_" . $v["type"];
      $text .= "<tr><td>" . $v["question"] . "</td>"
         . "<td>  </td><td>";
      if(isset($v["list"]))
         {
         $text .= $function($name, $v["list"], $v["default"]);
         }
      else
         {
         $text .= $function($name, $v["default"]);
         }
      $text .= "</td>";
      }
   return("<form action=\"" . $page . "\" method=\"post\">"
      . "<table>" . $text . "<tr><td></td><td></td>"
      . "<td><input type=\"submit\" name=\"submit\""
      . " value=\"Submit\"></td></tr></table></form>");
   }
```

Next you need the code to display the selection. The following code simply checks to see if a variable exists with the name **$destination** (as **destination** is the name you entered for the question in array **$question**), and then displays the variable:

```
if(!isset($destination))
   {
   print("<br>You selected " . $destination);
   }
```

When a form passes a value to the target page via the URL or the **GET** or **POST** mechanism, the PHP script in the target page sees the value in a variable named from the **name** parameter in the HTML tag that created the value. If you have

<input name="pet"> and someone types "dog" into that input field, the script will see **$pet** containing the value **dog**.

Selecting One of Many Choices with Radio Buttons

When you are out traveling in your car, you can instantly select a radio station by pressing a preset station button. One of your fellow commuters added that feature to HTML as the **<input>** tag type **radio**. Radio buttons are preferable to the **<select>** tag when displaying short lists, because you can see all the alternatives at once. On the other hand, a select list suits longer lists, because every option in a radio button list will take up page space.

To use radio buttons with the travel agency example from the previous Immediate Solution, you would start with a list of countries in an array:

```
$country[] = "Australia";
$country[] = "Austria";
$country[] = "Azerbaijan";
```

You need a function to display questions with radio buttons, and the function **form_radio( )**, shown next, does just that, accepting a name for the array, a list of options to present, and an optional **default** field in which you can specify the selection to be preselected by default. Here is **form_radio( )**:

```
function form_radio($name, $parameters)
    {
    $output = "";
    while(list($k, $v) = each($parameters["list"]))
        {
        if(strlen($output))
            {
            $output .= "<br>";
            }
        $output .= "<input name=\"" . $name . "\"" . " type=\"radio\""
            . " value=\"" . $v . "\"";
        if(isset($parameters["default"]) and $v == $parameters["default"])
            {
            $output .= " checked";
            }
        $output .= ">" . $v . "\n";
        }
    return($output);
    }
```

form_radio( ) is similar to **form_select( )** in that it accepts a name to name the answer field and a default value to prompt the user with the most likely answer. The rest is unique because it is creating a **<input>** tag. The Immediate Solution "Selecting Several of Many Choices" uses similar code to generate an **<input type="checkbox">** tag.

To display your new question, copy the question array from the previous Immediate Solution, as shown next, and feed it in to the **form( )** function, from previous solutions:

```
$question["destination"] = array("type" => "radio",
   "question" => "Which country do you want to visit?",
   "list" => $country);
```

The **$question** key names the answer in the script receiving the answers, **type** specifies the function that formats the question, and the element **question** provides the text for the question. You can add an optional element named **default** that provides the default answer for the question.

Selecting Several of Many Choices

In the previous Immediate Solution, when you opened up your own travel agency and asked your customers which countries they wanted to visit, you determined that it would be useful to have a form with a long selection list on which people could check off several of their desired destinations. This solution uses the HTML form checkbox to accept each selection, an array to contain the list of country names, and an array to receive the selections. The code is a slight modification of the code used in the "Selecting One of Many Choices" solution, and replaces **<select>** with **<input type=\"checkbox\">**. Using this code, when you receive the selection back from a customer's form, you will receive an array with a list of selections rather than a variable containing only one selection.

*NOTE: You may have guessed by now that I like PHP arrays, because they can be used in forms to return lists of values. Multiple-dimension arrays do not work; you just get one simple option, and that is to replace a standard HTML tag **name="fieldname"** with a PHP friendly **name="fieldname[]"** (although this limitation might change with future browsers and future versions of PHP).*

Start with a list of countries in an array:

```
$country[] = "Australia";
$country[] = "Austria";
$country[] = "Azerbaijan";
```

You need a function to display the selections from the array with an **<input type="checkbox">** around each array entry. The function **form_checkbox( )**, shown next, accepts a name for the array and a list of options to present in the selection list and an optional default field. The default sets the default for all selections, so you can create a list from which everything is selected and the customers turn off just the items they do not want.

Notice the **name=""** parameter in the **<input>** tag now contains **[]** after the field name to tell PHP to put the value in to the next entry in an array. The **[]** makes the **name** parameter equivalent to the PHP code, as in:

```
$destination[] = "_the name of the country_";
```

The **<input>** tag also contains a **value=""** parameter. In HTML, you can leave out the **value** parameter, and browsers will use the string between the **<input>** tag and the **</input>** tag. With PHP and some browsers, leaving out the **value** parameter will result in the array entry containing the value **on**. Avoid problems by using the **value** parameter.

For a checkbox, selected items have to be **checked** instead of **selected**, so remember to change that line in the code. Compared to previous solutions in this chapter, this function uses a linear method of building the output string, which is more suited to building large strings from many options. I add the tag components part by part so I can easily add future code and logic without disturbing the existing code or logic. I also added a **\n** to the end of the string so the HTML will be easier to read in the browser's "view source" screen. When you are writing other string-building functions in PHP, you might like to compare this approach to the one in **form_select( )**. Take a look at the following:

```
function form_checkbox($name, $parameters)
   {
   $output = "";
   while(list($k, $v) = each($parameters["list"]))
      {
      if(strlen($output))
         {
         $output .= "<br>";
         }
      $output .= "<input name=\"" . $name . "[]\""
         . " type=\"checkbox\""
         . " value=\"" . $v . "\"";
      if(is_array($parameters["default"])
      and in_array($v, $parameters["default"]))
         {
```

```
        $output .= " checked";
        }
    $output .= ">" . $v . "</input>\n";
    }
return($output);
}
```

form_checkbox( ) accepts a name for the question, a list of answers, and an optional list of default answers.

The **while( )** loop assembles the list in the variable **$output**, so the first thing to do is initialize **$output**. The **while( )** loop steps through the list and creates one **<input>** tag per entry. To separate the entries into a vertical list, a break, **
, is inserted before each **<input> tag. To prevent the break from producing an empty line before the first entry, the break is created only if there is text in **$output**; hence the **if(strlen($output))**.

The **<input>** tag gets a name to identify the answer in the target page and a type of **checkbox**. The **checkbox** produces the option list shown in Figure 9.11. Each checkbox is a separate entity, so visitors can click any number of checkboxes they want.

How do you display your new question? You modify the question array used throughout these form examples, so the country array becomes a **list** parameter for a question of type **checkbox**, as in:

```
$question["destination"] = array("type" => "checkbox",
    "question" => "Which country do you want to visit?",
    "list" => $country);
```

Once you do this, you can take the **form( )** function from the previous solution and use the function unmodified to display the country selection list. To do this, you would type:

```
function form($page, $question)
    {
    $text = "";
    while(list($name, $v) = each($question))
```

Figure 9.11   Form with multiple checkboxes.

```
        {
        if(strlen($text)) {$text .= "<br>";}
        $function = "form_" . $v["type"];
        $text .= "<tr><td>" . $v["question"] . "</td>"
            . "<td>  </td>"
            . "<td>" . $function($name, $v) . "</td></tr>";


        }
    return("<form action=\"" . $page . "\" method=\"post\">"
        . "<table>" . $text . "<tr><td></td><td></td>"
        . "<td><input type=\"submit\" name=\"submit\""
        . " value=\"Submit\"></td></tr></table>"
        . "</form>");
    }
```

form( ) accepts the name of a page to receive the answers and a list of questions. The **while( )** loop steps through the questions, building appropriate HTML. **Return( )** inserts a Submit button, and then wraps the HTML in form and table tags.

Although most people will love your form just the way you see it in Figure 9.11, some others may ask for forms with top-aligned questions, as shown in Figure 9.12. To make this one small change, and make it not only standard for all forms, but also easy to modify without having to change code, set up a common formatting option in **$option**, as shown here:

```
$option["form"]["valign"] = "top";
```

When making the change, you should add an extra line to control the space between the columns, so you can easily add and remove space as your Web site forms evolve. The **$option** array could be loaded from a common **include**, an administration database, or an XML file generated by a site administration page. To make this change, you would enter:

```
$option["form"]["separator"] = "  ";
```

After this, you should change **form( )** to apply the formatting to all table cells in the form and replace the hard-coded spacing column with the value loaded from

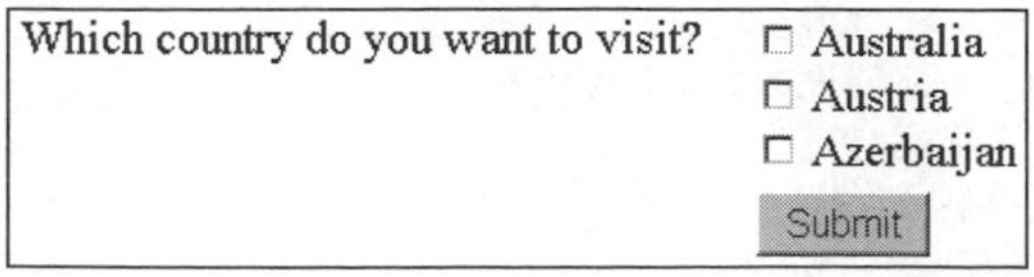

Figure 9.12   Form with a question neatly aligned next to multiple checkboxes.

9. Forms

$option. In other languages, global variables are declared once at the top of the script. In PHP, a variable is not global until you name the variable in a **global** statement within your function. This means it is easier to declare a single array in the **global** statement and store everything as entries in the array, rather than keeping all values in separate variables and then trying to add every variable to the **global** statement.

Before using a value from **$option**, first check to make sure the value is set by using PHP's **isset()**. Also, provide a workable default if someone has left out a value. In the case of the separator string, I changed the code to completely leave out the table's separator column if no separator value is defined. Last, but not least, I use the formatted **<td>** string, **$td**, in the separator column in case someone decides to add extra **<td>** formatting options, like **bgcolor**. To see how this works, take a look at the following:

```php
function form($page, $question)
    {
    global $option;
    $td = "<td";
    if(isset($option["form"]["valign"]))
        {
        $td .= " valign=\"" . $option["form"]["valign"] . "\"";
        }
    $td .= ">";
    $sep = "";
    if(isset($option["form"]["separator"]))
        {
        $sep = $td . $option["form"]["separator"] . "</td>";
        }
    $text = "";
    while(list($name, $v) = each($question))
        {
        if(strlen($text)) {$text .= "<br>";}
        $function = "form_" . $v["type"];
        $text .= "<tr>" . $td . $v["question"] . "</td>" . $sep . $td;
        $text .= $function($name, $v["default"])
            . "</td></tr>";
        }
    return("<form action=\"" . $page . "\" method=\"post\">"
        . "<table>" . $text . "<tr><td></td><td></td>"
        . "<td><input type=\"submit\" name=\"submit\""
        . " value=\"Submit\"></td></tr></table>"
        . "</form>");
    }
```

form( ) defines **$option** as a global variable, so **form( )** can access the **$option** defined outside **form( )**.

The code starting at **$td =** sets up a table cell definition. The **<td>** tag is built in detail from settings in **$option**, so you can use **$option** to completely control the formatting of your HTML. In this example, all I allowed is the **<td> valign** parameter to control the vertical alignment of the text in the table cell. You could expand it to cover colors and every other **<td>** option.

NOTE: *Why generate formatting this way instead of using CSS? Because some browsers do not process CSS. Other browsers do the wrong thing with CSS. Even the latest browsers disagree on the fine details of interpreting CSS.*

The code starting at **$sep =** simply sets up a table cell to separate the columns containing text. I use separator columns because screens are wide and humans need more horizontal space than vertical space to separate data.

The line of code starting with **$text = "<tr>"** is the older line of code enhanced to replace the fixed **<td>** tag with **$td** and replace "**<td> </td>**" with **$sep**.

The extra work in the **form( )** function, as you will see when you do this, produces a better, more flexible form. To process the result from this form, you would start with the following code. The data is in a variable named **$destination**, so first check that the variable exists, then check that it is an array, and then loop through the array displaying the values. Every item selected in the form will have the value from **value=""** placed as a value in the array. You can add any other processing you want, once you are happy that the data is arriving in your script. The code is as follows:

```
$d = "";
if(isset($destination))
   {
   $d = $destination;
   if(is_array($destination))
      {
      $d = "";
      while(list($k, $v) = each($destination))
         {
         $d .= "<tr><td>" . $v . "</td></tr>";
         }
      $d = "<table>" . $d . "</table>";
      }
   }
```

9. Forms

The code then sets a default value for **$d**, the variable that will receive the HTML and text. **if(Isset())** checks if **$destination** exists (on first entry to the page, the variable may not exist) and then sets **$d** to **$destination** (because **$destination** might be a formatted string). If **$destination** is an array, **$d** is cleared out, the **while()** statement steps through **$destination** adding table rows, and then **$d** is wrapped in **<table>** tags.

Retaining Answers and Highlighting Errors

The previous solution assumes your customer fills out a form and clicks Submit just once. But what happens when you want to either carry values from page one to page two of a multiple-page form or re-present page one with an error message? In this case, you would just add the extra fields to the **$question** array and the processing functions. You could, in this variation, add an extra column for error messages and also add red text to the front of each question so the horizontal spacing does not jump around from page to page. Essentially, you will use the same **$question** array you used in the previous solutions, adding extra values during processing. To allow easy testing of error messages, you could change the question to allow the selection of only two countries, as in:

```
$question["destination"] = array("type" => "checkbox",
   "question" => "Select up to two countries:",
   "list" => $country);
```

So you can match up answers with questions, each question is indexed by name. Then, when you are processing an answer field, such as **$destination**, you can refer to the question as **$question["destination"]** and easily insert answers and error messages as extra entries.

When there is an error in an answer and you want to return a message to the customer highlighting the error, all you need in your code is a line to add the error to the **$question** array. In the following example, you will see how this works in a situation when the customer has selected more than two counties. Of course, you can develop your own errors once your page is successfully displaying error messages. To add the error to the **$question** array, you would use:

```
if(count($destination) > 2)
   {
   $question["destination"]["error"] =
      "You selected more than two countries."
      . "<br><em>(Hint: Two is the number after one.)</em>";
   }
```

You also need to make sure you carry the previous answers into the new page in order to save people from having to retype everything. To do this, simply add previous answers to the question array as a new **default** value, as in:

```
if(isset($destination) and is_array($destination))
    {
    $question["destination"]["default"] = $destination;
    }
```

Both the default list and **$list** could be loaded from a database. If you have one database table containing both the data for **$list** and the data for the default list, you could combine both lists into one array and load the array from SQL. That would mean, in **form_checkbox( )**, **$paramter["default"]** would disappear and **$v** would become an array containing both the value for display and something to indicate the entry should be set to the default of **selected**. Then, you would apply a small change in the **form( )** function to add the error message to the front of the question, as in:

```
function form($page, $question)
    {
    global $option;
    $td = "<td";
    if(isset($option["form"]["valign"]))
        {
        $td .= " valign=\"" . $option["form"]["valign"] . "\"";
        }
    $td .= ">";
    $sep = "";
    if(isset($option["form"]["separator"]))
        {
        $sep = $td . $option["form"]["separator"] . "</td>";
        }
    $text = "";
    while(list($name, $v) = each($question))
        {
        if(isset($v["error"]))
            {
            $v["question"] = "<font color=\"Red\">" . $v["error"]
                . "</font><br>" . $v["question"];
            }
        $function = "form_" . $v["type"];
        $text .= "<tr>" . $td . $v["question"] . "</td>" . $sep . $td;
        if(isset($v["list"]))
            {
```

```
            $text .= $function($name, $v["list"], $v["default"]);
            }
        else
            {
            $text .= $function($name, $v["default"]);
            }
        $text .= "</td>";
        }
    return("<form action=\"" . $page . "\" method=\"post\">"
        . "<table>" . $text . "<tr><td></td><td></td>"
        . "<td><input type=\"submit\" name=\"submit\""
        . " value=\"Submit\"></td></tr></table></form>");
    }
```

The first change in **form( )** is the code that processes **$v["error"]**. The **error** element will exist only when the question is answered incorrectly, so the first step is to check if the element exists. When **error** does exist, the code takes the text from **error**, wraps the text in red (via the **<font>** tag), and adds the red text to the front of the question text.

Chapter 10

Functions

In Depth

Imagine designing a car. You would want to design the engine and the body together because you have to know that they fit each other. If you had a design team working for you, this team would work on and coordinate ideas for both the engine and the body. Now think about the CD player that will go into this car. Because it requires a totally different design technique and poses completely different design problems, it calls for an entirely different type of design team. A car design team would put together the car, leaving a standard-sized hole in the dashboard with a few wires ready for the CD player when it is completed. A CD player design team would construct the CD player so that it would fit the hole and match the wiring in the car when it was completed.

You can do the same with functions in PHP. Pick parts of your program that stand alone, and put those parts in functions. You can farm out the function development work to others and reduce development time by reusing the functions in other programs. When Australian industrial superhero Jacques Nassar was promoted to head Ford Motor Company's worldwide operations, he replaced 22 cigarette lighter designs with 1 design manufactured in 3 sizes. Jacques Nassar is now CEO of Ford. Just think where you could go with brilliant reuse of code.

This chapter explains functions and describes good uses for them, and also walks you through the process of learning how to apply them on your own. The functions specifically covered in this chapter are:

- **call_user_func( )**
- **create_function( )**
- **func_get_arg( )**
- **func_get_args( )**
- **func_num_arg( )**
- **register_shutdown_function( )**

When your code is rapidly changing, you might find development easier if you first leave the code mixed together, and then slice the code sections into functions. Later, you will be able to recognize what features fit best in a function, and create some functions before writing the code to use the functions.

Objects can provide a way of separating complex mixes of data and code into separate packages. When you have groups of useful functions and data, consider packaging them together in an object (for more information on using objects, see Chapter 17).

Functions give you immense flexibility. To provide all the details of how to write functions, the following sections work from the simplest function through all the options in PHP4.

The World's Shortest Function

Looking at some sample code is a good place to begin this discussion about functions. Functions are defined in one place, using the **function** statement, and then used throughout the rest of your code. The first step is to define the function, as shown here. The following is the world's shortest PHP function:

```
function a() {}
```

In this example, the keyword **function** starts the definition of a function. It is followed by a function name (in this case **a**), the parentheses, **( )**, which provide a space for optional input fields, and the braces, **{}**, which surround the function's code. You have to have a space between the word **function** and the function name, but you do not need a space between the function name and the **(**, or between the **)** and the **{**. Where you can use a space, you can also use a tab or skip to a new line. This is the outline for every function, and to this base, you add a mixture of input fields, processing code, and a means to output the result.

You use functions by writing the function name (in this case **a**) and the parentheses, as shown here:

```
a();
```

The example function **a( )** does nothing and returns nothing. It therefore produces false if you test **a( )** with **if( )**, as follows:

```
if(a())
```

Function names are not case sensitive. You can therefore use **a( )** by writing:

```
A();
```

NOTE: Input fields, parameters, *and* arguments *are three names for the same thing: the fields that let you supply information to a function.* Input field *is not technically correct, as the fields can be bidirectional.* Parameter *is used in some schools and* argument *in others.*

This function doesn't do anything in its current state, but the following sections discuss functions that do some work.

Returning Values

Function **a()**, in the preceding example, does nothing, and so has no actual use. Normally, you would want functions to perform work and be able to return values, which they do via the **return()** statement. PHP does not force typing on variables or functions, so you can return any type of value from your function.

If you are not familiar with the term *typing*, it is used in some programming languages to describe the process of forcing data into a particular data type. In PHP, data is not normally forced into a type when placed in a variable, but it can be, as shown in the following example. The value from **$b** is stored in **$a** as a floating-point number. To add to the confusion, *floating-point numbers* are also called *doubles* and *real numbers*; *double* is the most common term in PHP:

```
$a = (double) $b;
```

You might, for example, return an array when everything works right, but return the logical value false if something goes wrong. This section works through returning a value from a function, printing the returned value to verify that the return is correct, and then testing the returned value to detect special results and the case where the function indicates an error. The following sample illustrates a function that returns a **<font>** tag for the start of an error message. You will see a lot of simple formatting functions in this book, because they produce reliable HTML pages that work with any browser:

```
function red() {return("<font color=\"red\">");}
```

All this function does is create a string containing the HTML **<font>** tag, including the color red, and return the string to you. You use the example function **red()** in a **print** or **echo** statement (note the use of the dot concatenation character), as in:

```
print(red() . "my error message</font>");
```

The **print** statement creates a line on your Web page displaying the following in red letters:

```
my error message
```

If you use **print()** to send your value directly from the function to the browser, you cannot use the function within a larger page-formatting function to build whole pages. The next example shows how some programmers write message functions with built-in print statements. You get no control over the message display:

```
function warning_message()
   {
   print("<font color=\"red\">Warning!</font>");
   }
```

Instead, you should return the value from the function, and then have actions like **print()** wrapped around the function. The next example is a variation on the previous example, changed to move the **print()** outside of the function so you can use the warning message in a more flexible manner. Leaving the **print()** function until the last step in page generation means that you can nest unlimited text-processing functions:

```
function warning_message()
   {
   return("<font color=\"red\">Warning!</font>");
   }
print(warning_message());
```

By returning the value from the function, you can extend the usefulness of the function. The **warning_message()** function can be included in any other function that returns messages to the Web page, and gives you one simple central place where you can change the highlighting and message for all warnings. If **warning_message()** is called by several different functions, and you want to change the message from "Warning!" to "Look out!", you only need to make the change once.

In the following line, the warning message is enhanced with additional emphasis before it is printed:

```
print("<em>" . warning_message() . "</em>");
```

Another standard way of coding PHP functions is to make the function perform some work and return true for success or false for failure. The file functions, used later in this chapter, return either false or a file handle, which is an integer with a value greater than zero for an open file. Integers with a value of zero are interpreted as false, and all other integers, including negative values, are interpreted as true. This means you can test the file handle value for success or failure as if it were true/false.

In the following example, you can see how to use the PHP function **fopen()** and test the result for true/false. Note that the **@** in front of **fopen()** is used to suppress PHP's built-in error message for file not found, so you can produce your own message:

```
$file_handle = @fopen("atestfile.txt", "r");
if($file_handle)
   {print("<br>File open");}
else {print("<br>File did not open");}
```

PHP uses the results of a value assignment for the **if( )** test. This lets you simplify the previous example so that it reads as:

```
if($file_handle = @fopen("atestfile.txt", "r"))
   {print("<br>File open");}
else {print ("<br>File did not open");}
```

Note that the semicolon (;) disappears from the end of the **fopen( )** statement. One of the most common coding errors is to wrap the **if( )** around a statement and leave the semicolon on the end of a statement. In PHP4, this mistake produces an instant syntax error, so you can fix the mistake on the first test.

TIP: *Code contained in include files is not syntax checked until it is included somewhere. Write a test page that includes all your include files so they are all syntax checked.*

PHP interprets zero-length strings as false and other strings as true. If you build a function that returns a string, and you want to sometimes indicate an error, consider using a zero-length string as the error indicator. To further illustrate, in a function that generates text and returns a zero-length string on error, you can test the results of the function with the following:

```
if(generate_text())
```

The fact that the function returns a string causes a problem. Because PHP does not enforce typing of variables (typing of variables is discussed in Chapter 2), a string containing zero would be interpreted as an integer zero, and integer zero, in turn, would be interpreted as false. If your string-generation function could possibly return a single zero as a valid string, you have to use the following test to differentiate an empty string "" from "0":

```
if(generate_text() === "")
```

The comparison operator **==** (equal) checks that two fields have the same value but does not check if they are the same type, so PHP's automatic type conversion can make different values appear the same. The comparison operator **===**

(identical) checks that the fields are of the same type before checking the values, and does not confuse false with 0, "", or "0".

Supplying Values

Functions accept values via fields defined between the parentheses. In this example, the **red()** example is improved by accepting text and then wrapping both **<font>** tags around the text, to let you use the **red()** function with any text and ensure that the text ends up with the correct opening **<font>** tag and the matching closing **</font>** tag:

```
function red($text) {return("<font color=\"red\">$text</font>");}
```

The function **red()**, used in the following code sample, is now simpler to use, which will increase use of the function and reduce errors:

```
print(red("my error message"));
```

The result is still a line on your Web page displaying the following in red letters:

```
my error message
```

The PHP default passes parameters by value (makes a copy of the input field within the function). Changes to the input field will not appear outside of the function because any changes the function makes to the value are made to the copy within the function. The copy is described as being local to the variable or having a *scope* of local. Scope is covered in more detail later in this chapter.

If you want to change the original input field, however, add an ampersand (**&**) to the start of the input field. This makes PHP pass the value by reference, and the function works on the original variable instead of a copy. To illustrate this, try the following code:

```
function numbered_message(&$number, $text)
   {
   $number++;
   return("<br><font color=\"red\"><br>"
      . $number . " " . $text . "</font>");
   }
$message_number = 0;
print("<br>The message number is " . $message_number);
print(numbered_message($message_number, "bright red error message"));
print(numbered_message($message_number, "another error message"));
print("<br>The message number is now " . $message_number);
```

You will see the result shown next. The message number starts at 0 and then is incremented to 2 by the function **numbered_message( )**. If the number had been passed by value, **numbered_message( )** would have modified a copy of the variable, rather than the original; each message would be numbered 1; and the final line would display the value 0:

```
The message number is 0
1 bright red error message
2 another error message
The message number is now 2
```

Optional Values

If your function is used repeatedly for the same purpose, you might want to specify a default value for the function's input, and you might also want to be able to override that default under certain circumstances. You can add default values to the input fields, and then the person using the function can either enter a value or not. The function **date( )** has a default value of today's date and time, therefore making the input field optional. When you use **date( )**, you can choose to accept the default of today's date, or supply your own data to the function. Most times, you will accept the default so you can add today's date to a database record or to a Web page, but sometimes you will want to supply other dates, like a birthday or the first day of next month.

For example, the **red( )** function might have a default warning message, or you could let the user specify the color to use, with red as the default color.

TIP: *Why override the color red in a function that is supposed to produce red text? The standard HTML red has an red/green/blue (RGB) color of #ff0000, indicating 100 percent red, zero green, and zero blue, a color that cannot be seen by people with a certain type of color blindness. You might like to substitute #ff3333, a color that has some green and some blue, so that everyone can read the message. It is still safe in all browsers and still looks red. Visit* **http://petermoulding.com/colour/colourblindness.html** *for more details.*

The following code shows the **red( )** function with a default warning message:

```
function red($text="Warning, unidentified error!")
```

When you write in your script

```
print(red());
```

the result would be:

```
Warning, unidentified error!
```

You can mix compulsory and optional fields. Place the optional fields last, so people using the function can leave off the fields they are not using or fields for which they want to use the default. If the last parameter in a function is used, all the ones before it must be included. If the last parameter is not used, you can leave it out. If the preceding parameter is not used, you can leave that one out as well. By placing the least-used parameters last, you make it easier to leave them out.

In the example that follows, **$text** is compulsory, because you will always supply texrΔ A **<font>** tag without text does nothing on a Web page, so the text field is compulsory, but the **$color** parameter is optional, because most people will just use the default of red:

```
function message($text, $color="red")
   {
   return("<br><font color=\"" . $color . "\">" . $text . "</font>");
   }
print(message("bright red error message"));
```

The **$color** field gets a default that applies if the user does not supply **$color** to the function. The default is logically the same as making the first line of the function contain the following:

```
   if(!isset($color)) {$color = "red";}
```

The following code is not easy to use, because you cannot leave out a parameter if one of the following parameters is used. When you place the parameters in this order, you cannot leave out **$color**, because **$text** is always specified:

```
function message($color="red", $text)
   {
   return("<br><font color=\"" . $color . "\">" . $text . "</font>");
   }
print(message(, "bright red error message"));
```

print() prints the string returned by **message()**, and, because of the missing color parameter, **message()** will produce a syntax error.

Variable Number of Input Fields

Although optional values are useful, sometimes you may not know how many parameters will be passed into your function. PHP4 provides a way for the function to determine how many parameters have been passed and use them accordingly. You can use **func_num_args()**, **func_get_arg()**, and **func_get_args()** to handle a variable-length list of parameters in your function.

You might change the **red( )** function to:

```
function red()
   {
   $red_text = "";
   $red_count = func_num_args();
   for($i = 0; $i < $red_count; $i++)
      {$red_text .= func_get_arg($i) . "<br>";}
   return("<br><font color=\"red\">" . $red_text . "</font>");
   }
```

The modified **red( )** has no parameters specified in the heading line, **function red( )**, and all the decoding of parameters is performed manually. **func_num_args( )** provides the number of parameters supplied when the function **red( )** is used. The **for( )** loop steps through the parameter list, **func_get_arg( )** gets the next parameter, which is a line of text, and then all the input text is collected in **$red_text** and output within the one set of **<font>** tags. Each line of text has **
** added to the end to start a new line. Consider the following test:

```
print(red("red text", "more red text"));
```

This produces the following two lines of text:

```
red text
more red text
```

You can refer to specific parameters by ordinal value, as though each parameter was a member of an array:

```
$red_text = func_get_arg(3);
```

This feature was used in the previous example, with **$i** providing the number. Use numbers when you can relate the parameter position to something easy to remember and count. For example, you can use this feature in functions that accept numbered lists. Imagine a function that accepts a parameter for each gear in a car—parameter 1 would be first gear, parameter 2 would be second gear, and so on.

You can store all the parameters in an array, and then use array processing for those occasions that best suit array processing. **func_get_args( )** gets all the parameters into the array. You can then loop through the array any way you want. **func_get_args( )** works like this:

```
$red_array = func_get_args();
```

You can mix the fixed-style compulsory parameters with a variable list of optional parameters. If you specify three normal input fields, and then use the variable list processing, the first three input fields will be in the named fields and numbered zero to two. To access the fields in the variable part of the list, you jump past the first three entries in the parameter array.

The following example is the previous function **red( )** with three fixed-position parameters, **$date**, **$time**, and **$place**. The function uses the same **for( )** loop as before to loop through optional parameters, except that the loop starts at 3 instead of 0:

```
function red($date, $time, $place)
   {
   $red_text = $date . " " . $time . " " . $place . "<br>";
   $red_count = func_num_args();
   for($i = 3; $i < $red_count; $i++)
      {$red_text .= func_get_arg($i) . "<br>";}
   return("<br><font color=\"red\">" . $red_text . "</font>");
   }
```

Scope

The word *scope* is derived from the Greek word *skopós* and means "mark or aim." Scope is the root word for *microscope* and *telescope*, both good tools for zooming in on specific areas. When the term is applied to items like functions and variables, *scope* indicates where in the code you can see the items, and where they are available to use in your code. In PHP, the rules of scope are:

- Variables passed to a function via the parameter list are local to the function unless preceded by an ampersand (**&**).

- Variables defined inside a function are local to the function unless named in a **global** statement.

- Variables defined outside a function are not available inside a function unless passed as a parameter or defined in a **global** statement.

- Constants defined via **define( )** are always global, whether defined inside the function or outside the function.

- Functions are always global, so a function defined within another function is available everywhere.

Scope is one of the things people take a while to remember, because it varies from language to language. In Microsoft's Visual Basic, you make a variable global by defining the variable as global when you first define the variable at the start of your program. In PHP, you do not designate a variable as global in the main part of your program. Instead, you tell individual functions to access the variable of that name defined outside the function. The variable is global within that function but not in other functions unless they also define the variable as global.

The PHP approach is safer. If you use the Visual Basic approach, and then include another person's function in your code, you may break the new function because you defined a global variable of the same name as one of the new function's local variables. Visual Basic programmers sometimes adopt complex naming conventions to prevent this mistake. In PHP, the person writing the function decides if he wants the local or the global variable.

For example, consider the following code:

```
$a = "A short sentence";

$b = " ";  // the character that separates words
$c = 0;    // count of separation characters
$x = strlen($a);
for($y = 0; $y < $x; $y++)
    {
    if(substr($a, $y, 1) == $b) {$c++;}
    }
```

This code counts the number of spaces between words in a sentence. The variable **$a** contains the sentence, **$b** contains the space character, **$c** contains the count of spaces, and **substr( )** contains the function that finds each space. **$x** gets the count of characters in **$a**, and the **for( )** loop steps **substr( )** through the characters in **$a**. Although there are other ways to count spaces, this example serves to explain the scope of variables in PHP functions.

By separating code into a function, you can replace the code in the function at any time without having to search for several individual occurrences of the code. You also isolate the function's working variables from the code outside the function. If you find a long script with many uses of the variable **$x**, you can have a problem working out which code sets **$x** for each place where **$x** is used.

Try separating the code into functions. Keep each use of **$x** isolated within a function. In the previous example, the variables **$a**, **$b**, and **$c** are needed after the counting of spaces, so you need to keep them in the main code. The variables **$x** and **$y** are not needed after you count the spaces, so you can isolate them in the function. Therefore, the scope of **$x** and **$y** is confined to the function. With the function incorporated, the code looks like this:

```
$a = "A short sentence";
$b = " ";   // the character that separates words
$c = 0;     // count of separation characters
function count_spaces($input, $separator)
   {
   $x = strlen($input);
   $z = 0;
   for($y = 0; $y < $x; $y++)
      {
      if(substr($input, $y, 1) == $separator) {$z++;}
      }
   return($z);
   }
$c = count_spaces($a, $b);
```

In this example, **$a, $b, $c, $x, $y, for( )**, and **substr( )** all do exactly what they did in previous example. The only difference is where the variables are visible: in the scope of the main program (**$a, $b, $c**) or within the scope of the function (**$x, $y, $z**).

If you have lots of input fields that need to be modified, leave them out of the function heading and add them with a **global** statement. The **global** statement tells your function to use the existing variables defined outside your function. The variables are called *global variables*, and their scope is everywhere.

The next example shows part of the **numbered_message( )** function from a previous example and modifies it to use a global variable. Function **numbered_message( )** uses the variable **$message_count**, which is defined outside the function, and accesses the external **$message_count** via the **global** statement:

```
$message_count = 0;
function numbered_message($text)

   {
   global $message_count;
   $message_count++;
```

Global variables let you return multiple values from your function by simply listing all the variables in a **global** statement. The previous example defines one variable in the **global** statement but can name any number of variables. The function can modify any of the variables, return true or false to indicate success or failure, and allow the rest of your code to access all of the modified variables.

The previous example shows the standard way to make a global variable: Define the variable at the top of your script, and then define the variable as a global variable within each function that uses the variable. A variable does not have to exist at the point where it is named in a **global** statement. Your function can process data, then decide to create a new variable, and name the variable in a **global** statement. The variable does not have to exist before you define the variable in the **global** statement, and the **global** statement can be within a conditional statement such that the variable is created only with some uses of a function. You could have a function always return true for success, or false for failure, through a **return( )** statement, and create a global variable containing an error message only if the returned value is false.

Complicated use of global variables in functions not only can make the functions hard to learn and hard to remember but also can make your scripts difficult to troubleshoot. People using your functions will see variables change without being able to see where the variables are changed. Keep the use of the global variables well documented.

In PHP, all function names are global. Although you can nest functions, defining one function within another function, as shown in the following example, global functions make nesting illogical. In the following example, the inner function **bold( )** is available outside of **error_message( )**, so there is no point in placing **bold( )** within **error_message( )**:

```
function error_message($text)
    {
    function bold($text) {return("<strong>$text</strong>");}
    return("<br><font color=\"red\">" . bold($text) . "</font>");
    }
print(error_message("bright red error message"));
print(bold("bold message"));
```

The one area where you might use functions is in very long scripts that use half their functions for one process and the other half for a different process. You can slice and dice your script into smaller, more manageable units, as described in the following paragraphs, but you need to consider the scope of the variables you use. If a lot of common variables are passed between the sections, the code could become complicated, and tracking the use of variables could be complex. If a function has a lot of local variables, and few global variables or parameters, it will be an easy-to-understand slice. If most of the variables are global, you may have a difficult-to-understand slice, and you might be better off removing the code from the function and returning the code to the original position.

A script designed to help you order a custom-built car might use function set A for all cars, function set B for big sport utility vehicles, and function set C for convertible sports cars. You could split the function sets out in order to include the files a.html, b.html, and c.html, and then use a function something like the following code to include the right files:

```
function select_includes($model)
    {
    include("a.html");
    if($model == "Explorer")
        {
        include("b.html");
        }
```

The example shows only part of the code to give you an idea of how to manage big sets of functions. This example works because the functions will be available everywhere, even though they are included within another function.

When you are designing a large script, consider splitting the design into separate areas and making each area a function. Look at the scope of data and look for large numbers of variables with limited use. Just as you would split the design of a Web page into header and body, you can split your scripts the same way. You might have one function to gather all the data from a database, and a separate function to perform all the formatting on the page.

Static Variables

Suppose you have a function that is used several times in your script, and that has to carry a value from one usage to the next. Also suppose that the value is only used in that function. You could store the value in a global variable to be used each time the function is called. A simpler and more logical approach, however, is to use *static variables*. Here is an example of what you would have to do if you did not have static variables:

```
$message_count = 0; // message_count is used by numbered_message()
function numbered_message($text, $color="red")
    {
    global $message_count;
    $message_count++;
    return("<br><font color=\"" . $color . "\">"
        . $message_count . " " . $text . "</font>");
    }
```

You create the variable **$message_count** outside function **numbered_message()**, so **$message_count** survives from one use of **numbered_message()** to the next. Within **numbered_message()**, you access **$message_count** via a **global** statement.

With static variables, you throw away the external definition of **$message_count** and replace the **global** statement with a **static** variable definition, as shown in the highlighted line in the following example:

```
function numbered_message($text, $color="red")
   {
   static $message_count;
   $message_count++;
   return("<br><font color=\"" . $color . "\">"
       . $message_count . " " . $text . "</font>");
   }
```

What happens to **$message_count** when you call **numbered_message()** several times? Test the static variable by using **numbered_message()** in two print statements, as shown here:

```
print(numbered_message("bright red error message"));
print(numbered_message("another bright red error message"));
```

The result would be:

```
1 bright red error message
2 another error message
```

The value in **$message_count**, as a result, will be retained between uses of **numbered_message()** and will not appear outside of **numbered_message()**. A conventional variable is re-created every time the function is used, but a static variable remains unchanged. Everything else about static variables is the same as conventional variables. Static variables have a scope of local, and so are not shared among functions and are not available outside of the function.

If you write a function that performs lengthy processing to recalculate the same values every time the function is used, consider retaining the values in static variables to reduce processing overhead. If **$message_count** started with a number produced by lengthy code, you could save recalculating the start value by testing if the value is set. The **isset()** function returns true if the variable is set, and **!isset()** returns true if the variable is not yet set. The next example shows the test for a missing variable, and executes the length code (represented by the three dots):

```
If(!isset($message_count))
   {
   $message_count = …
   }
```

Recursion

Functions in PHP can call themselves, a practice known as *recursion*. Recursion can make your code hard to understand, so in general, you should avoid it. In PHP3, recursion is especially slow because scripts are interpreted line by line, and recursion of a function chews up CPU time in reinterpreting the function. PHP4 works more like a compiler, meaning that interpretation results are saved and reused, so recursion is less expensive in PHP4.

The next example uses recursion and, although it may be easier to code in other ways and may run more quickly if coded without recursion, it is the least complex example I can think of. (A really useful example of recursion when sorting files would require 18 cups of coffee and 200 pages of fine print text just to get to the first line of code.) This example removes one dot from the end of a string. If the next character is also a dot, the function calls itself to remove the next dot:

```
$string_with_lots_of_dots = "dots...............................";
function remove_dots($text)
   {
   if(substr($text, -1) == ".") {$text = substr($text, 0, -1);}
   if(substr($text, -1) == ".") {$text = remove_dots($text);}
   return($text);
   }
print(remove_dots($string_with_lots_of_dots));
```

The first **substr( )** finds the first dot and, if a dot exists, calls the second **substr( )**, on the same line, to remove the first dot. The third **substr( )**, in the highlighted line, detects a second dot and calls **remove_dot( )** to attack the second dot.

Functions Named in Variables

Function names can be stored in variables. Like recursion, it is an idea that has few benefits and makes code harder to understand. This section will work through an example, and then discuss advantages and documentation. Here is an example for a script that accesses several databases. The example contains functions to get error information from MySQL and Oracle:

```
function mysql_error() {…}
function oracle_error() {…}
```

You could fill your script with code to check which database you are accessing, and then select the appropriate function to use. Or you could check the database once, and put the result into a variable for subsequent use. In this next part of the example, some code, not shown, decides which database is in use. For the purposes of the example, the database used is MySQL, so the name of the MySQL error-processing function is placed in a variable:

```
$database_error = "mysql_error";
```

Now you can fill your code with references to **$database_error()** and not have to change the references when you add new databases. For example:

```
print($database_error());
```

Note the **$database_error()** part. PHP replaces **$database_error** with the contents of **$database_error** before trying to execute the function. PHP then executes **mysql_error()** because **$database_error** contains **mysql_error**.

The special function **call_user_func()** provides another way to call functions named in variables (an example appears in the "Immediate Solutions" section of this chapter). A new function, **call_user_func_array()**, goes a step further and lets you use an array to provide parameters for the called function. New variations pop up every few months to save a little code here and there. Use whatever is easiest to understand, maintain, and explain to others.

For some scripts, a sensible approach is to leave functions as ordinary functions used in the conventional manner, avoiding function names in variables or the likes of **call_user_func()**, and store status information in arrays, databases, or XML. The choice depends on the range of information and frequency of use. See the examples in Chapters 3, 5, and 20.

Placing function names in variables is a technique that works when the function names describe a status or action in a way that is easy to remember. The technique is scalable, because each function can be worked on by a different person, and is useful when there are many functions or large functions, and the total code would be unmanageable in **if()** statements or a **switch()** statement.

You need to document the use of a variable that contains a function name, because the usage is not obvious to the next person to work on the code. A string variable can easily accept an invalid entry, and your script will fail if the variable contains an invalid function name, so make sure the variable receives only valid function names.

Sequence

In PHP4, you can define functions in any sequence, whereas in PHP3, you were required to provide a definition of a function before you could use that function. Define all your functions in one place and consider placing all the commonly used functions in a separate file for inclusion into each page. If a function uses a variable, ensure the variable is created before the function uses it. When you call a function, check carefully check that you are providing all the values required in the parameters. But what about variables accessed through **global** statements? Make sure you have created all the variables the function accesses through its **global** statement and have created all the variables accessed by all the functions called by the function you are calling.

Immediate Solutions

Creating a Function

A function requires the keyword **function**, followed by the function name, some parentheses, and then brackets, as in:

```
function any_name()
   {
   }
```

The function name must be unique, and is not case-sensitive, so you cannot create function **Car()** when you have already defined **car()**. There must be a space between the word **function** and the name but you can have zero, one, or many spaces, tabs, or new lines between the name and the open parenthesis, and between the close parenthesis and the opening bracket.

You can return a value via the **return()** statement. To see how this works, take a look at how the following function returns the path to the current page in a Web site:

```
function path_to_page()
   {
   global $PATH_INFO,$PHP_SELF;
   if(isset($PATH_INFO))
      {
      return($PATH_INFO);
      }
   elseif(isset($PHP_SELF))
      {
 return($PHP_SELF);
      }
   }
```

After this, if you place the function in your index page for Web site directory php/, **path_to_page()** would display the following:

```
/php/index.html
```

You can supply any number of values, including zero, with parameters. You do not need parameters for the **date( )** function because **date( )** gets all input from the system clock, but a function to create a graphic image might have dozens of parameters to accept colors and coordinates. The following example continues with the previous example but adds some message text:

```
function path_to_page($part_a, $part_b)
   {
   global $PATH_INFO,$PHP_SELF;
   if(isset($PATH_INFO))
      {
      return("<p>" . $part_a . $PATH_INFO . $part_b . "</p>");
      }
   elseif(isset($PHP_SELF))
      {
return("<p>" . $part_a . $PHP_SELF . $part_b . "</p>");
      }
   }
```

Suppose you have a page named /php/index.html, and you place the following code in the page as a test:

```
print(path_to_page ("This page is ", "."));
```

The result will be:

```
This page is /php/index.html.
```

Declaring a Global Variable

If you have lots of input fields that need to be modified, leave them out of the function heading and add them with a **global** statement. These variables are called *global variables*, and their scope is everywhere.

In the following example, **$message_count** is defined outside the function **numbered_message( )**. To make **numbered_message( )** use the external

$message_count instead of creating a new local variable, name **$message_
count( )** in the highlighted **global** statement:

```
$message_count = 0;
function numbered_message($text, $color="red")
   {
   global $message_count;
   $message_count++;
   return("<br><font color=\"" . $color . "\">"
     . $message_count . " " . $text
     . "</font>");
   }
```

Test the global variable with the following two lines of code, and expect the test
to produce two messages numbered 1 and 2:

```
print(numbered_message("bright red error message"));
print(numbered_message("another bright red error message"));
```

A variable does not have to exist at the point where it is named in a **global** statement. Your function can create the variable. The **global** statement ensures that
the variable created by your function is stored in the global space available to
everyone instead of the space local to the function.

In the next example, the variable **$new_text** is created only if the function finds
text in variable **$text**. The **global** statement is used and the **$new_text** variable
created when the **if( )** is true:

```
function create_text($text)
   {
   if(isset($text) and strlen($text))
      {
      global $new_text;
      $new_text .= "<font color=\"red\">"
      . $text . "</font>";
      }
   return(true);
   }
```

If you copy the last example and define global variables only when they are about
to be filled with data, people will have a problem working out what variables are
used in your function. The **create_text( )** example could be improved, though,
by starting your script with something like the following:

```
$new_text = ""; // This variable is filled with text by create_text()
```

Declaring a Static Variable

Every time you use a function, everything in the function is created from scratch, a process that chews up time and means you cannot save values within the function. There are times when you want to save values from one use of a function to the next, and you would normally spend a lot of time defining variables outside your function, plus a lot of time coding **global** statements to make all the variables available in your function. Static variables eliminate all that.

The function **numbered_message( )** prints messages, with each message containing a unique number generated by **numbered_message( )**. The variable **$message_count** stores the unique number. If **$message_count** were a standard variable, it $would contain zero every time **numbered_message( )** started. By defining **$message_count** as static, the value in **$message_count** is retained from one invocation of **numbered_message( )** to the next:

```
function numbered_message($text, $color="red")
    {
    static $message_count;
    $message_count++;
    return("<br><font color=\"" . $color . "\">"
        . $message_count . " " . $text . "</font>");
    }
```

You would test the change with the following:

```
print(numbered_message("bright red error message"));
print(numbered_message("another bright red error message"));
```

And the result would be as follows:

```
1 bright red error message
2 another error message
```

Storing a Function in a Variable

Supposed you want to track the movement of your company's inventory with records that can be stored on a disk, or in a database. Here is the code to perform the same work with either a sequential Comma Separated Variable file (CSV) or a MySQL database table. This example automatically selects the right file and processing function by storing the processing function in a variable.

The example record contains two items, a part description (**$part**) and a quantity for that part (**$quantity**), as follows:

```
$part = "bolt";
$quantity = 3;
```

Here is the function to add the record to a file named movements.csv:

```
function add_file($part, $quantity)
   {
   $result = false;
   if($file = fopen("movements.csv", "a"))
      {
      $result = fwrite($file, $part . "," . $quantity);
      fclose($file);
      }
   return($result);
   }
```

The **fopen( )** function opens the file named in the first parameter of **fopen( )**, and the second parameter, "**a**", says to append new records to the end of the existing file. The variable **$file** receives an identifier for the open file, and **fwrite( )** uses the identifier to write a string to the end of the file. The **fclose( )** function closes the file to let other people access it. The variable **$result** receives true or false, indicating success or failure, for the file write, and that variable is returned to you so you can check the result.

Related solution:	Found on page:
Displaying a Text File	312

The following code adds the record to a MySQL table named **movements**. The MySQL connection is already established, and the database name is in global variable **$database**. Also, the table has an integer entry number as the key, and the key is set to **auto_increment**, so you do not need to specify the key value:

```
function add_mysql($part, $quantity)
   {
   $sql = "insert into movements set part='" . $part
   . "', quantity='" . $quantity . "'";
   return(mysql_db_query($database, $sql));
   }
```

Somewhere in your application defaults, you specify a variable to define whether to use **add_file( )** or **add_mysql( )**, as follows:

```
$add_stock = "add_mysql";
```

Once you do this, you can add stock movements to the right file type with:

```
$add_stock("bolt", 3);
```

Then, to put the right file processing into every function, you could instantly customize your whole stock application with a small piece of logic at the start, like this:

```
$file_type = "mysql";
$add_stock = "add_" . $file_type;
$delete_stock = "delete_" . $file_type;
$count_stock = "count_" . $file_type;
$print_stock = "print_" . $file_type;
```

Using Default Function Parameters

Default values for function parameters provide the value to be used if the user does not specify the function parameters. The next example, **red( )**, might have a default warning message, as follows:

```
function red($text="Warning, unidentified error!")
```

When you write in your script

```
print(red());
```

the result would be the following, a simple warning that something has gone wrong:

```
Warning, unidentified error!
```

A default like this indicates that the code reached function **red( )** but you forgot to supply a useful explanatory message, or you could not. At least your script identifies where the error occurred, even if it does not identify the cause.

You can mix compulsory and optional fields. The compulsory fields must go first so PHP can match up the fields. In the following example, **$text** is compulsory and **$color** is optional:

```
function message($text, $color="red")
    {
    return("<br><font color=\"" . $color . "\">" . $text . "</font>");
    }
print(message("bright red error message"));
```

The result would be as follows in bright red letters:

```
bright red error message
```

This demonstrates that the function worked happily without the second parameter and used the default value of **red** specified in the function definition.

The next example does not work because no value is provided for parameter one in **message()**. PHP will react like your neighbors react when you turn up the stereo at 3:00 A.M.: It will complain with an error message and stop interpreting your script. PHP requires every parameter up to the last parameter you supply; you cannot leave out a parameter if there is a following parameter:

```
function message($color="red", $text)
    {
    return("<br><font color=\"" . $color . "\">" . $text . "</font>");
    }
print(message(, "bright red error message"));
```

Checking that a Function Exists

If you create functions in files that are included into other files, you could create a function twice and cause an error that will stop your script from completing. This commonly happens when you create file a.html, and then a.html is included in b.html and c.html. Then, someone includes both b.html and c.html in d.html. The result is that a.html is included twice. You can avoid this problem by checking to see if your function already exists before you create your function.

Here is the definition of a simple **print** function with a safety check wrapped around it. The code creates the function **print_message()**. **function_exists()**

returns true if **print_message( )** is already defined. **!function_exists( )** returns true if **print_message( )** does not exist, as in:

```
if(!function_exists("print_message"))
    {
    function print_message($message)
        {
        print("<p>" . $message . "</p>");
        }
    }
```

There is a major difference between PHP3 and PHP4. To see this, try the following example:

```
if(function_exists("red"))
    {print("Function red exists.");}
else {print("Function red does not exist.");}
function red($text)
    {
    return("<font color=\"red\">" . $text . "</font>");
    }
if(function_exists("red"))
    {print("Function red exists.");}
else {print("Function red does not exist.");}
```

PHP3 compiles the functions as it reads through the script, so the function **red( )** is not compiled until after the first test; therefore, the result would be as follows:

```
Function red does not exist.
Function red exists.
```

PHP4, on the other hand, compiles all the functions before executing your code, so the result would be:

```
Function red exists.
Function red exists.
```

If a function may be created in several places—for example, in different included files—and you want to prevent errors, all definitions of the function must be wrapped within a test.

When you create an include file that contains many function definitions, and you do not want to put **function_exists( )** around every function, you can ask people to include your file using the new version of **include( )**, called **include_once( )**.

Using call_user_func()

The **call_user_func( )** function lets you use a function named in a variable. The parameters are as follows:

```
call_user_func($function_name, $function_parameter_1, ...)
```

$function_name is a string containing the name of the function you want to use. Because **$function_name** is a string variable, you can build the function name from components or load the name from a database.

$function_parameter is any parameter you want to pass to the function named in **$function_name**. There can be many function parameters or zero, but the number must be correct for the function you are using.

This example is a way of making your application work across operating systems. It lets you build file names of the correct format for each OS. First, define a variable to contain the name of the current operating system used on your test server, as follows:

```
$os = "unix";
```

Next, insert some code to determine the current OS. There are a number of complex ways to determine the operating system, but all that is needed in this case is a quick check that file names have a drive name of the format *x:* (a drive letter followed by a colon). The colon indicates Windows; everything else is Unix. The following test checks a common file name for a colon and sets **$os** to indicate Windows:

```
if(substr($DOCUMENT_ROOT,1,1) == ":")
    {
    $os = "windows";
    }
```

Now, write a formatting function for each OS. Take a look at the Unix and Windows versions of a function to join a path and file name with the correct separation character:

```
function file_name_unix($path, $file)
    {
    return($path . "/" . $file);
    }
```

```
function file_name_windows($path, $file)
   {
   return($path. "\\" . $file);
   }
```

> **NOTE:** *Windows NT accepts both characters. If NT is the only version of Windows used on your Web servers, you can use the Unix separation character.*

Now, you can use the correct formatting function by calling the function with **call_user_func()** and building the function name from the variable **$os**, like this:

```
$full_name = call_user_func("file_name_" . $os, "help", "index.html");
```

Using **create_function()**

You can build functions on the fly with **create_function()**. The function name is dynamically generated, so the name does not conflict with any other function in your code. The following is the syntax of **create_function()**:

```
create_function($parameters, $code);
```

This example builds a simple formatting function with **create_function()**. The **format_text()** function accepts two parameters, **$heading** and **$text**, and then wraps **$heading** in **<h1>** tags to create a level-1 HTML heading. The function then wraps the text in paragraph tags to complete the formatting:

```
function format_text($heading, $text)
   {
   $x = "<h1>" . $heading . "</h1>";
   $x .= "<p>" . $text . "</p>";
   return($x);
   }
```

The following is the same formatting function built using **create_function()**. **create_function()** accepts two strings; the first contains the list of parameters to go between the parentheses, (), at the head of the generated function, and the second string contains the code to go between the braces, {}:

```
$format_text = create_function('$heading, $text',
   '$x = "<h1>" . $heading . "</h1>";'
   . '$x .= "<p>" . $text . "</p>";return($x);');
```

> **TIP:** *Use single quotes (') instead of double quotes (") around the strings to avoid escaping all the special characters.*

To use the formatting function, type the following:

```
$formatted_text = $format_text("A poem", "The cat sat on the mat");
```

After you do this, you can dynamically build the formatting function using information from a database. You can let your customers with reading difficulties choose a larger font size in their profile, and then add the font size to the formatting function. The next example has the font size manually loaded in variable **$font_size**. You would load it into **$font_size** when the customer logs on, and then save **$font_size** as a session variable. The expanded formatting function build is as follows:

```
$font_size = "+2";
$t = '$text';
$t = '"<font size=\\"' . $font_size . '\\">" . ' . $t . ' . "<font>"';
$format_text = create_function('$heading, $text',
   '$x = "<h1>" . $heading . "</h1>";'
   . '$x .= "<p><font size=\"' . $font_size . '\">"'
   . ' . ' . $t . ' . "</p>";'
   . 'return($x);');
```

If all the backslashes and types of quotes confuse you, build an example function by hand first, and then try inserting the code into quotes.

Building functions dynamically may save you processing time if the end result is used many times within the script. The cost is the complexity of the generation code and the higher likelihood of error when someone has to change the code.

Using **func_get_arg()** and **func_num_args()**

The **func_get_arg( )** function lets you build a function that can accept unlimited parameters without having to define them in the parameter list. The **func_num_args( )** function lets you find the number of parameters to process. Both **func_get_arg( )** and **func_num_args( )** are limited to PHP4.

Here is a simple function that will be improved with **func_get_arg( )**:

```
function file_name ($directory, $file)
   {
   return($directory . "/" . $file);
   }
```

If you wanted the function to handle two levels of directory, you would have to define two directory parameters in the function, and then use both in the **return( )** statement. What do you do if there can be many directory levels, and the number of levels is variable? The answer is to count your way through the parameters, using **func_get_arg( )** and **func_num_args( )**.

The expanded version of the example **file_name( )** function has no parameters defined. The function accepts zero, one, or many parameters, as demonstrated here. The separator **/** is added between the components of the path, and the components of the path are collected by **func_get_arg( )**:

```
function file_name()
   {
   $path = "";
   $separator = "";
   for($i = 0; $i < func_num_args(); $i++)
      {
      $path .= $separator . func_get_arg($i);
      $separator = "/";
      }
   return($path);
   }
```

NOTE: *The separator variable is loaded with the separator character at the end of the first loop, so there will be no initial / . You could change this depending on the operating system and whether the file name is either relative to the current directory or absolute.*

Using **func_get_args( )**

The **func_get_args( )** function grabs all the function's parameters in an array so you can work through a long list of parameters using simple array processing. The **func_get_args( )** function is found only in PHP4.

The following example prints a list of healthy fruits and vegetables in alphabetical order:

```
function fruit_list()
   {
   $fruits =  func_get_args();
   $fruit_list = "";
   sort($fruits);
   $c = count($fruits);
   for($i = 0; $i < $c; $i++)
      {
      $fruit_list .= "<br>" . $fruits[$i];
      }
   return("<p>" . $fruit_list . "</p>");
   }
```

NOTE: *The separator variable is loaded with the separator character at the end of the first loop, so there will be no initial* **
**. *You could change this depending on the operating system and whether the file name is either relative to the current directory or absolute.*

Registering a Shutdown Function

If you create a huge script that updates lots of files and creates a huge Web page but which occasionally fails to finish, you may want to find some code that can always run at the end of the script no matter what happens. In this case, **register_shutdown_function( )** is made just for you.

In the following example, the function is named **special_code( )**:

```
function special_code()
   {
   // Code to terminate transactions.
   // Code to close files and databases.
   }
```

You register the function with the following:

```
register_shutdown_fuction("special_code");
```

In **special_code( )**, you can do anything except write to the browser. The HTTP session to the browser is closed before the shutdown function is started.

What should you do? You should terminate database transactions that are not complete and close files that have new records sitting in output buffers. You could troubleshoot abnormal occurrences, and log the results for later analysis.

Is anything not worth doing? At the end of a script, PHP automatically closes MySQL databases, saves session information, and cleans up memory. You only need to handle abnormal items. Check the documentation for the database you use.

10. Functions

Chapter 11

Images

In Depth

This chapter covers several file formats that include images: GIF, JPEG, PDF, PNG, and SWF. You will use some of the formats, and you will need to know them all so you can choose the best format, or argue against the wrong format if someone tries to force the use of a particular format in your next project. GIFs, JPEGs, and PNGs are created with the series of PHP functions prefixed by **image**, such as **imagecreate( )**. PDFs are created with **cpdf_**, **fdf_**, and **pdf_** functions, while SWFs are created with **swf_** functions.

GIF

The Graphics Interchange Format (GIF) was invented for CompuServe (now owned by AOL). This format allows various color depths, up to eight-bit, and included a compression technique named LZW (Lempel-Ziv-Welch), which was patented by Unisys. When Unisys demanded royalties for the use of LZW, an informal group of developers invented the Portable Network Graphics (PNG) format as a replacement, with enhancements, and it is slowly catching on as browsers are updated to include PNG support. GIF's eight-bit color limits GIFs to diagrams, cartoons, and text-based banners (JPEG is the format for photographs).

GIFs have the advantage of being small and having accurate color and pixel representation, but only one library was available in PHP for the creation of GIFs and that was withdrawn when Unisys demanded royalties. The image-read functions, such as **getimagesize( )**, can read GIFs without royalty infringement, but you cannot create new GIFs within your script. If, for some reason, you need to create GIFs from your script and you can use COM, you could look for a COM-compliant image editor that creates GIFs, but it is better to move to PNG.

You could create your images as PNG files and copy them to GIFs via an external batch program. (Chapter 7 covers external programs.) If you compiled your version of PHP, you could search the Web for an old source library that includes GIF support, and use that. You are faced with a lot of work to use GIFs, and most modern browsers support PNGs, so why bother? Most modern browsers support the features of PNG that were in GIF, but have trouble with new features like the alpha channel; so, a conversion from GIF to PNG works, but creating a brand new PNG with all the features of PNG may not work as well.

PNG

The Portable Network Graphics (PNG) format, from **www.libpng.org/pub/png**, is designed to replace GIFs, because part of the GIF format is patented. A related Multiple-Image Network Graphics (MNG) format, at **www.libpng.org/pub/mng**, is designed to replace animated GIFs.

PNG offers many advantages over GIFs: alpha channel transparency, 24-bit color, and text fields (like in JPEG). Several error-detection systems are built in, meaning you can transmit large images through newsgroups and email and detect the slightest corruption. PNG's 24-bit color with lossless compression means PNG is the ideal way to store your master images before conversion to JPEG (JPEG's higher level of compression is still useful for delivering images to browsers).

One advantage of GIF over JPEG is transparency, but GIF only supports solid transparency; one color is allocated to transparent, and that is all you get. With GIF transparency, you cannot have a semi-transparent shadow. PNG solves that with PNG's alpha channel transparency, a feature that lets you have graduated transparency. Try creating a GIF with blue text on a white background and use antialiasing to smooth out the edges. Next, make the white background transparent, and then put the image over a black page. Notice the white parts of the antialiasing. PNG lets the gradations along the edges fade to the color of the page background instead of the color used in the original image background.

JPEG

The Joint Photographic Experts Group (JPEG), formed as a joint effort by the European telecommunications standards organization (CCITT) and International Standards Organization (ISO), developed the JPEG standard as a way of presenting photographs online, no matter how large, or how slow the network. JPEG works by allowing you to specify the compression from 0 to 100 percent, giving you a file size ranging from the full native size of the image down to a few bytes. The "compression" works by destructively removing information in a linear fashion that gives you a gradual degradation toward useless blobs.

Compression systems that destroy information should not be called compression systems! JPEG's use of the term, like a lot of software advertisements, mislead people into thinking you can infinitely suck the life out of an image without reducing quality. JPEG compression also changes colors, replacing your original colors with a list of approximations that shrinks as compression increases. If you have to use a specific RGB color for a customer's trademark logo, use JPEG with zero compression, or any file format other than JPEG. Test your JPEGs at several compression levels before using them online (see a typical test at **petermoulding.com/jpegcompression.html**). The main things to remember are:

- JPEG compression suits low contrast images, not strong, bright colors.
- JPEG compression suits soft images and photographs, not sharp lines and edges.
- The more familiar the subject, the more compression is noticed.
- JPEG compression changes colors, and should not be used for logos.

PDF

PDF is the Portable Document Format from Adobe (**http://adobe.com**). You can create PDF files from PHP using either of two sets of functions. The **pdf_** functions use PDFlib, a library included in with PHP and written by Thomas Merz at PDFlib GmbH (**www.pdflib.com**). The **cpdf_** functions use the ClibPDF library from FastIO Systems (**www.fastio.com**). Both libraries, the time I last looked, are licensed for free nonprofit use, but require the purchase of a commercial license if you use the libraries for any project that makes a profit.

A recent addition to the PDF format is forms via Forms Data Format (FDF). There are theoretical advantages with PDF forms, but they do add one extra technology barrier between your customers and your Web site: The user must download a plug-in before accessing the site. Make sure your customers can contact you through conventional forms before using FDF, and provide a conventional form for each FDF form.

The documentation for ClibPDF says that PDF's unit of measure is PostScript points, 1/72 of an inch, and that it defaults to an initial measurement of 72 units, or 1 inch. I tried the default and found it used points all the time, so I defined a couple of constants for use when defining the defaults for a document. PDFlib defaults to using points, and if you wanted to write one set of graphics for both PDF and other formats, you could equate points to pixels on the average screen (screens are about 90 to 110 pixels per inch). The first **define( )**, for the residents of America, Liberia, and Myanmar, defines the points in an inch. The second **define( )**, for the rest of the world, defines the number of points in a millimetre (which is spelled *millimeter* in America):

```
define("inch", 72);
define("millimetre", 2.83464567);
```

Once you have your dimensions accurately defined, Adobe's Acrobat reader will display the document at a size unrelated to your careful measurements. I found a 4×5-inch page, when displayed at actual size, appeared about 2×2 inches. The default display size varied, with small images being magnified even if the default in the Acrobat reader is to display at actual size.

ClibPDF

The **cpdf_** functions use the commercial PDF library, ClibPDF, which the documentation says you have to download separately from PHP, but the PHP 4.0.5 Win32 binary had everything included. To install the ClibPDF option under NT 4 and Windows 2000, all you have to do is the following:

1. Stop Apache.
2. Copy php_cpdf.dll from php/extensions to c:/winnt/system32.
3. Edit php.ini to remove the **;** from the front of **extension=php_cpdf.dll**.
4. Restart Apache.

NOTE: *For other versions of Windows, use c:\windows\system instead of c:/winnt/system32.*

ClibPDF recently gained support for opening multiple documents, but the overhead of PDF when you generate documents suggests you would not want to use PDF to dynamically generate every Web page on the fly. At this stage, PDF document production is limited to one Web site administrator preparing PDF versions of new documents. The rest of this section is a quick run through the **cpdf_** functions, so you can relate them to the **pdf_** equivalents. The authors of these functions recommend you read the ClibPDF documentation before use. The PDF examples in the Immediate Solutions use the **pdf_** functions.

Document Functions

cpdf_open() opens a new document and returns a document id that you need as the first parameter in all other ClibPDF functions. You have the choice of building the document in memory or writing directly to a file, by naming a file in the function. In my examples, I build documents in memory and just allocate extra memory to PHP via the **memory_limit** parameter in php.ini. When you create a very long file, such as converting a database table into a report, you should write directly to a file. The current ClibPDF does not allow you to create more than one document at a time, but may do so in a future release.

cpdf_page_init() starts a new page, and is a page-level function, but I mention it here because PHP 4.0.5 crashes if you try to write to a document without initializing the first page. **cpdf_set_font()** is a text-level function that has to be used at least once per document; otherwise, at display time, the document will produce this warning:

```
Error processing a page. Font has not been set.
```

cpdf_finalize() accepts a document id and ends the building of the document. **cpdf_output_buffer()** outputs the document from the memory buffer to your screen, but using PHP 4.0.5, this function does not include the right headers to have the document processed as a PDF file; instead, the document appears as raw text. If you are sending a PDF page instead of a HTML page, precede **cpdf_output_buffer()** with the following code:

```
Header("Content-type: application/pdf");
```

cpdf_save_to_file() lets you save the document to a file and, if used, must be run before you close the document with **cpdf_close()**. The examples in this chapter leave the file name out of **cpdf_open()** and use **cpdf_save_to_file()**. **cpdf_close()** closes the document and deletes the document from memory.

Page Functions

cpdf_page_init() accepts a document id, page number, orientation indicator, height, width, and optional unit of measurement specified in PostScript points. A PostScript point is 1/72 of an inch, and the default unit of measurement is 72, so you should be able to specify all measurements in inches; but some measurements, like font size, still use points. You can specify millimeters using the **define** statements shown at the beginning of this section. The orientation can be 0 for portrait or 1 for landscape, and you can use the following definitions to make the settings easier to remember:

```
define("landscape", 1);
define("portrait", 0);
```

cpdf_save() saves the current environment in memory (not to disk), and **cpdf_restore()** restores a saved environment. You can save your settings, change a few settings, draw some figures, and then restore the settings as they were when you saved them. You could save the settings at the start of a page, create a non-standard page, and then restore the standard page settings for the next page.

Text Functions

Placing text in small documents with the following functions will drive you crazy, so if you decide to create little pop-up information screens using PDF, map them out in a PDF-capable browser first. Work out fonts, sizes, and everything else before trying to automate the task with PHP. Figure 11.1 is the typical screen I received when trying to display PDF pages that had simple mistakes, like setting the font size a little too big.

Here are some terms for those new to drawing pictures with the tools described next:

- *Path*—When you create a series of characters, they follow a path. A path is also used as the base line for drawing a wide line. Think of a path as the line

Figure 11.1 PDF document with incorrect text setup.

down the middle of a road, then imagine drawing the line down the middle first and then add the road and gutters around the line.

- *Outline*—An outlined character has lines around the outside of it, and may or may not have a fill in the middle. When you draw a shape, like a wide line, the drawing will create an outline around the path. Using the road analogy, the outline is a bit like the gutters at the edge of the road.

- *Fill*—The fill color is the asphalt on the road, the part that fills in the outline. If you use a fill color when drawing to create a solid shape or character, the fill color will be used for the whole shape, including the outline. If you draw an outline first and then fill the shape, you can use a different color for the fill. This gives you the ability to use characters with a black outline and a red center.

- *Stroke*—Another name for outline. When you stroke a line or a character, you are drawing an outline. Stroking lets you set options like stroke color and stroke width, so you can have a wide choice of outlines.

The following are the ClibPDF text functions:

- **cpdf_global_set_document_limits()**—Sets limits for all documents.
- **cpdf_set_char_spacing()**—Sets the spacing between characters.
- **cpdf_set_word_spacing()**—Sets the spacing between words.
- **cpdf_set_leading()**—Sets the spacing between lines of text.

- **cpdf_set_current_page()**—Sets the current page.
- **cpdf_set_font()**—Sets the font face and size.
- **cpdf_set_page_animation()**—Sets the duration (in seconds) between displaying each page.
- **cpdf_setdash()**—Sets the dash pattern for dashed lines.
- **cpdf_setflat()**—Sets the flatness.
- **cpdf_scale()**—Sets the scale for the X and Y axes of a document.
- **cpdf_set_horiz_scaling()**—Sets horizontal scaling of text.
- **cpdf_set_text_rise()**—Sets the text rise for the next text. A positive number creates a superscript, and a negative number creates a subscript.
- **cpdf_set_text_rendering()**—Sets the render for the text, with options like "fill character" to make solid-color text.
- **cpdf_set_text_matrix()**—Sets a matrix to transform the current text.
- **cpdf_stringwidth()**—Returns the width of text in the current font.
- **cpdf_setlinecap()**—Sets the **linecap** parameter, which makes the ends of lines square or round.
- **cpdf_setlinejoin()**—Sets the **linejoin** parameter, which makes intersections of lines mitered, rounded, or beveled.
- **cpdf_setlinewidth()**—Sets the line width.
- **cpdf_setmiterlimit()**—Sets the miter limit, which limits how sharp the point will be when two lines join at an acute angle.
- **cpdf_set_creator()**—Sets the creator field in the document.
- **cpdf_set_keywords()**—Adds keywords to the document.
- **cpdf_add_annotation()**—Adds an annotation to the document.
- **cpdf_set_subject()**—Sets the subject field of the document.
- **cpdf_set_title()**—Sets the title field for the document.
- **cpdf_begin_text()**—Begins a section of text.
- **cpdf_continue_text()**—Continues the text on the next line.
- **cpdf_end_text()**—Ends the text.
- **cpdf_show()**—Outputs text at the current position.
- **cpdf_show_xy()**—Outputs text at a position defined by coordinates x and y. Both coordinates have to be between **cpdf_begin_text()** and **cpdf_end_text()** functions to work. If you use **cpdf_show()** before **cpdf_begin_text()**, the Acrobat reader will report the error *Illegal operation 'Tj' outside text object*.

- **cpdf_set_text_pos( )**—Sets the text position for the next **cpdf_show( )**.
- **cpdf_text( )**—Outputs text to a position specified by coordinates.
- **cpdf_add_outline( )**—Adds a bookmark for the current page.

Color Functions

For those who prefer color, the following are the color functions:

- **cpdf_setrgbcolor( )**—Sets the drawing and fill color to an RGB color
- **cpdf_setrgbcolor_fill( )**—Sets the fill color to an RGB color
- **cpdf_setrgbcolor_stroke( )**—Sets the drawing color to an RGB color

Line Functions

The following are the line functions:

- **cpdf_translate( )**—Sets the origin of the coordinate system
- **cpdf_lineto( )**—Draws a line to an absolute point
- **cpdf_rlineto( )**—Draws a line to a relative point
- **cpdf_arc( )**—Creates an arc
- **cpdf_curveto( )**—Draws a curve
- **cpdf_circle( )**—Creates a circle
- **cpdf_rect( )**—Draws a rectangle
- **cpdf_setgray_fill( )**—Sets the fill color, which fills an outline created by drawing lines or shapes
- **cpdf_setgray( )**—Sets the drawing and filling color
- **cpdf_setgray_stroke( )**—Sets the drawing color
- **cpdf_rotate( )**—Sets the rotation to an angle specified in degrees
- **cpdf_newpath( )**—Starts a new path
- **cpdf_clip( )**—Clips to the current path
- **cpdf_closepath( )**—Closes the path
- **cpdf_fill( )**—Fills the current path
- **cpdf_fill_stroke( )**—Fills and strokes the current path
- **cpdf_stroke( )**—Draws a line along the path
- **cpdf_closepath_stroke( )**—Closes the path and draws a line drawn along the path
- **cpdf_closepath_fill_stroke( )**—Closes, draws a line along, and fills the path
- **cpdf_moveto( )**—Sets the current point to an absolute position
- **cpdf_rmoveto( )**—Sets the current point to a relative position

Image Functions

The following two functions work with images:

- **cpdf_import_jpeg()**—Lets you open a JPEG image for import into the document

- **cpdf_place_inline_image()**—Places an image on the page

FDF

To install the FDF option under Windows NT 4, all you have to do is the following:

1. Stop Apache.

2. Copy php_fdf.dll from php/extensions to c:/winnt/system32.

3. Copy FdfTk.dll from php/dlls to c:/winnt/system32.

4. Edit php.ini to remove the **;** from the front of **extension=php_fdf.dll**.

5. Restart Apache.

To fully understand Adobe's Forms Data Format (FDF), you might have to read the documents listed at **http://partners.adobe.com/asn/developer/acrosdk/ forms.html**. FDF covers a few areas. First you create an FDF document that attaches something similar to a HTML form to a PFF document, and then you use additional FDF functions to read the FDF data when the data is returned to your server.

Creating the FDF

The first step with FDF is to create an FDF file that can be sent to the browser. **fdf_create()** creates an FDF in memory and returns an id for use in the other FDF functions. **fdf_set_value()** adds a field and default value to the FDF. In the example that follows, there are two fields, for price and quantity.

fdf_set_file() connects the FDF with a PDF by inserting a URL reference to the PDF. The reference is a URL because the Adobe Acrobat reader reads the reference in the browser and then tries to read the PDF from the browser. You should replace the test URL in the example with something that works with your site.

fdf_save() saves the FDF to disk for later use. In this example, the FDF is immediately displayed, but because the FDF is a customer order form, you might want to keep it and continue using it for a while. Saving the file to disk also gives you more options for display and for testing. **fdf_close()** lets you free up the memory allocated to the FDF (not much, because most of the information is in the PDF):

```
$orders = "i:/orders/";
$fdf = fdf_create();
fdf_set_value($fdf, "price", "\$0.00", 0);
```

```
fdf_set_value($fdf, "quantity", "1", 0);
fdf_set_file($fdf, "http://test/order.pdf");
fdf_save($fdf, $orders . "order.fdf");
fdf_close($fdf);
```

Displaying the FDF

The FDF has to be displayed on a browser, and can be handled with a link, like any other file, if your Web server is set up to handle the file type. If your Web server is not set up, you can link to a page containing the following code. The **header( )** function sends a MIME type of application/vnd.fdf, and browsers that have Adobe Acrobat installed should recognize the file as an FDF. **fopen( )** returns the file as a string, and **fpassthru( )** sends the file out to the browser:

```
<?php
$orders = "i:/orders/";
Header("Content-type: application/vnd.fdf");
fpassthru(fopen($orders . "order.fdf", "r"));
?>
```

Reading the FDF Data

When the user fills out the form and returns the results to your Web site, the data is locked up in a special format, so recovering the data requires two steps. (I am sure somebody will write code to decode the data in one step.) Define a directory to receive the replies, or use a temporary directory. Open a new file using **fopen( )** with the **w** option to write a file, and if you want to keep the file as a record of an order, include something like the date and time in the file name. Use **fwrite( )** to write the string **$HTTP_FDF_DATA** into the file, and then close the file:

```
$replies = "i:/orders/replies/";
$fdf = fopen($replies . "areply.fdf", "w");
fwrite($fdf, $HTTP_FDF_DATA, strlen($HTTP_FDF_DATA));
fclose($fdf);
```

Now you have an FDF file you can read to supply the reply to your order form. Open the file for read with **fopen( )**, get the field values using **fdf_get_value( )**, and then close the file with **fdf_close( )**:

```
$fdf = fdf_open($replies . "areply.fdf", "r");
$price = fdf_get_value($fdf, "price");
$quantity = fdf_get_value($fdf, "quantity");
fdf_close($fdf);
```

In theory, you can loop through a long set of fields in an FDF document using the following sample code. **fdf_next_field_name( )** returns the name of the first field, if the second parameter in **fdf_next_field_name( )** is null. The next use of **fdf_next_field_name( )** will provide the next field, if you provide the previous field as the second parameter. What happens when the function goes past the last field is undefined, so it could change in the future:

```
$field = fdf_next_field_name($replies);
$values[$field] = fdf_get_value($fdf, $field);
while($field = fdf_next_field_name($replies, $field))
    {
    $values[$field] = fdf_get_value($fdf, $field);
    }
```

If you need to recall the name of the PDF set in the FDF with **fdf_set_file( )**, you can retrieve it with **fdf_get_file( )**. One possible use is when you attach one FDF to many PDFs, and you want to identify the PDF used in conjunction with the FDF. In the page that receives the reply from the FDF, the FDF name will be in the referrer string instead of the PDF, so either generate one FDF per PDF or use **fdf_get_file( )**.

The following functions set options described in the Adobe documentation:

- **fdf_set_ap( )**—Sets the appearance of a field.
- **fdf_set_flags( )**—Sets flags for a field.
- **fdf_set_opt( )**—Sets options for a field.
- **fdf_set_status( )**—Sets the value of the **/STATUS** key in the FDF document (see Adobe's documentation).
- **fdf_get_status( )**—Returns the value of the **/STATUS** key.
- **fdf_set_submit_form_action( )**—Sets an action field similar to the submit button on a HTML form (Adobe would have made life easier if they had just copied the HTML tag parameters).
- **fdf_set_javascript_action( )**—Lets you attach a JavaScript action to a field much like you would for some HTML tags. You could use the JavaScript to validate the data input in the field.

PDFlib

To install the PDFlib option under NT 4 and Windows 2000, do the following:

1. Stop Apache.
2. Copy php_pdf.dll from php/extensions to c:/winnt/system32.

3. Edit php.ini to remove the **;** from the front of **extension=php_pdf.dll**.

4. Restart Apache.

NOTE: *For other versions of Windows, use c:\windows\system instead of c:/winnt/system32.*

The PDF functions are shown in the Immediate Solution "Creating Text in a PDF Document with PDFlib" and are similar to the **cpdf_** functions.

Flash and Shockwave

The Shockwave file format (SWF) is described at OpenSWF (**www.openswf.org**). PHP SWF functions connect to Paul Haeberli's **libswf** module (**http:// reality.sgi.com/grafica/flash**) to let you create files that can be read by Macromedia's Flash (**www.macromedia.com/software/flash**) add-on for browsers. Macromedia produces two browser add-ons, Flash (**www.macromedia.com/ software/flashplayer**) and Shockwave (**www.macromedia.com/software/ shockwaveplayer**). (The Shockwave player also includes the Flash player.) Flash files are created with Macromedia's Flash, and Shockwave files are created with Macromedia's Director (**www.macromedia.com/software/director**). The file extension for Flash files is .swf; in HTTP, the document type for Flash files is application/x-shockwave-flash. The **libswf** library adopted the Flash file type, and the PHP functions adopted the same name. The SWF functions do not create the more complex Shockwave files.

Because Flash is commonly installed in many browsers and does not have all the hassles of launching PDF files, Flash is a better way of presenting the one-page brochures often presented in PDF. Flash also has better interactivity for navigating long documents, but at this stage, no major search engines are indexing the text within Flash files, so PDF has an advantage in that area.

Many Flash artists better than me are out there, so there is no point in my doing anything complicated in Flash to impress you. You need the **swf_** functions, **libswf**, and Unix, because the library is not currently available for Windows or Windows NT.

The File

Start by opening a Flash file with **swf_openfile()**. You have to use **swf_openfile()** as the first **swf** function, or the support library will produce an error. There is no equivalent to a file id returned from this function, so you cannot open several files at once.

The following **swf_openfile()** example opens a file to disk:

```
$flash["file"] = realpath("./veryflash.swf");
$flash["width"] = 400;
$flash["height"] = 500;
$flash["framerate"] = 20;
$flash["background"]["red"] = 20;
$flash["background"]["green"] = 20;
$flash["background"]["blue"] = 20;
swf_openfile($flash["file"], $flash["width"], $flash["height"],
    $flash["framerate"], $flash["background"]["red"],
    $flash["background"]["green"], $flash["background"]["blue"]);
```

The file setup code uses **realpath( )**, a function that accepts a relative file name of the type you use in a Web page, and converts the name to the absolute name used in PHP file functions. (On a Web page, file names are relative to the Web site's base address, but PHP uses file names relative to the operating system's base address for the server.)

If you replace the **swf_openfile( )** in the previous example with the **swf_openfile( )** from the following example, the SWF file will open on the screen, using the special file name php://stdout:

```
swf_openfile("php://stdout", $flash["width"], $flash["height"],
    $flash["framerate"], $flash["background"]["red"],
    $flash["background"]["green"], $flash["background"]["blue"]);
```

When you are finished with the Flash file, and before you can create a new file, you must close the existing file with **swf_closefile( )**. The following example simply closes the file to free up resources:

```
swf_closefile();
```

If you replace the previous **swf_closefile( )** with this next example, the optional **1** tells the function to return the Flash file as a string, so you can save the file to a database or create an email attachment:

```
$flash["data"] = swf_closefile(1);
```

The Frame

Within a file, you work with frames numbered from 0 and optionally labeled. Label the frame with **swf_labelframe( )** as shown in the following example. Once you have a label on a frame, you can add an action to cause the Flash presentation to go to that label via **swf_actiongotolabel( )**. **swf_actiongotolabel( )** displays the labeled frame, and then stops:

```
swf_labelframe("First frame");
swf_actiongotolabel("First frame");
```

swf_showframe( ) closes the current frame from input, sends the current frame to the display, and then opens a new frame for input. The next actions will be performed on the new frame. **swf_setframe( )** jumps to a specific frame, by number, and subsequent actions will occur on that frame. If you do not know the current frame number, **swf_getframe( )** returns the number of the current frame.

```
swf_showframe();
swf_setframe(5);
$flash["frame"] = swf_getframe();
```

The Color

When you add anything colored to a frame, you can adjust the colors using **swf_addcolor( )** and **swf_mulcolor( )**. Colors are stored as three sets of numbers, each ranging from 0 to 255. The first number represents red; the second number, green; and the third number, blue. Together the numbers are referred to as RGB colors. 0, 0, 0 is black, and in HTML is written as #000000. 255, 255, 255 is white, and in HTML is written as #FFFFFF (using hexadecimal notation). You can modify colors by performing arithmetic on the individual numbers.

swf_addcolor( ) lets you add (or subtract) color adjustments that make your image lighter (or darker). **swf_mulcolor( )** lets you multiply (or divide) colors to increase (or decrease) contrast. Both operate separately for red, green, and blue so you can perform adjustments, such as converting an image to sepia tones. Both functions include an alpha adjustment, so you can include transparency, and both affect the colors produced by **swf_placeobject( )**, **swf_modifyobject( )**, and **swf_addbuttonrecord( )**:

```
swf_addcolor(3, -1, 14);
swf_mulcolor(22, 22, 11, 60);
```

Objects

You can create image objects and place the objects in frame. Objects are identified by an id from 1 to 65535 and are placed on depth layers, also numbered 1 through 65535. **swf_placeobject( )** places the object and, in the next example, places an object at depth 5. You can find the next available object id with **swf_nextid( )** so you are not crashing into existing objects. You can remove objects with **swf_removeobject( )**, and the example removes the object at depth 5:

```
$frame["object"] = swf_nextid();
swf_placeobject($frame["object"], 5);
swf_removeobject(5);
```

swf_modifyobject( ) modifies the position or color of the object at the specified depth (which suggests you place each object at a separate depth so you can update them independently). The first parameter is the depth, and the second parameter specifies how to modify the object: It can be **MOD_COLOR** to modify the color with the current mulcolor and addcolor, **MOD_MATRIX** to use the current matrix to position the object, or both as **MOD_MATRIX|MOD_COLOR**:

```
swf_modifyobject(5, MOD_COLOR);
```

Objects are items like lines, and simple shapes are created with the functions **swf_defineline( )**, **swf_definepoly( )**, and **swf_definerect( )**. **swf_defineline( )** defines a line from x1, y1 (in this example, 1, 10) to x2, y2 (in this example, 101, 110), and lets you specify the line thickness (3, in this example):

```
$line = swf_nextid();
swf_defineline($line, 1, 10, 101, 110, 3);
```

swf_definepoly( ) accepts an array of x, y pairs, a parameter specifying the number of points to use, and the line width. The following example uses the array named **$points**, which happens to contain points used to draw an arrow in Immediate Solution "Creating a Diagram in a GIF, JPEG, or PNG Image", uses 7 points, and a line thickness of 2:

```
$polygon = swf_nextid();
$points = array(200, 200, 270, 140, 270, 170, 380, 170, 380, 230, _
    270, 230, 270 ,260);
swf_definepoly($polygon, $points, 7, 2);
```

swf_definerect( ) draws a rectangle from x1, y1 to x2, y2 and accepts a line width. The example uses the same coordinates as the line example but uses them as opposite corners of a rectangle. For both **swf_definepoly( )** and **swf_definerect( )**, you can set the width to 0.0 to make the function draw a solid color object by filling the outline:

```
$rectangle = swf_nextid();
swf_definerect($rectangle, 1, 10, 101, 110, 3);
```

You can build complex shapes using the shape commands, shown in the next code. A shape starts with **swf_startshape( )** and ends with **swf_endshape( )**.

swf_shapelinesolid( ) sets the line drawing color (50, 50, 50), alpha channel (0), and thickness (1). If you specify the thickness as 0.0, you will not get lines drawn. **swf_shapefillsolid( )** turns on shape filling for the shape and sets the fill color (75, 75, 75) and alpha channel (0). **swf_shapefilloff( )** turns off filling for the shape:

```
$shape = swf_nextid( );
swf_startshape($shape);
swf_shapelinesolid(50,50, 50, 0, 1);
swf_shapefillsolid(75,75, 75, 0)
swf_shapefilloff( );
swf_endshape( );
```

swf_shapefillbitmapclip( ) sets the fill to use a bitmap. **swf_shapefillbitmaptile( )** also fills the shape with a bitmap but tiles the bitmap image to fill the shape:

```
swf_shapefillbitmapclip($bitmap);
swf_shapefillbitmaptile($bitmap);
```

swf_shapemoveto( ) moves the current location to the x, y location. **swf_shapelineto( )** draws a line from the current location to the location given by parameters x and y (100, 100 in the example) and then moves the current position to the location given by x and y. **swf_shapecurveto( )** draws a quadratic Bézier curve from the current position, through the first x, y location (100, 100), to the second (250, 250), and then sets the current location to the second location. **swf_shapecurveto3( )** draws a cubic Bézier curve from the current position, through the first x, y location (300, 300), and the second (350, 350), to the third location (340, 340), and then sets the current location to the third location. **swf_shapearc( )** draws an arc of a circle using the first two parameters as the x and y coordinates of the circle's center, the third parameter as the radius, the fourth parameter as the starting angle, and the last parameter as the ending angle:

```
swf_shapemoveto(25, 40);
swf_shapelineto(100, 100);
swf_shapecurveto(100, 100, 250, 250);
swf_shapecurveto3(300, 300, 350, 350, 340, 340);
swf_shapearc(200, 200, 50, 30, 40);
```

swf_viewport( ) lets you place your drawing within a rectangular subset of the whole page. The parameters are in a different sequence from the normal rectangle functions: The first parameter is the minimum x, the second parameter the maximum x, the third parameter is the minimum y, and the fourth parameter is the maximum y:

```
swf_viewport(100, 200, 100, 300);
```

swf_ortho( ) defines a three-dimensional orthographic mapping of user coordinates into the current viewport. It accepts the minimum x, maximum x, minimum y, maximum y, minimum z, and maximum z:

```
swf_ortho(100, 200, 100, 300, 100, 200);
```

swf_ortho2( ) defines a two-dimensional orthographic mapping of user coordinates into the current viewport. It accepts the minimum x, maximum x, minimum y, and maximum y:

```
swf_ortho2(100, 200, 100, 300);
```

swf_perspective( ) transforms the perspective projection of the viewport. The first parameter is the field-of-view angle in the y direction, the second is the aspect ratio of the viewport, the third is the near clipping plane, and the fourth is the far clipping plane. **swf_polarview( )** defines the viewport viewer's position in polar coordinates. **swf_lookat( )** performs a view transformation that lets you do things like rotate text. **swf_scale( )** scales the current transformation in the x, y, and z axes, **swf_translate( )** performs another transformation on all three axes, and **swf_rotate( )** rotates the current transformation about all three axes.

swf_posround( ) changes the rounding used when placing or moving objects. Sometimes rounding helps image clarity and sometimes it does not.

swf_pushmatrix( ) pushes the current transformation matrix onto a stack so you can save it for later use. **swf_popmatrix( )** restores the previous transformation matrix from the stack.

Text

To write text, you start by defining a font using any PostScript font. The example **swf_definefont( )** function defines a serif font using the PostScript font Times-Roman. **swf_setfont( )** sets the current font to the specified font, **swf_fontsize( )** sets the size for the current font, and **swf_fontslant( )** sets the slant for the current font (which can be positive or negative). **swf_fonttracking( )** sets the spacing between characters in the current font, with a positive number increasing the space and a negative number decreasing the space. **swf_getfontinfo( )** returns an associative array containing **Aheight**, the height in pixels of a capital A, and **xheight**, the height in pixels of a lowercase x. **swf_definetext( )** creates an object containing the specified text and accepts an optional third parameter to center the text (as used in the example). To help you plan text placement, **swf_textwidth( )** returns the width of the specified text using the current font and current font size:

```
$font_serif = 1;
swf_definefont($font_serif, "Times-Roman");
swf_setfont($font_serif);
swf_fontsize(30);
swf_fontslant(-5);
swf_fonttracking(2);
$font_size = swf_getfontinfo();
$text = swf_nextid();
swf_definetext($text, "This text is Flash", 1)
$width = swf_textwidth("test string");
```

The font function requires PostScript type 1 fonts, and lots of people have True Type fonts, so you might need to convert. There is an open source converter at **http://ttf2pt1.sourceforge.net**, and many commercial ones are available for Windows and Mac.

Bitmaps and Symbols

Bitmaps are used in some of the functions, and are created with **swf_definebitmap( )**. You can use as input a JPEG, GIF, or RGB image, and it will be converted to a Flash format file. **swf_getbitmapinfo( )** returns an array containing **size**, the bitmap size in bytes; **width**, the bitmap width in pixels; and **height**, the bitmap height in pixels:

```
$image = swf_nextid();
swf_definebitmap($image, realpath("./test.jpeg"));
$image_info = swf_getbitmapinfo($image);
```

Symbols are tiny Flash movies used as objects in larger Flash movies. If you were setting up a Flash animation for General Motors' Web site, you might use a small animated symbol for each brand of car, and then assemble the symbols within the overall frame. You start a symbol definition with **swf_startsymbol( )**, end the symbol definition with **swf_endsymbol( )**, and in between, use Flash functions to define the symbol:

```
$symbol = swf_nextid();
swf_startsymbol($symbol);
swf_endsymbol();
```

Actions

Actions let you control the display of frames in the browser and are recorded in the Flash file as a script, in the order you insert the actions in the Flash file. In Flash terminology, playing a frame outputs the frame to the browser, and playing the movie puts the display into a continuous frame display mode.

swf_actionnextframe( ) jumps to the next frame in the file, and **swf_actionprev-frame( )** jumps to the previous frame so you can edit, display, or play the frame. **swf_actiongotoframe( )** jumps to the specified frame and displays the frame (frame 4 in the example). **swf_actionplay( )** plays the Flash movie starting at the current frame, and **swf_actionstop( )** stops the playing at the current frame.

How do you place an action on a frame, as opposed to making the action act? In the example, the code jumps to frame 4, places **swf_actionstop( )** on frame 4, and then jumps back to frame 1 and plays the movie. To indicate that you want **swf_actionstop( )** recorded on the frame instead of being executed immediately, wrap the function between **swf_startdoaction( )** and **swf_enddoaction( )**, as shown in the example:

```
swf_actionnextframe();
swf_actionprevframe();
swf_actiongotoframe(4);
swf_startdoaction();
swf_actionstop();
swf_enddoaction();
swf_actiongotoframe(1);
swf_actionplay();
```

You can mix URL information with Flash frames and movies. Grab the URL with **swf_actiongeturl( )**, shown in the next code, and display the URL in front of the movie using the parameter **_level1**. **_level0** replaces the current movie with the URL display:

```
swf_actiongeturl("http://test.com/test.html", "_level1");
```

The Flash reader displays frames at two levels of quality, and **swf_actiontog-glequality( )** switches between high and low quality. The next code checks to see if the quality is changed, and changes the quality if not changed:

```
if(!isset($flash["quality"]) or !$flash["quality"])
   {
   swf_actiontogglequality();
   $flash["quality"] = true;
   }
```

swf_actionwaitforframe( ) checks if a frame is loaded (in the next example it is frame 5), and if it is not loaded, skips the number of actions specified in the second parameter (in this case, 3). You could use this to display a message while frames are still loading. I find the logic the wrong way around; if the frame is not ready, it would be better to jump backward in the script. I hope that will be a future enhancement, as well as labels on actions so it is easier to skip to the right action:

```
swf_actionwaitforframe(5, 3);
```

swf_actionsettarget( ) lets you set a target of the actions, so you can control multiple Flash movies all playing at once. I have yet to see a good example of code using this feature, or of a Web site playing multiple movies. In fact, I find multiple moving images a real distraction that drives shoppers away and tends to leave Web sites with bored young visitors who are not going to buy anything.

Buttons

Buttons can be of type **TYPE_MENUBUTTON** or **TYPE_PUSHBUTTON**, where **TYPE_MENUBUTTON** allows the focus to travel from the button when the mouse is down, and **TYPE_PUSHBUTTON** locks the focus on the button when the mouse is down. **swf_startbutton( )** starts the button creation. **swf_addbuttonrecord( )** adds information about the use of the button with the first parameter, adding the button states (can be any or all of **BSHitTest**, **BSDown**, **BSOver**, or **BSUp**), an object id of the shape, and the depth of the button in the current frame. Various **swf_oncondition( )** and action functions provide the button actions, and **swf_endbutton( )** ends the button definition:

```
$button = swf_nextid();
swf_startbutton($button, TYPE_PUSHBUTTON)
swf_addbuttonrecord(BSDown, $shape, 20);
swf_oncondition(ButtonEnter);
swf_actiongeturl("http://test.com/test.html ", "_level1");
swf_oncondition(ButtonExit);
swf_actiongeturl("", "_level1");
swf_endbutton();
```

The **swf_oncondition( )** function accepts constants from one of two lists, depending on the button type. The constants represent actions similar to **mouseover** and **mouseout** in HTML. Refer to the documentation at **www.openswf.org** for more details. **TYPE_MENUBUTTON** accepts the following:

- **IdletoOverUp**
- **OverUptoIdle**
- **OverUptoOverDown**
- **OverDowntoOverUp**
- **IdletoOverDown**
- **OutDowntoIdle**

11. Images

- **MenuEnter (IdletoOverUp|IdletoOverDown)**
- **MenuExit (OverUptoIdle|OverDowntoIdle)**

TYPE_PUSHBUTTON accepts the following:

- **IdletoOverUp**
- **OverUptoIdle**
- **OverUptoOverDown**
- **OverDowntoOverUp**
- **OverDowntoOutDown**
- **OutDowntoOverDown**
- **OutDowntoIdle**
- **ButtonEnter (IdletoOverUp|OutDowntoOverDown)**
- **ButtonExit (OverUptoIdle|OverDowntoOutDown)**

Image Databases

If you store images within text in a document format, such as PDF or Microsoft Word, consider storing the text and images in parallel within a database, or storing the text within a searchable database and the images in a separate directory, with links to the images within the text. A well-designed database approach will give you better search options than a set of PDF documents and is easier than trying to add a database as an index over a collection of documents.

If you are building business diagrams from component images, and all the image components are tiny, you could store the diagram structure and all the components in a database without trouble. At this point I am thinking of the myriad flow charts and network diagrams, where image items are small standard icons re-used many times with varying text labels attached. A database representation of those diagrams may be a lot smaller than the eventual graphic representation, and it does not take much computer time to draw each diagram.

MySQL

MySQL is the easiest database for beginners and has fast read access, so it is well suited to a document system where most of the access is read access from a Web site. MySQL does have long binary fields for storing images, but you are better off keeping images as external files with the database storing just references to the images.

Other SQL Databases

Other databases, such as PostgreSQL, Oracle, and SQL Server, provide referential integrity and other features of value to commercial applications, like selling images. If you sell images online and your billing software uses Oracle, you might as well use Oracle for your image database. Because of the high database overhead from referential integrity (and the other goodies), store the images as external files, not as binary objects in the database. If someone insists on an image verification from within the database, store the image length and CRC within the database. CRCs are explained in Chapter 8.

Hyperwave

Hyperwave is a database designed for storing documents as searchable objects. The documents should be able to include all image formats, or references to external image files, because the searchable references are stored in parallel to the documents. Chapter 6 describes Hyperwave in more detail.

Installing the Image Module

For Unix systems, a list of downloads is in the installation instructions, including the source for the image module and various extras, such as the JPEG compression routines. A good Linux distribution has all the parts prepackaged as RPMs, but few install PHP as standard, and none that I know of include all the options in their PHP installation selection list.

For Windows and Windows NT, the image module is supplied in the download. All you have to do is copy php_gd.dll from php/extensions to c:/winnt/system32 for Windows NT or Windows 2000, or windows/system for other versions of Windows. While you're copying things, copy php_exif.dll so you can use function **read_exif_data()**. Then remove the semicolon (;) from the front of the following lines in php.ini:

```
extension=php_gd.dll
extension=php_exif.dll
```

If PHP is running as a module, you will have to restart your Web server to reread php.ini, and you might as well use the opportunity to install the PDF module.

Displaying Images

When you display images within a page, there are tricks to help make the page appear professional, and PHP has functions to help you make your page perfect. You can find out about image files using **getimagesize()**, a function that accepts a file name, including the path, and returns an array containing information about the file, if the file is an image of type GIF, JPEG, PNG, or SWF. You can use all sorts of file references including URLs (from PHP 4.0.5 onward), and you can feed **getimagesize( )** a string containing an image, which you might do if you are not using files for images—for instance when reading an image from an email attachment and saving the image into a database.

getimagesize( ) also has an optional second parameter that lets you access extra information from JPEG images. The extra parameter is shown in some documentation as a "call time pass by reference" parameter, as in **getimagesize($file, &$extra)**. When I tried that with PHP 4.0.5, I received the error message shown next. I tried the code without the **&**, as in **getimagesize($file, $extra)**, and it worked perfectly, indicating that **getimagesize( )** has the parameter internally identified as passed by reference:

```
Warning: Call-time pass-by-reference has been deprecated - argument
passed by value; If you would like to pass it by reference, modify the
declaration of getimagesize(). If you would like to enable call-time
pass-by-reference, you can set allow_call_time_pass_reference to true in
your INI file. However, future versions may not support this any longer.
```

Always Use Alt in Image Tag

The blind depend on text to read your Web pages, and the **alt** parameter in the **image** tag is their best guide to your image. If your page has a picture of Hillary Rodham Clinton, adding an **alt** parameter of **alt="Mrs. Clinton"** is of little help, whereas something like **alt="Hillary Rodham Clinton standing on the steps of the White House with her daughter, Chelsea Victoria Clinton, January 20, 2000"** is useful.

Descriptions for JPEG files can be stored in a database, and accessed with the functions described in Chapters 5 and 6, or stored within a text field in the JPEG file and retrieved with **getimagesize( )**. **getimagesize( )** returns an array containing a field named **extras**, which is usually empty, reflecting the vary small number of image editors that actually let you enter text into the field. If you do have an image editor that lets you add text to the **extras** field, add the **alt** text, and then a copyright statement.

GNU Image Manipulation Program (Gimp), available at **gimp.org** for Unix, Windows, and Windows NT, lets you change the JPEG comments when you perform a File, Save As. I mentioned a few other fields to the developers, so a future version of Gimp might have the ability to display and clear the **EXIF** field and others.

Use Size Information for the Image Tag

If you provide **height=""** and **width=""** parameters in your **<img>** tags, your visitor's browser will display the page with a rectangle reserved for each image and then insert the images as they download. If you leave out the parameters, the browser will place a small icon where each image should appear, size the page to suit the small icons, and then jump the page elements around as the images download. Your pages will appear more professional if you use **height** and **width**.

Create Thumbnail Images

When an image is so large that your Web page begins to scroll off an average size screen, look at replacing large images with thumbnail size representations and adding a click-through from the thumbnail image to a full-size image.

Creating Images

The following is a summary of the **image** functions and their use. After you read this, work through the two Immediate Solutions "Creating Text in a GIF, JPEG, or PNG Image" and "Creating a Diagram in a GIF, JPEG, or PNG Image," to see how easy it is to create basic images with these functions:

- **imagearc( )**—Draws a line along part of an ellipse. If you make two of the parameters, **height** and **width**, the same, you get the arc of a circle.

- **imagefilledarc( )**—Draws the same arc as **imagearc( )**, and fills the arc based on an additional parameter that lets you either make a pie slice for a pie chart or draw the chord between the start and end of the arc and fill within the chord.

- **imageellipse( )**—Draws an ellipse, and if the height and width are equal, draws a circle.

- **imagefilledellipse( )**—Draws an ellipse and fills the ellipse with the specified color. Like **imageellipse( )**, **imagefilledellipse( )** draws a circle if the ellipse's height and width are the same.

- **imagechar( )**—Writes one character horizontally.

- **imagecharup( )**—Writes one character vertically.

- **imagestring( )**—Writes a string of characters horizontally.

- **imagestringup( )**—Writes a string vertically.

- **imageAlphaBlending( )**—Lets you set the blending mode for a 24-bit image containing alpha channel information (PNGs). The setting affects subsequent functions involving two images. This function is new in PHP 4.0.6.

- **imagecolorallocate( )**—Allocates a color for an image. The first allocated color is applied to the background. If you want to set the background to something else, you can use **imagefill( )**.

- **imagecolordeallocate( )**—De-allocates a color so you can reallocate the color.

- **imagecolorat( )**—Lets you get the palette index of the color in a pixel so you can use the color elsewhere. When the image is built with true color (PHP 4.0.6) instead of a palette, **imagecolorat( )** should return the color.

- **imagecolorclosest( )**—Accepts an RGB color specification and returns the palette index of the closest color (which should not be necessary in true color mode).

- **imagecolorexact( )**—Accepts an RGB color and returns the index of the specified color, or –1 if the color is not found. It would make sense for these color functions to return zero on error, because zero is interpreted as false by PHP; but zero is a valid palette index, so –1 will have to do for a while. Perhaps in a future release these functions will be rewritten to return a genuine false.

- **imagecolorclosestalpha( )**—Accepts a color and an alpha value, and then returns the index of the closest color.

- **imagecolorexactalpha( )**—Accepts a color and an alpha value, and then returns the index of the color in the palette, or –1 if the color is not in the palette.

- **imagecolorresolve( )**—Accepts a color and returns the index of the color or its closest alternative. **imagecolorresolve( )** seems to perform the same function as **imagecolorclosest( )**, but may use a different selection method.

- **imagecolorresolvealpha( )**—Works the same as **imagecolorresolve( )** with the addition of an alpha parameter.

- **imagegammacorrect( )**—Lets you apply a gamma correction to an image so you can take an image from a Mac and correct the image for display on other computers, or the reverse. The function requires the gamma of the input image and the gamma to be applied to the output image. The Apple RGB specification includes a gamma setting of 1.8, and the RGB specification for PCs uses a gamma of 2.2. If you are building a Web site to deliver separate images for Macs and PCs, consider scanning all the images with a gamma of 1.0, and then writing a script to copy them into one directory (call it **images**) at 2.2, and into another directory (**imagesmac**) at 1.8. The single conversion will use fewer resources, and will introduce less color distortion than converting back and forth between formats. The worst case would be to get a

JPEG from a Mac, convert it to PC gamma, save the PC version in your **images** directory, and then convert back to Mac gamma on the fly, because this would introduce two conversions and more error.

- **imagecolorset( )**—Lets you set a color in a palette.

- **imagecolortransparent( )**—Lets you define a color as transparent. GIFs allow transparency, and PNGs give you better transparency control through alpha values.

- **imagecolorsforindex( )**—Returns a color from a palette as an array containing the separate red, green, and blue components.

- **imagecolorstotal( )**—Returns the number of colors in the palette, which should let you decide how to save an image, including how many bits per pixel. At this stage, **imagegif( )** and **imagepng( )** do not have options to save an image with a specific pixel size.

- **imagecopy( )**—Copies a rectangular part of an image from one location of the image to another.

- **imagecopymerge( )**—Copies the same as **imagecopy( )** with one extra feature: The copy is merged into the image based on a percentage specified by you. The merge percentage ranges from 0, where effectively nothing happens, to 100, where there is a complete image replacement.

- **imagecopymergegray( )**—Copies the same as **impagecopymerge( )** with one extra feature: The target area is converted to a gray scale first, so all the color comes from the copied image. This function is still in development, so I do not have examples.

- **imagecopyresized( )** and **imagecopyresampled( )**—These functions are discussed in the "Resizing and Resampling" section.

- **imagecreate( )**—Creates a palette-based image (8-bit color).

- **imagecreatetruecolor( )**—Creates an image using true color (24-bit).

- **imagetruccolortopalette( )**—Converts a true color (24-bit) image to a palette image (8-bit color), which you might do if an advertiser sends you a JPEG banner using simple flat colors. Rather than compress the banner and risk color inaccuracy, try copying the banner to PNG (or GIF).

- **imagecreatefromgif( )**—Creates images from a GIF file or URL. Even though copyright issues prevent the authors of PHP from including code to create GIFs, there is no restriction on reading them, and you can easily write a script to read every GIF on your site and then save as a PNG.

- **imagecreatefromjpeg( )**—Creates images from a JPEG file or URL.

- **imagecreatefrompng( )**—Creates images from a PNG file or URL.

- **imagecreatefromwbmp( )**—Create images from a Windows bitmap file or URL.
- **imagegif( )**—Sends the image to the browser, or saves the image to a file, in GIF format.
- **imagepng( )**—Sends the image to the browser, or saves the image to a file, in PNG format.
- **imagejpeg( )**—Sends the image to the browser, or saves the image to a file, in JPEG format.
- **imagewbmp( )**—Sends the image to the browser, or saves the image to a file, in Windows bitmap format.
- **imagedestroy( )**—Removes an image from memory when you are finished with it.
- **imagecreatefromstring( )**—Creates an image from an image stored in a string, so you can read images saved in databases or decoded from email attachments. This is a new function still in development, so I have not tested what image formats work with this function.
- **imagesetpixel( )**—Lets you write to a single point.
- **imageline( )**—Draw a line from one x, y reference to another.
- **imagedashedline( )**—Draws a line of dashes from one point to another.
- **imagerectangle( )**—Draws a rectangle between two corner points.
- **imagefilledrectangle( )**—Draws a rectangle and fills the rectangle with the selected color.
- **imagepolygon( )**—Draws a polygon from a list of points supplied in an array.
- **imagefilledpolygon( )**—Draws a polygon and fills the polygon with the selected color. Rectangles, polygons, and ellipses are shown in the Immediate Solution "Creating a Diagram in a GIF, JPEG, or PNG Image."
- **imagesetbrush( )**—This function is still in development; it lets you select a "brush image" for drawing lines. The image can be any image in memory and is defined as a pseudo color, so you can select the brush, in line and polygon drawing, via a function's color parameter.
- **imagesetthickness( )**—This is another new function, which lets you select the line thickness for line drawing functions.
- **imagepsloadfont( )**—Loads a PostScript font from a file.
- **imagepsbbox( )**—Returns the dimensions of a rectangle bounding text built with PostScript Type1 fonts.

- **imagepsencodefont( )**—Alters the character encoding vector of a PostScript font.

- **imagepsfreefont( )**—Frees memory used by a PostScript font, which you might want to do if you are using a lot of fonts in one script and using them one at a time.

- **imagepsextendfont( )**—Extends or condenses a PostScript font.

- **imagepsslantfont( )**—Adds a slant to a PostScript font.

- **imagepstext( )**—Writes string of text on an image using a PostScript font.

- **imageloadfont( )**—Loads a bitmap font from a file using a special format.

- **imagefontheight( )**—Returns the height of a font.

- **imagefontwidth( )**—Returns the width of a font.

- **imagettftext( )**—Writes text using a TrueType font.

- **imagettfbbox( )**—Returns the size of the rectangle bounding the text written by **imagettftext( )**.

- **imagefill( )**—Fills the whole image with one color.

- **imagefilltoborder( )**—Starts filling the image with a specified color, to the border specified by a color.

- **imagesettile( )**—This is a new function, like **imagesetbrush( )**, that lets you set a pseudo fill color for an image and have the image used as a tile to fill shapes. To use tiling in functions like **imagefilltoborder( )**, simply select the special color **IMG_COLOR_TILED**.

- **imageinterlace( )**—Tells you if the image interlace option is on for an image, and lets you set the option on or off. For some images, interlace lets users see the gist of the image before the image is completely downloaded; but many images will have no meaning until fully downloaded, so this function may be of no use. With some file formats, interlacing the image actually makes the image larger, so test interlacing before use on your production Web site.

- **imagesx( )**—Returns the image width.

- **imagesy( )**—Returns the image height. **imagesx( )** and **imagesy( )** enable you to perform calculations based on the image size. This is great for images you loaded with functions like **imagecreatefromjpeg( )**.

- **imagetypes( )**—Returns a list of the image types supported by PHP. This lets you write dynamic code that will use GIFs on sites with an old version of PHP, and will use PNGs with the later versions of PHP that support PNG.

Changing Images

Every change to an image has the potential to turn a carefully crafted work of art into an embarrassingly bad image. Prior to PHP 4.0.6, the image functions worked in 8-bit mode, so they worked with GIFs and the 8-bit mode of PNG but not with JPEGs. PHP 4.0.6 introduces **imagecreatetruecolor( )** to let you work in full 24-bit color with PNG's 24-bit mode and JPEGs.

Changing Colors

GIFs use 8-bit color (allowing 256 colors), JPEGs use 24-bit color (24 million colors), and PNGs allow both but when you use 8-bit color, both GIFs and PNGs use a palette system where each of the 256 colors can have a 24-bit value. This means your customer can request a specific RGB color, like #f2334c, and you can use the color in any file format. Will the color remain accurate?

GIFs and PNGs store exact colors, so your customer will get #f2334c displayed. JPEGs store an approximation (that becomes less accurate as you increase the compression), so the color will be wrong but may not be noticeably wrong at low levels of compression. If you use **imagejpeg( )** and set the optional quality parameter to anything less than 100 (it defaults to 100), you will lose color accuracy. For images like company logos, show the customer the results first.

Macs and PCs have different gamma settings, so images prepared on a PC will look too light on a Mac, and images prepared an a Mac will look too dark on a PC. LCD displays generally produce far fewer than 24 million colors, which will make colors look inaccurate. With all the technical problems preventing your customer from seeing the right color all the time, what can you do to help?

Always work from an original image. If you are continually changing an image, especially a JPEG, keep the original file and a list of cumulative changes. Then create new images by applying the accumulated changes to the original. Set up one directory in your Web site named **images** and another, outside the Web site, named **originals**. The public can access **images** but not **originals**, and PHP can access both. When you want to make a change, like opening a map of Canada and writing city names and temperatures on the map, you open the original and then write everything. It is tempting to open the original, write the city names on the map, and then save the changes and only write the temperatures on a daily basis, but with JPEG and any level of compression, changing the image twice will increase the image distortion.

Another approach is to store the originals as PNG, perform the updates, such as adding city names, and then save as PNG. Your daily update can then use **imagecreatefrompng( )** to open the PNG image from **originals**, add the temperatures, and use **imagejpeg( )** to create the JPEG in **images**.

Resizing and Resampling

Resizing an image is easy. What is not so easy is producing the optimal image. Simple geometric graphics with sharp edges tend to get ragged edges, and colors in photographs become washed out. What do you do to get the perfect image?

Pixel resizing works with sharp vertical and horizontal edges where the new size is an even fraction of the original, such as exactly half the original size. Other techniques favor diagonal lines and color graduations. Figure 11.2 shows text before resizing. Figure 11.3 shows the same text after resizing to one-third the original size and then magnifying back to original size. You can see the difference between the clean, sharp, straight edges of Figure 11.2 and the ragged curves of Figure 11.3. PHP image functions include **imagecopyresized( )** to resize images.

Figure 11.4 shows the text resized with bilinear resampling, and Figure 11.5 shows the text after bicubic resampling. Bicubic resampling makes your images fuzzy, in an attempt to hide ragged edges, but all it really does is make me want to clean my reading glasses. As I write this, PHP 4.0.6 is under development, and includes the new function **imagecopyresampled( )**, which will provide resizing similar to either Figure 11.4 or 11.5.

Figure 11.2   Text before resizing.

Figure 11.3   Text after pixel resizing.

Figure 11.4   Text after bilinear resizing.

Figure 11.5   Text after bicubic resizing.

External Programs

You can perform mass conversions of images using a variety of utility programs. Chapter 7 covers running external programs. The batch programs let you convert images, so all images become one standard size or have the same compression levels. If you let one program, like Gimp, perform a batch conversion, you can settle for an average result across all images, or use Gimp's scripting language to modify individual conversions, or call Gimp once per image to perform the conversion most suitable for that image. I prefer to keep all the scripting within PHP and call external programs once per image.

The **image** functions are transforming into a true color toolkit to make full use of the PNG format. Newer 3D image formats are likely to become very popular as broadband Internet access makes 3D virtual showroom walkthroughs practical. Based on experience with many programming languages, when support for a new technology appears in a scripting language, it appears in PHP first.

Choosing the Right Format

You are now ready to choose the right image file format for a specific application and argue the relative benefits of competing formats. Flash support is limited to Unix, which gives you a quick deciding point for some sites. Browser support will influence some decisions, as will your choice of font types.

Ease of coding is often a deciding factor, but there is not a lot to choose between the various formats unless you decide to tackle something complex. As soon as you do that, you are likely to be limited to one file format.

Immediate Solutions

Listing Images

This solution is a simplified version of solutions developed in Chapter 8, where image information is displayed as part of an overall file display. The code shows how to step through files, listing the attributes of files that are images.

getimagesize( ) accepts a file name and an optional extra parameter, here named **$extra**, and returns an array, named **$att** in the example, containing information about the image. **$att** receives four standard values, plus two extras for JPEG images. None of the test images had the extra information, and only two of the standard values (height and width) are of use, so I included code to store all the values, but displayed only height and width. **$extra** receives an array containing information stored within the image—information that is currently only in JPEGs. There were none in the test files, so, although I included code to collect and place the information into a string ready for display, I did not place the string in the output HTML table.

Collecting Image Information

The following function is a modification of a function developed in Chapter 8 for reading file attributes. This function accepts a path to a directory and returns an array containing information about the images in the directory. The first part of the code removes any slash at the end of the path, and then opens the directory the path points to. The code loops through files, finding any with a file extension of .jpg, .jpeg, .gif, .png, or .swf, and then gathering from the files the information returned by **getimagesize( )**. The information is added to an array and returned at the end of the function:

```
function get_directory_file($path)
    {
    if(substr($path, -1) == "/")
        {
        $path = substr($path, 0, -1);
        }
    $path_id = opendir($path);
    while($file_name = readdir($path_id))
        {
```

```
      if($file_name != "." and $file_name != "..")
         {
         $file["type"] = @filetype($path . "/" . $file_name);
         if($file["type"] == "dir")
            {
            $file_array = get_directory_file($path. "/" . $file_name);
            print("<br>found type: " . gettype($found) );
            if(isset($found))
               {
               $found = array_merge($found, $file_array);
               }
            else
               {
               $found = $file_array;
               }
            }
         else
            {
            $file["size"] = filesize($path . "/" . $file_name);
            $x5 = strtolower(substr($file_name, -5));
            $x4 = substr($x5, -4);
            if($x4 == ".jpg" or $x5 == ".jpeg" or $x4 == ".gif"
            or $x4 == ".png" or $x4 == ".swf")
               {
               $att = getimagesize($path . "/" . $file_name,
                  $file["extra"]);
               if(isset($att[0])) {$file["width"] = $att[0];}
               if(isset($att[1])) {$file["height"] = $att[1];}
               $found[$path][$file_name] = $file;
               }
            }
         }
      }
   closedir($path_id);
   if(!isset($found))
      {
      $found = array();
      }
   return($found);
   }
```

Related solution:	*Found on page:*
Listing Files with Attributes	294

Displaying Image Information

The following code uses table formatting functions introduced in Chapter 8 and saved in a separate file named table.html:

```
include("./table.html");
```

The following code gets the array of images from **get_directory_file( )** and then loops through the array, decoding information from the array and formatting the information into a table:

```
$found = get_directory_file($path, "");
reset($found);
$print_limit = 10;
print("<table border=\"3\">" . tr("<td colspan=\"7\">"
    . "<font color=\"Green\"><em>Directory</em></font></td>"));
while(list($d, $dv) = each($found))
    {
    if(is_array($dv))
        {
        print(tr("<td colspan=\"7\">"
            . "<font color=\"Green\"><em>" . $d . "</em></font></td>")
            . tr(tde("File") . tde("Size") . tde("Height") . tde("Width")
            . tde("Channel") . tde("Bits") . tde("Extra")));
        while(list($f, $fv) = each($dv))
            {
            if(is_array($fv))
                {
                if($print_limit)
                    {
                    if(!isset($fv["channel"])) {$fv["channel"] = " ";}
                    if(!isset($fv["bits"])) {$fv["bits"] = " ";}
                    if(!isset($fv["extra"])) {$fv["extra"] = " ";}
                    if(is_array($fv["extra"]))
                        {
                        $e = "";
                        reset($fv["extra"]);
                        while(list($ek, $ev) = each($fv["extra"]))
                            {
                            if(strlen($e))
                                {
                                $e .= "<br>";
                                }
                            if($ek == "APP13")
                                {
                                $e .= $ek . ": " . iptcparse($ev);
                                }
```

433

```
          else
            {
            $e .= "k: " . $ek . ", v: " . $ev;
            }
          }
        }
      else
        {
        $e = $fv["extra"];
        }
      print(tr(tdl($f) . tdl($fv["size"])
        . tdl($fv["height"]) . tdl($fv["width"])
        . tdl($fv["channel"]) . tdl($fv["bits"])
        . tdl($e)));
      $print_limit--;
      }
    }
  }
 }
}
```

The function **iptcparse( )** decodes information formatted to the International Press Telecommunications Council (IPTC) standard described at **www.iptc.org**.

Figure 11.6 shows the output of the previous code, and demonstrates that in most images, there are no channels, bits, or extra values. I looked through 40,000 images from the Internet and found only a few mentioning Adobe image editor as the last editor used on the image.

Related solution:	Found on page:
Listing File Image Attributes	308

Figure 11.7 shows the same array from **get_directory_file( )** displayed with the image instead of the image attributes.

Directory						
i:/petermoulding/web/root/phpblackbook/images/images						
File	Size	Height	Width	Channel	Bits	Extra
bs.gif	255	22	61			
kingparrot.jpg	60810	500	250			
me.jpg	6530	100	80			
notme.jpg	50024	250	280			
PHPSydney.com.gif	6405	100	190			

Figure 11.6   List of images with attributes.

Directory				
i:/petermoulding/web/root/phpblackbook/images/images				
File	*Size*	*Height*	*Width*	*Image*
bs.gif	255	22	61	Backspace
kingparrot.jpg	60810	500	250	
me.jpg	6530	100	80	

Figure 11.7   Image list with images full size.

Sometimes you need to list the images neatly for your customers and visitors. The next code shows you how to correctly display images using the information gathered from functions like **getimagesize()**.

The code loops through the same array formatting the same type of table but with images displayed inline. **iptcparse()** is dropped, because it does not supply anything useful. The image is included via an **<img>** tag. The image size information is used to tell the browser how much space should be allocated for the image. The **alt** information is the image file name and, if you were using an image editor that let you place text in a JPEG text field, you could place the text from there into the **alt** field. The alternative is to look up the **alt** text on a database. Chapters 5 and 6 describe the databases you can use:

```
$found = get_directory_file($path, "");
reset($found);
```

```
$print_limit = 10;
print("<table border=\"3\">" . tr("<td colspan=\"5\">"
   . "<font color=\"Green\"><em>Directory</em></font></td>"));
while(list($d, $dv) = each($found))
   {
   if(is_array($dv))
      {
      print(tr("<td colspan=\"5\">"
         . "<font color=\"Green\"><em>" . $d . "</em></font></td>")
         . tr(tde("File") . tde("Size") . tde("Height") . tde("Width")
         . tde("Image")));
      while(list($f, $fv) = each($dv))
         {
         if(is_array($fv))
            {
            if($print_limit)
               {
               print(tr(tdl($f) . tdl($fv["size"])
                  . tdl($fv["height"]) . tdl($fv["width"])
                  . tdl("<img src=\"./images/" . $f . "\""
                  . " width=\"" . $fv["width"] . "\""
                  . " height=\"" . $fv["height"] . "\""
                  . " border=\"0\" alt=\"" . $f . "\">")));
               $print_limit--;
               }
            }
         }
      }
   }
print("</table>" );
```

Figure 11.8 shows the image list taken one step further with every image listed in a controlled size. Because some images are far bigger than others, the large ones have their size constrained to a maximum that leaves them readable but that allows many more images per page. Note the image files are not resized, just constrained in the display—something perfectly reasonable for an intranet application.

The following code makes a few small additions to the previous code. **$image_limit** specifies the maximum height and width for images. The code in the middle finds the largest dimension out of the image's height and width, divides the dimension down to **$image_limit**, and then uses the same ratio to divide the other dimensions down to a proportional size. The two lines in the **print** statement are changed to use the calculated size instead of the original size:

Directory				
i:/petermoulding/web/root/phpblackbook/images/images				
File	*Size*	*Height*	*Width*	*Image*
bs.gif	255	22	61	Backspace
kingparrot.jpg	60810	500	250	
me.jpg	6530	100	80	
notme.jpg	50024	250	280	
PHPSydney.com.gif	6405	100	190	

Figure 11.8 Image list with images thumbnail size.

```php
$found = get_directory_file($path, "");
reset($found);
$print_limit = 10;
$image_limit = 100;
print("<table border=\"3\">" . tr("<td colspan=\"5\">"
   . "<font color=\"Green\"><em>Directory</em></font></td>"));
while(list($d, $dv) = each($found))
   {
   if(is_array($dv))
      {
      print(tr("<td colspan=\"5\">"
         . "<font color=\"Green\"><em>" . $d . "</em></font></td>")
         . tr(tde("File") . tde("Size") . tde("Height") . tde("Width")
         . tde("Image")));
      while(list($f, $fv) = each($dv))
         {
         if(is_array($fv))
            {
            if($print_limit)
               {
```

```
        $h = $fv["height"];
        $w = $fv["width"];
        if($w > $image_limit)
            {
            $div = $w / $image_limit;
            $h = $h / $div;
            $w = $w / $div;
            }
        print(tr(tdl($f) . tdl($fv["size"])
            . tdl($fv["height"]) . tdl($fv["width"])
            . tdl("<img src=\"./images/" . $f . "\""
            . " width=\"" . $w . "\""
            . " height=\"" . $h . "\""
            . " border=\"0\" alt=\"" . $f . "\">")));
        $print_limit--;
        }
    }
  }
 }
}
print("</table>" );
```

If you are presenting many files over the Internet, consider copying and resizing the images using the **image** functions shown elsewhere in this chapter. What you could do to reduce overhead is to have image directory **/image/** containing the originals and **/imagesmall/** containing the thumbnail versions. In your administrative display of images, gather the array of images in **/image/** and compare it to **/imagesmall/**. If a file is in **/image/** but not in **/imagesmall/**, read in the file using the appropriate **image** functions, resize the image, and then save under the same name in **/imagesmall/**.

You could modify the previous image display to calculate the new size, call the **image** functions to copy, resize, and save the result, and then display the result in the thumbnail browse list.

Creating Text in a PDF Document with ClibPDF

Creating a PDF file from a Web site script makes sense when you want to output text with special fonts that aren't available in a normal browser. The code that follows shows you how to produce text using the standard Times Roman font, and you can then add any font and text you like. The font name is any name valid in PostScript, and the font size has to be specified in points no matter what you specify as the document's unit of measure:

```
define("portrait", 0);
$doc_name = "clibpdftest.pdf";
$doc_path = dirname($PATH_TRANSLATED) . "/";
$font["face"] = "Times-Roman";
$font["size"] = 40;
if($doc = cpdf_open(0))
   {
   print("<br>Opened." );
   cpdf_page_init($doc, 1, portrait, 288, 360);
   cpdf_begin_text($doc);
   cpdf_set_font($doc, $font["face"], $font["size"], "NULL");
   cpdf_show($doc, "test text");
   cpdf_show_xy($doc, "test at xy", 1, 1);
   cpdf_end_text($doc);
   cpdf_finalize($doc);
   if(cpdf_save_to_file($doc, $doc_path . $doc_name))
      {
      print("<br><a href=\"./" . $doc_name . "\">"
         . $doc_name . "</a>");
      }
   cpdf_close(\$doc);
   }
```

The code creates a PDF file in the current directory, and then produces a link to the file, an approach that will help you with testing by letting you save examples for reference. You can also use this approach in an administrative panel that creates new pages for your site, or recreates pages using updated data.

cpdf_open() opens the document and returns the document id, **$doc**, for use as the first parameter in all other ClibPDF functions. **cpdf_page_init()** sets the page orientation and size (in points). **cpdf_begin_text()** starts a block of text, and **cpdf_end_text()** ends the block. Within the text block, you need to set a font with **cpdf_set_font()**, and then use **cpdf_show()** or **cpdf_show_xy()** to produce the text. **cpdf_show()** uses the current location, whereas **cpdf_show_xy()** accepts a location as x and y coordinates from the bottom-left corner. The units for the coordinates default to 1 inch because nothing else was set in **cpdf_page_init()**.

cpdf_finalize() finishes the document, **cpdf_save_to_file()** writes the document to disk in the same directory as the script, and **cpdf_close()** removes the document from memory. The code produces the link shown next and the PDF document displayed in Figure 11.9:

clibpdftest.pdf

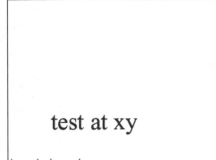

Figure 11.9   PDF showing text from cpdf_show().

Creating Text in a PDF Document with PDFlib

This example uses the same approach as the previous Immediate Solution, but uses PDFlib functions instead of ClibPDF functions. The most noticeable changes are the creation of an object for the document, **pdf_new( )**, and the use of standard font names instead of PostScript font names. By standard, I mean the ones in your operating system. **pdf_findfont( )** returns false if it cannot find the font:

```
$doc_name = "pdflibtest.pdf";
$doc_path = dirname ($PATH_TRANSLATED) . "/";
$font["face"] = "Times New Roman";
$font["size"] = 40;
$doc = pdf_new();
pdf_open_file($doc, $doc_path . $doc_name);
pdf_begin_page($doc, 288, 360);
$serif = pdf_findfont($doc, $font["face"], "host", 1);
if($serif)
    {
    pdf_setfont($doc, $serif, $font["size"]);
    }
else
    {
    print("<br>Could not find font: " . \$font["face"] );
    }
pdf_set_value($doc, "textrendering", 1);
pdf_show($doc, "test text");
```

```
pdf_show_xy($doc, "test at xy", 40, 40);
pdf_end_page($doc);
pdf_close($doc);
pdf_delete($doc);
print("<br><a href=\"./" . $doc_name . "\">" . $doc_name . "</a>" );
```

pdf_set_value() sets a value, named in parameter two, to the value supplied in parameter three. **textrendering** changes the way text is drawn. (Table 11.1 lists values for **textrendering**.) Figure 11.10 shows the results from experimenting with two different values. On the left is filled text from value 0, and on the right is stroked (outlined) text from value 1.

Table 11.1   Values for textrendering.

Value	Name	Description
0	Fill	Solid color text.
1	Stroke	Outlined text.
2	Fill and stroke	Solid color with different color outline.
3	Invisible	
4	Fill and add to clipping path	The clipping path is used to shape text into curves.
5	Stroke and add to clipping path	
6	Fill, stroke, and add to clipping path	
7	Add to clipping path	

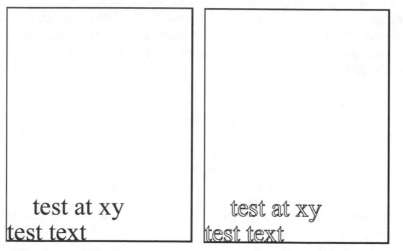

Figure 11.10   PDF showing filled text (left) and stroked text (right) from **pdf_show()**.

Creating Text in a GIF, JPEG, or PNG Image

This example uses the same approach as the previous Immediate Solution but uses image functions instead of PDFlib functions.

The image functions can read True Type fonts, but that requires extra installation work, so the example uses one of the five built-in fonts; it's set in **$font["size"]**, and used in **imagechar()**. The file setup code is changed to use **realpath()** to convert the relative file name, the type you use in a Web page, to an absolute name for the PHP file functions.

imagecreate() creates an image in memory using the supplied width and height. There is no option to save directly to disk, and the image is unlikely to be used for long multipage PDF-style documents, so you do not need the option. The first **imagecolorallocate()** defines a color that can be used anywhere in the image and also becomes the default background. **imagepng()** saves the image to disk and **imagedestroy()** removes the image from memory. That is all you need to create a blank image file.

The second **imagecolorallocate()** defines the color **black** for the text, and is used in the two text writing functions. The first text writing function is **imagechar()** and writes one character to the image file, no matter how much text is supplied. The second text writing function, **imagestring()**, writes a full string of text in one hit, and has all the other parameters the same as **imagechar()**. Both functions accept the image id from **imagecreate()** and a font id, where 1 through 5 are built-in fonts and all others are user-defined fonts. Both accept an x and y coordinate to start the text; the top-left corner of the image is 0,0, and the x and y coordinates count from the bottom-left corner of the first text character. The functions accept a text string, and then the color id from an **imagecolorallocate()**:

```
$image["name"] = "imagetest.png";
$image["path"] = realpath("./" . $image["name"]);
$font["size"] = 5;
$image["id"] = imagecreate(288, 360);
$white = imagecolorallocate($image["id"], 0xff, 0xff, 0xff);
$black = imagecolorallocate($image["id"], 0, 0, 0);
imagechar($image["id"], $font["size"], 10, 10, "test text", $black);
imagestring($image["id"], $font["size"], 40, 40, "test at xy", $black);
imagepng($image["id"], $image["path"]);
imagedestroy($image["id"]);
print("<br><a href=\"./" . $image["name"] . "\" target=\"_blank\">"
   . $image["name"] . "</a>" );
```

imagecolorallocate( ) accepts the image id and three numbers representing the red, green, and blue components of the color. In the example, black is defined in decimal as 0, 0, 0 and white, in decimal, would be 255, 255, 255. Instead of decimal, white is defined using hexadecimal notation, where colors range from 0x0 to 0xff, and equate to the HTML color parameter used in **<font>** and other tags. Aquamarine, in a font tag, is **color="#7fffd4"**, and that equates to the **imagecolorallocate( )** shown next:

```
$aquamarine = imagecolorallocate($image["id"], 0x7f, 0xff, 0xd4);
```

That is the PNG example. How complicated is it to create a GIF, JPEG or Windows BMP? Simply replace the **imagepng( )** line with one of the following:

```
imagegif($image["id"], $image["path"]);
imagejpeg($image["id"], $image["path"]);
imagewbmp($image["id"], $image["path"]);
```

Now for a tricky part. The base library behind the image functions is based on 256-color rendering, as used in GIFs. There is a new version of the library with 24-bit color (as used in JPEGs and the like), and a new **imagecreatetruecolor( )** function to start the image creation using the higher resolution. I tested a beta copy, so it should all be working cleanly by the time you read this.

NOTE: *Some browsers cache images no matter what settings you set, so when you are testing images, you often have to refresh images separate from pages to get an updated image.*

Figure 11.11   Diagram of a target in a PNG image.

Creating a Diagram in a GIF, JPEG, or PNG Image

The example diagram in Figure 11.11 is a simple target with an arrow pointing to the center; if you combine it with the text functions from the previous Immediate Solution, it creates a useful business graphic. The diagram could have your sales target for the month, or a demographic analysis with age groups on each circle. Most important of all, the code demonstrates the creation of the basic rectangles, circles and polygons you can use to build any diagram.

The code looks similar to the PNG image-creation code used for the text example. The image size is changed to 400×400 in **imagecreate()**, and there are two extra **imagecolorallocate()** functions so the arrow can be pepper red with a yellow edge.

Because these functions do not have shading and 3D, you might prefer to draw the base diagram using a fancy 3D drawing package, import the result into the image, and then just add words and numbers. Other diagrams, like flow charts, are best prepared with the flat layout that is easy to create with this type of code.

imagerectangle() creates a black rectangle of one pixel thickness around the outside edge so the diagram can have a nice border. In PHP 4.0.6 onward, you will be able to set the line thickness using **imagesetthickness()**; but in earlier versions, use the technique used in this example, where the 5-pixel-thick border was created by drawing five borders each 1 pixel smaller. **imagerectangle()** accepts the id of the image, the x and y coordinates of one corner of the rectangle, the x and y coordinates of the opposite corner, and a color.

A circle is an ellipse with equal height and width, so you can draw the circular target with the **imagefilledellipse()** function, which accepts the image id, the x and y coordinates for the center of the ellipse, and a height and width. The outer circle is black filled with black, the next circle is white filled with white, and the last black-filled circle completes the target. If you need to create a pattern with many lines, such as many concentric circles, you could convert the code to a **for()** loop to step from the outer circle to the inner circle.

The arrow is a polygon with seven points, input through an array. The outer yellow arrow is defined in array, **$outer_arrow**, which is then input to **imagefilled-polygon()** with the second parameter set to the name of the array, and the third parameter specifying the number of point pairs to use from the array. Each point in the polygon is entered as an x, y pair.

The inner pepper-colored arrow uses an array similar to the outer arrow with each point moved in one or two pixels. One trick you can use to draw neat borders is to draw the polygon twice, once filled with the central color and then a second time using the border color but not filled. The results depend on line thickness and the accuracy of the software. The straight vertical and horizontal lines tend to work no matter how you create the image, but the diagonal lines always tend to look jagged. The technique I used in this example gives you more control over the relative line strengths, especially along the diagonal edges.

The rest of the code saves the image for later display. When testing, it is easier to write the images to disk so you can save a series of tests for comparison, including both your successes and any failures that help show the behavior of the various image functions:

```php
$image["name"] = "imagediagram.png";
$image["path"] = realpath("./" . $image["name"]);
$image["id"] = imagecreate(400, 400);
$white = imagecolorallocate($image["id"], 0xff, 0xff, 0xff);
$black = imagecolorallocate($image["id"], 0, 0, 0);
$yellow = imagecolorallocate($image["id"], 0xff, 0xff, 0x00);
$pepper = imagecolorallocate($image["id"], 0xff, 0x33, 0x00);
imagerectangle($image["id"], 0, 0, 399, 399, $black);
imagerectangle($image["id"], 1, 1, 398, 398, $black);
imagerectangle($image["id"], 2, 2, 397, 397, $black);
imagerectangle($image["id"], 3, 3, 396, 396, $black);
imagerectangle($image["id"], 4, 4, 395, 395, $black);
imagefilledellipse($image["id"], 200, 200, 300, 300, $black);
imagefilledellipse($image["id"], 200, 200, 200, 200, $white);
imagefilledellipse($image["id"], 200, 200, 100, 100, $black);
$outer_arrow = array(200, 200, 270, 140, 270, 170, 380, 170, 380, 230,
    270, 230, 270 ,260);
imagefilledpolygon($image["id"], $outer_arrow, 7, $yellow);
$inner_arrow = array(202, 200, 268, 144, 268, 171, 379, 171, 379, 229,
    268, 229, 268 ,256);
imagefilledpolygon($image["id"], $inner_arrow, 7, $pepper);
imagepng($image["id"], $image["path"]);
imagedestroy($image["id"]);
print("<br><a href=\"./" . $image["name"] . "\" target=\"_blank\">"
    . $image["name"] . "</a>" );
```

Now you have all the tools you need to use dynamic graphics on your Web site. If you need a more complex image, you probably need to prepare it offline using Gimp, Paint Shop Pro, or Adobe Photoshop, and more importantly, an experienced image editor. Of course, you can always watch a professional in action and then translate their actions to PHP image functions for later incorporation into your code.

11. Images

Chapter 12

International Iconography

In Depth

You have a Web site, and 400 million visitors from 80 countries drop in for a quick read of your Web pages. How many can read the language you used—the acronyms and technical terminology, the local words and slang? Have you used colors that mean "good luck" or "death"? If you used a special character set for a language, should the characters run right to left, left to right, or vertically? What about displays of dates, numbers, currency, and copyright symbols?

When you take your Web site to the world, you have many things to consider. I checked the logs of one site and found that, within one month, visitors from 82 countries had hit the site. The site is in English and has a high visit rate to the home page, so I looked at one of the lower-level information pages. People from most of the 82 countries visited the information pages, but most of the 82 countries had a very high exit rate from the home page. What does this mean?

There are over 200 countries in the world, but some have restricted access to the Internet, so you are unlikely to get a casual visit to your site from them. In some countries, the access costs are so high that the only visits from those countries are exporters trying to find customers for their products. Retail sites seem to get visits from 80 different countries, so that is probably the number of countries where Internet access costs are low enough to attract a wide range of customers for your site.

Visitors from 15 countries will explore an English-language site, but the rest visit the home page and then leave. The high drop-off rate for more than 60 countries reflects the fact that few people in those countries know enough English to shop at your site. They know just enough to use an English-language search engine to find words like *software* or *PlayStation* but not enough to navigate your site, select the right model PlayStation, and complete your checkout procedures. A few researchers from universities will work their way right through your site, as will Web crawler software from that country's local search engines, but not enough to sustain a business.

To retain the visitors from those countries, you need to display text in their local languages. You need to explain acronyms, slang, and local terminology in their language. Is gas called *gasoline* or *petrol*? I tried to use the word *pram* in this book, only to be told that in the United States, everyone calls the same device a *stroller*. A biscuit is not a biscuit in every country, nor is a muffin. In Yosemite

National Park, a kind person behind the counter at the deli (which was a completely different type of shop from delicatessens in other parts of the world), explained that I had to ask for wheat bread if I wanted wholemeal. What a strange term to use, considering that all the breads available where made of wheat.

Cultural differences go beyond just languages; they can even extend to the colors you use on your site. In some countries, white is worn by the bride at a wedding, but in China, white is worn when mourning the dead. Australians are happy wearing large splashes of orange or green, or both, but would green be a wise choice in Northern Ireland or orange in the rest of Ireland? (When you do have just the right colors for your Web site, please also be sure to test them with the colorblind.)

This chapter helps you build the code that lets you choose the words, colors, and other options to suit every visitor from all countries. The solutions cover the basics required to deliver your choices consistently and efficiently, while remaining open to easy future enhancements.

Detecting the Language and Country

In your browser, look at Edit|Preferences|Language, or the equivalent. You can select several languages and set the order of priority. If you read English and Korean, you could set the list to **en ko** or **ko en**, depending on which language you prefer. The **www.w3.org/WAI/ER/IG/ert/iso639.htm** site has a list of two- and three-letter language codes you might see used in browsers. The language code can also have a country code added. The official list of country codes is at **www.din.de/gremien/nas/nabd/iso3166ma/codlstp1/en_listp1.html**. English is represented by the code **en**, but English as used in the United States can be represented by **en-US**. The language codes are usually written in lowercase and the country codes in uppercase, but not all browsers comply with the standard.

Detecting the Language and Country from the Browser

Once a browser is set up with one or more language codes, the browser includes the codes with each page request. Your scripts, or your Web server, can respond with a page in the appropriate language. If the visitor is using a corporate network, or is in an Internet café, the visitor may not be able to change the country code in the browser, so use the code just as a guide. Deliver your home page in the language selected by the browser, and then provide links to any other languages you have available, so the user can select the best choice and store their choice in their session record. If they provide a list but you cannot deliver the first choice, work through the list until you find a match. If there are no matches, default to English, because various standards specify English as the default.

You can detect some visitors' countries of origin by looking at their HTTP referrer string and getting the country code from their domain name or IP address. This technique is so full of errors, however, that you should treat it as a rough guide. Here is one simple example: In the same week that I was planning a trip overseas, AltaVista started using the technique to direct people to country-specific sites. When I tried to access **altavista.com**, they bounced me to **altavista.com.au**. When I tried to view **altavista.co.uk**, they bounced me back to **altavista.com.au**. At that time, **altavista.com.au** did not give me an easy way to check the weather overseas, so I switched to Yahoo and AltaVista lost a long-term user.

If you categorize your customers solely by their domain or IP address, you are often making a mistake and preventing people from choosing what they want. When you find someone visiting your site from a domain ending in .de, the visitor might be a German visiting from Germany, but might also be a resident of France accessing the Internet through a company network that just happens to have a connection to the Internet in Germany. One of my customers, a multinational financial institution, has its head office Internet connection directed through a branch office in another country because the connection costs are lower. Your CompuServe customer connecting through a U.S.-based proxy could be an Australian business person working in Italy and trying to visit Greek sites to practice reading Greek, because part of his family is from Greece and Greece is the next stop on his itinerary. AltaVista's forced redirection will cost it a lot of customers.

Detecting the Language and Country with Apache

Apache is a great product with great features, and, if you are only using HTML, you can use Apache's language redirection to serve the right page. The visitor sets their language preference in their browser, you set some options in Apache, and Apache delivers a page. If you have page index.html in English and Italian, you call the English version index.html.en and the Italian version index.html.it. In the Apache .conf file, you insert the following entries:

```
AddLanguage en .en
AddLanguage it .it
LanguagePriority en it
```

If you have a good book on Apache, such as *Apache Server Commentary* by Greg Holden and Nick Wells (The Coriolis Group, Inc.), or you are using another Web server with equivalent facilities, you can perform other tricks to guide people around your site based on the language in their browser—but it is not the ultimate customer service. Your visitors from Japan might have their browsers set to **jp**, but may want the English-language version of your site so they can practice reading English. Even if they want to read your site in Japanese, they might be in the office of a subsidiary in Ireland, and may not be able to set the language option in their browser because the local network administrator has locked down all the browser settings.

Ultimate Choice with PHP

Take control of country and language settings in your PHP code. You can give your visitors the ultimate choice completely free of browser problems. Give your visitors the option of a free logon so they can configure their access to your site to suit them and store their preferences in their profile. By free logon, I mean a logon they can create themselves, without a registration process, free from restrictions and intrusive marketing surveys. The idea is to encourage them to use the logon to customize their view of the site.

What choices should they get?

- *Language*—Visitors should be able to specify the language in which they want to read your site.

  - *Character set*—Some languages require special character sets, but not all browsers have these characters. Provide a fall-back option.

  - *Direction of display*—Some languages are displayed right-to-left, and some are displayed vertically.

- *Country*—If your site provides country-specific information, let the visitor choose the default country. Display both the country name and country code, because some countries have more than one code, and some codes are shared by several countries.

  - *Date format*—Show your customers the date format you will use when they select a country: MM-DD-YYYY, DD-MM-YYYY, or YYYY-MM-DD.

  - *Number format*—Show your customers the number format you will use for their country: both the character you will use for the decimal point (**.** or **,**) and the character you will use to separate thousands (**,** or **.**).

- *Search defaults*—If you have a search facility, save options like parental control, country, type of search, and number of results per page.

- *Colors*—If you use colored backgrounds, give visitors the option to turn off the color. Some colored backgrounds do not work with some LCD screens, clash with technologies like WebTV, and might have negative cultural meanings in other countries.

- *User name*—If your page starts with "Hello Pete," or has a similar use of the user's logon name, remember that common names will run out fast and "Pete" might have to log on as "Pete110." Give visitors an option to specify a friendly name.

- *Email address*—If you collect a visitor's email address, give them the option to change it when they change their address. They will often give you a fake address, or one at **yahoo.com**, when they start, and then switch to a real address when they trust your site.

- *Password*—Many sites use passwords but provide no option to change the password. Let people change their passwords, and be clear about how you handle special characters from country-specific keyboards. If someone types in their password on a kana keyboard and then flies from Tokyo to Helsinki, can they still log on?

- *Other information*—If you collect age, sex, and other junk that marketing departments ask for, expect people to lie until they trust your site, and then correct their entries if they see some useful result. You might provide a better selection of banner advertising if they provide the right age. If you tell your visitors about the use of the information and the benefit, they will likely become more honest and open. Your visitor's desire for privacy varies greatly based on both culture and country.

Language Requirements

The language display options for HTML are described at **www.w3.org/TR/ html401/struct/dirlang.html**, and include the two-character language codes, language variations by country, and a direction to display the text.

The browser first looks for a **lang=** parameter in the tag surrounding text, such as a quotation tag. If not is supplied, the browser reads outward through the tags and may find a **lang=** parameter in a paragraph or division tag. If no tag is found, the browser next looks for an **HTTP "Content-Language"** header, and finally uses any defaults set in the browser. You could display an English-language page, and include a paragraph from a French philosopher displayed in French. If the French philosopher quotes a Greek philosopher, the Greek quotation could be displayed in Greek within the French paragraph.

If the language is specified as a country-specific variation of a language, such as **en_US**, the browser may do something special, or may just ignore the country code and use the base language. Browsers have varying levels of support for language facilities, and have to wade through sometime conflicting requirements from Cascading Style Sheet (CSS) and extensible style language (XSL) formatting.

HTML includes the **dir = LTR** and **dir = RTL** options to specify that text displays right-to-left or left-to-right. If your page uses a Unicode (**www.unicode.org/ index.html**) character set, the Unicode settings override **dir=**. Some character sets are displayed vertically, and the latest browsers support vertical display. To format a page for vertical text, you need to read the latest information on CSS, XSL, and XLT (XML-based formats for lexicons and terminologies).

Application-Specific versus Site-Specific

If your Web site integrates several application packages, each application will have a way of customizing output. Your customers will be upset if they set preferences on one page, and then have to repeat the settings on another page. How do you fix the mess?

On a few sites, I tried fixing applications to use a common method of retrieving and storing the settings, only to find that a lot of the code has frequent updates, and each update wipes out all the improvements you make. You can contribute your changes back to an open source project, but a popular open source application might have 200 people, each wanting to use a particular method. You have little hope of making major changes quickly, and you might find that someone immediately changes your changes.

I found the best approach is to leave each application to distribute and use settings through their existing mechanism, and focus on each application's init.inc file. Each application normally has an initialization file named init.inc or init.php. This file normally has definitions for settings relevant to the application, and code to retrieve overrides from profiles. At the start of the code, you can seed the application's variables with values from your common site initialization code, or you can add a little code at the end of the init.inc file to replace their values with the site values.

Having one common setting for your whole site is best, but wholesale modifications to an application mean you are stuck with maintaining the application. Try to wrap your code around the application's code, or wrap its code around your code, to get the perfect fit and leave you with the minimum work to implement a new release. Your customers may not compliment you for having one central setting, but they will complain loudly if you have more than one. The extra changes required to integrate applications are well worth the effort.

GNU recode

The GNU recode software translates one character set to another, and currently translates between 150 character sets. Although the translations are not perfect, that is mostly because many characters do not have exact translations in every character set. recode is mentioned at **www.gnu.org/software/recode/**, but you will have to search the Web for the user manual.

recode is at least 10 years old, and well tested, so the translations are the best available. You still need to check translations by hand. When you translate to another language and another character set, have the result tested by a person who uses the target language all the time, so they will pick up both technical inaccuracies and common usage problems that would give the translation the wrong meaning.

You can specify ASCII with several names, including **ascii** and **us**. The Latin character sets contain several character sets related to one another, with Latin-1, or **l1**, the base character set for Western Europe.

PHP has two recode functions, **recode_string( )** and **recode_file( )**. **recode( )** is an alias for **recode_string( )**. The following code shows **recode_string( )** recoding a string from ASCII to a screen representation with special characters removed:

```
print(recode_string("ascii..flat", "Test code with diacritical marks"
    . " &aacute;, &Aacute;, &Atilde;, &Aring;, and a EURO &euro;"));
```

The following code shows **recode_file( )** recoding from an input file to an output file, from ASCII to the Latin-1 character set:

```
$test = fopen('test.txt', 'r');
$recoded = fopen('recoded.txt', 'w');
recode_file ("ascii..latin-1", $test, $recoded);
fclose($test);
fclose($recoded);
```

GNU gettext

GNU's gettext is described at **www.gnu.org/software/gettext/gettext.html**, and the manual is at **www.gnu.org/manual/gettext/html_mono/gettext.html**. gettext uses the term *domain* to associate translations with an area of your Web site, usually an application. If your Web site has an email facility and a shopping cart, combining all the shopping terms with the mail terms in one big translation list could be a lot of work. It is usually easier for the mail developers to maintain their translation table, and for the shopping cart authors to maintain a separate list. You give the mail list a name of mail.mo and access the list using a domain of **mail**. The shopping card gets a file name like shop.mo and a domain of **shop**. The domain name has to match the bit in front of **.mo**.

There are five gettext functions:

- **bindtextdomain( )**—Associates a domain with the directory that contains the files for that domain
- **textdomain( )**—Sets the domain to be used by the next **gettext( )**
- **gettext( )**—Requests a translation

- **dgettext( )**—Performs a translation using a domain other than the selected domain

- **dcgettext( )**—A version of **dgettext( )** that includes a category selection.

Setting a domain is slow, because the code has to find files, so set the domain once and leave it. If you occasionally need a special domain, perhaps for error messages, use **dgettext( )**. If you have to continually swap between two domains on a busy Web site, consider merging their MO files.

As of PHP 4.0.7dev, the Unix version of gettext is working reliably, and the Windows version works in CGI mode; however, the Windows version has a "single use" problem when used as an Apache module. The Win32 module version accepts the first language request, and then ignores subsequent requests. It also checks files for availability once and refuses to check again. If you set the language to German, and then set it to Spanish, you will continue to get translations to German until you restart the Web server. If you install a directory with a wrong name, and then use **gettext( )**, the translation will fail. Renaming the directory will not fix the problem, because the gettext code will keep the old directory information in cache. The only solution is to restart the Web server or use the CGI version (where every setting is set afresh for every script). If you are testing a new installation of the gettext language directories and files, use PHP in CGI mode.

Spelling

For many Web site authors, their first need to check spelling occurs when they write an email application, and the second is when they write a system to let customers, such as nonprogramming content writers, enter content directly into Web pages. Both applications present different challenges that are worth considering before tackling spelling.

If your Web site sells teddy bears to teddy bear collectors, the content writers writing for your site will have a specific set of technical terms to use. You can set up their dictionary well in advance and make all the writers use the same dictionary. If you are setting up a public email facility, you cannot dictate a dictionary to your customers, so will have to set up a basic dictionary, and then let each customer have a customer dictionary for their own words.

The teddy bear Web site will be written in one base language and translated to others, so you can set one language for the writers, and have each translator maintain his or her own language-specific dictionary. The public mail site will need a dictionary for every language, a way for the public to select a different dictionary for each email, and a custom dictionary for each language.

What does your spelling checker do if your customer writes in Afrikaans and quotes Zulu text? Do you attempt to check spelling by paragraph?

There are four choices with PHP:

1. Use an off-the-shelf open source application and whatever spelling checker is used by the application, including Java- and JavaScript-based systems.

2. Write your own word-matching application.

3. Use Apsell.

4. Use Pspell.

Word Matching

You can match words using soundex indexes, metaphone equivalents, and match phrases based on Levenshtein comparisons (as described in this section). All three can be used to find alternatives for misspelled words. Because my brain thinks in SQL, I would set up a database with a word list as one index and the results of one word-matching function as another index. Then I would search for similarities based on using the same function on incoming words. If your customer types in *monie* instead of *money*, soundex and metaphone should indicate that *money* sounds like *monie* and is a good choice for your spelling correction prompt. Look at the functions first, and then their use.

soundex()

soundex( ) produces an indicator of how a word sounds, and can be used to match words in a dictionary based on sound similarities. The following example compares several words using **soundex( )**. The code is on the left, and the resultant **soundex( )** indexes are on the right. *dia* is the name of a software product; **soundex( )** uses the *d* from dia as the first letter of the soundex index. **soundex( )** throws away vowels, so dia scores a 000 after the letter. *Diablo* is the name of a fun, fast car, and scores a 14 after the d because of the *b* and *l* in the name. The remaining two words are given soundex indexes that are sufficiently different to indicate that the words are not a good match:

```
print("<br>" . soundex("dia"));          D000
print("<br>" . soundex("diablo"));       D140
print("<br>" . soundex("dialectric"));   D423
print("<br>" . soundex("diacritical"));  D263
```

metaphone()

metaphone( ) is the alternative to **soundex( )**, and is explained at **www.lanw.com/java/phonetic**. **soundex( )** support is built into some databases, so **soundex( )** may be the preferred choice if you use one of those databases. If not, use any database and **metaphone( )**.

Like **soundex( )**, **metaphone( )** produces an indicator of how a word sounds. It can be used to match words in a dictionary, and because of the similarities with **soundex( )**, the following code reproduces the **soundex( )** example using **metaphone( )**. Comparing **metaphone( )** values is more difficult than comparing **soundex( )** values unless you limit the length for your comparisons. In the following example, limiting the comparison to the first five, or even three, characters of the metaphone value would not produce a match:

```
print("<br>" . metaphone("dia"));              T
print("<br>" . metaphone("diablo"));           TBL
print("<br>" . metaphone("dialectric"));       TLKTRK
print("<br>" . metaphone("diacritical"));      TKRTKL
```

levenshtein()

The Levenshtein distance is a count of the number of characters you would have to add, delete, or change to make two phrases the same. Although it is not of much use in finding matching words in a spelling checker, it is useful for tasks such as matching names and addresses. **metaphone( )** and **soundex( )** are heavily oriented to the first few letters in a word, and would not match the place name *The Great Sandy Desert* with *Great Sandy Desert*. Use **levenshtein( )** for matching phrases and place names. I provide an example in the "Immediate Solutions" section under "Matching Phrases and Place Names with **levenshtein( )**."

The Match

Suppose you are setting up an online travel agency. You have a list of cities, and you want to help your customers book flights to the correct city. How can you match a mistyped city to a list of cities? Place the cities and entries in a database, once city per row. As you insert each city, calculate the city's metaphone, or soundex, and store that in another field. Index the other field for speedy retrieval. When your customer types in a city name, first look up the name in the database, because it might be spelled correctly. If the first lookup fails, try for a match with the metaphone, or soundex, by passing the customer's spelling through **metaphone( )** or **soundex( )**, and then query the database for an exact match.

If exact matches fail, you then search for a prefix of the metaphone using the SQL **like** facility. You can perform the equivalent of a binary search based on the number of characters in the metaphone and the number of rows returned. If too few rows are returned, use fewer letters. If too many rows are returned, increase the number of characters used for the search. Because a soundex is always four characters, you minimize the number of searches, but nothing stops you from beginning your second metaphone search (after the exact match search), with four characters, which would give you the same result after one extra search. The commissions on extra flights sold because of your extremely good search facility will soon pay for the faster disks and processor you need to drive multiple database searches, and from then on the extra sales are pure profit.

Aspell

A is for Auld (what an awful pun). Aspell works only with older Aspell spelling libraries, and Pspell is the replacement. If you find Aspell in existing code, and you can update the related libraries, convert to Pspell.

Aspell uses a small selection of functions to check spelling of a word:

- **aspell_new( )**—Loads a new dictionary for use in the other functions.
- **aspell_check_raw( )**—Checks a word as typed, which means it will match on case. This function is the first choice for technical terms.
- **aspell_check( )**—Attempts a generic check for a word, by altering the word's case and trimming spaces. This function is a good choice for general text that contains no technical terms.
- **aspell_suggest( )**—Suggests words that might match a supplied word. You would use this function to provide alternatives when a word is rejected by **aspell_check( )**.

Pspell

Pspell stands for *Portable spelling checker* and is the replacement for Aspell. Pspell is the recommended interface to Aspell libraries. The Aspell libraries are available at **http://aspell.sourceforge.net**, and the Pspell libraries are at **http://pspell. sourceforge.net** (you need both). The PHP 4.0.7dev Win32 binary does not include Aspell or Pspell.

To use Pspell in your script, start by opening a dictionary for a language, as shown next:

```
$country["language"]["code"] = "en";
if(!$dictionary = pspell_new($country["language"]["code"]))
    {
    print("<br>pspell_new failed.");
    }
```

Some languages have variations, so the optional second parameter of **pspell_new** lets you specify variations. The following example checks the country code, and then varies the parameters for some countries. In a full production system, you would expand the overall code so your visitor can specify the language variation option. A salesperson in America may want to use the British variation when sending email to Britain, and then may want to use the Canadian option for Canadian prospects:

```
$country["language"]["code"] = "en";
$country["country"]["code"] = "US";
switch($country["country"]["code"])
    {
        case "CA":
            $option = "canadian";
            break;
        case "EN":
            $option = "british";
            break;
        case "US":
            $option = "american";
            break;
    }
if(isset($option))
    {
    $dictionary = pspell_new($country["language"]["code"], $option);
    }
else
    {
    $dictionary = pspell_new($country["language"]["code"]);
    }
if(!$dictionary)
    {
    print("<br>pspell_new failed.");
    }
```

The following code is a longer version of the same action, using additional functions to set additional options. **pspell_config_create()** defines a new dictionary configuration, **pspell_new_ignore()** tells the configuration to ignore words shorter than *n* letters (in this case, 3), and **pspell_new_mode()** tells the dictionary to work longer and bring back more recommendations for possible words. **pspell_config_personal()** defines a custom dictionary to supplement the main dictionary. **pspell_config_repl()** defines a file to store word pairs used to suggest replacements for words that fail the spell check. **pspell_config_runtogether()** turns on an option to allow "run together" words, like *sourceforge*, the name of a useful Web site:

```
$country["language"]["code"] = "en";
$configuration = pspell_config_create($country["language"]["code"]);
pspell_config_ignore($configuration, 3);
pspell_config_mode($configuration, PSPELL_BAD_SPELLERS);
pspell_config_personal($configuration, "/home/me/spell/custom.pws");
pspell_config_repl($configuration, "/home/me/spell/replace.repl");
pspell_config_runtogether($configuration, true);
```

```
if(!$dictionary = pspell_new_create($configuration))
   {
   print("<br>pspell_new failed.");
   }
```

When you have the right dictionary, check a word's spelling with the following code:

```
$word = "PHP";
if(pspell_check($dictionary, $word))
   {
   print("<br>Ok: " . $word);
   }
else
   {
   print("<br>Reject: " . $word);
   }
```

If the word is a new word that you want to save to a custom dictionary, use either of the next two lines. These functions are new as of PHP 4.0.2. There are several parallel functions and little end-user experience to guide you to the best choice between the various dictionary configurations. The simplest seems to be the **session** option. After you add to a word list, remember to save the word list with **pspell_save_wordlist( )** before your script ends:

```
pspell_add_to_personal($dictionary, $word);
pspell_add_to_session($dictionary, $word);
pspell_save_wordlist($dictionary);
```

pspell_clear_session( ) clears everything from your session wordlist. You could provide this as an option for people who make a mistake with adding words and want to start again. It would be better to have an option to backtrack, like the multilevel undo with optional selection list, in some office applications, but Pspell does not provide the right functions for a selectable wordlist undo:

```
pspell_clear_session($dictionary);
```

pspell_store_replacement( ) lets you save a misspelled word and the correct replacement. Use **pspell_save_wordlist( )** to permanently save the updated replacement list:

```
pspell_store_replacement($dictionary, "frieght", "freight");
```

pspell_suggest( ) accepts a word and returns a list of probable matches in an array. You can then display the list in a HTML select list and let your customer choose the right replacement. Also give them the opportunity to type in their own replacement and save their replacement using **pspell_store_replacement()**:

```
$list = pspell_suggest($dictionary, $word);
```

pspell_new_personal() is an alternative to **pspell_new_create()** for use with a personal dictionary. **pspell_config_save_repl()** is an alternative to **pspell_config_repl()**.

Multibyte Characters

The standard computer character occupies one byte, and one byte can represent 256 characters. What do you do when your language has 50,000 characters? You use two bytes, for a total range of 65,536 characters. PHP supports multibyte characters through the **mb_** series of functions. These functions are experimental, and the first experiments use the various Japanese character sets.

The Japanese and Chinese written languages use pictograms, which roughly represent a word, part of a word, or a phrase. A newspaper may use 5,000 pictograms, and a book may use 50,000. Think how hard it is to distinguish *1* (the number one) from *l* (the lowercase letter L) in most western character sets, and then multiply the problem by 1,000. Pictograms need more space to display clearly, and there are several character sets in use within Japan to attempt to present their characters clearly on different media.

A special character set exists that is designed for use with their mobile communication devices, principally phones, so the characters will be readable on small LCD screens. Before you launch into the Japanese market, think about their 11,000,000 commuters reading the Internet on mobile phones. They are not using the Wireless Application Protocol (WAP); they walked right past WAP and chose a newer way to access the Internet, a version of HTML access named *i-mode*.

The multibyte functions (currently listed at **www.php.net/manual/en/ref. mbstring.php**) include **mb_send_mail()**, a version of the standard mail function that encodes mail in the Japanese ISO-2022-JP character set. **mb_send_mail()** wraps itself around **mail()**, performs the encoding, and then passes the mail to **mail()** for normal delivery.

PHP has functions to handle multibyte characters in HTTP requests, including **POST** and **GET** input, plus functions to translate output. There are replacements for standard string functions that count each multibyte character as one character, which can be complex because a string can include sections of multibyte characters and control characters to switch in and out of multibyte mode.

When you send and receive pages, or anything that looks like a file to HTTP, there is a MIME header at the front to describe the file. The receiver can find out that a file is text/html or image/jpeg and process the file appropriately. There are multibyte functions to convert MIME headers to and from the ISO-2022-JP character set used in MIME headers in Japan.

HTML lets you code special characters to numeric references so you can transmit the special characters to a browser without running into problems in the network or browser. The special characters appear as plain old text until the browser interprets them. The multibyte functions include a function for encoding multibyte characters in HTML numeric format and for returning HTML numeric format numbers as multibyte characters.

Immediate Solutions

Creating Country Information

Where do you begin with all the information for the 239 countries in the world? Start with one entry for your own country, and then add entries as you develop content for other countries. This example creates an entry for Australia, and you can modify the example for any country.

The following list displays all the international information discussed earlier in this chapter for Australia, which has a country code of **AU**. If PHP receives no country code, most of the defaults will work for Australia, and **number_format( )** will display numbers in the correct format of **nn,nnn.nn**. I included the definitions with **null** just to show you the full range of data used in this example:

```
$country["characterset"]["direction"] = null;
$country["characterset"]["name"] = null;
$country["color"]["bg"] = null;
$country["color"]["edge"] = null;
$country["country"]["code"] = "AU";
$country["country"]["name"] = "Australia";
$country["date"]["full"] = "l F j, Y";
$country["date"]["mysql"] = "Y-m-d";
$country["date"]["standard"] = "F j, Y";
$country["language"]["code"] = "en";
$country["language"]["name"] = "English";
$country["number"]["decimal"] = null;
$country["number"]["thousands"] = null;
$country["time"] = "H:i";
```

The method for interpreting fields is important. In this list, unused fields are set to **null** to indicate the field is not set and that subsequent code should use a default value. If a field is not specified, or null, the field is stored in a database as **null**, so you can distinguish between a field that is needed and one that is not. When a null entry is retrieved from a database and stored in a PHP, PHP deletes the field, as you will see in the solution entitled "Retrieving Country Information." By carrying the null/unused concept throughout the code, you can indicate that items should not be set or transmitted to a browser, so the browser can use local defaults.

The number formatting can be left as **null** in the database, not read into a variable. Any code that includes **number_format( )** can use the defaults simply by leaving format parameter out of **number_format( )**. **number_format( )** has one peculiarity: It requires you to specify both the decimal point separator and the thousands separator, or neither of them. To check that the incoming profile selections are valid, you need verification code something like the following code. The example checks to see if either the decimal or thousands separator is specified without the other, and then sets the missing one to a reasonable value. (If the decimal separator is a period, the thousands separator should probably be a comma.) The example also deletes **$country["number"]** if both decimal and thousands are missing, so later code only has to check for the presence of **number**. I suggest placing this code after any form that lets a user override the settings, or where the Web site administrator updates country settings:

```
if(isset($country["number"]["decimal"])
or isset($country["number"]["thousands"]))
    {
    if(!isset($country["number"]["decimal"]))
        {
        if($country["number"]["thousands"] == ",")
            {
            $country["number"]["decimal"] = ".";
            }
        else
            {
            $country["number"]["decimal"] = ",";
            }
        }
    if(!isset($country["number"]["thousands"]))
        {
        if($country["number"]["decimal"] == ",")
            {
            $country["number"]["thousands"] = ".";
            }
        else
            {
            $country["number"]["thousands"] = ",";
            }
        }
    }
elseif(isset($country["number"]))
    {
    unset($country["number"]);
    }
```

Once your data is clean, you can test the data by using it the way it will be used in a script. The following example displays a number using **number_format()** and settings from **$country**:

```
function numf($number, $decimals=2)
    {
    global $country;
    if(isset($country["number"]))
        {
        return(number_format($number, $decimals, _
            $country["number"]["decimal"], _
            $country["number"]["thousands"]));

        }
    else
        {
        return(number_format($number, $decimals));
        }
    }
print("<br>" . numf(50985.7273, 4));
print("<br>" . numf(50985.7273, 6));
print("<br>" . numf(50985.7273));
print("<br>" . numf(50985.7237));
print("<br>" . numf(12345678901234567890.1234567890, 10));
```

The results are displayed next. Note the second parameter in **number_format()**, which is the number of decimal places you require. **number_format()** fills numbers to the right with zeros when you specify a number greater than the decimal digits contained in the input data, as shown in the second line. The third line shows **number_format()** rounding the result up when it has to truncate decimal places. The fourth line shows **number_format()** rounding down. The fifth line is a quick test of how many digits would pass through the formatting:

```
50,985.7273
50,985.727300
50,985.73
50,985.72
12,345,678,901,234,567,000.0000000000
```

Little things, like rounding errors, can cause problems for sites displaying financial data, so make sure your contract excludes responsibility for verifying the accuracy of a number or the way a number is displayed. Ask your customer to test data with a list just like the one used here.

As the Internet and Web sites develop, you will need to store more information, like which adult content rating system is used in a country. The structure presented here, and in the following solutions, is designed to let you add a new field without breaking the existing code.

Storing Country Information

MySQL is the easiest database for multiple platforms and fast reading of data, so MySQL is used in this example to store the country information. MySQL is explained in Chapter 5, and alternate databases are explained in Chapters 5 and 6.

The example starts with the data from the previous solution, stored in the array named **$country**. The database representation inherits the two-level naming structure in the array, using the underscore character (_) as a delimiter. That means you need to keep underscores out of any new keys you add to the array:

```
$country["country"]["code"] = "AU";
$country["country"]["name"] = "Australia";
$country["date"]["full"] = "l F j, Y";
$country["date"]["mysql"] = "Y-m-d";
$country["date"]["standard"] = "F j, Y";
$country["language"]["code"] = "en";
$country["language"]["name"] = "English";
$country["time"] = "H:i";
```

The data goes into the general database associated with the Web site, the one where sessions and user profiles are stored. In the test Web site, the database is selected by the session code, so a database selection step is not needed in this code. The following code drops any existing table named **country** so that you can create a new table. While you are testing, you might like to keep the **drop table** and **subsequent create table** code handy so you can recreate the table any time one of your experiments messes up the database.

mysql_query() runs an SQL query, returns a result identifier for queries that return data, and requires an existing connection to a database, which is set up at the start of your script when you initiate database based sessions. Chapter 5 explains the **mysql_** functions, and Chapter 19 explains sessions:

```
$sql = "drop table if exists country";
if(mysql_query($sql))
    {
    print("<br>SQL worked.");
    }
```

```
else
  {
  print("<br>SQL failed: " . $sql . ", error: " . mysql_error());
  }
```

Note that the code has the SQL built into a variable, and the variable is fed to the database query function and the later error message. That ensures that the error message displays exactly the same SQL that is used in the query. I am surprised how many professional applications, after months of testing, display hand-typed SQL in the error message—SQL that is not the same as the SQL used in the query.

Related solution:	*Found on page:*
Using Databases for Sessions	181

The database table is keyed on **$country["country"]["name"]**, because the country name is the most practical identifier and the one the visitors will use to select country related settings. The following SQL code creates the table, named **country**, with a field for every value of **$country** and the primary index on the country name. Note the fields names are the array key names joined with an underscore where there are two levels of names. That will let the code automate the input and output of data, so any new field added to this table will automatically be added to **$country**. The SQL defines the primary index as **not null** because that is required in some databases, including MySQL:

```
$sql = "create table country"
  . "("
  . "country_name varchar(60) not null, "
  . "characterset_direction enum('ltr','rtl'), "
  . "characterset_name tinytext, "
  . "color_bg tinytext, "
  . "color_edge tinytext, "
  . "country_code char(2) not null, "
  . "date_full tinytext, "
  . "date_mysql tinytext, "
  . "date_standard tinytext, "
  . "language_code tinytext, "
  . "language_name tinytext, "
  . "number_decimal tinytext, "
  . "number_thousands tinytext, "
  . "time tinytext, "
  . "primary key (country_name) "
  . ")";
if(mysql_query($sql))
  {
```

```
        print("<br>SQL worked.");
    }
else
    {
    print("<br>SQL failed: " . $sql . ", error: " . mysql_error());
    }
```

Once you have the database table created, you need data. The following code shows an automated insertion from the existing **$country** array. You could read Chapter 9 and then create an administration form to let you add entries for other countries, or use one of the data sources mentioned at the start of this chapter. (SQL can read an external file, or you can read an external file, including Web pages at other sites, using PHP, and then feed the data into SQL.)

The code loops through the array **$country** and converts each entry into a **name='value'** pair for use in SQL. If an entry is an array, the code loops through the lower-level array creating a name/value pair using the two-part name in the form **name1_name2**. Pairs are joined to the SQL with a comma-space ("**, **"), except for the first join, and then the SQL is fed into a query (read Chapter 3 for more array tricks):

```
$sql = "insert into country set";
$sep = " ";
reset($country);
while(list($k1, $v1) = each($country))
    {
    if(is_array($v1))
        {
        while(list($k2, $v2) = each($v1))
            {
            if(!is_null($v2))
                {
                $sql .= $sep . $k1 . "_" . $k2 . "='" . $v2 . "'";
                $sep = ", ";
                }
            }
        }
    elseif(!is_null($v1))
        {
        $sql .= $sep . $k1 . "='" . $v1 . "'";
        $sep = ", ";
        }
    }
print("<br>SQL: " . $sql);
if(mysql_query($sql))
```

```
   {
   print("<br>Inserted.");
   }
else
   {
   print("<br>Insert failed with error: " . mysql_error());
   }
```

What happens if you try to insert the record twice? Add this code to produce an error.

```
if(mysql_query($sql))
   {
   print("<br>Inserted." );
   }
else
   {
   print("<br>Insert failed with error: " . mysql_error());
   }
```

Here is the result:

```
Insert failed with error: Duplicate entry 'Australia' for key 1
```

Retrieving Country Information

How do you retrieve all the information for a country? The following code selects the entry from a database, inserts the data into the **$country** array, and then displays the data to verify that the retrieval code is working.

The code selects the entry for Australia from a database named **international**. I added the database selection for those sites with one central administration server and a series of Web servers. You can hold the country table in a single database on the central server, access a country entry from the central server, and then save the country information in the visitor's session record. That means you have just one country table to maintain, and the bulk of the I/O activity is in the session database. If you keep the data in discrete fields within the session database, you can analyze your online population by country across the day:

```
$database["database"] = "international";
if(mysql_select_db($database["database"]))
   {
```

```
    print("<br>Select worked." );
    }
else
    {
    print("<br>SQL failed: " . $sql . ", error: " . mysql_error());
    }
```

The select SQL selects every field and retrieval code, shown next, and brings the country record into memory as an array named **$row**. The array has an entry for each field with a name that can be translated to the name in **$country**. The MySQL function can return a row as an indexed array, associative array, or both, and the associative array is perfect for this code. Because the query is selecting an entry by the primary key, there can be only one matching entry, or no matching entries; you do not have to worry about duplicates:

```
$country["country"]["name"] = "Australia";
$sql = "select * from country where country_name='"
    . $country["country"]["name"] . "'";
if($result = mysql_query($sql))
    {
    if($row = mysql_fetch_assoc($result))
        {
        print("<br>Fetch worked.");
        }
    else
        {
        print("<br>Fetch failed: " . $sql . ", error: " . mysql_error());
        }
    }
else
    {
    print("<br>SQL failed: " . $sql . ", error: " . mysql_error());
    }
```

$row has the data keyed by names in the form of **name1** or **name1_name2**. The next code loops through the array, splitting up the names and adding the appropriate entries to **$country**. Each entry is printed for verification, and null values are translated to **null**. When you are happy the code is working on your site, just delete the **print** statements:

```
print("<table><tr><td><em>Field</em></td><td> </td>"
    . "<td><em>Value</em></td></tr>");
while(list($k, $v) = each($row))
    {
    $n = explode("_", $k);
```

```
        if(isset($n[1]))
           {
           if(is_null($v))
              {
              print("<tr><td>" . $n[0] . "</td><td>" . $n[1] . "</td>"
                 . "<td><em>Null</em></td></tr>");
              }
           else
              {
              print("<tr><td>" . \$n[0] . "</td><td>" . $n[1] . "</td>"
                 . "<td>" . $v . "</td></tr>");
              $country[$n[0]][$n[1]] = $v;
              }
           }
        else
           {
           if(is_null($v))
              {
              print("<tr><td>" . $n[0] . "</td><td> </td>"
                 . "<td><em>Null</em></td></tr>");
              }
           else
              {
              print("<tr><td>" . $n[0] . "</td><td> </td>"
                 . "<td>" . $v . "</td></tr>");
              $country[$n[0]] = $v;
              }
           }
        }
print("</table>");
```

Here is the result, complete with the null fields displayed. Compare this result with the result, later in the section, of reading the values back from **$country**:

```
Field                    Value
country       name       Australia
characterset  direction  Null
characterset  name       Null
color         bg         Null
color         edge       Null
country       code       AU
date          full       1 F j, Y
date          mysql      Y-m-d
date          standard   F j, Y
```

```
language    code      en
language    name      English
number      decimal   Null
number      thousands Null
time                  H:i
```

Time to test **$country**. The following code reads the **$country** array, displaying every entry and expanding entries where the entries are arrays:

```
reset($country);
print("<table><tr><td><em>Field</em></td><td> </td>"
  . "<td><em>Value</em></td></tr>" );
while(list($k1, $v1) = each($country))
   {
   if(is_array($v1))
      {
      while(list($k2, $v2) = each($v1))
         {
         print("<tr><td>" . $k1 . "</td><td>" . $k2 . "</td>"
            . "<td>" . $v2 . "</td></tr>");
         }
      }
   else
      {
      print("<tr><td>" . $k1 . "</td><td> </td>"
         . "<td>" . $v1 . "</td></tr>" );
      }
   }
print("</table>");
```

The following is the result from displaying **$country**. Compare this to the data inserted in the previous result. All the fields that were set to null are nicely cleaned out. When you want to test if a field is set to something other than the default, you can test the field with **isset( )**:

```
Field               Value
country   name      Australia
country   code      AU
date      full      l F j, Y
date      mysql     Y-m-d
date      standard  F j, Y
language  code      en
language  name      English
time                H:i
```

Using Sessions for Country Information

The best way to carry country data from page to page is with sessions (which are described in Chapter 19). You need to register **$country** with the session manager using the following code. I suggest that your pages just use the language code from the browser until the visitor logs on, or clicks on a language-specific link. If the visitor chooses the link first, open a session and use the session to carry the language. If the visitor logs on, start the session and restore the values from their profile:

```
if(!session_is_registered("country"))
    {
    session_register("country");
    }
```

When a session starts, the session sends out an HTTP header containing a cookie (the cookie contains the session ID). HTTP headers have to be sent before your code sends any data, so your script needs a little planning. If no session is started for a page, **session_register( )** will start a session, which means sending out a cookie. You can change php.ini to automatically start sessions, start a session manually at the top of your script before sending output, or make sure your **session_register( )** code is before your first output. If you leave your session code too late, you will get messages like these:

```
Warning: Cannot send session cookie - headers already sent

Warning: Cannot send session cache limiter - headers already sent

Warning: open(/tmp\sess_03258d2598ba860e4883a8331ef434c4, O_RDWR)
    failed: No such file or directory (2)
```

Finding a Message in Another Language with GNU Gettext

To use gettext, you need to install it. Using the Windows binary version of PHP under NT 4, all that is required is:

1. Copy php_gettext.dll from c:/Program Files/php/extensions to c:/winnt/system32.

2. Copy gnu_gettext.dll from c:/Program Files/php/dlls to c:/winnt/system32.

3. Change one line in c:/winnt/php.ini from **;extension=php_gettext.dll** to **extension=php_gettext.dll**.

4. Restart your Web server (if PHP is running as a module).

NOTE: *For Windows, use c:\windows\system instead of c:/winnt/system32.*

You need some translation files to test gettext, and because none were supplied with PHP, I downloaded the source library for gettext and used files from the source package. There are utilities to create MO files from text format PO files. You create the PO files using any text editor you like, and then run a utility to convert the PO file to a MO file. There are also collections of MO files named GMO, and I found you can just rename GMO files to MO for use with gettext.

In the Win32 version of PHP, a directory named tools/gettext contains the conversion utility. In Unix, the utilities are installed when you install gettext. I did not test the utilities because I favor the database-based translation shown in a later Immediate Solution.

You need a directory structure for all the files, starting with the name locale. I had my test pages in a directory named /international, so I created /international/locale. The next level requires a directory for every language in use at your site, and the directory name is the two-character language code. I created /locale/de, /locale/en, and /locale/es. Within each language, you need a directory named LC_MESSAGES, and within LC_MESSAGES, you need files named ___.mo, where ___ is the name of your domain.

The domain name is used to identify lists for specific applications. Your email application might have all its special text in mail.mo and use a domain name of **mail**. The example below uses a domain name of **test**, so there is a test.mo file in each language directory.

The first step in the example is to set the environmental values **LANG** to **de**. gettext also requires the locale **LC_ALL** to be set to **null**, although the requirement varies from system to system and between releases of gettext. The function **bindtextdomain()** connects domain test to the directory structure starting at ./locale. **textdomain()** selects domain text, and **gettext()** requests a translation of a string and returns the result:

```
if(putenv("LANG=de"))
    {
    print("<br>putenv worked.");
    }
```

```
else
   {
   print("<br>putenv failed. ");
   }
if(setlocale(LC_ALL, "") === null)
   {
   print("<br>Language not supported");
   }
print("<br>Bind text domain: " . bindtextdomain("test", "./locale"));
print("<br>Text domain: " . textdomain("test"));
print("<p>Test text: " . gettext("Unknown system error"));
```

The result is shown next. Note that **bindtextdomain( )** returns the path to the directory structure but not to the language. The language can be set after the **bindtextdomain( )** command, but it must be set before the **gettext( )** function:

```
putenv worked.
Bind text domain: i:/usr/home/international/locale
Text domain: test
Test text: Unbekannter Systemfehler
```

The domain selection process is slow, so it is separated from the translation function. If you perform most of your translation with one domain, and the occasional translation with another domain, use **dgettext( )** for the other domain, as shown here:

```
print("<br>d test text: " . dgettext("test", "Unknown system error"));
```

The result is:

```
d test text: Unbekannter Systemfehler
```

There is also a **dcgettext( )** command that adds a category selection to **dgettext( )**, but I did not have a working sample of categorized MO files when I tested this code, so I ended up with a result left in English. When anything goes wrong with your files, gettext defaults to returning your text untranslated:

```
print("<br>dc test text: " . dcgettext("test", "Unknown system error",
   6));
```

Finding Text in Other Languages with SQL

Sometimes you want to translate text messages and content, but no existing system, like **gettext( )**, fits your need. That is the time for an SQL-based database solution. Use any database you like; the enclosed code can be translated to all SQL-based databases. The application suits databases with fast read access, like MySQL, and does not need the transactions or any of the other special features of databases like PostgreSQL.

The first step is to define a table of languages, using the SQL shown next. The table is keyed by language code and has a second index on the language name, so you can quickly search either way. If you decide to use this table to feed language presentation functions, you can add fields to supply character set and other language display characteristics. You can type the SQL direct into database administration applications like phpMyAdmin, or insert it into a database function in your own script. Chapter 5 explains SQL and database functions:

```
drop table if exists language;
create table language
    (
    code char(2) not null,
    name varchar(60) not null,
    primary key (code),
    key name (name)
    );
```

You need a reference table of text, and this example uses **English** stored in table **en**. It does no matter which base you use for your site, as long as you nominate a specific table. The *nominated* table is the table that receives all text, before translation, and is the one that allocates the entry number used to identify the text across all translations. Because **en** is the nominated table, **en** has **auto_increment** on the primary key, entry, and the others do not have **auto_increment**, so you can control updates to the other tables.

The **text** field has unlimited length, so you can put whole pages in the field, if you want. The **comment** field is a smaller text field where translators can leave a quick note about the accuracy of a translation. If you want translation management, you can create a parallel table for extensive notes and a log file to track changes. The **translator** entry is the key to a table listing the last person to change the text, and the **date** is the date of last change:

```
drop table if exists en;
create table en
    (
```

```
entry int(10) unsigned default '0' not null auto_increment,
text text not null,
translator int(10) unsigned default '0' not null,
date timestamp(14),
comment mediumtext not null,
primary key (entry),
key text_key (text(20))
);
```

Copy table **en** as **de**, **es**, and any other language you want to use. All tables, other than the nominated reference table, have **auto_increment** removed from the entry field. If your Web site has half the text entered in German, the system still has to allocate an entry in the **en** table first and use the entry number from **en** when inserting into the **de** table.

A large translation project might have several translators per language, and some translators translating several languages. You need to identify who made each translation, and the table called **translator** does exactly that. Each translator gets an entry number, name, email address, and any other contact information you need. The timestamp called **date** records when the entry was last updated so you can check that old email addresses and other details are still current:

```
drop table if exists translator;
create table translator
    (
    entry int(10) unsigned default '0' not null,
    name tinytext not null,
    email tinytext not null,
    date timestamp(14),
    primary key (entry)
    );
```

If you want to build forms to update the language tables, Chapter 9 explains forms. Add sample entries using the following SQL. MySQL will use a timestamp of zero on inserts, and add the current date for an update. You can check the currency of translations by comparing dates, and you can write a script to list items that do not have translations or have translations with dates older than the reference text:

```
insert into en (entry, text) values ('1', 'memory exhausted');
insert into de (entry, text) values ('1',
   'virtueller Speicher erschöpft');
insert into en (entry, text) values ('2', 'Written by');
insert into de (entry, text) values ('2', 'Geschrieben von');
insert into en (entry, text) values ('3', 'untranslated message');
insert into de (entry, text) values ('3', 'unübersetzte Meldung');
```

The following code finds a translation for **$text**, translating from language **$from** to language **$to**. The SQL performs a **join**, taking data from two tables and matching records on a common value, in this case **en.entry=de.entry**. Because the two tables are indexed on entry, the join is almost instantaneous. The search for the **$from** text will be fast because there is an index on the first characters of the text field, and the index has enough characters to find the correct entry. When your database is huge, you can tune the search by adjusting the number of characters replicated by the database from field text to the index of text:

```
$text = "untranslated message";
$from = "en";
$to = "de";
$sql = "select " . $to . ".text from " . $to . ", " . $from
    . " where " . $to . ".entry = " . $from . ".entry"
    . " and " . $from . ".text='" . $text . "'";
if($result = mysql_query($sql))
    {
    if($row = mysql_fetch_assoc($result))
        {
        print("<br>" . $from . ": " . $text
            . "<br>" . $to . ": " . $row["text"] );
        }
    else
        {
        print("<br>Not found: " . $text);
        }
    }
else
    {
    print("<br>SQL failed: " . $sql . ", error: " . mysql_error());
    }
```

The result is shown next. To make the translation display in an appropriate way for all languages, you need to use the right character set:

```
en: untranslated message
de: unübersetzte Meldung
```

You can use this example system to perform a translation from German to English, but in some cases, the English translation will not be the best result. Translations are not always bidirectional, because the translator chooses the best words to suit the context of the original. The German-to-English translation will work for common short phrases on Web sites because everyone agrees on simple terms, like *right click on mouse,* and because a lot of English words have a derivation common to the equivalent German words. Words without a common derivation create more problems. The Inuktitut language contains many words for *snow.* You can translate the English word *snow* to Inuktitut, but you can't perform a single translation back. To provide that type of translation, you need to fill your English list with words like *powder snow, icy snow,* and so on.

This is the reason the example is keyed on entry number, rather than the actual text: You can have multiple entries of the same text. If you wanted a German-to-English translation table with increased accuracy, you could set up a table named **de_en** and use it to store the exact English translation for text that does not translate back to the same English as the forward translation. You would only resort to the more complex double-translation facility if you had content arriving in multiple languages, and even then, you might be better off to hand-translate page by page and reserve the translation tables for short, common messages.

You cannot always build sentences from translated phrases. If you have three phrases that make a logical sentence in your language, and you translate each of the three phrases into another language and then concatenate the translated phrases, you are likely to break rules for grammar and meaning in some languages.

Last, but by no means least, visit **http://petermoulding.com/languagecodes.html** and look up Inuktitut.

Checking Character Types

Can your customers print all the characters in your text? Will the same text be printable in another language? The PHP character-checking functions help you check a string's suitability for several purposes. The functions use the **locale** setting to ensure they are checking the right characters for a given country.

To test the functions, you need data, and the following list is a good sample. The first line is alphabetic, the second includes numbers, the third adds punctuation, the fourth line has a random selection of characters from the top row of the keyboard, and the last row includes a nonprint character, **chr(5)**:

```
$text[] = "PHP";
$text[] = "PHP4";
$text[] = "PHP 4.0.7";
$text[] = "PHP %^&*(*_";
$text[] = "PHP %^&*(*_" . chr(5);
```

Before you send a word off to a dictionary-checking routine, you want to know if the word has characters other than alphabetic characters, because other characters indicate technical terms, chemical formulae, and other text not in basic dictionaries. **ctype_alpha( )** checks every character in a string of text and returns false if any of the characters is not alphabetic. The next code loops through the previous array of text and returns the results for each entry:

```
reset($text);
while(list($k, $v) = each($text))
    {
    if(ctype_alpha($v))
        {
        print("<br>Passed: " . $v);
        }
    else
        {
        print("<br>Failed: " . $v);
        }
    }
```

The results show that only the first line passed:

```
Passed: PHP
Failed: PHP4
Failed: PHP 4.0.7
Failed: PHP %^&*(*_
Failed: PHP %^&*(*_
```

If your dictionary check is set to allow numeric characters in words (a common option), you need to replace the alphabetic check with an alphanumeric check as shown next. **ctype_alnum( )** returns true if every character is a letter or a number:

```
reset($text);
while(list($k, $v) = each($text))
    {
    if(ctype_alnum($v))
        {
        print("<br>Passed: " . $v);
        }
    else
        {
        print("<br>Failed: " . $v);
        }
    }
```

Here are the results of the **ctype_alnum( )** check:

```
Passed: PHP
Passed: PHP4
Failed: PHP 4.0.7
Failed: PHP %^&*(*_
Failed: PHP %^&*(*_
```

The most basic check is just to see if characters are printable. Because they are the only ones that make sense when you use the new PHP **print** functions (which are being tested as I type), they are the only ones you want on a page that a customer will print (like a form to be signed and faxed back), and they are the only ones that make sense in a text-translation system. **ctype_print( )** returns true if it considers every character printable. The next code tests **ctype_print( )** against the test array:

```
reset($text);
while(list($k, $v) = each($text))
    {
    if(ctype_print($v))
        {
        print("<br>Passed: " . $v);
        }
    else
        {
        print("<br>Failed: " . $v);
        }
    }
```

The results are shown next. The **chr(5)** is the only character rejected as not printable. **ctype_print( )** uses the **locale** setting, but does not know the capability of an individual browser or printer. The function might occasionally be wrong:

```
Passed: PHP
Passed: PHP4
Passed: PHP 4.0.7
Passed: PHP %^&*(*_
Failed: PHP %^&*(*_
```

The **ctype** series will check other character types. If you program in C, you will recognize these from their C equivalents.

ctype_cntrl( ) checks for control characters, so it helps indicate text that will display or print in unusual ways on some browsers and printers. If your text contains control characters, and you store the text in a database, you need to make sure you are using binary-compatible field types and functions.

ctype_digit( ) checks for numeric characters so you can safely put the text into a numeric function or database field. **ctype_xdigit( )** checks for a character string that represents hexadecimal digits, and can be used to check text before storing the text in a hexadecimal field or before conversion to a number.

ctype_lower( ) checks for lowercase text, and **ctype_upper( )** checks for uppercase text. If a word contains uppercase characters, the word may be an acronym, and you might want to give your customers the option of excluding acronyms from spell checking. You might also check Web page content for that annoying style of writing where text has a random mix of upper- and lowercase letters.

ctype_graph( ) tests for any printable characters except space, and I have not thought of a use for it. **ctype_print( )** seems to be a more useful function.

ctype_punct( ) checks for any printable character that is not white space or an alphanumeric character, which might help differentiate between text that will display with simple fonts and text that will require more extensive fonts.

ctype_space( ) checks for whitespace characters and helps you find the mystery characters that sometimes print or display as a space, sometimes do neither, and often make a character count appear wrong. If you have a limit of 100 on a field, but you never seem to be able to get 100 characters in the field, your text could have whitespace characters on the end of the text. (When a browser interprets a HTML-based page, the browser is supposed to count and display all white space characters as spaces, but the browser has rules about not displaying more than one consecutive space. If you only count space characters and not what a browser considers whitespace, your count will appear wrong.)

Matching Phrases and Place Names with **levenshtein( )**

The Levenshtein distance, as returned by **levenshtein( )**, is a count of the number of characters that are different between two phrases. **metaphone( )** and **soundex( )** are heavily oriented to the first letters in a word and would not match the two versions of the place name shown in the following example:

```
$text1 = "The Great Sandy Desert";
$text2 = "Great Sandy Desert";
```

These two text strings are typical of the problem you encounter when matching names that are written is several forms, like places starting with *Saint* on some maps and *St.* in other maps. In the test, the Levenshtein distance is low for a text string of this length, whereas the **soundex( )** results are totally different:

```
print("<br>" . levenshtein($text1, $text2));
print("<br>" . soundex($text1));
print("<br>" . soundex($text2));
```

This code produces the results that follow. The Levenshtein distance of 4 is low for a 22-character string and indicates a good match. The **soundex( )** codes have no similarity, and just do not work for this type of match, because of the emphasis on the first letter of the text:

```
4
T263
G632
```

How do you use **levenshtein( )** to search a table from a file or database? Define your list of place names, phrases, or countries as in this example, with a name field (indexed for speed). The following snippets from an SQL **create table** statement show the field definition plus the index definition. Chapter 5 describes SQL in more detail. Create your table and include the field:

```
country_name varchar(60) not null
KEY countryname (country_name)
```

When you search the country table, first perform a search for an exact match. If the exact match search fails, read the list of countries into an array and search the array as shown next. The example shows example entries entered into array **$countries**, an item for matching in **$match**, then a loop to perform a match:

```
$countries[] = "Australia";
$countries[] = "Saint Kitts and Nevis";
$countries[] = "USA";
$match = "St Kitts and Nevis";
$best_ld = 9999999;
$best_match = "";
while(list($k, $v) = each($countries))
    {
    $new_ld = levenshtein($match, $v);
    if($new_ld < $best_ld)
        {
        $best_ld = $new_ld;
        $best_match = $v;
        }
    }
print("<br>Best match: " . $best_match);
```

The result is, of course, **Saint Kitts and Nevis**. How could you implement this as a database lookup? If your database had a **levenshtein( )** function, you could use that, but would be committed to a permanent computationally intensive search. The better solution would be to create a translation table. When your exact match fails, read the database table into memory, perform the search shown here, and let the user verify the match. As soon as the user clicks OK, save the mistyped name and the correct name in a lookup table. Whenever a new search fails the exact match on the original table, perform an exact match on the translation table to see if the string was found on a previous occasion. If the translation table matches, you have a result using only a few I/O operations on a database index. After a while, the translation table will fill with all the common variations, misspellings, and typographical errors.

Chapter 13

Internet

In Depth

The whole Internet is available from your browser. Can PHP give you the same freedom to read Web pages, gather information, and move files around? Yes — PHP can read anything a browser reads, and can also work as a Web crawler, or *spider*, gathering information just like the crawlers and spiders used by search engines.

In this chapter, you will find the tools to read from other Web sites, communicate between servers, and start building management facilities for multiple Web servers. If you manage one Web site or multiple Web sites, or if you are an Internet service provider (ISP) hosting thousands of Web sites, here are PHP functions and code you will need somewhere in your Web site administration system.

You will find more than one way to perform many of the tasks you need. If you are working on a large project, take time to write out everything you need in your site, and then select the simplest solution for all your requirements. If you need everything mentioned in this chapter, you might find PHP's Curl functions the best choice because the underlying Curl library has so much power. If you need only a small portion of Curl's capability, you might choose a simpler route using PHP's standard network, socket, or file functions.

One other consideration is the range of platforms on which you can use particular functions. If you want complete cross-platform flexibility, write out all your target platforms and check the availability of each function against each platform. The same applies for hosted sites—you need to write out your requirements and talk with your ISP, or ISPs, about their support for those options, potential security problems, and any lead time if they have to upgrade and test their servers.

URL

Uniform Resource Locators (URLs) are the connections between information that makes the Internet into the World Wide Web. URLs are described in full at **www.w3.org/Addressing/**. The people who set the standards refer to URLs as a particular type of Uniform Resource Identifier (URI), and go into great detail. You only need to know the main parts, because PHP helps you split a full URL into components, and your first projects will use only a few components. Here is a sample URL:

```
http://www.google.com/search?q=sun+sand+surf
```

parse_url( ) returns **scheme**, **host**, **port**, **user**, **pass**, **path**, **query**, and **fragment**. The following lists the **google.com** URL components by returned by **parse_url( )**:

```
scheme: http
host:   www.google.com
path:   /search
query:  q=sun+sand+surf
```

Scheme or Protocol

The first part of the URL is the *scheme*, the part before the colon, also called the *protocol*. **http** indicates a normal Web page request. **ftp** indicates the File Transfer Protocol. If a visitor forgets to type in the scheme, most modern browsers default to http. You can get the protocol in a few ways. **$SERVER_PROTOCOL** contains the scheme, a slash, and then the release of the protocol. **$HTTP_REFERER** contains the URL used to request a page, so the script in that page can grab the scheme from the front of the referrer string with code as simple as the line shown next:

```
$referrer_parts = parse_url($HTTP_REFERER);
print($referrer_parts["scheme"]);
```

Host

The second part of the URL is the *host*, which also contains the *domain*. You can get the host from **parse_url( )**, as described in the previous section. If you need to extract the value by hand, it is the part between the initial *://* and the first single slash.

The domain is the generic name of a Web site, and the host is the name of a server within the domain. **www.coriolis.com** is a useful Web site when you want books. **coriolis.com** is the domain name, and **www** is the name of a Web server within the domain. In the dark ages of the Web, a Web site with three Web servers, a mail server, and an FTP server, would have **www.petermoulding.com**, **ww2.petermoulding.com**, **ww3.petermoulding.com**, **mail.petermoulding.com**, and **ftp.petermoulding.com**. Then people discovered how to have multiple servers behind one Web address, so the site's host addresses were reduced to **www.petermoulding.com**. Now people have their domain name default to an unnamed server, so their host name reduces to **petermoulding.com**, the same as their domain name.

Path

The *path* is the sequence of directory names and page name required to find a page. In the example **google.com** URL, the path contains one directory name, **/search**. The path is important in PHP scripts because you need to translate the URL relative path names to absolute server names for use in PHP file functions. **realpath( )** performs some but not all translations, so extracting the path from the URL is useful. The path runs from the first single forward slash to the last single forward slash, if there is one. The part between the last **/** and the question mark (**?**) may be a part of the path or a page name. Often, the only way to tell is to look for a page extension, such as .html, and if there is no page extension, to treat the last part as a directory name that is part of the path.

Page

The *page* is usually the part of the URL between the last forward slash and the question mark (**?**) and contains the name of a page. This part of the URL does not have to be a page name, because Web servers, such as Apache, can automatically match this part of the URL to a directory name and then construct an index of the directory contents or perform an automatic redirect to a special page. In the **google.com** example, there is no page name; Google is relying on its Web server's facility to direct incomplete URLs to a default page. In theory, the URL should have been entered as "http://www.google.com/search/?q=sun+sand+surf," with a trailing slash, but most Web servers will work without the last slash.

You will need to know the name of the page using your script, and you can get the current **path/page** combination from **$PHP_SELF** and the page name from **basename($PHP_SELF)**, as shown here:

```
print("<br>" . $PHP_SELF);
print("<br>basename(): " . basename($PHP_SELF));
```

The result is:

```
/phpblackbook/internet/url.html
basename(): url.html
```

Fragment

A *fragment* is an extension to a page to access a specific location in a page. If page **xyz.html** contains an anchor tag, **<a>**, with a name parameter, **name=abc**, you can ask the browser to begin displaying the page from the anchor tag downward by requesting page **xyz.html#abc**. The fragment did not appear in PHP when I tested it with Netscape 4.76. The best explanation I can think of is that the browser extracts the fragment before transmission, and uses it when the page returns. Not all browsers work that way, because I found fragments in some URL requests at the server.

Query

The *query* part of the URL is everything after the question mark. PHP places the query string in a variable named **$QUERY_STRING**. In the **google.com** example, the query is **q=sun+sand+surf**. The equal sign indicates a **name=value** pair, **q** is the name of the query, and **sun+sand+surf** is the value. The plus signs represent spaces. If there are multiple name/value pairs, they are joined with an ampersand (**&**). You rarely need to know the query string in PHP, because PHP decodes the name/value pairs into PHP variables. In the **google.com** example, your script that processes the query will start as if PHP had generated the next line of code:

```
$q = "sun sand surf";
```

Special Characters

If you have special characters in the value part of a query name/value pair, you can encode the special characters using **urlencode()**. The encoding replaces each special character with a three-character representation, a percent sign (%), and the hexadecimal representation of the character. An example is shown next:

```
$x = urlencode("special characters like & and =");
print("<br>" . $x);
print("<br>" . urldecode($x));
```

The result is:

```
special+characters+like+%26+and+%3D
special characters like & and =
```

PHP automatically decodes URL encoding when PHP sets up the variables at the start of your script. URL encoding is also used in cookies, and is automatically decoded when PHP reads the cookies into memory. If you place long binary strings in URLs, base64 encoding produces a shorter string than URL encoding; but it is not automatically decoded, and URL encoding is more efficient when there are a few special characters in a long string of regular characters.

PHP also contains **rawurlencode()** and **rawurldecode()**, which both convert special characters just like **urlencode()** and **urldecode()**, but translate spaces to **%20** instead of **+**. **rawurlencode()** is technically correct, but **urlencode()** encodes the way most people encode URLs.

Base64 Encoded Text Strings

The theory behind encoding is that computers and network devices use selected characters to indicate control strings and other special functions. Therefore you cannot use every one of the 256 characters that can be represented within the 8 bits of a byte. That means you need to convert the 256 characters to another form.

The theory behind base64 encoding is that you can represent the 256 combinations of 8 bits with 64 combinations of 6 bits if you can join 3 groups of 8 bits together into 24 bits, and then split the 24 into 4 sets of 6 bits. Base64 encoding uses the letters A to Z and a to z, the numbers 0 to 9, and the special characters **+** and **/** to form the 64-bit character set that makes base64-encoded data printable and safe to go through any medium, such as email.

Figure 13.1 shows the theory applied to the string *abc*. The string is converted to binary, and then split into four sets of six bits. Each group of six bits is converted to a readable character. The characters used to represent the six bits are not consecutive characters in the ASCII character set, so a translation is required to produce the final result.

The input data does not come neatly packed into sets of three bytes, so the base64 encoding has to include a way of rounding up the last characters. The following example shows, on the left, the character strings, *aaa*, *aa*, and *a*. On the right are the base64 encodings, with the first containing **YWFh** as the encoding of *aaa*. The second has **YWE** as the encoding of *aa* and a trailing **=** to indicate that there were only two bytes in the input string. The third example has **YQ** as the encoding of *a* and two trailing **=** signs to indicate the input contained only one byte:

```
aaa   YWFh
aa   YWE=
a    YQ==
```

By now you might be thinking of uses for base64 encoding, including sending binary data through URLs. You already realize the problem of having **=** and **+** in URLs where **=** and **+** have special meanings. The answer is URL encoding. You wrap a URL encode function around a base64 encoded string. (You can use URL encoding without base64 encoding, but URL encoding converts three input characters into as many as nine characters in the output, something that is too expen-

a	b	c
0 1 1 0 0 0 0 1	0 1 1 0 0 0 1 1	0 1 1 0 0 0 1 1

0 1 1 0 0 0	0 1 0 1 1 0	0 0 1 1 0 1	1 0 0 0 1 1
Y	W	J	j

Figure 13.1 Base64 encoding converts from 8-bit to 6-bit.

sive for binary data.) The following line shows *aa* base64 encoded, and then URL encoded. Note that **=** became **%3D**:

```
YWE%3D
```

Browsing Other Servers

How do search engines find out what is in your site? They browse your site just like a curious visitor, clicking on every link and image to see what happens. You can browse the Web using the same techniques; an example is presented in the Immediate Solution "Browsing the Web with PHP," later in this chapter.

When search engines browse your site, they emulate a browser, decoding HTML and other tags the same way. As each tag is decoded, the information is saved and indexed, or thrown away. If one of the tags contains a link to another site or page, the link is scheduled for a subsequent browse. If your site is a portal to other sites, you can use the same techniques to index the right pages on the other site. There are several open source search engine projects in existence, and one is likely to suit your needs.

If all you need to do is check that links are still valid, you can request a page or you can request information about a page, thus verifying the link with far less network traffic.

The PHP socket functions, Curl, **fopensock( )**, and the normal file-handling functions can read a file from a URL, so you have several choices depending on the complexity of your requirement and the flexibility you desire to allow future enhancements.

Socket Functions

The socket functions let you write your own Web server or browser using PHP. I do not recommend either activity as your first project for practicing PHP, but there are occasions when you might want part of the function of a Web server or part of a browser, so it is worth reading about the functions.

Imagine you are an ISP, running lots of virtual Web sites on your server and planning to offer your customers (the ones who own the virtual Web sites) an advertising placement service from an outside agency. The agency has a server that provides a selection of banners and associated commissions for use on Web sites. The banners are categorized by type, so sports-oriented sites can select sports-oriented advertisers and sites oriented to school children can avoid banner advertisements for adults-only sites.

Your customers get access to a selection of banner advertising to generate revenue from their site, and you get a commission on each ad placement. You could connect your customers to the agency's server, and trust the agency to pay you full commissions and not deal directly with your customers. An alternative is to reproduce the agency's Web pages on your Web site, keep your customers visiting your Web site, and pass their requests on to the agency using PHP's socket functions. The customers deal with you, not the agency. The agency sees all the activity under your account and never finds out the contact information for your customers. You receive one big commission check, and pass the money back to your customers as rebates on their hosting fees.

To install sockets in PHP on Unix, configure PHP with **--enable-sockets**, and then compile PHP. For Windows NT (or Windows), just copy **c:\Program files\php\extensions\php_sockets.dll** to **c:\winnt\system32** (or **c:\windows\system** on Windows), and then add **extension=php_sockets.dll** to php.ini. Restart your Web server if you are not running PHP as CGI. Note that socket support is still experimental in PHP, and even if socket support were not experimental, it still has security and firewall issues.

An alternative to loading extensions in php.ini is to load them dynamically using **dl( )**. The following code shows you how to use **dl( )**, including checking to see if an extension is loaded before you load the extension. php.ini contains **extension_dir** to tell PHP the location of the extensions, or you can add the file path to the file name in **dl( )**. In Unix, the file extensions are .so instead of .dll:

```
if(extension_loaded("sockets"))
    {
    print("<br>Sockets loaded.");
    }
else
    {
    print("<br>Sockets not loaded.");
    dl("php_sockets.dll");
    }
```

There is just one problem. Using Apache 1.3.20 on Windows NT, I get the following error. Perhaps when Apache 2 is in common use, PHP will use Apache 2's superior multithreading support to allow dynamic loading. Windows NT has both multithreading and multitasking, but some operating systems have only multithreading, not multitasking, and so cannot use Apache or PHP features dependant on multitasking:

```
Fatal error: dl() is not supported in multithreaded Web servers - use _
    extension statements in your php.ini
```

socket( ) accepts a domain, a type parameter, and a protocol, and then returns a resource id for a socket. The domain is not the name of the domain you want to reach, but is either **AF_INET** or **AF_UNIX**. The type parameter is one of **SOCK_STREAM**, **SOCK_DGRAM**, **SOCK_SEQPACKET**, **SOCK_RAW**, **SOCK_RDM**, or **SOCK_PACKET**:

```
$sock = socket(AF-INET, SOCK_STREAM, 0);
```

bind( ) connects an Internet address to the socket, for **AF_INET**, or to the path name of a Unix domain socket, if the socket was defined with **AF_UNIX**. The first parameter is the socket from **socket( )**. The second parameter is the IP address or pathname. The third address is an optional port number, if the socket is of type **AF_INET**. **bind( )** returns zero when successful and a negative error number if an error occurs. **strerror( )** will convert the error number to a meaningful message:

```
$result = bind($sock, "127.0.0.1");
```

strerror( ) accepts an error number returned from a socket function, and returns an explanation. The following code shows **strerror( )** in use with the **bind( )** code just shown:

```
if($result != 0)
   {
   print("<br>" . strerror($result));
   }
```

listen( ) listens for an incoming connection on a socket that is bound to an address by **bind( )**. The first parameter is the socket id, and the second parameter is the maximum number of incoming connections to queue. **listen( )** returns zero on success and a negative error number on failure. The error number can be fed through **strerror( )** as shown in the following example:

```
$heard = listen($sock, 20);
if($heard != 0)
   {
   print("<br>" . strerror($heard));
   }
```

accept_connect( ) accepts a socket id for a socket primed with **bind( )** and **listen( )**, and accepts an incoming connection request. **accept_connect( )** returns a new socket id just for the accepted connection. The original socket id remains open for subsequent accepts. When you are finished with this connection, you have to close it. When you are finished with all connections, you have to close the original socket:

```
$accepted = accept_connect($sock);
if($accepted != 0)
    {
    print("<br>" . strerror($accepted));
    }
```

connect( ) accepts a socket id for a socket created by **socket( )**, an IP address, and an optional port number, if the socket is of type **AF_INET**. If the socket is of type **AF_UNIX**, the second parameter is the pathname of a Unix domain socket. **connect( )** returns zero when successful and a negative error number if an error occurs, as shown in the following code:

```
$result = connect($sock, "127.0.0.1");
if($result != 0)
    {
    print("<br>" . strerror($result));
    }
```

read( ) accepts a socket id, the name of a buffer, and the maximum length to read, and then returns the number of bytes actually read. An optional fourth parameter lets you specify the type of read. The options for this fourth parameter are currently:

- **PHP_SYSTEM_READ**—Uses the system **read( )**
- **PHP_BINARY_READ**—Uses binary safe **read( )**
- **PHP_NORMAL_READ**—The default, where reading stops at \n or \r

The following code reads up to 1,000 bytes from **$sock** into **$data** and returns the number of bytes read, or returns false if the read fails:

```
$data = "";
$read = read($sock, $data, 1000);
print("<br>Bytes read: " . $read);
```

write( ) accepts a socket id, the name of a buffer containing data, and the length to write:

```
$data = "The cow jumped over the moon"
    . " while the dish and spoon learnt HTML";
$result = write($sock, $data, strlen($data));
print("<br>Write result: " . $result);
```

socket_get_status( ) returns the status of a socket used with **connect( )**, but gives unpredictable results for a socket created by **accept_connect( )**. **socket_get_status( )** accepts a socket id and returns an associative array containing **"timed_out"**, **"blocked"**, **"eof"** and **"unread_bytes"**. The first three are true/false values, and the last is an integer. The following code tests the status of the socket used by **connect( )** and prints the results of the test as an array. You can add code to test for timeouts or a blocked port and produce appropriate messages or loop back to the socket for another **read( )** or **write( )**:

```
$status = socket_get_status($sock);
while(list($k, $v) = each($status))
    {
    print("<br>" . $k . ": " . $v);
    }
```

close( ) accepts a socket id and closes the socket. The socket id is from **socket( )** or **accept_connect( )**. **close( )** returns true if the close works and false if the socket id is invalid:

```
if(!close($sock))
    {
    print("<br>Socket close failed!");
    }
```

SNMP

For an overwhelming list of documents about, and companies working on, the Simple Network Management Protocol (SNMP), see **www.ibr.cs.tu-bs.de/ietf/snmpv3/**. In the simplest terms, SNMP lets you talk with every intelligent item in your network, whether hardware or software. You can ask routers if they have enough memory, and plan an upgrade for those running short.

Many of the intelligent devices on your network will be able to send alerts when they are running out of resources, but their thresholds might not be set to useful levels. There is no point getting a warning 30 minutes before a failure if it takes 30 hours to order, acquire, and install an upgrade.

Why use PHP to browse SNMP when so much software is available for rich graphic displays of network status? Imagine arriving in the Maldives or Australia's Great Barrier Reef for a few days of scuba diving. You know that once you dive to full depth with a full tank of air, you cannot jump on a commercial jet back to your office for at least 24 hours after the dive. At high altitude, the low air pressure would make your blood fizz like a warm can of cola. Not many dive shops are likely to have direct connections to your corporate network—a simple Internet connection is about all you can expect. An Internet connection is all you need to access PHP on your server, so that is all you need to check the status of your network, before committing to the dive and another 24 hours in paradise.

Before you leave for anywhere, write a few PHP-based screens to browse your SNMP devices, and add SSL and a disposable logon. You can then access SNMP and manage your network from any Internet café in the world.

TIP: *If you do get to scuba dive in Australia's Great Barrier Reef, the first thing to do, on arrival, is to send your boss an email explaining that the Internet has not yet reached Australia.*

SNMP is available in Unix, Windows NT, and Windows 2000 but not Windows 98. You have to follow the installation instructions for SNMP, and you need to have documentation about the SNMP-capable devices in your network. Make sure the documentation can be browsed from a Web site so you can bring it up alongside the SNMP information. The PHP functions use net-snmp, formally named ucd-snmp, from **http://net-snmp.sourceforge.net/**. PHP functions require that you set the **net_snmp** option **NO_ZEROLENGTH_COMMUNITY** to 1 before you compile.

If you have a non-SNMP device in a network, you may not be able to track a problem end to end. In a well-laid-out network, the cheaper, nonintelligent, unmanaged devices are out at the edge of the network and the critical backbone links are fully managed with SNMP, so you can manage the most expensive bits.

snmpwalk() is the starting point for using SNMP. **snmpwalk()** accepts a hostname or IP address, a community name, an object id, an optional timeout parameter, and an optional number of retries. It returns an array of SNMP objects available through the object specified in the function. The following code starts a walk through the objects on a test server supplied by the developers of net-snmp. The community name is the one they set up for public access. The object id is left as a zero-length string to start the walk from the top level of the object's information structure:

```
$host = "ucd-snmp.ucdavis.edu";
$objects = snmpwalk($host, "demopublic", "");
if($objects)
    {
    while(list($k, $v) = each($objects))
        {
        print("<br>" . $v );
        }
    }
```

```
else
  {
  print("<br>snmpwalk error." );
  }
```

The first three lines of the output are displayed next. A lot of the output from the demo system is meaningless to me because it is not a Cisco router or something similar. Several lines of the output are repeated many times. You need to know the device you are interrogating and the normal levels for the device so you can see changes:

```
"HP-UX ucd-snmp B.10.20 A 9000/715"
OID: .iso.3.6.1.4.1.2021.250.6
Timeticks: (170055755) 19 days, 16:22:37.55
```

snmpget( ) accepts a hostname or IP address, a community name, an object id, an optional timeout parameter, and an optional number of retries. It returns an SNMP object. You can get the id from the list returned by **snmpwalk( )**. The contents of the object depend on the type of device supplying the information for the object. **snmpwalk( )** lets you see everything from the device, and **snmpget( )** lets you quickly see one item of information from the device, so use each according to the type of research you are conducting. Chapter 17 describes objects and how to browse them.

snmpset( ) accepts a hostname or IP address, a community name, an object id, the value type, the value, an optional timeout parameter, and an optional number of retries. It sets the SNMP object. The type parameter is **i** for integer, **s** for string, and other options depending on the object.

snmpwalkoid( ) is an older variation of **snmpwalk( )**, but I cannot see any useful difference.

snmp_get_quick_print( ) returns the current value (under Unix) of net-snmp's quick_print setting, and **snmp_set_quick_print( )** changes the value. The visible difference is the formatting of the results from **snmpget( )** and **snmpwalk( )**; the default is verbose, with descriptions wrapped around values, whereas the quick print makes the functions return raw values.

How do you make real use of SNMP from the Cairns Internet Café (on the edge of the Great Barrier Reef)? Set up a database. Table one lists the IP addresses, device types, and SNMP capability of everything in, on, under, or just lying on the floor next to your network (including all the spares and backup devices). Table two has a description of all the attributes or value types you find across all the devices, indexed by device and object id within each device. Table three contains all the values, and is indexed by device, object id, date, and time. You need to identify devices by make, model, asset/serial number, and IP address so you can track an item when the item's IP address changes, and so you can compare several devices when they are swapped in and out of the same network address. Then you can build screens to show device X at this time today versus this time on the same day last week.

You need to poll the devices regularly to find their normal operating values. You want the device display formatted to suit a device, and you should have help panels to explain the meaning of each value. You also want a list of what each device connects to, so you can see all the hubs connected to a switch.

It is a fun project, and your boss will probably pay for it if it helps your boss keep track of the organization's assets. You therefore need a screen that lists items not in use and the reason they are not in use (produced a puff of smoke/caught fire/still on fire). If your boss asks for pictures, a lovely little open source diagram application named Dia (**www.lysator.liu.se/~alla/dia**) can save your diagrams as PNG files for display via PHP on the same pages that list the device attributes. (Dia works on Unix, and there is a Windows 32 bit binary version at **http://hans.breuer.org/dia/**. I installed Gimp [**http://gimp.org**] then Dia on my Windows NT workstation and both work like a beauty.)

Curl

Curl does everything except make cappuccino. To quote the Curl Web site:

> *Curl is a tool for transferring files with URL syntax, supporting FTP, FTPS, HTTP, HTTPS, GOPHER, TELNET, DICT, FILE and LDAP. Curl supports HTTPS certificates, HTTP POST, HTTP PUT, FTP uploading, kerberos, HTTP form based upload, proxies, cookies, user+password authentication, file transfer resume, http proxy tunneling and a busload of other useful tricks.*

The underlying Curl library is available at **http://curl.haxx.se/**. To use Curl in Unix, compile PHP with **--with-curl[=*DIR*]** (point *DIR* at the downloaded Curl library). In Windows NT and Windows 2000, copy **php\dlls\Libeay32.dll**, **php\dlls\Ssleay32.dll**, and **php\extensions\php_curl.dll** to **c:\winnt\system32**. In php.ini, remove the semicolon from the front of **;extension=php_curl.dll**. Use the Windows NT instructions for Windows 98, changing c:\winnt\system32 to c:\windows\system.

curl_init( ) starts a Curl session, **curl_setopt( )** sets options for the current session, **curl_exec( )** performs an action, and **curl_close( )** closes the session. You need a current version of Curl to use all the latest features, and you can check the Curl version with **curl_version( )**.

FTP

You are probably already accessing files on servers using FTP, so you know FTP is a simple way of performing basic file transfers. The formal description of FTP is at **www.normos.org/en/summaries/ietf/rfc/rfc959.html**. Parts of FTP, especially security and the **site** command, are extensions that depend on the operating system and FTP software installed on the remote server.

FTP programs tend to lack sophistication, so replacing an FTP program with a PHP script would give you more control and the opportunity to add your own logic for file selection. I often transfer sites between Windows NT and Unix servers, so I would like an FTP program that could accept lists of files for exclusion, and rules for renaming files.

Before jumping into the PHP FTP functions, consider using other functions, such as **fopen( )**, that accept FTP requests. **fopen( )** accepts a file name prefixed with **ftp://**, which lets you read files from and write files to a remote machine. **fopen( )** would be of particular value if you wanted to validate or transform the file contents during the transfer, such as converting Windows-style line ends, **\r\n**, or Macintosh style line ends, **\n\r**, to Unix-style **\n**. FTP has handy directory functions that make FTP an easy way to look through multiple directories on a remote server.

Immediate Solutions

Base64 Encoding

When you want to write your own email system, you will need base64 encoding for the attachments, the same for attachments in newsgroups. You can use base64 to encode binary data for storing in databases that do not have binary string fields (**blobs** or Binary Long Objects). To demonstrate base64 encode and decode, type the following data into a script:

```
$data[] = "Hello Jennifer";
$data[] = "Here are funny characters: ?+&'\"|[]{}~<>";
$data[] = "Here are binary characters: " . chr(5) . chr(250);
```

Add the following code to encode the strings from array **$data** into array **$encoded**, and print the encoded strings for visual verification:

```
reset($data);
while(list($k, $v) = each($data))
   {
   $encoded[$k] = base64_encode($v);
    print("<br>encoded: " . $encoded[$k]);
   }
```

Here is the visual verification:

```
encoded: SGVsbG8gSmVubmlmZXI=
encoded: SGVyZSBhcmUgZnVubmkgY2hhcmFjdGVyczogPysmJyJ8W117fX48Pjs=
encoded: SGVyZSBhcmUgYmluYXJ5IGNoYXJhY3RlcnM6IAX6
```

Decode each string in **$encoded** with the function **base64_decode()** and print the result to verify that the data matches the original:

```
reset($encoded);
while(list($k, $v) = each($encoded))
   {
   print("<br>decoded: " . base64_decode($v));
   }
```

Here is the decoded data:

```
decoded: Hello Jennifer
decoded: Here are funny characters: ?+&'"|[]{}~<>;
decoded: Here are binary characters: ú
```

The base64 functions accept any string as input, so you could use a file function to read a file into memory and then encode the file. You cannot concatenate encoded strings unless the original strings had a length that is an even multiple of three. If you were to read a file 99 bytes at a time, encode each string of 99 bytes, and then concatenate the result, it would work. Performing the same process while reading the file 100 bytes at a time would not work. The following code displays text base64 encoded in one hit, then encoded three bytes at a time, and then decoded for verification:

```php
$poem = "Roses are red, violets are blue,"
    . " PHP is sweeter than those two";
print("<br>" . base64_encode($poem) );
$c = "";
while(strlen($poem))
    {
    $c .= base64_encode(substr($poem, 0, 3));
    $poem = substr($poem, 3);
    }
print("<br>" . $c );
print("<br>" . base64_decode($c) );
```

The results are next and show that both forms of encoding match (note that both encoded lines exceed one print line in this book's layout format; in both cases the *B* on the second line immediately follow the *i* at the end of the previous line):

```
Um9zZXMgYXJlIHJlZCwgdmlvbGV0cyBhcmUgYmx1ZSwgUEhQIGlzIHN3ZWV0ZXIgdGhhbi_
    B0aG9zZSB0d28=
Um9zZXMgYXJlIHJlZCwgdmlvbGV0cyBhcmUgYmx1ZSwgUEhQIGlzIHN3ZWV0ZXIgdGhhbi_
    B0aG9zZSB0d28=
Roses are red, violets are blue, PHP is sweeter than those two
```

If you take the previous code and replace 3 with 11, you get the result shown next. The decode function decodes up to the first = (or ==), and then stops:

```
Um9zZXMgYXJlIHJlI=ZWQsIHZpb2xldHM=IGFyZSBibHVlLCA=UEhQIGlzIHN3ZWU=dGVyIH_
    RoYW4gdGg=b3NlIHR3bw==
Roses are r
```

Browsing the Web with PHP

PHP can act as a browser of other sites, and relay the information from another site through your site to your visitors. There are many examples where people use this technique to rip off information from other sites, including meta search engines that relay your search to other search engines, and then merge the results back to your browser. The technique is used to browse other sites for the best available prices, daily news, and all sorts of valuable information (if it were not valuable, people would not want to rip it off). Eventually the people spending the money to create the original content sued the pirates copying the content and drove most of the pirates out of business. Some pirates paid licensing fees, turned into respectable business people, and continue their Web site relay/merge activities.

Why did I write this solution if it is illegal, immoral, and will make your Web site unnecessarily fat? This approach is of most use for people managing intranets. If your intranet blocks access to most Web sites because of pornography or time-wasting games, you can write a PHP server-based relay to present parts of sites and suppress others. You can relay a search engine, but delete any search engine results that contain words you think might not be appropriate. Ask the search engine for permission before relaying their site and check if they have a content rating system, because they may already have a content filter that fits your requirement.

If your intranet is in a school for younger children, you might want to pick out large and complex words on each page and add links to a dictionary that explains the words. Dictionary functions are described in Chapter 12 and contain everything you need to match words to simpler words, or even to translate complex phrases to simpler phrases.

If your intranet is used by the visually impaired and you do not want to spend a lot of money installing special browsers on every computer, you can relay incoming pages through a script that increases font sizes and increases contrast by removing page background colors. If your visually impaired users are trying to access the Internet through Internet cafés, and cannot change the browser to suit, you can set up a relay site to work through Web pages at the HTML level, increasing font sizes, performing text-to-sound conversions, and placing links to the sound files around the text.

Think of the third-world students using older, less capable browsers on machines with limited resources. You could help them build a relay that reduces the complexity of graphics, converts convoluted bandwidth-wasting animations to simple still images and deletes everything that uses Java. (Hey, that last one could make a lot of sites more useful!)

Before you access items across a network, increase PHP's time limit to allow for network delays. The code is shown next, and the limit will be used again in the later code:

```
$time_limit = 30;
set_time_limit($time_limit);
```

The code is next. **fsockopen( )** opens a Web page as if it were a file, **fputs( )** initiates an HTTP request, and the rest of the code is almost exactly the same as you would write to transfer a file to the screen. The code reads the Web page into an array, so you can add code to modify the page. You can read the page into an array or a string, depending on the modifications you want to make:

```
$page = "www.yahoo.com";
$file = fsockopen($page, 80, $errno, $error, $time_limit);
if($file)
    {
    fputs($file, "GET / HTTP/1.0\r\n\r\n");
    while(!feof($file))
        {
        $data[] = fgets($file, 1000);
        }
    fclose($file);
    }
else
    {
    print("<br>Error: " . $errno . " " . $error);
    }
```

fsockopen( ) accepts the name of a Web site, a port, the name of two variables to receive an error number and an error message, and a timeout value in seconds. **fsockopen( )** returns a file handle that can be used with any of the functions used to process files. **fputs( )** writes to the file (hence to the Web site) and sends an HTTP **GET** request followed by a blank line, to indicate the end of the request.

The next code simply prints the data to the screen. There are no special tricks for a standard Web page. When you want to modify the page before printing the page, you should insert the modification code as a standalone section before the print loop. That way, you can add multiple filters to modify the page, have them all start with the data in an array (or string), and return the modified data to the same variable. You can stack the filters in any sequence without interdependencies:

```
reset($data);
while(list($k, $v) = each($data))
    {
    print($v);
    }
```

Yahoo! is a great site for many reasons. I find their exchange rate feature the most useful. Try planning a business trip without a site like Yahoo! to find everything you need. Figure 13.2 shows **yahoo.com** relayed through a test page on my site. I chose Yahoo! because, as a site, it is so useful and, as a series of Web pages, it uses such simple implementations of HTML and other technologies that it would be one of the easiest sites to modify for the visually impaired. The home page contains no redirects, Java, or anything else to impair your access. You could easily work through the Web page at the HTML level and increase font sizes, make light colors darker, perform text-to-sound conversions, and place links to the sound files around the text. Perhaps Yahoo! would sponsor a relay site for the visually impaired.

After Yahoo!, I tried an ASP site and struck the following error. The page is trying to load a JavaScript file from the relay server instead of the originating server. If you want to relay those sorts of pages, you have to relay the reference files, alter the references from relative references to absolute references, or just drop the references. Some sites fall apart when you remove all the JavaScript, some become more reliable, and well-written sites work as usual:

```
Not Found
The requested URL /jscript/fpi-init.js was not found on this server.
Additionally, a 404 Not Found error was encountered while trying to use
  an ErrorDocument to handle the request.
```

If I had another 100 pages, I could list all the JavaScript coding errors found on expensive "professional" Web sites, but then I would need another 300 pages to

Figure 13.2   Browsing another site.

show you the correct way to code JavaScript. Well, here is the whole secret in one line:

• *Test for the existence of an object before using the object.*

The solution uses HTTP, and HTTP is defined in RFC2068 at **www.w3.org/Protocols/rfc2068/rfc2068**. There are just two versions of HTTP, HTTP 1 and 1.1.

Verifying Links

fsockopen( ) lets you check if a link is still valid, and it is perfect for sites built around links to other sites. If you run a directory site listing all the pet shops in the world, you can write a script to check every link to every pet shop every day. Portal sites lose customers fast if the links click through to dead pages. A little script, coupled to a list of links, can warn you of problem links before customers become aggravated.

The following code checks one link to one article, but it could be reading a list of 1,000 links from a database. **fsockopen( )** opens a link to a site, **fputs( )** sends a request for the header information for the page (you only need the headers to verify that the file exists), and then **fgets( )** reads the headers. In the example, the headers are printed so you can see the result, but you could easily add code to check the contents and display a message only if the result indicates a page is missing:

```
$site = "www.phpbuilder.com";
$page = "/columns/peter20000629.php3";
$file = fsockopen($site, 80, $errno, $errstr, $time_limit);
if($file)
    {
    fputs($file, "HEAD " . $page . " HTTP/1.0\r\n\r\n");
    while(!feof($file))
        {
        $data[] = fgets($file, 1000);
        }
    fclose($file);
    }
else
    {
    print("<br>Error: " . $errno . " " . $errstr );
    }
```

```
reset($data);
while(list($k, $v) = each($data))
    {
    print("<br>" . $v );
    }
```

The result is shown next, and verifies that the page exists:

```
HTTP/1.1 200 OK
Date: Sun, 17 Jun 2001 04:42:42 GMT
Server: Apache/1.3.17 (Unix) PHP/4.0.4pl1 AuthMySQL/2.20
X-Powered-By: PHP/4.0.4pl1
Connection: close
Content-Type: text/html
```

When you use the same code to request a page that does not exist, you get the following result. Notice that the result code changes from 200 to 404:

```
HTTP/1.0 404
Date: Sun, 17 Jun 2001 09:11:15 GMT
Connection: close
Content-Type: text/html
```

Some Web sites implement a "page not found" facility in their Web server, named **ErrorDocument** in Apache's configuration file. The facility redirects the browser to a generic error message page or a page search facility, as shown next. 302 means redirect, and the **Location:** statement provides the new location. When you find a redirect, hand-check that the new page is the correct replacement, and then update your links:

```
HTTP/1.1 302 Found
Date: Sun, 17 Jun 2001 04:46:24 GMT
Server: Apache/1.3.17 (Unix) PHP/4.0.4pl1 AuthMySQL/2.20
X-Powered-By: PHP/4.0.4pl1
Location: /search/?feedback=Page+Not+Found
Connection: close
Content-Type: text/html
```

How old is the page? Page age is an important question if you want to provide current information, like weather reports, and you have to know the currency of your source information. In the previous code, replace the **fputs( )** line with the following line, to check if the page has a modified date of June 17, 2001, or later. Insert your own date and time where needed. If you need a page that is less than seven days old, insert a date from seven days ago. Current pages will be found and return a code of 200. If the page is older than your cut-off date, you will get a "page not found" error:

```
fputs($file, "HEAD " . $page . " HTTP/1.0\r\n"
    . "If-Modified-Since: Sunday, 17 Jun 2001 01:00:00\r\n\r\n\r\n");
```

You can automate as much of this task as you need. Generally you want to automate the repetitive checking and only handle the exceptions, such as checking if a redirection leads to an appropriate replacement page. Exceptions can be sent to you by email, so you can run the check overnight and see the result in the morning. Chapter 15 covers email in depth.

Using FTP Functions

All the FTP functions are demonstrated in this solution, so you can do anything and everything that FTP allows. Some functions have operating-system-dependent considerations because the operating systems have specific ways of handling files. One function, **ftp_site( )**, depends entirely on the FTP server software in use on the remote server.

ftp_connect( ) accepts a host name and an optional port number and returns a resource identifier, just like a file handle or the resource id returned by **fsockopen( )**. The port number defaults to 21:

```
$host = "ftp.gnu.org";
if(!$ftp = ftp_connect($host))
    {
    print("<br>Error: " . $errno . " " . $errstr);
    }
```

After opening a connection to the FTP server, you need to log in using a user id and password. I attempted an anonymous user logon by leaving out the user id and password, as shown here, but I just received a message about *Wrong parameter count for ftp_login*:

```
ftp_login($ftp);
```

I tried an anonymous logon using empty strings, as shown next:

```
ftp_login($ftp, "", "");
```

The result was:

```
Warning: ftp_login: 'USER': command not understood
```

When I tried a made-up user name with no password, I received the previous message with **USER** replaced by **PASS**. The code that worked is shown next, complete with an error check. In your own version of the script, you could place each part of this code within the appropriate brackets of the preceding code, so the logon will execute only when the connect works, or you could place an **exit( )** statement after the error message so the script stops:

```
if(!ftp_login($ftp, "anonymous", "x@y.com"))
    {
    print("<br>Login error: " . $errno . " " . $errstr );
    }
```

If you want to know the type of system behind the FTP server, use the following code. For most parts of FTP, you do not need to know the system type, but it can help you decide if you should translate spaces in file names to underscores, and other operating system-dependent variations:

```
if($type = ftp_systype($ftp))
    {
    print("<br>systype: " . $type);
    }
else
    {
    print("<br>Systype error: " . $errno . " " . $errstr);
    }
```

The result of this code on **ftp.gnu.org** is:

```
systype: UNIX
```

When you use FTP from behind a firewall, you may need the following command to use FTP successfully:

```
if(ftp_pasv($ftp, true))
    {
    print("<br>passive mode on.");
    }
else
    {
    print("<br>Systype error: " . $errno . " " . $errstr);
    }
```

ftp_nlist( ), new in PHP 4, gives you a list of the files in a directory on the FTP server. The following code uses **ftp_nlist( )** and generic code to list an array, complete with keys and values:

```
if($array = ftp_nlist($ftp, $directory))
    {
    reset($array);
    while(list($k, $v) = each($array))
        {
        print("<br>k: " . $k . ", v: " . $v);
        }
    }
else
    {
    print("<br>ftp_nlist() failed.");    }
```

The result is shown here. The values resemble the result of the Unix command **ls**, except for the double slashes at the beginning of the file and directory names (the slashes will have to be removed before using the names in other functions):

```
k: 0, v: //pub
k: 1, v: //welcome.msg
k: 2, v: //bin
k: 3, v: //lib
k: 4, v: //gnu
k: 5, v: //ls-lrR.txt
k: 6, v: //ls-lrR.txt.gz
k: 7, v: //non-gnu
k: 8, v: //README
k: 9, v: //lpf.README
k: 10, v: //old-gnu
k: 11, v: //find-ls.txt
k: 12, v: //find-ls.txt.gz
k: 13, v: //md5sums.txt
k: 14, v: //md5sums.txt.gz
k: 15, v: //var
k: 16, v: //third-party
```

TIP: *One of the most unbelievably frustrating typographical errors is to type "**while(list($k, $v) = each($array));**".* *That semicolon at the end of the line does not show up as a syntax error, and the code appears to work, but the array always appears empty. Grrrr! It takes two cups of coffee and 185 new gray hairs before I notice my stupid typo.*

---

ftp_rawlist( ), new in PHP 4, will give you an unmodified, unfiltered list of directories and files in a directory on the FTP server. The following code uses

ftp_rawlist() on the same directory used for **ftp_nlist()**, and prints just the values from the resultant array:

```
if($raw = ftp_rawlist($ftp, $directory))
    {
    reset($raw);
    while(list($k, $v) = each($raw))
        {
        print("<br>" . $v);
        }
    }
else
    {
    print("<br>ftp_rawlist failed.");
    }
```

The result is shown here. It resembles the result of the Unix command **ls -l**:

```
-rw-r--r-- 1 ftp ftp 1516 Aug 18 2000 README
drwxr-xr-x 2 ftp ftp 4096 Jan 1 1999 bin
-rw-r--r-- 1 ftp ftp 2131267 Jul 6 13:28 find-ls.txt
-rw-r--r-- 1 ftp ftp 208066 Jul 6 13:28 find-ls.txt.gz
drwxr-xr-x 193 ftp ftp 8192 Jul 3 03:03 gnu
drwxr-xr-x 2 ftp ftp 4096 Jan 1 1999 lib
-rw-r--r-- 1 ftp ftp 90 Feb 16 1993 lpf.README
-rw-r--r-- 1 ftp ftp 1342751 Jul 6 13:28 ls-lrR.txt
-rw-r--r-- 1 ftp ftp 137580 Jul 6 13:28 ls-lrR.txt.gz
-rw-r--r-- 1 ftp ftp 997585 Jul 6 13:33 md5sums.txt
-rw-r--r-- 1 ftp ftp 293249 Jul 6 13:33 md5sums.txt.gz
lrw-r--r-- 1 ftp ftp 11 Feb 23 03:55 non-gnu -> gnu/non-gnu
drwxr-xr-x 10 ftp ftp 4096 May 29 14:50 old-gnu
lrw-r--r-- 1 ftp ftp 1 Feb 23 03:19 pub -> .
drwxr-xr-x 2 ftp ftp 4096 Mar 5 20:28 third-party
-rw-r--r-- 1 ftp ftp 128800 Mar 25 03:03 var
-rw-r--r-- 1 ftp ftp 980 Aug 18 2000 welcome.msg
```

TIP: *If you like using the Unix command **ls** and its relatives, but are using NT, install Cygwin. Cygwin adds dozens of POSIX-compliant Unix commands to NT.*

To change a directory, use **ftp_chdir()** as shown next. If the directory does not exist, **ftp_chdir()** puts a message out to the browser, so suppress that with **@** in front of the function name and perform your own error processing (which, in the example, is just a message):

```
if(@ftp_chdir($ftp, "pub"))
   {
   print("<br>chdir worked");
   }
else
   {
   print("<br>chdir failed");
   }
```

To change to the parent directory of the current directory, equivalent to a **cd ..** command, use **ftp_cdup( )** as shown next (for the next few examples, add appropriate error messages similar to what I added in the previous example):

```
if(@ftp_cdup($ftp))
```

Create a directory on the FTP server using **ftp_mkdir( )**, as shown next, and **ftp_mkdir( )** should return the name of the new directory:

```
if($new_dir = ftp_mkdir($ftp, "new"))
```

Rename a directory (or a file) on the FTP server using **ftp_rename( )**, as shown here (copy the rest of the code from the **ftp_chdir( )** example):

```
if(ftp_rename($ftp, "new", "test"))
```

Delete a directory on the FTP server using **ftp_rmdir( )**, as shown in the following code. The result is true on success, or false on failure (copy the rest of the code from the **ftp_chdir( )** example):

```
if(ftp_rmdir($ftp, "new"))
```

Delete a file on the FTP server using **ftp_delete( )**, as shown here. The result is true on success, or false on failure (copy the rest of the code from the **ftp_chdir( )** example):

```
if(ftp_delete($ftp, "new.txt"))
```

You may need to check a file size before download, just in case there is a 650MB CD image in among the tiny text files you intend to download. **ftp_size( )** returns the size of a file, as shown next. Because zero is valid as a file length, and zero can be confused with false if you do not perform the right type of comparison, **ftp_size( )** returns –1 to indicate failure. The first time I tried this, I received –1 because I typed *welcome* instead of *Welcome*. Doh! **ftp_systype( )** did return UNIX:

```
$size = ftp_size($ftp, "Welcome");
if($size < 0)
    {
    print("<br>ftp_size error.");
    }
else
    {
    print("<br>size: " . $size);
    }
```

The result for Welcome is:

```
size: 364
```

Is a file current? **ftp_mdtm( )** returns a Unix timestamp containing the date/time a file was last modified. Because zero is a valid date/time, and zero can be confused with false if you do not perform the right type of comparison, **ftp_mdtm( )** returns –1 to indicate failure. The following code is a modification of the **ftp_size( )** code to display the date/time of modification instead of size:

```
$time = ftp_mdtm($ftp, "Welcome");
if($time < 0)
    {
    print("<br>ftp_mdtm error.");
    }
else
    {
    print("<br>date/time: " . date("Y-m-d H:i:s", $time));
    }
```

The result for Welcome is:

```
time: 2001-08-09 03:14:51
```

You get files from a remote server with **ftp_get( )**. The first parameter is the FTP connection id, the second parameter is the local file name, the third parameter is the remote file name, and the last parameter tells FTP to work in ASCII text or binary mode. By default, the file ends up in the same directory as the script containing **ftp_get( )**, but if you prefix the local file name with a full path, the file can be placed anywhere on the machine containing the script (that is, anywhere where you have write permission). You cannot use **ftp_get( )** to direct the file to the computer that requests the script execution (the machine with the browser). The following example has the local file going to a test partition, **t:/**:

```
if(ftp_get($ftp, "t:/welcome", "Welcome", FTP_BINARY))
   {
   print("<br>Get worked.");
   }
else
   {
   print("<br>Get failed.");
   }
```

You copy a file to a remote server with **ftp_put( )**. The first parameter is the FTP connection id, the second parameter is the remote file name, the third parameter is the local file name, and the last parameter tells FTP to work in ASCII text or binary mode. The following example has a local file going to the Netscape FTP server that was opened earlier, but that server does not allow uploads, so you will have to find your own test server:

```
if(ftp_put($ftp, "Welcome", "t:/welcome", FTP_BINARY))
   {
   print("<br>Put worked.");
   }
else
   {
   print("<br>Put failed.");
   }
```

You can display remote files direct to your browser using **ftp_fget( )**. The first parameter is the FTP connection id, the second parameter is a file handle for a local file, the third parameter is the remote file name, and the last parameter tells FTP to work in ASCII text or binary mode. You can make the local file a temporary file and direct the content of the temporary file to your browser with **fpassthru( )**, as shown next. **tempnam( )** allocates a temporary file, **fopen( )** opens the file in read/write mode, **ftp_fget( )** writes the remote file to the local file, **rewind( )** resets the file pointer back to the start of the file, and **fpassthru( )** writes the file contents to the browser. File functions are described in detail in Chapter 8:

```
$temp_file = tempnam("", "");
if($file = fopen($temp_file, "w+"))
   {
   if(ftp_fget($ftp, $file, "Welcome", FTP_BINARY))
      {
      print("<br>Fget worked." );
      rewind($file);
```

```
        fpassthru($file);
        }
    else
        {
        print("<br>Fget failed.");
        fclose($file);
        }
    }
else
    {
    print("<br>Fopen failed.");
    }
```

The **ftp_fget( )** example could be modified to save a permanent copy to disk, or to modify the file contents in between the read from the remote server and the display to the browser. By replacing **fpassthru( )** with more controlled code, you could format the file contents on the way to the screen. In the Immediate Solution entitled "Browsing the Web with PHP," I describe how to help visually impaired people browse sites by relaying the browse through a server that improves the visual formatting of a site. You could apply the same principle to documents available through FTP, by representing the documents with better formatting.

ftp_fput( ) uploads a file from an open file handle to a remote server. All the parameters are the same as **ftp_put( )**, except the local file is specified as a file handle instead of a file name. An obvious use is to combine **ftp_fput( )** with **ftp_fget( )** to relay files from one server to another when you are managing several servers, and that is the example shown next. The only difference to the example code is the replacement of **fpassthru( )** with **ftp_fput( )**. In a production application, you would test the result of **ftp_fput( )**, much like the **ftp_put( )** example earlier in this section:

```
$temp_file = tempnam("", "");
if($file = fopen($temp_file, "w+"))
    {
    if(ftp_fget($ftp, $file, "Welcome", FTP_BINARY))
        {
        print("<br>Fget worked." );
        rewind($file);
        ftp_fput($ftp2, "Welcome", $file, FTP_BINARY))
        }
    else
        {
        print("<br>Fget failed.");
        fclose($file);
```

```
        }
    }
else
    {
    print("<br>Fopen failed.");
    }
```

To change permissions or group ownership for a file on the FTP server, use **ftp_site( )**, as shown below. The result is true on success, or false on failure. (Copy the rest of the code from the **ftp_chdir( )** example.) There is just one problem with the **site** command: The format and content depend on the type of system that receives the command. You have to use **ftp_systype( )** to find out the system type, then look up the site for that system, and then format the command to suit. Some systems allow Unix commands in the form of **site** followed by the command you would type in at a command-line console, such as **site chmod 777**:

```
if(ftp_site($ftp, $command))
```

When you finish using the connection to the host, close the connection with **ftp_quit( )**, as shown next:

```
if($ftp)
    {
    ftp_quit($ftp);
    }
```

Now you can use FTP to access any FTP server in any way you need.

Using Curl

Use Curl instead of the PHP FTP and socket functions, and test and twist all the approaches until you decide which is the best for you. If you need to use Curl for some of its features, you might find life easier if you use Curl for everything that it can do.

The following example initializes a connection to a Web site via **curl_init( )**, opens a file with **fopen( )**, and then tells Curl the id of the file via **curl_setopt( )**. Curl can read the page from the remote server and write the page into the file. To stop Curl from placing the HTTP headers in the file, **CURLOPT_HEADER** is turned off. **curl_exec( )** executes the request, and then **curl_close( )** closes the connection to the remote server. **fclose( )** closes the output file:

```
if($curled = curl_init("http://petermoulding.com/"))
    {
    if($file = fopen("t:/testpage.txt", "w+"))
        {
        curl_setopt($curled, CURLOPT_FILE, $file);
        curl_setopt($curled, CURLOPT_HEADER, 0);
        curl_exec($curled);
        curl_close($curled);
        fclose($file);
        }
    else
        {
        print("<br>fopen() failed." );
        }
    }
else
    {
    print("<br>curl_init() failed." );
    }
```

The example code could be extended to display the received page in the browser, extract information, and perform all sorts of other activities as outlined in the example using **fsockopen()**. There appears to be little difference between **fsockopen()** and **curl()** for such a simple example.

Curl handles SSL and https pages, which is of definite interest when you are sharing information between servers. If you are selling content to other sites, you want to secure the exchange of information so your information cannot be copied, and to prove that your customers received the content. The same applies when you buy content; you want to make sure it is legitimate and that your competitors cannot rip off the information for free. They probably have my book too, so they can use Curl to copy the same pages, unless you secure the pages.

Curl will help you perform a secure copy between servers. Set **CURLOPT_SSLCERT** and **CURLOPT_SSLCERTPASSWD** before the copy and use https as the protocol.

Some people report that Curl is faster. I have not tested them side by side because Curl has different options, and I tend to choose function sets based on ease of use and flexibility over speed. A large proportion of network time is consumed establishing connections, so if you can reuse a connection for a second request, you will save time. Another way to save time is to request headers only when you do not need the contents of a page. Your performance results will vary. Read through all the Curl options to see if they will help you optimize the performance of Curl.

Curl Options

Curl's actions depend on the options you set with **curl_setopt( )** and the format of the URL you supply, particularly the first part of the URL, the scheme or protocol. Curl uses the scheme to decide if Curl should perform an HTTP or an FTP activity. The options are listed here, with examples, but every update to Curl brings more options and refinements to existing options.

CURLOPT_COOKIE

Set **CURLOPT_COOKIE** to a string containing your content for a cookie in the next HTTP header.

CURLOPT_COOKIEFILE

Set **CURLOPT_COOKIEFILE** to the name of a file containing cookie data. The cookie file can use the Netscape format, or HTTP-style headers:

```
curl_setopt($curled, CURLOPT_COOKIEFILE, "test.txt");
```

CURLOPT_CUSTOMREQUEST

Set **CURLOPT_CUSTOMREQUEST** to replace **GET** or **HEAD** with another option, like **DELETE**, when performing a HTTP request. This will work only if the remote server accepts the command:

```
curl_setopt($curled, CURLOPT_CUSTOMREQUEST, "DELETE _string value_");
```

CURLOPT_FAILONERROR

Set **CURLOPT_FAILONERROR** to a non-zero value if you want PHP to stop when Curl returns a HTTP code greater than 300. The default is to return all pages, no matter what the HTTP code:

```
curl_setopt($curled, CURLOPT_FAILONERROR, 1);
```

CURLOPT_FOLLOWLOCATION

Set **CURLOPT_FOLLOWLOCATION** to a non-zero value to make Curl follow **Location:** headers (redirections) found among HTTP headers received from a server. It is possible to get location loops, because Curl will follow every redirect, and a redirect from a missing page may redirect to the same missing page:

```
curl_setopt($curled, CURLOPT_FOLLOWLOCATION, 1);
```

CURLOPT_FTPAPPEND

Set **CURLOPT_FTPAPPEND** to a non-zero value to make an FTP file copy append to the remote file instead of overwriting the file:

```
curl_setopt($curled, CURLOPT_FTPAPPEND, 1);
```

CURLOPT_FTPLISTONLY

Set **CURLOPT_FTPLISTONLY** to a non-zero value to make an FTP directory list include names but nothing else:

```
curl_setopt($curled, CURLOPT_FTPLISTONLY, 1);
```

CURLOPT_FTPPORT

Set **CURLOPT_FTPPORT** to a string containing the IP address for an FTP **POST**. The value may be an IP address, a hostname, a network interface name (under Unix), or a dash (-) to use the system's default IP address:

```
curl_setopt($curled, CURLOPT_FTPPORT, "192.168.0.1");
```

CURLOPT_HEADER

Set **CURLOPT_HEADER** to a non-zero value when you want HTTP headers included in the output:

```
curl_setopt($curled, CURLOPT_HEADER, 1);
```

CURLOPT_INFILESIZE

Before you upload a file to a remote server, set **CURLOPT_INFILESIZE** to the size of the file:

```
$size = filesize("test.txt");
curl_setopt($curled, CURLOPT_INFILESIZE, $size);
```

CURLOPT_LOW_SPEED_LIMIT

Set **CURLOPT_LOW_SPEED_LIMIT** to the transfer speed, in bytes per second, at which you want Curl to abort transfers:

```
curl_setopt($curled, CURLOPT_LOW_SPEED_LIMIT, 300);
```

CURLOPT_LOW_SPEED_TIME

Set **CURLOPT_LOW_SPEED_TIME** to the time, in seconds, that a transfer should wait before aborting because of a transfer speed lower than **CURLOPT_LOW_SPEED_LIMIT**:

```
curl_setopt($curled, CURLOPT_LOW_SPEED_TIME, 20);
```

CURLOPT_MUTE

Set **CURLOPT_MUTE** to a non-zero value to make PHP silent when executing Curl functions:

```
curl_setopt($curled, CURLOPT_MUTE, 1);
```

CURLOPT_NETRC

When you are connecting to a remote site, set **CURLOPT_NETRC** to a non-zero value to make Curl scan your ~./netrc file for your username and password to use with that remote site:

```
curl_setopt($curled, CURLOPT_NETRC, 1);
```

CURLOPT_NOBODY

Set **CURLOPT_NOBODY** to a non-zero value if you don't want the body of a page included in the output. Make sure you change **CURLOPT_HEADER** if you are after headers without a body:

```
curl_setopt($curled, CURLOPT_NOBODY, 1);
```

CURLOPT_NOPROGRESS

Set **CURLOPT_NOPROGRESS** to zero if you want PHP to display a progress meter for Curl transfers. You can turn the meter back off by setting **CURLOPT_NOPROGRESS** to a non-zero value:

```
curl_setopt($curled, CURLOPT_NOPROGRESS, 0);
```

CURLOPT_POST

Set **CURLOPT_POST** to a non-zero value when you want to perform an HTTP **POST**, as used by HTML forms:

```
curl_setopt($curled, CURLOPT_POST, 1);
```

13. Internet

CURLOPT_POSTFIELDS

Set **CURLOPT_POSTFIELDS** to a string containing the full data for an HTTP **POST**.

CURLOPT_PROXYUSERPWD

Set **CURLOPT_PROXYUSERPWD** to a string formatted as [*username*]: [*password*], for a connection to a proxy server:

```
curl_setopt($curled, CURLOPT_PROXYUSERPWD, "freda:ero4509");
```

CURLOPT_PUT

Set **CURLOPT_PUT** to a non-zero value when you want to perform an HTTP **PUT**. Also set **CURLOPT_INFILE** and **CURLOPT_INFILESIZE**:

```
curl_setopt($curled, CURLOPT_PUT, 1);
```

CURLOPT_RANGE

Set **CURLOPT_RANGE** to the range you want for HTTP transfers. You can use the format **X-Y**, or several ranges in the format **X-Y,N-M**.

CURLOPT_REFERER

Set **CURLOPT_REFERER** to a string containing the referrer header for a HTTP request. The referrer is the page requesting information from a server and is provided to a PHP script in **$HTTP_REFERER**. If you want to tell the remote server the truth, you can construct the referrer field as shown next, or you might prefer to supply the name of a contact page or just your domain name:

```
curl_setopt($curled, CURLOPT_REFERER,
   "http://" . $HTTP_HOST . $PHP_SELF);
```

CURLOPT_RESUME_FROM

Set **CURLOPT_RESUME_FROM** to the offset, in bytes, for the start of a transfer. This can be used to resume a previous transfer that failed, but you should check that the output file is okay before resuming:

```
curl_setopt($curled, CURLOPT_RESUME_FROM, 500);
```

CURLOPT_SSLCERT

Set **CURLOPT_SSLCERT** to the filename of a PEM (privacy-enhanced mail)-formatted certificate (PEM is an attempt to make encryption, like PGP, part of the MIME standard for mail attachments):

```
curl_setopt($curled, CURLOPT_SSLCERT, "test.pem");
```

CURLOPT_SSLCERTPASSWD

Set **CURLOPT_SSLCERTPASSWD** to the password required for the **CURLOPT_SSLCERT** certificate:

```
curl_setopt($curled, CURLOPT_SSLCERTPASSWD, "testingpw");
```

CURLOPT_SSLVERSION

Set **CURLOPT_SSLVERSION** to the SSL version, 2 or 3, that you use. PHP can determine the version by itself, but in some cases, you have to set the value manually:

```
curl_setopt($curled, CURLOPT_SSLVERSION, 3);
```

CURLOPT_TIMECONDITION

Set **CURLOPT_TIMECONDITION** to control how the **CURLOPT_TIMEVALUE** is treated. It is a HTTP feature and can accept the values **TIMECOND_IFMODSINCE** or **TIMECOND_ISUNMODSINCE**:

```
curl_setopt($curled, CURLOPT_TIMECONDITION, TIMECOND_IFMODSINCE);
```

CURLOPT_TIMEOUT

Set **CURLOPT_TIMEOUT** to the maximum time, in seconds, that you will let the Curl functions wait to complete:

```
curl_setopt($curled, CURLOPT_TIMEOUT, 30);
```

CURLOPT_TIMEVALUE

Pass a **long** as a parameter that is the time in seconds since January 1, 1970. The time will be used as specified by the **CURLOPT_TIMEVALUE** option, or **TIMECOND_IFMODSINCE** will be used by default.

13. Internet

CURLOPT_UPLOAD

Set **CURLOPT_UPLOAD** to a non-zero value when you are about to upload a file:

```
curl_setopt($curled, CURLOPT_UPLOAD, 1);
```

CURLOPT_URL

Set **CURLOPT_URL** to the URL that you want to read. This option can be set as part of **curl_init( )**, and usually is:

```
curl_setopt($curled, CURLOPT_URL, "http://petermoulding.com/");
```

CURLOPT_USERAGENT

Set **CURLOPT_USERAGENT** to the user-agent you want to emulate when browsing other Web sites. Some Web sites change their page content based on the assumed capabilities of a browser, so if you do not want the incoming page flooded with useless Java, set the agent field to indicate an older, pre-Java browser. PHP receives the agent field in **$HTTP_USER_AGENT**. I set the following example to Netscape 4.77, English, but you could include any language and any browser name. If you want pure text with no images, use an agent string containing the browser name of Lynx:

```
curl_setopt($curled, CURLOPT_USERAGENT, "Mozilla/4.77 [en] (WinNT; U)");
```

CURLOPT_USERPWD

Set **CURLOPT_USERPWD** to a string formatted as **[*username*]:[*password*]**, for a connection to a server:

```
curl_setopt($curled, CURLOPT_USERPWD, "joe:dg09xy");
```

CURLOPT_VERBOSE

Set **CURLOPT_VERBOSE** to a non-zero value to make Curl report everything that happens:

```
curl_setopt($curled, CURLOPT_VERBOSE, 1);
```

Chapter 14

LDAP

In Depth

Visit **yahoo.com**, click on Arts & Humanities, click on Artists, then Animation@, and then Cartoonists@. You have just used a directory to look up cartoonists. Figure 14.1 shows the structure you worked through. LDAP lets you perform exactly the same type of directory lookup.

An LDAP database can be set up as a Yahoo!-style directory, or as a directory like the telephone white pages. LDAP suits data that has many more reads than writes, very small chunks of data, and data that has a hierarchical structure.

LDAP stands for Lightweight Directory Access Protocol, and is the "lite" version of the X.500 Directory Access Protocol (DAP). How lite is the lite version? DAP uses the OSI network model, whereas LDAP uses the simple TCP/IP protocol. TCP/IP has much less overhead over the Internet, because TCP/IP is the native protocol of the Internet. DAP uses all sorts of complex data structures, whereas LDAP uses simple strings for almost all fields. The use of simple data structures means the database behind LDAP can be almost any database. OpenLDAP uses the small, efficient Berkeley DB, available at Sleepycat Software (**www.sleepycat.com**).

In conventional relational databases, data is stored in organized lists called *tables*, the database software builds separate indexes, and the whole arrangement is designed to accommodate very fast updates. LDAP uses an older style of database structure, called *hierarchical*, where the data is the index. Hierarchical databases allow fast read access to data when you know the index structure, such

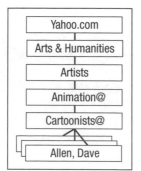

Figure 14.1   Directory structure from the Yahoo! lookup.

as when you click down through the categories at Yahoo!. Hierarchical databases tend to be slower for updates and inserts of new data, because a change to the database is more likely to require the building of new pages and new links from existing pages.

XML databases, like Software AG's Tamino, use the same hierarchical approach to allow storage of structured documents. In theory, LDAP could use an XML database for data storage, and structured documents could be stored in LDAP. LDAP databases could be set up to conform to the Document Object Model (DOM) and could be used to serve your whole Web site content. In practice, LDAP databases have proved too slow to use for anything other than simple directories.

Both Unix and Apache can be configured to authenticate users from an LDAP directory. The temptation is to store the user id and password in an LDAP directory, and add contact information and user-profile information, such as the user's preferred font size. As soon as you add frequent profile updates to the LDAP database, you get slow response, upset customers, and loss of business to your Web site.

A better approach for most sites is to use LDAP just for the user authentication, and store everything else in a conventional database. If you use MySQL in your site, use MySQL to store everything the users can update themselves. If you do store user profile information in LDAP, and you use the information to format each Web page, avoid constant reading of the profile from LDAP by copying the profile to the user's session record. Only return to LDAP when a user updates something in his or her profile.

Installation

I list an Immediate Solution in this chapter that covers installing LDAP under Windows NT, including installing the OpenLDAP server. Windows 2000 installation is the same as Windows NT. I did not find a good, comprehensive solution for Windows 95 and 98 users. Unix users must install an LDAP client library from **www.openldap.org/** or **http://developer.netscape.com/tech/directory/**, and then compile PHP with the option **-with-ldap** (LDAP may be on their Unix distribution CD).

Terminology

LDAP terminology has unique meanings you need to know before reading detailed descriptions of LDAP. Navigation through an LDAP directory depends on your understanding the LDAP usage of terms like *attribute* and *object*.

14. LDAP

DN

LDAP uses distinguished names (DN) as a basic unit of identification. A DN is a collection of identifiers that build the path you want to access. In the Yahoo! cartoonists example, the DN of the top level is shown here. **dc** is the abbreviation of *domain component.* Yahoo.com has two domain components, **yahoo** and **com**:

```
dc=yahoo, dc=com
```

My test site is **test.petermoulding.com**, so I access the test site with the following DN, using three domain components:

```
dc=test, dc=petermoulding, dc=com
```

If your site name has more components, use more instances of **dc=**. **mail.test.petermoulding.com.au** requires five domain components.

The standard components of a DN have predefined ids. The name of a country is identified as **c=**. The name of a company or organization is identified as **o=**. User names are identified as **cn=** (common name). You can add your own field ids, but do not override the commonly used ids, because that would cause a clash if you connected your LDAP directory to other LDAP directories.

For the Yahoo! example, call the various levels **ca** (category), **sc** (subcategory), **ss** (subsubcategory), **nl** (next level), and **cn** (common name). A request at the category level would use the following DN:

```
ca=Arts & Humanities, dc=yahoo, dc=com
```

Notice one difference from the Yahoo! category display and other structured directory information, such a path to a file. The LDAP DN is read right to left, so the top-level directory entry is placed at the right and lower levels are added at the left. A request at the subcategory level would use the following DN:

```
sc=Artists, ca=Arts & Humanities, dc=yahoo, dc=com
```

A request at the common name level would use the following DN:

```
cn="Allen, Dave", nl=Cartoonists@, ss=Animation@, sc=Artists, ca=Arts & _
    Humanities, dc=yahoo, dc=com
```

In the Yahoo! directory, the final entry is a link to a site with a description of the site, and so it is a little different than the common LDAP directory usage, where the final entry is oriented to contact information such as name and telephone number. Note also the double quotes, ", around field values that contain special characters, like commas. There are a few other things to remember when using distinguished names. Any field can contain a list of values; a request for "Allen, Dave" might return several entries for people named "Allen, Dave". The database might be set up to store "Allan, Dave" as **fn=Dave, sn=Allen** (first name and surname, respectively).

RDN

DNs become RDNs (relative distinguished names) when used within the structure of an LDAP directory. You are probably used to referring to a page as **./index.html** when requesting the page from within a Web site subdirectory (if you are in directory **/test/**, and request **./index.html**, you get **/test/index.html**). An RDN works the same way. If you select **sc=Artists, ca=Arts & Humanities, dc=yahoo, dc=com**, you can then request **cn="Allen, Dave", nl=Cartoonists@, ss=Animation@**.

Levels

Just as you can step down through the categories in **yahoo.com**, or step down through the directories on a disk partition, you can step down through the *levels* of an LDAP directory. You request a list of identifiers at each level, and select one identifier to take you down to the next level.

There are differences between an LDAP directory and stepping through file directories. When you step through file directories, each level contains the same types of items: directories and files. In LDAP, every level can be completely different. In the disk file structure, a directory can contain a list of files and directories, but a file name cannot refer to more than one file. If the disk file structure were replaced with LDAP, a file entry would also be allowed to contain lists, which could lead to duplicate file entries, which would make accurate file retrieval impossible.

Entries

Each point of reference in an LDAP directory is called an *entry, node,* or *distinguished service entry* (DSE). It is similar to a record in a relational database, because it has a unique identity and contains fields; but in an LDAP entry, each field can contain lists of values, and may be a lower-level entry.

In the Yahoo! example, the node identified as **sc=Artists, ca=Arts & Humanities, dc=yahoo, dc=com** can contain fields and lower-level entries, including the example **ss=Animation@**. When you look through Yahoo! categories, you find descriptive text and advertising banners for each page, a list of subcategories, and a list of entries at that level. LDAP can store that rich variety of information, but navigating through the information can be a problem because every time you retrieve an entry, you then have to check every field to find if it is a list or contains lower-level entries.

Attributes

Each entry has *attributes*, just as relational database records have fields. In the Yahoo! example, cartoonist "Allen, Dave" has the common name attribute of **Allen, Dave**. He could also have the attributes of email address or Web site, or he could have first name and surname attributes that replace the common name. In fact, there is no reason why he could not have first name, surname, common name, and other forms of name like salutation (sl). His entry could be a line like the following:

```
fn=David, sn=Allen, cn=Dave Allen, sl="Mr D. Allen"
```

You can add attributes at any time, you can leave out attributes for individual entries, and you can vary the type of attributes you use for each entry. If you created a white pages for the whole world, there would be 6.5 billion entries, of which only a few hundred million entries would have email addresses and only some would have postal codes, and the format of the postal codes would vary by country.

Object

An *object* in an LDAP directory defines the attributes in an entry for all entries that share the same object class. All the cartoonists in the Yahoo! example have the same object, defining what can be in an entry for a cartoonist. Of course, most of the fields can be optional, and several fields can have similar and confusing values, so you could set up an object definition to be extremely flexible, to the point of being vague. Object definitions need to be planned, a bit like normalizing database records, to ensure there is no duplication of data.

DIT

The structure of the LDAP directory, including all objects, is named the *Directory Information Tree* (DIT).

Schema

A *schema* is the formal definition of an LDAP DIT and the objects in the DIT. The following is a quick whip through an LDAP schema, **core.scheme**, supplied with OpenLDAP. If you want to know all about LDAP schemas, you will have to trace through all the links from the **http://openldap.org** site.

The following code is the basic definition of a attribute type, using an **attributetype** statement. **2.5.4.41** is an identifier unique within a schema. **NAME** indicates the name of this type. **EQUALITY** supplies the name of a routine that is used when comparing the value in this type of field with another value, to determine if they are a match. **caseIgnoreMatch** means the matching routine will ignore case when comparing values. **SUBSTR** is the routine to use for matching based on substrings of the values. Most of **SYNTAX** seems meaningless and identical across all fields. The last bit of SYNTAX, **15{32768}**, means a length of 15 with a variable length up to 32768:

```
attributetype ( 2.5.4.41 NAME 'name'
   EQUALITY caseIgnoreMatch
   SUBSTR caseIgnoreSubstringsMatch
   SYNTAX 1.3.6.1.4.1.1466.115.121.1.15{32768} )
```

Attribute types can be reused and extended. **NAME** is reused in the following two **attributetype** definitions. Notice that both of these have a short name and a long name:

```
attributetype ( 2.5.4.3 NAME ( 'cn' 'commonName' ) SUP name )
attributetype ( 2.5.4.4 NAME ( 'sn' 'surname' ) SUP name )
```

The next **attributetype** adds **SINGLE-VALUE** to prevent the field receiving a list of values.

```
attributetype ( 2.5.4.6 NAME ( 'c' 'countryName' ) SUP name SINGLE-VALUE )
```

The schema also contains **objectclass** definitions, but I hope you will not have to learn about them. You should be able to just extend **attributetype**s to get the fields you need.

LDIF

When you send entries to, or retrieve entries from, an LDAP directory, you format the entries in LDAP Data Interchange Format (LDIF), a text-based format. If your LDAP entry includes an attribute that contains binary information, the binary information has to be base64 encoded.

An alternative to LDIF is the XML-based Directory Services Markup Language (DSML) described at **http://dsml.org**. The LDAP servers can talk to each other or to clients using the LDAP protocol. When you use **ldap_bind( )** (as explained in the Immediate Solution entitled "Connecting to LDAP") and point to an LDAP server with a URL, you specify the protocol as **ldap://**.

Server Features

Does LDAP have advantages over alternative databases? Can you expand an LDAP directory beyond one server? The following LDAP server features let you expand your LDAP server out to a worldwide network of LDAP servers. In addition, few databases offer an equivalent to LDAP's referral feature.

14. LDAP

Referral

One LDAP server can share work with another by referral. If **yahoo.com** used LDAP and had a **yahoo.com.an** handling all the entries for the Netherlands Antilles, **yahoo.com** could refer all requests containing **c=an** (country = Netherlands Antilles) to **dc=yahoo, dc=com, dc=an** (**yahoo.com.an**).

Several **yahoo.com** servers could share the work through referral, based on the workload each server received, or based on a node within the DIT. If the Arts & Humanities portion of Yahoo! had a vastly different structure and usage from the rest of Yahoo!, the Arts & Humanities requests could go to a server with a different configuration from the server handling the rest of Yahoo!.

Replication

If you have more than one LDAP server sharing the work, you need to replicate the data between the LDAP servers. If you have 20 active servers, add a 21st server for all your updates. Have all the people performing updates to the directory make all the changes on server 21. Then replicate from server 21 to the other servers. The replication might take only three minutes to one server, letting you replicate once per hour to each of the other servers.

Security

The base protocol for LDAP is LDAP, but if your LDAP server has Secure Sockets Layer (SSL) or the newer Transport Layer Security (TLS) installed, you can replace LDAP with LDAPS for security. If you have worked with HTTP and HTTPS, you already know everything you need to know about LDAPS. If you have not used HTTPS, you may want to tackle HTTPS before LDAPS.

Both HTTPS and LDAPS require the installation of SSL, a security certificate, and a way of controlling which protocol you use in your site. If someone accesses your site using HTTP, you should be accessing LDAP with LDAP. When your visitor logs on and starts accessing your site with HTTPS, you should consider using LDAPS. The visitor could be accessing public information from within their logon, and so would not need secure access to LDAP, or the visitor could be accessing a members-only part of your LDAP directory, and would need secure access.

LDAP Functions

This section describes LDAP functions not featured in the "Immediate Solutions" section.

ldap_compare( ) accepts a connection id, a distinguished name pointing to an entry in the directory, the name of an attribute, and a value to compare to the attribute found in the directory. The function returns true if the supplied value matches the value in the directory, false if the values do not match, and **–1** if an error occurs.

ldap_delete( ) accepts a connection id and the distinguished name of an entry. **ldap_delete( )** deletes the entry and returns true if the delete is successful and false if the delete fails.

ldap_dn2ufn( ) accepts a distinguished name and returns the values in a formatted string with the type names removed. I tested **ldap_dn2ufn( )** with the following code:

```
print(ldap_dn2ufn("dc=test, dc=petermoulding, dc=com"));
```

The result was the line shown next, a line that does not look user-friendly to me. perhaps in a future version, the code will be able to construct site names from multiple dc components:

```
test, dc=petermoulding, dc=com
```

ldap_explode_dn( ) accepts a distinguished name and a format option. It returns the distinguished name split into components, with each component stored as an entry in an array. The second parameter, when set to 0, leaves each component with the attribute name, like **c=FR**, whereas setting the parameter to 1 chops off the attribute name and leaves just the value, as in **FR**.

The following code explodes **$dn** into the array **$array**, with the second parameter set to 0, and prints the resultant array:

```
$dn = "dc=test, dc=petermoulding, dc=com";
$array = ldap_explode_dn($dn, 0);
while(list($k, $v) = each($array))
    {
    print("<br>k: " . $k . ", v: " . $v );
    }
```

The result is shown next, and shows that this form of the array is the most useful when you want to use the distinguished name components to build other distinguished names:

```
k: count, v: 3
k: 0, v: dc=test
k: 1, v: dc=petermoulding
k: 2, v: dc=com
```

14. LDAP

The following code explodes the same **$dn** into the array **$array**, with the second parameter set to 1, and prints the array:

```
$array = ldap_explode_dn($dn, 1);
while(list($k, $v) = each($array))
   {
   print("<br>k: " . $k . ", v: " . $v );
   }
```

The result is shown next, and shows that this form of the array is the most useful when you want to display the values for the user:

```
.k: count, v: 3
k: 0, v: test
k: 1, v: petermoulding
k: 2, v: com
```

ldap_search( ) is used in the "Immediate Solutions" section, and is described here because the value returned by the function is needed by the following **ldap_first_entry( )**. **ldap_search( )** accepts a connection id, a distinguished name to indicate the starting point for the search, and a search string. It returns a search result id for **ldap_first_entry( )**, or false if the search fails. The following code shows **ldap_search( )** in action searching for any country, using the search string **c=***:

```
$ldap["dn"] = "dc=test, dc=petermoulding, dc=com";
$ldap["search"] = "c=*";
if($search = ldap_search($ldap["connection"], $ldap["dn"],
   $ldap["search"]))
   {
   // Insert code here:
   }
else
   {
   print("<br>LDAP search failed for " . $ldap["search"]);
   }
```

The **ldap_search( )** search string has a flexible syntax, but unfortunately it is not a standard format, unlike the **where** clause in **SQL**, which is understood by millions of programmers. You may have to read the LDAP documentation a few times to get even simple searches working. The latest PHP has several optional parameters to let you limit the number of entries returned, select which attributes are returned, and handle some other controls. I think it would be easier if they had used the SQL structure, with search terms like SQL's **start** and **limit**. Instead, you have yet another syntax to learn. The problems with the search string mean a conventional relational database is a better choice unless you are forced to use LDAP for compatibility with other sites.

When you test search strings, you may find you are missing entries and attributes because the LDAP directory has built-in limitations on what you can retrieve. Some LDAP software defaults to returning everything unless you limit the request using the optional parameters. Other databases have limits built in that have to be overridden by the optional parameters, and some of the limits may be set so you cannot override them.

ldap_count_entries() counts the number of entries returned by a search and can be used to plan your strategy for handling a search. If the input to the search was a request from an online form, you could returns the first 10 results followed by a message stating the total number of entries found, so the user could choose to refine the search or to broaden the search if there were not enough results. **ldap_count_entries()** accepts a connection id and a search result id from **ldap_search()** and returns the count, or false if an error occurs.

ldap_first_entry(), **ldap_next_entry()**, **ldap_first_attribute()**, and **ldap_ next_attribute()** let you step through large LDAP directories entry by entry and attribute by attribute, without the memory overhead you would encounter with the **ldap_get** series of functions. The **ldap_get** functions read everything in one hit into one big array, so a wide-ranging search could chew up available memory. The **ldap_first** and **ldap_next** functions let you step through search results choosing just a few attributes for each entry, and varying the selection for each entry.

ldap_first_entry() accepts a connection id and a search result id from **ldap_search()** and returns the entry identifier for the first entry in the result, or false if the function cannot return an entry identifier. **ldap_next_attribute()** accepts a connection id and the entry identifier returned by **ldap_first_entry()** and returns the id of the next entry. The following code shows **ldap_first_entry()** and **ldap_next_entry()** in use to step through the search result, **$search**, returned from **ldap_search()**. **$entry** carries the result from one iteration of **ldap_next_entry()** to the next until **ldap_next_entry()** returns false. **display_ entry()** is a function I made up to display each entry. You can insert any code you like at that point, including the later code containing **ldap_first_attribute()** and **ldap_next_attribute()**:

```
$entry = ldap_first_entry($ldap["connection"], $search);
while($entry !== false)
   {
```

```
print("<br>ldap_first_entry search: " . $search );
display_entry($ldap["connection"], $entry);
$entry = ldap_next_entry($ldap["connection"], $entry);
}
```

ldap_first_attribute( ) and **ldap_next_attribute( )** let you step through the attributes of an entry returned by **ldap_first_entry( )** or **ldap_next_entry( )**. **ldap_first_attribute( )** accepts a connection id, the entry id from **ldap_first_entry( )** or **ldap_next_entry( )**, and a work field that in this example is named **$next**. It returns a string containing an attribute, or false if there are no more attributes. **ldap_next_attribute( )** accepts a connection id, the entry id from **ldap_first_entry( )** or **ldap_next_entry( )**, and the work field named **$next**. It returns a string containing an attribute, or false if there are no more attributes. **$next** provides the communication from **ldap_first_attribute( )** to **ldap_next_attribute( )**, and from one iteration of **ldap_next_attribute( )** to the next:

```
$next = "";
$attribute = ldap_first_attribute($ldap["connection"], $entry, $next);
while(isset($attribute) and $attribute !== false and isset($next))
    {
    print("<br>ldap_first_entry search: " . $attribute);
    $attribute = ldap_next_attribute($ldap["connection"], $entry, $next);
    }
```

The work field named **$next** is referred to as a **ber_identifier** in the LDAP documentation and described as an internal memory location pointer. I tried all sorts of Web sites to find an exact definition of a **ber_identifier**, but found none. When I tested the code, the Apache task crashed. **ldap_first_attribute( )** returned something meaningless to **ldap_next_attribute( )**. Avoid these functions and use **ldap_get_attributes( )**.

ldap_free_result( ) frees the memory allocated to a search result. You do not have to free the result set if you use only one in a script, because the result set will be freed automatically when the script terminates. Using **ldap_free_result( )** is a good idea if you create several large result sets in one script and do not need all the result sets open at the same time.

Immediate Solutions

Installing LDAP in Windows NT

To install LDAP in Windows NT, you need an LDAP server and the LDAP extension for PHP. Start with the PHP LDAP extension, and then try one option for an LDAP server.

PHP Extension

My Windows NT workstation has PHP 4.0.7dev installed in the c:/Program Files/ php/ directory, so the PHP subdirectories are relative to that directory. The first step is to copy the PHP LDAP extension from the PHP extensions subdirectory to c:/winnt/system32/. PHP LDAP requires one extra DLL, so copy Libsasl.dll from the PHP dlls subdirectory to c:/winnt/system32/.

If you run PHP as an Apache module, stop Apache. Edit php.ini, remove the semicolon (;) from the front of the line shown next, and then save the change to php.ini. (The semicolon at the front of a line in php.ini makes the line a comment.) If you had to stop Apache, then start Apache again:

```
extension=php_ldap.dll
```

If you use IIS or another Web server, follow the instructions supplied with PHP for installing extensions your Web server.

OpenLDAP Server

Some distributions of NT Server include LDAP as part of a mail server. Microsoft's Small Business Server used to be a quick, low-cost way of installing everything for a business using just one server. Microsoft also sells Microsoft's ActiveServer Directory, which is similar LDAP but is not accessible through PHP's LDAP functions. If you do not want Microsoft's mail package, or, like me, you need a solution that matches the LDAP installed on your customers' Unix servers, the solution is OpenLDAP from **openldap.org**.

Read the readme.txt file in the PHP directory **php/tools/ldap/**. There is a link for **www.fivesight.com/downloads/openldap.asp**, which contains a download for a Windows NT/Windows 2000 binary and instructions on how the binary was compiled. The download is compressed into a tar.gz file, and can be expanded with WinZip. Expand the contents of the file c:/Program Files/OpenLDAP/.

14. LDAP

Edit slapd.conf to change the library names to fit your system. The four lines that need changing are shown next (and could change in future releases). **%SYSCONFDIR%** points to a subdirectory of the directory containing OpenLDAP. **%LOCALSTATEDIR%** could point to a subdirectory of the directory containing LDAP or, for testing, could point to a new directory on a test disk:

```
include    %SYSCONFDIR%/schema/core.schema
pidfile    %LOCALSTATEDIR%/slapd.pid
argsfile   %LOCALSTATEDIR%/slapd.args
directory  %LOCALSTATEDIR%/openldap-ldbm
```

The following lines show the configuration I used, with **%LOCALSTATEDIR%** pointing to a new directory on the disk array I use for testing Internet-related software and Web sites:

```
include    "c:/program Files/OpenLDAP/schema/core.schema"
pidfile    i:/OpenLDAP/slapd.pid
argsfile   i:/OpenLDAP/slapd.args
directory  i:/OpenLDAP/openldap-ldbm
```

The next change to the configuration file is to add your site name to the following line:

```
suffix "dc=my-domain, dc=com"
```

My production site is **petermoulding.com**, so I set up slapd.conf with:

```
suffix "dc=petermoulding, dc=com"
```

My test site is **test.petermoulding.com**, so I set up the test workstation with the following line, using three sets of **dc=**. If your site name has more components, use more instances of **dc=**. **mail.test.petermoulding.com.au** would require five instances of **dc=**:

```
suffix "dc=test, dc=petermoulding, dc=com"
```

Set up a shortcut to start the LDAP server, slapd.exe. The shortcut properties shown in Figure 14.2 start the server from the LDAP directory, so any special DLLs in the LDAP directory will override DLLs of the same name in the system directories.

Start the LDAP server by clicking on the shortcut. slapd will pop up in a command prompt window, as shown in Figure 14.3. When you are finished with slapd, just close the command prompt window.

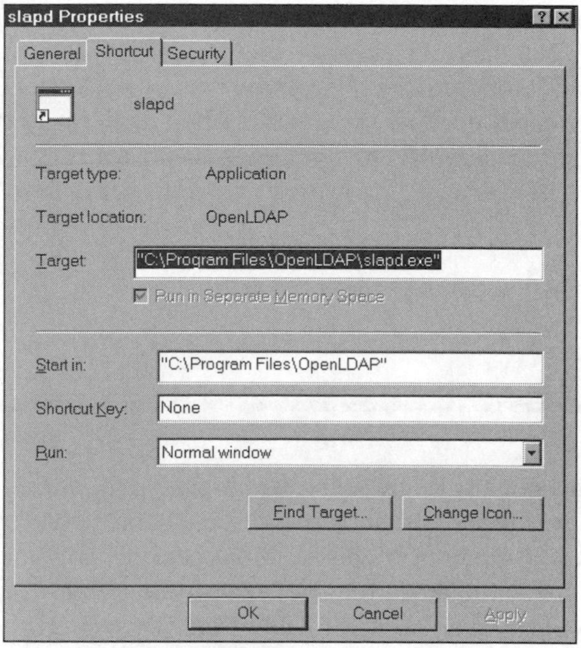

Figure 14.2   LDAP server startup shortcut properties.

Figure 14.3   LDAP server starting in a command prompt window.

Testing the Server

Test the LDAP server with the following code. **ldap_connect( )** returns a connection id, or false if the connection fails:

```
if($connection=ldap_connect("localhost"))
   {
   print("<br>LDAP connection: " . $connection);
   }
else
   {
   print("<br>LDAP connection failed.");
   }
```

The result is:

```
LDAP connection: Resource id #2
```

537

You can compile the LDAP binary yourself if you have Visual C++. Half the open source software for Windows NT uses an open source C compiler, and the other half uses Visual C++. I try to avoid compiling the software that uses Visual C++, because the software tends to use special versions of DLLs that are already in my system directories. The **http://fivesight.com** Web page has a warning about msvcrt.dll and instructions on how to avoid the problem by starting LDAP's slapd from within the LDAP directory.

The next solution expands on connecting to LDAP servers.

Connecting to LDAP

To use LDAP, you need a connection to an LDAP server. In the previous Immediate Solution, the connection was to **localhost**, and the LDAP server was configured to point to **test.petermoulding.com**. In this solution the connection will be to the same server, but using the site name of **test.petermoulding.com**. You can use the connection facilities to reach any server visible from the server running your PHP script, and LDAP servers can be configured to relay requests to other servers, so you can search an entire network of servers from one connection.

An LDAP connection starts with **ldap_connect()** to reach a server, followed by the **ldap_bind()** command, which is effectively the same as logging on to the LDAP server. You perform the LDAP operations you need, and then use **ldap_close()** or **ldap_unbind()** to close the connection to the LDAP server. This solution covers the connect, bind, and close procedures. Later solutions describe the operations you can perform once you are connected and bound to a server.

The first step is connecting. The following code makes a simple connection using **ldap_connect()** and the name of a site:

```
$ldap["site"] = "test.petermoulding.com";
if($ldap["connection"] = ldap_connect($ldap["site"]))
    {
    print("<br>LDAP connected to " . $ldap["site"]);
    }
else
    {
    print("<br>LDAP connection failed for " . $ldap["site"]);
    }
```

The only option for **ldap_connect()** is a second parameter containing a port number, which defaults to 389. The next code is the first two lines of the previous code, expanded to include a port number, which you might have to do if you have several LDAP servers on the same machine:

```
$ldap["port"] = 1389;
$ldap["site"] = "test.petermoulding.com";
if($ldap["connection"] = ldap_connect($ldap["site"], $ldap["port"]))
```

From PHP 4.0.4 onward, **ldap_connect( )** accepts a URL as a site name, so you can reach LDAP servers anywhere across the Internet. The following code is the first connect code changed to a URL:

```
$ldap["site"] = "http://test.petermoulding.com";
if($ldap["connection"] = ldap_connect($ldap["site"]))
```

http://test.petermoulding.com is not valid for an LDAP server, so you will see the following error you get when your site name or URL is wrong. The error can also occur if the response across the network is too slow:

```
Warning: Could not create LDAP session handle (3): Time limit exceeded
```

ldap://test.petermoulding.com is the valid URL for an LDAP server. The URL **scheme** (also called **protocol**) has to be **ldap**, as shown in the following code:

```
$ldap["site"] = "ldap://test.petermoulding.com";
```

If your LDAP server has SSL installed for security, replace **ldap** with **ldaps**, as in:

```
$ldap["site"] = "ldaps://test.petermoulding.com";
```

Once you have a valid connection, you need to bind with the LDAP server using **ldap_bind( )**. The following code is the minimum you can specify for **ldap_bind( )**, and only if the LDAP server is configured for an anonymous bind. Public LDAP servers, set up as yellow-pages or white-pages–style directories, are often set up with anonymous access for reading, but require a password to perform updates:

```
if($ldap["connection"])
   {
   if(ldap_bind($ldap["connection"]))
      {
      print("<br>LDAP anonymous bind worked.");
      }
   else
      {
      print("<br>LDAP anonymous bind failed.");
      }
   }
```

The result is:

```
LDAP anonymous bind worked.
```

When you need to log on as a user, use the following code. The second parameter is referred to as the relative distinguished name (RDN), and the third parameter is the password. The RDN normally contains a user name in the form **cn=username**, and can contain other identifiers, like the part of the directory you are allowed to access. The documentation for **ldap_bind( )** says you can provide a user name without a password, but when I tested this with PHP 4.0.7, I received a wrong parameter count. OpenLDAP has a default user named Manager that can do anything, and has a default password of secret. Use Manager for the initial database setup and testing, but change the name and password before placing the LDAP database on a public server:

```
$ldap["user"] = "Manager";
$ldap["rdn"] = "cn=" . $ldap["user"] . ", dc=test, dc=petermoulding,
    dc=com";
$ldap["password"] = "secret";
if($ldap["connection"])
    {
    if(ldap_bind($ldap["connection"], $ldap["rdn"], $ldap["password"]))
        {
        print("<br>LDAP bind worked for " . $ldap["user"]);
        }
    else
        {
        print("<br>LDAP bind failed for " . $ldap["user"]);
        }
    }
```

If the user id or password is wrong, you get the following message. The message will also occur if the RDN is missing other identifiers. You might be authorized to access only part of a database, in which case you have to identify that part of the database as part of the RDN:

```
Warning: LDAP: Unable to bind to server: Invalid credentials
```

If you get the format of the RDN wrong, you will get this message:

```
Warning: LDAP: Unable to bind to server: Invalid DN syntax
```

If the LDAP database contains information for several countries, individuals are authorized to update specific countries, and you are authorized to update Scotland, you may need to add **c=Scotland** to the RDN, as shown in the following code. The code is the first part of the previous code with the country added as an extra parameter:

```
$ldap["user"] = "Manager";
$ldap["country"] = "Scotland";
$ldap["rdn"] = "cn=" . $ldap["user"] . ", dc=test, dc=petermoulding,
    dc=com, c=" . $ldap["country"];
```

Most LDAP servers are set up with the country field containing a two-character country code instead of the country name. The country codes are explained in the solution "Adding Country Codes" later in this chapter. Scotland does not have a country code; it is included in GB (Great Britain or the United Kingdom).

When you are finished with the connection, you can close it with **ldap_close()**, as shown next. All the function needs is the connection id. The function returns true on success or false if the close fails:

```
if($ldap["connection"])
    {
    if(ldap_close($ldap["connection"]))
        {
        print("<br>LDAP close worked.");
        }
    else
        {
        print("<br>LDAP close failed.");
        }
    }
```

The result is:

```
LDAP close worked.
```

An alternative to **ldap_close()** is **ldap_unbind()**. Both functions accept the same parameter, perform the same action internally, and return the same result. I tend to use **ldap_close()** because it is easier to remember, because many PHP function groups that have a connect or open function also have a close function. **ldap_unbind()** is shown next:

```
if($ldap["connection"])
    {
    if(ldap_unbind($ldap["connection"]))
        {
        print("<br>LDAP unbind worked.");
        }
```

14. LDAP

```
else
   {
   print("<br>LDAP unbind failed.");
   }
}
```

All the other Immediate Solutions use this connect code and start with a test for **$ldap["connection"]**. The updates assume you are using the Manager id, set up by default in OpenLDAP, and will assume the default global read for all other code. If you use a different LDAP server, change the update code to use the appropriate authorized user.

Adding Country Codes

The highest levels of an LDAP directory are typically the domain and then a country code. This solution adds all the country codes in one hit, so you can create a truly international site and use the country code list for things like selection boxes in HTML forms. The featured functions are **ldap_add( )** and **ldap_mod_add( )**.

Although you would not, for performance, have HTML pages reading the country codes directly from the LDAP directory, you could use the LDAP directory to generate a file to be included elsewhere. If your site or business is based around an LDAP directory, it is easy to keep the country codes up to date in the LDAP directory and use the directory as the source for your site.

Connecting

This code assumes you are connected to LDAP, using the code from the solution "Connecting to LDAP," and using the user id of Manager. The following code is inserted between **ldap_bind( )** and **ldap_close( )**. The rest of this solution is inserted within the brackets of the **if( )**, so the code is executed only when there is a valid connection:

```
if($ldap["connection"])
   {
   // The rest of the code
   }
```

Getting Country Codes

Get your list of country codes from this book's CD-ROM(/examples/ countrycodes.txt), and place the file where you can read it from PHP. If you want an up-to-date list, or way too much information about country codes, visit **www.din.de/gremien/nas/nabd/iso3166ma/** and look for the ISO 3166 list.

The following example shows the first few lines of the 239 entries in the current file. Each line has a space and **newline** at the end, so they will have to be trimmed using the **trim( )** function. The name and two-letter country code can be separated with **explode( )** and then placed in an array for subsequent formatting and usage. The two-letter country codes are kept in capital letters to distinguish them from the two-letter language codes in common use. The language codes are used in lowercase, and the two are sometimes combined when a browser requests a Web page in a specific language. An American might request English-language pages as **en-US**, indicating a preference for *catalog* spelled as *catalog*, whereas a British person might request **en-GB** so *catalog* will be spelled *catalogue*:

```
AFGHANISTAN;AF
ALBANIA;AL
ALGERIA;DZ
AMERICAN SAMOA;AS
```

Formatting Country Codes

The first step is to clean up the input file and place the result in an array that can be used anywhere, including input to databases and HTML creation programs. Place countrycodes.txt in the same directory as your script, and place the file name in **$file**, as shown next, or point **$file** to the location you chose for the file:

```
$file = "./countrycodes.txt";
```

In the following code, **file( )** reads the text file into an array with each array entry containing one line of input. (File functions are explained in Chapter 8.) The **while( )** loop loops through the entries in **$text**. The rest of the code reads an entry, formats the entry, and adds the formatted content as a new entry in the array called **$codes**. Each entry is split in two by **explode( )**: The country name goes in **$name** and the country code goes in **$code**. **$name** is uppercase, so it is converted to lowercase. Eventually **ucwords( )** will make the first letter of each word a capital, but **ucwords( )** only works only on words delimited by white-space characters, and this file needs capitals after the open parenthesis and the period. The first two **str_replace( )** functions change (and . to distinct white-space characters, **ucwords( )** converts the right letters to uppercase, and then the next two **str_replace( )** functions convert the white-space characters back to their original values. The remaining **str_replace( )** functions perform manual adjustments for unique names and all the names containing **of** as the last word. The result is printed for visual verification and placed in **$codes**:

```
if($text = file($file))
   {
   print("<br>File worked for " . $file);
   while(list($k, $v) = each($text))
      {
      $v = trim($v);
      list($name, $code) = explode(";", $v);
      $name = strtolower($name);
      $name = str_replace("(", "\n", $name);
      $name = str_replace(".", "\r", $name);
      $name = ucwords($name);
      $name = str_replace("\r", ".", $name);
      $name = str_replace("\n", "(", $name);
      $name = str_replace(" And ", " and ", $name);
      $name = str_replace("D'ivoire", "d'Ivoire", $name);
      $name = $name . " ";
      $name = str_replace(" Of ", " of ", $name);
      $name = str_replace(" of The ", " of the ", $name);
      $name = trim($name);
      print("<br>" . $code . "   " . $name);
      $codes[$code] = $name;
      }
   }
else
   {
   print("<br>File failed for " . $file);
   }
```

Related solution:	*Found on page:*
Displaying Any Data	311

Adding the First Country Code

This section of code reads the first entry of **$codes** and adds the entry to the LDAP directory using **ldap_add( )**. The first line resets the array entry pointer in **$codes** back to the start of the array, which is worth doing if there is other code between the array creation and the array use (arrays are explained in Chapter 3):

```
reset($codes);
```

To access the right location in the LDAP directory, you need a distinguished name pointing the place where you want to insert the new entry. Because country is at the top of the directory, all you need is the domain name, as follows:

```
$ldap["dn"] = "dc=test, dc=petermoulding, dc=com";
```

ldap_add( ) adds the first entry for a class of entries and adds the **objectClass** definition for the entry. Because the entry is added from an array, start the array by adding the **objectClass** definition, in this case **country**, to the entry's array, as shown in the following line:

```
$entry["objectClass"] = "country";
```

You then need the country code in the entry array, and that is done in the next line of code, where the country code is placed into **$entry["c"]**. Note that the array entry key is the name of the field when inserted into the directory. The default LDAP directory schema supplied with OpenLDAP does not have an attribute allocated for country name, so that is left out in this example:

```
list($entry["c"], $v) = each($codes);
```

Add the entry, with the **objectClass**, using **ldap_add( )** as shown in the following code. The first parameter is the LDAP connection id, the second is the distinguished name where you are adding the entry, and the third is the array containing the entry. **ldap_add( )** returns true on success and false on failure:

```
if(ldap_add($ldap["connection"], $ldap["dn"], $entry))
    {
    print("<br>LDAP add worked for " . $entry["c"]);
    }
else
    {
    print("<br>LDAP add failed for " . $entry["c"]);
    }
```

Adding Subsequent Country Codes

One you have one country code in the directory, the directory does not need the object class, so remove the object class from the entry array using the following code:

```
unset($entry["objectClass"]);
```

The following code loops through the **$codes** array and adds each entry to the LDAP directory using **ldap_mod_add( )**. Because the previous code accessed the array using **each( )**, the array pointer is now pointing at the second entry, and the loop will proceed from the second entry to the last. The parameters for **ldap_mod_add( )** are the same as for **ldap_add( )**:

```
while(list($entry["c"], $v) = each($codes))
    {
    if(ldap_mod_add($ldap["connection"], $ldap["dn"], $entry))
      {
      print("<br>LDAP add worked for " . $entry["c"] );
      }
    else
      {
      print("<br>LDAP add failed for " . $entry["c"] );
      }
    }
  }
```

If **country** had been defined with other attributes, like **capital** or **population**, you would add the other attributes to the entry array, as shown in the following code, before using **ldap_add( )** or **ldap_mod_add( )**. The example uses China's capital and population:

```
$entry["capital"] = "Beijing";
$entry["population"] = "1300000000";
```

LDAP allows multiple values for every attribute for every entry, unless multiple values are turned off for an attribute within the schema. How do you enter multiple values for an attribute in the entry array? Just use the regular PHP array-entry addition technique shown next. The example assumes **airport** is added as an attribute of **country**, and **airport** does not have multiple values turned off. The airports listed are some of China's international airports:

```
$entry["airport"][] = "Shanghai Pudong";
$entry["airport"][] = "Guangzhou Baiyun";
$entry["airport"][] = "Xinzheng";
$entry["airport"][] = "Hong Kong";
```

What happens when you get the entry array wrong? You receive the following message. The generic message covers a dozen errors, from misspelling an attribute name to using **ldap_add( )** when you should be using **ldap_mod_add( )** and vice versa:

```
Warning: LDAP: add operation could not be completed.
```

Adding a User

When you add a user to the default LDAP directory configuration, you add a country, then an organization, and then the person. All the country codes were added by the previous solution, so this example adds an organization and a person. You can configure an LDAP directory any way you like by changing the schema, but given the limited documentation available on LDAP schema construction, I suggest you practice using the PHP LDAP functions on the default schema before you tackle your own design.

This solution adds one intermediate level, **organization**, and one final level, **person**, to illustrate the process. You could step through as many intermediate levels as you need, and could add a little code to step through an input file to add multiple entries.

Adding Intermediate Levels

When you add an entry, you need a start point, a distinguished name that points to the entry that will be the parent of your new entry. This step adds **organization** to **country**, so the DN points to the right country, as shown next:

```
$ldap["dn"] = "c=AU, dc=test, dc=petermoulding, dc=com";
```

The entry is added via an array that is fed into **ldap_add( )**. The array is named **$entry**, and is shown next. The **objectClass** entry in the array **$entry** names **organization** as the object class used for the entry. The objectClass **organization** has one compulsory attribute, **o**, and a small number of optional attributes. All that is needed for the demonstration is the attribute **o**. I named my company as the organization, because **<free plug>** it is the only organization you need for great Web site architecture**</free plug>**:

```
$entry["objectClass"] = "organization";
$entry["o"] = "petermoulding";
```

ldap_add( ) adds the entry, using the connection id, the DN, and the entry array:

```
if(ldap_add($ldap["connection"], $ldap["dn"], $entry))
    {
    print("<br>LDAP add worked for " . $ldap["dn"]);
    }
else
    {
    print("<br>LDAP add failed for " . $ldap["dn"]);
    }
```

The result is next:

```
LDAP add worked for c=AU, dc=test, dc=petermoulding, dc=com
```

Adding the Final Level

This step adds the final level of the person entry, the level with an object class of **person**, and the attributes defined in the **person** object. The attributes are common name (**cn**) and surname (**sn**). When you add an entry, you must include all the compulsory attributes (those attributes listed in the schema under **MUST**), though you can leave out the optional attributes listed in the schema under **MAY**:

```
$ldap["dn"] = "o=petermoulding, c=AU, dc=test, dc=petermoulding,
   dc=com";
unset($entry);
$entry["cn"] = "Pixie";
$entry["sn"] = "Moulding";
$entry["objectClass"] = "person";
if($ldap["connection"])
   {
   if(ldap_add($ldap["connection"], $ldap["dn"], $entry))
      {
      print("<br>LDAP add worked for " . $ldap["dn"]);
      }
   else
      {
      print("<br>LDAP add failed for " . $ldap["dn"]);
      }
   }
```

The result is:

```
LDAP add worked for o=petermoulding, c=AU, dc=test, dc=petermoulding,
   dc=com
```

Handling Errors

You want code that handles all errors so your Web site visitors never see an error message break the nice layout of your Web pages. There are three functions to help you: **ldap_errno()**, **ldap_err2str()**, and **ldap_error()**. You also need to use **@**.

@ is the PHP function prefix that suppresses built-in error messages. One step in this example will use **ldap_bind( )** to create an error so that you can see the error message that will be suppressed, and then see the error handled.

The following code connects to LDAP the way that was shown in the Immediate Solution "Connecting to LDAP." Because the LDAP error functions require a connection to LDAP, you cannot use the LDAP error functions to diagnose LDAP connection errors:

```
$ldap["site"] = "test.petermoulding.com";
if($ldap["connection"] = ldap_connect($ldap["site"]))
    {
    print("<br>LDAP connected to " . $ldap["site"]);
    }
else
    {
    print("<br>LDAP connection failed for " . $ldap["site"]);
    }
```

The next line is the standard **ldap_bind( )** code used for access to LDAP, but with one little change. The second parameter, the distinguished name, contains invalid information that does not form a distinguished name:

```
if($ldap["connection"])
    {
    if(ldap_bind($ldap["connection"], "aa", "bb"))
        {
        print("<br>LDAP bind worked.");
        }
    else
        {
        print("<br>LDAP bind failed.");
        }
    }
```

The error produces the following message, a message that does not help your visitors:

```
Warning: LDAP: Unable to bind to server: Invalid DN syntax
```

The following code has **@** added to the front of the **ldap_bind( )** function to suppress the built-in error messages. Test the previous code with the **@** added as shown here:

```
if(@ldap_bind($ldap["connection"], "aa", "bb"))
```

Once you have the built-in error messages suppressed, you can detect the errors with your script, handle the errors in a less disruptive way, and log important errors so you can view them later and take action to prevent their occurring again.

ldap_errno( ) accepts a connection id and returns the error number for the last action performed via the connection. You can perform an action based on the error number, or convert the number to a displayable message using **ldap_err2str( )**. The following code retrieves the error number via **ldap_errno( )** and selects an action via **switch( )**:

```
$error = ldap_errno($ldap["connection"]);
switch($error)
   {
   case 0:
      print("<br>No error.");
      break;
   case 34:
      print("<br>There is a syntax error in the Distinguished Name.");
      break;
   default:
      print("<br>Error number: " . $error);
   }
```

How did I know the syntax error was error 34? I found out by listing all the errors using **ldap_err2str( )**. The error numbers are standard across all LDAP software and directories, but each implementation of LDAP has its own set of error messages. When you are deciding what action your script should take, base the decision on the error number, not the error text. Actions might include returning a user to an input form to retype search strings, or sending yourself an email to warn you about a more dramatic error.

ldap_err2str( ) accepts an LDAP error number and returns an error message. The following code displays the first 100 possible error messages so you can see what each message means (and plan ahead to handle each one):

```
for($i = 0; $i < 100; $i++)
   {
   print("<br>Error number: " . $i . ", message: " . ldap_err2str($i) );
   }
```

The following list is the first part of the error message list to help you start planning. The time and size limits in messages 3 and 4 are likely to occur with wide-ranging searches of large directories:

```
Error number: 0, message: Success
Error number: 1, message: Operations error
Error number: 2, message: Protocol error
Error number: 3, message: Time limit exceeded
Error number: 4, message: Size limit exceeded
Error number: 5, message: Compare false
Error number: 6, message: Compare true
```

When this code reaches a high enough number, you will see messages like the following two, indicating you have passed the available error messages. There are gaps in the middle of the list, so with each new release of LDAP, you need to display the list a long way past the last known message just to check that no new ones are lurking after a gap in the sequence:

```
Error number: 99, message: Unknown error
Error number: 100, message: Unknown error
```

ldap_error() accepts a connection id, returns the error message for the last action performed via the link, and is equivalent to using **ldap_err2str (ldap_errno())**. The following code displays the error message from the **ldap_bind()** error:

```
print("<br>Error: " . ldap_error($ldap["connection"]));
```

The result is shown next. Just remember that this is the message from OpenLDAP and may not be the same text issued by Netscape's directory product or any other LDAP server:

```
Error: Invalid DN syntax
```

Listing All Entries

There are times when you want to list every entry and every attribute in a test directory, such as when you are adding the first entries for a new branch of a directory. You might add emergency services contact information, using a new **objectClass** of **emergency**, for each location, and want to verify that these entries are 100 percent perfect. This is the solution for you.

The code is in three versions. The first version grabs entries using **ldap_read()** and **ldap_get_entries()** to return one level of entries at whatever distinguished name you choose. The data is listed in a table so you can see the format and understand subsequent parts. The second version reads every entry from every level (up to the number of lines you want to print) and displays the data with a little structure, so you can see how to handle multiple levels. The third version attempts a little beautification of the output so the output is more readable.

If you want to take the formatting further, you can build the equivalent of a Windows Explorer or another other sophisticated reader for structured data. When you take the presentation to that level, the fine detail depends on how you structure your directory, what data you use, and what you want to show the browser. Do you want some people to get quick access to email addresses? Do you want the display to remember where the person was when they last browsed the directory? How many options do you want to give them for searching? No matter what degree of development you put into the directory structure, contents, and interface, you will always need the option to display everything when diagnosing problems.

The code in this solution uses the connect and bind shown in the solution "Connecting to LDAP." The code starts by testing for a connection id.

Listing All Entries at One Level

The highest-level entry in the default OpenLDAP directory setup is **country**, so the first code lists countries. The **country** entry has one compulsory attribute, the country name, abbreviated to **c**. All the LDAP directories in public use have the ISO-standard two-letter country code in the country name.

LDAP stores the entries in the order in which you add them, and the standard retrieval functions do not provide a sort facility. If you want all the values in a sequence, the easiest approach is to place the values in a PHP array and sort the array. If you are always sorting the data after retrieving it, consider simply replacing the LDAP database with a conventional relational database and using SQL views of the data to return the data the way you need it.

Reading the Data

The following code retrieves the data, using **ldap_read( )** to select all the entries in the directory and **ldap_get_entries( )** to retrieve all the entries into an array called **$entries**. The rest of the code prints status messages to help you see what the functions achieve. The starting point in the directory is the distinguished name in **$ldap["dn"]**. If **ldap_read( )** succeeds in creating a result, **ldap_free_result( )** is run to free the result set in case your script chews up memory by creating several result sets:

```
$ldap["dn"] = "dc=test, dc=petermoulding, dc=com";
if($ldap["connection"])
    {
    if($result = @ldap_read($ldap["connection"], $ldap["dn"],
```

```
        "objectClass=*"))
        {
        if($entries = ldap_get_entries($ldap["connection"], $result))
            {
            print("<br>LDAP_get_entries returned " . count($entries)
                . " for " . $ldap["dn"]);
            }
        else
            {
            print("<br>LDAP_get_entries failed for " . $ldap["dn"]);
            }
        ldap_free_result($result);
        }
    else
        {
        print("<br>LDAP read failed for " . $ldap["dn"]);
        }
    }
```

Displaying the Data

The array **$entries** is created by the previous code, and the next code displays all
the contents of **$entries** in a straightforward HTML table. The array contains a
mixture of entries; some are arrays and some are not. The arrays run up to three
levels deep, so similar code is nested three levels deep. The **while( )** statements
loop through the array at one level. The **if( )** statements detect fields and output
them, or find arrays and pass the arrays to the next level of **while( )** statement:

```
if(isset($entries))
    {
    print("<table border=\"3\">\n" );
    while(list($k1, $v1) = each($entries))
        {
        if(is_array($v1))
            {
            while(list($k2, $v2) = each($v1))
                {
                if(is_array($v2))
                    {
                    while(list($k3, $v3) = each($v2))
                        {
                        print("<tr><td>" . $k1 . "</td><td>" . $k2 . "</td>"
                            . "<td>" . $k3 . "</td><td>" . $v3 . "</td>"
                            . "</tr>\n");
                        }
                    }
```

```
                   else
                     {
                     print("<tr><td>" . $k1 . "</td><td>" . $k2 . "</td>"
                        . "<td>" . $v2 . "</td><td> </td></tr>\n");
                     }
                  }
               }
         else
            {
            print("<tr><td>" . $k1 . "</td><td>" . $v1 . "</td>"
               . "<td> </td><td> </td></tr>\n");
            }
         }
      print("</table>\n");
      }
```

Figure 14.4 shows the result. There are 239 countries in the directory, so I cut the middle 233 from the figure. The highest level of the array contains a single entry, **count**, which is a count of the arrays at the next level. I ran a lot of tests, and they all produced the same top level.

Entry 0, at the top level, is an array that contains what looks like a jumble of entries. To read the second level correctly, start with the entry named **dn**. **dn** contains the distinguished name that points to the entries within the array. **count** contains the number of entries in that level, so you can step through the numbered entries with a **for( )** loop. The entries numbered 0 through 1 are the next entries to read.

count	1		
0	objectclass	count	1
0	objectclass	0	country
0	0	objectclass	
0	c	count	238
0	c	0	AU
0	c	1	AL
0	c	2	DZ
0	c	235	YU
0	c	236	ZM
0	c	237	ZW
0	1	c	
0	count	2	
0	dn	dc=test, dc=petermoulding, dc=com	

Figure 14.4   Raw data from **ldap_get_entries( )**.

Entry 0 contains the name **objectclass**. **objectclass** is an entry at that level, and is an array containing entries to be read another level down. Entry 1 contains the name **c**, which points to an entry named **c**, which is an array to be processed the next level down. **country** is the **objectclass** for the entry, whereas **c** and **objectclass** are attributes of **country**.

c is an array containing a count of the numbered entries in the array **c** and the numbered entries. **c** is an example of an attribute with multiple values.

Listing All Entries at All Levels

To read through all levels of an LDAP directory, the following code uses a function to process one level, and the function then calls itself to process lower levels. The function returns data as print lines in an array, and includes in the print lines all the lines from the lower levels. Every level prefixes the print with varying lengths of non-blank spaces, ** **, that will be recognized by browsers and make the print lines indent.

If you use this code on anything other than a test directory, be sure to include a count of the lines queued for printing and terminate the retrieval before reaching the practical limit for your browser.

The Function

display_one_entry( ) uses **ldap_read( )** to read all the entries at one level. **ldap_read( )** needs a connection id, the distinguished name for the starting point, and a search string. The string **objectClass=*** searches for every entry with an attribute of **objectClass**. Entries have to have an **objectClass** before they can go in an LDAP directory, so the search string will find every entry.

ldap_read( ) returns a result id that is fed into **ldap_get_entries( )**. **ldap_get_entries( )** then returns an array that is processed into print lines using code that is different from the code used earlier in this solution. This version of the code decodes the array using the information discovered when looking at the earlier display of the array.

Each level of the array has a count, so the count is placed in a count field, **$c1** and so on, and is used as the limit in a **for( )** loop. The **for( )** loops step through the array and subarrays, reading the numbered array entries that represent LDAP entries (level 1), attributes for an entry (level 2), and multiple values for an attribute (level 3).

$s provides a standard indentation for lines, and **$s1** and so on apply the cumulative indentation to lines. The lines end up in the array **$print** and are returned to the higher-level code for printing. Each line of output consists of a description followed by the value:

```
function display_one_entry($connection, $dn)
    {
    if($result = @ldap_read($connection, $dn, "objectClass=*"))
        {
        $entries = ldap_get_entries($connection, $result);
        $c1 = $entries["count"];
        $s = "   ";
        for($i1 = 0; $i1 < $c1; $i1++)
            {
            $v2 = $entries[$i1];
            $print[] = "dn: " . $v2["dn"];
            $c2 = $v2["count"];
            for($i2 = 0; $i2 < $c2; $i2++)
                {
                $a2 = $v2[$i2];
                $print[] = $s . "attribute: " . $a2;
                $v3 = $v2[$a2];
                $c3 = $v3["count"];
                for($i3 = 0; $i3 < $c3; $i3++)
                    {
                    $a3 = $v3[$i3];
                    $print[] = $s . $s . "value: " . $a3;
                    if($pr = display_one_entry($connection,
                        $a2 . "=" . $a3 . ", " . $dn))
                        {
                        while(list($k, $v) = each($pr))
                            {
                            $print[] = $s . $s . $s . $v );
                            }
                        }
                    }
                }
            }
        ldap_free_result($result);
        }
    else
        {
        $print = false;
        }
    return($print);
    }
```

Retrieving and Displaying the Data

The following code simply checks that a connection exists to LDAP, and then calls **display_one_entry( )** with an appropriate distinguished name. The array, **$print**, that is returned from **display_one_entry( )**, is printed one entry at a time with a HTML break (**
) at the start of the line and a **newline (**\n**) at the end. The break forces a new line in the page when displayed in the browser, and the **newline** forces a new line when you view the source for the page through the browser. Viewing the source helps you debug Web pages, and the **newline**s in the source help you read the source without time-consuming horizontal scrolling:

```
$ldap["dn"] = "dc=test, dc=petermoulding, dc=com";
if($ldap["connection"])
   {
   if($print = display_one_entry($ldap["connection"], $ldap["dn"]))
      {
      while(list($k, $v) = each($print))
         {
         print("<br>" . $v . "\n");
         }
      }
   else
      {
      print("<br>LDAP search failed for " . $ldap["search"]);
      }
   }
```

The following output shows the code stepping through the entries and stepping down through the levels. Each time the code finds a value for an attribute, the code tries to read that value as a lower-level entry. Because there are hundreds of countries in the directory, the output is cut off after a few countries. Note the sequence of the countries; if you want a different sequence, you would have to restructure the **$entries** array to let you sort the entries:

```
dn: dc=test, dc=petermoulding, dc=com
   attribute: objectclass
      value: country
   attribute: c
      value: AU
         dn: c=AU, dc=test, dc=petermoulding, dc=com
            attribute: objectclass
               value: organization
            attribute: o
               value: petermoulding
                  dn: o=petermoulding, c=AU, dc=test, dc=petermoulding, _
                     dc=com
```

```
                    attribute: cn
                        value: Peter
                    attribute: sn
                        value: Moulding
                    attribute: objectclass
                        value: person
        value: AL
        value: DZ
        value: AS
        value: AD
```

Interpreting the Entries within the Listing

The next code is a step toward interpreting the data retrieved from an LDAP directory. The previous **display_one_entry( )** function is modified to interpret fields and values common to all entries in an LDAP directory. You can add code to interpret values specific to your directory.

The first change is to pick up the **objectclass** name in **$o** and append the name to the display of the distinguished name. That saves two lines of output per entry and makes it easier to see where the distinguished name leads. I thought a blue font tag would make it easier to tell which field is which on the screen.

Because the **objectclass** is extracted before looping through the numbered array elements, the code contains the statement **if($a2 != "objectclass")** to skip the **objectclass** entry in the numbered elements. You can make this part of the change conditional, so you can run the code in a test mode where every field and all the counts are displayed to help your testing, but perhaps are displayed in a smaller font and in a color like gray or silver. The objective is to reduce the space used by the repetitive elements of the array so you can focus on the changing values.

There are fewer **print** statements, so the remaining **print** statements have their indentation reduced. When you are reaching down to the lower depths of a deep directory, the simple spacing system used in this code will push some information off the right side of the screen. At that point, consider suppressing the higher levels and letting people know where they are with the distinguished name:

```
function display_one_entry($connection, $dn)
    {
    if($result = @ldap_read($connection, $dn, "objectClass=*"))
        {
        $entries = ldap_get_entries($connection, $result);
        $c1 = $entries["count"];
```

```
        $s = "   ";
        for($i1 = 0; $i1 < $c1; $i1++)
            {
            $v2 = $entries[$i1];
            $o = $v2["objectclass"][0];
            $print[] = "<font color=\"Blue\">" . $v2["dn"] . "</font>: "
                . $o;
            $c2 = $v2["count"];
            for($i2 = 0; $i2 < $c2; $i2++)
                {
                $a2 = $v2[$i2];
                if($a2 != "objectclass")
                    {
                    $v3 = $v2[$a2];
                    $c3 = $v3["count"];
                    for($i3 = 0; $i3 < $c3; $i3++)
                        {
                        $a3 = $v3[$i3];
                        $print[] = $s . $a2 . ": " . $a3;
                        if($pr = display_one_entry($connection,
                            $a2 . "=" . $a3 . ", " . $dn))
                            {
                            while(list($k, $v) = each($pr))
                                {
                                $print[] = $s . $s . $v );
                                }
                            }
                        }
                    }
                }
            }
        ldap_free_result($result);
        }
    else
        {
        $print = false;
        }
    return($print);
    }
```

The result is displayed next. The 22 lines are reduced to 12, without reducing usefulness:

```
dc=test, dc=petermoulding, dc=com: country
    c: AU
        c=AU, dc=test, dc=petermoulding, dc=com: organization
```

```
    o: petermoulding
        o=petermoulding, c=AU, dc=test, dc=petermoulding, dc=com:
            person
            cn: Peter
            sn: Moulding
c: AL
c: DZ
c: AS
c: AD
```

Your next challenge, should you decide to use LDAP, is to read about forms in Chapter 9, and then add a facility to type in the top-level distinguished name. You could change some of the attribute names from short names, like **sn**, to long names, like **surname**, using a lookup array. You could also convert the lower-level fields into links, so one click on a lower level would produce a new display starting from that point. The result would be a map of the directory where you can move through the whole directory. Remember to provide links back up to higher levels, and give the user an input field to specify how many levels he or she wants displayed on the page.

Related solution:	*Found on page:*
Creating a Form	343

Chapter 15

Mail

In Depth

If you have ever been frustrated by email clients, now is your chance to get even and dump those second-rate applications for your own smooth, sophisticated PHP-based client. Read the "Modes of Operation" section, and then write your own client to suit your needs.

When you want to send mail, PHP's **mail( )** function is the best choice. This chapter has Immediate Solutions showing you how to send one mail or many. If incoming mail is your focus, PHP's LDAP support is the best choice, but you should read through the **mail( )** examples to see how mail headers and message parts are constructed.

You will want extra information on specific mail protocols, and you can spend a couple of days reading all the following references, or just choose those that you need:

- *Common Internet Message Headers*—**www.faqs.org/rfcs/rfc2076.html**
- Internet Message Access Protocol (IMAP)—**www.faqs.org/rfcs/rfc2060.html**
- *Internet Message Format*—**www.faqs.org/rfcs/rfc2822.html**
- *Multipurpose Internet Mail Extensions (MIME)*—**www.faqs.org/rfcs/rfc2045.html; www.faqs.org/rfcs/rfc2046.html; www.faqs.org/rfcs/rfc2047.html; www.faqs.org/rfcs/rfc2048.html; www.faqs.org/rfcs/rfc2049.html**;
- *Network News Transfer Protocol (NNTP)*—**www.faqs.org/rfcs/rfc977.html**
- *Post Office Protocol Version 3 (POP3)*—**www.faqs.org/rfcs/rfc1939.html**
- *Simple Mail Transfer Protocol (SMTP)*—**www.faqs.org/rfcs/rfc2821.html**

PHP's mail support includes the **mail( )** function plus the IMAP functions listed later in this section. There is also an **ezmlm_hash( )** function for users of the EZMLM mailing list manager.

IMAP

PHP's IMAP functions handle the IMAP protocol plus POP3, SMTP, NNTP, and local mailbox access. IMAP is the standard protocol for accessing many mail servers, but is overkill if you only want to send mail. The IMAP functions are listed next.

Mailbox Functions

The mailbox functions handle access to your mailboxes. The later mail functions handle access to individual items of mail. You have to select a mailbox, and then select mail. With news servers, a news group is equivalent to a mailbox:

- **imap_open( )**—Accepts the name of a mailbox, a user name, a password, and optional flags. It returns a resource id for a connection to a mailbox on an IMAP server, or a POP3 connection, or an NNTP server. The mailbox name includes a server name, an optional port name, and a mailbox name. The user's default mailbox is INBOX, so the mailbox on the local server would be {localhost}INBOX. If the port number is needed, the same name would be {localhost:143}INBOX. You can access POP3 with {localhost:110/POP3}INBOX. The flags allow read-only access, anonymous access for news (NNTP), and an option to open a connection without opening a mailbox.

- **imap_close( )**—Accepts the resource id returned by **imap_open( )**, and closes the connection.

- **imap_getmailboxes( )**—The function to use as soon as you open a connection. The function accepts the connection id from **imap_open( )**, a reference string, and a pattern string. It returns an array of objects, with each object containing information about a mailbox. The reference string is the starting point for the list, so you can start a list from a point down in a hierarchy of names. The pattern lets you select a subset of names and works like file searching, so * returns everything, and **s*** returns names starting with *s*. You can use the returned array as the base for a drop-down selection list, so the user can select another mailbox. You can find the number of messages in a mailbox and, more importantly, the number of messages flagged as unseen— the new messages you have not yet read.

- **imap_listmailbox( )**—A short version of **imap_getmailboxes( )**. It accepts the same parameters, but returns an array containing just the names of the mailboxes.

- **imap_scanmailbox( )**—Accepts a connection id, a reference string, a pattern, and a search string. It returns an array listing the mailboxes that have the search string in the data within the mailbox. The previous section on **imap_getmailboxes( )** explains the reference string and pattern.

- **imap_search( )**—Accepts a connection id, search criteria, and a flag. It searches the current mailbox and returns an array of messages matching the search criteria. The criteria string can contain keywords separated by spaces. Keywords containing spaces must be enclosed in quotes. The flag can be **SE_UID** if you want the array to contain UIDs instead of message numbers. The keywords are listed in RFC2060 (**www.faqs.org/rfcs/rfc2060.html**), section 6.4.4, and include single keywords, like **ANSWERED**, to get all messages that have been answered, and also keyword string pairs like **CC "john"**, to find all mail copied to addresses that contain the string **john**.

- **imap_reopen( )**—If the user selects a different mailbox, **imap_reopen( )** accepts the connection id, the name of the selected mailbox, and optional flags. It then changes the connection to the new mailbox. The optional flags are the same as for **imap_open( )**.

- **imap_check( )**—Accepts a connection id and returns an object containing information about the current mailbox, including the number of messages.

- **imap_status( )**—Returns an object containing information about a mailbox. The function requires the connection id, the mailbox name, and some options, of which **SA_ALL** is the most useful. The mailbox name format is described under **imap_open( )**.

- **imap_num_msg( )**—Accepts a connection id and returns the number of messages in the current mailbox.

- **imap_num_recent( )**—Accepts a connection id and returns the number of recent messages in the current mailbox. Recent mail is mail that is new to a mailbox, either because the mail is new or because it is old mail recently copied into this mailbox.

- **imap_mailboxmsginfo( )**—Similar to **imap_status( )**, **imap_mailboxmsginfo( )** takes longer to run because it reads through messages gathering more information than **imap_status( )**. The information is returned in an object, and includes the date of last change, the number of messages, the number of recent messages, the number of unread messages, the number of deleted messages, and the mailbox size. You might use this function instead of **imap_status( )** when you want people to clear out old mail to conserve disk space.

- **imap_expunge( )**—Removes all deleted messages from the current mailbox. Use **imap_delete( )** to delete individual messages.

- **imap_createmailbox( )**—Creates a shiny new mailbox for you when you are tired of your old ones. The function accepts a connection id and a mailbox name in the format described in **imap_open( )**.

- **imap_deletemailbox( )**—Deletes the mailbox when you finish using it. The function accepts a connection id and a mailbox name in the format described under **imap_open( )**.

- **imap_renamemailbox( )**—Gives your mailbox a brand new name. The function accepts a connection id, the name of the mailbox, and the new name for the mailbox. Both mailbox names are in the format described in **imap_open( )**.

Mail Functions

Mail functions read individual items of mail, or newsgroup posts, and assume you previously selected a server and a mailbox or newsgroup:

- **imap_headers( )**—Accepts a connection id, once the user is happy with the mailbox selection, and returns an array of the mail headers for all the mail in the mailbox.

- **imap_headerinfo( )**— Accepts a connection id, a message number from **imap_headers( )**, and some optional parameters. It returns an object full of the headers for the mail.

- **imap_header( )**—An alias for **imap_headerinfo( )**.

- **imap_fetch_overview( )**—Accepts a connection id, a string containing a sequence of message numbers, and optional flags. It returns an array of objects with one object per mail. Each object contains information including subject, from, seen, size, and date.

- **imap_sort( )**—Returns an array of mail headers sorted in order. The function accepts a connection id, a criteria string, a reverse sequence parameter, and an options parameter. The criteria string can contain a value like **SORTDATE**, to sort the headers by one of the header fields. If the reverse sequence parameter is set to **1**, the sort sequence is reversed.

- **imap_body( )**—Accepts a connection id, a message number, and optional flags. It returns the message body as a string. If the message is a multipart MIME message, use **imap_fetchstructure( )** to see the structure of the message, and then use **imap_fetchbody( )** to get each part of the message.

- **imap_fetchstructure( )**—Fetches the structure of multipart MIME messages. Use **imap_fetchbody( )** to get each part of the message.

- **imap_fetchbody( )**—Fetches part of a multipart MIME message.

- **imap_mail_compose( )**—Creates a message in a string for use in **imap_append( )**. The input is an array of message headers and an array containing the parts of the message body. Each part can be an array of headers and text, which makes the building of a multipart message just that little bit easier. You might consider using this function for non-IMAP MIME mail.

15. Mail

- **imap_append( )**—Adds a message to a mailbox. The function accepts a connection id, a mailbox name similar to the one used in **imap_open( )**, a string containing a message, and optional flags. It returns true if successful, or false if the append fails. The format of the message string is similar to the mail you will see in the examples for **mail( )**. In **imap_append( )**, the mail headers, like To and From, are included in the message string instead of being passed as a separate parameter.

- **imap_delete( )**—Accepts a connection id and a message number, and deletes the message. A deleted message is marked as deleted and remains in the mailbox until you use **imap_expunge( )** on the mailbox.

- **imap_undelete( )**—The reverse of **imap_delete( )**. It accepts a connection id and a message number, and removes the deletion indicator from the message. A message marked as deleted remains in the mailbox until you use **imap_expunge( )** on the mailbox. Once you expunge the mailbox, you cannot undelete.

- **imap_mail( )**—Read about **mail( )** in the "Sending One Mail" Immediate Solution, and then try **imap_mail( )** with an IMAP server. **imap_mail( )** takes almost identical parameters to **mail( )** and produces the same results.

- **imap_mail_copy( )**—Accepts a connection id, a string containing a list of message numbers, the target mailbox name, and a few optional flags. It copies the messages from the current mailbox to the target mailbox.

- **imap_mail_move( )**—Accepts identical parameters to **imap_mail_copy( )**, and moves the messages from the current mailbox to the target mailbox.

Subscription Functions

An IMAP subscription is a way of highlighting a few mailboxes among many. Suppose your company gives you read access to hundreds of mailboxes containing various product enquiries from customers, and buried in the list are your few private mailboxes. You can simply subscribe to your mailboxes; when you want your private mail, replace the standard functions with the subscription functions:

- **imap_subscribe( )**—Accepts a connection id and a mailbox name, and places that mailbox in your subscription list. The mailbox name format is described in **imap_open( )**.

- **imap_getsubscribed( )**—Nearly identical to **imap_getmailboxes( )**. Where **imap_getmailboxes( )** returns all mailboxes, **imap_getsubscribed( )** returns only mailboxes in your subscription list.

- **imap_listsubscribed( )**—Nearly identical to **imap_listmailbox( )**. Where **imap_listmailbox( )** returns all mailboxes, **imap_listsubscribed( )** returns only mailboxes in your subscription list.

- **imap_unsubscribe( )**—Accepts a connection id and a mailbox name, and removes that mailbox from your subscription list. The mailbox name format is described in **imap_open( )**.

String Conversion Functions

The functions in this section encode strings into various representations, such as UTF, and include matching decode functions.

UTF means UCS transformation formats. UCS refers to the Unicode 16-bit character sets that allow representation of all the world's written languages, including the various pictograms used in ideographic languages like Mandarin (China), Korean, and Japanese.

imap_8bit()

imap_8bit( ) accepts a string, and returns the string formatted as a quoted-printable string for inclusion in mail as per RFC 2045. Longer strings are wrapped at 76 characters, so use this function only for strings that will go in the body of the mail.

The following code tests **imap_8bit( )**, and the result shows you what quoted-printable code looks like. In the example, the array **$before** is loaded up with samples of text including single and double quotes, carriage returns, and newlines. RFC 2045 recognizes new lines only when they are represented by a carriage return–new line pair (as used by Windows and NT), but not a single **newline** (as used by Unix). There is a line each for a return, newline, and a line with the pair. RCF 2045 requires the breaking of lines at 76 characters, so there are test strings containing more than 76 characters. The second long string contains newlines, and the third long string contains carriage return–newlines.

The code loops through the array, converting the strings and saving the conversions to an array for a later test. The **before** and **after** strings arc printed. Because the carriage returns and newlines in the **before** string would not be visible, the **before** string is URL-encoded. Spaces turn to **+** signs, and special characters turn into a percent sign followed by the hexadecimal representation:

```
$before[] = "test of quote, ', doublequote, \", and equal, =.";
$before[] = "test of doublequote \"";
$before[] = "test of quote carriage return \r";
$before[] = "test of quote newline \n";
$before[] = "test of quote carriage return and newline \r\n";
$before[] = "test of long, long, long, long, long, long,"
   . " long, long, long, long, long, long, long, long,"
   . " long text without newlines.";
```

```
$before[] = "test of long, long, long, long, long, long,\n"
   . " long, long, long, long, long, long, long, long,\n"
   . " long text with newlines.";
$before[] = "test of long, long, long, long, long, long,\r\n"
   . " long, long, long, long, long, long, long, long,\r\n"
   . " long text with carriage returns and newlines.";
while(list($k, $v) = each($before))
   {
   $after[$k] = imap_8bit($v);
   print("<br><font color=\"blue\">" . urlencode($v) . "</font><br>"
      . $after[$k] . "<br>" );
   }
```

The result is shown next with comments on each conversion. In the first test, single quotes (**%27**) and double quotes (**%22**) do not change, whereas equal (**=**) changes to **=3D**. The equal sign is used as part of the encoding, so it has to be encoded if found in the input string. Encoded characters are encoded to the equal sign followed by the character represented as two hexadecimal characters with letters in uppercase. During the decode, the decoder looks for the equal sign, and then decodes the two characters after the equal sign. The decoder should accept the letters whether they are upper- or lowercase:

```
test+of+quote%2C+%27%2C+doublequote%2C+%22%2C+and+equal%2C+%3D.
test of quote, ', doublequote, ", and equal, =3D.
```

The next test shows the carriage return converted to **=0D** the way RFC 2045 requires for nonprintable characters. The preceding space is also converted, producing **=20**. RFC 2045 has long, complicated provisions for converting spaces if the spaces are at the end of a line, because some mail programs drop spaces at the end of lines. RFC 2045 would be at least a page shorter if the RFC 2045 authors had decided just to encode all spaces:

```
test+of+quote+carriage+return+%0D
test of quote carriage return=20=0D
```

The next test shows the newline encoded as **=0A**, but the preceding space is not encoded, indicating that the code thinks the space is not at the end of the line and so does not need encoding. Why is this different from a carriage return at the end of the line? RFC 2045 is so convoluted that I could not work out if the difference is a requirement of RFC 2045 or a fault in **imap_8bit( )**:

```
test+of+quote+newline+%0A
test of quote newline =0A
```

The next test includes a carriage return-newline pair. The result shows that carriage return–newline pairs are retained unencoded. The preceding space is encoded to stop removal of the space. RFC 2045 is a little unclear about how unencoded carriage return–newline pairs should be decoded, because the RFC allows addition and removal of newlines by mail servers:

```
test+of+quote+carriage+return+and+newline+%0D%0A
test of quote carriage return and newline=20
```

The next test is a line longer than 76 characters, and the result includes an = sign, followed by a space, at the break. The space is actually a carriage return–newline pair, which will cause a break in the text when traveling through mail servers, and will then be removed in your mail client. Mail clients have the option to wrap text in the display if a line exceeds a given length, but they are usually more intelligent and look for a break between words. The 76-character lines here would not fit within the book's layout, so I chopped two "longs" (12 characters) from each line, but you can still see the result with the = inserted in the last line of the display:

```
test+of+long%2C+long%2C+long%2C+
  long%2C+long%2C+long%2C+long%2C+long%2C+long%2C+long%2C+
  long+text+without+newlines.
test of long, long, long, long, long, long, long, long,
  long, l= ong, long text without newlines.
```

The next test has the long line split up with newlines. The result shows the newlines encoded, and also has new breaks inserted at 76 characters. This display also has two sets of "longs" edited out of each line to fit the width of the book's layout:

```
test+of+long%2C+long%2C+long%2C+long%2C%0A+long%2C+long%2C+long%2C+long%
  2C+long%2C+long%2C%0A+long+text+with+newlines.
test of long, long, long, long,=0A long, long, long, long, long= , long,
  =0A long text with newlines.
```

The next test has the long line split up with carriage return–newline pairs. The result shows that the carriage return–newline pairs are not encoded, but are used to split the lines for transmission. Even though the trick works, the encoding, decoding, and RFC 2045 would all be far easier if all carriage returns and newlines in the string were encoded, and new breaks were inserted by the encoding:

```
test+of+long%2C+long%2C+long%2C+long%2C+long%2C+long%2C%0D%0A+long%2C+
  long%2C+long%2C+long%2C+long%2C+long%2C+long%2C%0D%0A+long+
  text+with+carriage+returns+and+newlines.
test of long, long, long, long, long, long, long, long, long, long,
  long, long, long, long, long text with carriage returns and newlines.
```

imap_qprint()

imap_qprint( ) does the reverse of **imap_8bit( )**, converting a quoted-printable string back to a normal string. The following code decodes and prints the first entry in **$after**:

```
print("<br>" . imap_qprint($after[0]));
```

The result is:

```
test of quote, ', doublequote, ", and equal, =.
```

quoted_printable_decode()

quoted_printable_decode( ) is an alternative to **imap_qprint( )**. It is supposed to perform the same conversion but is reported as having slight differences. **quoted_printable_decode( )** does not require the IMAP extension, so it could be useful when reading mail collected by an external program.

The following code resets **$before**, loops through **$before**, decodes the matching value in **$after**, and prints the decoded value next to the original value. Both values are URL-encoded so you can see special characters. If the decoded string matches the original, the decoded value is highlighted in green; if not, the nonmatching string is highlighted in red:

```
reset($before);
while(list($k, $v) = each($before))
   {
   $decoded = quoted_printable_decode($after[$k]);
   print("<br><font color=\"blue\">" . urlencode($v) . "</font>" );
   if($decoded == $v)
      {
      print("<br><font color=\"green\">" . urlencode(\$decoded)
         . "</font><br>" );
      }
   else
      {
      print("<br><font color=\"red\">" . urlencode($decoded)
         . "</font><br>" );
      }
   }
```

The following four result comparisons show that the decoded strings match the originals:

```
test+of+quote%2C+%27%2C+doublequote%2C+%22%2C+and+equal%2C+%3D.
test+of+quote%2C+%27%2C+doublequote%2C+%22%2C+and+equal%2C+%3D.

test+of+quote+carriage+return+%0D
test+of+quote+carriage+return+%0D

test+of+quote+newline+%0A
test+of+quote+newline+%0A

test+of+quote+carriage+return+and+newline+%0D%0A
test+of+quote+carriage+return+and+newline+%0D%0A
```

The following two result comparisons show that the decoded strings do not match
the originals (to fit this book's layout, I split the long displayed lines into shorter
print lines):

```
test+of+long%2C+long%2C+long%2C+long%2C+long%2C+long%2C+long%2C+long%2C+
    long%2C+long%2C+long%2C+long%2C+long%2C+long%2C+long+text+without+
    newlines.
test+of+long%2C+long%2C+long%2C+long%2C+long%2C+long%2C+long%2C+long%2C+
    long%2C+long%2C+long%2C+l%0Aong%2C+long%2C+long%2C+long+text+without+
    newlines.

test+of+long%2C+long%2C+long%2C+long%2C+long%2C+long%2C%0A+long%2C+
    long%2C+long%2C+long%2C+long%2C+long%2C+long%2C%0A+long+text+
    with+newlines.
test+of+long%2C+long%2C+long%2C+long%2C+long%2C+long%2C%0A+long%2C+
    long%2C+long%2C+long%2C+long%0A%2C+long%2C+long%2C+long%2C%0A+long+
    text+with+newlines.
```

In both cases, newlines are not removed from the result string. Is the problem
with **quoted_printable_decode()** or a hole in RFC 2045? I think the RFC is
overly complex, to the point where writing reliable encoders and decoders is
difficult.

The following result comparison shows that the decoded string matches the
original:

```
test+of+long%2C+long%2C+long%2C+long%2C+long%2C+long%2C%0D%0A+long%2C+
    long%2C+long%2C+long%2C+long%2C+long%2C+long%2C%0D%0A+long+text+
    with+carriage+returns+and+newlines.
test+of+long%2C+long%2C+long%2C+long%2C+long%2C+long%2C%0D%0A+long%2C+
    long%2C+long%2C+long%2C+long%2C+long%2C+long%2C%0D%0A+long+text+
    with+carriage+returns+and+newlines.
```

15. Mail

imap_utf7_encode()

imap_utf7_encode( ) accepts a string, and returns the string encoded according to modified UTF-7 encoding as described in RFC 2060 (**www.faqs.org/rfcs/ rfc2060.html**). (**imap_utf7_decode( )** decodes the encoded string back to the original string.) The encoding is used for mailbox names that contain international characters outside of the standard printable character set.

URL and other forms of existing encoding would make sense for encoding the names, but might slow down some forms of software access. RFC 2060 encoding keeps directory structure characters, like the slash, unencoded to suit mail systems that store each mailbox as a separate directory. The following data shows what modified UTF-7 encoding looks like. The data contains common directory characters, like slash (/), tilde (~), ampersand (**&**), dash (-) and the Greek character **ß**:

```
$before[] = "mail/in";
$before[] = "~john";
$before[] = "amper&sand";
$before[] = "new-mail";
$before[] = "Basic Greek: ß";
$before[] = "Basic Greek: ßß";
```

The data is fed through the same code used to test **imap_8bit( )**, with just one change, as shown next. **imap_8bit( )** is replaced by **imap_utf7_encode( )**:

```
$after[$k] = imap_utf7_encode($v);
```

The results including /, ~, and – were no different than the input, so I left them out. The **&** was translated to **&-**, as shown next:

```
amper&-sand
```

The Greek character, **%DF** in the next result, is translated to **&3w-**. **&** is used to indicate the start of an encoded string, and the – indicates the end. **3w** indicates the actual character:

```
Basic+Greek%3A+%DF
Basic Greek: &3w-
```

imap_utf7_decode()

imap_utf7_decode( ) accepts a string and returns the string decoded according to RFC 2060. (**imap_utf7_encode( )** performs the encoding.)

To test the decode function, feed the encoded data through the same code used to test **quoted_printable_decode( )**, with just one change, as shown next. **quoted_printable_decode( )** is replaced by **imap_utf7_decode( )**. Print the result to see the decoded text:

```
$decoded = imap_utf7_decode($after[0]);
```

All the output strings matched the original strings in **$before**; the encode and decode worked perfectly.

imap_utf8()
imap_utf8( ) accepts a string and returns the string encoded to UTF8 (RFC 2044).

imap_base64()
Base64 encoding is covered extensively in the "MIME" section of this chapter. **imap_base64( )** is the IMAP function equivalent to **base64_decode( )**, accepting an encoded string and returning a decoded string.

imap_binary()
imap_binary( ) is the IMAP function equivalent to **base64_encode( )**, accepting a string and returning a string encoded to the base64 standard.

Other Functions
The previous sections covered functions to access a mailbox and functions to access mail items within a mailbox. This section lists all the other IMAP functions including error-handling functions, functions used for testing, and functions that provide a more manual approach than the functions described earlier.

imap_alerts()
imap_alerts( ) returns an array of alert messages from the IMAP server. The server's list of alerts is cleared, so you receive an alert just once.

imap_clearflag_full() and imap_setflag_full()
Flags on each mail indicate if the mail has not been seen, is a draft, or is deleted. The **imap_clearflag_full( )** and **imap_setflag_full( )** functions set and clear the flags. Normally the delete flag is set by **imap_delete( )**, and the unseen flag is cleared when you fetch the mail, so you do not need these two functions.

imap_errors()
Read about **imap_alerts( )**, because the alerts can indicate situations that will lead to an error. **imap_errors( )** returns an array of previous error messages and clears the server's error list so you receive an error message just once. When testing new IMAP code, check for alerts and errors after every IMAP function until you are confident that everything works.

imap_last_error()

imap_last_error() returns the last IMAP error message and does not alter the IMAP server's error list (the one returned by imap_errors()). This function returns just one error message, so you could miss important clues if the last error was actually caused by a previous error. If you use imap_last_error(), occasionally use imap_errors() to check and clear out all errors.

imap_fetchheader()

imap_fetchheader() is a simplified version of imap_header(), which accepts a connection id, a message number, and a few flags. It returns a raw header string conforming to RFC 2822 (www.faqs.org/rfcs/rfc2822.html). It is up to you to decode the headers. Use imap_header() unless you are stuck with strange results, and then resort to imap_fetchheader() to find if the problem is caused by new, unusual, or incorrect headers.

imap_mime_header_decode()

imap_mime_header_decode() decodes MIME header strings into an array where each array element has two values, charset and text. If the text is in the default us_ascii character set, charset contains default. You can quickly test MIME headers with the following code, which prints the charset and text in a simple list. htmlentities() prevents unusual characters from upsetting the page's HTML. To get the correct representation of each character set, you need to set up the HTML for whatever works in your browser. The code assumes you created $header with imap_header():

```
$strings = imap_mime_header_decode($header);
while(list($k, $v) = each($strings))
    {
    print("<br>charset: " . $v["charset"] . ", text: "
        . htmlentities($v["text"]));
    }
```

imap_uid()

imap_uid() accepts a connection id and a message number, and returns the message's UID. imap_msgno() returns a message number from a UID. The UID is a 32-bit message identifier that is unique within a mailbox and should remain unique across deletions and all other mailbox maintenance. You can use the UID to match mail from an offline session back to the mail on the server.

imap_msgno()

imap_msgno() accepts a connection id and a UID, and returns the message number that matches the UID. imap_uid() returns a UID from a message number. See imap_uid() for an explanation of UID.

imap_ping()

If you suspect an LDAP server has dropped offline, or you just want to remind the server you are around, issue **imap_ping( )**. All **imap_ping( )** needs is the connection id, and the function returns true if the connection is still alive.

You might use this if you wrote a PHP batch program to sit in the background and perform some long-term mail function, like checking for unsolicited commercial email or redirecting mail for people on leave. The program could sit there and check mailboxes for new mail every few minutes. To keep the session alive between mailbox checks, issue **imap_ping( )**.

imap_rfc822_parse_adrlist()

imap_rfc822_parse_adrlist( ) accepts an address string and a default host name. It returns an array of objects containing four values for each address: **mailbox**, **host**, **personal** (the person's name), and **adl** (at domain list; that is, addresses of the form **@petermoulding.com**). The following code parses an address string and prints the result. This function is useful for strings that can contain multiple addresses, like the fields **To**, **Cc**, and **Bcc**:

```
$addresses = imap_rfc822_parse_adrlist($address, "a_test_domain.com");
while(list($k, $v) = each($addresses))
    {
    print("<br>mailbox: " . htmlentities($v->mailbox)
        . ", host: " . htmlentities($v->host)
        . ", personal: " . htmlentities($v->personal)
        . ", domain: " . htmlentities($v->adl));
    }
```

imap_rfc822_parse_headers()

imap_rfc822_parse_headers( ) is a simplified version of **imap_header( )** that accepts a string containing headers and a default host name, and returns an object containing the header values.

imap_rfc822_write_address()

imap_rfc822_write_address( ) accepts a mailbox name, the name of a host, and a personal name. It returns a mail address formatted to RFC 2822. You can test it with the following code:

```
print("<br>address: " . htmlentities(imap_rfc822_write_address(
    "peter", "petermoulding.com", "Peter M")));
```

The result is:

```
address: Peter M <peter@petermoulding.com>
```

Mail Headers

Mail consists of header, header, body. There are many types of headers in use, with a small number required in every mail and the rest optional. MIME headers are required only when the mail contains attachments.

Minimum Headers

Here is an example of the minimum headers for mail and news, using headers you will see generated in the "Sending Mail" solution. The **To** header directs the mail to the right mailbox. The **From** header lets the recipient reply to you. The **Date** header lets them know which of your mail is the most recent, and the **Subject** header gives them an indication of what the mail is for. To, From, and Subject are the minimum identifiers you supply to functions like **mail()**, and the mail system inserts the date:

```
Subject: PHP Sydney meeting
   Date: Sun, 01 Jul 2001 19:51:48 -1000
   From: address@the_mail_server.com.au
     To: peter@a_web_site_somewhere.com
```

Additional Headers

Here are other headers you can use in your experiments. Their availability and interpretation depend on the mail client and server software. Some software is case sensitive and so requires that you type the headers as they are shown here:

- **Mailing-List**—This header lets you name the mailing list used to supply addresses for mail. This is one way of letting people know why they received the mail, but not the best way, because many people do not know how to view the headers.

- **Bcc**—This header accepts multiple mail addresses and sends a copy to every address, but does not list any of the **Bcc** addresses in the mail. If you send mail to an employee, you might copy the human resources department with **Bcc**. Eventually an employee will hear about secret copies of emails and spread rumors, and your staff will begin to distrust email. **Cc** is more honest, open, and preferable to **Bcc**.

- **Reply_To**—This header gives people an address for replies when the **From** address is inappropriate, such as when a salesperson sends you a message but wants you to reply through a generic sales mail address when he or she is on vacation.

- **Return_Path**—This header tells the mail system where to send error messages.

- **X-Mailer**—This header names the product used to send the mail. You might want to put in an advertisement for PHP (or for yourself).

- **X-Priority**—**1** gives your mail the highest priority, but rarely makes any difference. The problems that slow down mail tend to slow down all mail. Do not mark your mail urgent if it is not urgent, because that is one trait of the scum who silt up the mail system with unsolicited commercial email.

MIME

MIME is a group of Multipurpose Internet Mail Extensions that extend the original RFC 822 definition of mail. In fact, RFC 822 does little more than tell you how guide a text string around the Internet. The MIME extensions add the rules and guidelines for using different character sets and attaching files.

MIME headers are required for attachments and special character sets. The MIME headers are listed in the following sections.

MIME-Version

MIME-Version is required if there is anything MIME-encoded in the mail, and provides the MIME version number. The current and only version is 1.0, as shown in the following header:

```
MIME-Version: 1.0
```

You can have comments in the **MIME-Version** header, but the receiving software should ignore the comments:

```
MIME-Version: 1.0 (Produced by my PHP script)
```

Content-Type

Content-Type defaults to **text/plain; charset="us-ascii"**, and can be set to many other values, including **text/html; charset=iso-8859-1**, if you include HTML in your mail. The next code example is from an email that contains a small number of fancy characters, like ®. Some **Content-Type** headers have quotes around the value assigned to **charset**, and others do not. Note that this header uses a semicolon (;) as a separator between values, whereas some other mail headers use a comma:

```
Content-Type: text/plain; charset="iso-8859-1"
```

If the mail includes multiple attachments, the **Content-Type** header looks like the following header (all on one line). The **boundary** value is some sort of pseudo-random string that marks the beginning and end of each attachment:

```
Content-Type: multipart/mixed;
    boundary="------------53B3198E1AEEC7DDA5896006"
```

Each attachment includes a set of headers specific to the attachment. The following three headers were in front of an attachment containing a program. Note that the encoding of the attachment is base64, an encoding scheme covered in Chapter 13:

```
Content-Type: application/octet-stream; name="test.exe"
Content-Transfer-Encoding: base64
        Content-Disposition: attachment; filename="test.exe"
```

Content-Transfer-Encoding

Content-Transfer-Encoding is included in most mail containing a **Content-Type** header. It has options such as **7bit**, **8bit**, **base64**, **quoted-printable**, and **binary**, and it allows custom encoding types. The default is 7bit, so this header is usually left out for standard 7bit ASCII email, and included for everything else. There is an example under **Content-Type**.

Content-ID

Content-ID was implemented before the Web. It let people send mail with references to attachments instead of including the attachments. The recipient could then select some of the attachments for a separate delivery, without having to receive all the attachments. The idea had few implementations and then was made obsolete by the modern method of including links to files on Web sites.

Content-Description

Would you like to describe attachments in your mail? Most people describe attachments by simply typing a paragraph about the attachment. **Content-Description** lets you provide a formal description, similar to the **alt** text in an HTML image tag. The following example shows the sort of description you might add to an attachment if you were the author of the Happy Virus:

```
Content-Description: The attachment is not a virus. Ha! Ha! Ha!
```

Content-Disposition

Content-Disposition is an experimental header that can tell your mail viewer if an attachment should be viewed inline or not, as shown in the following example. If a message contains a couple of screen shots and a program, the author might want the recipient to view the screen shots inline, but not the program. Your mail viewer should give you the power to override the **Content-Disposition** so you can view nothing except the mail text and then decide if you want to view anything else, especially with attachment types that can carry viruses or link to nasty Web sites with dozens of annoying pop-up advertisements:

```
Content-Disposition: inline
```

Modes of Operation

You can access electronic mail in at least three ways. Your current mode helps you decide the best approach for using PHP with mail.

Offline

In offline mode, your mail client, or mail user agent (MUA), fetches all new mail from a mail server and stores the mail on your workstation. You browse the mail on your workstation, compose replies or new mail, on the same workstation, and then send the new mail and replies to a mail server for injection into the Internet.

The default protocol for offline mail collection is POP3, because POP3 does everything you need for offline mode and has no overhead you do not need. SMTP is used to send mail, and pairs well with POP3. An alternative to POP3 and SMTP is IMAP, but IMAP does more than what is needed, has overhead and installation problems, and is supported by few email clients. Most ISPs choose the POP3/SMTP combination over IMAP.

If you want to write your own mail client using PHP, install Apache, PHP, and MySQL on your workstation, and use PHP to retrieve, display, and send email from your workstation. The PHP socket functions, covered in Chapter 13, can be used to retrieve email via POP3, the IMAP functions will retrieve and send email via IMAP, and the mail function will send mail via SMTP.

The real disadvantage of offline mode becomes obvious when you are away from your workstation and want to read important information, like the name of a hotel, from an email locked up in your workstation. If your workstation is a notebook, you can carry your email everywhere, and so can any thieves who take your workstation off the luggage trolley at the airport.

15. Mail

One of my mates arrived in a large Asian city late one evening, only to find his luggage had arrived elsewhere, perhaps not even in Asia, and all his contact telephone numbers had traveled inside the luggage. The backup list was on a floppy disk on a desk in an office not in Asia, and the people who work in the office were all home in bed, asleep. Luckily, when you work for a company that automatically books you into a Hilton, no matter which city you are in, the solution is simple. Jump into a taxi, and every taxi driver knows the Hilton. My mate stood there at the airport wishing he worked for a company that booked people into the Hilton.

Online

When you access mail online, you browse your email much the same as you browse any a file on a Web server. The mail stays on the mail server. The client is just a browser and can be on any workstation, anywhere in the world. It could even be a ghastly lime-green iMac in the Quetzal Internet Café in San Francisco. The undersized iMac keyboards might slow down typing, but they do not completely stop access to a server that is three meals and six movies away (by air).

POP3 and SMTP do not work for online access. The protocol between the server and your workstation is a combination of HTTP and IMAP. Here is how you use each.

If you want pure IMAP from your workstation to the mail server, you install an IMAP-capable mail client application on your workstation, or install Apache and PHP on your workstation and let PHP talk IMAP with the mail server. Windows users can use Personal Web Services (PWS) instead of Apache, but getting applications working with PWS is just as hard as installing the Apache/PHP combination. The PHP scripts use the PHP IMAP functions to talk IMAP with consenting servers.

If you don't want to install PHP on your workstation (sort of like an actor turning down an Oscar), you can set up your Web server to act as the mail client and browse the pages from any browser, anywhere. The mail stays on the server, the Web server talks IMAP with the mail server, and your browser talks HTTP with your Web server.

Disconnected

Disconnected mode is for notebooks and dialup. The mail client on the notebook dials the ISP, connects to the mail server, collects the mail, and hangs up. The original mail remains on the mail server, you work with copies on the notebook, and you dial in every so often to synchronize your client with the server. Outgoing mail waits for the connection. Mail deletions do not affect the mail on the server until you connect. If a thief takes your notebook, you buy a new notebook and dial in, and your new notebook springs to life with all the email still on the server.

You cannot easily use disconnected mode from an Internet café because you are generally not allowed to change the software configurations at Internet cafés. There is little point in writing a PHP replacement for a mail client when using disconnected mode, because the client often has to know peculiarities specific to the server accepting the dial-in, and hassle with dialing. You might as well dial manually and start PHP as a conventional mail client.

Temporary

If you have a notebook and a need for extreme security, you can configure mail clients not to store mail on the notebook. Mail is downloaded when you switch the notebook on and thrown away when you close the mail client. If a thief steals your notebook when the notebook is switched off, the thief ends up with an empty inbox and none of your mail about secret bank accounts in the Bahamas.

The PHP equivalent to temporary mode is placing your mail scripts on your server and using the notebook purely as a Web browser. Just make sure you have the browser set to empty its cache when you close the browser session.

Immediate Solutions

Installing PHP Mail Functions

PHP has **mail( )** and **ezmlm_hash( )** built in. You have to install the IMAP functions. You may also need to configure the **SMTP** setting in php.ini.

Windows NT

To activate IMAP in Windows NT, stop Apache, copy c:/Program Files/php/extensions/php_imap.dll to c:/winnt/system32/, remove the semicolon (;) from the following line, and start Apache:

```
;extension=php_imap.dll
```

If you use PHP as CGI, you do not have to restart your Web server. Windows 2000 should install the same way as Windows NT. Windows 98 uses slightly different directory names.

You may need to change two lines in php.ini to make **mail( )** work. Look for the following lines in php.ini:

```
SMTP = localhost
sendmail_from = me@localhost.com
```

Change **localhost** to the name of your mail server. Change **me@localhost.com** to a valid email address to use as the default **From** address in outgoing mail.

Unix

To install IMAP on Unix, Get the C client library from the University of Washington (**ftp://ftp.cac.washington.edu/imap/**).

Copy c-client/c-client.a to a directory in your link path, like /usr/local/lib/. Copy c-client/ rfc822.h and mail.h to a directory in your include path, like /usr/local/include/. Compile PHP with the following option:

```
--with-imap
```

You may need to change one line in php.ini to make **mail( )** work. Look for the following line in php.ini, remove the semicolon, and change the line to point to your **sendmail**. You can include parameters; the default is **sendmail -t -i**:

```
;sendmail_path =
```

Sending Mail

Have fun sending mail from your PHP scripts, but be sure to test mail to your address before inflicting the results on unsuspecting friends. The "Sending One Mail" section that follows shows you the minimum required to send mail, but not enough to be practical. The next section, "Sending the **From** Header," shows you the additional **From** header required for useful mail. The "Sending Many Headers" section shows you how to add many headers, and you can experiment with what you need. Finally, the "Sending One Message to Many" section shows you how to send one mail to many people with individual salutations.

Sending One Mail

When you're sending one mail, all you need is the address you are sending the mail to, a subject, a message, and the function **mail( )**. The following example shows a cryptic message to members of PHP Sydney. (The real messages contain the date and location, plus information on subscribing and unsubscribing.) The newlines (**\n**) create breaks to new lines in the mail. Your customer's mail viewer may add extra breaks to long lines:

```
$to = "peter@a_web_site_somewhere.com";
$subject = "PHP Sydney meeting";
$message = "A reminder.\n"
    . "The next meeting of PHP Sydney is Tuesday night.\n"
    . "The meeting starts at 7:00pm.\n"
    . "\n"
    . "Peter\n";
```

The following code sends the message using **mail( )**, and returns true if **mail( )** was able to talk with the mail transport agent (MTA). If the MTA fails to send the mail, you will still get a true response from **mail( )**, but you may have to check the MTA's log to find if the mail was really sent. When testing MTAs, you can include a **Cc** or **Bcc** (explained later) to your own address:

```
if(mail($to, $subject, $message))
   {
   print("<br><font color=\"green\">Mail sent to " . $to . ".</font>" );
   }
else
   {
   print("<br><font color=\"red\">Mail failed.</font>" );
   }
```

Sendmail is the usual MTA in Unix. There are alternatives, but you should not need to know the name of the MTA, because the system should handle the process. A variety of MTAs exist for Windows NT and Windows 9*x*. I have so much software installed on my workstation, including POSIX extensions, that I do not know what is currently providing the MTA service. The default in the Win32 php.ini is **localhost**, which works for some system setups, and the alternatives are to install a mail server on your machine, or point SMTP to a server containing a mail server.

Some originating MTAs insert a header that lets you identify the source software, but not the one I am using. Here is the message as viewed in the Netscape 4.77 browser with View Headers set to Normal:

```
Subject: PHP Sydney meeting
   Date: Sun, 01 Jul 2001 19:51:48 -1000
   From: address@the_mail_server.com.au
     To: peter@a_web_site_somewhere.com


A reminder.
The next meeting of PHP Sydney is Tuesday night.
The meeting starts at 7:00pm.


Peter
```

What does View Headers look like when set to All? The following shows all the headers from the same mail. When mail has traversed the world, there will be many **Received:** headers, one for each server. You can use the **Received** headers to both check the configuration of your mail server and trace the origin of unsolicited commercial email. Unfortunately you will catch only the stupid that way, because the experienced manufacture fakes headers (the way they fake everything else in the mail):

```
   Return-Path: <address@the_mail_server.com>
Delivered-To: peter@a_web_site_somewhere.com
     Received: from a800 (CPE-144-132.nsw.bigpond.net.au
```

```
                        [144.190.50.132]) by a_web.com (Postfix)
                        with SMTP id 9257D17A08 for
                        <peter@a_web_site_somewhere.com>;
                        Sun, 1 Jul 2001 19:51:32 +1000 (EST)
                        Date: Sun, 01 Jul 2002 19:51:48 -1000
                From:   address@the_mail_server.com
             Subject:   PHP Sydney meeting
                  To:   peter@a_web_site_somewhere.com
          Message-ID:   <20010701095132.9257D17A08@a_web.com>
              Status:
     X-Mozilla-Status:   8001
    X-Mozilla-Status2:   00000000
               X-UIDL:   3aad41fa00000403
```

The **To** field can contain multiple addresses, and an example of multiple addresses, with **Cc**, appears later in this solution. I receive many email messages from vendors complete with their whole marketing mail list as one long multiple address string in the **To** field. Some people do not know how to send mail, and they give away their company's most valuable asset, their mailing list, in one message. You can also upset recipients when they find their email address published to many other people. Instead of using multiple **To** addresses, use the "Sending One Message to Many" approach discussed later in this solution.

Sending the From Header

You may have noticed that the example in the previous section has a weird **From** address. If you leave out the **From** address in mail, one of the MTAs will insert an address. Some businesses and Web site owners prefer to have staff leave out individual **From** addresses and have the mail server insert a generic address. Other businesses prefer individual or departmental **From** addresses. This section shows you a small number of modifications to the previous example that enable you to include a **From** address. First you need a **From** address:

```
$from = "everyone@thatusesphp.com.au";
```

The **From** address is inserted into a parameter designed to handle several additional mail headers. The following code sets up a field, **$additional**, for the additional headers, and adds the **From** address, **$from**, with the prefix **"From:"** if there is data in **$from**:

```
$additional = "";
if(isset($from) and strlen($from))
    {
    $additional .= "From: " . $from;
    }
```

Make one change to the previous code: Add **$additional** to the parameters in **mail( )**, as shown next:

```
if(mail($to, $subject, $message, $additional))
```

When the mail arrives, the **From:** line will contain the **From** address, as shown next:

```
From: everyone@thatusesphp.com.au
```

The hidden headers contain the server address, and that can be addressed with additional headers in your message, but usually the **From** address is sufficient to let your recipients reply:

```
Return-Path: <address@the_mail_server.com>
        Sender: address@the_mail_server.com
```

There are two other ways to set the **From** value. PHP has an option in php.ini to set a default **From** address, which is a good way to set a default if your site shares an MTA with other sites. You can also override php.ini with .htaccess files if your site is one virtual site among many.

I used an alternative for a while on one system, because adding **From:** to the additional headers parameter was not working reliably. The default from php.ini can be overridden with **ini_set( )**, as shown next. When I tested this option on my current configuration, **ini_set( )** produced a syntax error:

```
ini_set("sendmail_from", $from);
```

Sending Many Headers

There are times when you need to use additional headers. **Cc** accepts multiple email addresses and sends a copy to each address. The **To** recipient and every **Cc** recipient will see the **To** address and all the **Cc** addresses. **Cc** is case sensitive, as are some other headers. **Cc** is used here as the example of headers that allow multiple mail addresses. A list of other headers appears at the end of this solution.

The following addresses will be used for the example code. **$cc** is an array containing multiple **Cc** addresses, to show the techniques for processing multiple addresses. **$cc** includes an empty string because empty strings can cause problems:

```
$cc[] = "info@some_other_site.com";
$cc[] = "";
```

```
$cc[] = "info@yet_another_test.com";
$from = "everyone@thatusesphp.com.au";
```

To allow for multiple headers, the individual headers will be built into an array called **$add**, and **$add** will be joined to the string **$additional** for the mail function. The **From** address is added to the array **$add**, with the prefix **"From:"** if there is data in **$from**:

```
if(isset($from) and strlen($from))
    {
    $add[] .= "From: " . $from;
    }
```

The following code checks that **$cc** is an array, steps through the array removing entries that contain zero-length strings, and then joins all the entries into string **$c** using **implode**. When you use multiple entries in fields like **Cc** and **Bcc**, the entries are separated by a comma-space, so **implode** includes a comma-space. If **$cc** is not an array, the code treats **$cc** as a string containing a single entry and adds the single entry. It is important to keep the input addresses clean, because an error in one entry can prevent the mail from reaching everyone. If you have problems with a list, try sending mail to each address by itself:

```
reset($cc);
if(isset($cc))
    {
    if(is_array($cc))
        {
        while(list($k, $v) = each($cc))
            {
            if(!strlen($v))
                {
                unset($cc[$k]);
                }
            }
        $c = implode(", ", $cc);
        if(strlen($c))
            {
            $add[] = "Cc: " . $c;
            }
        }
    elseif(strlen($cc))
        {
        $add[] = "Cc: " . $cc;
        }
    }
```

You can add handlers for any number of other headers using a copy of the single-address **From** code or the multiple-address **Cc** code. The next step is to join together all the text in array **$add** as one long string of headers in **$additional**. The following code checks that **$add** is a valid array, and concatenates the text in **$add** using the value in **$separator**. **$separator** is set to **\r\n** for Windows and Windows NT, and to **\n** for Unix. Notice that the separator is also added to the end of the string of headers. I found that if **$additional** contains any separators, there must be a separator at the end of **$additional**. When **$additional** contains only one header, you can add the separator or leave it off; the mail software does not care if the separator is **\n** or **\r\n** or not there at all:

```
$additional = "";
$separator = "\r\n";
if(isset($add) and is_array($add))
    {
    $additional = implode($separator, $add) . $separator;
    }
```

Note that the body of an email is separated from the headers by a blank line. If you let a blank line sneak into your headers, the part of the header after the blank line will appear in the body of your email. Add all the extra safety checks you need to ensure your code does not add zero-length or blank entries to the headers. You might want to add the following code, as a final safety check, just before you implode **$add** into **$additional**:

```
reset($add);
while(list($k, $v) = each($add))
    {
    if(!strlen($v))
        {
        unset($add[$k]);
        }
    }
```

The code around **mail()** does not have to change. If **$additional** is empty, **mail()** still sends the mail.

Sending One Message to Many

The best way to send one mail to many people is to send an individual mail to each person so they do not see their mail address published on a giant **To** list in a single mail. Individual mail also lets you customize the mail. The following example sends one mail to everyone on a list.

The list can start anywhere: a file, a database, or a form. To let you fit the code in with every source, the following code creates a list, **$mail_list**. Subsequent code converts the list to an array, and the mail send function is placed in a loop feeding from the array. You can replace one or two steps with your own code to build an array from your own source. The list has one entry per line, containing a name and an address separated by the pipe character (I). The code uses a simple way of entering large amounts of text within PHP code. You can replace **endoflist** with any text string that does not occur within the data:

```
$mail_list = <<<endoflist
John S Brown|jsb@somewhere_or_another.com
Peter|peter@a_web_site_somewhere.com
endoflist;
```

The following code converts the list, **$mail_list**, to an array, **$to**, structured in a way that makes sending the mail easy, and makes building the array from a database equally easy:

```
if(isset($to))
    {
    unset($to)
    }
$x = explode("\n", $mail_list);
while(list($k, $v) = each($x))
    {
    list($name, $address) = explode("|", $v);
    $to [] = array("address" => $address, "name" => $name);
    }
```

explode( ) takes the list, splits it into an array of lines, **$x**, and then loops through the array, creating the final array, **$to**. Every line in **$x** is split at the I by **explode**, with the first part of the line going into **$name** and the second part going into **$address**. The two fields are placed into an entry in **$to**. (Just a reminder about arrays: If **$to** is previously defined as a string, PHP will complain about your trying to convert **$to** to an array. If **$to** is already an array, the code would append entries to the existing entries. I added the **unset($to)** to prevent both problems.)

You could have the **$mail_list** entries in the extended address form **Peter <peter@a_web_site_somewhere.com>**, use the extended address for the mail address, and extract the first part of the address as the name. I found that some MTAs do not accept the extended address, or accept only limited variations of the extended address, so keep to the short form of the mail address until you have everything else working.

The header processing code is the same as the previous section. The mailing code changes, as shown in the following code, to loop through **$to** and use each entry to create one mail. **while( )** loops through **$to** and returns the entry in **$v**, which contains the addressee's name and address. The line starting with **$message** adds the salutation to the front of the message, in this case **Dear John,**. The **if(mail( ))** line has the address replaced by **$v["address"]**, as do the two print lines:

```
while(list($k, $v) = each($to))
   {
   $message = "Dear " . $v["name"] . ",\n" . $message;
   if(mail($v["address"], $subject, $message, $additional))
      {
      print("<br><font color=\"green\">Mail sent to " . $v["address"]
         . ".</font>" );
      }
   else
      {
      print("<br><font color=\"red\">Mail failed to " . $v["address"]
         . ".</font>" );
      }
   }
```

If the mail contains addresses in the extended format, including **<, >**, the **print** statements will not work because part of the output will be interpreted as HTML. To prevent the display problem, wrap **htmlentities( )** around the address, as shown next. Use **htmlentities( )** around all mail fields before display to avoid the same problem. If you are displaying the mail body and you want to retain the line breaks, use **nl2br(htmlentities( ))** because **nt2br( )** adds a **
** to each newline:

```
print("<br><font color=\"green\">Mail sent to "
         . htmlentities($v["address"]) . ".</font>" );
```

When sending large mail several times, or small mail many times, PHP will time out. Change the default PHP time limit from 30 seconds to the number of seconds required using **set_time_limit( )**, as shown in the following code. You can set the time limit to **0** to let the script run forever, but that is inherently dangerous, because your script will run forever if in a loop. The safest approach is to allocate a certain number of seconds per email, **2** in the example, and multiply by the number of messages:

```
set_time_limit(count($to) * 2);
```

You now have the code to send everything except attachments. You can handle 99.8 percent of the mail-sending requirements for mail lists.

Sending Mail with Attachments

This solution presents the 0.2 percent of mail-sending not covered in previous solutions. This is the most complex part, the part you have to either trust, or be prepared to spend a lot of time experimenting on. This is where you add MIME to your mail and include attachments. Once you start, your mail will not work until everything is working perfectly. That is why you should get your mail working without attachments first. Work your way through the previous solutions, and when you can send mail with all headers, you are ready to experiment with MIME.

Selecting Test Data

The following list is the test message for a single mail. The test message will be matched with two test files representing the common types of files attached to mail: text files with unusual characters, and image files. The next most popular group is executable files, but they seem to be less trusted because of the number of viruses hiding in executable files. When you are testing your MIME code, start with one file type and then add one more file type per test until you have tested every file type you want to use.

Note that the first definition is the separator string of carriage return-newline, **\r\n**. In the previous mail solutions, you only had to worry about the sending program's requirements; everything else on the Internet worked with a single **\n**. MIME messages will fail if you use a single **\n**, or the Mac's **\n\r** variation. Some messages may get through, but not all. It depends on all the mail software on all the servers between you and the recipient:

```
$separator = "\r\n";
$from = "everyone@thatusesphp.com.au";
$to = "peter@a_web_site_somewhere.com";
$salutation = "Peter";
$subject = "Test mail attachments";
$message = "The enclosed files are tests." . $separator;
```

Next, you need test files. I found a very small GIF and created a small text file containing a couple of sentences with special characters, like ®. The files will be attached to the one message, so placing the names in an array makes for easier processing later. The code will add other attributes to the entries for each file, so the entry for each file is also an array, with the file name entry named **["file"]**:

```
$attachments[]["file"] = "./backspace.gif";
$attachments[]["file"] = "./test.txt";
```

Gathering File Information

The code is broken up into small chunks for easy testing and modification. Once the code is working, you can bring the parts closer together to save processing overhead, but the main overhead will be the actual transmission of the mail. The following code simply loops through the attachments array, **$attachments**, splitting the file name, **["name"]**, from the full file path in **["file"]**. **./backspace.gif** becomes **backspace.gif** and **./test.txt** becomes **test.txt**:

```
reset($attachments);
while(list($k, $v) = each($attachments))
   {
   $attachments[$k]["name"] = basename($v["file"]);
   }
```

When you read each file, you will need the file size, so use the following code to find the file size and add the size to the array. This is the first code that will break if the file is missing, so add your standard site error reporting to this section:

```
reset($attachments);
while(list($k, $v) = each($attachments))
   {
   $attachments[$k]["size"] = filesize($v["file"]);
   }
```

If you are writing a form to let people select files for attachment to email, forms are described in Chapter 9 and file functions are described in Chapter 8.

Related solution:	Found on page:
Uploading Files	318

MIME processing depends on the type of file you attach to the message. The following code is a quick and unreliable way to determine file types—the code is dependent on file suffixes, but not all files or operating systems use suffixes, and some file types have several suffixes:

```
reset($attachments);
while(list($k, $v) = each($attachments))
   {
   switch(substr(strrchr($v["file"], "."), 1))
      {
      case "gif":
         $attachments[$k]["type"] = "image/gif; name=\""
            . $attachments[$k]["name"] . "\"";
```

```
        break;
    case "txt":
        $attachments[$k]["type"] = "text/plain; charset=iso-8859-1";
        break;
    Default:
        $attachments[$k]["type"] = "application/octet-stream";
    }
    $attachments[$k]["encoding"] = "base64";
}
```

You can add additional checks using file functions or, in the case of image files, using image functions from Chapter 11. You can also let people type in a file type, or select a file type from a drop-down list, if the type is unusual. The MIME type has to be accurate if you want the recipient to open the file in their mail browser, because the browser has to know which file viewer should be launched. When the recipient is only going to save the file to disk, the MIME type can be any generic value that helps the mail browser make the right choice between text and binary mode.

The code loops through the attachment array, grabbing the file suffix (everything after the last period) from the file name, via **substr( )** and **strrchar( )**. The **switch( )** function takes an action depending on the file suffix, and the actions set the file type, **["type"]**, for use in the MIME headers. There is a default action, **application/octet-stream**, which I did not test in this example. You will find dozens of MIME types out there, and the easiest way to work out what headers they need is to send yourself mail with the files attached. In Netscape mail, use View Page Source to see the headers.

Related solutions:	Found on page:
String Functions	63
Collecting Image Information	431

Building MIME Headers

MIME requires additional headers at the start of the message, additional headers at the start of each attachment, and a boundary marker between the attachments. The additional mail headers can go in the array **$add**, which is used for headers in the previous solutions; you can reuse the previous code for this solution. Some headers will go in **$message_prefix**, which can then be concatenated onto the front of the mail body, and the rest of the MIME headers can go in **$message_ suffix**, along with the encoded attachments. The reason for keeping the headers and attachments separate from **$message** is to leave you free to build a custom message for each recipient, if you are using the code for a mailing list:

15. Mail

```
$message_prefix = "";
$message_suffix = "";
```

You could be building a system with a lot of code between the start of the script and the point where you add the attachments, so the following code includes a check that the attachments array exists, is an array, and has entries to process:

```
if(isset($attachments) and is_array($attachments)
   and count($attachments) > 0)
   {
```

The code then creates a boundary field, as shown next. The boundary field needs a unique string that will separate encoded attachments. All the encoding performed in this example is base64 encoding, and base64 encoding does not contain dashes, so any dashes will work. I added the time to make the boundary a little more unique and to avoid the situation where someone has underlined a heading with a row of dashes, which is common in text attachments. You can safely use base64 encoding for everything, with little overhead, and thus avoid having to generate unique boundary strings:

```
list($x, $y) = explode(" ", microtime());
$boundary = "boundary--" . $y . substr($x, 2);
```

Two MIME headers are added to the message, to tell the mail system that the message contains MIME encoding. Once you add MIME, the whole message must conform to MIME standards, and any error can make the whole message fail:

```
$add[] = "MIME-Type: 1.0";
$add[] = "Content-Type: multipart/mixed; boundary=\"" . $boundary
  . "\"";
```

The boundary string is used once with the two trailing dashes. All subsequent uses require two dashes added at the front, so add the dashes next:

```
$boundary = "--" . $boundary;
```

The message body needs MIME headers to indicate the message has text in the body. The following code adds the right headers, and little can go wrong here, unless you include special characters (if you do need special characters, change the **Content-Transfer-Encoding** to **8bit** and the **charset** to **iso-8859-1**):

```
$message_prefix .= $boundary . $separator
   . "Content-Type: text/plain; charset=us-ascii" . $separator
```

```
. "Content-Transfer-Encoding: 7bit" . $separator
. $separator;
```

Note that there are two separators at the end of these headers, because that tells the mail browser where headers finish and the message body begins. If you leave out the second header, your text will not display. If you think a mail script may contain that mistake, add a double separator in the middle of the mail message and see if the text disappears just after the double separators in the message.

If the message does not end with a separator, add one so that the message is not messed up with the headers for the attachments. I added the extra separator to the message suffix so the message would not be changed. If you are building a custom message, move this check to the end of the custom message build and add the separator to the custom message:

```
if(substr($message, -1) != $separator)
    {
    $message_suffix .= $separator;
    }
```

Building MIME Message Parts

The rest of the code steps through the list of attachments. If there is any code between the creation of an array and the use of an array, reset the array to the start with **reset( )**:

```
reset($attachments);
while(list($k, $v) = each($attachments))
    {
```

The next code adds the headers for the start of an attachment. The headers go in **$message_suffix** and start with a boundary line to indicate a new attachment. The **Content-Type** header is required, and uses the type from the array entry. **Content-Transfer-Encoding** is required, and in this example, everything is encoded with base64. There are some slightly more efficient ways of encoding some data, but nothing worth worrying about. Base64 encoding turns a 12MB file into 16MB, whereas other encoding techniques might use only 14MB, or up to 17MB. Look at other encoding techniques only if you frequently send large files of a specific type and can verify that the recipient has a mail browser that can decode the special encoding. The **Content-Disposition** header made no difference in Netscape 4.77. Feel free to experiment and find out which mail readers do understand the header:

```
$message_suffix .= $boundary . $separator
    . "Content-Type: " . $v["type"] . $separator
    . "Content-Transfer-Encoding: base64" . $separator
    . "Content-Disposition: inline; filename=\"" . $v["name"]
    . "\"" . $separator . $separator;
```

Time to read the attachment. Open the file in read mode, read the whole file in one hit using the size you gathered earlier, and then close the file. On Windows and Windows NT, add the binary attribute to the file read (use **"rb"** instead of **"r"**), or you will miss parts of binary files such as images. You will not see an error at your end; it will be the recipient who gets a strange result, including files that half display. You can check for the error by saving the received file and comparing the length of the received file to the original. The binary read problem will produce short files:

```
$f = fopen($v["file"], "rb");
$x = fread($f, $v["size"]);
fclose($f);
```

The string containing the file needs to be base64-encoded via **base64_encode( )** and then split into manageable lines via **chunk_split( )**, as shown next. **chunk_split( )** adds **\r\n** every 76 characters and has optional parameters to modify both the number of characters and the separator, if you wish to use the function for some other split:

```
$message_suffix .= chunk_split(base64_encode($x));
    }
```

After you attach all the attachments, attach one more boundary line. This line has a slight difference: It has an extra two dashes at the end. The extra dashes are important when forwarding a MIME-encoded mail, because the mail software has to then nest one set of MIME boundaries within another. Nesting boundaries also requires a unique boundary value, which is where the microtime part of the boundary line becomes useful:

```
$message_suffix .= $boundary . "--" . $separator;
    }
```

Building Non-MIME Headers

The following code is similar to the equivalents in the previous solutions, with a small change to use one **To** address and the standard separator string:

```
if(isset($from) and strlen($from))
    {
    $add[] = "From: " . $from;
    }
$additional = "";
if(isset($add) and is_array($add))
    {
    $additional = implode($separator, $add) . $separator;
    }
```

Sending the Mail

Now it's time to send the mail. The following code sends the message complete with the message prefix and message suffix fields. The only custom work performed on this message is the salutation. You might want to add custom information about the attachments, especially if you are sending Word documents or executable files. You might start the script by running the files through a virus checker, and then put the results into a custom message for each attachment:

```
$m = $message_prefix . "Dear " . $salutation . ",\n"
    . $message . $message_suffix;
if(mail($to, $subject, $m, $additional))
    {
    print("<br><font color=\"green\">Mail sent to "
        . htmlentities($to) . ".</font>" );
    }
else
    {
    print("<br><font color=\"red\">Mail failed to "
        . htmlentities($to) . ".</font>" );
    }
```

You can now send anything via mail. The world is waiting, but please take the journey one tiny step at a time. MIME mail is not self-healing; the smallest error can break the whole mail and leave you scratching your head for hours. Your results will vary based on the first and last links in the chain. Your sendmail program, the one that receives the mail from the PHP functions, may have a few peculiarities that will stop your mail. The last link is the recipient's mail browser, and the browser might not support the more ambitious features of MIME, so test everything first. Ask the recipient to forward the mail back to you so you can save the attachments on your machine and compare the saved files with the original files.

Verifying Mail Addresses

If you accept email addresses through a form, you want to verify that the email addresses are correct while the visitor is sitting at the screen. The only safe way guarantee a mail address is correct is to send a confirmation mail. Ask the visitor to check that the confirmation mail arrives.

What if the user cannot wait? There are a million suggestions on how to use things like regular expressions to validate mail addresses, and every one is wrong. Mail addresses are so flexible that you cannot validate the whole address by any useful means; you can only check parts of the address, and every part you check is subject to change.

I use the following list of mail addresses, good and bad, to test validation suggestions. Mail from mailing list managers, like unsubscribe addresses, is far more complex than this, but fortunately those are not normally typed into an enquiry form. The extensions .com, .net, and .org are gaining seven siblings soon, so any validation routine that includes a check for .com must include all the other possibilities. There are also at least 239 country codes to check:

```
$e[] = "";
$e[] = "peter";
$e[] = "peter@";
$e[] = "peter@petermoulding";
$e[] = "peter@petermoulding.";
$e[] = "peter@petermoulding.com";
$e[] = "x@y.z";
$e[] = "x@y.z.au";
$e[] = "Peter Moulding <peter@petermoulding.com>";
```

The following two regular expressions are suggestions for verifying email. The first appeared in a newsgroup somewhere. The second is one of a number of modifications I tried, just so I could experiment with regular expressions. (There are two types of regular expressions in PHP: POSIX and Perl style.) I found, in newsgroups, a dozen other variations of this regular expression, with just one or two characters different:

```
$f[] = "^[_a-z0-9-]+(\.[_a-z0-9-]+)*@[a-z0-9-]+(\.[a-z0-9-]+)*$";
$f[] = "^[_a-z0-9-]+(\.[_a-z0-9-]+)*@[a-z0-9-]+(\.[a-z0-9-]+)+$";
```

The results of using the two regular expressions against all the test addresses are shown in Figure 15.1. Notice that the second version is better than the first, but it is still not perfect, and neither is looking up domain types or country codes.

The following is the code used to produce the comparison. Use it to experiment with regular expressions, but do not get hung up if the result does not work reliably:

Eregi pattern	
^[_a-z0-9-]+(\.[_a-z0-9-]+)*@[a-z0-9-]+(\.[a-z0-9-]+)*$	
Email address	**Result**
	No
peter	No
peter@	No
peter@petermoulding	Ok
peter@petermoulding.	No
peter@petermoulding.com	Ok
x@y.z	Ok
x@y.z.au	Ok
Peter Moulding <peter@petermoulding.com>	No
^[_a-z0-9-]+(\.[_a-z0-9-]+)*@[a-z0-9-]+(\.[a-z0-9-]+)+$	
Email address	**Result**
	No
peter	No
peter@	No
peter@petermoulding	No
peter@petermoulding.	No
peter@petermoulding.com	Ok
x@y.z	Ok
x@y.z.au	Ok
Peter Moulding <peter@petermoulding.com>	No

Figure 15.1   Mail addresses checked by regular expressions.

```
print("<table border=\"3\"><tr>"
    . "<td><font color=\"Green\"><em>Eregi pattern</em></font></td>"
    . "<td> </td></tr>" );
while(list($k, $fv) = each($f))
    {
    print("<tr><td><font color=\"Green\">" . $fv . "</font></td>"
        . "<td> </td></tr><tr><td><em>Email address</em></td>"
        . "<td><em>Result</em></td></tr>" );
    reset($e);
    while(list($k, $ev) = each($e))
        {
        print("<tr><td>" . htmlentities($ev) . "</td>" );
        if(eregi($fv, $ev))
            {
            print("<td>Ok<td>" );
            }
        else
            {
            print("<td><font color=\"Red\">No</font></td>" );
            }
```

```
        print("</tr>" );
        }
    }
print("</table>" );
```

How can you take verification a step further? Cut the problem down into manageable chunks. Start by inserting the following code in the loop through the test mail lists. Suddenly you have a smaller problem. If **$e2** has fewer than two entries, the mail address is incomplete. If **$e2** has more than two entries, the mail address is invalid:

```
$e2 = explode("@", $ev);
```

You can now validate **$e2** as two separate problems. The part of the address on the left of the **@** symbol, the username, can be validated using fancy regular expressions, or just tested for illegal characters. With the advent of non-English mail addresses, there is probably nothing you can reject as illegal. The right-hand part of the address, the domain, can be validated with one more **explode**, as shown next:

```
$d = explode(".", $e2[1]);
```

$d contains the domain name split by parts of the name. If the last part of **$d**, the highest entry, is two characters long, it can be checked for a country code. The next entry down, or the last entry if the last entry is not a country code, can be checked for domain type, and an error produced if it is invalid. Some countries have their own domain types, so you need to vary the code for some countries.

Once you have validated the country code and type, you can perform a domain lookup, to determine if the domain exists. Another trick is to use some of the functions from Chapter 13 to request a page, or page headers, from a domain to find out if the domain is active. At this point, you are performing a lot of work, and sending a verification email looks far easier and more reliable. Just don't get talked into accepting the results of a regular expression, to the point of letting a potential customer leave your site without leaving a valid email address. Up to one in three email addresses are mistyped into forms, and few people revisit a site if their email enquiry is not returned. Grab their address, send them a message, and ask them to please check that the message arrived.

Related solution:	Found on page:
Regular Expressions	Chapter 1

Chapter 16

Networks

In Depth

Do you know the meaning of *IP address*, *host name*, and *DNS*? When you know, or want to know, you are ready to experiment with network-aware scripts and in-depth access to Internet facilities. This chapter covers the network-related functions that are not used in other chapters. Many are new, experimental, and definitely not for use on your production server.

PHP has functions to retrieve Domain Name Service (DNS) records so you can search for available domains and Web Distributed Data Exchange (WDDX) serialization so you can exchange information with remote servers. PHP is gaining a debugger, and you will need very good debugging when trying to trace problems with network interactions.

System and private logging are included because network-oriented scripts can be long-running. A script to collect articles from several content servers around the world might run for 10 minutes and be kicked off every hour. You cannot be there for exactly the right 10 minutes each hour, so logging errors (and successes) becomes critical to ongoing support and diagnosis.

Debugger

The PHP debugger is still in development, so you will need to use logging and other techniques to follow your code until the debugger is ready. I work with dozens of debuggers, and every one has high system overhead, so be selective when debugging. Just switching on a debugger usually adds to processing overhead, even without debugging a single line of code. A common reason for atrocious performance in production online systems is the remnant of a test debugging or logging system; so in your instructions for quality assurance testing, before moving the test system into production, include a step to remove all debugging code. The following are the functions for use with the debugger:

- **debugger_on( )**—Accepts an address and connects the debugger to the address. This function is still in development, so there are no examples to show you.

- **debugger_off( )**—If you want to debug the first part of your code, but not all of your code, turn off the debugger with **debugger_off( )**.

DNS and MX Records

URLs contain names, but the Internet addresses everything by numbers; so DNS translates the names to Internet numbers. The following functions help you get the raw records used for the translation:

- **checkdnsrr( )**—This Unix-only function checks if a host name or IP address appears in DNS records, and is used in the solution entitled "Checking DNS Records."

- **getmxrr( )**—Returns Mail Exchange (MX) records for an Internet host name. It performs a similar function to **checkdnsrr( )** with the MX option.

Host Names

When you need to get a host name, there are three functions to help you. The *host name* is the name of a server within a domain. For example, in the URL **www.petermoulding.com**, **www** is the name of the server and **petermoulding.com** is the name of the domain. Many modern sites have multiple servers sharing one host name, using technology invisible to the person looking up a host name. In fact, a domain name may have no distinct host names, with all activity allocated to server groups by protocol. People used to set up something like **www.petermoulding.com** to service HTTP requests, and **mail.petermoulding.com** to service mail requests. Today's site has **petermoulding.com** set up to service everything, and the Web server, or intelligent front-end router, directing mail requests to the mail servers and HTTP requests to the Web servers. The following are the functions that get a host name:

- **gethostbyaddr( )**—Accepts an IP address, and returns the name of the host that is allocated that IP address. If no host is allocated to the IP address, the function returns the IP address.

- **gethostbyname( )**—Accepts a host name, and returns the IP address of the host. If there is no host of that name, the function returns the host name unchanged.

- **gethostbynamel( )**—Accepts a host name, and returns an array of IP addresses allocated to that host. If there is no host of that name, the function returns false. A host can have multiple IP addresses during transition from one address to another or when the host is set up to provide multiple services.

IP Addresses

The Internet currently uses IP addresses based on IP version 4 (IPv4), and an address looks like this: **125.3.0.7**. IPv4 addresses are processed as 32-bit unsigned integer numbers within the Internet. IP version 6 (IPv6) is on the way, and IPv6 uses a 128-bit address featuring 8 segments of 16 bits each. IPv6 addresses look like this: **f4c0:101:10:b05:110:2c0e:11c4:a014**. PHP will have to handle 128-bit unsigned integers to cope with IPv6.

ip2long()

The **ip2long( )** function converts an IP address to the IPv4 internal network number, an integer in a range from 0 to 4 billion. The following code converts the IP address 125.3.0.17 to an internal number and displays the result:

```
print("<br>" . ip2long("125.3.0.17"));
```

The result is:

```
2097348625
```

What happens when your address is a high number? The next conversion uses an address near the top of the IP address range:

```
print("<br>" . ip2long("255.3.0.17"));
```

The following result shows a negative number because PHP treats the number as a signed 32-bit integer:

```
-16580591
```

Overriding the field format with type specifications does not help, which indicates that the number is converted to a signed integer within **ip2long( )**. The next approach is to manually convert the number back by adding the maximum possible 32-bit integer value, which is 2 to the power of 32, or 256 to the power of 4, a number slightly over 4 billion. The following code defines the number in two different ways (use whichever is easiest to remember):

```
define("fourbillion", 4294967296);
$four_billion = 256 * 256 * 256 * 256;
```

The following code adds the defined **fourbillion** to the **ip2long( )** result if the result is less than zero:

```
$x = ip2long("255.3.0.17");
if($x < 0)
    {
    $x += fourbillion;
    }
print("<br>" . $x);
```

The result is:

```
4278386705
```

To help you understand IP addresses a little better (in their dotted format, like 255.3.0.17), the following code expands the address into an integer in a different way from the previous code. Logically, each segment of the IP address (the digits between dots) is a number in the range of 0 to 255, and each segment represents 8 bits of a 32-bit number starting with the high-order bits. The following code splits the dotted-format IP address into the segments, then moves through the segments multiplying the previous value by 256, and then adds the next segment to the value:

```
$a = explode(".", "255.3.0.17");
$b = (double) 0;
while(list($k, $v) = each($a))
    {
    $b = (double) ($b * 256) + $v;
    }
print("<br>" . $b );
```

Again the result is:

```
4278386705
```

To make the last piece of code handle IPv6 addresses, replace the period in **explode( )** with a colon, and change **$b * 256** to **$b * 256 * 256**, as shown here:

```
    $b = (double) ($b * 256 * 256) + hexdec($v);
```

You will also have to convert **$v** from hexadecimal to integer, by wrapping **hexdec( )** around **$v**. For way too much information on IPv6, visit **www.ipv6.org/**.

long2ip()

The **long2ip( )** function converts an IP internal network number to a conventional IP address, as follows:

```
print("<br>" . long2ip(2097348625));
```

The result is:

```
125.3.0.17
```

Protocol Names and Numbers

Few PHP functions require protocol specifications and, of those I have used, all use protocol names. You might need a protocol number if you are buried deep in the internals of networking software or a transmission log. The following two functions let you translate between protocol names and numbers, and both functions refer to the /etc/protocols file found on Unix systems (which also means Windows and Windows NT systems cannot use the functions):

- **getprotobyname()**—Accepts a protocol name (in upper- or lowercase) and returns the protocol number, or returns false if the protocol name is not found

- **getprotobynumber()**—Accepts a protocol number and returns the protocol name, or returns false if the protocol number is not found

Service Names and Port Numbers

Occasionally you need the port number for use with a service, or the service available on a port. The following functions let you find a port number for a service, and a service name for a port.

getservbyname()

The **getservbyname()** function accepts a service name and a protocol name, and returns the port number for the combination.

getservbyport()

The **getservbyport()** function accepts a port number and a protocol name. It returns a service name, or false if the protocol number is not found. The following code hunts through ports 0 to 199 looking for services that use the User Datagram Protocol (UDP):

```
for($i = 0; $i < 200; $i++)
    {
    if($n = getservbyport($i, "udp"))
      {
      print("<br>" . $i . ": " . $n);
      }
    }
```

Sockets

The following sections cover socket functions and related functions not covered in Chapter 13.

pfsockopen()

pfsockopen() is the persistent version of **fsockopen()**. It accepts a host name, a port number, an error number field, an error string field, and a time limit (in seconds). It returns a resource id identifying a socket. For an Internet connection, the function opens a TCP socket to a port on a host (domain name or IP address). For Unix connections, the host name is the path to the socket, and the port number is 0. UDP connections can be made using the host name in the form **udp://host**.

The resource id from **pfsockopen()** can be used as a file id in file functions like **fgets()**. If there is an error, the error number will go into the error number field, and the error message will go into the error string field:

```
$hostname = "a.host.com";
$errno = 0;
$error ="";
if($socket =  pfsockopen($hostname, 80 , $errno , $error , 90))
   {
   print("<br>Socket open for " . $hostname);
   }
else
   {
   print("<br>pfsockopen error. Host: " . $hostname
      . ", error: " . $errno . ": " . $error);
   }
```

socket_get_status()

socket_get_status() can be used with **pfsockopen()**, **fsockopen()**, or **socket()**. It is best suited to **pfsockopen()** and **fsockopen()**, rather than the passive listening applications you would often use with **socket()**.

socket_get_status() accepts a socket id from **pfsockopen()** or **fsockopen()**, and returns the socket status in an array, as shown in the following code:

```
$array = socket_get_status($socket);
while(list($k, $v) = each($array))
   {
   if($k == "unread_bytes")
      {
      print("<br>Unread bytes: " . $v);
      }
   elseif($v)
```

```
        {
        print("<br>" . $k);
        }
    }
```

Three of the array values are Boolean values mainly of interest when they are true, and the fourth value is the length of data remaining in the socket, which you will want most of the time.

socket_set_blocking()

The following examples of **socket_set_blocking()** first set blocking on (true) and then set blocking off (false):

```
socket_set_blocking($socket, true);
socket_set_blocking($socket, false);
```

When blocking is on, **fgets()** and similar functions will wait for a socket to return data before control is passed back to the PHP script. Blocking is a good idea if your script does nothing but wait for data from a content server. When blocking is off, **fgets()** and similar functions return immediately, even if there is no data ready. Turn blocking off if you want your script to check for a new record, and then go away and do something else with or without a record.

Blocking confuses people, so I'll run through the options again. You set up a script on your server to get content from another server, set your script to never time out, start the script, and walk away. You want the script to run forever and do nothing but get content. Therefore, turn blocking on in the script, and the script will wait until there is data in the socket before processing the data. The script might spend hours, or all night, waiting for the next data, so you have to set all the timeouts to 10,000 or 100,000 seconds to cope.

The alternative is to leave blocking turned off so the script regains control when there is no data. Program the script to complete if there is no data. Set up **cron** or some other task-scheduling system to fire off your script at a regular time interval, like five minutes, and have your script pick up whatever data is available each time your script connects. With this approach, you have to make sure the source can buffer data for the time between connections. You also need a source that can deliver data as fast as you can read the data from the source, or else you will get continual dropouts.

socket_set_timeout()

If my math is correct, the following **socket_set_timeout()** code sets the socket timeout to 2.5 seconds:

```
socket_set_timeout($socket, 2, 500000);
```

socket_set_timeout( ) accepts a socket id, a timeout value in seconds, and a timeout value in microseconds. It adds the two timeout values together, and then sets the timeout. A microsecond is one millionth of a second, so 500,000 microseconds should be half a second.

System Log

How do you record the use of network facilities and errors? One way is to write to the system log. Check that you have access to read the system log before you begin testing. If you do have access to the system log, or if the system administrator regularly analyzes the system log, you can write to the log messages about problems connecting between sites, servers, and systems. The administrator can then tackle dropouts, timeouts, and all the other outages interrupting your scripts. On Windows NT, the syslog messages go to Windows NT's Event Log.

If you cannot access the system log, and no one is analyzing the log, you may have to write your own log using the file functions from Chapter 8. There is a short version, with little error checking, in the Immediate Solution entitled "Writing a Private Log."

define_syslog_variables()

define_syslog_variables( ) declares the constants used by the other system log functions. Thus function has to be run once before the first use of **openlog( )** or **syslog( )**.

openlog()

openlog( ) opens a connection to your system's log, but the **syslog( )** function opens the connection automatically, so **openlog( )** is not needed unless you are changing the default values. If your Web server or PHP is writing to the same system log, you might end up changing the values for them as well. I prefer to keep Apache and PHP errors out of system logs, so that leads to a problem only when your Web site is buried in many other Web sites on one server and you cannot change any configuration files.

openlog( ) accepts a string identifier, an option, and a facility parameter. The option parameter accepts **LOG_CONS** to direct messages to the system console when the system log fails, **LOG_NDELAY** to open a connection to the system log immediately, and **LOG_ODELAY**, the default, to delay opening the connection to the system log until a message is logged. Test with the facility parameter set to **LOG_USER**:

```
openlog("My test: ", LOG_NDELAY, LOG_USER);
```

syslog()

syslog( ) accepts a priority parameter and a message string. The priority is combined with the facility parameter from **openlog( )** to decide how the message will be handled. The following list shows the priorities in order. Ask your system administrator how they check each priority. If you are reporting that a remote content server is not available, perhaps they will want you to report the error at a level where the system will send a message to the administrator's pager:

- **LOG_EMERG**
- **LOG_ALERT**
- **LOG_CRIT**
- **LOG_ERR**
- **LOG_WARNING**
- **LOG_NOTICE**
- **LOG_INFO**
- **LOG_DEBUG**

The following code is a simple test to make sure **syslog( )** works and gives you the change to test your access to syslog (make sure you test each priority level that you intend to use):

```
syslog(LOG_INFO, "I am about to flood this log with messages");
```

closelog()

You do not need to use **closelog( )** to close the system log, but if you want to close the log early, just insert the following line. **closelog( )** has no parameters:

```
closelog();
```

NFS

The Network File System (NFS) version 3 is defined at **ftp://ftp.isi.edu/in-notes/rfc1813.txt**. News of the next version, version 4, is at **www.nfsv4.org/**. NFS lets Unix systems share disk partitions. If you have disk 1 on system b, you can mount disk 1 on system c as if disk 1 is part of system c. Samba is a product that lets Windows users join in the sharing.

Note that sharing files via disk partition sharing is a little more complicated. If someone has unrestricted access to your whole disk partition or a directory, they can delete everything on that partition or directory, load viruses onto the disk, and generally wreak havoc. You need to be extra careful with security.

Disk sharing can cause disk performance to acquire characteristics often referred to by technical terms like "totally whacked." Suppose you share your disk to allow another site to take a once-per-day copy of your 200-byte file containing the latest price for alluvial mud, and the person at the other site decides to grab your disk as extra workspace for a 30,000-player Quake 3 deathmatch. Transferring that much data back and forth across a network (the Quake 3 data, not the 200-byte alluvial mud file) does as much damage to your network as 300 teenagers would do to a medium-size pizza. There would not be much left for you.

NFS is safest when you control all the servers on the network and can use the disk sharing to distribute data intelligently. If the data is really needed on several servers, and all servers need frequent access, look at replication of data across the servers, with NFS used only to facilitate the replication, not the ongoing data access.

NIS

Network Information Service (NIS) lets you share information between servers. NIS used to be known as YP (Sun Yellow Pages); but Yellow Pages is a registered trademark in some countries, so Sun changed the name to NIS. To install NIS with PHP under Unix, compile PHP with **--enable-yp**.

The new NIS+ has extra added security, but it is less mature at this time, so you may have problems implementing NIS+ reliably.

Map

An NIS map contains the instructions for retrieving selected data in a specific sequence, similar to a view in a relational database. The example NIS map used in this section is **passwd.byname**, a map that retrieves passwords in the sequence of the related user's name:

```
$nis_map = "passwd.byname";
```

yp_get_default_domain()

yp_get_default_domain( ) gets the NIS domain name used by the server for NIS lookups. Every server (or host) binds to an NIS domain before using NIS. The value returned from **yp_get_default_domain( )** is the NIS domain name used in the bind, and is used in turn in the other NIS functions. If **yp_get_default_domain( )** fails, the function returns false:

```
if($nis_domain = yp_get_default_domain())
    {
    print("<br>" . $nis_domain);
    }
else
    {
print("<br>yp_get_default_domain() failed.");
    }
```

yp_master()

yp_master( ) accepts the NIS domain name and an NIS map name, and returns the machine name for the master machine serving the map:

```
if($nis_master = yp_master($nis_domain, $nis_map))
    {
    print("<br>" . $nis_master);
    }
else
    {
    print("<br>yp_order() failed to find: " . $nis_map);
    }
```

yp_order()

Once you have an NIS domain, you can get an NIS map. **yp_order( )** accepts an NIS domain name and an NIS map name, and returns the map order number. If **yp_order( )** fails to find the map, **yp_order( )** returns false:

```
if($nis_order = yp_order($nis_domain, $nis_map))
    {
    print("<br>" . $nis_order);
    }
else
    {
    print("<br>yp_order() failed to find: " . $nis_map);
    }
```

yp_match()

yp_match( ) finds an entry in an NIS domain using an NIS map and a value for the match. The match must be an exact match, or **yp_match( )** returns false:

```
$user = "fred"
if($nis_entry = yp_match($nis_domain, $nis_map, $user))
    {
    print("<br>" . $nis_entry);
    }
else
    {
    print("<br>yp_match() failed to find: " . $user);
    }
```

yp_first()

yp_first( ) finds the first entry in a map, or returns false. The entry is returned as an array containing the entry's value and key, as shown here:

```
if($entry = yp_first($nis_domain, $nis_map))
    {
    print("<br>Key: " . $entry["key"] . ", value: " . $entry["value"]);
    }
else
    {
    print("<br>yp_first() failed with map: " . $nis_map);
    }
```

yp_next()

yp_next( ) finds the first entry in a map after a key, or returns false. The key is supplied as the third parameter, and is normally the key from the previous use of **yp_next( )** or **yp_first( )**. The entry is returned as an array containing the entry's value and key, the same as from **yp_first( )**. The following code could be added immediately after the **yp_first( )** code to loop through all entries in the NIS map:

```
while($entry = yp_next($nis_domain, $nis_map, $entry["key"]))
    {
    print("<br>Key: " . $entry["key"] . ", value: " . $entry["value"]);
    }
```

WDDX

Web Distributed Data Exchange (WDDX), described at **www.openwddx.org/**, lets you convert data to an XML format for transmission across a network. You can convert integers, strings, arrays, and objects into a simple string that can be stored as a session record, placed in a database, included in an email, or transmitted via any Internet protocol. The receiving application can use WDDX to convert the data back to the original form. Converting from a data structure to a string is called *serializing*, and converting from the string back to the original data is called *deserializing*.

To install WDDX in Windows, copy c:\Program Files\php\dlls\expat.dll to c:\windows\system\. For Windows NT, copy expat.dll to c:\winnt\system32\. WDDX uses XML, and XML is compiled into the Win32 binaries. For Unix, install the expat library, supplied with the current release of Apache, and then compile PHP with **--with-xml** and **--enable-wddx**.

You do not need WDDX for sessions, because PHP has a serializer built in, but you can choose to use WDDX instead of the PHP serializer. I have not yet found a good reason for replacing the PHP serializer with WDDX, and there are several disadvantages. WDDX is dependent on an external library, WDDX produces longer session records, the WDDX XML tag structure is not optimized for session data, and WDDX is not yet GPL licensed open source, because Macromedia still holds the copyright.

WDDX Packet

The string containing WDDX serialized data is referred to as a *WDDX packet*. In theory, a WDDX packet can be embedded in a larger string and retrieved independently of the larger string. You could have a WDDX packet within a Web page, or a file, or an email, and have **wddx_deserialize()** extract the packet contents without your having to separate the packet from the rest of the string. In practice, **wddx_deserialize()** calls PHP's XML facility, which uses the expat library, and the result depends on the quality of the XML in the overall string. If the whole Web page/file/string has well-formed XML and none of it conflicts with WDDX, the WDDX packet will survive. If XML errors occur before the packet is extracted, the extraction will fail:

- **wddx_serialize_value()**—Accepts one value, and returns the value encoded in a WDDX packet within a string.
- **wddx_serialize_vars()**—Accepts one or more variables, and returns the variables encoded in a WDDX packet within a string.
- **wddx_packet_start()**—Accepts an optional comment, and returns a packet id for use in building a WDDX packet.
- **wddx_add_vars()**—Accepts a packet id and one or more variables, and adds the variables to the WDDX packet.
- **wddx_packet_end()**—Accepts a packet id, and returns a string containing the WDDX packet.
- **wddx_deserialize()**—Accepts a string containing a WDDX packet, and returns the content of the packet as an associative array.

The Immediate Solution "Serializing Data with WDDX" shows examples of all the WDDX functions and a comparison with the PHP **serialize( )** function.

CORBA

CORBA is the Common Object Request Broker Architecture (**www.corba.org/**). When you want objects to talk to each other, but do not want to keep rewriting objects to be compatible, you can rewrite each object once to talk to other objects via CORBA, and then let CORBA handle translation between objects. In theory, objects can be on different machines, but, of course, performance would be lousy and network use would be reclassified as abuse if you placed a network access in the busiest parts of applications.

ORBit is an Object Request Broker designed for the GNOME project (**http://gnome.org/**). GNOME is free open source software to create a desktop environment for UNIX. The project uses CORBA to build its component model, named Bonobo. ORBit is used as the prefix for some PHP CORBA functions; others are prefixed **satellite_**.

PHP has experimental functions to connect to CORBA objects via very new code. How experimental? Imagine a person walking up to you and asking if you would like to buy the first ever, disposable, paper parachute. The sales person assures you that no one has ever been hurt by the paper parachute. A lot of people died from hitting the ground, but none were harmed by the actual parachute.

The following function descriptions are based on current documentation, but not on live experiments with my Web site. If you like working with objects, these functions will keep you happy. For a lot of other people, the functions will be overkill. Why use something like CORBA when ODBC and other approaches offer a simpler communication between applications? CORBA should automate some types of complex communication between applications written by different vendors and can work across networks, so your human resources application can pass an employee's mortgage application to a bank's mortgage processing server, answer questions about the employee's salary, marital status, bonuses, sick leave, DNA, drug history, and everything else the bank wants, and then receive the rejection notice, all without human intervention.

Also remember that CORBA was started before XML became popular, and many business-to-business data-sharing schemes are already in place using simple XML (Chapter 20). Look at your industry's current data-sharing systems before diving into the complexities of CORBA.

orbitobject()

orbitobject( ) creates a new instance of an ORBit object using the Interoperable Object Reference (IOR) as the parameter. The following code shows how it should work, once you have your IOR defined in **$ior**:

```
$object = new orbitobject($ior);
```

orbitenum()

Once you can access your object, you need to access a reference within the object, and that is where you use **orbitenum( )**. The following code returns an enumeration id for an identifier; your CORBA object supplier will provide the list of identifiers:

```
$enumeration = new orbitenum("nameofsomething");
```

The identifiers have a longer, formal name as used in the following code. IDL is a reference to Interface Definition Language, and the **:1.0** at the end of the name gives you a form of version control:

```
$enumeration = new orbitenum("IDL:nameofsomething:1.0");
```

orbitstruct()

orbitstruct( ) returns a structure you can then use to access a remote object:

```
$structure = new orbitstruct("structure");
```

You can load the structure with values and add the structure to the object returned by **orbitobject( )**, or use the structure to get values from the object.

satellite_caught_exception()

satellite_caught_exception( ) returns true if a previous orbit function produced an error. Test the function as follows:

```
if(satellite_caught_exception())
    {
    print("Error occurred.");
    }
```

satellite_exception_id()

satellite_exception_id( ) returns a reference for the error from the object repository. It is roughly equivalent to the error number returned by other PHP error functions like **mysql_errno( )**:

```
if(satellite_caught_exception())
   {
   print("<br>" . satellite_exception_id());
   }
```

satellite_exception_value()

satellite_exception_value( ) returns a structure containing data about the latest error:

```
if(satellite_caught_exception())
   {
   $error_object = satellite_exception_value();
   }
```

The function is roughly equivalent to using **mysql_error( )** or a similar error message function. You have to make up the code to work through the error object based on the type of object that returned the error and the object vendor's documentation on error handling.

Compression

Compression increases CPU usage in order to save disk space or network transmission time. The extra CPU processing overhead of compressing and decompressing data is usually not justified for local disk storage or local network transfer, but becomes a cost saver when you have to pay money to transmit data around the world or to store data on another person's server.

What is the best type of compression? Popularity helps. If you choose a popular compression technique at your end, the receiver is more likely to have the decompression software. If not, you have to send the decompression software with the compressed data.

Speed helps too, and compression techniques aimed at networks usually have both fast compression and fast decompression times. Compression software aimed at publishing may put up with very slow compression, because the compression occurs just once if the resultant file is extra small, and lets the publishers fit more files on a CD. Publishing compression techniques also emphasize decompression speed over compression speed because their paying customers are only decompressing.

Copyright problems limit the use of some techniques, so you have to check that the compression software is copyright-free and that the techniques used within the software are copyright-free.

bzip2

bzip2 must be a new compression technique, because I had not heard of it until I found a page at **http://sources.redhat.com/bzip2/**. The source code is open source with a BSD-style license and competes with GNU-Zip.

bzcompress()

bzcompress( ) accepts a string, and returns the string compressed by the bzip2 technique:

```
$compressed = bzcompress($data);
```

The optional second parameter supplies the number of blocks to use for compression in a range of 1 through 9; the default is 4. The optional third parameter supplies a value called **workfactor** in a range of 0 through 250; the default is 30.There is little information on the effect of the **workfactor** and no immediate reason to change either the number of blocks or the **workfactor**.

bzdecompress()

bzdecompress( ) accepts a string and returns the string decompressed by the bzip2 technique:

```
$data = bzcompress($compressed);
```

The optional second parameter tells bzip2 to use less memory and run at half speed (which is generally not a good idea).

bzopen()

bzopen( ) works much the same as **fopen( )**, discussed in Chapter 8, and accepts a file name to open for reading or writing. The second parameter, **r** or **w**, decides if the file will be read or written. The function returns a resource id, also called a file id, for use in other bz functions:

```
if($file = bzopen("test.nz", "r"))
    {
    print("<br>bzopen worked.");
    }
else
    {
    print("<br>bzopen failed.");
    }
```

bzread()

bzread() accepts a file id and an optional length to read, and returns data from the file. The length defaults to 1,024 bytes:

```
$data = bzread($file);
```

bzwrite()

bzwrite() accepts a file id, data, and optional length, and writes the data to the file. If length is specified, **bzwrite()** writes just the specified length and then stops. **bzwrite()** would not work with the example file opened with **bzopen()** in the previous section, because the file was opened for read access:

```
if(!bzwrite($file, $data))
    {
    print("<br>bzwrite failed.");
    }
```

bzclose()

bzclose() works much the same as **fclose()**; it accepts a file id and closes the file:

```
if(!bzclose($file))
    {
    print("<br>bzclose failed.");
    }
```

bzflush()

bzflush() accepts a file id, and forces the write of any data queued for a write to the file:

```
if(!bzflush($file))
    {
    print("<br>bzflush failed.");
    }
```

bzerrno()

bzerrno() accepts a file id and returns an error number, if there was an error on the last access to the file:

```
print("<br>bzerrno: " . bzerrno());
```

bzerrstr()

bzerrstr( ) accepts a file id and returns an error message, if there was an error on the last access to the file:

```
print("<br>bzerrstr: " . bzerrstr());
```

bzerror()

bzerror( ) accepts a file id and returns an array containing an error number and an error string, if there was an error on the last access to the file:

```
$array = bzerror();
print("<br>bz error  " . $array["errno"] . ", " . $array["errstr"]);
```

gzip

gzip is the open source compression software from GNU (**www.gnu.org/software/gzip/gzip.html**) that started the trend to use .gz compressed files. PHP gets the same functionality from zlib (**www.gzip.org/zlib/**). zlib seems to be taking over, with gzip and other applications moving to use the zlib library. Both work well and let you read zipped files (.zip) as well as GZ (.gz) files. PHP's GZ functions can also be used on strings prior to transmission across a network.

To activate zlib in Windows NT and Windows 2000, stop Apache, copy c:/Program Files/php/extensions/php_ zlib.dll to c:/winnt/system32/, remove the semicolon from the following line in php.ini, and then start Apache:

```
;extension=php_zlib.dll
```

If you use PHP as CGI, you do not have to restart your Web server. For other versions of Windows, copy c:\Program Files\php\extensions\php_zlib.dll to c:\windows\system\.

If you have the latest PHP, try using **fopen( )** as shown next:

```
$file = fopen("zlib:/test.gz", "r");
```

The PHP file functions now accept **zlib:** as a file path prefix, and use the zlib compression automatically.

The Immediate Solution "Compressing Data with zlib" shows examples of zlib use, and shows a quick test using a standard file function with the **zlib:** option.

Immediate Solutions

Checking DNS Records

You can check the existence of a domain in a number of ways. Checking the DNS records tells you that a domain is defined, but does not tell you if a server is online in that domain. The best way to check if a server is online is to use a network or file function to open a file on the server. Checking DNS records is more useful to find out if a domain name is already registered.

The following example uses **checkdnsrr( )** to find if anyone has registered the site **yahoo.com**:

```
if(checkdnsrr("yahoo.com"))
    {
    print("<br>checkdnsrr() worked.");
    }
else
    {
    print("<br>checkdnsrr() failed.");
    }
```

The result in Windows and Windows NT follows:

```
Warning: checkdnsrr() is not supported in this PHP build
```

One of the Windows modules is missing the code to check DNS records, so this function does not work. The following result, from Unix, says that someone has already registered that domain:

```
checkdnsrr() worked.
```

What happens if you check a name like **yahxxxx.com**? You get the following result, which you would expect:

```
checkdnsrr() failed.
```

Now run the test yourself using **yah00.com**. Did Yahoo! think to register a domain name that is so easy to type accidentally, given that the 0 key is close to the o key and looks similar?

16. Networks

checkdnsrr( ) accepts a second parameter, **type**, which defaults to a value of **MX**. The first parameter can also be an IP address instead of a domain or host name. The following code runs through a list of the possible types, in array **$type**, and a list of test host/domain names, in array **$host**, to show you what results you can expect:

```
$host[] = "yahoo.com";
$host[] = "216.115.108.243";
$type[] = "MX";
$type[] = "A";
$type[] = "NS";
$type[] = "SOA";
$type[] = "PTR";
$type[] = "CNAME";
$type[] = "ANY";
print("<table border=\"3\">");
print("<tr><td> </td><td>" . $host[0] . "</td><td>" . $host[1]
   . "</td></tr>");
while(list($kt, $t) = each($type))
   {
   print("<tr><td>" . $t . "</td>");
   reset($host);
   while(list($kh, $h) = each($host))
      {
      print("<td>");
      if(checkdnsrr($h, $t))
         {
         print("checkdnsrr() worked." );
         }
      else
         {
         print("checkdnsrr() failed.");
         }
      print("</td>");
      }
   print("</tr>");
   }
print("</table>");
```

Figure 16.1 shows you the results from the test. Note that there were no successes with the IP address. Yahoo has hundreds of servers and few would have their IP addresses registered.

	yahoo.com	216.115.108.243
MX	checkdnsrr() worked.	checkdnsrr() failed.
A	checkdnsrr() worked.	checkdnsrr() failed.
NS	checkdnsrr() worked.	checkdnsrr() failed.
SOA	checkdnsrr() worked.	checkdnsrr() failed.
PTR	checkdnsrr() failed.	checkdnsrr() failed.
CNAME	checkdnsrr() failed.	checkdnsrr() failed.
ANY	checkdnsrr() worked.	checkdnsrr() failed.

Figure 16.1   Testing domains with **checkdnsrr()**.

Getting MX Records

MX records are the Internet's way of redirecting traffic. Imagine going from A to B by train, say from Hornsby to Sydney. Sydney has a station on that line named Wynyard; to get to Sydney, you have to go to Wynyard. Simple.

The Internet equivalent uses MX records. If you want traffic to go to server B but server B is not directly connected to the Internet, and B is indirectly connected through C, you can set up an MX record to direct traffic for B to C so C can pass the traffic to B.

getmxrr( ) accepts a host name and returns an array the MX entries for that host. The following code loops through a list of host names, one valid and one invalid. The code receives an array from each pass through **getmxrr( )**, and lists the contents of each array. **getmxrr( )** returns false if the host name is not found:

```
$host[] = "yahoo.com";
$host[] = "yahxxxx.com";
while(list($kh, $vh) = each($host))
   {
   $array = array();
   if(getmxrr($vh, $array))
      {
      while(list($k, $v) = each($array))
         {
         print("<br>getmxrr(" . $vh . "): " . $v);
         }
      }
   else
      {
      print("<br>getmxrr(" . $vh . ") failed.");
      }
   }
```

The results are shown next, four for **yahoo.com**, and a failure for the invalid domain name. Note the MX records are pointing to mail servers. MX records are often used to point to mail servers, and the MX record values are used with SMTP:

```
getmxrr(yahoo.com): mx2.mail.yahoo.com
getmxrr(yahoo.com): mx3.mail.yahoo.com
getmxrr(yahoo.com): mta-v18.mail.yahoo.com
getmxrr(yahoo.com): mx1.mail.yahoo.com
getmxrr(yahxxxx.com) failed.
```

Getting the Host Name

A *host name* is the name of a server within a domain, and the functions in this solution all help you find the name of a host.

Getting the Host Name by Address

The following code takes a list of IP addresses and looks up the host name for each:

```
$ip[] = "216.115.108.243";
$ip[] = "1.115.18.23";
while(list($k, $v) = each($ip))
   {
   if($host = gethostbyaddr($v))
      {
      print("<br>gethostbyaddr(\"" . $v . "\"): " . $host);
      }
   else
      {
      print("<br>gethostbyaddr\"" . $v . "\") failed.");
      }
   }
```

The first address is an IP address returned by a ping of **yahoo.com**, so that address should have a valid host name. The second address was made up using a prefix allocated in the early days of the Internet, but not allocated to a host.

The result shows a successful lookup plus a failed lookup that just returns the IP address:

```
gethostbyaddr("216.115.108.243"): img3.yahoo.com
gethostbyaddr("1.115.18.23"): 1.115.18.23
```

Note that you would not type in "img3" as a server name when accessing Yahoo! You type in just "yahoo.com", and Yahoo's load-balancing software, or hardware, allocates your request to the appropriate server.

Getting the Host Address by Name

The following code looks up two host names via **gethostbyname()**, and returns their IP address:

```
$name[] = "img3.yahoo.com";
$name[] = "xyzyx.yahoo.com";
while(list($k, $v) = each($name))
    {
    if($address = gethostbyname($v))
        {
        print("<br>gethostbyname(\"" . $v . "\"): " . $address);
        }
    else
        {
        print("<br>gethostbyname\"" . $v . "\") failed.");
        }
    }
```

The first name is a name from the previous test, so you would expect it to work. The second is a name that does not yet exist at Yahoo!, even though they have many servers.

NOTE: *When I first wrote the "Getting the Host Address by Name" code, I tried to reuse **$host** as an array, using **$host** where I now have **$name**. PHP complained about using a string as an array, so I changed the name. The alternative is to use **unset($host)**.*

The result is shown here:

```
gethostbyname("img3.yahoo.com"): 216.115.108.243
gethostbyname("xyzyx.yahoo.com"): xyzyx.yahoo.com
```

Like **gethostbyaddr()**, **gethostbyname()** simply returns the input if the function cannot find the right answer.

A better solution would be to return false on failure, and that is what the next code does. The user-defined function **getip()** simply compares the value returned by **gethostbyname()** to the input and returns false if the values are the same. The value from **gethostbyname()** is returned, of course, if the value is different from the input. This modification to the function of **gethostbyname()** is valuable if your script has to highlight lookup failures:

```
$name[] = "img3.yahoo.com";
$name[] = "xyzyx.yahoo.com";
function getip($name)
   {
   $address = gethostbyname($name);
   if($address === $name)
      {
      return(false);
      }
   else
      {
      return($address);
      }
   }
while(list($k, $v) = each($name))
   {
   if($address = getip($v))
      {
      print("<br>gethostbyname(\"" . $v . "\"): " . $address);
      }
   else
      {
      print("<br>gethostbyname\"" . $v . "\") failed.");
      }
   }
```

The result is as follows:

```
gethostbyname("img3.yahoo.com"): 216.115.108.243
gethostbyname"xyzyx.yahoo.com") failed.
```

The **getip( )** structure can be applied to the other **gethost** functions, and similar functions, to make them return false when required. A few older functions return zero as a valid value and -1 as an indication of error, which is useful in PHP3, but not needed in PHP4 because -1 can be replaced with false, and PHP4 can distinguish false from 0 with the new comparison operator **===**. You could use the **getip( )**-style wrapper to convert a few of the older functions to return false instead of –1 on error.

Getting a Host Address List by Name

If you are looking up the IP addresses for a domain name, rather than a server, or if you are looking up the IP addresses for a multihomed server, you will often get more than one IP address. **gethostbynamel( )** is the function to get you that

IP address list. **gethostbynamel( )** accepts a host name or a domain name, and returns an array of IP addresses. The function also returns false on failure, which is usually more useful than the result returned by **gethostbyname( )**. That's enough to make me use **gethostbynamel( )** in preference to **gethostbyname( )** even when I expect only one IP address.

The following code processes three names, the two used in the last example, plus **yahoo.com**, a domain name sure to return more than one address:

```
set_time_limit(100);
$site[] = "img3.yahoo.com";
$site[] = "xyzyx.yahoo.com";
$site[] = "yahoo.com";
while(list($k, $v) = each($site))
    {
    if($list = gethostbynamel($v))
        {
        while(list($ks, $vs) = each($list))
            {
            print("<br>gethostbynamel(\"" . $v . "\"): " . $vs);
            }
        }
    else
        {
        print("<br>gethostbynamel\"" . $v . "\") failed.");
        }
    }
```

The code is similar to the code used for **gethostbyname( )**, and is expanded because the output of **gethostbynamel( )** is an array. The extra lookups made the script run out of time, so I added **set_time_limit( )** to give the script extra time.

The result is shown next, with two IP addresses returned for **yahoo.com**. Note that the failed result returned false instead of just passing the input through to the output:

```
gethostbynamel("img3.yahoo.com"): 216.115.108.243
gethostbynamel"xyzyx.yahoo.com") failed.
gethostbynamel("yahoo.com"): 216.115.108.243
gethostbynamel("yahoo.com"): 216.115.108.245
```

Listing Protocol Numbers

When you want to know the protocol number for a protocol, just run up a page with the following code. The code loops through numbers from 0 to 200, printing any protocol names found:

```
for($i = 0; $i < 200; $i++)
    {
    if($n = getprotobynumber($i))
        {
        print("<br>" . $i . ": " . $n);
        }
    }
```

The result is shown here:

```
0: ip
1: icmp
2: igmp
3: ggp
4: ipencap
5: st
6: tcp
8: egp
12: pup
17: udp
20: hmp
22: xns-idp
27: rdp
29: iso-tp4
36: xtp
37: ddp
39: idpr-cmtp
41: ipv6
43: ipv6-route
44: ipv6-frag
50: ipv6-crypt
51: ipv6-auth
58: ipv6-icmp
59: ipv6-nonxt
60: ipv6-opts
73: rspf
81: vmtp
89: ospf
94: ipip
98: encap
```

You can do the reverse, finding protocol numbers from protocol names, using the following code. This example tests the one protocol name in both lower- and uppercase to make sure both work:

```
$protocol[] = "tcp";
$protocol[] = "TCP";
while(list($k, $v) = each($protocol))
   {
   if($n = getprotobyname($v))
      {
      print("<br>getprotobyname(" . $v . "): " . $n);
      }
   else
      {
      print("<br>getprotobyname(" . $v . ") failed.");
      }
   }
```

The result follows, and shows that the function **getprotobyname( )** ignores case:

```
getprotobyname(tcp): 6
getprotobyname(TCP): 6
```

Serializing Data with WDDX

The WDDX functions give you two approaches to serializing data: a single-step process, or a three-step packet building process. For a single-step process, use either **wddx_serialize_value( )** or **wddx_serialize_vars( )**. When you want to serialize a large set of data into one string, use the three-step process: Create a WDDX packet using **wddx_packet_start( )**, add variables to the packet using **wddx_add_vars( )**, and close the packet and produce the string using **wddx_packet_end( )**.

wddx_serialize_value()

The following code serializes a string, an integer, and a floating-point number, which are different field types in PHP. All three are serialized and then printed, with the print passing the result string through **htmlentities( )**, because the result string contains XML, and your browser would attempt to interpret the XML tags:

```
$value[] = "a string \" <>";
$value[] = 99;
$value[] = 99.99;
```

```
while(list($k, $v) = each($value))
   {
   $string = wddx_serialize_value($v);
   print("<br>" . $v . "<br>   "
      . htmlentities($string));
   }
```

The result, shown here, demonstrates that WDDX produces a huge overhead of tags and treats both types of numbers the same. When your script decodes a WDDX string, PHP has to guess what type of number is stored between the **<number>** and **</number>** tags:

```
a string <>
   <wddxPacket version='1.0'><header/><data><string>a string
   " &lt;&gt;</string></data></wddxPacket>
99
   <wddxPacket version='1.0'><header/><data><number>99</number>
   </data></wddxPacket>
99.99
   <wddxPacket version='1.0'><header/><data><number>99.99</number>
   </data></wddxPacket>
```

wddx_deserialize()

How do you get the data back from **wddx_serialize_value( )**? Add the following code to decode the last string produced in the **wddx_serialize_value( )** example:

```
print("<br>" . htmlentities(wddx_deserialize($string)));
```

The result is the last value in the variable **$string**, shown here:

```
99.99
```

serialize()

How does PHP's serialize stack up against the WDDX serialize function? The following code runs the same array of data through the PHP **serialize( )** function:

```
reset($value);
while(list($k, $v) = each($value))
   {
   $string = serialize($v);
   print("<br>" . $v . "<br>   "
      . htmlentities($string));
   }
```

The following result shows two advantages of the PHP **serialize( )** function: The resultant string takes up less space, and the function differentiates between an integer, **i:**, and a floating-point number (double), **d:**. If you only plan to serialize and deserialize within PHP, PHP's functions are the better choice:

```
a string " <>
   s:13:"a string " <>";
99
   i:99;
99.99
   d:99.99;
```

wddx_serialize_vars()

wddx_serialize_vars( ) has one difference from **wddx_serialize_values( )**: **wddx_serialize_vars( )** encodes the variable complete with variable name, so the deserialize function restores the variable, rather than just returning the variable's value. The following code serializes one variable, the string from the earlier WDDX examples:

```
$a = "a string \" <>";
$string = wddx_serialize_vars("a");
print("<br>" . htmlentities($string) );
```

Note that you have to pass the variable name as a string. If you provided the variable instead, **wddx_serialize_vars($a)**, the function would look at the value in **$a**, and try to use the value as a variable name. It would find nothing, serialize nothing, and not produce an error.

The result is:

```
<wddxPacket version='1.0'><header/><data><struct><var name='a'>
<string>a string "&lt;&gt;</string></var></struct></data></wddxPacket>
```

The result shows the value within **<string>** tags, as in the **wddx_serialize_ value( )** example, but this time with **<var>** tags wrapped around the **<string>** tags, and **<struct>** tags wrapped around the **<var>** tags.

The next test includes several variables, including an array. **wddx_serialize_ vars( )** accepts an unlimited number of parameters, so you can serialize all the variables you need in one string:

```
$b = 99;
$c = 99.99;
```

```
$value = array($b, $c);
$string = wddx_serialize_vars("b", "c", "value");
print("<br>" . htmlentities($string) );
```

The result, shown next, has one set of **<struct>** tags containing several sets of **<var>** tags. The **<var>** tag containing the array contains **<array>** tags to identify the variable as an array:

```
<wddxPacket version='1.0'><header/><data><struct><var name='b'>
<number>99</number></var><var name='c'><number>99.99</number></var>
<var name='value'><array length='2'><number>99</number>
<number>99.99</number></array></var></struct></data></wddxPacket>
```

wddx_deserialize() with Variables

To get variables back from **wddx_serialize_vars( )**, add the following code to decode the previous **wddx_serialize_vars( )** example:

```
var_dump(wddx_deserialize($string));
```

The result is shown next and demonstrates that **wddx_deserialize( )** returns an array containing the original variables within the array:

```
array(3) { ["b"]=> int(99) ["c"]=> float(99.99) ["value"]=> array(2)
  { [0]=> int(99) [1]=> float(99.99) } }
```

You would have to write code to separate the original variables into discrete variables. Clearly **wddx_serialize_vars( )** would be best suited to serializing a single variable or an array that you can then name during the deserialization.

wddx_packet_start()

When you want to serialize a large set of data, create a WDDX packet using **wddx_packet_start( )**, as shown here:

```
$packet = wddx_packet_start("Another test");
```

The only parameter is an optional comment inserted into the packet. The result is a resource id, the packet id, that is used in **wddx_add_vars( )** and **wddx_packet_end( )** to identify the packet.

wddx_add_vars()

Add all your variables to a WDDX packet using **wddx_add_vars( )**, as shown here:

```
$a = "a string \" <>";
wddx_add_vars($packet, "a");
$b = 99;
$c = 99.99;
$value = array($b, $c);
wddx_add_vars($packet, "b", "c", "value");
```

The first parameter for **wddx_add_vars( )** is the packet id from **wddx_packet_start( )**. You can then specify as many variable names as you like, similar to **wddx_serialize_vars( )**.

wddx_packet_end()

When you finish adding variables to the WDDX packet using **wddx_add_vars( )**, convert the packet to a serialized string using **wddx_packet_end( )**, as follows (the example code also prints the string so you can see the result):

```
$string = wddx_packet_end($packet);
print("<br>" . htmlentities($string));
```

The next example is the string from **wddx_packet_end( )**, which demonstrates that the packet-building process builds the same packet you would have received had you collected all the variables into one **wddx_serialize_vars( )**:

```
<wddxPacket version='1.0'><header><comment>Another test</comment>
</header><data><struct><var name='a'>
<string>a string " &lt;&gt;</string></var><var name='b'>
<number>99</number></var><var name='c'><number>99.99</number></var>
<var name='value'><array length='2'><number>99</number>
<number>99.99</number></array></var></struct></data></wddxPacket>
```

The only extra feature is the optional comment; the comment is not returned by **wddx_deserialize( )**, it so serves little purpose outside of testing.

Compressing Data with zlib

The gz functions include both file functions and raw data functions. This Solution starts from the raw data functions, so you can compress for encapsulation within a message or database, and then expands to full file compression, so you can reduce the size of files before transmission across a network.

The following code takes a string, compresses the string using **gzcompress( )**, and prints the result:

```
$compressed = gzcompress("Clarinet Quintet K.581 - 1st Movement");
print("<br>" . htmlentities($compressed));
```

Here is the result to give you a quick idea what the compression ratio is and how you can use the compressed data:

```
xœsÎI,ÊÌK-Q,ÍÌ+Ò_z|† º †Å% _ùe©ı©y%
```

Clearly the compressed string is not much different in size from the original, mainly because of the compression overhead. Compression of a long string would show savings because the space saved would become greater than the compression overhead. Note also that the character set includes characters that would not survive transmission via email or a similar transmission method. The compressed string would have to be base64 encoded, and that would destroy most of the savings achieved through compression.

To prove the compression is easily reversible, here is the code to uncompress string **$compressed**:

```
$uncompressed = gzuncompress($compressed);
print("<br>" . htmlentities($uncompressed));
```

Here is the result of the uncompression, a string identical to the original test string:

```
Clarinet Quintet K.581 - 1st Movement
```

zlib also supports deflation, something similar to compression, but not as reliable, as shown in the following quick test:

```
$deflated = gzdeflate("Clarinet Quintet K.581 - 1st Movement");
print("<br>" . htmlentities($deflated));
```

The code deflates the same string used for **gzcompress()**. **gzdeflate()** accepts an optional second parameter where you can specify a compression level from 0 (no compression) to 9 (maximum compression). The higher levels of compression use more CPU time.

The result, shown here, is similar to the compressed string from **gzcompress()**:

```
sÎI,ÊÌK-Q,ÍÌ+Ò_z|† º †Å% _ùe©ı©y%
```

The following code should inflate the deflated string back to the original and print the result:

```
$inflated = gzinflate($deflated);
print("<br>" . htmlentities($inflated));
```

gzinflate() has an optional second parameter that accepts a length, and produces a warning message if the data exceeds the length, presumably to stop overruns because of inflation errors, or data that deflates extremely well and wants to inflate back to a size exceeding available memory.

The result was the following error message:

```
Warning: gzinflate: buffer error
```

The error occurred using a development edition of PHP 4.0.7, so it may be fixed by the time you try **gzinflate()**.

The following code tests the zlib file functions:

```
$data = "Clarinet Quintet K.581 - 1st Movement";
$gz = "./test.zip";
if($file = gzopen($gz, "w"))
   {
   gzwrite($file, $data);
   gzclose($file);
   if($file = gzopen($gz, "r"))
      {
      print("<br>File size: " . filesize(realpath($gz)));
      $text = gzread($file, 100000);
      print("<br>" . $gz . " contained:<br>" . htmlentities($text));
      gzclose($file);
      }
   else
      {
      print("<br>gzopen failed for " . $gz );
      }
   }
else
   {
   print("<br>gzopen failed for " . $gz);
   }
```

The code creates a new compressed file with **gzopen()**, writes data to the file with **gzwrite()**, closes the file with **gzclose()**, opens the file for read with **gzopen()**, reads the data with **gzread()**, and finally displays the data for comparison to the original. The code also contains **filesize()** to get the size of the GZ file for comparison.

The results are as follows:

```
File size: 58
./test.zip contained:
Clarinet Quintet K.581 - 1st Movement
```

The 37 bytes of test data produced a 58-byte file. The data read back in is the same as the date written out.

Read about file functions in Chapter 8, and just substitute the equivalent zlib function. You can also experiment using the file functions with the **zlib:** path prefix to save using the zlib functions. Either way, you can reduce the size of some files before moving the files across the network, particularly large text-based files, using zlib compression.

Writing a Private Log

This solution is for those occasions when you cannot access system logs, a common occurrence when your Web site is hosted by an ISP. The following code assumes you are logging to file log.txt on partition t:/, which is a throw-away test partition on my Windows NT workstation:

```
function privatelog($message)
   {
   if($file = fopen("t:/log.txt", "a"))
      {
      fwrite($file, $message . "\n");
      fclose($file);
      }
   else
      {
      return(false);
      }
   }
```

Your Windows machine usually has a directory called c:\temporary files\, and your ISP's Unix hosting server has a directory for your Web site with a name like /usr/home/petermoulding/.

The code opens the log file (and creates a new one if the file does not exist), appends the message, and closes the file to guarantee the message is written before a subsequent error can terminate your script. If you are testing tricky code that blows up your script, write a log record before and after each doubtful line of code. The **\n** is to make the text break to a new line when you view the log file in a text editor; change the formatting to suit your preferred display method. If you wanted to make the function perfect, you could prefix the message with the date and time using **microtime( )** from Chapter 2.

Related solution:	*Found on page:*
rand(), **srand()**, and **microtime()**	69

Chapter 17

Objects

In Depth

Objects are the next step up from functions, and they also use functions, so you should read Chapter 10 before reading this chapter.

Objects are code encapsulated in a way that lets you split up large development projects into groups of smaller projects, and reuse code from other projects. If you invent a really good calendar for one site, you can package the calendar in an object and use the object on other sites.

My favorite comparisons are mobile telephones (called cell phones in some countries) in a car. Car manufacturers design cars with a standard-size hole in the dashboard for a radio or CD player, but not for a mobile phone. If you want great reception, hands-free operation, and no annoying cables everywhere, you have to buy a car kit to suit your phone, get the car kit fitted, and throw the whole kit away when you upgrade to a new phone. Objects are the equivalent in software.

A PHP object can be used in any PHP script in the world, but every calendar object has a different *interface,* so you cannot just unplug one calendar object and plug in another. A *class* is a prototype for an object, and contains all the code to assemble an object, so objects of the same class have the same interface, and objects of different classes have different interfaces even if the objects are designed to perform the same function. An object's interface is the collection of *properties* and *methods* within the object. You assemble an object from a class using the keyword **new** and a special function in the class called a *constructor*.

Classes

When the factory builds a mobile phone, it starts with a plan that says "put part A there," "put part B next to part A," and "glue part C on top of A and B." A *class* is exactly that for objects—a class contains all the parts for the object (static code that goes into an object) and instructions for building the object (dynamic code that modifies the object's parts when the object is built).

The following code is the world's shortest class. It does nothing except create a container, named **a**, for code. This class is the cardboard box you fill with parts and instructions for building an object of type **a**:

```
class a
    {
    }
```

new

Here is how you use class **a** to create an object, in this case named **$b**, using the special keyword **new**:

```
$b = new a;
```

Like a Variable

All shiny and new/Like a variable/Constructed for the very first time (Madonna singing about object-oriented programming)

You treat an object almost like a variable: You can compare objects just like any other PHP resource, even if the comparison does not make sense, and you can serialize objects for storing in session records, even though it is a bad idea to store objects in session records.

Why does the comparison of objects often not make sense? One advantage of objects over variables is the ability to manage multiple variables as one object, with each variable becoming a property. Comparisons of like properties make sense, just as you could compare the color of two suitcases. The comparison of two objects is more difficult, just as is the problem of comparing suitcases by an overall characteristic like weight. The lightest suitcase seems like the best selection because you can easily carry it, but it may be empty. The heaviest suitcase might be filled with lead, whereas the middle-weight suitcase is filled with diamonds. To usefully compare objects, you need to evaluate which are the relevant properties.

Why is it dangerous to serialize objects? PHP throws away code and serializes all data when you pass an object to **serialize( )** or register the object with PHP sessions. The object might contain 20 bytes of useful information and 300,000 bytes of working variables that are not needed in a session record. If the object is coded to detect serialization and throw away the 300,000 bytes of junk, you can safely serialize the object but otherwise just extract the needed value and serialize that value without the object. PHP's facility to help objects optimize themselves for serialization is new, so few off-the-shelf classes will generate optimizing objects.

The following code creates object **$c** with the same class as **$b**, compares **$c** to **$b**, and returns the message that **c equals b**:

```
$c = new a;
if($c === $b)
   {
   print("<br>c equals b.");
```

17. Objects

641

```
    }
else
    {
    print("<br>c does not equal b.");
    }
```

In real-life code, creating two objects from the same class may not produce identical objects, because the objects may configure themselves differently during creation. You need to look through their *constructor* code, described in the "Constructor" section of the chapter, to find out the differences between two new objects of the same class.

You cannot create an object from another object via the **new** command. The following code does not work:

```
$d = new $c;
```

Here are the error messages from that command:

```
Warning: Object to string conversion
Fatal error: Cannot instantiate non-existent class: object
```

You can copy objects and delete objects just like normal variables, as shown in the following two code lines:

```
$d = $c;
unset($c);
```

When you copy an object, you get a copy of the object as it exists at the time of the copy, which is usually not the same as creating an object with **new**. Object creation via **new**, or *instantiation* if you want to impress the object-oriented crowd, creates a new set of variables within an object, and may change the variables, or the code, based on date, time, or the existence of an object of the same class.

stdClass

stdClass is a special class definition reserved for use by PHP4, so do not use **stdClass** in your code.

——

In PHP4, the double-underscore (__) is reserved as a special function name prefix. Two special functions, __**sleep()** and __**wakeup()**, are already in use, and the developers reserve the right to make up other functions starting with __ at any time.

__sleep

__**sleep( )** is a special function within PHP4 to help you serialize objects. Why would you want to do that when PHP already has the **serialize( )** function? The **serialize( )** function (see Chapter 16) is used primarily to save things in session records, and session records are not good places for objects. If you are stuck with software that requires an object to go in the session record, you can use __**sleep( )** within the object's class to make the object safer to **serialize( )**.

When **serialize( )** is about to serialize an object, **serialize( )** looks for and executes __**sleep( )** within the object. __**sleep( )** can close files and database connections, and returns an array of variables to be serialized so anything not identified in __**sleep( )** does not take up space in the serialization string.

If **serialize( )** runs automatically after the completion of the script, as is the default for sessions, __**sleep( )** runs too late to use **print( )** or echo; therefore, all messages have to be transmitted via logs or some other means. Chapter 7 shows how to log errors without using **print( )**.

Large variables hanging around in objects is also a bad idea. The variables should be **unset( )** when no longer needed. If you read a set of rows from a database into an array, and then make several passes through the array to build elements of your page, **unset( )** the array immediately after the last pass. Your object may not know when the rest of the script will finish with the data—for example, if several methods use the array and a script can use the methods in any order—you are stuck with creating a __**sleep( )** function to delete the array before the object is serialized. You may also need __**wakeup( )** to re-create the array when the object is unserialized.

There is an example of __**sleep( )** in the Immediate Solution "Saving Objects in Sessions and Using __**sleep( )**."

__wakeup

__**wakeup( )** is a special function within PHP4 reserved for a function reserved to reset an object when the object is retrieved from a session record. When the **unserialize( )** function unserializes an object, usually from a session record, the object may need to read files or run SQL against databases to re-create or refresh data within the object. __**wakeup( )** is the special function for that purpose. When **unserialize( )** unserializes an object, **unserialize( )** looks in the object for __**wakeup( )** and executes the function.

Suppose your object supplies exchange rates for display on a Web page. The visitor expects current exchange rates on each new page, but the person writing the script simply registers the object as a session variable, rather than creating the object from scratch on each page. It is left to the object to read the latest exchange rates for each new page, which means reading the exchange rates each time the object is unserialized.

Personally, I would not register the object. Once the object is registered as a session variable, the object is serialized and unserialized for every page, even if it is not used. If exchange rates are displayed on only one page within your site, and your visitors pass that page only a few times among many page views, the object will be unserialized many more times than the data is used on a page.

Another approach is to serialize the object but leave the data out of **__sleep( )** and **__wakeup( )**. Only retrieve the data when a function first requests the data. If several functions use the exchange rate array, have each function check for the existence of the exchange rate array and retrieve the exchange rate data if the array is missing. By deferring data retrieval until the data is needed, the data retrieval will not occur on pages that do not need the data. Although **__sleep( )** make sense to clean out unused data before serializing an object, automatic re-creation of the data via **__wakeup( )** can produce unnecessary processing overhead.

You need to remember one more thing about unserializing objects: **serialize( )** stores the variables from the object, plus the name of the class, but not the object's code. When **unserialize( )** unserializes the object, **unserialize( )** attempts to read the object's code from the class definition, so the class definition has to be included in your script before **unserialize( )**. Because the most useful place to restore session information is right at the start of a script, the class definition is best included via **require( )** at the head of your script. Your script could blow up if the code in the class is changed but is used with an existing object. That is another reason not to store objects in session records.

Properties

A *property* of an object is a value you can access with the object name followed by a dash and a greater-than (**->**), followed by the property name. If object **$b** has a property of **length**, the property is named **$b->length**, and you treat **$b->length** as a variable you can read or set. The following line of code attempts to print the property **length** from the object **$b**, created earlier, even though there are no properties in **$b**:

```
print("<br>" . $b->length);
```

The result is this error:

```
Warning: Undefined property: length
```

What happens if you just add **$length = 29;** to the middle of class **$a**? You get the following error message, an indication that raw PHP code does not work the same way within class definitions (if you try **$length;** you get the same error):

```
Parse error: parse error, expecting 'T_OLD_FUNCTION' or 'T_FUNCTION'
or 'T_VAR' or ''}"
```

var

The correct code to define a property in a class is shown next, complete with the keyword **var** to indicate you are declaring a variable. **var** creates the space for the variable, and the addition of the variable value creates a property you can display:

```
class a
    {
    var $length = 29;
    }
```

Constructor

In PHP4, defining a property with **var** works only with constants. The next step is to add a function called a *constructor* function, which is identified by having the same name as the class. A constructor function can do anything to variables and executes at the time you create an object from a class, which means every object created from a class can be different from every other object made from that class.

PHP4 constructors behave differently than PHP3 constructors, and this chapter is written for PHP4. The best of the prewritten open source PHP code available for download is PHP4-compatible, so you are unlikely to run into problems with PHP3 code.

There are no destructor functions in PHP. If your constructor function opens a new file for writing, you need a matching destructor function to close the file. You could add a destructor function to a class and call the destructor manually before destroying an object manually. If you want an automatic destructor, you could create the destructor function and register the destructor as a shutdown function, as shown in the "Methods" section.

$this

Inside a class, **$this** is a reference to *this object*. **$this->x** is a reference to the variable named **x** within this object. Using **$this** gets around a simple problem: The person writing the class does not know what the object will be called when the object is created from the class. **$this** is the special name that remains constant within an object no matter what the object is named.

The following code defines class **k**, variable **$start** within class **k**, and the constructor function **k** within class **k**:

```
class k
    {
    var $start;
    function k()
        {
        $m = explode(" ", microtime());
        $this->start = $m[1] . substr($m[0], 1);
        }
    }
$1 = new k;
print("<br>" . $1->start );
```

Within function **k**, **$this** is a reference to the object created from class **k**. **$this->start** is a reference to the variable named **start** within this object. The code then creates object **$1** from class **k**, and prints **$1->start**. Within **$1**, **$this** refers to **$1**, and **$this->start** means **$1->start**.

The result follows:

```
995012077.37157100
```

microtime( ) is explained in Chapter 2 and returns the same as **time( )**, plus the time in microseconds. The result represents the number of seconds and microseconds since January 1, 1970. You could use **$1->start** to help time a script or to time code within objects created from class **k**.

Property names are case-sensitive. The following code tries to access **$1->start** by the name **$1->Start**:

```
print("<br>" . $1->Start);
```

The result is the following warning message:

```
Warning: Undefined property: Start
```

Methods

Methods are functions within a class that perform actions within an object. All functions defined within a class are available as methods, and you need to consider what will happen if someone uses a method in a random manner.

The following class is an extension of the previous class **k**. This version includes function **start()** to print **$this->start**. **start()** then becomes a method of every object created from class **k**:

```
class k
    {
    var $start;
    function k()
        {
        $m = explode(" ", microtime());
        $this->start = $m[1] . substr($m[0], 1);
        }
    function start()
        {
        print("<br>Start: " . $this->start);
        }
    }
```

The following test creates object **$q** from class **k** and executes method **$q->start()**. Note that methods are differentiated from properties by the **()** at the end of the method name and are, to all intents, ordinary PHP functions with a slightly more complex name:

```
$q = new k;
$q->start();
```

The result is:

```
Start: 995085968.38211500
```

Method names, like function names, are not case-sensitive. The following line tests a change of case for the name:

```
$q->Start();
```

The result follows:

```
Start: 995085968.38211500
```

To demonstrate that class methods are just like any other function, replace **function start()** in the previous class definition with the following **function start**:

```
function start($text)
    {
    print("<br>" . $text . ": " . $this->start);
    }
```

Test the change with the following code:

```
$q = new k;
$q->start("Time");
```

The result is shown here:

```
Time: 995085968.38211500
```

Methods work like any other functions and, like other functions, need global statements to access external variables, with one exception: External variables within the same object are accessed via **$this->**.

Destructor

There are no destructor functions in PHP, so you have to add a destructor function to a class and use the function as a method before destroying the object. The following class **p** contains a constructor **p** that records a start time, and a destructor **destroy( )** that calculates and prints the time elapsed since the start time:

```
class p
    {
    var $start;
    function p()
        {
        $m = explode(" ", microtime());
        $this->start = $m[1] . substr($m[0], 1);
        }
            function destroy()
        {
        $m = explode(" ", microtime());
        $end = $m[1] . substr($m[0], 1);
        $duration = $end - $this->start;
        print("<br>Duration: " . $duration);
        }
    }
```

The following code defines the new object **$q** from class **p**, executes the destructor function **$q->destroy( )**, and then unsets **$q**. This manual destructor is the best option in PHP when you want a destructor function to manually destroy a function:

```
$q = new p;
$q->destroy();
unset($q);
```

The result is shown next (and is accurate to only six decimal places, a problem with floating-point arithmetic):

```
Duration: 0.00010406970977783
```

If you wanted to automate the destruction process a little, you could invent the function **destroy( )** as follows:

```
function destroy($object)
    {
    eval("global \$" . $object . ";");
    ${$object}->destroy();
    unset($GLOBALS[$object]);
    }
```

The three lines of code in the function access the object through a global statement, execute the **destroy( )** function in the object, and then unset the object. **${$object}** is an alternative notation to writing an **eval( )** for the method execution. Unsetting **$GLOBALS** is necessary when using **unset( )** within a function, because a straight unset of the object, or a global variable, does not work within a function.

The test code is shown next:

```
$q = new p;
destroy("q");
```

The code creates the object **$q**, and then destroys **$q** with the **destroy( )** function. The result is a line of print showing a duration.

What if you want the destructor to run automatically at the end of your script without manual intervention? There is one option that works, if your destructor does not use **print( )** or **echo**, and that is **register_shutdown_function( )**. Shutdown functions are run at the end of the script after the last output is sent to the browser, and just prior to destroying all variables. You can use shutdown functions to close files, end transactions, log messages to files or databases, and clean up anything that will not be cleaned up by PHP. The code shown next attempts to register **$q->destroy( )**. **$q->destroy( )** will run at shutdown but will not complete because the function attempts to print:

```
register_shutdown_function("q->destroy");
```

Extending Classes

What if you want to use an existing class but just add an extra method or make some slight change? If there are no existing objects based on that class, you can change the class. Once the existing class is in use in your Web site or elsewhere, the safest approach is to maintain the original class untouched and define a new class based on the existing class. This approach works well when the existing class is supplied by someone else and they supply updates, because you can replace their class without having to reapply your changes.

Adding Functions

Start with the following class **p** used earlier in the chapter. The class will be extended with an extra method that returns **$start** with formatting:

```
class p
    {
    var $start;
    function p()
        {
        $m = explode(" ", microtime());
        $this->start = $m[1] . substr($m[0], 1);
        }
    }
```

The following code extends class **p** into class **q** and adds function **start_time( )** to display the start time with a formatted hour, minute, and second:

```
class q extends p
    {
    function start_time()
        {
        $m = explode(" ", $this->start);
        print("<br>" . date("H:i:s", $m[0]) . "." . $m[1] );
        }
    }
```

Test the extended class with the following code to create an object **$r** with the class and then execute the method **$r->start_time( )**:

```
$r = new q;
$r->start_time();
```

The result follows:

```
17:09:09.10376000
```

Constructors in Extended Classes

Note that the class extension from **p** to **q** left function **p( )** as the constructor for the class. In PHP3, that would not happen; PHP3 would look for function **q( )** in class **q**, and then stop. PHP4 looks for function **q( )** in class **q**, and if **q( )** is missing, PHP4 looks for **p( )** in class **p**. The following code extends class **p** as class **s**, and includes the constructor function **s( )**. **s( )** formats and prints **$this->start**:

```
class s extends p
    {
    function s()
       {
       $m = explode(".", $this->start);
       print("<br>" . date("H:i:s", $m[0]) . "." . $m[1] );
       }
    }
```

Test the extended class with the following code to create object **$t**:

```
$t = new s;
```

The result follows and shows that function **s( )** did work. It did print something, but the variable **$this->start** contained nothing because the constructor **p( )** in class **p** did not execute:

```
10:00:00.
```

To get both constructors from both classes working when the object is created, you have to execute the original class constructor from the new class constructor. The following code extends class **p** into class **s** the same as the previous class extension, and it has one extra line to execute constructor function **p( )** before the code in constructor function **s( )**:

```
class s extends p
    {
    function s()
       {
       $this->p();
       $m = explode(".", $this->start);
       print("<br>" . date("H:i:s", $m[0]) . "." . $m[1]);
       }
    }
```

Test the extended class with the following code to create object **$t**:

```
$t = new s;
```

The result follows, and shows that both functions **s( )** and **p( )** executed. The result is the nicely formatted time you received from some previous tests:

```
17:09:09.10376000
```

Replacing Functions

When you extend a class and want to replace the code within a function, just define in the new class a new function with the same name as the old function. This is the only time you can replace a function; once PHP has compiled the function into an object, there is no way to replace a function or the code within a function.

The following code is a simple class definition, class **a**, that includes function **print_time( )** to provide a time print method:

```
class a
    {
    var $start;
    function a()
        {
        $m = explode(" ", microtime());
        $this->start = $m[1] . substr($m[0], 1);
        }
    function print_time()
        {
        global $helpnet;
        $m = explode(".", $this->start);
        print("<br>The time is " . date("H:i:s.", $m[0]) . $m[1]);
        }
    }
```

The next code extends class **a** as class **b** and replaces function **print_time( )** with slightly different code:

```
class b extends a
    {
    function print_time()
        {
        global $helpnet;
        $m = explode(".", $this->start);
        print("<br>Replacement time " . date("H:i:s.", $m[0]) . $m[1]);
        }
    }
```

The following code tests the function replacement in class **b** by creating object **$c** from **b** and then executing the method **$c->print_time( )** to see which function is used:

```
$c = new b;
$c->print_time( );
```

The result follows, and shows that the function **print_time( )** in class **b** replaced function **print_time( )** in class **a**:

```
Replacement time 08:24:16.16906100
```

Deleting Functions

There are times when you want to delete a function when extending a class. However, PHP does not allow the deletion of functions, and that applies when extending classes. Instead, you can replace a function with a new function that does nothing, so the function effectively becomes inactive.

Multiple Extensions

There are times when you want to extend an extended class. PHP allows the extending of an extended class with full inheritance of methods and properties. You cannot have multiple inheritance—that is, inheritance from two classes at once—but you can have class **u** extend class **s**, where **s** is an extension of class **p**, as shown next. The following test code extends **s** as **u** and adds a new constructor named **u( )**:

```
class u extends s
   {
   function u()
      {
      $this->s();
      $m = explode(".", $this->start);
      print(date(" a", $m[0]) );
      }
   }
```

Test the extended class with the following code to create object **$v**:

```
$v = new u;
```

The result follows, and shows that class **u** inherited and used both function **s()** from class **s** and function **p()** from class **p**. The result is the formatted time from class **s** with an added A.M./P.M. indicator.

```
17:09:09.10376000 pm
```

::

The double colon (::) is a weird operator that does not appear to have an obvious use. It lets you execute a function from a class without creating an object from the class. Because there is no object from the class, **$this** is not valid within the function and no class variables are valid. That means that the most you can use is a generic function, like a data-formatting function, and those functions should not be in classes anyway.

The following code is a generic function, **time_format()**, to return a formatted **microtime()** for use anywhere in your Web site. Suppose **time_format()** is buried within class **p** but you want to use the function without creating an object from class **p**:

```
function time_format($time)
    {
    $m = explode(".", $time);
    return(date("H:i:s", $m[0]) . "." . $m[1]);
    }
```

The function can be accessed as follows, with the class name **p** followed by ::, and then the function name **time_format()**:

```
print("<br>" . p::time_format(time()));
```

If your classes do contain neat and useful functions that can stand alone, consider moving the functions outside the class definitions so the functions can be used by everyone as regular functions.

parent

parent is a keyword that makes sense and suddenly makes the :: operator useful. **parent** lets you refer to the parent class of an extended class without naming the parent class. When you extend class **p** to create class **s**, code in class **s** can refer to functions in class **p** as **parent**. If you rename class **p** to **p2**, the only place you have to rename **p** is in the class statement **s extends p;**. You no longer have to rename **$p** in **$p->()**; each time you rename class **p**; instead you make a one-off change to **parent::p();**.

Software Distribution and Documentation

When you distribute an application or an application extension, you can distribute a block of raw code as an include file, a set of functions, or an object. The object offers the most code isolation, but the most complex interface. Think about the complexities of your code before choosing an object as a package.

Raw code provides the most opportunities for people to learn about code, so it is a good way to package small selections of code for educational examples. Raw code has the least integrity because people will make changes to it, so raw code is the least useful when you need to provide ongoing support.

Functions accept many inputs and easily produce one output, so they suit some kinds of code. Functions are easy to explain because you can show a table of input values and the exact output for each input combination. If you cannot explain a function with a simple state table, you most likely have an overly complex function that needs a rethink. When you try to build a function with multiple outputs, you get real problems explaining the function's actions and testing the function. Objects suit the packaging of code where there are multiple outputs or complex state requirements.

Multiple Data Items and State

If there are many data items to carry from one use of a function to another, consider using an object and storing the data in the object. The data values represent the state of the processing between uses of the code. If the data can be fully stored in the object or cleanly divided between the object and the surrounding code, the object can control the data within the object. The items within the object can then be relied on to carry information from one code use to the next.

If you have an object **$n** created from class **news**, which manages newsgroups, you can safely read the list of available newsgroups when the object is created, and refer to that list in subsequent uses of the object. The object contains the list and controls additions, deletions, and refreshes from the news server. The object does not have to verify the list each time the object uses the list. If you then add a list of subscribed groups to class **news**, object **$n** will also control the subscriptions.

Imagine adding the subscription list as a list external to object **$n**. Every time you send a request to **$n** based on an item in the subscription list, the code in **$n** would have to verify the request is valid. Every refresh to the newsgroup list in **$n** would leave the subscription list out of sync.

The best solution would be to extend class **news** with a new class that incorporates the subscription list and related code so the subscription list can be locked in sync with the newsgroup list. An object should control all data that affects the state of the object.

Multiple Outputs

When you write code that creates 22 types of output, you can use 22 functions, or a far smaller number of objects. Objects provide the best savings when you minimize the number of objects the end user has to learn, but they are a waste if you incorporate several unrelated items of data in the one object. Objects become hard to explain when the object's properties are unrelated and there are many methods but many of the methods perform duplicate actions on unrelated data.

If you created an object to create a whole Web page but then returned the page as lots of small segments, like separate paragraphs and headings, and demanded 75 different inputs, each through a different method, most people would throw out the object. A better approach would be to create a nested structure where objects or functions create items such as headings, and an overall object or function brings the whole lot together.

I would approach the development of a page-creation class by starting with individual formatting functions, such as paragraphs, bringing them together into the sections of a page, and then writing an overall function to return the finished page. I might not get around to making the functions into a class because there is only one output, the formatted page.

Try writing the documentation for the object before writing the code. List the inputs, list the outputs, and list what is stored from one use of the object to the next. Use an object when there is more than one output, or where many data items can live within the object.

Immediate Solutions

Saving Objects in Sessions and Using __sleep()

This solution sets up a primitive session tracking object to demonstrate the use of objects and **__sleep()**. You could develop this object into a custom visitor tracking system complete with custom presentation to the visitor based on their browser. If the visitor then logged on as a customer, you would want some of the same information and some presentation based on their profile. That suggests three objects working together.

The first object would trace their session, when and where the visitor entered your site, where they visited, what they typed into query and search screens, and where they exited. If they logged on, the trace would show where they logged on and where they logged off, if they did log off.

The second object would be used when the visitor first hit the site, and would decide if the page presentation should be altered based on the visitor's browser configuration. The best way to arrange your pages for specific browser configurations is to start with browser object detection, something that requires a couple of smart pages working together and JavaScript to test the browser. This example skips the intelligent approach, the second object, and the page configuration and settles for just recording the browser's agent string for later analysis.

The third object would kick in when someone logs in, and handle information from his or her user profile, such as language preference overrides. If you are going to add things like user profiles and language preferences later, read Chapter 12 and then enhance this object to record **HTTP_ACCEPT_LANGUAGE** and other relevant fields for analysis. When you are ready to add extra languages, you will be able to see which languages are most popular.

This object starts with the class **session_logger**:

```
class session_logger
    {
    var $agent;
    var $log_file;
    var $messages;
    var $remote;
```

```
            function __sleep()
               {
            if(isset($this->messages) and strlen($this->messages))
                  {
               if($file = fopen($this->log_file, "a"))
                     {
                  fwrite($file, $this->messages);
                  fclose($file);
                  }
                  }
            return(array("agent", "log_file", "remote"));
               }
         function add_message($text)
               {
            if(!isset($this->messages))
                  {
               $this->messages = "";
                  }
            $m = explode(" ", microtime());
            $this->messages .= session_id() . " " . date("Y-m-d H:i:s", $m[1])
               . substr($m[0], 1) . " " . $text . "\n";
               }
         function session_logger()
               {
            if(!isset($this->agent))
                  {
               $this->log_file = "t:/sessionlog.txt";
               $n = "HTTP_USER_AGENT";
               $this->agent = getenv($n);
               $this->add_message($n . " " . $this->agent);
                  }
            if(!isset($this->remote))
                  {
               $n = "REMOTE_HOST";
               $this->remote = getenv($n);
               if(!isset($remote) or !strlen($remote))
                     {
                  $n = "REMOTE_ADDR";
                  $this->remote = getenv($n);
                     }
               $this->add_message($n . " " . $this->remote);
                  }
               }
            }
```

session_logger contains the variables **$agent**, **$log_file**, **$messages**, and **$remote**, with **$messages** required only within one script and the three other fields required across the whole session. This class has to be included before the session code starts so the class will be readable before the session code retrieves an object based on this class. That means you cannot automatically start the session using the **session.auto_start** setting in php.ini.

$agent receives the **HTTP_USER_AGENT** field when the visitor enters the first page. You could add decoding of the agent field to reduce page displays to the capability of the browser, such as suppressing images for text-based browsers.

$log_file contains the name of the log file, passes the name from instance to instance, and makes the name available as a property so test code can display the log file.

$messages receives messages for the log via the **add_message()** function, available as the **$this->add_message()** method, and supplies **__sleep()** with the messages for transfer to the log at the end of the script. It is not retained from page to page because the contents are in the log.

$remote collects the visitor's remote host name or IP address on their first entry, and retains the value from page to page in case you want to use the host name for something. In real life you would, on first entry, check if the host name indicates a country or some other significant factor, save the significant factor, and drop **$remote**. The IP address might be useful if you give preferential treatment to another site or server, and again you would determine the privilege on first entry and retain the privilege status rather than the IP address.

The function **__sleep()** is activated by the session code when serializing variables at the end of a script, and returns an array containing the name of the variables to serialize. Because **__sleep()** runs once per script at the end of every script, you can use it to output all log messages in one efficient hit to the log file. Note that script failures can prevent the script from ending in a normal session termination, which means that serialization does not occur and **__sleep()** is not activated, so no messages are written to the log file. If you want critical messages processed, make your code perform an immediate write as shown in other examples in this book. Chapter 8 describes file functions.

add_message() adds one message to **$this->message**, complete with a prefix including the session id, date, and time to the nearest millisecond so you can time parts of your code. If you are testing new code, write lots of messages and check the time required to process new parts of your code. As the code becomes stable, pull out the pure timing messages and keep the code indicating abnormalities.

17. Objects

Related solutions:	Found on page:
Error Logging	269
Writing a Private Log	636

You need to include the class before you can create an object, or before the session code can decode an object of that class, so wrap the class code in PHP tags, place the class code in a file named session_logger.html, place the file in a directory in your include path, and place the following **require( )** at the top of your script, followed by the **session_start( )**. On first entry to your script, the class is not used until an object is defined. On subsequent entries to your script, the class definition will be read by the session start code:

```
require("session_logger.html");
session_start();
```

Your page will look something like the following page with the class code, the session start, an include of the code common to all your pages, and the code specific to the individual page. Once you are happy with the class code and session start, incorporate both in the common HTML file:

```
<?php
require("session_logger.html");
session_start();
require("common.html");
// Processing code here
?>
```

To get an object created and into the session record, use the following code to test for the existence of object **$session_log** and create **$session_log** from class **session_logger** if the object does not exist:

```
if(isset($session_log))
    {
    print("<br>Agent from session record: " . $session_log->agent );
    $session_log->add_message("message");
    }
else
    {
    $session_log = new session_logger;
    print("<br>Agent: " . $session_log->agent );
    print("<br>Remote: " . $session_log->remote );
    session_register("session_log");
    }
```

To help you test the **session_log** object, the code prints some of the object's properties after creation, and one property on those occasions when the object exists from the session record. **session_log** creates a message automatically when defined, because of the code in the class's constructor function **session_logger( )**, and a message is added manually via **$session_log-> add _message( )** on subsequent entries so you can see the progress of the object.

On the first entry, you will see the following messages printed to confirm the object is working. Of course the *Agent* string will contain the agent string from your browser, and the IP address or host name will be the IP address or host name for your Host or proxy server.

```
Agent: Mozilla/4.77 [en] (WinNT; U)
Remote: 192.168.0.100
```

On subsequent entries to your script, you will see the following message to indicate that your script picked up object **$session_log** from the session record:

```
Agent from session record: Mozilla/4.77 [en] (WinNT; U)
```

To track the contents of the log file, add the following code to the bottom of your test page (remember that on each page this will display the log file as of the end of the previous script):

```
if(file_exists($session_log->log_file))
   {
   $lines = file($session_log->log_file);
   while(list($k, $v) = each($lines))
      {
      print("<br>" . htmlentities($v));
      }
   }
```

Your log file will look something like the following display (the lines have been wrapped here to fit the book's layout):

```
652ad60c11ab3d7457e56c39aaa5c7fa 2001-07-16 17:16:01.74908700
    HTTP_USER_AGENT Mozilla/4.77 [en] (WinNT; U)
652ad60c11ab3d7457e56c39aaa5c7fa 2001-07-16 17:16:01.74932100
    REMOTE_ADDR 192.168.0.100
652ad60c11ab3d7457e56c39aaa5c7fa 2001-07-16 17:17:12.47705700 message
652ad60c11ab3d7457e56c39aaa5c7fa 2001-07-16 17:19:37.90405100 message
```

17. Objects

I would like to say this is a sexy technique for testing code, but *sexy* is not always an acceptable adjective for programming in some cultures, so I will use the word *sophisticated*. You could do everything shown in this solution using functions and an array, but then you would have to ensure several functions and one array all have names unique within your script. By using an object, you need only two unique names: the class name and the object name. References to variables (properties) and functions (methods) are a little more tedious because of the longer names, but it is easier to make the names unique.

You can now add anything you like to the code, and the code will work with hosted sites because it does not need access to system logs or anything fancy. It really only needs the latest PHP because **__sleep( )** was added in about PHP 4.0.6. (Personally, I think you should always use the latest stable PHP and look for a host ISP that considers the latest PHP far more important than Perl or anything else except Apache and security.)

Using Object Functions

Object functions let you use classes, object methods, and properties based on information available when your script is active. You might have to open a file, read a sample of the data from the file, and then decide which class will be used to create the right processing object for the file. These functions let you build a dynamic environment and check all classes, methods, and properties before use.

call_user_method()

There are times when you want to execute a method of an object, but the object has many methods, or there are many objects, and you want to build the object-method name dynamically. **call_user_method( )** accepts both the method name and object name as strings so your can build both from data.

As a simple HTML example, you might have a heading-level counter to decide if your are displaying heading level 1, 2, or 5, and you might have a formatting object with a method for each heading. You may then want to add the heading counter to the end of the method. The following code shows manual use of a formatting object with two levels of headings:

```
$format->heading1("Portugal");
$format->heading2("Algarve");
```

Now set up the same headings in an automated fashion, perhaps with data read from a database into an array. Simulate the process with the following quick array:

```
$headings[1] = "Portugal";
$headings[2] = "Algarve";
```

Now pump the array through the formatting object using a **while** loop, **list()**, **each()**, and **call_user_method()**. **call_user_method()** accepts the method name as a string, the object name as a string, and any number of parameters as required by the method:

```
while(list($k, $v) = each($headings))
    {
    call_user_method("heading" . $k, "format", $v);
    }
```

call_user_method_array()

call_user_method_array() is a slight modification of **call_user_method()** added in PHP 4.0.5, so this example builds on the previous example. Imagine a method that accepts multiple parameters in one hit similar to the following example:

```
$format->heading("Portugal", "Algarve");
```

call_user_method() could use decidedly boring code like the following to handle the situation, but think of what the code would look like with six levels of headings:

```
if(count($headings) == 2)
    {
    call_user_method("heading", "format", $headings[1], $headings[2]);
    }
elseif(count($headings) == 1)
    {
    call_user_method("heading", "format", $headings[1]);
    }
```

The following is a simpler way of handling multiple parameters, provided they are in an array:

```
call_user_method_array("heading", "format", $headings);
```

class_exists()

class_exists() is an alternative to **include_once()** when used with classes. **class_exists()** accepts the name of a class, and returns true when the class is defined or false when the class is not defined. You can use this code to create a class when the class does not exist in your script. The simplest way to create a class is to include the class from a file, via **include( )**, make sure the class is not included twice by testing for the class with **class_exists( )**, and include the class only if it does not exist. That used to make sense, but now there is **include_once( )** to ensure inclusions happen just once. That is a simpler way of ensuring your class definition files are included just once.

The following code includes class **session_logger** from file session_logger.html:

```
include("session_logger.html");
```

The following code includes class **session_logger** just once from file session_logger.html, by checking if class **session_logger** exists before inclusion:

```
if(!class_exists("session_logger "))
    {
    include("session_logger.html");
    }
```

The following code includes class **session_logger** just once from file session_logger.html by using **include_once( )**:

```
include_once("session_logger.html");
```

get_class()

If you have an object, and want to know the object's class, use the following code. The example uses the object **session_log** created from class **session_logger** created in the "**class_exists( )**" section:

```
print("<br>" . get_class("session_log"));
```

The result is shown next:

```
session_logger
```

get_class_methods()

When you want to know all the methods for a class or object, use **get_class_methods( )**. Feed the function a class name or, as of PHP 4.0.6, an object name, and the function will return an array of method names. The following code example feeds **get_class_methods( )** the name of the class from the previous solution. The code would work equally well if you fed in **session_log** (the object name from the "**get_class**" section):

```
$list = get_class_methods("session_logger");
while(list($k, $v) = each($list))
   {
   print("<br>" . $v);
   }
```

The result is the following list of method names:

```
__sleep
add_message
session_logger
```

get_class_vars()

When you want to know all the properties for a class, use **get_class_vars( )**.
Feed the function a class name, and the function will return an associative array
of variables and values, representing all the properties of the class. The array
contains only initialized variables, so test it with your classes to see what it returns.

The following code example feeds **get_class_vars( )** the name of the class from
the previous solution and prints the resulting array. The code accepts one level of
array within a value:

```
$list = get_class_vars("session_logger");
while(list($k, $v) = each($list))
   {
   if(is_array())
      {
      while(list($k2, $v2) = each($v))
         {
         print("<br>" . $k . ": " . $k2 . ": " . $v2);
         }
      }
   else
      {
      print("<br>" . $k . ": " . $v);
      }
   }
```

When the code runs against **session_logger**, the code produces no output, because none of the variables are initialized. To prove the output works, change **var
$messages;** to **var $messages = "test text";** and run the code again. You will
get the following output:

```
messages: test text
```

get_declared_classes()

To find out the names of all the classes in your script, use **get_declared_classes( )**, as shown in the following code, which gets an array from the function and prints the array:

```
$list = get_declared_classes();
while(list($k, $v) = each($list))
   {
   print("<br>" . $v);
   }
```

The results are shown for the script used to test class **session_logger**:

```
stdClass
OverloadedTestClass
Directory
COM
VARIANT
session_logger
```

stdClass and **OverloadedTestClass** were introduced as special classes in PHP 4.0.1pl2. **COM** is defined because I have the COM extension installed, and the other two are mysteries I have yet to research, but are probably from some of the other extensions currently loaded.

get_object_vars()

The **get_object_vars( )** function works like **get_class_vars( )**, but it works for an object. The following code feeds an object to **get_object_vars( )** and prints all the variable name/value pairs:

```
$list = get_object_vars($session_log);
while(list($k, $v) = each($list))
   {
   if(is_array())
      {
      while(list($k2, $v2) = each($v))
         {
         print("<br>" . $k . ": " . $k2 . ": " . $v2);
         }
      }
   else
      {
      print("<br>" . $k . ": " . $v);
      }
   }
```

An alternative print mechanism, if you do not care how your print looks, is **print_r( )**. **print_r( )** dumps a variable or array straight to the browser with minimal formatting:

```
print_r(get_object_vars($session_log));
```

get_parent_class()

get_parent_class( ) accepts the name of a class and returns the name of the class's parent class. It also accepts the name of an object and returns the name of the class that is the parent of the class used to build the object. The following code prints the class name returned from object **$session_log**:

```
print("<br>" . get_parent_class($session_log));
```

is_subclass_of()

Suppose class **a** is extended to class **b**, and class **b** is extended to make class **session_logger**. You want to know if object **$session_log** is built on class **a**. Use the following code to feed an object and a class name to **is_subclass_of( )**, and get back true if class **a** is a superclass of object **$session_log**, or false if not:

```
if(is_subclass_of($session_log, "a"))
    {
    print("<br>True");
    }
```

method_exists()

Does object **$session_log** contain method **print_list**? You can test for a method in a class with **method_exists( )**, as shown in the following code:

```
$method = "print_list";
if(method_exists($session_log, $method))
    {
    print("<br>Method " . $method . " exists.");
    }
else
    {
    print("<br>Method " . $method . " does not exist.");
    }
```

In this case, **print_list** does not exist.

Customizing Your Web Page with an Object

When you are ready to customize your Web pages using information from the visitor's browser or items discussed in Chapter 12, the following class generates an object you can use as the base for your special code:

```
class agent
   {
   var $agent;
   var $browser;
   var $cookies = false;
   var $frames = false;
   var $images = false;
   var $language;
   var $version = 0;
   var $words;
   function agent()
      {
      $this->agent = getenv("HTTP_USER_AGENT");
      $this->language = getenv("HTTP_ACCEPT_LANGUAGE");
      $this->decode_agent($this->agent);
      $this->get_language($this->language);
      global $HTTP_COOKIE_VARS;
      if(isset($HTTP_COOKIE_VARS))
         {
         $this->cookies = true;
         }
      }
   function decode_agent($agent)
      {
      $x = explode(" ", $agent);
      $y = explode("/", $x[0]);
      switch($y[0])
         {
         case "Mozilla":
            $this->browser = $y[0];
            $this->version = $y[1];
            break;
         default:
         }
      if(substr($x[1], 0, 1) == "[" and substr($x[1], -1) == "]")
         {
         if(!strlen($this->language))
            {
            $this->language = substr($x[1], 1, -1);
```

```
                }
            }
        }
    function get_language($language)
        {
        if(file_exists("./words" . $language . ".html"))
            {
            include_once("./words" . $language . ".html");
            $this->words = $words;
            }
        }
    function local($word)
        {
        if($this->words and isset($this->words[$word]))
            {
            $word = $this->words[$word];
            }
        return($word);
        }
    }
```

The class **agent** is named agent because it starts by reading the browser's agent string. The agent string is available to every script, and could change during the life of a session if the visitor changes a browser setting such as language.

Class **agent** starts with a list of variables including **$cookies**, **$language**, and **$words**. Some default to empty, and some have default settings. Why have two approaches? Consider how you will test a variable, and if you want a default value. In the case of cookies, it would be useful just to test for the option to use cookies with **if($this->cookies)**, which means the variable must exist and must be set to true or false. (If you have PHP warnings turned off, you can be less accurate, but that will also let through more typographical errors.)

Function **agent()** executes when the class is turned into an object and grabs the browser's agent string. If there is an incoming cookie, PHP stores the cookie in **$HTTP_COOKIE_VARS**, so a simple test for the variable's existence means that the browser is accepting cookies.

Function **decode_agent()** is a prototype for code to pull relevant information from the agent string so you can make decisions based on the type of browser. The code checks for a language field in the agent string, and sets **$this->language** based on the language field. The language value in **HTTP_ACCEPT_LANGUAGE** overrides anything found in the agent string. This code could go in **agent()**, but that would make life harder when you want to replace the **agent** decode code with more detailed code. By keeping the decode

code in a separate function, you can easily extend class **agent** into a new class, and replace **decode_agent( )** at the same time.

You also have the option of using **get_browser( )** to decode the agent string into an object full of theoretical information about a browser. **get_browser( )** could be easily applied when extending class **agent**. If you use the overhead of **get_browser( )**, then perform the decode once and save the results in a session record.

Related solution:	Found on page:
Browser-Based Code	272

Function **get_language( )** is another block of code you could place in **agent( )**, but it is better left separate so you can replace the function when the class is extended. **get_language( )** reads language information from include files. My first change to a site that uses lots of dynamic text and many languages would be to replace **get_language( )** with a database read. One other advantage of having this function separate is that, for testing, you can change the value in **$language**, and execute **get_language( )** again to get the language you need for testing.

Function **local( )** translates words or phrases from English to another language using a table loaded by **get_language( )**. English would be replaced by your local language, the language used on your Web pages, and the translation would be made to whatever local language is indicated by the browser.

To test the class, use the following code to create an object from the class:

```
$a = new agent;
```

Test the object with the following code:

```
print("<br>Agent: " . $a->agent);
if($a->cookies)
    {
    print("<br>Cookies true.");
    }
if($a->language)
    {
    print("<br>Language: " . $a->language);
    }
```

The **agent** string is always there, so just print the string. The **cookies** variable is used only to indicate whether cookies are used, so the code tests if the variable is true and prints a message. Language translation occurs only if a language is requested, so use of the language field includes a test to see if the field is set.

The following output is the result of testing the code so far:

```
Agent: Mozilla/4.77 [en] (WinNT; U)
Cookies true.
Language: en
```

The next test is to change the language. All you need do is add the following code to the end of the script to force function **get_language( )** to read a new language translation file:

```
$a->get_language("de");
```

Test the language change by modifying the previous test prints as follows:

```
print("<br>" . $a->local("agent") . ": " . $a->agent);
if($a->cookies)
    {
    print("<br>" . $a->local("cookies") . " " . $a->local("true") . ".");
    }
if($a->language)
    {
    print("<br>" . $a->local("language") . ": " . $a->language);
    }
```

Each text string is wrapped in function **$a->local( )** to return the text in the local language. The test files used for this page contain only words, so the phrase *cookies true* is split into two words with each separately translated. In a production system, you would have whole phrases entered in a translation system to ensure accuracy of meaning.

The result follows (if the German translation is wrong, blame the Babel Fish translation facility at AltaVista):

```
mittel: Mozilla/4.77 [en] (WinNT; U)
plätzchen zutreffend.
sprache: en
```

What does the translation file look like? The following file is loaded for German and contains just a few test words translated by the Babel Fish software (Babel Fish translates *cookies true.* to one phrase, and *cookies true* to a different phrase, which is a good illustration of problems with computer translation):

```
<?php
$words["agent"] = "mittel";
```

```
$words["cookies"] = "plätzchen";
$words["dog"] = "hund";
$words["true"] = "zutreffend";
$words["language"] = "sprache";
?>
```

You could arrange the translation a lot of different ways, including using XML files and databases. The important thing is to arrange the structure of the object so you can make changes without rewriting the original structure. Class **agent** has sufficient structure that you can replace parts like the translation when extending the class.

Reading the News

To read information from newsgroups, you need the names of news servers, a list of the newsgroups on each server, a list of articles in a newsgroup, a way of reading the article headings, and the article bodies, including attachments. If it all sounds too complicated, don't worry; you do not have to tackle everything from scratch.

News is based on the Network News Transfer Protocol (NNTP), described in RFC 977 (**www.faqs.org/rfcs/rfc977.html**), and a set of RFCs shared with mail. Some news servers can be easily accessed with PHP's IMAP functions, but the IMAP functions do not let you see what is happening behind the scenes so you can understand news. You can use PHP's experimental socket functions to access news servers, but they are overkill. PHP's ordinary **fsockopen( )** and normal file functions (see Chapter 8) are sufficient to read newsgroups and learn about NNTP, so **fsockopen( )** is used in this solution.

You can access any news server that is public, but you will find real problems with some servers because of the server's configuration or software. You can download PHP objects for handling mail and news, but you may not understand the complexities of their code until you experiment with a little code of your own. You can download whole news applications, but again you have the problem of understanding the code if you want to make any changes or strike a problem news server.

The code in this solution lets you start off with simple reads from news servers, then from newsgroups, and then progress to news items. Attachments are not covered here, because attachments are stored with MIME encoding, and MIME is described in Chapter 15.

The following code defines class **news** to read a list of newsgroups into **$groups** from a list of servers in **$servers**. To make testing practical, I will use just one server at a time and limit the newsgroups to just 10 of the 50,000 available newsgroups:

```
class news
    {
    var $servers;
    var $groups;
    var $limit = 10;
    function get_groups()
        {
        $limit = 0;
        if(isset($this->groups))
            {
            unset($this->groups);
            }
        if(isset($this->servers))
            {
            while(list($k, $server) = each($this->servers))
                {
                if($file = fsockopen($server, 119, $errno, $error, 2))
                    {
                    $x = fgets($file, 10000);
                    if(substr($x, 0, 3) != 200)
                        {
                        print("<br>fgets not 200: " . $x );
                        }
                    fputs($file, "list\r\n");
                    $x = fgets($file, 10000);
                    if(substr($x, 0, 3) != 215)
                        {
                        print("<br>fgets not 215: " . $x );
                        }
                    while(substr($x, 0, 1) != "." and !feof($file)
                    and $limit < $this->limit)
                        {
                        $limit++;
                        $a = explode(" ", fgets($file, 10000));
                        $this->groups[$server][] = array("name" => $a[0],
                            "start" => intval($a[2]), "end" => intval($a[1]));
                        }
                    fclose($file);
                    }
                else
                    {
```

```
                        print("<br>Cannot fsockopen server " . $server );
                    }
                }
            }
        }
    }
```

The limit is defined in **$limit**. Function **get_groups( )** reads through **$servers**, opens each server, and gets all the newsgroups from the server. In a real-life system, you would need a way to select or exclude newsgroups with specific prefixes, and select or exclude newsgroups containing specific words, and then let people subscribe to the ones they want to read.

The subscription list could be in the user's profile and then be copied to the session record for easy access. You could expand this class to use **__sleep( )** and **__wake( )** to make the object suitable for storing in the user's session record, but be careful about the volume of data stored in the session record. When there are thousands of newsgroups and tens of thousands of article entries in the object, the session record is not appropriate. Look at storing the newsgroups and articles in a database with large attachments possibly stored as discrete files. If you have many users subscribing to newsgroups, you can use the unique id in each article to store the article once and share the article with all the users subscribed to the newsgroup.

fsockopen( ) opens the news server using the server name, port 119, two error fields, and a timeout value in seconds. Both the timeout value and port number should be stored separately for each server because some servers do not use port 119 and some will take longer to reply than the two seconds specified here. (Two seconds is based on broadband access at a quiet time in the morning; this value used to be from 10 seconds to 60 seconds during the day when using a modem.)

fgets( ) reads a line from the news server because news servers send an identification line when you connect. The first three characters of the line should be 200 to indicate a successful connection; anything else indicates an error. The message numbers are described in RFC 977.

fputs( ) sends a line containing a **list** request. **list** can be in any case you like including **liSt**. You can have parameters after some requests, and there can be spaces or tabs between and after parameters. All lines have to end with a carriage return and **newline**, **\r\n**. All incoming lines end with **\r\n**, so remember to remove the **\r\n** when you are converting strings to data. The **fgets( )** immediately after the **fputs( )** is to get the response from the list request and make sure the response is 215, indicating that a list of newsgroups follows the response line.

The **while( )** loop reads the subsequent lines until it finds a line starting with a period, which indicates the end of the list. The period line should be **.\r\n**, but I have not rigorously tested responses from all servers; one server did give problems suggesting the server delivered some lines with the **\n** but not the full **\r\n** as specified in RFC 977.

explode( ) splits the article lines into an array based on spaces, places the first three parts of the line in **$groups**, and converts two of the values from strings to integers. The final step is to close the link using **fclose( )**, and the remaining code is to display error messages if a function returns false. There are more opportunities to include error checking and error messages than implemented in this code.

The newsgroup lines look like the following:

```
php.announce 0000000029 0000000001 m\r\n
php.beta 0000000161 0000000001 n\r\n
php.cvs 0000006251 0000000001 n\r\n
php.db 0000010539 0000000001 y\r\n
php.dev 0000060198 0000000001 y\r\n
php.doc 0969336294 0969332401 y\r\n
```

The first column is the newsgroup name, followed by a space. The second column is the end article number. The third column is the start article number, and the last column—with a value of **m**, **n**, or **y**— indicates your access to the newsgroup. In RFC 977, **y** indicates that you can post articles to the newsgroup and **n** indicates you cannot post articles. **m** is not defined, but most likely indicates the newsgroup is moderated, which means you can post articles, but the articles will not be displayed until a moderator has approved them for display. The **\r\n** is a manual translation of the normally invisible carriage return and newline characters. Note that one row of numbers has unusually large values likely to be caused by an error in the news server software.

Test the class with the following code:

```
$a = new news;
$a->servers[] = "news.php.net";
$a->get_groups();
```

The class is used to create object **$a**, the object is set to use news server **news.php.net**, and then the code reads the newsgroup list via method **get_groups( )**.

The following code simply lists the newsgroups stored in array **$a->groups** and wraps an HTML table around the data to display the data in neat columns:

```
if(isset($a->groups))
   {
   print("<table><tr><td>Server</td><td>Group</td>"
      . "<td>Start</td><td>End</td></tr>");
   while(list($s, $vs) = each($a->groups))
      {
      while(list($k, $v) = each($vs))
         {
         print("<tr><td>" . $s . "</td><td>" . $v["name"] . "</td>"
            . "<td>" . $v["start"] . "</td>"
            . "<td>" . $v["end"] . "</td></tr>" );
         }
      }
   print("</table>");
   }
```

The next list contains all the newsgroups retrieved from **news.php.net**. Note that the start values were the second number in the rows returned from the server, and here are displayed first. If you extend this code to post articles to newsgroups, you will need to include the **y/n/m** indicator in this table so people can see which newsgroups accept posts:

```
Server          Group          Start       End
news.php.net    php.announce   1           29
news.php.net    php.beta       1           161
news.php.net    php.cvs        1           6251
news.php.net    php.db         1           10532
news.php.net    php.dev        1           60193
news.php.net    php.doc        969332401   969336293
news.php.net    php.general    1           58379
news.php.net    php.gtk        1           2255
news.php.net    php.i18n       1           164
news.php.net    php.install    1           3598
```

The following class **news2** extends class **news** with the function **get_articles( )** to read all the article headings from a newsgroup:

```
class news2 extends news
   {
   function get_articles($server, $group)
      {
      $limit = 0;
      if($file = fsockopen($server, 119, $errno, $error, 2))
```

```
        {
        $x = fgets($file, 10000);
        if(substr($x, 0, 3) != 200)
            {
            print("<br>fgets not 200: " . $x);
            }
        fputs($file, "group " . $group . "\r\n");
        $x = fgets($file, 10000);
        if(substr($x, 0, 3) == 211)
            {
            do {
                $limit++;
                fputs($file, "head\r\n");
                $head = fgets($file, 10000);
                print("<br>head: " . $head );
                $y = fgets($file, 10000);
                while(substr($y, 0, 1) != "." and !feof($file))
                    {
                    print("<br>   " . htmlentities($y) );
                    $y = fgets($file, 10000);
                    }
                fputs($file, "next\r\n");
                $head = fgets($file, 10000);
                } while(substr($head, 0, 3) == 223
                    and $limit < $this->limit);
            }
        else
            {
            print("<br>fgets not 211: " . $x);
            }
        fclose($file);
        }
    else
        {
        print("<br>Cannot fsockopen server " . $server);
        }
    }
}
```

Some newsgroups have 10,000 or more articles, so this code limits the number retrieved. Note than news servers retain articles for a limited time; an active newsgroup might receive 1,000 articles per day, and your ISP might limit the newsgroup to 10 days' retention. A newsgroup oriented to adult audio/video files might have a retention of only a few hours because of the huge file sizes.

The code has four lines emphasized because they stand out as different from the code in function **get_groups( )**. The first **fputs( )** sends a group request to select a newsgroup, and the news server remembers the selected newsgroup for the life of the connection. The next **fputs( )** sends a **head** request to get the heading lines from the selected newsgroup. You can send a **body** request to get the article body, or an **article** request to get the whole article, including headings and body. The **print( )** statement is to help you see the contents of the heading lines while you develop code to extract any values you need. The final **fputs( )** sends a **next** request to get the next article in the newsgroup. **next** works equally well for head, body, and article requests.

Test the class with the following code:

```
$b = new news2;
$b->servers[] = "news-server";
$b->limit = 1;
$b->get_articles($b->servers[0], "alt.php");
```

Replace **news-server** with the name of the news server you currently use and manually specify the newsgroup as **alt.php** to pick up a useful newsgroup. Note that the class does not yet contain code to step through all the newsgroups from all servers and retrieve all article headings because the volume of headings would be difficult to handle. Instead, add code to display the **$groups** array, add a button to each row to let people subscribe, and then retrieve article headings for the subscribed newsgroups.

Here is the print of the first line returned from the first article in the newsgroup (221 is the message number and indicates that headings, but not body text, follow):

```
head: 221 19081 <3b4240a1@news.kos.net>
```

Here are the head records from the first article in the newsgroup (lines have been broken here to allow for the layout of this book):

```
Path: news-server.bigpond.net.au!intgwpad.nntp.telstra.net!
    news.stealth.net!news.maxwell.syr.edu!newsfeed.slurp.net!
    news.kos.net
From: "Online Creator Inc" <jobs@theonlinecreator.com>
Newsgroups: alt.php,ca.jobs,can.jobs,comp.jobs,
    kingston.jobs,linux.jobs,ont.jobs,ott.jobs,tor.jobs
Subject: Web Programmer / Web Designer
Lines: 61
X-Priority: 3
```

```
X-MSMail-Priority: Normal
X-Newsreader: Microsoft Outlook Express 5.50.4133.2400
X-MimeOLE: Produced By Microsoft MimeOLE V5.50.4133.2400
X-Original-NNTP-Posting-Host: 216.13.93.203
Message-ID: <3b4240a1@news.kos.net>
X-Original-Trace: 3 Jul 2001 18:01:05 -0500, 216.13.93.203
Organization: Kingston Online Services
Date: Tue, 3 Jul 2001 18:09:55 -0400
NNTP-Posting-Host: 216.13.25.103
X-Trace: newsfeed.slurp.net 994197876 216.13.25.103 (Tue, 03 Jul 2001
    17:04:36 CDT)
NNTP-Posting-Date: Tue, 03 Jul 2001 17:04:36 CDT
Xref: news-server.bigpond.net.au alt.php:19081 ca.jobs:153181
    can.jobs:505434 comp.jobs:276301 kingston.jobs:11067
    ont.jobs:436593 ott.jobs:208118 tor.jobs:392964
```

RFC 977 provides some information about headings, and some are made up by the people developing news servers. The **X-MimeOLE** heading looks like an advertisement for Microsoft. The **Path** heading can help you track down problems with news servers. **Newsgroups** tells you this article is duplicated across several newsgroups, and **Message-ID** gives you an id, unique across all newsgroups, that can be used to eliminate duplicates. **Subject** gives you the article name for display on your Web page, and **From** gives you the email address for replies. **Lines** tells you how many lines are in the article, which is helpful for people on dial-up connections so they can choose to read or ignore long articles, but is not needed to read the lines. You can use **Date** or **NNTP-Posting-Date** to delete and ignore old postings. Print several sets of headings from several news groups to get an indication of which headings are consistent and useful.

Retrieving news articles is similar to retrieving headings, and the requests are described in RFC 977. Attachments are similar to attachments in mail (see Chapter 15), and posting articles is almost the reverse of retrieving articles. Experiment with the code shown here, and then visit **http://freshmeat.net** or **http://sourceforge.net** and download a fully developed news application. The time required to fully develop a news or mail application, complete with attachment handling, is beyond most people, and the object of developing your own news class is to learn how NNTP works, so have code you can rip apart and reconstruct for experiments or diagnostic work. Experimenting with this code will help you to understand the prewritten PHP-based news applications.

Related solution:	Found on page:
Sending Mail with Attachments	591

17. Objects

Chapter 18

Search

In Depth

The World Wide Web offers the chance to search a huge range of documents and databases but most of the search engines focus on one area, Web pages. If you want to search anything else, you need to know and understand special search tools and techniques.

If you want to search for images, try the **altavista.com** facility. I tested the AltaVista image search many times, and few searches bring back relevant results. The software does not know what is in an image, so it makes a guess based on text surrounding the image, a technique that works for only a small percentage of images.

There is a huge range of information sources available across the Internet, but not all the information is available as Web pages, and some sources require special access facilities. The Z39.50 protocol gives you access to a huge range of special databases, many in libraries, that contain content, or index content, from historical paper-based sources. If you want to search old newspapers, search the Z39.50 sources using PHP's YAZ functions.

Searching Search Engines

You can search a site like **yahoo.com** using PHP's **fsockopen( )** and file functions, or socket services. Every Internet directory and search site can be accessed by your server just by emulating a browser. You can write experimental code to pass a search on to **google.com** or **excite.com**, and then retrieve and display the results. If you do this as a one-time experiment, no one will jump on you. If you set up your personal machine with a Web server, and have the Web server act purely as your personal browser, that is no different than using a conventional browser. As soon as you pass retrieved information to a third party, however, you breach copyright, and you can expect a visit from the FBI, or your local equivalent, at 5:00 A.M.

When you write code that goes into a loop hitting one server, you can expect the server to report the incident. Hitting servers in the wrong way can be interpreted as a denial of service (DoS) attack, and DoS attacks attract fines up to $500,000. You might also score several years' accommodation at a location determined by the courts. Think of that backup floppy disk you stored in a smelly old shoe box at the bottom of a cupboard 10 years ago, and then think of yourself spending the next 10 years in about the same-sized space.

If you still want to proceed and think there is commercial merit in your venture, contact the target search site about licensing their information. Google and other search engines will provide special interfaces in return for a share of your revenue. Some search sites provide paid-for placement advertising and share their revenue in return for extra exposure of the advertisements. The solution entitled "Searching **google.com**" shows you how to set up a quick interface to **google.com** for testing your own search theories. Expand the code with your new ideas, and then sell the new interface to Google. (Their existing interface could do with a more logical way of handling search phrases, in my opinion.)

LDAP

You can search LDAP databases using the PHP LDAP functions described in Chapter 14. LDAP is used to list people in a way similar to a yellow pages search, but many yellow-pages-style applications use conventional relational databases and SQL-based searches behind the scenes so LDAP adds little that you could not perform directly in SQL.

Z39.50

Z39.50 is an American National Standard Institute (ANSI) standard approved by the National Information Standards Organization (NISO) in 1988, and maintained by the Library of Congress Z39.50 International Standard Maintenance Agency (**http://lcweb.loc.gov/z3950/agency/**). The International Standards Organization (ISO) ISO 23950 standard, "Information Retrieval (Z39.50): Application Service Definition and Protocol Specification," is technically the same as ANSI/NISO Z39.50.

Z39.50 is a protocol to let one computer search another computer and retrieve information without knowing the search syntax used by the other computer. Both computers must have Z39.50 software installed.

The Interlibrary Loan Application Standards Maintenance Agency (**www.nlc-bnc.ca/iso/ill/main.htm**) developed extensions to Z39.50 to handle loan requests. The extensions are described in PDF documents at **www.nlc-bnc.ca/iso/ill/stanprf.htm**. Look for "Profile for the Use of Z39.50 Item Order Extended Service to Transport ILL Protocol APDUs (Z39.50/ILL Profile 1)" and "Profile for the Use of Parameters from the ILL-Request APDU in Z39.50 Item Order (Z39.50/ILL Profile 2)." The YAZ function **yaz_itemorder( )** is designed to handle the extensions.

18. Search

YAZ

The YAZ (Yet Another Z39.50 Toolkit) software and the PHP YAZ functions are from Index Data (**www.indexdata.dk**). Index Data specializes in Z39.50-based applications and uses PHP for its Web site, so the marriage of Z39.50 and PHP seems logical.

Installing YAZ

YAZ is a recent addition to PHP, including additions in PHP 4.0.6, so update to the latest PHP: First install the latest PHP, then test existing code with PHP, and then install YAZ.

Windows 98 ME, and Later

To install YAZ under Windows 98 ME, and later, follow these steps:

1. Copy c:\Program Files\php\extensions\php_yaz.dll to c:\windows\system\.

2. Stop your Web server.

3. In php.ini, remove the semicolon from the front of the following line:

```
extension=php_yaz.dll
```

4. Start your Web server.

Windows NT and Windows 2000

To install YAZ under Windows NT and Windows 2000, follow these steps:

1. Copy c:/Program Files/php/extensions/php_yaz.dll to c:/winnt/system32/.

2. Stop your Web server.

3. In php.ini, remove the semicolon from the front of the following line:

```
extension=php_yaz.dll
```

4. Start your Web server.

Unix

To install YAZ under Unix, follow these steps:

1. Download the latest YAZ from Index Data (**www.indexdata.dk/yaz/**).

2. Compile and install YAZ.

3. Compile PHP with **--with--yaz**.

Data Sources

A YAZ data source is a database that you can search—the database is usually in a library, and a library can have several data sources. BookWhere has a list of data sources at **www.bookwhere.com/library.htm**, and the list appears to be old. Index Data maintains a list at **www.indexdata.dk/targettest/**, and the sources are regularly tested for availability.

Part of the Index Data test target list is shown in Figure 18.1, and includes an entry for Bell Labs. Bell Labs conducts primary research into the things that make our technology tick, so it should have fascinating documents listed in its databases. Bell Labs invented handy gadgets like the transistor and laser and, for all I know about physics, probably invented the electron.

Testing

Many of the YAZ functions in this chapter are new in PHP 4.0.6, so there is little documentation and few comprehensive examples of their use. You will need to test your code more than you would when you are using older and better-known functions.

There is a list of test sites at **http://lcweb.loc.gov/z3950/agency/resources/ testport.html**. The following sample entry describes one of the sources I use for the examples in this chapter. I chose this source in part because it offers a diverse range of information to search and in part because South Australia is an interesting part of the world and home to some of the world's best wines. I will search for people like Dr. Christopher Rawson Penfold, developer of the world-famous Penfolds wines (**www.penfolds.com.au/**) and Max Schubert, developer of Penfolds magnificent Grange:

```
The State Library of South Australia
    Address: 143.216.21.3
    Port: 210
```

Target Name	Db Name	Access	Address Port	Record Syntaxes	Services	Explain Categories	Bib-1 Use Attributes
Bavarian State Libraries	BVBSR011	100%	193.174.96.24 31310	SUTRS Unimarc	search, present, delSet, resourceReport, scan, namedResultSets	None	1-6, 8, 12, 20-29, 34-35, 37-41, 44, 46, 48, 53, 59, 1003-1006, 1008-1009, 1018
Belgorod State Universal Scientific Library	liber	97%	liber.bgunb.ru 210	SUTRS USmarc	search, present, scan	None	1-4, 7-8, 21, 30-32, 59, 63, 1003, 1011-1012, 1018, 1035
Bell Laboratories Library Network	books	97%	z3950.bell-labs.com 210	SUTRS USmarc GRS-1	search, present, accessCtrl, scan, extendedServices, level-2Segmentation, namedResultSets	CategoryList, TargetInfo, DatabaseInfo, SchemaInfo, AttributeSetInfo	1-63, 1000-1028, 1030-1036

Figure 18.1   Index Data list of available Z39.50 servers.

18. Search

```
Databases available for testing:
   innopac
   arch
   pict

Searching:
   MAIN : author,title,subject,word
   PICT : word,title,name
   ARCH : word,title,name
```

MAIN : Books, newspapers, magazines, periodicals, non-print and electronic
library materials held in the Bray Reference Library, Mortlock Library of
South Australiana and Rare Books and Named Collections

PICT: Photographs and other pictorial material from the Mortlock Library's
collections, and references to articles and other citations from selected
South Australian published material held in the Library

ARCH: This database contains Personal, business and society archives and the
J.D.Somerville Oral History Collection

Contact: Elvio Pederzolli

RPN

Reverse Polish Notation (RPN) is a notation used in early HP calculators to make some types of calculations faster. In RPN, you enter **A + B** as **A B +**. In the YAZ functions, references to RPN actually mean a reverse RPN where **A + B** is entered as **+ A B**. Note that the operation goes first, followed by the operands. YAZ uses the reversed RPN for search strings, and it is the one illogical part of YAZ that is bound to create problems.

Searching with YAZ

YAZ lets you search a database for references using the Z39.50 protocol, search several databases at one time, and request the results in several formats. The types of searches depend on what a database accepts, and the format of the results depends on what a database can produce. The Z39.50 protocol does not remove the need to match search types and result format requests to data sources. YAZ, or X39.50, does not provide a means of interactively discovering the acceptable search types and result formats. That is the next improvement needed in YAZ.

Unsupported Search

Unsupported search is the common error message you get when performing your first searches on a data source. The cause can be an invalid search type or an invalid syntax. There is a facility to provide extra information for an error, but the sources I tried did not use the extra information facility to provide a list of supported search types.

YAZ Functions

The PHP 4.0.6 YAZ functions are described in this section. The recent expansion of YAZ and the current lack of self-discovery functions suggest the YAZ function range will grow. Index Data, the author of YAZ, could help the world by making its online list of Z39.50 data sources a YAZ searchable database so YAZ users can acquire lists of YAZ sources via YAZ.

yaz_connect()

yaz_connect( ) sets up a control structure to be filled by other functions, and then connects to a server for a search by function **yaz_wait( )**. The second parameter is an optional authorization string, and some examples of this function show multiple strings including user name and password. The first string, as shown here, contains the name of a server or an IP address, followed by a port number and the name of a database. The port number is optional and defaults to 210; most servers use port 210, so the port number is rarely needed. When you leave out the port number, also leave out the colon. The database is optional, and the connection will default to using the site's default database.

yaz_connect( ) returns a connection id when successful and zero when the function fails, so save the result from **yaz_connect( )** and produce an error message if the connection fails. The connection id is the first parameter for all the other YAZ functions:

```
if($connection = yaz_connect("143.216.21.3:210/pict", "auth"))
```

Here is the same connection without wasting space on port number 210:

```
if($connection = yaz_connect("143.216.21.3/pict", "auth"))
```

yaz_close()

yaz_close( ) closes the connection created by **yaz_connect( )**, and the only parameter is the connection id returned by **yaz_connect( )**:

```
yaz_close($connection);
```

yaz_syntax()

yaz_syntax( ) accepts a connection id and a string nominating the syntax for the search results. If you provide an invalid syntax string, the default appears to be

usmarc. Other options include **grs1**, **sutrs**, and **xml**. This function returns the same result no matter what happens, so there is no point in testing the result:

```
yaz_syntax($connection, "xml");
```

yaz_search()

yaz_search() accepts a connection id, a string containing **rpn**, and a search string, as follows:

```
if(yaz_search($connection, "rpn", $search))
```

The result returns an indication of success or failure. The second parameter specifies the type of query, but currently accepts only **rpn**. The RPN search parameter format is described at **www.php.net/manual/en/function.yaz-search.php**.

You can test with simple search strings like **penfolds** and **"new york"**:

```
$search = "@and penfolds \"new york\"";
```

Search values containing spaces must be enclosed in quotes. You can combine multiple search criteria using strange RPN notation. **@and** means the subsequent criteria are joined by **and**, **@or** joins the criteria with **or**, and **@not** joins the criteria with **and not**.

yaz_wait()

yaz_wait(), shown next, requires no parameters, and waits for all searches to complete. You can make multiple connections, start multiple searches, and then wait for all the searches to complete. In **yaz_wait()**, there is no option to wait for one search and leave the others running:

```
yaz_wait();
```

yaz_error()

After waiting for a search, check for an error using either **yaz_error()** or **yaz_errno()** (see "**yaz_errno()**"). **yaz_error()** accepts the connection id and returns the error message for the most recent error. A zero-length string indicates no error, and anything else indicates an error. Save the error string, test the string's length, and display the string if the length is greater than zero:

```
$error = yaz_error($connection);
if(strlen($error))
    {
```

```
    print("<br><font color=\"red\">" . $error . "</font>");
    }
```

yaz_errno()

yaz_errno( ) accepts the connection id and returns the error number for the most recent error. Zero indicates no error, positive numbers indicate simple errors like syntax errors, and negative numbers indicate dramatic errors like a lost connection. Save the error number, test the number, and display the number if it is not zero. Display the error string from **yaz_error( )** with the error number:

```
$errno = yaz_errno($connection);
if($errno != 0)
    {
    print("<br><font color=\"red\">" . $errno . " " . $error
        . "</font>");
    }
```

yaz_addinfo()

yaz_addinfo( ) is supposed to return additional error information if there is an error, or return a zero-length string. I found that **yaz_addinfo( )** sometimes repeated what is returned by **yaz_error( )**. The following code shows a simple way to add **yaz_addinfo( )** to the **yaz_error( )** string for those servers that do return useful information via **yaz_addinfo( )**:

```
$error = yaz_error($connection);
if(strlen($error))
    {
    $error .= "<br>" . yaz_addinfo($connection);
    print("<br><font color=\"red\">" . $error . "</font>");
    }
```

yaz_hits()

yaz_hits( ) accepts a connection id and returns the number of hits found by the search in the selected database, or zero when there are no hits. Use the following code, after **yaz_wait( )** and your error-checking code, to display the number of hits (when there are hits):

```
$hits = yaz_hits($connection);
if($hits > 0)
    {
    print("<br>Hits: " . $hits);
    }
```

yaz_record()

When you find hits from a search, use **yaz_record( )** to get the result records. **yaz_record( )** accepts a connection id, a hit number, and a string specifying the format of the result ("**string**" or "**array**"). Hits are numbered from 1 up to the number returned by **yaz_hits( )**, and you can step through the result records with the following **for( )** loop. Not all hits will contain results, so check the length of the result record and drop zero-length records:

```
for($h = 1; $h <= $hits; $h++)
  {
  $hit = yaz_record($connection, $h, "string");
  }
```

yaz_range()

yaz_range( ) accepts a connection id, a search result record start number, and the maximum number of records to retrieve. Use **yaz_range( )** after **yaz_search( )** and before **yaz_present( )** to change **yaz_present( )**'s default start number of 1 or the default of returning 10 records. The following example tells **yaz_present( )** to get results starting at result record 25 and return a total of 20 result records:

```
yaz_range($connection, 25, 20);
```

yaz_present()

yaz_present( ) is used after **yaz_range( )** and before **yaz_wait( )** to prepare a set of results for retrieval. The combination of **yaz_range( )** and **yaz_present( )** is used only if you want to change a range selection option through **yaz_range( )**:

```
yaz_present();
```

yaz_database()

yaz_database( ) lets you override the database specified in **yaz_connect( )**. **yaz_database( )** accepts a connection id and a list of databases in a string with the database names separated by plus sign (**+**). The following code executes **yaz_database( )** using a list of databases stored in an array. This function returns true on success and false on error:

```
$db[] = "books";
$db[] = "newspapers";
if(!yaz_database($connection, implode("+", $db)))
  {
```

```
print("<br><font color=\"red\">yaz_database failed. " . $error
    . "</font>");
}
```

yaz_element()

yaz_element( ) accepts a connection id and an element set indicator of **F** (full) or **B** (brief). The following example code sets the element set to full. Use **yaz_element( )** after **yaz_search( )** and before **yaz_present( )**:

```
if(!yaz_element($connection, "F"))
    {
    print("<br><font color=\"red\">yaz_element failed. " . $error
        . "</font>");
    }
```

yaz_scan()

You can use **yaz_scan( )** in a similar way to **yaz_search( )**, and get the results with **yaz_scan_result( )**. **yaz_scan( )** accepts a connection id, a scan parameter type, which is currently only **rpn**, a scan start parameter, which is of the same format as the **yaz_search( )** search parameter, and optional flags. I have not found an example to explain the optional flags. The following scan starts at the word *cat:*

```
yaz_scan($connection, "rpn", "cat");
```

yaz_scan_result()

This function accepts a connection id and an optional array and returns an array containing the results produced by **yaz_scan( )**. The optional array receives a few fields from the scan: **number** contains the number of result entries, **stepsize**, **position**, and a **status** field:

```
$array = yaz_scan_result($connection);
```

yaz_ccl_conf()

This function configures the CCL query parser but not many details are available about the CCL parser and I have not found a use for it, so you can safely skip this function and **yaz_ccl_parse( )** while the developers work on examples of use. CCL is the Common Command Language defined in ISO 8777; some Z39.50 software translates CCL to the Z39.50 version of RPN:

```
$config[] = "";
yaz_ccl_conf($connection, $config);
```

yaz_ccl_parse()

yaz_ccl_parse( ) converts a CCL-format **find** query to the RPN format for **yaz_search( )**:

```
$array = array();
if(yaz_ccl_parse($connection, "query", $array))
   {
   yaz_search($connection, "rpn",$search);
   }
else
   {
   print("<br>ccl_parse error.");
   }
```

yaz_itemorder()

yaz_itemorder( ) implements an extension to Z39.50 for interlibrary loans. A heap of parameters is placed in an array, and then the array is fed into **yaz_itemorder( )**. The example shows just a book's ISBN number going into the array. If you need to use this feature, you will most likely have document references provided by the library supplying the books:

```
$order["item-id,ISBN"] = "1588800539";
yaz_itemorder($order);
```

Database-Based Searches

How would you set up a search engine if you were inventing one from scratch? Here are some ideas based on inventing search engines for several Web sites and many online systems before the Web was invented.

Keep Data Original

Some people like to squeeze everything into one mold, to take a database and rename everything to suit their ideas. When you receive data, keep the data as close to the original format and classification as possible.

Take a simple example of CRC32 data. 32-bit CRCs are stored as unsigned 32-bit integers or as unsigned 32-bit hexadecimal numbers. PHP uses signed 32-bit integers and displays CRC32 data differently from what most people expect of CRC32 data. The results of processing CRC32 data can be unpredictable unless you can personally check the code. You need to ensure that the incoming data is kept in the original format when stored in a database, even if you have to use a field type that will use up more disk space than the theoretical minimum size field for that database.

Now look at the name of the original data. Was the original name something like CRC32h? The person setting up the data might have added an *h* to indicate that the CRC is stored as hexadecimal. Both the name of a field and the format of the field can have meaning that needs to be stored along with the data.

How can you store CRC32 data from several sources complete with the original formats? One approach is to store the data and format in a string. This is the approach used in **serialize( )** (see Chapter 17), and is one way of coping with data formats that do not fit exactly into a neat data storage format. A hexadecimal CRC32 field could be stored as **h:ef014ec2**, with the **h:** indicating it is hexadecimal. When the input is an integer, the integer can be stored as **i:12345678**. Another approach is to have two fields, on named CRC32i and the other CRC32h. When the input is an integer, store the value in CRC32i, and when the input is hexadecimal, store the value in CRC32h.

CRC32 seems a silly field to store in two different formats, so why waste that space? I have seen CRCs damaged by incorrect conversion to or from hexadecimal, by PHP's signed 32-bit integers, and by signed 32-bit integer representations in databases. The representation problems become far more complex with telephone numbers, where every country has different formats. Valid email addresses are rejected by systems that assume they know the correct format for an email address. People's names are corrupted by systems that limit the length of names and assume things about the order and number of people's names.

You need to design your database to store the data as closely as possible to the way data exists before you acquire it, and then store any translations or simplifications as new separate data.

Keep Data Flexible

When you fill out a survey, how often do you find a job title or job classification that matches your actual job? The form should have an Other field where people can suggest new and more accurate values for the form's selection list. In the resultant database, you should store both the selected job classification and the Other field so someone can analyze the alternative suggestions to help improve your survey's accuracy.

How do you classify an agricultural motorcycle that has six wheels, carries more than one person, has a rain-proof fold-up roof better than that on many convertible cars, and is equally good at motoring across a lake as it is over grass? When a person searches the database, should they click motorcycle or boat?

You need to think about the data going into your database and how your visitors can retrieve the data. Get people to perform searches on a test database and log all the searches. Give the testers a way to indicate a successful search. Sit there and watch some of the searches. Work out what data characteristics users want and how you can maintain those characteristics within your database.

Keep Searches Flexible

Many Web site search engines ignore the HTML and other markup in Web pages and extract just the content. That makes it hard to search for Web pages that contain examples of JavaScript, Flash, and other technology. Some search engines use metadata, and others ignore metadata in favor of titles. Why not retain both, and have both available as discrete fields and as aggregated page text content?

When I was single and searching for silk lingerie as presents, I wanted to exclude metadata from searches because the meta tags in more than a million pages of Web pornography had either the word *lingerie* or the word *silk*. When I search for Web sites created with specific technology or designed by specific people, I want to include metadata, particularly tags like **<meta name="author">**. I do not know of any search sites that let me select the meta tags I want included.

Classify Data

There are endless attempts to reduce data to a meaningless cloud of information, and then extract entries by matching string by string. The technique works, but not as well as matching based on fully classified data, and neither approach works as well as using both approaches together. When someone searches for an author to find books by that particular author, the fact that the target of the search is an author field in a database is a help. The author's job title does not help if the searcher is looking for a biography of the author, because a search for the author's name under Author will not find the author of the biography.

When you can classify incoming data, go ahead and classify. You do not have to get the classification perfect or invent the one true classification for every data item. In an autobiography, an author can appear as the author of the work, as a character in the work, and in the list of researchers. The author might also have a father or son of the same name mentioned in the same book. When a person searches for an author by name, return the results from the author search and, if there are few or no results, give the searcher the option to perform a generic search of all string data for the same value. Start with the specific and work out toward the less specific until the searcher indicates success.

Reduce but Do Not Remove

When people set up a database for cars and motorcycles, the inexperienced leave out the Number of Wheels field because all cars have four wheels and all motorcycles have two wheels. Once the database is in wide use and hard to change, someone has to enter motorcycles with 3, 4, and 6 wheels, plus cars with up to 10 wheels.

You want to reduce the information flowing through your server, but not remove data that happens to have no apparent current use. When the vehicle information is entered into your database, set up one database to contain everything, and another to contain just the fields and records you want available online. The full database goes on to a cheap, slow server with huge, slow, cheap disks. The online subset goes on a fast server with expensive, fast disks. The online subset is used to serve Web pages to your visitors, and the offline database is used to experiment with new Web site facilities that use the information you thought was worthless.

Use Free Text Associations

Are food bars food? When you set up an online grocery store, someone will point out that some food bars are so high in sugar, they count as confectionery. You want all your formal classifications of grocery items, and a free text field where people can add comments to help visitors find the right products. Someone will complain that tomatoes, a fruit, are listed in your vegetable category, so provide a way of listing tomatoes as both fruit and vegetables. Do you have a No Added Salt checkbox in your grocery search? If not, let your staff add No Added Salt as a comment in the free text comment field and add that to the strings people can search.

Your customer service staff should be able to use end-user comments about products and categories as additional free-form input to your database until you can produce a formal database facility to handle the extra information.

Build a Big Index

There is no reason why your database index should be smaller than your database. You build the index for a page once, and then people search the index many times, so the time taken to update the index is immaterial. When you index a page titled *PHP and Web Site Architecture*, you want to let people find the page by a direct index lookup, not an index scan. That means avoiding the slow, costly SQL **like** parameter. Avoid resorting to searching the page title with SQL containing **where title like '%php%'**.

Place the title *PHP and Web Site Architecture* in the index as:

```
php and web site architecture
php and web site
php web site
php
web site architecture
```

```
web site
architecture php
architecture web site
```

Generate all the combinations you can think of, so they can be found by an exact match. Leave SQL's slow **like** scan as the last resort if the exact match fails. Log all requests that fail to make a match, then try to work out what users were looking for and how you can help them find it. Refine your index build routine to minimize the percentage of searches that resort to an SQL **like**.

Immediate Solutions

Searching One Server

YAZ lets you search or scan one or many servers and databases at one time. This solution tackles one database and uses **search()**, because some data sources allow only **search()**, not **scan()**.

search()

Step one is to create a function or object to search a database using the search string, search string syntax type, server name or IP address, port, and database. The only result required is the search result ready to print, or an error message ready to print. Because of the single-output requirement, I chose a function instead of an object. The following code is the result and is tested against a database at both the State Library of South Australia and Bell Labs:

```
function search($site, $database, $search, $syntax = "", $port = "")
   {
   $result = "";
   $target = $site;
   if(strlen($port))
      {
      $target .= ":" . $port;
      }
   $target .= "/" . $database;
   if(!strlen($syntax))
      {
      $syntax .= "sutrs";
      }
   if($connection = yaz_connect($target))
      {
      yaz_syntax($connection, $syntax);
      if(yaz_search($connection, "rpn", $search))
         {
         yaz_wait();
         $errno = yaz_errno($connection);
         if($errno == 0)
            {
            $hits = yaz_hits($connection);
```

```
            $result .= "Hits: " . $hits;
            if($hits > 0)
                {
                $record = "array";
                if($syntax == "sutrs" or $syntax == "xml")
                    {
                    $record = "string";
                    }
                $result .= "<table cellspacing=\"0\" cellpadding=\"0\">"
                    . "<tr><td>Hit</td><td> </td></tr>\n";
                for($h = 1; $h <= $hits; $h++)
                    {
                    $hit = yaz_record($connection, $h, $record);
                    if(is_array($hit))
                        {
                        $result .= "<tr><td align=\"right\""
                            . " valign=\"top\">" . $h . "</td><td>"
                            . array_display($hit) . "</td></tr>\n";
                        }
                    elseif(strlen($hit))
                        {
                        $result .= "<tr><td align=\"right\" "
                            . " valign=\"top\">" . $h . "</td><td>"
                            . htmlentities($hit) . "</td></tr>\n";
                        }
                    }
                $result .= "</table>\n";
                }
            }
        else
            {
            $result .= "Wait failed. Error: " . $errno . " "
                . yaz_error($connection);
            $add = yaz_addinfo($connection);
            if(strlen($add))
                {
                $result .= "<br>  " . $add;
                }
            }
        }
    else
        {
        $result .= "Search failed.";
        }
yaz_close($connection);
}
```

```
    else
        {
        $result .= "Connection failed.";
        }
    return($result);
    }
```

The first part of the code combines the server name, port number, and database into one string, **$target**, for use in **yaz_connect( )**. The port number is optional because it defaults to 210, and most data sources use port 210. **yaz_connect( )** returns **$connection**, which becomes the first parameter in all the other YAZ functions.

The **$syntax** field is optional, and defaults to **sutrs** because the YAZ documentation suggests that is the most common syntax. A look though a variety of sources suggests **usmarc** is more common. **yaz_syntax( )** tells the connection the correct syntax.

yaz_search( ) passes the search type, **rpn**, and search string to the connection. **yaz_wait( )** waits for the search completion, **yaz_errno( )** indicates any errors, and **yaz_hits( )** tells you the number of hits found by the search.

You get the hits by reading through the results with **yaz_record( )**—you must wrap **yaz_record( )** in a **for( )** loop to get records from 1 to the number of hits. The search defaults to returning the first 10 results unless you expand the number by using **yaz_range( )**, which is not attempted in this solution. Note that **yaz_range( )** can be used with **yaz_present( )** to create a result display system where you present the first 10 results on the first page, and then step forward and backward through the results page by page. You need to read Chapter 19 and store the visitor's search profile in a session record to create a reliable search facility. You could also store the user's selection of data sources in their profile to save frequent reentry.

yaz_error( ) provides an error message to go with the error number from **yaz_errno( )**, and **yaz_addinfo( )** adds extra error information. Not every server supplies extra error information, and some repeat the error message in the extra info field. Test the sources you use, or add a compare to suppress the additional information if it is exactly the same as the standard error message.

yaz_close( ) closes the connection when you are finished with it. With normal Web pages you would run one search, display the results, and close the connection immediately. If you want to develop an iterative search procedure, use **yaz_range( )** to request all the results, save the results in the session record, and work from the saved results rather than re-requesting the same information across the network for every page.

array_display()

Some of the results are arrays instead of strings, so the following function converts an array to a string. If an array element is a string, this function calls itself to format the array. Each array is placed in a table with the keys in the left-hand column and the values in the right-hand column. There is no spacing or formatting, so add borders and coloring to suit your taste:

```
function array_display($array)
   {
   if(is_array($array))
      {
      $return = "<table cellspacing=\"0\" cellpadding=\"0\">\n";
      while(list($k, $v) = each($array))
         {
         $return .= "<tr><td align=\"right\" valign=\"top\">" . $k
            . "</td><td valign=\"top\">" . array_display($v)
            . "</td></tr>\n";
         }
      return($return . "</table>\n");
      }
   else
      {
      return(htmlentities($array));
      }
   }
```

State Library of South Australia

The first test uses the State Library of South Australia innopac database and a search of type **usmarc**. I tried the syntax field with **usmarc** in uppercase, lowercase and mixed case with the same result. The search keyword **@attr** means a search by attribute, and **1=4** means a search by title. The search is returning references to books and documents that have the word *penfold* in the title:

```
$site = "143.216.21.3";
$database = "innopac";
$search = "@attr 1=4 penfold";
$syntax = "USmarc";
print(search($site, $database, $search, $syntax));
```

The following is a selection of entries from the results, but the entries are meaningless to me without a document listing the fine details of the **usmarc** standard:

```
Hits: 12
Hit
  1   0 0 (3,001)
      1 0 (3,001)(3,@)
         1 000022215008
     23 0 (3,245)(3,04)(3,a)
         1 The Penfold Cottage story.
     41 0 (3,600)(3,10)(3,a)
         1 Penfold, Christopher Rawson,
  3 23 0 (3,245)(3,14)(3,c)
         1 Story by Oswald L. Ziegler.
     36 0 (3,500)(3, )(3,a)
         1 Wines industries. Australia. Penfolds Wines Australia Ltd,
           1844-1974 (ANB/PRECIS SIN 0037818)
```

The first line of text is probably the title. The line starting *Story by* gives the author, and there were other lines with just the author's name by itself. The last lines seem to be a categorization of the book.

Clearly you need to know the syntax of the output and the meaning of the various identifying fields. In a real public application of this data, you would simplify the output to useful fields like title, author, and ISBN.

Bell Labs

The State Library site would not accept a syntax of **sutrs**, so I tried **sutrs** with Bell Labs, using the following parameters (syntax defaults to **sutrs**):

```
$site = "z3950.bell-labs.com";
$database = "books";
$search = "new york";
print(search($site, $database, $search));
```

The result follows, and is more human-readable but has less break-up for analysis by your script. How would you extract publication date from this lot?

```
Hits: 1375
Hit
  1 Conference on Optical Fiber Communication (7th :. Digest of
    technical papers of t 1984. 621.38275/062f 1984 v.1 100112T
  2 Electronic Components Conference (23rd :. 1973 proceedings : 23rd
    Electronic Components Con 1973? 621.3815/E38c1 1973 100553X
  3 International Electron Devices Meeting . Technical digest of the
    1976 IEDM. 1976. 621.3815/I614e 1976 101177A
  4 Product Liability Prevention Conference (9th : 1978 : Philadelphia.)
    Proceedings 1978. 658.026/P49 1978 101185J
```

```
5 IEEE Power Engineering Society. Winter Meeting (1977 : New York.)
  Conference papers 1977. 621.319/I21 1977 103080S
6 IEEE Vehicular Technology Group. Annual Conference (22d : 1971 :
  Detroit.) Technical digest 1971. 629.2/I11 22d/1971 104463X
```

The lesson is to experiment with data sources and syntaxes. A format that gives you lots of discrete fields gives you more search options, like author, publisher, and date of publication, but is hard to read without formatting for display.

XML

A test of Bell Labs with syntax of **xml**, as shown here, produced exactly the same output as **sutrs**. Bell Labs software may just ignore the syntax setting:

```
$site = "z3950.bell-labs.com";
$database = "books";
$search = "new york";
$syntax = "xml";
print(search($site, $database, $search, $syntax));
```

GRS1

A test of Bell Labs with syntax set to **grs1** produced a different result. The Bell Labs server must be set to ignore just those syntax types it does not understand:

```
$site = "z3950.bell-labs.com";
$database = "books";
$search = "new york";
$syntax = "grs1";
print(search($site, $database, $search, $syntax));
```

The results with **grs1** look a bit like **usmarc** results with the addition of a tilde and a vertical bar (~|) to delineate strings within strings. Here is a selection from the result:

```
10 0 (3,388)
   1 ~|+ 20 ~|a Conference on Optical Fiber Communication ~|n (7th : ~|d
     1984 : ~|c New Orleans, La.)
```

USMARC

Bell Labs accepted **usmarc** as a syntax in the following code:

```
$site = "z3950.bell-labs.com";
$database = "books";
```

```
$search = "new york";
$syntax = "usmarc";
print(search($site, $database, $search, $syntax));
```

Here is a selection from the result to match up with the **grs1** result:

```
21 0 (3,111)(3,20)(3,a)
   1 Conference on Optical Fiber Communication
22 0 (3,111)(3,20)(3,n)
   1 (7th :
23 0 (3,111)(3,20)(3,d)
   1 1984 :
24 0 (3,111)(3,20)(3,c)
   1 New Orleans, La.)
```

Unknown

To test what Bell Labs' server does with a completely unknown syntax, I tried **zzzz**:

```
$site = "z3950.bell-labs.com";
$database = "books";
$search = "new york";
$syntax = "zzzz";
print(search($site, $database, $search, $syntax));
```

Here is part of the result, which shows that the server defaults to **usmarc**. It would be nicer to have part of the protocol and YAZ functions work together to retrieve a list of acceptable syntaxes from the server:

```
21 0 (3,111)(3,20)(3,a)
   1 Conference on Optical Fiber Communication
```

Searching Multiple Servers

This solution expands on the previous solution, and performs one search of multiple sources. The code also contains extra formatting of search requests. You could read all about forms in Chapter 9, and then create a page that lets people type in fields such as author, and feed the values into this solution.

18. Search

Data Source

The **search( )** function is expanded to accept data sources in an array. The following example shows an array containing the two data sources used in the first solution:

```
$source["State Library of South Australia"] =
    array("site" => "143.216.21.3", "database" => "innopac",
    "syntax" => "usmarc");
$source["Bell Labs"] = array("site" => "z3950.bell-labs.com",
    "database" => "books");
```

The array, **$source**, is keyed by source name so you can sort the array by name and present your visitors with a neat source selection list. You can then present the results in the same order as their source selection.

The source's syntax is also included in the array. Some sources accept multiple syntax types, so you could add code to give the visitor a choice of syntax by source. This code assumes that **$source** contains the visitor's selection, rather than the multiple choice you give to your Web site visitors.

The Search Parameters

The **$search** array accepts multiple search parameters of various sorts. You can grab one of the Z39.50 documents, or bibliographic references from the Z39.50 site, and add as many fields as you like. All you need do is add matching code in the **search( )** function to process each field type:

```
$search[] = array("title" => "penfold");
```

search()

The following **search( )** function accepts the two arrays and returns multiple results in the same sequence the sources are listed in **$source:**

```
function search($source, $search)
    {
    if(is_array($source))
        {
        $s = $source;
        }
    elseif(is_string($source) and strlen($source))
        {
        $x = explode("/", $source);
        $y = explode(":", $x[0]);
```

```
        $s[$y] = array("site" => $source);
        }
    else
        {
        $s["Bell Labs"] = array("site" => "z3950.bell-labs.com",
            "database" => "books");
        }
```

The first part of the code checks that **$source** is an array, and converts **$source** to an array if it is not. This lets you specify one data source as a preformed string for ease of testing. The contents of **$search** end up in **$s**. You could modify this part of the code to perform services including looking up the source's site name/ IP address and port number from a database so the information does not have to be known outside this function.

The second part of the code converts the **$search** array to an RPN string. Because of my engineering background, I made the code provide for all circumstances, including receiving a preformed query string. After you build your search input page, you can remove unneeded code and add any refinements that will help the people using the search. You could move the translation between common field names, like **title**, and attribute references, like **1=1003**, to an array, so you can add extra field types with little effort and then use the array to generate the questions on your search input form:

```
if(is_array($search))
    {
    $t = "";
    if(count($search) > 1)
        {
        $t .= "@and ";
        }
    while(list($k, $v) = each($search))
        {
        if(isset($v["author"]))
            {
            $t .= "@attr 1=1003 " . $v;
            }
        if(isset($v["title"]))
            {
            $t .= " 1=4 " . $v;
            }
        }
    }
```

18. Search

705

```
elseif(is_string($search))
    {
    $t = $search;
    }
else
    {
    $t = "";
    }
```

The next code creates the result string, and subsequent code adds to this string:

```
$result = "<br>Search string: " . $t;
```

The code makes two passes through array **$s**, once to generate the searches, and then a second time to gather the results. The first pass is shown next, and steps through the array using a **while( )** loop:

```
reset($s);
while(list($k, $v) = each($s))
    {
    $s[$k]["source"] = $v["site"];
    if(isset($v["port"]) and strlen($v["port"]))
        {
        $s[$k]["source"] .= ":" . $v["port"];
        }
    if(isset($v["database"]) and strlen($v["database"]))
        {
        $s[$k]["source"] .= "/" . $v["database"];
        }
    if(!isset($s[$k]["syntax"]) or !strlen($s[$k]["syntax"]))
        {
        $s[$k]["syntax"] = "sutrs";
        }
    if($s[$k]["connection"] = yaz_connect($s[$k]["source"]))
        {
        yaz_syntax($s[$k]["connection"], $s[$k]["syntax"]);
        if(yaz_search($s[$k]["connection"], "rpn", $t))
            {
            }
        else
            {
            $result .= "Search failed for " . $s[$k]["source"]
                . " and search " . $t;
            }
        }
```

```
    else
        {
        $result .= "Connection failed for " . $s[$k]["source"];
        }
    }
```

Within the loop, some references are to the **$v** array extracted from **$s**, and some are directly to **$s**. The references to **$s** are to save values in **$s** for use in the second pass through **$s**. For some people, the code may be easier to follow if you replace references to **$v** with **$s[$k]**. For other people, the code will be easier to follow if the code is split into two passes: one to format the fields, and another to use the fields in connections.

yaz_connect( ) accepts one source and creates a connection for that source. You can have multiple connections, and a server accepts multiple connections, so you can have connections to several databases on one server. **yaz_syntax( )** specifies the result syntax for the source, and **yaz_search( )** passes the search string to the connection. The rest of this code produces error messages if a connection does not work, but does not stop the rest of the search.

yaz_wait( ) waits for all sources to complete all searches before proceeding. That lets you run multiple searches in parallel, but lets one data source slow down the whole search. If you have a large list of sources with overlapping information, you could benefit from setting up a script that searches one source at a time and lists the time for each search so you can cull out the excessively slow sources:

```
yaz_wait();
```

The next section of code loops through each data source and gathers the results:

```
reset($s);
while(list($k, $v) = each($s))
    {
    $errno = yaz_errno($v["connection"]);
    if($errno == 0)
        {
        $hits = yaz_hits($v["connection"]);
        $result .= "<br>" . $hits . " hits for " . $k . " "
            . $v["database"];
        if($hits > 0)
            {
            $record = "array";
            if($v["syntax"] == "sutrs" or $v["syntax"] == "xml")
                {
```

```
                        $record = "string";
                        }
                $result .= "<table cellspacing=\"0\" cellpadding=\"0\">"
                    . "<tr><td>Hit</td><td>" . $v["syntax"]
                    . "</td></tr>\n";
                for($h = 1; $h <= $hits; $h++)
                    {
                    $hit = yaz_record($v["connection"], $h, $record);
                    if(is_array($hit))
                        {
                        $result .= "<tr><td align=\"right\""
                            . " valign=\"top\">" . $h . "</td><td>"
                            . array_display($hit) . "</td></tr>\n";
                        }
                    elseif(strlen($hit))
                        {
                        $result .= "<tr><td align=\"right\""
                            . " valign=\"top\">" . $h . "</td><td>"
                            . htmlentities($hit) . "</td></tr>\n";
                        }
                    }
                $result .= "</table>\n";
                }
            }
        else
            {
            $result .= "Wait failed. Error: " . $errno . " "
                . yaz_error($v["connection"]);
            $add = yaz_addinfo($v["connection"]);
            if(strlen($add))
                {
                $result .= "<br>  " . $add;
                }
            }
        yaz_close($v["connection"]);
        }
```

The last part of the function returns the result string ready for display:

```
    return($result);
    }
```

yaz_errno( ) indicates errors for a connection, and **yaz_hits( )** reports the number of hits for the connection. Collect the hits by reading through the results with

yaz_record( ) with the **for( )** loop collecting from one to the number of hits. If there is an error, **yaz_error( )** provides an error message, and **yaz_addinfo( )** adds extra error information. See the notes about **yaz_addinfo( )** in the previous solution. **yaz_close( )** closes each connection.

A lot of this code is table formatting and can be replaced with the table formatting functions used in other chapters. Develop your own table formatting functions to suit your needs, because they will be among your most-used tools.

array_display()

Some of the results are arrays instead of strings, so they are converted from an array to a string using function **array_display( )** from the previous solution.

Testing the Search

All you need to do to test the **search( )** function is to type in the next line of code. All changes to data sources and search parameters are made in the input arrays:

```
print(search($source, $search));
```

The Results

Here are the first few lines of results from the State Library of South Australia:

```
Search string: @attr 1=4 Array
1 hits for State Library of South Australia innopac
Hit usmarc
   1 0 0 (3,001)
     1 0 (3,001)(3,@)
       1 flu00032526
```

Here are the first few lines of the Bell Labs results:

```
2 hits for Bell Labs books
Hit sutrs
  1 cn 621.395/I613a 1990 ti Application specific array processors :
    proceedings of the international conference, September 5-7, 1990,
```

There is one obvious problem with presenting results from multiple sources. If each source presents results in a different format, you are faced with the challenge of presenting all the results in a single useful list.

Searching google.com

This code will make your personal Web server into a browser using the Google search engine. You can use this code as a base for developing a meta-search engine, searching many search engines at once, or the base for a revolutionary new search engine interface to replace the existing interfaces.

How could you improve on Google's current interface? Its standard interface is too limited, its advanced interface has too many options, and neither implements an iterative search refinement. What you want is a search that automatically takes the narrowest view of the search request, tests the view with a search, broadens the search until there are sufficient results, and then presents the results from the narrow to the broad.

The code I will show you performs one search using the Google defaults, and then performs limited editing of the defaults for display. If you wanted the perfect search, you would edit the results to count the number of results and try the search in other ways if there were not enough results. The test search string is *PHP and web site architecture*. Google stupidly drops the word *and*, and treats the other words as unrelated. What a good search engine would do is search for the exact phrase first, followed by all the terms joined by logical **and**, and then repeat the search, dropping one word at a time from the right, until it reaches the desired minimum result count. If the search engine is prefect, it will list **phptect.com** first, but that is just my own bias.

The Form

The following code is an enhancement of a form from Chapter 9:

```
$x = "";
if(isset($keywords))
   {
   $x = " value=\"" . $keywords . "\"";
   }
print("<form action=\""  . $PHP_SELF . "\" method=\"post\">"
   . "Please enter your search keywords:"
   . "<br><input type=\"text\" name=\"keywords\" size=\"60\"" . $x . ">"
   . "<br><input type=\"submit\" name=\"submit\ value=\"Submit\">"
   . "</form>" );
```

The search string goes into the field **$keywords**, and that form loops back to itself, so the code uses the existence of **$keywords** to decide if you are using the page for the first time or a subsequent time. The value in **$keywords** becomes the default value for the one input field.

```
Please enter your search keywords:
PHP and web site architecture
  Submit Query
```

Figure 18.2   The search input form.

Figure 18.2 shows the form with the search phrase used to test this solution.

The following code is all you need to perform a search of **google.com** using its simple search:

```
if(isset($keywords))
    {
    $search = "http://www.google.com/search?q=" . urlencode($keywords);
    print("<br>" . htmlentities($search) );
    $page = file($search);
    }
```

The URL would be longer if you used the site's advanced search. The **file( )** function sends the URL to the site and returns the page containing the search results in array **$page**.

Here is the URL sent to Google:

```
http://www.google.com/search?q=web+site+architecture+and+PHP
```

I tried the same search phrase in the Exact Phrase field of Google's advanced search, and the following URL is the result. Many of the extra fields can be left off if they are defaults. Despite requesting an exact phrase match, Google still produced the warning "The **AND** operator is unnecessary:"

```
http://www.google.com/search?as_q=&num=10&btnG=Google+Search&as_epq=PHP+
and+web+site+architecture&as_oq=&as_eq=&lr=&as_qdr=all&as_occt=any&as_dt
=i&as_sitesearch=&safe=off
```

Related solution:	*Found on page:*
Creating a Form	343

The Raw Results

You want to pull apart the retrieved page, so you can use just the parts you need. The following code displays the raw result page so you can look for markers that distinguish the parts you want:

```
if(isset($page))
   {
   reset($page);
   while(list($k, $v) = each($page))
      {
      print("<br>k: " . $k . ", " . htmlentities($v) );
      }
   }
```

Here are excerpts from the result page showing the start of the page, line 0, the start of a style in line 3, the end of the style in line 13, the start of the results in line 18, and the start of the bottom navigation bar in line 53:

```
k: 0, <html>
k: 3, <style><!--
k: 4, body {font-family: arial,sans-serif}
k: 5, div.nav {margin-top: 1ex}
k: 12, //-->
k: 13, </style>
k: 14, </head>
k: 15, <body bgcolor=#ffffff text=#000000 link=#0000cc vlink=#551A8B
k: 16, <form name=gs method=GET action=/search><INPUT TYPE=hidden
   valign=middle><input type=text name=q size=31 maxlength=256 value="web
   site architecture and PHP"> <input type=submit name=btnG value="Google
   Search"><input type=submit name=btnI value="I'm Feeling
   Lucky"><br></form>
k: 17, </td></tr></table>
k: 18, <table border=0 cellspacing=0 cellpadding=2><tr><td
k: 53, <div class=nav>
k: 54, <p><table border=0 cellpadding=0 width=10% cellspacing=0><tr
k: 71, <p><center><table width=100% cellpadding=2 cellspacing=0
Google</font></center></body></html>
```

The Results Edited

The following code displays the raw results again with a few lines left out:

```
$nav = "<div class=nav>";
if(isset($page))
   {
   reset($page);
   while(list($k, $v) = each($page) and substr($v, 0, 7) != "<style>")
      {
      }
   print("<br>k: " . $k . ", " . htmlentities($v));
```

```
    while(list($k, $v) = each($page) and substr($v, 0, 8) != "</style>")
        {
        print("<br>k: " . $k . ", " . htmlentities($v));
        }
    print("<br>k: " . $k . ", " . htmlentities($v));
    print("<br>");
    while(list($k, $v) = each($page) and substr($v, 0, 6) != "<table")
        {
        }
    print("<br>k: " . $k . ", " . htmlentities($v));
    while(list($k, $v) = each($page)
        and substr($v, 0, strlen($nav)) != $nav)
        {
        print("<br>k: " . $k . ", " . htmlentities($v));
        }
    }
```

The first line defines the marker for the start of the navigation bar, so you can
easily change the marker. You could use the same approach for all the other markers. The code checks that **$page** exists, resets **$page** just in case other code has
used **$page**, and then performs a series of loops through **$page** to print the desired portions and skip the undesired portions.

The first **while( )** loop skips entries through to the first line starting with **<style>**.
Because the line starting with **<style>** is needed in the output, there is a one-off
print of the current entry. The next **while( )** loop prints until it finds the end tag
for **<style>**. The end tag is printed, and then a break, and then a **while( )** loop
looks for the start of a **<table>** tag. Printing starts, and then stops when the next
while( ) loop finds the tag in **$nav**. One advantage of having the marker tags in
variables is the ability to get the tag length with **strlen( )** so comparisons can be
of an exact length. You can also use the tags in variables if you include error
messages to indicate missing tags.

The following result shows the first lines returned from **$page** by the selection
loops. The style is included, although not all the results are displayed here:

```
k: 3, <style><!--
k: 4, body {font-family: arial,sans-serif}
k: 5, div.nav {margin-top: 1ex}
k: 10, A.l:link {color: #6f6f6f}
k: 11, A.u:link {color: green}
k: 12, //-->
k: 13, </style>

k: 18, <table border=0 cellspacing=0 cellpadding=2><tr><td width=200>
```

The Results Displayed

You want to see the edited results displayed in the Web page, so you can easily relate the results to the editing. The next code displays the HTML from the Google page within your Web page, using all the same selection loops as before but now printing the HTML as part of the page rather than the format produced by **htmlentities( )**:

```
if(isset($page))
    {
    reset($page);
    print("<br>");
    while(list($k, $v) = each($page) and substr($v, 0, 7) != "<style>")
        {
        }
    print($v);
    while(list($k, $v) = each($page) and substr($v, 0, 8) != "</style>")
        {
        print($v);
        }
    print($v);
    while(list($k, $v) = each($page) and substr($v, 0, 6) != "<table")
        {
        }
    print($v);
    while(list($k, $v) = each($page)
        and substr($v, 0, strlen($nav)) != $nav)
        {
        print($v);
        }
    }
```

The first part of the displayed result is shown in Figure 18.3. 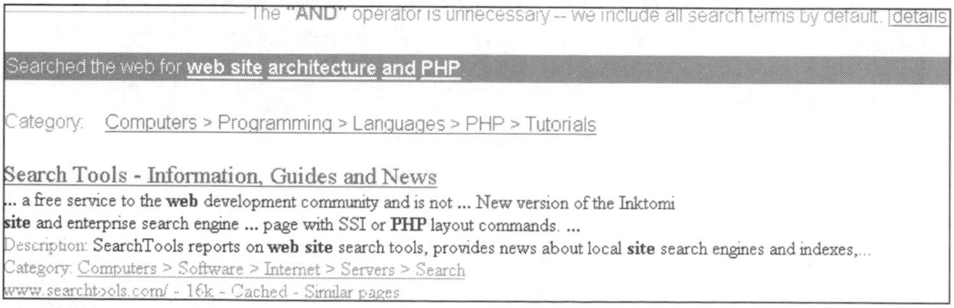

Figure 18.3   The Google results.

You can add code to refine the search string input facility, to use the Google advanced search, to search several search engines at once, to extract information from the results and display them your way, or to merge the results with other data sources. Share your improvements, or invent a whole new search engine. Google is one of the best search engines but is still in need of refinement, and you could invent that refinement.

Indexing Data

When you set up your own database for searching, you will be faced with building a lookup index. The better the index, the more your visitors will find with a straight lookup, and the less you will have to revert to slow searches using SQL's **like** operator. This solution works through a simple index build using a small number of generic examples. You can expand this example based on the specific range of name and description conventions in your data.

The following list contains a couple of strings representing common ways of presenting titles of books and movies. They will test the index build code:

```
$data[] = "PHP and web site architecture";
$data[] = "Test with Punctuation, The";
```

The following list contains words and phrases that will be excluded if, and only if, a potential index string is an exact match:

```
$exclude["and"] = true;
$exclude["the"] = true;
```

The following code steps through the **$data** entries, creating index entries in **$index** that point back to entries in **$data**. In a Web page indexing function, the entries in **$index** would point back to the page containing the input data:

```
while(list($k, $v) = each($data))
   {
   $v = trim($v);
   $index[$v] = $k;
   if(strtolower($v) != $v)
      {
      $index[strtolower($v)] = $k;
      }
   $x = str_replace("|", " ", $v);
   $x = str_replace(" and ", "|", $x);
```

```
$x = str_replace(",", "|", $x);
$y = explode("|", $x);
while(list($yk, $yv) = each($y))
    {
    $yv = trim($yv);
    if(!strlen($yv))
        {
        unset($y[$yk]);
        }
    }
if(count($y) > 1)
    {
    reset($y);
    while(list($yk, $yv) = each($y))
        {
        $yv = trim($yv);
        if(!isset($exclude[strtolower($yv)]))
            {
            $index[$yv] = $k;
            if(strtolower($yv) != $yv)
                {
                $index[strtolower($yv)] = $k;
                }
            }
        }
    }
}
```

The first step is to place the exact phrase, trimmed of leading and trailing spaces, from **$data** into **$index**. The second step is to translate the phrase to lowercase and enter the lowercase version into the index. That lets you search for an exact-case match for acronyms, and then perform a case-insensitive match.

The code with all the **str_replace()** functions converts various separators to a common I character. Then **explode()** separates the parts of the string into array **$y**. You can add code to split the string based on quotes, semicolons, and whatever else appears in your text.

If **$y** has only one entry, that entry is essentially the same as the original entry already in the index. When **$y** has more than one entry, each entry is added to the index. I added a loop through **$y** to remove null and blank entries before performing the count just in case the data has double separators somewhere.

The **while()** loop through **$y** skips any entry that is in **$exclude** and places the survivors in **$index**. Before an entry is tested in **$exclude**, the entry is trimmed and translated to lowercase. The entries added to **$index** are trimmed of leading and trailing spaces, and then added in both mixed case and lowercase.

It is time to test the index. The following code prints **$index** as a table with the left-hand column containing the index entry, and the right-hand column containing the string identified by the index entry:

```
print("<table>");
while(list($k, $v) = each($index))
    {
    print("<tr><td>" . $k . "</td><td>" . $data[$v] . "</td></tr>");
    }
print("</table>");
```

Here is the output from the index build:

```
PHP and web site architecture PHP and web site architecture
php and web site architecture PHP and web site architecture
PHP                           PHP and web site architecture
php                           PHP and web site architecture
web site architecture         PHP and web site architecture
Test with Punctuation, The    Test with Punctuation, The
test with punctuation, the    Test with Punctuation, The
Test with Punctuation         Test with Punctuation, The
test with punctuation         Test with Punctuation, The
```

Your challenge is to locate the identifiers in your data and arrange them to satisfy your visitors. If you want to help people find streets, removing the word *Grove* from *Rose Grove* helps people find *Rose* among a mass of avenues, groves, and streets. When they type in *Rose Street* by mistake, show them all the Rose Streets and then, if there are few or no Rose Streets, the Rose Groves.

If your database contains restaurants, flower shops, and plant nurseries, removing the word *Grove* might return thousands of flower shops with the word *Rose* in their names. You might find that a useful feature of SQL is the **limit** clause to limit how many results are returned from the database. Set a range of results from a minimum of 10 to a maximum of 50 results, and place the 50 limit in the SQL. If the visitor's search returns fewer than 10 results, try a wider-range search, like dropping the *grove* from *rose grove*. When the results exceed the limit, suggest the searcher use a more specific search, and prompt them with the options you can offer, like the addition of a state or city selection. To make that sort of prompt useful, make sure your results contain the prompt field for the entries returned to the searcher. If they can see there are many entries per state, they will attempt to select the right city. Without some sort of visual feedback, they might just select a state and still end up with more than 50 results. Google tells you how many entries it found. If you are looking at results 1 through 10, and you see that there are a total of 23 results, you just step through the pages. However, a total of 29,858 results would prompt most people to be more specific with their search.

Do your visitors type in *chips corn* when they want *corn chips*? How many shoppers could remember the correct sequence of *lemon, lime, orange, and ginger marmalade*? You can easily add code to split identifiers into words and reassemble the words in different sequences. If you split the string of words into an array using **explode( )**, you can loop through the array producing every combination of words.

You can also add equivalents of common words. Add *jam* when you see *marmalade*. Make sure you do not replace words, like some dumb search engines; just add the extra references.

Chapter 19

Sessions

In Depth

Sessions change the World Wide Web from random page reads to a coordinated, focused interaction between the user and the Web site. Compare visiting a naturopath to learning about natural health from the back of packets in supermarkets. The bottle of vitamin C on the supermarket shelf features a little sales pitch on how vitamin C cures everything from dandruff to cancer. The jar of zinc tablets at the supermarket features the information that zinc helps you with everything from cancer to dandruff. The information is isolated and uncoordinated.

Now visit the naturopath for a session. The naturopath will take you through a coordinated discussion and point out things like the health benefits of vitamin C, but will warn you that chewing vitamin C tablets can lead to the ascorbic acid eating holes in your teeth. The naturopath will tell you that zinc is good for your skin and it can help with dandruff, but your diet contains enough zinc, and the zinc is leached away by all that coffee. Each time you visit the naturopath, he or she will write down the things you say, and before the next visit, will read what happened at the previous sessions. Web site sessions help in a similar manner.

The Internet was designed to be a series of random unrelated events so the failure of one event would not damage another event. A file transfer by FTP is a single *event*. One event occurs when your Web browser requests a page and the Web site server delivers that page. If the Web page contains images and your browser requests the images, each image request and delivery is a separate event. In the same way, the label on one product at the supermarket has nothing to do with the label on the next product. The rules of the Internet make sure there are minimum standards and formats for data so the data does not get lost, just as the government says the packaging on supermarket products must state a minimum weight and not make any claims that the product can cure cancer.

The World Wide Web inherited the randomness of the Internet and tried to add a little order through the query string added to URLs. If you search a site for the word *dandruff*, the word goes into the URL, or a **GET** header or a **POST** header, and is passed to the site. Usually, the search term goes back to your browser within the Web page as a query string added to URL links in the page. When you search the site again, the search entry box is preloaded with the word *dandruff*, so you can start there and add qualifying words to refine your search—words like *itchy*, *real bad*, or *snowstorm*.

The Web site might have 300 servers answering your questions, and none of them know what you did on the previous page except for that query string. What if you tried 20 search terms and left the site in disgust because the site did not answer your question or sell you a cure? *Sessions* can help.

Sessions add an identifier that is passed between browser and server to link one page request to all previous requests in the same session. If the identifier is used intelligently, it can be used to do just about everything except cure cancer.

Benefits to the Owner

Sessions provide many benefits to the site owner and the site's visitors. The site owner can use session records to find that you asked 20 questions about dandruff, and did not proceed to buy vitamin C or whatever the site is selling. The site owner can then use that feedback to improve the search engine so you find the right pages. If the Web site sells bicycle parts, the site owner has the choice of adding vitamin C tablets to the site's product range. The site owner can also research the first pages you visited before you searched for information about dandruff, and find out why a page about bicycle parts induced your search for dandruff cures.

Those fancy Web analyzer tools that cost thousands of dollars are just decoration without sessions. They just show you the pages people looked at, not the pages that brought people into your site or the pages that made people leave. Add sessions, and suddenly the data becomes information. You can find the first page in sessions, the last page in sessions, and the average read time per page.

Benefits to the Visitor

The visitor gets to visit a better quality Web site when the owner uses sessions to analyze and improve the site. The visitor also gets the opportunity to log on, automatically use a custom profile, maintain a shopping cart, review cumulative search terms, and use many other useful features.

The session can link to one small record in a file or a whole database of information about the visitor and his or her likes and dislikes.

Session Identifier

The link between sessions is an *identifier* (or key) that is sent to the browser with each page, then sent by the browser back to the Web server with the next page request. You can generate your own identifier or let PHP generate it. The identifier can be used as the key to a database of session information or as a unique string within a session file name. The identifier is passed to the browser and back in either a cookie or link URLs.

Cookies

Heaps of people confuse cookies with sessions. Cookies are one of two ways you pass a session id from page to page, but that is all. Sessions do not need cookies and do not store anything other than the session id in the cookie.

You will find shopping cart software that stores the cumulative shopping list in a cookie. Install the software on your site and ask people to test the cookie-based shopping cart. It will be a race as to what will send you insane first. There will be people editing the prices in the cookie so the $19.95 book costs them only $4.95. There will be people losing half their shopping cart contents because the cookie exceeds the 4KB cookie size limit in their browser. As they shop and pop up links to manufacturers' sites to read about products, their cookie count will go up and will finally make the browser drop the first cookie—the one with the shopping cart.

If there is information in a cookie, the information is as fragile as a snowflake in a microwave oven. When you read information from a cookie, trust it like you trust "no new taxes" or "your check is in the mail." Good cookie-based sessions not only keep important information out of the cookie, they also go to great lengths to make sure the session id is legitimate. What can you do to trust a cookie? Place the session id in the cookie in plain text so the returning cookie can be automatically routed by server management software in your primary server or an intelligent router. Add an encrypted secret, something unique about each page request, so you can decrypt the secret to verify that the incoming page request is the result of the Web site's previous reply to the same session.

Everything sent out in a cookie should be recorded on your server and checked whenever a cookie comes back in. The result is a safe, reliable connection from page to page.

There are other things to avoid when using cookies for sessions. You can encrypt the visitor's IP address within the session cookie, or store the IP address in the session record, and then reject a request that comes from another address. Users of WebTV and some proxies supply a different IP address for every request, so they are not able to shop at sites using IP addresses for session verification.

When your visitor clicks the Back button on his or her browser, the information returned to the server depends on how the browser's authors interpreted the rules for writing Back buttons, but right or wrong, the information is almost certainly the wrong information for a shopping application. What you want in a shopping application is to send a person back to a previous product page or shopping category, but not to change the contents of the shopping cart. That means keeping the shopping cart constant in the session record and accepting older Web page requests, including ones that break your special rules for cookie content verification.

HTTPS

One approach to verifying cookies while allowing steps back is to use HTTPS, the secure version of HTTP. During logon, you switch from HTTP to HTTPS, and it encrypts the data flowing between a browser and a Web site.

Security experts can tell you much more about HTTPS than I can with my limited experience. I did, on one occasion, help a friend with his Web site and find out I knew more about HTTPS and security than the senior technical officer at the ISP hosting my friend's Web site. Oops. Check your Web site's security with your ISP, and then get a second opinion.

I worked as security administrator for several large online systems, and all the concepts behind HTTPS existed before the Web, are well researched, and are thoroughly hacked. An expert can take you through all the steps needed to securing your site and, based on recent experience, the main problems will be proxy servers and firewalls.

Cookies versus URLs

Cookies keep the messy-looking session id string out of your URLs and let people bookmark pages without getting a session id locked into the bookmark. URLs keep the messy-looking session id string visible in your URL while you are testing, and let people use your site when they have cookies turned off.

Cookies can be thrown at the visitor and rejected by the user, with your script detecting the rejection. When a visitor first hits your site, the field **$HTTP_REFERER** contains a URL pointing to a different Web site, and **$REMOTE_HOST** contains a different server name. You can use the difference to identify their first visit and sent session information by both a cookie and the link URLs. When the visitor requests the next page from your site, look for an incoming cookie to determine if their browser is set to accept cookies. Set a field in their session record to a cookie or URL, and then deliver subsequent pages with the session id stored via the method specified in the session record.

Files versus Databases

Session information is stored on the Web server using files or a database. In a database, there is one record per session; with files, there is one file per session. Files are the easiest way to set up sessions, so they make sense for your first experiments with sessions in PHP. I use a database instead of files because I already know how to use databases. Your decision may depend on which chapter you read first, this chapter or Chapter 5.

I use MySQL for sessions because MySQL is easy to install, runs on every operating system I use for Web sites, is easy to administer, lets me add session analysis, and does not have the overhead of transaction-based databases. You can choose another database or stick with files, but consider the following items when selecting a method for a large site.

Files have large space overhead for small amounts of data in file systems like Linux's ext2, whereas space-efficient file systems like Reiser and NTFS are optimal only for certain ranges of sizes. Databases have very little space overhead, no matter what the size of your session record.

Files have low processing overhead, but have problems when shared among multiple servers. Databases have a higher processing overhead, but come ready-built for access from multiple servers.

MySQL gives you the choice of tables built with transaction support or simpler, faster tables without transaction support, which are ideal for sessions. You could leave all your other databases in PostgreSQL (discussed in Chapter 5) or DB2 (discussed in Chapter 6) , and set up a MySQL database just for session management. MySQL tables can be easily administered using phpMyAdmin, a PHP-based administration system for MySQL. Chapter 5 tells you how to write your own MySQL scripts. PostgreSQL does have an equivalent to phpMyAdmin, but it does not yet have the option of turning off transaction support for a table. Your choice depends on your operating system and the requirements of your other applications.

When you want to list or analyze current sessions, you need your session records in a database. To analyze the records from files, you would have to read a directory, then read every file in the directory, and allow for files disappearing between the time you read the directory and the time you read individual files. With a database, all you need is one line of SQL and a query.

PHP Facilities

PHP has built-in session-handling facilities that work in most circumstances and can be turned off, or bypassed, for those occasions when you need more control over sessions. Start by understanding the settings in php.ini, leave the session records in files, and practice with the session functions. Once the sessions are working, experiment with changes in php.ini and then move on to session records in a database. Keep notes about your changes to php.ini and their results.

php.ini

The following code example is the **Session** section of php.ini as installed by default from PHP 4.0.5:

```
[Session]
session.save_handler = files
session.save_path = /tmp
session.use_cookies = 1
session.name = PHPSESSID
session.auto_start = 0
session.cookie_lifetime = 0
session.cookie_path = /
session.cookie_domain =
session.serialize_handler = php
session.gc_probability = 1
session.gc_maxlifetime = 1440
session.referer_check =
session.entropy_length = 0
session.entropy_file =
;session.entropy_length = 16
;session.entropy_file = /dev/urandom
session.cache_limiter = nocache
session.cache_expire = 180
session.use_trans_sid = 1
url_rewriter.tags =
    "a=href,area=href,frame=src,input=src,form=fakeentry"
```

This section is a quick explanation of the settings you may need to change. The latest php.ini has far more settings than when sessions were first released, so you can presume that the additional settings were created to solve problems, but not problems you get when first using sessions.

session.save_handler defaults to storing sessions in files and lets you specify **user**, in which case you have to use **session_set_save_handler()** to define the functions that handle the reading and writing of session records. The following code shows the change you make to php.ini when placing sessions in a database like MySQL:

```
session.save_handler = user
```

session.save_path defines where PHP should write the session files when you are using files. Use **/tmp** for Unix and Linux, **c:/temp** or **c:\temp** for Windows NT/ Windows 2000, and **c:\temp** for Windows 98 or later. Once sessions are working, create a special directory for session files and restrict access to the directory so other users of the system cannot access the session records, because it is possible someone could steal a session for fun or profit.

session.use_cookies lets you turn off cookies, but do not try this when you are first testing cookies. **session.name** provides the name for the cookie. Set

session.auto_start to **1** to start cookies for every page, and then, when cookies are working, turn off automatic mode to experiment with manual control, such as only starting a session when someone logs on.

Leave **session.cookie_lifetime** alone; it defaults to sessions running as long as the browser is active. Leave **php** as the **session.serialize_handler** and leave all the other settings at their defaults until you have cookies working.

session.gc_probability sets the percentage of times PHP session garbage collection runs. Each time a page request starts a PHP session-handling routine, PHP checks if garbage collection is required. Leave **session.gc_probability** set to 1 so garbage collection runs just once for each 100 pages. Although theoretical reasons exist for changing this value, there are as many reasons for making the value smaller as there are for making the value larger. The result of a change is hard to measure and is dependent on your type of database, server configuration, and volume of traffic. On a site that is extremely busy for several hours per day then quiet for the rest of the day, you might want to take the garbage cleanup out of PHP's control by removing the cleanup code from the garbage handler and place the cleanup code in a batch job run by a scheduler like cron.

session.gc_maxlifetime sets the number of seconds a session record survives after last use. The default is 1440, allowing 24 minutes from the last time a person presses Enter to the point where the PHP session garbage collection routine deletes the session record as too old. Someone at your site will complain that this duration is too short and they have to log back on too often, so you will make this setting larger and larger, until someone complains that their session was hijacked after they went home. You cannot get all 225,000 users to agree on the one time, so pass the responsibility back to the site owner and let them cop the flack.

session.referer_check lets you restrict cookies to visitors from certain sites, but the check is not reliable because the source data is not a reliable guide to who is visiting your site. Leave this inaccurate security check out of sessions. Instead, let every visitor have a session, and then restrict access through conventional security; but leave other visitors with somewhere else to go—somewhere with information about your site and an inquiry form so you do not lock out potential customers.

session.entropy_file lets you specify a file that supplies extra data to the session id generation routine. On many Unix systems you can use /dev/random or /dev/urandom. I have yet to see a site that needs this setting. When sites grow to many servers and begin to push PHP's random id generation to the limit, the sites often switch to intelligent routers to perform session id allocation and management. You can also replace PHP's id with one generated from a database autoincrement field, which will guarantee an id that is unique across the range of servers using the database. **session.entropy_length** specifies the number of bytes read from the external file, and 0 disables reads from the external file.

url_rewriter.tags defines which HTML tags will receive the session identifier when cookies are turned off. The default is fine for your initial tests and may never need changing.

PHP Session Functions

The following functions are used to manually control sessions, including overriding php.ini settings. When you replace PHP's default session files with a database, you will define session record-handling functions as shown in the "Starting a Session Using MySQL" Immediate Solution.

session_cache_limiter()

php.ini contains the **session.cache_limiter** setting to control caching via HTTP headers. **session_cache_limiter()** lets you display the current setting and alter the setting for the current script. Naturally, this has to run before the headers are sent, and the headers are sent when you use **session_start()** or **session_ register()**, or when you send any data to the browser. The following code prints the current value, and then changes the value to **private** (the options are **private**, **nocache**, and **public**):

```
print("<br>" . session_cache_limiter());
session_cache_limiter("private");
```

session_decode()

If you want to manually decode session record information when testing sessions, use **session_decode()**. The following code decodes a string and reports any errors:

```
if(!session_decode($data))
   {
   print("<br>Decode failed for " . htmlentities($data));
   }
```

Where does the data end up? In the global variable pool. Even if you use **session_decode()** in a function, the data ends up in the global variable pool, and that is one of the reasons for not using session decode for anything other than testing.

session_destroy()

session_destroy() removes all data associated with a session. You have to use **session_start()** before **session_destroy()**, and the session cookie remains in the browser. The following code starts a session, so the session can be destroyed, then destroys the session:

```
session_start();
if(!session_destroy())
   {
   print("<br>session destroy failed.");
   }
```

What happens if in one script you destroy a session and then create a new session? The following error messages occur when you use **session_start( )** or **session_register( )** a second time in the one script:

```
Warning: Constant sid already defined
Warning: Cannot send session cache limiter - headers already sent
Fatal error: Failed to initialize session module
```

To avoid the duplicate SID define, you would have to create the new session by hand, issue the cookie yourself, and create the new session record yourself. To avoid the header error, you would have to destroy and re-create the session while the page is still in the HTTP header stage. Instead of destroying and re-creating the session, you could leave the session intact and perform a manual call to **session_unset( )** to remove all variables from the session. On the next page, the visitor will have a session id and no variables, and the script should build new variables as if the visitor is visiting for the first time.

session_encode()

session_encode( ) grabs all the registered variables, encodes them in PHP's proprietary way, and returns a string containing the encoded variables. You can use this for testing, and decode with **session_decode( )**. The following code contains a quick test with one variable:

```
$title = "Articles for sale";
session_register("title");
$string = session_encode();
print("<br>Session string: " . htmlentities($string));
```

session_end()

Session processing is automatically ended when your script ends, but you might want to reduce overhead by ending the session processing early. This is extra important when using frames, because frame updates have to wait on the same session record. For frames, leave **session_start( )** until the last minute in your script, then perform all session updates as fast as possible, and then issue **session_end( )**

to end use of the session record. Your script then frees up the session record for other frames. This function will appear in PHP after version 4.0.6:

```
session_end();
```

session_get_cookie_params()

When you are testing your session code with cookies, use **session_get_cookie_params()** to check the values contained in the incoming cookie, as follows:

```
$p = session_get_cookie_params();
while(list($k, $v) = each($p))
    {
    print("<br>Cookie parameter: " . $k . ", value: " . $v);
    }
```

The function returns an array containing **lifetime**, the time the cookie expires, **domain**, which should match the domain of your Web site, and **path** when the cookie applies to a subdirectory of your Web site. The cookie can also contain **secure** if it has to be sent via Secure Sockets Layer (SSL).

session_id()

session_id() returns the current session id and optionally sets a new id. The following code prints the current id, uses **microtime()** to build a new id, sets the new id, and prints the new id:

```
print("<br>" . session_id());
$x = explode(" ", microtime());
$id = session_id("id" . $x[1] . substr($x[0], 2));
print("<br>" . $id);
```

The session id is also available through the constant SID, if there is no cookie, and SID can be used to build URLs if automatic building of URLs is turned off:

```
if(defined("SID"))
    {
    print("<br>Session id: " . SID);
    }
```

You will see endless code for producing unique session ids. Most is based on fantasy. You want one thing with a session id: uniqueness. Random numbers work most of the time, but because they are random numbers, they can still come up with the same value on two consecutive selections. The way to get a unique number is to save session records in a database and use the database's **auto_increment** facility to generate a new key for each session.

If you are not using a secure network like a secured Virtual Private Network, you want the session id to be hard to guess, so people will not break in through trial-and-error techniques. That means mixing the unique id with other text, and encrypting part or all of the result. Chapter 4 contains a pile of encryption techniques you can use.

session_is_registered()

session_is_registered( ) accepts the name of a variable as a string and returns true if the variable is registered or false if it is not registered:

```
$reg = "title";
if(session_is_registered($reg))
    {
    print("<br>" . $reg . " is registered.");
    }
else
    {
    print("<br>" . $reg . " is not registered.");
    }
```

session_module_name()

You can use **session_module_name( )** to find out if **session.save_handler** is set to **files** or **user**, as shown in the first line of code that follows:

```
print(session_module_name());
print(session_module_name("user"));
```

You can also change the handler, as shown in the second line of code. Changing the handler would be done only in testing, would have to occur before using any code that starts a session, and would have to remain the same for the life of a session. It is easier to test using a test Web site than try to dynamically change the session handler module.

session_name()

session_name( ) returns the session name defined by **session.name** in php.ini. If you supply a new name as a parameter, **session_name( )** will set a new name. The name has to be set before you start session processing in the script, before you use **session_start( )** or **session_register( )**. When you change the name, a new cookie is set. To read the new cookie, you have to set the new name for every script in the session. One reason you might set a special name is to initiate a second session when a visitor logs in. After they log off, you can drop the new session name and let them revert to the original cookie and session. The following code prints the current name and then sets and prints a new name:

```
print("<br>" . session_name());
print("<br>" . session_name("supersession"));
```

The result is:

```
PHPSESSID
supersession
```

session_readonly()

When you use frames, you have all the frame updates sharing the same session record and locking each other out. You can reduce the interference by starting the script with **session_readonly( )** to retrieve session variable values. When everything is in place, quickly open the session record for update, and then close the record again with **session_end( )**. **session_readonly( )** will improve session handling within frames by allowing some frames to read the session record without updating the session record.

session_readonly( ) has not been released at the time I am writing this so I am guessing at how it will fit together. The function was mentioned in PHP documentation, and then removed. A **read only** option could be added to **session_start( )** to achieve the same result. **session_readonly( )** will need a matching **session_update( )**, or a way of synchronizing updates through a regular **session_start( )**:

```
session_readonly();
```

session_register()

session_register( ) registers variables to be saved in session records. If you do not run **session_start( )** before **session_register( )**, **session_register( )** will start the session. This function accepts an unlimited number of parameters. Each parameter can be a string containing the name of a variable, an array containing strings containing variable names, or an array of arrays containing names of variables:

```
$title = "Articles for sale";
$reg = "title";
if(!session_register($reg))
   {
   print("<br>Register failed for " . $reg);
   }
```

Once a variable is registered, you can check the registration using **session_is_registered( )**, and unregister the variable with **session_unregister( )**.

session_save_path()

session_save_path( ) returns the path used to store the session files, if you are using files, and optionally sets a new path. The following code shows **session_save_path( )** setting a temporary directory for session files under Windows NT and Windows 2000. You could use c:\temp\session under Windows 98:

```
print(session_save_path("t:/session"));
```

The directory has to exist before you use **session_save_path( )**, and to be effective, you have to set the save path before you start a session through **session_start( )** or **session_register( )**.

session_set_cookie_params()

session_set_cookie_params( ) sets a session cookie, but session cookies are set automatically, so why use this function? Manual control of cookies lets you set special cookies for specific directories and override other cookie parameters such as the expiry time:

```
session_set_cookie_params(time()+90000);
session_set_cookie_params(time()+90000, "/test");
session_set_cookie_params(time()+90000, "/test", "test.com");
```

You can override the session lifetime, as shown in the first of the code lines. You can override the time and path, as shown in the second line, or the time, path, and domain, as shown in the third line. Note that time is in seconds and there are 86,400 seconds in a day. Also note that if the browser has the wrong time or date, because of daylight savings time or some other reason, the browser may expire your cookie with the manually set time. It is better not to set a time in order to let the cookie last the life of the browser session.

session_set_save_handler()

session_set_save_handler( ) accepts the name of all the session record processing routines, and registers them ready for use during the script. You use this function before **session_start( )** and the first **session_register( )**, so the session open and read functions will be ready for the start of the session processing. In the following example, I named the session-handling functions by their function:

```
function session_open($path, $name)
   {
   return(true);
   }
function session_close()
   {
   return(true);
   }
```

```
function session_read($id)
    {
    return($data);
    }
function session_write($id, $data)
    {
    return(true);
    }
function session_remove($id)
    {
    return(true);
    }
function session_gc($life)
    {
    return(true);
    }
session_set_save_handler("session_open", "session_close",
    "session_read", "session_write", "session_remove", "session_gc");
```

session_open() accepts the path to the session files and the session name, and does little of use. **session_close()** again does little. **session_read()** accepts the session id and reads in the session data, returning the data undecoded. **session_write()** accepts the session id and session data already encoded, and returns true. **session_remove()** accepts a session id and destroys the session record. **session_gc()**, garbage cleanup, runs every so often and deletes expired session records for sessions that just timed out and were never destroyed.

session_start()

session_start() starts or resumes a session. A session is automatically started by **session_register()**, so **session_start()** may be unnecessary in some scripts, although I make a habit of always putting in **session_start()**, just in case someone moves or deletes the **session_register()** code. **session_start()** has to occur before any output to the browser, including accidental white space characters:

```
session_start();
```

session_unregister()

This function removes a variable from the registration list. In PHP 4.0.6, the function had not gained the **session_register()** feature of multiple parameters and arrays of parameters. The function returns false if unregistration fails, as shown here:

```
$reg = "title";
if(!session_unregister($reg))
    {
    print("<br>Unregister failed for " . $reg);
    }
```

session_unset()

This function is equivalent to running **unset( )** against all the variables registered for the session. If you are destroying a secure session during a logoff, you could run *(unset)* to remove all the private values, such as passwords, in one hit. The code would then go on to populate just those variables that are used by a person not logged on:

```
session_unset();
```

setcookie()

setcookie( ) accepts a cookie name and a set of optional parameters, and sets a cookie to be delivered with the current HTML headers. **setcookie( )** has to run before you output any HTML, because HTML stops you from sending headers, including cookies. Use **setcookie( )** to set cookies when you want additional cookies or want standard session cookies but do not want to use the PHP automatic cookies. The following code outputs an empty cookie that deletes a cookie of the same name:

```
setcookie("mycookie");
```

The next code sets a new cookie with all parameters:

```
setcookie("mycookie", "pizza", time()+90000, "/php/", "phptect.com", 1);
```

The first parameter is the name ("**mycookie**"), the second parameter is the value ("**pizza**"), and the third parameter is an expiry time set to just over one day. The fourth parameter makes the cookie apply to directory /php/ and the fifth parameter makes the cookie work only for domain phptect.com. The last parameter makes the cookie work only over HTTPS, the secure form of HTTP. The expiry parameter and the security parameter can be skipped with 0, and the string parameters can be skipped with an empty string ("").

The cookie will appear in the next page request from the same browser if the page request is within the same domain and directory. The value will appear in a variable of the same name as the cookie. When PHP receives the previous cookie, PHP will place the value in variable **$mycookie** and the value can be displayed with:

```
print("<br>My Cookie: " . $mycookie);
```

The result will be:

```
pizza
```

You delete a cookie by sending a cookie with the same name, an empty value, an expiry time in the past, the same directory, and same domain. To delete the previous cookie, use:

```
setcookie("mycookie", "", time()-90000, "/php/", "phptect.com", 1);
```

Customer Service

Sessions and cookies are to provide a service, not security, not shopping carts, and not a barrier to entry. People with cookies turned off should still be able to visit your site and reach a contact page containing information about your use of cookies. Allow sessions to switch from cookies to URLs when cookies are off, and consider not placing cookies on your home page unless the visitor enters the page with an existing cookie.

Make sure your cookies are set to return to your domain and, if possible, to your server. All browsers should have the option to allow only cookies that return to the issuing domain, but current browsers either do not give you the choice, bury the choice so it is impossible to understand, or give you the wrong choices. Unfortunately, the original cookie specifications seem to be the result of a snap decision by some kid on work experience leave from a school that did not teach professional programming or logic, so you are stuck with fighting a system full of browsers lacking even the most basic cookie usage protocol.

Never store your shopping cart contents in a cookie; leave cookies with just the session id and keep the rest on the server. When you see an online shopping system that places prices in a cookie, you are looking at a system wide open to fraudulent modification of prices, and plenty of companies are suffering financial losses because they cannot secure the cookie.

When you spot JavaScript in the application, you have found a trouble spot. I charge $10,000 to teach Web site developers the following secret: *Do not use JavaScript.*

You can look through 90 percent of major Web sites, backed by millions of dollars of development, and still find several coding errors in their most basic image rollover scripts. Think about how unlikely it is that a JavaScript "wizard" can get a shopping cart to work in JavaScript if the wizard's rollover code is full of holes. Before you add any JavaScript to your site, commit to a full and systematic multiple-browser testing program that will take several days and several people, and will cost thousands of dollars.

Immediate Solutions

Starting a Session Using Cookies and Files

This solution presents the minimum you need to use sessions. Get this working first, and then experiment with registering variables and the examples in the other solutions:

```
[Session]; Handler used to store/retrieve data.
session.save_handler = files
session.save_path = t:/session
session.use_cookies = 1
session.auto_start = 0
session.cookie_lifetime = 0
session.use_trans_sid = 1
url_rewriter.tags =
"a=href,area=href,frame=src,input=src,form=fakeentry"
```

Your php.ini file should have the right defaults for a test Unix system. **session.save_handler** is set to **files**. **session.save_path** is set to **/tmp** by default for Unix. Set it to **c:\temp** for Windows. My NT workstation has drive t: allocated to disposable test files so I allocated a discrete directory **t:/session**, as highlighted. **session.use_cookies** defaults to 1 to use cookies, but **session.auto_start** defaults to 0, so the session is not started until you use **session_start( )**. This is the ideal test configuration so you can change settings before the session starts, it's ideal for frames where you want to minimize the time the session file is open, and it's ideal for sites that perform tricks like changing sessions when people log on. **session.cookie_lifetime** defaults to 0, which indicates the session cookie will remain until the browser is closed.

session.use_trans_sid is set to add the session id to your URLs and links if cookies are not used, so test this setup at least once with cookies turned off in your browser. **url_rewriter.tags** lists the HTML tags that will receive the session id automatically. Test this with cookies off using pages that have things like HTTP redirection headers, and note what does not automatically receive the session id. You can then work on functions to generate the missing session id.

HTTP relocation headers are generated by the following code:

```
header("Location: /test/index.html");
```

If HTTP relocation headers are issued at the start of the headers, they make a browser request a different page (HTTP headers are not HTML tags, so they are not rewritten by the URL rewriter).

The following function accepts a location string and returns the string with the SID added if it is defined:

```
function session_header($location)
   {
   $location = "Location: " . $location;
   if(defined("SID"))
      {
      if(strpos($location, "?") === false)
         {
         $location .= "?";
         }
      else
         {
         $location .= "&";
         }
      $location .= "session=" . SID;
      }
   return($location);
   }
```

The code checks for an existing query string, indicated by **?**, and adds the session parameter with **?** or **&** as appropriate.

To use sessions in your script, add the following code to your script:

```
<?php
session_start();
?>
```

The code will send headers, so it must be inserted in your script before you produce any non-header output. That means no **print** or **echo** statements before session start and no blank lines, carriage returns, or newlines before the **<?php** tag.

The session save path directory will look like Figure 19.1, with one file per session. The first part of each file name is a common prefix, so the file can be distinguished

Contents of 'T:\session'

Name	Size	Type	Modified	Attributes
sess_512adcdefd83a32460661ee39d92077f	0KB	File	7/27/01 12:44 PM	A

Figure 19.1 Session file in session save path.

if it is placed in a general shared directory. The second part of the file name is the SID. Note that the length of the file is zero because no variables are registered.

Test **session_register( )** next. The following code sets up variables of various types, including multiple dimension arrays. All are registered so you can see what they look like in a session record:

```
$integer = 235;
$string = "test text";
$special = "special character:" . chr(245);
$array[] = "test";
$array[] = "test2";
$again["DE"] = "Germany";
$again["JP"] = "Japan";
$multiple[1][1] = "a";
$multiple[1][2] = "b";
$multiple[2][1] = "c";
if(!session_register("integer", "string", "special", "array", "again",
   "multiple"))
   {
   print("<br>session register failed");
   }
```

The registration happens when you use **session_register( )**, but the variables are actually written to the session record after your script finishes. The variables must exist at the end of the script and still contain the values you want saved. The one exception is in scripts that write the session record early with **session_end( )**, because **session_end( )** writes the variables to the session record immediately.

What does a session record file look like? The following line (broken to fit the book's layout) shows the content of a file with the previously assigned variables registered, and using the default PHP encoding, not the optional WDDX encoding:

```
integer|i:235;string|s:9:"test text";special|s:31:"quote " and special
character:õ";array|a:2:{i:0;s:4:"test";i:1;s:5:"test2";}again|a:2:{s:2:"
DE";s:7:"Germany";s:2:"JP";s:5:"Japan";}multiple|a:2:{i:1;a:2:{i:1;s:1:"
a";i:2;s:1:"b";}i:2;a:1:{i:1;s:1:"c";}}
```

integer is the name of the first variable. **l** indicates that a type follows. **i** is the type for integer, **s** for string, **a** for array, and **o** for object. **:** means an attribute follows, and the first attribute, **235**, is the value for the integer. Strings have the string length as their first attribute and the string value as the second attribute.

The double quote ("), and special character in string **$special** are not escaped or given special treatment because the string is preceded by a length, and the length is all that is needed to define the string. In fact, the quotes around the string are merely decorative because of the length field.

The braces ({}), are used to define lists of entries within arrays, and any entry can be another array, as shown in the array **multiple**. Each entry in an array is a pair of values, with the first indicating the key name for the entry, and the second indicating the value for the entry.

When you have lots of code in a script and you are creating variables on the fly, you might want to know if a session is registered. Use **session_is_registered( )**, as follows, to test for an existing registration:

```
if(session_is_registered("integer"))
    {
    print("<br>integer is registered" );
    }
```

You will not get an error if a variable is registered twice in one script, or is reregistered in the next script in the same session. The only reason for testing the registration process is to skip a long registration process for a huge variable list if it is not needed.

The following code is a test to explain how registration works:

```
if(isset($zzzz))
    {
    unset($zzzz);
    print("<br>zzzz unset");
    }
else
    {
    $zzzz = "Sounds like a mosquito.";
    print("<br>zzzz set");
    }
if(session_is_registered("zzzz"))
    {
    print("<br>xxxx is already registered");
    }
else
    {
    session_register("zzzz");
    print("<br>registered zzzz");
    }
```

The code uses variable **$zzzz**, checks if the variable exists, sets the variable if it does not exist, and unsets the variable when the variable does exist. The code also registers the variable if it is not registered. The status is printed every time so you can see what happens.

The first time you run the script, you get the following result because the variable is not set and not registered:

```
zzzz set
registered zzzz
```

The second time you run the code, you get the following result because the variable is set by **session_start( )**, and is indicated as registered:

```
zzzz unset
xxxx is already registered
```

When you run **session_start( )**, every variable in the session record is set in memory and registered. You do not have to register the variable in every script. A variable that is created during logon can be registered once during logon and then forgotten, and will remain registered for the life of the session. When you reach the logoff page, unregister the variable to stop it from being saved for future scripts in that session.

The following result shows the third run of the script. The variable is reset, because the variable is missing, but it is still recognized as registered. How does PHP manage that trick?

```
zzzz set
xxxx is already registered
```

The following line is the contents of a session record when a variable is registered but not set:

```
!zzzz|
```

Note that there is an exclamation mark (!) in front of the variable name, but there are no attributes after the l. This is PHP's way of carrying a variable registration from page to page even if the variable is not set.

To complete the test, here is the code to unregister variable **$zzzz**:

```
if(!session_unregister("zzzz"))
   {
   print("<br>session_unregister failed.");
   }
```

Experiment with unregistration on your logout page. Note that unregistration does not unset the variable in the current script; unregistration stops the variable from carrying over to the next script.

You can now do anything you like with sessions, no frames, and a single server. There is more work to do when you have multiple frames in one browser sharing the one session record, or multiple servers sharing the one session record.

Starting a Session Using MySQL

If you use session files for just a few variables, the session files waste space in file systems like FAT and ext2; so look at file systems like NTFS or Reiser, or jump straight to session records in a database. MySQL makes sense for session records because it has the minimum overhead for storing session records and is available on every platform that runs PHP.

You will have problems sharing files between servers, with both performance and access issues, and the problems increase geometrically as you increase the number of servers. Databases tend to make data sharing easier and performance problems increase at a linear rate, rather than exploding geometrically.

For optimum performance on a single server, keep the files in memory. MySQL lets you store tables in memory using a table type of **heap**. When you define a heap table using SQL, add **type=heap** after the table name, as shown in the following SQL fragment. Heap tables have limited indexing and SQL lookup facilities, but you do not need the missing bits for session records:

```
create table test type=heap
```

For this solution, use the default MySQL table creation, which will produce a table type of MyISAM. The table will have no transaction processing overhead, so you get optimum performance for a disk-based table. The following SQL creates a table named **session** for session records, with field **id** receiving the session id, **time** acquiring the current date time for use in expiring sessions, and **data** receiving the encoded session data:

```
create table session
    (
    id varchar(32) not null,
    time timestamp(14),
    user tinytext not null,
```

```
data text not null,
primary key (id)
);
```

user is an extra field thrown in to receive the visitor's name if the visitor is logged in, and gives you a quick way of displaying who is logged in. Enter the SQL through an application like phpMyAdmin or through **mysql_query( )**. Chapter 5 describes the MySQL functions.

Related solution:	*Found on page:*
Displaying Table Data	171

The **id** field is a fixed-length character field of 32 bytes, because that is the size of the PHP-generated session id. The record will be found through a binary search of the primary index, and will be fast. If you have a database that allows fixed record allocation, you can devise a slightly faster access method, but you will be limited in what you can store in a session record because each record will be a fixed length.

The timestamp field is one to watch in many databases. Earlier versions of MySQL left timestamp fields empty on row inserts; the timestamp was updated only for row updates. Using the latest version of MySQL, the timestamp is set on insert. Check your database—you need the timestamp field set every time, because a row with an empty timestamp field will appear to be expired, and will be deleted by the garbage cleanup routine.

Tell your test script you are using user-defined session code by adding the following code at the start of your script (this line must precede **session_set_save_handler( )**, and **session_set_save_handler( )** must precede **session_start ( )**):

```
session_module_name("user");
```

Add the following functions to your script. The functions provide the name of the session or site **database**, and the name of the database session **table** to the remaining code:

```
function session_db()
    {
    return("petermoulding");
    }
function session_table()
    {
    return("session");
    }
```

session_db( ) could be expanded to select the database via **mysql_select_db( )**, and you could write a matching function to reselect the database that was selected before selecting the session database. In the system used to test this code, all the tables are in one site-specific database so reallocation is not necessary, and the ISP hosting the production version of the test site currently has one database per virtual Web site, so there is no reselection code included. The MySQL functions include an older **mysql_db_query( )** where you could include a database name as a parameter, but that function is deprecated and will disappear.

The next function gives you a way to see messages from the session functions, even from **session_write( )**, which runs after the browser output is closed. You can change this function to send the messages anywhere you want, including system logs, but make sure you have easy access during testing. I suggest you use this approach until you are happy that the sessions are working, and then remove all information messages, leaving just the error messages, and direct the error messages to your normal error log:

```
function session_log($message)
    {
    if($file = fopen("t:/session.txt", "a"))
        {
        fwrite($file, date("Y-m-d H:i:s ") . $message . "\n");
        fclose($file);
        }
    }
```

Here is a modification of the log function that replaces the date/time display with a **microtime( )** display so you can see the exact time a database connection is open. I dropped the data to save space, and show the result from this version later in this solution:

```
function session_log($message)
    {
    if($file = fopen("t:/session.txt", "a"))
        {
        $m = explode(" ", microtime());
        fwrite($file, date("H:i:s", $m[1]) . substr($m[0], 1) . " "
            . $message . "\n");
        fclose($file);
        }
    }
```

You need a function to open the session processing, and another to close the session processing. All these functions do is produce a log message. Your functions can do anything, including connecting to a remote database server. When you have 45 servers receiving connections distributed by an intelligent router, you can have all the servers connecting to a common database server that has just one database and one table purely for session records. (Choose a database that lets you expand to at least two hot-swappable database servers in case one server dies.) When you use connections to shared database servers, minimize connection times by delaying **session_start()** until the latest possible point in your script. Also use the new **session_end()**, when the function is available, to end the connection at the earliest point in your script. Also look at permanent connections as explained in Chapter 5:

```
function session_open($path, $name)
   {
   session_log("session_open");
   return(true);
   }
function session_close()
   {
   session_log("session_close");
   return(true);
   }
```

Immediately after you run **session_start()** and PHP runs **session_open()**, PHP runs **session_read()** to read in the current session record, if the record exists.

The following user-written function, **session_read()**, accepts the session id and returns a string containing the session data. If the data is not available, the function returns a zero-length string. This function assumes a database connection, and you can establish a connection in this function or back in **session_open()**:

```
function session_read($id)
   {
   session_log("session_read");
   if(!mysql_select_db(session_db()))
      {
      session_log("session_read select database error: "
         . mysql_error());
      return(false);
      }
   $sql = "select * from " . session_table()
      . " where id='" . $id . "'";
   if(!$result = mysql_query($sql))
      {
      session_log("MySQL error: " . mysql_error()
         . " with SQL: " . $sql);
      return(false);
```

```
        }
    if(mysql_num_rows($result))
        {
        session_log("MySQL query returned " . mysql_num_rows($result)
           . " rows.");
        $row = mysql_fetch_assoc($result);
        session_log("session_read returned " . $row["data"]);
        return($row["data"]);
        }
    else
        {
        session_log("session_read found zero rows with SQL: " . $sql);
        return("");
        }
    }
```

The function starts by selecting the right database, **mysql_select_db( )**, and the database name is provided by **session_db( )**. Every database function is checked for an error (a value of false), and on error the code logs a message, and then exits (**return( )**) from the function that returns false.

The SQL query, **$sql**, is built using the table name from **session_table( )** and the session id supplied as a parameter to **session_read( )**. **mysql_query( )** executes the SQL query and returns a result id on success or false on failure. **mysql_num_rows( )** returns the number of rows found by a **select** query, and you want one returned. Zero rows is the preferred result at the start of a session, and an error on subsequent reads. There is no check for a missing session record because there is no indication of when a session record should exist. Even if the session is started, the record could have expired and been removed by the garbage cleanup routine. There is no check for a duplicate row because the id is the primary key and the database will prevent duplicates.

This code could check if the record has expired, but that will be left to the garbage cleanup routine. In secure systems where timeouts are very short, add an expiration check here because the garbage collection might not happen for several minutes after the session expires.

mysql_fetch_assoc( ) returns the row as an associative array with the keys being the field names. The encoded session data is in string **$row["data"]**, and you return the string still encoded. If you want to analyze sessions by user id or other variables, you have the choice of adding the variables as extra fields in the row, as I did with **user**, and leaving the same variables in the encoded data, or leaving the variables out of the encoded data. When you store the variables twice, as discrete fields and as encoded data, you waste space, but you save having to restore the variables during this read. When you store the variables once as discrete fields and do not register them for encoding as session variables, it is your responsibility to restore the variables during this read.

session_write() accepts the session id and the encoded session data as shown in the code below. It writes the session data to the database and returns true on success or false on error. **mysql_select_db()** selects the database as described for **session_read()**. The SQL, **$sql**, is prepared using the table name form **session_table()** and the session data. The session data is enclosed in **addslashes()** because the data might contain single quotes and upset the SQL. MySQL removes the added slashes when entering the data into the database, so you do not have to remove the slashes when you retrieve the data. If your php.ini has automatic slashes set on, and you cannot turn them off, leave **addslashes()** out of this code.

$PHP_AUTH_USER supplies the user id so you can see which users have active sessions. **mysql_query()** updates the database and returns true if the SQL is syntactically correct. **mysql_affected_rows()** returns the number of rows actually changed by this update: 0 indicates an error, 1 indicates success, and a number greater than 1 indicates your SQL or database table definition is wrong.

When zero records are updated, the code assumes this is the first update for a session and inserts the record instead, using SQL **insert** and another **mysql_query()**. Some databases let an update perform the insert automatically, or let you perform an insert that replaces any existing record. MySQL has a **replace** command that updates existing records and inserts new records. Check your database and consider using **replace** instead of **update** if the database vendor recommends **replace** as faster than **update**.

One advantage of using a separate update and insert is the ability to cross check fields between updates from multiple windows within frames, but that is way beyond the scope of this solution. For frames, wait until the new **session_end()** and **session_readonly()** functions are available, or send me a note asking for the full explanation of handling frames with the existing functions:

```
function session_write($id, $data)
   {
   session_log("session_write");
   if(!mysql_select_db(session_db()))
      {
      session_log("session_write select database error: "
         . mysql_error());
      return(false);
      }
   $sql = "update " . session_table()
```

```
         . " set data = '" . addslashes($data) . "'";
    if(isset($PHP_AUTH_USER))
        {
        $sql .= ", user='" . addslashes($PHP_AUTH_USER) . "'";
        }
    $sql .= " where id='" . $id . "'";
    if(!$result = mysql_query($sql))
        {
        session_log("session_write error " . mysql_error()
            . " with SQL: " . $sql);
        return(false);
        }
    if(mysql_affected_rows())
        {
        session_log("session_write update affected "
            . mysql_affected_rows() . " rows with SQL: " . $sql);
        return(true);
        }
    session_log("session_write updated zero rows with SQL: " . $sql);
    $sql = "insert " . session_table()
        . " set data = '" . addslashes($data) . "', id='" . $id . "'";
    if(!$result = mysql_query($sql))
        {
        session_log("session_write error " . mysql_error()
            . " with SQL: " . $sql);
        return(false);
        }
    else
        {
        session_log("session_write inserted with SQL: " . $sql);
        return(true);
        }
    }
```

This code seems perfect until you test it. A strange thing can happen in the current MySQL (and some other databases). If you update a record and the new values happen to match the previous values, MySQL does not count the update as an update. That remains true even if a timestamp is, or should be, automatically updated. When the previous code performs an update that produces a zero update count, the code tries to perform an insert and produces an error. There is a simple solution. Replace one line, **set data=**, in the previous code with the following line. This modified line sets the timestamp field to null, which forces MySQL to both update the timestamp field and count the update as an update:

```
    . " set data = '" . addslashes($data) . "', time = null";
```

session_remove( ) removes an existing session record, and is initiated by **session_destroy( )**. **session_destroy( )** could also be used to remove a session during a logoff. All the secret stuff in the secure session record would be wiped, and a new session would be created for the logged-off visitor. **session_remove( )** receives the session id, deletes the session record via SQL **delete** and **mysql_query( )**, and then returns true to indicate success or false to indicate failure. The only time your code should try to delete a deleted record is when the user logs off, clicks the Back button in his or her browser, and then tries to log off again.

All the logging and error messages are the same as in **session_read( )** and **session_write( )**. The only thing you might choose to do in this code is add a check that the user is logged off, has **$PHP_AUTH_USER** removed, and has logged off LDAP or any other connected system. This function could force a logoff of all the other systems or just report an error if the session is destroyed before the user is logged off the other systems:

```
function session_remove($id)
   {
   session_log("session_remove");
   if(!mysql_select_db(session_db()))
      {
      session_log("session_remove select database error: "
         . mysql_error());
      return(false);
      }
   $sql = "delete " . session_table() . " where id='" . $id . "'";
   if($result = mysql_query($sql))
      {
      session_log("MySQL query delete worked.");
      return(true);
      }
   else
      {
      session_log("MySQL update error: " . mysql_error()
         . " with SQL: " . $sql);
      return(false);
      }
   }
```

Garbage collection is a no-brainer with a database, intelligent database design, and one line of SQL. What you want to do is perform a **session_remove( )** for all the sessions that did not have a **session_destroy( )** because the session timed out or the user closed his or her browser. If **session_remove( )** has logoff code, and there are sessions where the user closed the browser without logging off, you need to run **session_remove( )** for each expired session. I will describe that first, and then walk through the simpler code that follows.

In **session_gc( )**, you could select every expired session, read all the results into an array, step through the result array, and feed the session ids one at a time to **session_remove( )**. **session_remove( )** would delete the session record and perform associated logoffs.

The following code assumes there is no reason to run **session_remove( )**, and simply deletes all the expired session records with one SQL **delete**:

```
function session_gc($life)
   {
   session_log("session_gc");
   if(!mysql_select_db(session_db()))
      {
      session_log("session_gc select database error: " . mysql_error());
      return(false);
      }
   $sql = "delete " . session_table() . " where time < '"
      . date("YmdHis", time() - $life) . "'";
   print(p(red("session_gc sql: " . $sql)) );
   if($result = mysql_query($sql))
      {
      session_log("session_gc deleted " . mysql_affected_rows()
         . " rows.");
      return(true);
      }
   else
      {
      session_log("session_gc error: " . mysql_error()
         . " with SQL: " . $sql);
      return(false);
      }
   }
```

Most of the code—**mysql_select_db( )**, **mysql_query( )**, and the error reporting—is the same as in **session_read( )**. The SQL, **$sql**, uses SQL **delete** and the table name from **session_table( )**, and selects all the rows that have a time field earlier than the expiration time. The expiration time is the current time minus the session life value supplied by PHP to **session_gc( )**.

Notice that this approach requires very little thinking or calculation. Some people try to drive expiration via the expiration time set in a cookie, but the expiration time in the cookie can fail when the visitor's browser is in a different time zone and the browser does not use exactly the time-based expiration system you expect. Using this garbage collection to remove expired session means the sessions are expired by exactly the same date/time used to create and update the session records. You can then use the lack of a session record as the opportunity to expire cookies. In fact, there is never any need to expire the cookie because the worst that can happen is someone returning to a browser after a long absence, clicking on a link that sends an old cookie to your server, and then receiving a new empty session. They will not revive a logged-on session because your script will not receive the session values required to continue a secure session.

The following code ties together the preceding functions:

```
session_set_save_handler("session_open", "session_close",
    "session_read", "session_write", "session_remove", "session_gc");
```

session_set_save_handler( ) tells PHP which user-written functions will perform each session function. This function has to execute before **session_start( )** to have an effect. In one development version of PHP, **session_set_save_ handler( )** worked even if you forgot **session_module_name( )**.

The next code, **session_start( )**, uses all the preceding code:

```
session_start();
```

As soon as you use **session_start( )**, PHP runs **session_open( )** and **session_read( )**. If you have a special connection to a session database, resources are allocated and the connection is opened. The resources will remain in use until the end of your script, and no matter how your script ends, short of the server bursting into flames, PHP will run **session_write( )** and **session_close( )**.

The following code tests the session by creating a variable, registering the variable, and printing messages to tell you what happened:

```
if(!isset($zzzz))
    {
    $zzzz = "Sounds like a mosquito.";
    print("<br>zzzz set" );
    }
if(!session_is_registered("zzzz"))
    {
    session_register("zzzz");
    print("<br>registered zzzz" );
    }
```

Here are the results of the test code for the first page in a session:

```
zzzz set
registered zzzz
```

The variable is set and registered. Subsequent scripts in the session produce no messages because the variable is restored and marked registered by PHP's session code.

What does a session record look like in the MySQL table? See Figure 19.2 for a session record from MySQL displayed through phpMyAdmin.

What does the session log look like? The following list is a session log for one page using the **microtime( )** version of the log:

```
13:57:16.64906100 session_open
13:57:16.64980800 session_read
13:57:16.65543500 MySQL query returned 1 rows.
13:57:16.65623200 session_read returned zzzz|s:23:"Sounds like a
    mosquito.";
13:57:16.95838700 session_write
13:57:16.96103100 session_write update affected 1 rows with SQL: update
    session set data = 'zzzz|s:23:\"Sounds like a mosquito.\";' where
    id='9b7078927131c3a1edb1fcbecf47e4af'
13:57:16.96346100 session_close
```

Notice that the order is open, read, write, and then close. The read occurs immediately after the open, and the close occurs immediately after the write. If you opened a page containing frames, the first open and read would be for the main page, and all the remaining opens, reads, and writes would be jumbled together. The only thing that will serialize the access is a file or row lock, but a lock slows down the access and subsequent page display. You can speed up that access by deferring the **session_start( )** to the last minute, and you can use the microtime log to look at the results of your efforts.

Once your sessions are working, comment out the information entries in the log and drop the data display because the data field can grow to be huge.

id	time	user	data
9b7078927131c3a1edb1fcbecf47e4af	20010728121954		zzzz|s:23:"Sounds like a mosquito.";

Figure 19.2   Session record in MySQL table.

Displaying Current Users

When you are using the session functions listed in the preceding solution, you can easily list current active users online. The following list is ordered by user and shows the user's id, the time they last requested a page, and the session id:

```
user       time            id
Agnetha    20010728121954  9b7078927131c3a1edb1fcbecf47e4af
Anni-Frid  20010728183450  cd95db833aa0a98b72a673108892349c
Benny      20010728180308  df5bc09dd416e42f3044d86e90f0db51
Björn      20010728183216  628720e1e48457e94d28a4664e0b0987
Others:    2
```

You could order the list by time to gauge the best cutoff point for your session lifetime. If, during logon, you retrieve a longer name and a contact email address or telephone number for each user, you can add those items to the session record and to this list to produce a contact list. When you want to call users and tell them the server is going offline for a grease and oil change, bring up this list including telephone numbers:

The following is the code for the list:

```php
$sql = "select user, time, id from session order by user";
if($result = mysql_query($sql))
    {
    $others = 0;
    print("<table>");
    while($row = mysql_fetch_assoc($result))
        {
        if(!isset($heading))
            {
            $heading = "<tr>";
            while(list($k, $v) = each($row))
                {
                $heading .= "<td>" . $k . "</td>";
                }
            print($heading . "</tr>");
            reset($row);
            }
        if(strlen($row["user"]))
            {
            print("<tr>");
            while(list($k, $v) = each($row))
                {
                print("<td>" . $v . "</td>");
                }
```

```
        print("</tr>");
        }
    else
        {
        $others++;
        }
    }
    print("<tr><td>Others:</td><td>" . $others . "</td></tr>");
    print("</table>");
    }
else
    {
    session_log("MySQL error: " . mysql_error() . " with SQL: " . $sql);
    return(false);
    }
```

The SQL performs a simple request ordered by user. **mysql_query()** sets up a cursor full of results, and **mysql_fetch_assoc()** retrieves the rows one at a time. The code following **if(!isset($heading))** sets up a heading using the field names. The outer **while()** loop steps through the rows, and the inner **while()** loop steps through the fields. There are variations of this code in Chapter 5 that produce prettier results and allow easier modification.

Related solution:	*Found on page:*
Displaying Table Data	171

One thing to note is the calculation of **$others**. If a row has a user field of zero length, the row is not printed and is just added to the count in **$others**. The last line of the table row code includes the other count so you can see how many visitors are visiting but not logged on. You might like to buffer the table output and print the **$others** count first.

If your garbage collection is set to run infrequently and the activity rate is low, you could improve this list by running garbage collection before reading the database. If you are using the session code from the previous solution, you can call function **session_gc()** at any time to delete expired sessions.

Using **session_end()**

session_end() does not exist in PHP 4.0.6, so I will make up **session_end()** and assume the eventual PHP **session_end()** will do the same as the function included in this solution. The important point is that **session_end()** reduces your connection time to databases, and can be used to reduce the time files are locked when displaying frames.

Files

If you want to use files for session records, either wait for the official PHP **session_end( )** function or replace PHP's built-in file processing using the code shown in the solution entitled "Starting a Session Using MySQL," but with file reads and writes replacing the MySQL functions. To ensure the file is locked for the duration of use, open the file for update with **session_open( )** and close the file in **session_close( )**.

Databases

Get the code from the solution entitled "Starting a Session Using MySQL" working, and then apply the following modifications to replace the normal end-of-script session end with the user-written **session_end( )**:

```
function session_filler_close()
    {
    session_log("session_filler_close");
    return(true);
    }
```

Step one of the change is to add two dummy functions to pretend they are writing the session record and closing the session. The following function pretends to be **session_close( )**, but does nothing. **session_close( )** does nothing in the example code, but can be modified to close connections and clean up anything elaborate you set up in **session_open( )**. **session_filler_close( )** merely replaces **session_close( )** in **session_set_save_handler( )** so **session_close( )** can be used in **session_end( )**.

The following **session_filler_write( )** does the same nothing as **session_filler_close( )**, with the only difference being the parameters accepted by this function:

```
function session_filler_write($id, $data)
    {
    session_log("session_filler_write");
    return(true);
    }
```

Change **session_set_save_handler( )** to replace **session_close** with **session_filler_close** and **session_write** with **session_filler_write** as shown next:

```
session_set_save_handler("session_open", "session_filler_close",
   "session_read", "session_filler_write", "session_remove",
   "session_gc");
```

Now you need **session_end( )** to perform the real session write and close. The following function does everything you need. One line runs the real **session_write( )** with the session id and encoded session data. Another line runs **session_close( )**, and then a line returns the value returned by **session_write( )**:

```
function session_end()
   {
   session_log("session_end for id " . session_id());
   $result = session_write(session_id(), session_encode());
   session_close();
   return($result);
   }
```

If your version of **session_close( )** performs useful work, you could expand this **session_end( )** as follows to return the individual function values if there is a problem. You also have to decide if you want **session_close( )** to run even when there is an error in **session_write( )**:

```
function session_end()
   {
   session_log("session_end for id " . session_id());
   if(!session_write(session_id(), session_encode()))
      {
   return(false);
      }
   return(session_close());
   }
```

Test the altered code with the following code:

```
if(isset($zzzz))
   {
   print("<br>zzzz: " . $zzzz );
   }
else
   {
   $zzzz = "Sounds like a mosquito.";
   print("<br>zzzz set" );
   }
if(!session_is_registered("zzzz"))
   {
```

```
            session_register("zzzz");
            print("<br>registered zzzz" );
            }
    session_end();
    $zzzz = "My brain after herbal tea.";
```

The code sets a value in variable **$zzzz**, registers **$zzzz**, runs **session_end( )**, and then changes the value in **$zzzz**. Run the page several times, and look in the session log each time to check the session record through phpMyAdmin or a similar utility.

On the second and subsequent viewings of the page, you will get the following line:

```
zzzz: Sounds like a mosquito.
```

The variable will never retain the second value because **session_end( )** saves the session values before the change.

How much time do you save on session connections and the like? The following is an edited session log from a live page:

```
14:51:22.62918300 session_open
14:51:22.62982100 session_read
14:51:22.76881400 session_end
14:51:22.76935400 session_write
14:51:22.77387100 session_close
14:51:23.32397000 session_filler_write
14:51:23.32454800 session_filler_close
```

The time from session open to session close is only 20.8 percent of the total time from session open to the PHP session close. If your page has long page formatting routines, you might save far more than this example.

If you are using remote connections to databases and not using permanent connections, as explained in Chapter 5, then use **session_end( )** to minimize the time resources are tied up. If you are storing session records in files and using frames, minimize the lockout time between scripts within the one frameset by using **session_end( )**.

When PHP's **session_readonly( )** is working, you can further minimize resource usage and lockout time for some kinds of scripts, but you may have to perform a lot of work to fully utilize **session_readonly( )**. Among other things, you would still tie up resources connecting to a database for the read in **session_readonly( )**, so you might as well perform a normal read and write. Instead, focus on minimizing the time from **session_start( )** to **session_end( )**, and when everything is minimized, send me a note, through my Web site, about your success. I will set up a page with guidelines for using **session_readonly( )** to help you on those odd long scripts where **session_readonly( )** will produce additional benefit.

If you use **session_readonly( )** in frames, then another frame updates your data, and then you attempt a normal **session_write( )**, you will override the update from the other frame. The solution includes using **session_end( )** to minimize each frame's usage of the session record, discrete fields in the session record to hold interframe messages, discrete frame-specific variables or frame-specific encoded variables, and the dreaded JavaScript to force refreshes of other frames to make them pick up their messages. Here is the best plan. The script in the main page will execute first. Lock the session record for update in the main page. Set up all the data needed for each frame using the main script. Save the data to the session record using **session_end( )**. Let all the other frames take their turn at using the session record. If a frame wants to send a message back to another frame, the sending frame updates the session record, and then uses JavaScript to refresh the receiving frame. The receiving frame can reduce resource usage when the receiving frame knows if the refresh requires an update of the session record or just a read. You can have the receiving frame lock the record for update, read the record, decide on a read versus an update, and then unlock the record. A lock, read, unlock, is quicker than a lock, read, update, unlock.

Chapter 20

XML

If you need an immediate solution to:	See page:

In Depth

What Is XML?

XML is the Extensible Markup Language. XML is a child of Standard Generalized Markup Language (SGML) and the brother/sister of HTML, another SGML-based markup language. SGML is the child of Generalized Markup Language (GML), a project started at IBM in 1973.

I worked with one of the first commercial implementations of GML, on one of the first attempts at a simplification of GML. My main contribution was an interface between two computer systems—a large-scale online information system and a huge data repository—by implementing real-time data conversion from a proprietary format to a GML-based format. Today, using PHP, this book, and little practice, you could write and test in two weeks what required a very experienced Assembler programmer two months to write in Assembler code. You could bypass the whole real-time conversion problem by performing a one-time conversion of the database to an XML format. Most of the two weeks of work would be analyzing the data, and there might be only two days of actual programming.

The Web site **www.w3.org/XML/** lists numerous links containing way too much information on XML. Read this chapter first, practice with the Immediate Solutions, and then read the official documents that tell you how to dot the i's and cross the t's.

Why is XML magic? What does it do? What does it not do?

Why Is XML Magic?

Before XML, people argued over how data should be shared. Simple formats like Comma Separated Variable (CSV) files provided a simple and effective means of transferring data, but were limited to transferring the equivalent of one database table per file. To transfer structured data, like a whole database or a document, the transfer involved a complicated mess of CSV files. To make matters worse, some people could not understand the C in CSV and used tabs instead. Quoting strings is easy, and escaping quotes within quoted strings is also easy, but CSV files end up containing different quotes, or different methods of escaping quotes, and some files contain no quotes around strings. Add to the dozens of CSV file formats the hundreds of software makers who ignored CSV files, and you get endless unique file formats.

XML removed one layer of difficulty by providing one common file structure. The structure covers what the CSV file was intended to cover, does not allow arbitrary changes like replacing commas with tabs, and allows both a regular table type structure and an irregular document-type structure. XML provides a means for including a file definition with a file so a computer can understand the file structure and verify that new data is acceptable within the structure.

What Does XML Do?

XML delimits data by separating data items with tags. The tags give you the chance to provide long, meaningful names to identify each data element, or short cryptic tags to save space. The tags can contain attribute parameters, and the file can contain an overall structure definition called a Document Type Definition (DTD), or a reference to an external DTD, named a Document Type Declaration. A Declaration names an external file containing a Definition, and a Definition defines the file structure.

What Does XML Not Do?

XML does not make a good cappuccino, provide world peace, or help you analyze data. You are still stuck with data analysis and developing an XML structure to define your data. If you have an industry-standard XML structure for your data, you still have to fit your data to the standard. If you manufacture shoes, and there is an international XML standard for orders from shoe makers to leather suppliers, you still have to work out how the definition matches your data. You have to find out which field accepts the grade of leather, what grades can be specified in the file, and how those grades match up to the grades listed in your computer system. There is little use in sending the XML file containing grades like *fine* and *superfine* if the receiving computer expects grades A, B, and C.

When an XML file contains a structure definition or a reference to an external definition, a computer can automatically perform some validation of new data before inserting the data into the file, but you still have to ensure the definition is complete and understand what is missing. The missing definition parts will allow the insertion of invalid data.

The Web site **www.xml.org/xml/registry.jsp** contains a registry of XML definitions from various industries. Look for the closest standard definition for your data, and then work out if you can use the standard, if you need to change your data to fit the standard, or if you need a new standard. Some standards were created by industry committees, so they could be great representations of what your industry needs, a poor average, or a monolithic overkill far too complicated for real-life use. Study what XML can do, what your industry's existing XML definitions do, and what your data needs, and then choose the solution.

XML Does Not Replace HTML

In Benoît Marchal's excellent book on XML, *XML By Example*, Benoît suggests XML *is* a replacement for HTML. That is a slight over simplification. XML replaces *part* of HTML (the form definition), but not the content (the individual tags). XML tells you how to form a **<h1>** tag, but not what a **<h1>** tag does. XML gives you a way of dynamically adding new tags without breaking old browsers but does not tell the browser if a tag should force a new line on the page or what color to use for text in the tag, or even if the tag should display text. Tag content is defined in XHTML, a version of HTML rewritten in XML format.

Data

The following is a simple line of XML data from an example used in the Immediate Solutions. The less-than sign (**<**) starts an XML tag, and the greater-than sign (**>**) ends an XML tag. The start tag contains a tag name surrounded by **<** and **>**, and the matching end tag contains a forward slash (**/**), after the opening **<**. It looks a lot like HTML, and XML files can be easily edited by most HTML editors:

```
<p>mustard seed</p>
```

How does XML handle the special characters that create problems with CSV files? I typed the following test text into AbiWord, a word processor that stores documents in an XML file:

```
Start tag: <
End tag: >
Tab:
Single quote: '
Double quote: "
```

Here is the text as stored in the XML file. The **<** and **>** became HTML-style special character implementations with an ampersand (**&**) at the start and a semicolon (**;**) at the end. The tab, single quote, and double quote stayed themselves:

```
<p>Start tag: &lt;</p>
<p>End tag: &gt;</p>
<p>Tab:        </p>
<p>Single quote: '</p>
<p>Double quote: "</p>
```

You can give tags almost any name you want, with a small range of names reserved for special cases. XML comments, similar to HTML comments, are indicated with an exclamation point dash dash (**!--**) following the opening **<**, and two dashes (**--**) preceding the closing **>**, like this:

```
<!-- This file is an AbiWord document. -->
```

There is only one version of XML, so there is just one way to handle XML data; but in case that ever changes, the XML developers included a special tag to identify the XML version used to create a file:

```
<?xml version="1.0"?>
```

Notice the tag starts with **<?** and the language name, just like a PHP script. It is important to start PHP scripts with **<?php** instead of just **<?** so the PHP scripts are XML-compliant and can be mixed with other XML-compliant languages. When your PHP is XML compliant, you can store PHP code fragments with other page content in XML databases. Eventually all editors and Web servers will use XML.

Tags can be presented in several ways. A break tag, as defined in XHTML, can be written in any of the three following forms. All three are legal in XML, but XML-compliant browsers may not work with the first or last versions:

```
<br/>
<br />
<br></br>
```

The little details are killers. Is there a space before the trailing **/**? Can a tag pair be empty? **
</br>** can be empty, but in XHTML the paragraph tag is defined as not empty, so **<p></p>** is illegal (not illegal in XML, just illegal in XHTML).

The rules for the data structure and content are in the DTD, so the DTD should be read by everything that creates the XML data to ensure that the data is correctly formed.

Text lines do not impact XML tags. The following example contains the first two lines and last two lines from a very long comment tag in one of the XHTML DTDs. When XML reads in data with line breaks, the line breaks are thrown away before interpreting the tags:

```
<!--
    Extensible HTML version 1.0 Strict DTD

-->
```

The following example is another multiline tag from XHTML:

```
<!ENTITY % focus
 "accesskey    %Character;      #IMPLIED
  tabindex     %Number;         #IMPLIED
  onfocus      %Script;         #IMPLIED
  onblur       %Script;         #IMPLIED"
  >
```

Notice the exclamation in front of the tag name, the percent signs (%), and the use of the pound sign (#). DTDs contain weird tags and attributes that together act almost like a programming language. If you have to write a DTD and find yourself using all the complexities allowed in DTDs, you probably missed something in the data analysis stage and you need to reduce the data validation rules.

I mentioned the HTML **<h1>** tag earlier. Here is the XHTML definition of **<h1>**:

```
<!ELEMENT h1 %Inline;>
<!ATTLIST h1
   %attrs;
   >
```

The **<h1>** definition refers to **%inline**, and the % means substitution. **%inline** means the string **%inline** should be replaced with the string defined in an **ENTITY** definition named **inline**. **%attrs** is replaced by the string contained in the definition of **attrs**. Here is the definition for **inline**:

```
<!ENTITY % inline "a | %special; | %fontstyle; | %phrase; |
   %inline.forms;">

<!-- %Inline; covers inline or "text-level" elements -->
<!ENTITY % Inline "(#PCDATA | %inline; | %misc;)*">
```

Oops, there are two. The names are case-sensitive, and the creators of XHTML used the one name type in two representations. (I hope you never do that in your DTDs.) **<h1>** needs **%Inline**, not **%inline**. **%Inline** then includes **%inline**. Grrr. Naming confusions like that create errors that produce problems after the Web site goes live, when millions of people are using the site, and every error makes your company lose a $100 sale.

External Entities

XML entities described within an XML file are referred to as *internal entities*. *External entities* are entities that point to an external definition in a file on the local system or on another server. The previous code shows an internal entity and the following entity is an external entity pointing to a local file:

```
<!ENTITY heading1 SYSTEM "heading1.ent">
```

The next entity is an external entity pointing to a file via a URL:

```
<!ENTITY heading1 SYSTEM "http://petermoulding/heading1.ent">
```

Unparsed Entities

Entities can refer to non-XML data via an *unparsed entity*. *Unparsed* means data you do not want to parse as XML. It is used to include image files, multimedia files, and anything else that is not XML compliant, but can be used by your program or passed through to a browser. When you parse XML data for inclusion in a page and find an unparsed entity, you might insert the reference in to a HTML image (**<img>**) or anchor (**<a>**) tag and let the browser do the work:

```
<!ENTITY image SYSTEM "earth.jpg" NDATA JPEG>
```

Writing Complex DTDs

Before you tackle DTDs, finish this chapter, work through the examples, and then grab a good book on XML (such as *XML Black Book* 2nd edition, by Natanya Pitts [The Coriolis Group, Inc.]). Remember, if you are confused by a construct in a DTD, a mere mortal will have no hope of understanding the construct, and some of the software using the DTD will have the same problem. Keep your data and DTDs simple.

Structure

AbiWord files contain a **<section>** tag that contains **<p>** tags. The DTD provides the rules, and the AbiWord DTD's definition of **<section>** says **<section>** can contain **<p>** as follows:

```
<section><p>A paragraph.</p></section>
```

The DTD may or may not say that the following **<section>** within **<p>** is legal, but if it does, that means in turn that a paragraph is legal within a paragraph, which would be hard to format in a logical way. When you create a DTD, you need to impose rules to prevent situations where the data cannot be interpreted:

```
<p><section>A paragraph.</section></p>
```

The following structure is definitely not legal. The first part establishes **<section>** as the parent of **<p>**, and you cannot end a tag outside the tag's parent:

```
<section><p>A paragraph.</section></p>
```

Names

XML tag names can start with a letter or the underscore character (_). The rest of the name can be letters, numbers, the underscore, a period (.), or a hyphen (-). **xml** is a reserved name prefix, and the colon (:), although legal in names, is reserved for XML namespaces. Names are case-sensitive, but please do not confuse anyone by using mixed or uppercase.

Attributes

An XML tag can have attributes. If you specified a **font** tag in XML, you could allow a **color** attribute and type the tag as **<font color="green">**. XML requires quotes around attributes. HTML does not require the quotes, but it does allow them; so always use the quotes in HTML, and your HTML will be XML-and XHTML-compatible.

CDATA

Sometimes your XML data will contain what looks like XML to the XML processor, so you will want the special data delimited by something other than the standard XML delimiters. If your data contains a formula like **A <B> C**, you read it as *A is less than B and B is greater than C*. However, the XML processor tries to interpret **<B>** as an XML tag named **B**. CDATA is delimited by the characters **<[CDATA[** and **]]>**, and all other special characters and delimiters within the CDATA data, including <B>, are ignored.

DTD

The DTD (Document Type Declaration) is the schema for an XML file. You need to draw up a schema before creating an XML file so you know what will and will not be allowed in the file. When you read an XML file, it is up to you to decide if you will accept the data as valid or validate the data against the schema.

The DTD specifies every element and every attribute allowed in the XML file. You specify which elements are nested within each element. You can make elements and attributes compulsory or optional. Think of a file containing a catalog of products. You might make the *weight* field compulsory so you can always calculate shipping charges. You might make the *color* field optional because some items come in only one color.

Remember, there are actually two types of DTDs. The Document Type Definition is the schema defined within an XML file. A Document Type Declaration is a **<!DOCTYPE>** tag that points to an external Document Type Definition file. The external declaration lets many files share the one definition.

DTDs can be far more complicated than needed. If you cannot explain the schema to the person preparing data for your file, you probably made the schema too complicated. Short tag names save file space, but can lead to similar names across related files and can result in people confusing the names. If you send out one XML file containing news reports and another XML file containing the weather reports, make sure tags with the same name have exactly the same definition and meaning, whereas elements with different meaning have distinct names. That will stop people confusing the meaning of elements in the weather report with similar elements in the news report.

An element id is defined with an **<!ELEMENT>** tag like the following. The line contains an element name, the name that will be in the element's tag, and then the list of elements nested within this element:

```
<!ELEMENT product (name, price, weight, color)>
```

The example element definition lets you enter the following product entry:

```
<product><name>truck</name><price>$120,000</price>
    <weight>5 tons</weight><color>Red</color></product>
```

Once you know element definitions, you can usually read enough of a DTD to find out the range of fields in an XML file. When you create an XML file, you need detailed knowledge of all the rules embedded in DTDs, and than means finding a good book or Web site. Send me a note via my Web site if you are looking for the best and most up to date books on XML. I read every one I find just in case one of them has a clearer explanation or a better diagram.

A few more rules will help you read a DTD so you can understand the structure of an XML file. In the element definition for **product**, **name** appears without modification, which means the **<name>** tag must appear exactly once within **<product>**. The same applies to the other tags in the list. If an element name ends with a plus (**+**), the element can appear one or more times. If the definition of **product** contained **color+**, **product** could contain several **<color>** tags as follows:

```
<product><name>truck</name><price>$120,000</price>
    <weight>5 tons</weight><color>Red</color><color>Green</color>
<color>Blue</color></product>
```

If the element name ends with an asterisk (*), the element can appear zero or many times. If the element name ends with a question mark (?) the element can appear zero or one times.

If element names are separated by a vertical bar (|), that means you choose one element. When the **product** element has the following definition, the **product** can have a **color** element or a **fabric** element, but not both:

```
<!ELEMENT product (name, price, weight, (color | fabric))>
```

Note the brackets (()) used to group subsets of elements. You can also add modifiers to brackets. If both **color** and **fabric** were allowed in **product**, and both could appear zero or many times, you can enter them as **(color, fabric)***.

The last things you need to read are attribute definitions so you can work out what attributes will appear in the data. There is no use processing 30,000,000 records and discovering new attributes on record 29,897,465. DTDs can contain ATTLIST definitions to say what attributes appear in an element and define the characteristics of an attribute so you know what to expect when you begin reading an XML file. Attributes can also have a default value, so you can use the defaults in place of the attributes for the first 29,897,464 records.

The following attribute definition says element **fabric** has an attribute named **fire-proof** that can contain true or false, and has a default of false. The default applies whenever you find a **fabric** tag without a **fire-proof** attribute. When you are reading XML files, you only need the element name and the attribute name. Once you have the two names, you can find and display the attribute value. That is all you need for most data:

```
<!ATTLIST fabric fire-proof (true | false) "false">
```

Namespace

When you define an XML tag in your file and send your file to me, I can invent my own tags, add data using my tags, and send the file on to a third person, and the third person does not know who to blame for each tag. Solve the problem of identifying XML tag owners with XML namespaces. At the top of your document, you place a namespace reference to the page on your Web site that documents your tags. You give the URL a small prefix, and add the prefix to each of your tags. Your **<heading>** tag becomes **<your:heading>**, and when I add a tag named **heading**, I add **<my:heading>**. The following **xmlns** parameters sit in a tag at the top of the XML file and relate each prefix to the right Web page:

```
<tag_name xmlns:your=" http://your_web_site.com/tags/"
          xmlns:my="http://petermoulding.com/tags/">
```

The **xmlns** parameters are inserted into a tag that surrounds the tags using the prefixes. That means you can use a different set of prefixes in each part of your document.

XLink and XPointer

XML Linking Language (XLink) lets you insert elements into XML documents to link within a document or to other documents, similar to HTML links. The specification is at **www.w3.org/TR/2001/REC-xlink-20010627/**. The XML Pointer Language (XPointer) lets you write the equivalent of URLs in XML, including paths within the structure of an XML document. Together they let you link from one document to the middle of another document, right down to individual XML tags.

XML Functions

This section covers the PHP functions prefixed by **xml_**.

Installation

Use Apache 1.13.9 or later, because Apache includes the expat library (**www.jclark.com/xml/**) needed by PHP.

For Unix systems, compile PHP using **--with-xml**. If you do not have expat installed, or a version of Apache containing expat, go to **www.jclark.com/xml/**, install expat, and then compile PHP.

For Windows 98, Windows NT, and Windows 2000, the Win32 binary has XML support compiled in.

Functions

You access XML data sequentially using functions prefixed by **xml_**. The process is similar to reading a file record by record, gives you fine control over processing, ensures your code sees all the data, and lets you read huge files with little overhead. Separate **domxml_** functions access XML data in a tree structure, but that requires all the XML data in memory at once.

When using the **xml_** functions, you create a parser to process the data and then pass the data through the parser via **xml_parser()**.

xml_parser_create()

xml_parser_create() accepts an optional character set and returns a parser id that is needed in the other XML functions. If you use the optional character encoding parameter, the legal values are ISO-8859-1, US-ASCII, and UTF-8. ISO-8859-1 is the default. An example follows:

```
if(!$parser = xml_parser_create())
    {
    print("<br>parser create failed!");
    }
```

xml_parser_free()

xml_parser_free( ) frees resources by removing a parser. The parser disappears at the end of your script, so this function is of most use when your script has a lot of resource-hungry processing after the last use of the XML parser:

```
if(!xml_parser_free($parser))
    {
    print("<br>Parser not free!");
    }
```

xml_set_object()

xml_set_object( ) is used when you use XML functions in objects. **xml_ set_ object( )** accepts a parser id from **xml_parser_create( )** and a reference to the object name, as shown in the following example. Use this function after **xml_ parser_create( )** and before any of the set handler functions:

```
xml_set_object($parser, &$this);
```

xml_set_element_handler()

xml_set_element_handler( ) accepts a parser id, the name of the start element handler, and the name of the end element handler. It registers the element handlers in the parser and returns true on success or false on failure. The start element handler has to accept the parser id, the tag name, and an array containing a list of attributes from the tag (if there are any). Try to minimize tag usage in XML. Many DTDs use tag attributes to store data that should be in a child tag. The end element handler has to accept the parser id and the tag name:

```
function start_element_handler($parser, $tag, $attributes)
    {
    }
function end_element_handler($parser, $tag)
    {
    }
```

```
if(!xml_set_element_handler($parser, "start_element_handler",
   "end_element_handler"))
   {
   print("<br>xml_set_element_handler failed!");
   }
```

xml_set_character_data_handler()

xml_set_character_data_handler( ) accepts a parser id and the name of the character data handler. It registers the handler and returns true on success or false on failure. The character data handler has to accept the parser id and the character data:

```
function character_data_handler($parser, $data)
   {
   }
if(!xml_set_character_data_handler($parser, "character_data_handler"))
   {
   print("<br>xml_set_character_data_handler failed!");
   }
```

xml_set_default_handler()

xml_set_default_handler( ) accepts a parser id and the name of a default handler. It registers the handler and returns true on success or false on failure. The default handler has to accept the parser id and data and take some sort of action. For a start, I recommend just dumping the data to print:

```
function default_handler($parser, $data)
   {
   }
if(!xml_set_default_handler($parser, "default_handler"))
   {
   print("<br>xml_set_default_handler failed!");
   }
```

xml_set_external_entity_ref_handler()

xml_set_external_entity_ref_handler( ) accepts a parser id and the name of the external entity reference handler. It registers the handler and returns true on success or false on failure. The external entity handler receives the parser id, a string containing a list of entity names separated by spaces, a string named **base** that is currently left empty, the system id, and the public id. I recommend you just leave this function out until you have all the other XML stuff working, and let the default handler handle this tag:

```
function external_entity_ref_handler($parser, $entity_names, $base,
   $system_id, $public_id)
   {
   }
if(!xml_set_external_entity_ref_handler($parser,
   "external_entity_ref_handler"))
   {
   print("<br>xml_set_external_entity_ref_handler failed!");
   }
```

xml_set_notation_decl_handler()

xml_set_notation_decl_handler( ) accepts a parser id and the name of the notation handler. It registers the handler and returns true on success or false on failure. The notation handler has to accept information about a notation declaration of the form **<!NOTATION name {systemId | publicId}>**. The notation handler receives the notation name, a string named **base** that is currently left empty, the system id, and the public id. I recommend you just leave this out until you have all the other XML stuff working, and let the default handler handle this tag:

```
function notation_handler($parser, $notation_name, $base, $system_id,
   $public_id)
   {
   }
if(!xml_set_notation_decl_handler($parser, "notation_handler"))
   {
   print("<br>xml_set_notation_decl_handler failed!");
   }
```

xml_set_processing_instruction_handler()

xml_set_processing_instruction_handler( ) accepts a parser id and the name of the processing instruction handler. It registers the handler and returns true on success or false on failure. The processing instruction handler has to accept the parser id, a target name, and the target's data. Processing instructions are of the form **<? target data ?>**. I recommend you just leave this out until you have all the other XML stuff working, and let the default handler handle processing instructions:

```
function processing_instruction_handler($parser, $target, $data)
   {
   }
if(!xml_set_processing_instruction_handler($parser,
   "processing_instruction_handler"))
```

```
   {
   print("<br>xml_set_processing_instruction_handler failed!");
   }
```

xml_set_unparsed_entity_decl_handler()

xml_set_unparsed_entity_decl_handler( ) accepts a parser id and the name of the unparsed entity declaration handler. It registers the handler and returns true on success or false on failure. The unparsed entity declaration handler has to accept information about an external entity declaration with an **NDATA** parameter. External entity declarations are in the form **<!ENTITY name {publicId | systemId} NDATA notationName>**. The handler receives the entity name, a string named **base** that is currently left empty, the system id, the public id, and the notation name from the entity declaration. I recommend you just leave this out until you have all the other XML stuff working, and let the default handler handle this tag:

```
function unparsed_entity_decl_handler($parser, $entity_name, $base,
   $system_id, $public_id, $notation_name)
   {
   }
if(!xml_set_unparsed_entity_decl_handler($parser,
   "unparsed_entity_decl_handler"))
   {
   print("<br>xml_set_unparsed_entity_decl_handler failed!");
   }
```

xml_parse()

xml_parse( ) accepts the parser id, a string of data for processing, and an optional value of true to indicate the string is the last string for processing. The function returns true if everything works, and returns false if the parser id does not identify a valid parser or the parser fails:

```
if(!xml_parse($parser, $data))
   {
   print("<br>xml_parse failed with " . htmlentities($data));
   }
```

xml_get_error_code()

xml_get_error_code( ) accepts the parser id and returns an error code for the latest error or false if the parser id is not valid. The following code uses the error code and **switch( )** to take action, which in this short example is just to print a message. Note that you do not have to memorize error numbers because the PHP XML support includes a list of names defined for the error codes:

```
switch(xml_get_error_code($parser))
   {
   case XML_ERROR_NONE:
      break;
   case XML_ERROR_NO_MEMORY:
      print("<br>Out of memory.");
      break;
   default:
      print("<br>Oops, unknown error!");
   }
```

Here are the names defined for the error codes from **xml_parse( )**:

```
XML_ERROR_NONE
XML_ERROR_NO_MEMORY
XML_ERROR_SYNTAX
XML_ERROR_NO_ELEMENTS
XML_ERROR_INVALID_TOKEN
XML_ERROR_UNCLOSED_TOKEN
XML_ERROR_PARTIAL_CHAR
XML_ERROR_TAG_MISMATCH
XML_ERROR_DUPLICATE_ATTRIBUTE
XML_ERROR_JUNK_AFTER_DOC_ELEMENT
XML_ERROR_PARAM_ENTITY_REF
XML_ERROR_UNDEFINED_ENTITY
XML_ERROR_RECURSIVE_ENTITY_REF
XML_ERROR_ASYNC_ENTITY
XML_ERROR_BAD_CHAR_REF
XML_ERROR_BINARY_ENTITY_REF
XML_ERROR_ATTRIBUTE_EXTERNAL_ENTITY_REF
XML_ERROR_MISPLACED_XML_PI
XML_ERROR_UNKNOWN_ENCODING
XML_ERROR_INCORRECT_ENCODING
XML_ERROR_UNCLOSED_CDATA_SECTION
XML_ERROR_EXTERNAL_ENTITY_HANDLING
```

Most of these errors are self-explanatory; a duplicate attribute occurs when you have a specific attribute twice in one tag. When you find an error that is not obvious, print the last string supplied to **xml_parse( )** and remember to wrap the string in **htmlentities( )**.

xml_error_string()

xml_error_string( ) accepts an error code and returns a string describing the error. The following code prints a readable message from an XML error:

```
print("<br>" . xml_error_string(xml_get_error_code($parser)));
```

xml_get_current_line_number()

xml_get_current_line_number( ) accepts a parser id and returns the line number for the current line passing through **xml_parser( )**. The following code prints the line number. Display the line number when displaying errors about an XML input file, so you can easily browse the file and find the right line:

```
print("<br>Current line number: "
   . xml_get_current_line_number($parser));
```

xml_get_current_column_number()

xml_get_current_column_number( ) accepts a parser id and returns the column number within the current line passing through **xml_parser( )**. The following code prints the line and column number. Display these numbers when displaying errors about an XML input file:

```
print("<br>Current line number: "
   . xml_get_current_line_number($parser). " and column number: "
   . xml_get_current_column_number($parser));
```

xml_get_current_byte_index()

xml_get_current_byte_index( ) accepts a parser id and returns the number of the current byte in the parser's input buffer. The following code prints the byte index, and would only be of use if you also print the input data buffer when printing XML data (remember to use **htmlentities( )** to make the XML tags visible):

```
print("<br>Current byte index: " . xml_get_current_byte_index($parser));
```

xml_parse_into_struct()

xml_parse_into_struct( ) accepts a parser id, a string of XML data, and two arrays to receive a data structure decoded from the XML data. Both arrays have to be prefixed with an ampersand to be passed by reference; this technique is going away, so the function may be changed to accept the arrays by reference without using the ampersand. One array receives the data and the other array becomes an index into the data:

```
if(!xml_parse_into_struct($parser, $data, &$values, &$index))
    {
    print("<br>Error during parse.");
    }
```

This function requires all the data in memory at once, so it is not suited to large XML files. If you want to extract just a small amount of data from a large XML file and then process the data using a structure, you could use a modified version of the code from the Immediate Solution entitled "Parsing XML Data" to read a large file and create a subset for feeding into **xml_parse_into_struct( )**.

xml_parser_set_option()

xml_parser_set_option( ) accepts a parser id, the name of a parser option, and a new value for the option, and returns true on success or false if the value cannot be set. The function lets you set and unset the small number of XML processing options mentioned here but may gain extra options as the XML processing code develops. **XML_OPTION_CASE_FOLDING** controls how the XML functions treat the case of tag names. The XML functions default to the intelligent option of translating all tag names to a single case so you do not get errors from mistyping a tag name, meaning you do not miss a tag just because the input contains a tag name typed as "headingOne" instead of "headingone". Unfortunately, XML allows duplication of names using different cases, and XHTML actually contains two fields named **inline** and **Inline**. To process those XML files with design faults like the **inline/Inline** name duplication, turn case folding off, like this:

```
if(!xml_parser_set_option($parser, XML_OPTION_CASE_FOLDING, 0))
    {
    print("<br>Error setting option.");
    }
```

XML_OPTION_TARGET_ENCODING lets you specify a string containing the encoding for the target data; the current options are ISO-8859-1, US-ASCII, and UTF-8. The default is to use the source encoding for the target encoding. During testing of a new XML source, you want the output to be traceable directly to the input. Test without this option, get the tag processing and everything else working, and then experiment with encoding changes.

XML_OPTION_SKIP_WHITE lets you turn on an option for skipping whitespace characters. I did not test this because the default works fine for most files. In addition, when you do need to skip whitespace characters, you often need to accept the whitespace characters during testing so you can find out if the incoming file is formed the correct way.

xml_parser_get_option()

xml_parser_get_option( ) returns the current setting for an XML option. See **xml_parser_set_option( )** for a list of options. The following code prints the current setting for one option:

```
print("<br> XML_OPTION_TARGET_ENCODING: "
    . xml_parser_get_option($parser, XML_OPTION_TARGET_ENCODING));
```

utf8_encode()

utf8_encode( ) encodes ISO-8859-1 string data to UTF-8 format string data to let you mix 16-bit Unicode data within 8-bit data. UTF-8 is described in RFC 2279 (**www.faqs.org/rfcs/rfc2279.html**). You can include Unicode data within XML tags without upsetting XML decoding, and return the data to 16-bit Unicode data using **utf8_decode( )**. The following example encodes a string and then wraps XML tags around the string to indicate the data is UTF-8 encoded. When the data is parsed by the XML functions, the end element handler can detect the **<utf8>** tag and decode the string:

```
$data .= "<utf8>" . utf8_encode($string) . "</utf8>";
```

utf8_decode()

utf8_decode( ) matches **utf8_encode( )**, and decodes the 8-bit string into 16-bit Unicode:

```
$data = utf8_decode($utf8_data);
```

XSLT

eXtensible Stylesheet Language Transformations are possible using the experimental PHP XSLT functions (experimental in PHP4 and still experimental in 4.0.6). You will need a good book that describes XML style sheets (XSL) and the XSL transformation language (XSLT). The PHP XSLT functions feed the XML and XSL files through Sablotron software, and the result is another XML file, an XHTML file, or a plain HTML file depending on the instructions in the XSL file.

HTML, DHTML, or XSLT?

XSL is an XML-based style sheet language that is available in some new browsers. XSLT is a language for transforming one XML document into another XML document, and can be used to transform XML data into XHTML. XHTML is a version of

HTML 4 defined in XML DTDs, and is usable in some newer browsers. If you put them all together, you can take XML data and present the data as a Web page.

HTML 4 is the standard HTML in most current browsers, and is great for static data, but does not let you incorporate dynamic data. By adding PHP to HTML, you can merge dynamic data into HTML at the server. With PHP and HTML, you can format the HTML to suit any browser and merge in any data. The various XML technologies let you perform the merge and formatting at the server or browser, but they require the data in XML format, and, if you use browser-based facilities, they require the latest browser.

Dynamic HTML (DHTML) is an attempt to update HTML into a dynamic new language by adding JavaScript, but JavaScript is a poorly defined language with limited capability, spotty support in browsers, and limited access to server-based data. You need PHP to build the appropriate JavaScript for each browser, so it is much easier to bypass JavaScript and use PHP to build the whole page. JavaScript cannot read a database on your server; you need PHP to feed data to JavaScript, and PHP can feed the data within fully built HTML. I think the D in DHTML stands for *Doh!*

HTML and PHP is a great combination. PHP and XML on the server is a great combination. Any technology that depends on intelligence in the browser is unpredictable, and will limit your customer base. Perform transformations and formatting at the server.

Installing XSLT

XSLT uses Sablotron, and Sablotron uses the expat library but does not pick up the version used by the XML functions.

To install Sablotron under Unix, follow these steps:

1. Install the latest Sablotron and expat from **www.gingerall.com/**.
2. Compile PHP with **--with-sablot**.

To install Sablotron on Windows or Windows NT, follow these steps:

1. Stop Apache or your Web server.
2. Remove the semicolon (;) from the front of the following line in php.ini:

```
extension=php_sablot.dll
```

3. Copy php_sablot.dll from c:\Program Files\php\extensions to c:\windows\system (or c:/winnt/system32 in Windows NT and Windows 2000).

4. Copy sablot.dll and expat.dll from c:\Program Files\php\dlls to c:\windows\system (or c:/winnt/system32 in Windows NT and Windows 2000).

5. Restart Apache.

XSLT Functions

XSLT processing starts with **xslt_create()** to create an XSLT process, **xslt_run()** to process the XSLT file, and then **xslt_fetch_result()** to retrieve the results. You can alter processing, including processing groups of files in one hit, by alternative combinations of functions.

xslt_create()

xslt_create() creates a new XSLT resource id for use in all other XSLT functions. The following code sets up **$x** as the XSLT resource. **$x** is the first parameter in the subsequent examples:

```
$x = xslt_create();
```

xslt_openlog()

The XSLT processing will output errors to a log of your choice, and you open the log with **xslt_openlog()**. **xslt_openlog()** accepts an XSLT resource id, a file name, and an integer log level. Specifying a resource id means there can be a separate log for every XSLT process. The log level is not documented at the time of this writing, so experiment with it. To control processing, you have to test for errors within your code, so you will know about errors before looking at the log and can match the log contents to the errors returned by **xslt_error()**:

```
if(!xslt_openlog($x, "t:/xslt.txt", 1))
    {
    print("<br>xslt_openlog failed.");
    }
```

xslt_errno()

xslt_errno() returns an error number for the last XSLT error. If you supply an XSLT resource id, the error is the last error for that XSLT process. If you leave the resource id out, the error is the last error across all processes. The following code prints the most recent error number from **$x**:

```
print("<br>xslt error " . xslt_errno($x));
```

The following is the result when there is no error:

```
xslt error 0
```

xslt_error()

xslt_error( ) returns the error text for the latest XSLT error. When you supply an XSLT resource id, the error is the latest error for that XSLT process. The following code prints the text from the most recent error in XSLT process **$x**:

```
print("<br>xslt error " . xslt_error($x));
```

Here is the message you get when there is no error:

```
xslt error OK
```

xslt_run()

xslt_run( ) accepts an XSLT resource id, an input XSL file name in a URL, an input XML file name in a URL, the optional name of a result buffer, an optional array of XSLT parameters, and an optional array of XSLT arguments. The output goes into the buffer and is retrieved by **xslt_fetch_result( )**. The buffer name defaults to "/_result" in both **xslt_run( )** and **xslt_fetch_result( )**. The following code runs **xslt_run( )**, checks for an error, and then fetches and displays the result within as a HTML page:

```
if(xslt_run($x, "./test.xsl", "./test.xml"))
    {
    print("<br>" . xslt_fetch_result($x));
    }
else
    {
    print("<br>xslt_failed failed.");
    }
```

xslt_fetch_result()

xslt_fetch_result( ) is the function that fetches the results produced by **xslt_run( )**. The following code fetches the results, and instead of displaying them as a Web page, displays them as uninterpreted HTML so you can see all the tags within the results:

```
$string = xslt_fetch_result($x);
print("<br>XSLT data: " . htmlentities($string));
```

xslt_output_begintransform()

xslt_output_begintransform( ) lets you perform a series of transformations using the one style sheet. Specify the style sheet in **xslt_output_begintransform( )**, and all transformations will use that style sheet until you run **xslt_output_endtransform( )**:

```
xslt_output_begintransform("./test.xsl");
```

xslt_output_endtransform()

xslt_output_endtransform( ) ends the use of the current XSLT file specified in **xslt_output_begintransform( )**:

```
xslt_output_endtransform();
```

xslt_set_sax_handler()

When you read about XSL and XSLT at the W3 Web site and others, you will find references to Simple API for XML (SAX), the method of transforming XML documents before the Sablotron code became available. You can use SAX handlers within XSLT processing by creating an array containing the SAX handlers and supplying the array as the second parameter to **xslt_set_sax_handler( )**. The following code assumes that the SAX array is already set up, runs **xslt_set_sax_handler( )**, and then checks for an error and prints a message on failure (I have not seen SAX in use at sites using the newer XSLT functions and Sablotron, so you may never need this function):

```
if(!xslt_set_sax_handler($x,$array))
    {
    print("<br>xslt_set_sax_handler failed.");
    }
```

xslt_transform()

xslt_transform( ) performs a single transformation, and lets you specify all the advanced Sablotron parameters you need. Grab the documentation supplied with Sablotron and read about the parameters. The following code shows **xslt_transform( )** within a check for errors:

```
if(!xslt_transform("./test.xsl", "./test.xml", $result, $parameters,
    $arguments, $result_buffer))
    {
    print("<br>xslt_transform failed.");
    }
```

xslt_process()

xslt_process( ) is a simplified version of **xslt_transform( )** that accepts strings for both inputs and the output. There are no parameter or argument options. This is the choice if your data is already in a string and the XSL file can perform the transformation without extra parameters:

```
if(!xslt_process($xsl, $xml, $result))
   {
   print("<br>xslt_process error " . xslt_errno() . " " . xslt_error());
   }
```

xslt_closelog()

xslt_closelog( ) closes the log for a specific XSLT process, as shown in the following code. You can then check the log to ensure that the transformation worked:

```
if(!xslt_closelog($x))
   {
   print("<br>xslt_closelog failed.");
   }
```

xslt_free()

Free all the resources for an XSLT process with **xslt_free( ),** as shown in the following code:

```
xslt_free();
```

WDDX

Web Distributed Data Exchange (WDDX) from OpenWDDX (**www.openwddx. org**) lets you encapsulate programming information, like variables, in a string for transmission via email and other character-based transmission techniques. Read Chapter 16 for an explanation and examples.

WDDX suits program-to-program communication where the source and target programs are closely related. I do not recommend WDDX as a way of transferring values from a PHP script to JavaScript or similar browser-based technologies. WDDX has limited data definition facilities, and it is possible to create data that will be incorrectly interpreted at the target. Even if the format is interpreted the correct way, the meaning can be messed up if the source and target are not in close synchronization. WDDX suits sharing data between servers you control, but not between your servers and foreign servers.

DOM

The Document Object Model (DOM) lets you access the structure and parts of a complete document in a semi-random fashion similar to stepping through a Web page within a browser using JavaScript, or through a Word document using Visual Basic for Applications, or through an LDAP directory. You need to know the top parts of a structure to access the lower parts, and you need to know all the components of a path to an entry to get an entry. The DOM XML functions have the prefix **domxml_**.

Because DOM requires the whole document to be in memory first, DOM suits smaller documents or big servers. If you want to traverse a large XML file, use the conventional XML functions.

Because you need to step through a structure, you need to know the structure in advance, or have functions that reveal the structure. The DOM XML functions include functions to discover a document structure and to build a new structure. Building a new structure is similar to building a multilevel array, so building an XML file with the DOM XML functions is an alternative to building a complex array with WDDX. You still end up with an XML string for transmission.

When do you use DOM XML? If your source or target document is something like an AbiWord word-processing document or an XSL-type style sheet, use the structured approach of DOM. If the source or target is a database table, forget the DOM tree structure and use the sequential approach of the conventional XML functions.

The PHP DOM functions are experimental, so they will frustrate your efforts to build a reliable Web site. Do not bet money on DOM XML becoming reliable within the lifetime of your current and future projects. DOM XML experience is purely for bragging rights and to satisfy those employment agencies that will immediately begin demanding five years experience with DOM XML.

Installing DOM XML

To install DOM XML under Unix, follow these steps:

1. Install the latest GNOME XML library from **www.xmlsoft.org**.
2. Compile PHP with **--with-dom=[DIR]**.

To install DOM XML under Windows and Windows NT, follow these steps:

1. Stop Apache or your Web server.
2. Remove the semicolon (;) from the front of the following line in php.ini:

```
extension=php_domxml.dll
```

3. Copy php_domxml.dll from c:\Program Files\php\extensions to c:\windows\system (or c:/winnt/system32 in Windows NT and Windows 2000).

4. Copy Libxml2.dll from c:\Program Files\php\dlls to c:\windows\system (or c:/winnt/system32 in Windows NT and Windows 2000).

5. Restart Apache.

DOM XML Functions

Use **xmldoc( )** to create a new document object and **xmldocfile( )** to read an existing file in as an object. All the other functions work with an object from **xmldoc( )** or **xmldocfile( )**.

xmldoc()

xmldoc( ) creates a DOM XML object and is the starting point for all the other DOM XML functions when creating a new document or using a file already imported into a string. The following example creates an object from a simple text string and dumps the object to print:

```
$object = xmldoc("<doc><title>Test</title><text>The cholesterol laden"
  . " cow tried to beat NASA to the moon.</text></doc>");
print_r($object);
```

Here is the print of the object (note that the class is **DomDocument**):

```
DomDocument Object ( [name] => [url] => [version] => 1.0
  [standalone] => -1 [type] => 9 [compression] => -1
  [charset] => 1 [0] => 2 [1] => 74523584 )
```

xmldocfile()

xmldocfile( ) creates a DOM XML object and is the starting point for all the other DOM XML functions when reading XML data direct from a file. The following example creates an object from the AbiWord document (an AbiWord document is used in other examples). The file access is read-only, so updates to the object are not reflected in the file. The function needs a full path to the file, so **realpath( )** is wrapped around the relative file name. This may not work if your document uses anything other than the basic XML type declaration, so double check files for character set parameters in the file's **<?xml version="1.0" >** tag:

```
$file_object = xmldocfile(realpath("./fishcurry.abw"));
print_r($file_object);
```

Here is a print of the object:

```
DomDocument Object ( [doc] => Resource id #3 [url] =>
   i:\usr\home\petermoulding\web\root\phpblackbook\xml\fishcurry.abw
   [version] => 1.0 [standalone] => -1 [type] => 9 [compression] => -1
   [charset] => 1 )
```

Note the resource id and URL of the input file despite the fact that **xmldocfile( )** currently provides only read access. The URL contains the full path of the file relative to the server. Also note that the object contains only the root node of the file, not the whole tree structure of the file. This may mean that the function brings into memory only the parts you access, which means you could access part of a huge file without swamping memory.

xmltree()

xmltree( ) creates a structure of DOM XML objects and is an isolated function for looking at the contents of an XML-based document. The following example creates an object structure from a simple text string, and then prints the structure using **print_r( )**:

```
$tree_object = xmltree("<doc><title>Test</title><text>The cholesterol laden"
   . " cow tried to beat NASA to the moon.</text></doc>");
print_r($tree_object);
```

Here is the result, which contains every node in the input string:

```
DomDocument Object ( [name] => [url] => [version] => 1.0 [standalone] =>
   -1 [type] => 9 [compression] => -1 [charset] => 1 [0] => 4 [1] =>
   75945888 [children] => Array ( [0] => DomElement Object ( [type] => 1
   [tagname] => doc [0] => 5 [1] => 75932784 [children] => Array ( [0]
   => DomElement Object ( [type] => 1 [tagname] => title [0] => 6 [1] =>
   75932720 [children] => Array ( [0] => DomText Object ( [content] =>
   Test [0] => 7 [1] => 75932656 ) ) ) [1] => DomElement Object ( [type]
   => 1 [tagname] => text [0] => 8 [1] => 75945184 [children] => Array (
   [0] => DomText Object ( [content] => The cholesterol laden cow tried
   to beat NASA to the moon. [0] => 9 [1] => 75945104 ) ) ) ) ) ) )
```

domxml_root()

domxml_root( ) accepts a DOM XML object and returns an object containing the root element of the document. The following code should work, but caused an error in Apache using PHP 4.0.6. Adding an **<?xml version="1.0"?>** tag did not solve the problem. **domxml_root( )** still has errors to be fixed before you can use it reliably across all servers:

```
$root = domxml_root($object);
```

The alternative is to use the following code:

```
print_r($object->root());
```

This version is quicker for a one-time code line. The previous code is shorter when you want to make many references to the root element. This version has the advantage of working.

Here is the output from **$object->root()**. Note the class of **DomElement** and the **tagname** of **doc**, the first tag in the document:

```
DomElement Object ( [type] => 1 [tagname] => doc [0] => 3 [1] =>
    73711360 )
```

domxml_add_root()

domxml_add_root() accepts a DOM XML object and a string containing an element name. It returns an object containing a new root element of the document. The following example adds a new root element to the object from **xmldoc()**, but sadly just makes PHP 4.0.6 blow up:

```
$root = domxml_add_root($object);
```

The alternative follows and works:

```
$root = $object->add_root("doc");
print_r($root);
```

Here is object **$root** with a class of **DomElement** and a **tagname** of **doc**, the first tag in the document:

```
DomElement Object ( [type] => 1 [tagname] => doc [0] => 3 [1] => 8945680
    )
```

domxml_dumpmem()

domxml_dumpmem() dumps the current DOM XML object back into a string and is the reverse of **xmldoc()**. The following code creates a string from the current DOM XML object when the function is working, which it does not in the PHP 4.0.6 Win32 version:

```
$xml_string = domxml_dumpmem($object);
```

Here is the same action using conventional object method notation and a **print** statement to let you see the result:

```
$xml_string = $object->dumpmem();
print("<br>" . htmlentities($xml_string));
```

Here is the output (after coding hundreds of thousands of **print** statements, I still occasionally leave out **htmlentities()** and wonder why the output is missing critical items):

```
<?xml version="1.0"?> <doc><title>Test</title><text>The cholesterol
    laden cow tried to beat NASA to the moon.</text></doc>
```

domxml_attributes()

domxml_attributes() should accept an object containing a node of a document and return the attributes for the node as an array. The following example causes an error in PHP 4.0.6:

```
$attributes = domxml_attributes($root);
while(list($k, $v) = each($attributes))
    {
    print("<br>" . $k . ": " . htmlentities($v));
    }
```

domxml_get_attribute()

domxml_get_attribute() accepts an object containing a node of a document and the name of an attribute. It returns the attribute for the node as an object. The following example should return the **font** attribute for the document's root node and print the result. There are no attributes in the example **xmldoc()**, so this function should return an empty object. In PHP 4.0.6, this function fails:

```
$attribute = domxml_get_attribute($root, "font");
```

domxml_set_attribute()

domxml_set_attribute() should accept an object containing a node of a document, the name of an attribute, and the value for the attribute. It returns the attribute as an object. The following example creates the **font** attribute for the document's root node. Unfortunately, PHP 4.0.6 complains about the parameter count with three parameters, and terminates the task with two parameters:

```
$font = domxml_set_attribute($root, "font", "times roman");
```

Here is a working version using conventional object notation plus a **print_r( )** to show you the contents of the result:

```
$font = root->set_attribute("font", "times roman");
print_r($font);
```

Here is the result with a class of **DomAttribute**:

```
DomAttribute Object ( [name] => font [value] => times roman [0] => 4
   [1] => 74570560 )
```

domxml_children()

domxml_children( ) accepts a document or node object and returns an array listing all the children of the node, or it will when it works, which it does not in PHP 4.0.6:

```
$children = domxml_children($root);
```

Here is a working version using conventional object notation and **print_r( )** to print the result:

```
$children = $root->children();
print_r($children);
```

The following result shows an array of two objects, each object of class **DomElement**, and the element name in the **tagname** entry. **$root** has two children named **title** and **text**, which matches the example string fed into **xmldoc( )**:

```
Array ( [0] => DomElement Object ( [type] => 1 [tagname] => title
   [0] => 4 [1] => 73443472 ) [1] => DomElement Object ( [type] => 1
   [tagname] => text [0] => 5 [1] => 73443344 ) )
```

domxml_new_child()

domxml_new_child( ) should accept an object containing a node of a document, the name of a child, and the value for the child. It should then return the child as an object. The following example creates the **author** attribute for the document's root node, but the result is a message about a wrong parameter count, and changing the number of parameters makes PHP terminate the task:

```
$child = domxml_new_child($root, "author", "Peter");
```

Here is a working version using object notation and a line to print the result:

```
$child = $root->new_child("author", "Peter");
print_r($child);
```

Here is the result with a class of **DomElement** and a **tagname** of **author**:

```
DomElement Object ( [type] => 1 [tagname] => author [0] => 4
   [1] => 8703120 )
```

domxml_new_xmldoc()

domxml_new_xmldoc( ) is another way of creating a new XML document. The function accepts an XML version and returns a document object. I suspect some of these overlapping functions will disappear, and the remaining functions will gain extra parameters for things like the XML version:

```
$object = domxml_new_xmldoc("1.0");
print_r($object);
```

Here is the result from **domxml_new_xmldoc( )**:

```
DomDocument Object ( [name] => [url] => [version] => 1.0
   [standalone] => -1 [type] => 9 [compression] => -1 [charset] => 1
   [0] => 4 [1] => 74013248 )
```

xpath_new_context()

xpath_new_context( ) accepts a document object and creates a new context for use in **xpath_eval( )**, but the function is new. It only arrived in PHP 4.0.4, changed in 4.0.6, and it is likely to change again. The following example creates a context object and dumps the object with **print_r( )**. The function was not compiled into the PHP 4.0.6 Win32 binary, so I do not have an example of the output:

```
$context = xpath_new_context($object);
print_r($context);
```

xpath_eval()

xpath_eval( ) accepts a context object and a string for evaluation. It returns a result object. The following example uses **$context** created by **xpath_new_context( )**, and looks for **"/doc/title"** (the function was not compiled into the PHP 4.0.6 Win32 binary, so I do not have an example of the output):

```
$result = xpath_eval($context, "/doc/title");
print_r($result);
```

Immediate Solutions

Displaying XML Files

XML files are text files containing tags. To display the contents of an XML file for testing and diagnosis, simply combine a simple text file display with **htmlentities( )** as shown in the following code:

```
$line_length = 70;
$xml = file("./fishcurry.abw");
while(list($k, $v) = each($xml))
   {
   while(strlen($v) > 0)
      {
      print("<br>" . htmlentities(substr($v, 0, $line_length)));
      $v = substr($v, $line_length);
      }
   }
```

file( ) reads the XML file into an array with one array entry for each line of the input (based on newline characters). XML contains SGML tags that are interpreted by Web browsers as unknown HTML tags, so the tags are swallowed by the browser. **htmlentities( )** changes the tag's opening less-than sign (**<**) and closing greater-than sign (**>**) into the display-safe **<** and **>**. The code has one **while( )** loop to read through the array, and an extra **while( )** loop to chop lines down to size with the limit set at 70 characters per line.

The following is the display of a recipe ingredients list prepared in AbiWord, a word processor for Windows and Unix that uses XML to store, delimit, and indicate formatting of documents:

```
<?xml version="1.0"?>
<abiword version="0.7.14" fileformat="1.0">
<!-- ================================================================ -->
<!-- This file is an AbiWord document.                                -->
<!-- AbiWord is a free, Open Source word processor.                   -->
<!-- You may obtain more information about AbiWord at www.abisource.com -->
<!-- You should not edit this file by hand.                           -->
<!-- ================================================================ -->
```

```
<!-- Build_ID = (none) -->
<!-- Build_Version = 0.7.14 -->
<!-- Build_Options = LicensedTrademarks:Off Debug:Off BiDi
:Off Pspell:Off -->
<!-- Build_Target = /home/tom/release/abi/src/WIN32_1.1.8
_i386_OBJ/obj -->
<!-- Build_CompileTime = 14:34:43 -->
<!-- Build_CompileDate = Mar 30 2001 -->

<pagesize pagetype="Letter" orientation="portrait" width="8.500000" he
ight="11.000000" units="inch" page-scale="1.000000"/>
<section>
<p>1 teaspoon of chili flakes</p>
<p>1 soup spoon of capsicum</p>
<p>1 can coconut cream</p>
<p>500 gm light, boneless fish.</p>
<p>1 packet of green vegetables</p>
<p>1 packet of corn</p>
<p>mustard oil</p>
<p>mustard seed</p>
<p>ground mild chili</p>
<p>turmeric</p>
<p>cumin</p>
<p>medium onion chopped fine</p>
<p>fennel seed</p>
<p></p>
</section>
</abiword>
```

Note the AbiWord document has all the basics of XML except a DTD. The **\<abiword\>** tag delimits a document. **\<p\>** delimits a paragraph. There are comment tags (**\<!-- --\>**) to describe the software, and the **\<pagesize\>** tag to describe the page size and format. To save paper and your reading time, the document does not contain the full recipe or the full range of formatting that AbiWord provides. Download AbiWord to experiment further. To get the full recipe, send me a note via my Web site.

To display a continuous data stream or a very large file, read the Immediate Solution entitled "Displaying XML Data." To see the file parsed by the PHP XML functions, see the Immediate Solution entitled "Parsing XML Data."

20. XML

Displaying XML Data

There are times when you want to display the contents of an XML data stream for testing and diagnosis, but you cannot simply load a file into memory and print it as shown in the previous solution, because the file is too long to fit memory or the data is in a continuous stream from a network port. This solution shows a longer way of processing and displaying the data, a way that does not require all the data to be present when you start displaying. To emulate a data stream, the code reads the same file as the previous solution but line by line. You could replace the file read with any of the functions for network access explained in other chapters.

The following code reads the input file line by line using **fgets( )**, parses each line for tags delimited by **<** and **>**, and accumulates the tags in array **$tags**:

```
$line_length = 70;
$file_name = "./fishcurry.abw";
$data = "";
if($file = fopen("./fishcurry.abw", "r"))
   {
   while(!feof($file))
      {
      $data .= fgets($file, $line_length);
      if(substr($data, -1) == "\\n")
         {
         $data = substr($data, 0, -1);
         }
      if(substr($data, -1) == "\\r")
         {
         $data = substr($data, 0, -1);
         }
      $offset = 0;
      while($offset < strlen($data))
         {
         $pos = strpos($data, "<", $offset);
         if($pos === false)
            {
            $offset = strlen($data);
            }
         elseif(substr($data, $pos, 2) == "</")
            {
            $end = strpos($data, ">", $pos);
            if($end === false)
               {
               $offset = $pos + 1;
               }
```

```
        else
           {
           $tags[] = substr($data, 0, $end + 1);
           $data = substr($data, $end + 1);
           $offset = 0;
           }
        }
     elseif($pos == 0)
        {
        $offset = $pos + 1;
        }
     else
        {
        $tags[] = substr($data, 0, $pos);
        $data = substr($data, $pos);
        $offset = 0;
        }
     }
  }
fclose($file);
}
if(strlen($data))
  {
  $tags[] = $data;
  }
while(list($k, $v) = each($tags))
  {
  while(strlen($v) > 0)
     {
     print("<br>" . htmlentities(substr($v, 0, $line_length)));
     $v = substr($v, $line_length);
     }
  }
```

fopen( ), **fgets( )**, **feof( )**, and **fclose( )** are the normal file-handling functions described in Chapter 8 and could be replaced by network read functions. **fgets( )** adds all new data to **$data**, and **$data** is parsed to extract any complete tags. The data left over in **$data** is then augmented with the next segment of data from **fgets( )**.

The extraction of tags from **$data** is essentially the same as the extraction used in the previous solution with one extra piece of logic. When the code finds an end tag, indicated by **</**, the data is extracted up to the end of the end tag, **>**, so individual end tags are placed in separate array entries. There is no extra logic to handle the single tags that act as both start and end tags in one. If there is any

20. XML

data left in **$data** after the main file-reading **while( )** loop, the data is placed in a **$tags** entry.

The code ends with a **while( )** loop to read through the array printing the tags and data up to 70 characters per line.

Related solution:	*Found on page:*
Displaying a Text File	312

Here is the last part of the output showing the tag separation, particularly the separation of the single end tags:

```
<p>medium onion chopped fine</p>
<p>fennel seed</p>
<p></p>
</section>
</abiword>
```

The accumulation of tags in **$tags** and the subsequent display is unlikely to suit long-running scripts reading data fragments from networks, because there is too much danger of a network timeout. In those cases, the data would be written to a file or database with each entry becoming one line in the file or one row in the database table. You could then read Chapter 9 and write a nice form to step through the file or table section by section, where a section is an arbitrary number of lines or based on finding certain tags.

Part of this code will be the base for the Immediate Solution "Parsing XML Data." The file functions are well established, and the XML functions are relatively new, so you might like to get this solution running first, and then tackle the XML functions in the next solution.

Parsing XML Data

This solution parses XML documents using PHP's XML functions and uses the AbiWord document plus the basic file processing functions from the previous solution.

The first step is to create a parser. The following code creates the parser using **xml_parser_create( )**. The parser id, in **$parser**, is used in all the other XML functions:

```
if(!$parser = xml_parser_create())
    {
    print("<br>xml_parser_create failed.");
    }
```

The parser requires various processing handlers to process parts of the incoming XML stream. The most basic are the start and end element handlers. The following code is the start element handler. This example prints the start element. The next Immediate Solution ("Matching XML Start and End Tags") adds processing to group tags together:

```
function start_element_handler($parser, $tag, $attributes)
    {
    print("<br>start_element " . htmlentities($tag));
    }
```

The inputs include a string containing the name of the start tag and an array containing a list of attributes. In the AbiWord document, the only tags that have attributes are tags not relevant to a Web page.

The following code is the end element handler. This handler receives the name of the tag so this processor can match the end tag with a start tag. This example just prints the tag so you can see what is happening:

```
function end_element_handler($parser, $tag)
    {
    print("<br>end_element " . htmlentities($tag));
    }
```

When you create XML processing handlers, you have to register the handlers in the parser that uses the handlers. The following code registers both the start and end element handlers. In all the XML **set_handler** functions, you can choose to not run a registration if there is no handler to register, or leave an individual handler out by using an empty string:

```
if(!xml_set_element_handler($parser, "start_element_handler",
    "end_element_handler"))
    {
    print("<br>xml_set_element_handler failed.");
    }
```

The character data handler handles the data sitting between tags. The following example just prints the data, but a production processing system would accumulate the data up to the matching end tag for that data, and then perform whatever the tag requires:

20. XML

```
function character_data_handler($parser, $data)
    {
    print("<br>character_data " . htmlentities($data));
    }
```

Register the character data handler with the following code. The character data handler is required for all XML processing functions, or there would be no point in parsing the XML:

```
if(!xml_set_character_data_handler($parser, "character_data_handler"))
    {
    print("<br>xml_set_character_data_handler failed.");
    }
```

The default handler is the handler that gets whatever is not processed elsewhere. Initially set the handler up to print everything. Once you have everything important processed through other handlers, the remainder left in the default handler is most likely of no interest to your Web page processing:

```
function default_handler($parser, $data)
    {
    print("<br>default " . htmlentities($data));
    }
```

Register the default handler with the following code:

```
if(!xml_set_default_handler($parser, "default_handler"))
    {
    print("<br>xml_set_default_handler failed.");
    }
```

An external entity reference may be useful, but I have yet to see an example that needs to be processed for a Web page. If someone is shipping news articles to you in XML, and the XML or DTD is full of references back to their site, you will have problems processing their data reliably. The following code prints any external entity references found in the data just in case there are some in your test files (there are none in the AbiWord example):

```
function external_entity_ref_handler($parser, $entity_names, $base,
    $system_id, $public_id)
    {
    print("<br>external_entity_ref " . htmlentities($entity_names));
    }
```

Register the external entity reference handler using the following code:

```
if(!xml_set_external_entity_ref_handler($parser,
    "external_entity_ref_handler"))
    {
    print("<br>xml_set_external_entity_ref_handler failed.");
    }
```

The notation declaration handler handles notation declarations. The following code prints the notation just in case there are notation declarations in your files:

```
function notation_decl_handler($parser, $notation, $base, $system_id,
    $public_id)
    {
    print("<br>notation_decl " . htmlentities($notation));
    }
```

Register the notation declaration handler using the following code:

```
if(!xml_set_notation_decl_handler($parser, "notation_decl_handler"))
    {
    print("<br>xml_set_notation_decl_handler failed.");
    }
```

A processing instruction contains the name of a target process and data for the process. The following handler accepts and prints the target and data:

```
function processing_instruction_handler($parser, $target, $data)
    {
    print("<br>processing_instruction " . htmlentities($target, $data));
    }
```

Register the processing instruction handler using the following code:

```
if(!xml_set_processing_instruction_handler($parser,
    "processing_instruction_handler"))
    {
    print("<br>xml_set_processing_instruction_handler failed.");
    }
```

The following is another handler just in case your data contains unparsed entity declarations:

```
function unparsed_entity_decl_handler($parser, $entity, $base,
    $system_id, $public_id, $notation)
    {
```

```
print("<br>unparsed_entity_decl " . htmlentities($entity,
   $notation));
}
```

Register the unparsed entity declaration handler using the following code:

```
if(!xml_set_unparsed_entity_decl_handler($parser,
   "unparsed_entity_decl_handler"))
   {
   print("<br>xml_set_unparsed_entity_decl_handler failed.");
   }
```

You are now past the boring bit and on to the real work. The following code loops through the fishcurry.abw file the same way as the code in the previous solution, but this time it passes data to **xml_parse( )**:

```
$line_length = 70;
if($file = fopen("./fishcurry.abw", "r"))
   {
   while(!feof($file))
      {
      $data = fgets(\$file, $line_length);
      if(substr($data, -1) == "\n")
         {
         $data = substr($data, 0, -1);
         }
      if(substr($data, -1) == "\r")
         {
         $data = substr($data, 0, -1);
         }
      if(!xml_parse($parser, $data))
         {
         print("<br>xml_parse failed with " . htmlentities($data));
         }
      }
   if(!xml_parse($parser, "", true))
      {
      print("<br>xml_parse failed on eof.");
      }
   fclose($file);
   }
```

Each incoming line ends in a newline, or a return/newline pair, so the code needs the two occurrences of **if(substr($data, -1)** to remove the newline and carriage return. **xml_parse( )** accepts the parser id and the data up to end of file. After end of file, **xml_parse()** is called again to finish processing, and this time it has a third parameter set to true to indicate the end of file.

Once the parsing is finished, close the parser with the following code to free up resources. There seems to be nothing wrong with PHP closing the parser at the end of the script other than the resource overhead until your script completes:

```
if(!xml_parser_free($parser))
    {
    print("<br>xml_parser_free failed.");
    }
```

The following output is a trimmed-down version of the output with a few of the repetitious lines chopped out:

```
default <?xml version="1.0"?>
start_element ABIWORD
default <!-- This file is an AbiWord document. -->
default <!-- Build_CompileTime = 14:34:43 -->
default <!-- Build_CompileDate = Mar 30 2001 -->
start_element PAGESIZE
end_element PAGESIZE
start_element SECTION
start_element P
character_data 1 teaspoon of chili flakes
end_element P
start_element P
end_element P
end_element SECTION
end_element ABIWORD
```

You can see that the default handler was called for the XML version number and some comments. The start and end element handlers kicked in, as did the character data handler. Note that the tag names are translated to uppercase to prevent case mismatches. Think about matching up the **ABIWORD** start element and end element across the whole file.

Matching XML Start and End Tags

The previous Immediate Solution lets you parse an XML file and see the components returned to you in the order chosen by XML. The next step is to match up and process a few tags. This Solution takes the previous solution and adds tag matching code.

To match end tags to data and start tags, you need an array to store accumulated start tags and data. The following array, **$elements**, provides the link between the start element handler, the end element handler, and the character data handler. After you read Chapter 17, you can implement **$elements** and some of the following processing as an object:

```
$elements = array();
```

The character data handler has to change to accumulate data for a tag. The character data handler could be called with part or all of the data for a tag, and there is no way of knowing within this handler when the data is complete. The current element in **$elements** is always entry zero, and within the current element, the data is accumulated in element **"data"**. **"data"** is always created by the start element handler, so this character data handler can just append data:

```
function character_data_handler($parser, $data)
   {
   global $elements;
   $elements[0]["data"] .= $data;
   }
```

The start element handler starts the processing for a tag and contains all the attributes so both the tag name and attributes are added to a new entry in array **$elements**. To make the code easier to understand, the new element is inserted as element zero by **array_unshift()**, a function that pushes the new element onto the start of the array and moves all the other elements up one level. **"data"** is set to a zero-length string so the character data handler can append data. Single tags, of the form **<x />**, are interpreted by the XML code as double tags, **<x></x>**, with the first going through the start element handler and the second going through the end element handler. For all tags, this example code processes the tags in the end element handler when the tags are complete. Note that the tags are translated to lowercase for easier processing. The PHP XML functions translate the XML tags to a single case, but they choose uppercase, which looks annoying to me, a bit like shouting, so I translate back to lowercase:

```
function start_element_handler($parser, $tag, $attributes)
   {
   global $elements;
   $x["attributes"] = $attributes;
   $x["data"] = "";
   $x["tag"] = strtolower($tag);
   array_unshift($elements, $x);
   }
```

The following end element handler performs all the tag-specific processing as each tag is closed. The handler matches the incoming end tag to the current start tag in **$elements**, and produces an error message if the match fails. When you have one extra end tag, this code will drop the end tag and continue. When you have one extra start tag, this code will produce a mass of error messages because the end tags will not get back in sync with the start tag. Both situations indicate an error in the input XML file. If you want to avoid excessive processing of faulty files and the occasional browser error because a mass of error messages, include an error message count and exit after a certain number of errors, perhaps 10 errors. Remember to display anything that will help you find an error within a huge file, including byte and record counts.

Some tags include attributes but others do not, so the processing of the attribute element is wrapped in **isset( )** to avoid errors. The tag's attributes and data are removed from the **$elements** array via **array_shift( )**, and are placed in the local variables **$data** and **$attributes** for easier coding. **switch( )** selects the correct processing for each tag, and has a default of just printing the tag name in a message about unknown tags.

The first cases in the **switch( )** statement, from "**abiword**" to "**pagesize**", contain all the tags that are deliberately not processed by this code. (Note that **switch( )** drops through from one **case** to another if there is no **break** statement, so you can have several **case** statements leading to one action.) All those tags are dumped into the page as HTML comments complete with attributes. You can use this part of the code to absorb the tags not relevant to data display and tags you are not yet ready to process. When you are developing XML processing for a particular XML file, it is often easier to test the first stages if you can process through to the end of the XML file and just drop tags that do not have an appropriate process.

The **section** case translates a **section** tag to a HTML **<div>** tag. I do not know if that is what the AbiWord people intend long-term, but it does fit the HTML structure and shows an example of translating from one tag to another. If you had many tags of the same form and some required translation, you could set up a translation array and translate only those tags in the translation array.

Case **p** shows the complexity of processing individual tags. In this case, the AbiWord developers placed a lot of formatting parameters in a tag named **props** rather than in discrete attribute tags. This part of the code has to decode the key/value pairs out of **props**, and, for convenience, it places the pairs into the **$attributes** array. One key, **text-align**, looked like it would translate directly to the paragraph **align** parameter, so that is performed while transferring the key/value pairs from **props** to **$attributes**. There is a check for duplicate entries in **$attributes** and a warning message so you can discover cases where the two overlap:

```
function end_element_handler($parser, $tag)
    {
    global $elements;
    $tag = strtolower($tag);
    if($tag == $elements[0]["tag"])
        {
        if(isset($elements[0]["attributes"]))
            {
            $attributes = $elements[0]["attributes"];
            }
        $data = $elements[0]["data"];
        array_shift($elements);
        switch($tag)
            {
            case "abiword":
            case "c":
            case "field":
            case "l":
            case "lists":
            case "pagesize":
                print("<!-- " . $tag . " ");
                while(list($k, $v) = each($attributes))
                    {
                    print(" " . strtolower($k) . "=\"" . $v . "\"");
                    }
                print($data . " -->\n");
                break;
            case "section":
                $tag = "div";
                print("<div" . $tag);
                while(list($k, $v) = each($attributes))
                    {
                    print(" " . $k . "=\"" . $v . "\"");
                    }
                print(">" . $data . "</" . $tag . ">\n");
                break;
            case "p":
                if(isset($attributes["PROPS"]))
                    {
                    $props = explode("; ", $attributes["PROPS"]);
                    while(list($k, $v) = each($props))
                        {
                        $att = explode(":", $v);
                        if($att[0] == "text-align")
                            {
                            $att[0] = "align";
```

```
                }
            if(isset($attributes[$att[0]]))
                {
                print("<br>Duplicate attribute; " . $att[0]
                    . "\n");
                }
            else
                {
                $attributes[$att[0]] = $att[1];
                }
            }
        unset($attributes["PROPS"]);
        }
    print("<" . $tag);
    while(list($k, $v) = each($attributes))
        {
        print(" " . $k . "=\"" . $v . "\"");
        }
    print(">" . $data . "</" . $tag . ">\n");
    break;
default:
    print("<br>end_element " . $tag . " not processed.\n");
    }
    }
else
    {
    print("<br>end_element " . $tag . " does not match "
        . $elements[0]["tag"]);
    }
}
```

The following shows part of the printed result, including the right-aligned paragraph:

```
1 teaspoon of chili flakes

                                                1 soup spoon of capsicum
1 can coconut cream
```

Here is a section of the HTML behind the printed result (note the **pagesize** tag reproduced as an HTML comment and the **paragraph** tag including **align="right"**):

```
<!-- pagesize  pagetype="Letter" orientation="portrait" width="8.500000"
   height="11.000000" units="inch" page-scale="1.000000" -->
<p>1 teaspoon of chili flakes</p>
<p align="right">1 soup spoon of capsicum</p>
<p>1 can coconut cream</p>
```

The example decoding of an AbiWord document shows you a number of steps you can make toward decoding your favorite XML document. Some of the tags and attributes do not translate to Web page parameters, so there is no point in decoding them. Some XML tags and parameters are designed to prevent the insertion of invalid data, so these are not needed when you are just decoding the data for display. Try applying the code to your XML files. Pick short files so the file size does not blow up the browser. Where the code converts tags to HTML comments, you could convert them to light gray text so you can see the tags in context.

AbiWord documents appear to be unnecessarily complex and use too many attributes where discrete tags would be more useful. The attributes look like they could be compatible with style sheets, which are outside the scope of this book. I will continue developing the decoding of AbiWord documents as Web pages. If you are interested in the updated code, drop me a note via my Web site.

Index

G

What's on the CD-ROM

The *PHP Black Book's* companion CD-ROM contains elements specifically selected to enhance the usefulness of this book, including:

- *Apache 1.3.20*—A full version of the Apache Web server, complete with source code from the Apache Software Foundation (**http://apache.org**).
- *CygIPC 1.09*—A free open source NT 4.0 program to connect PostgreSQL and CygWin.
- *CygWin 1.09*—A free open source NT 4.0 program to help Unix programs run on NT 4.0 by extending NT's POSIX compliance (**http://sources.redhat.com/ cygwin/**).
- *Dia 0.88.2*—A free open source diagram drawing tool for NT, Windows 9x, Windows ME, Windows 2000, Unix, and Linux from the developers listed at **www.lysator.liu.se/~alla/dia/**.
- *Gimp 1.22*—A free open source image editing tool for NT, Windows 9x, Windows ME, Windows 2000, Unix, and Linux from Gimp.org (**www.gimp.org/**).
- *MySQL 3.23.41*—A free open source relational database for NT, Windows 9x, Windows ME, Windows 2000, Unix, and Linux from MySQL AB (**http:// mysql.com/**).
- *PHP 4.0.6*—The free open source Web-site scripting and programming language for NT, Windows 9x, Windows ME, Windows 2000, Unix, and Linux from The PHP Group (**http://php.net/**).
- *PostgreSQL 7.1.3*—A free open source relational database for NT, Windows 2000, Unix, and Linux from PostgreSQL, Inc. (**www.pgsql.com/**).
- *Source code for the book's projects*—You can insert this working code directly into your Web site.

System Requirements

Software

- **Windows 98, NT 4, Windows 2000, Windows ME, and later** or **Linux/Unix**.

Hardware*

- Intel (or equivalent) Pentium processor
- 128MB
- 200MB of disk storage space
- 24-bit color

*Consult individual Web sites for specific requirements.